W9-BNV-709

Katharine Gibbs
BUSINESS WORDBOOK

Katharine Gibbs BUSINESS WORDBOOK

BEA SCALA AND JOAN NICHOLSON

THE FREE PRESS
A Division of Macmillan Publishing Co., Inc.
New York

COLLIER MACMILLAN PUBLISHERS
London

The Free Press
A Division of Macmillan Publishing Co., Inc.
866 Third Avenue, New York, N.Y. 10022

Collier Macmillan Canada, Inc.

Library of Congress Catalog Card Number: 82-16019

Printed in the United States of America

1 2 3 4 5 6 7 8 9 10

Library of Congress Cataloging in Publication Data

Main entry under title:
Katharine Gibbs business wordbook.

1. English language—Business English. 2. Business —Dictionaries. 3. Spellers. I. Katharine Gibbs School.
PE1115.K37 1982 428.2'08865 82-16019
ISBN 0-02-911670-8

TABLE OF CONTENTS

FOREWORD

The Katharine Gibbs School has changed in many ways since it was founded in 1911. However, one constant throughout the school's seventy-one-year history has been an unflagging commitment to proficiency in the English language as the most important prerequisite to a successful career in business. Katharine M. Gibbs believed that the business of business is communication. Her belief became the foundation stone on which the rigorous grammar, usage, and spelling curriculum of the Katharine Gibbs School is built.

Because it is not possible for every conscientious business person to benefit from the instruction and experience of the Katharine Gibbs School, we have made this book and our grammar and usage text available to the public. The *Katharine Gibbs Business Wordbook* is a companion volume to the *Katharine Gibbs Handbook of Business English*. The two books complement each other in a unique way: Whereas the *Handbook* deals with English grammar and usage, the *Wordbook* provides the reader with a comprehensive guide to the spelling, hyphenation, and definition of words most commonly used in business today. In addition, the "Reference Sections" of the *Wordbook* have a wealth of helpful facts and information that should be at arm's reach in the day-to-day conduct of business.

I hope that you will find the *Katharine Gibbs Business Wordbook* to be a valuable addition to your business reference library.

Eleanor P. Vreeland

Eleanor P. Vreeland

President
The Katharine Gibbs School

ACKNOWLEDGMENTS

The following people are gratefully acknowledged for their contributions to this book: Rosanna Hansen and Curtis Cox, for their editorial guidance and hard work throughout the project; Eve Rouke of the Katharine Gibbs School, for her constant support and helpful comments on the manuscript; David B. Guralnik, dictionary editor in chief, Simon & Schuster, for permission to reprint, with modifications, *Webster's New World Speller/Divider*; Phyllis Winant, for her contributions to the "Glossary of Business Terms"; Sally R. Bell and Robert A. Bell, for their contributions to the "Glossary of Business Terms" and the "Reference Sections"; David Falk, for compiling the "Guide to Reference Sources"; Nick Pease and Foerster-Forlini Associates for their contributions to the "Glossary of Business Terms"; Celia McTague, for editorial assistance; and Lynn Levine, for typing.

PART I
SPELLER/DIVIDER

Guide to the Speller/Divider

The "Speller/Divider" contains approximately 26,000 words and is based on *Webster's New World Speller/Divider*, which in turn, is based on *Webster's New World Dictionary of the American Language*, Second College Edition.

Variant spellings are included in the "Speller/Divider," but preferred spellings are shown first; for example: add·a·ble *or* add·i·ble.

Capsule definitions are included with words that, because of similar spellings and/or similar pronunciations, may be confused with other words. If the confusing words are listed very near each other, only the short definition appears; for example: ad·join (*to be next to*), ad·journ (*suspend*). When confusing words are listed some distance apart, the capsule definitions are followed by cross-references; for example: au·ral (*of the ear*; SEE oral), o·ral (*of the mouth*; SEE aural). The capsule definitions are not intended to replace dictionary definitions.

Parts of speech and **stress marks** are shown when such indications are helpful in distinguishing one word from another; for example: re·cord′ *v.*, rec′ord *n.*; re·fuse′ *v.*, ref′use *n.*

Syllabification is indicated by a centered dot, stress mark, or hyphen; for example: cus·to·di·al, ref′use, cus·tom-made. Note that whenever a hyphen appears, that hyphen is part of the actual spelling of the word.

A

ab·a·cus
·cus·es *or* ·ci
a·ban·don
a·base
·based ·bas·ing
a·bash
a·bat·a·ble
a·bate
·bat·ed ·bat·ing
ab·a·tis
ab·at·toir
ab·ax·i·al
ab·bess
ab·bre·vi·ate
·at·ed ·at·ing
ab·bre·vi·a·tion
ab·bre·vi·a·tor
ab·di·cate
·cat·ed ·cat·ing
ab·di·ca·tion
ab·di·ca·tor
ab·duct
ab·duc·tion
ab·duc·tor
ab·er·rant
ab·er·ra·tion
a·bet
·bet·ted ·bet·ting
a·bey·ance
ab·hor
·horred ·hor·ring
ab·hor·rence
ab·hor·rent
a·bide
·bode *or* ·bid·ed
·bid·ing
a·bil·i·ty
·ties
ab·ject
ab·jec·tion
ab·ju·ra·tion
ab·jure
·jured ·jur·ing
ab·la·tive
a·blaze
a·ble
·bler ·blest
a·ble-bod·ied
ab·lu·tion
ab·ne·gate
·gat·ed ·gat·ing
ab·ne·ga·tion
ab·nor·mal
ab·nor·mal·i·ty
·ties
ab·nor·mi·ty
·ties
a·board
a·bode
a·bol·ish
ab·o·li·tion
a·bom·i·na·ble
a·bom·i·nate
·nat·ed ·nat·ing
a·bom·i·na·tion
a·bom·i·na·tor
a·bort
a·bor·ti·cide
a·bor·tion
a·bor·tive
a·bound
a·bout-face
-faced -fac·ing
a·bove·board
ab·rade
·rad·ed ·rad·ing
ab·ra·sion
ab·ra·sive
ab·re·act
ab·re·ac·tion
a·breast
a·bridge
·bridged
·bridg·ing
a·bridg·ment
or ·bridge·ment
a·broad
ab·ro·gate
·gat·ed ·gat·ing
ab·ro·ga·tion
ab·ro·ga·tor
a·brupt
ab·scess
ab·scessed
ab·scond
ab·sence
ab′sent *adj.*
ab·sent′ *v.*
ab·sen·tee·ism
ab·sent-mind·ed
ab·so·lute
ab·so·lu·tion
ab·so·lut·ism
ab·solve
·solved ·solv·ing
ab·solv·ent
ab·sorb
·sorbed ·sorb·ing
ab·sorb·a·ble
ab·sorb·en·cy
ab·sorb·ent
ab·sorp·tion
ab·stain
ab·ste·mi·ous
ab·sten·tion
ab·sti·nence
ab·sti·nent
ab′stract *n.*
ab·stract′ *v.*
ab·strac·tion
ab·struse
ab·surd
ab·surd·i·ty
·ties
a·bun·dance
a·bun·dant
a·buse
·bused ·bus·ing
a·bus·er
a·bu·sive
a·but
·but·ted ·but·ting
a·but·ment
a·but·ter
a·bys·mal
a·bys·mal·ly
a·byss
a·ca·cia
ac·a·de·mi·a
ac·a·dem·ic
ac·a·dem·i·cal
a·cad·e·mi·cian
ac·a·dem·i·cism
a·cad·e·my
·mies
A·ca·pul·co
ac·cede
·ced·ed ·ced·ing
(*agree;* SEE exceed)
ac·cel·er·ant
ac·cel·er·ate
·at·ed ·at·ing
ac·cel·er·a·tion
ac·cel·er·a·tor
ac·cel·er·om·e·ter
ac·cent
ac·cen·tu·al
ac·cen·tu·ate
·at·ed ·at·ing
ac·cen·tu·a·tion
ac·cept
(*receive;* SEE except)
ac·cept·a·bil·i·ty
ac·cept·a·ble
ac·cept·a·bly
ac·cept·ance
ac·cep·ta·tion
ac·cept·ed
(*approved;* SEE excepted)
ac·cep·tor
ac·cess
(*approach;* SEE excess)
ac·ces·si·bil·i·ty
ac·ces·si·ble
ac·ces·sion
ac·ces·so·ry
or ·sa·ry
·ries
ac·ci·dent
ac·ci·den·tal
ac·claim
ac·cla·ma·tion
ac·cli·mate
·mat·ed ·mat·ing
ac·cli·ma·tize
·tized ·tiz·ing
ac·co·lade
ac·com·mo·date
·dat·ed ·dat·ing
ac·com·mo·da·tion
ac·com·pa·ni·ment
ac·com·pa·nist
ac·com·pa·ny
·nied ·ny·ing
ac·com·plice
ac·com·plish

ac·com·plished
ac·cord
ac·cord·ance
ac·cord·ant·ly
ac·cord·ing
ac·cor·di·on
ac·cost
ac·count
ac·count·a·bil·i·ty
ac·count·a·ble
ac·count·a·bly
ac·count·ant
ac·count·ing
ac·cou·ter·ments
ac·cred·it
ac·cred·it·a·tion
ac·cre·tion
ac·cru·al
ac·crue
·crued ·cru·ing
ac·cul·tu·rate
·rat·ed ·rat·ing
ac·cul·tu·ra·tion
ac·cu·mu·la·ble
ac·cu·mu·late
·lat·ed ·lat·ing
ac·cu·mu·la·tion
ac·cu·mu·la·tive
ac·cu·mu·la·tor
ac·cu·ra·cy
ac·cu·rate
ac·cu·rate·ly
ac·cus·al
ac·cu·sa·tion
ac·cu·sa·tive
ac·cu·sa·to·ry
ac·cuse
·cused ·cus·ing
ac·cus·tom
ac·cus·tomed
a·cer·bi·ty
·ties
ac·e·tate
ac·e·tone
a·cet·y·lene
ache
ached ach·ing
a·chiev·a·ble
a·chieve
·chieved
·chiev·ing
a·chieve·ment
ach·ro·mat·ic
a·chro·ma·tize
·tized ·tiz·ing
a·cid·ic
a·cid·i·fi·er
a·cid·i·fy
·fied ·fy·ing
a·cid·i·ty
a·cid·u·late
·lat·ed
·lat·ing
ac·knowl·edge
·edged ·edg·ing
ac·knowl·edge·a·ble
ac·knowl·edg·ment
or ·edge·ment
ac·me
ac·o·lyte
a·cous·tic *or* ·ti·cal
ac·quaint
ac·quaint·ance
ac·qui·esce
·esced ·esc·ing
ac·qui·es·cence
ac·qui·es·cent
ac·quir·a·ble
ac·quire
·quired ·quir·ing
ac·quire·ment
ac·qui·si·tion
ac·quis·i·tive
ac·quit
·quit·ted
·quit·ting
ac·quit·tal
ac·quit·tance
a·cre
a·cre·age
ac·rid
a·crid·i·ty
ac·ri·mo·ni·ous
ac·ri·mo·ny
ac·ro·bat
ac·ro·bat·ic
ac·ro·nym
ac·ro·pho·bi·a
a·crop·o·lis
a·cross
a·cros·tic
a·cryl·ic
act·ing
ac·tin·i·um
ac·tion
ac·tion·a·ble
ac·ti·vate
·vat·ed ·vat·ing
ac·ti·va·tion
ac·ti·va·tor
ac·tive
ac·tiv·ism
ac·tiv·ist
ac·tiv·i·ty
·ties
ac·tiv·ize
·ized ·iz·ing
ac·tor
ac·tu·al
ac·tu·al·i·ty
·ties
ac·tu·al·ize
·ized ·iz·ing
ac·tu·al·ly
ac·tu·ar·i·al
ac·tu·ar·y
·ies
ac·tu·ate
·at·ed ·at·ing
ac·tu·a·tion
ac·tu·a·tor
a·cu·i·ty
·ties
a·cu·men
ac·u·punc·ture
a·cute
a·cute·ly
ad
(*advertisement*)
ad·age
ad·a·mant
a·dapt
(*fit;* SEE adept, adopt)
a·dapt·a·bil·i·ty
a·dapt·a·ble
ad·ap·ta·tion *or* a·dap·tion
a·dapt·er *or* a·dap·tor
a·dap·tive
add
(*addition*)
add·a·ble *or* ·i·ble
ad·den·dum
·da
ad·dict
ad·dic·tion
ad·dic·tive
ad·di·tion
(*an adding;* SEE edition)
ad·di·tion·al
ad·di·tive
ad·dle
·dled ·dling
ad·dle·brained
ad·dress
ad·dress·ee
ad·duce
·duced ·duc·ing
ad·duc·i·ble
ad·duc·tion
ad·ept
(*skilled;* SEE adapt, adopt)
ad·e·qua·cy
ad·e·quate
ad·e·quate·ly
ad·here
·hered ·her·ing
ad·her·ence
ad·her·ent
ad·he·sion
ad·he·sive
ad hoc
a·dieu
ad in·fi·ni·tum
ad in·ter·im
ad·ja·cen·cy
ad·ja·cent
ad·jec·tive
ad·join
(*to be next to*)
ad·journ
(*suspend*)
ad·judge
·judged
·judg·ing
ad·ju·di·cate
·cat·ed ·cat·ing

ad·ju·di·ca·tion
ad·ju·di·ca·tor
ad·junct
ad·ju·ra·tion
ad·jure
·jured ·jur·ing
ad·just
ad·just·a·ble
ad·just·er *or*
·jus·tor
ad·just·ment
ad·ju·tant
ad-lib
-libbed -lib·bing
ad·man
·men
ad·min·is·ter
ad·min·is·tra·ble
ad·min·is·trate
·trat·ed ·trat·ing
ad·min·is·tra·tion
ad·min·is·tra·tive
ad·min·is·tra·tor
ad·mi·ra·ble
ad·mi·ra·bly
ad·mi·ral
ad·mi·ral·ty
·ties
ad·mi·ra·tion
ad·mire
·mired ·mir·ing
ad·mir·er
ad·mis·si·bil·i·ty
ad·mis·si·ble
ad·mis·si·bly
ad·mis·sion
ad·mit
·mit·ted ·mit·ting
ad·mit·tance
ad·mit·ted·ly
ad·mix
ad·mix·ture
ad·mon·ish
ad·mo·ni·tion
ad·mon·i·to·ry
ad nau·se·am
a·do
ad·o·les·cence
ad·o·les·cent
a·dopt
(*choose;* SEE adapt, adept)
a·dop·tion
a·dop·tive
a·dor·a·ble
ad·o·ra·tion
a·dore
·dored
·dor·ing
a·dorn
a·dorn·ment
ad·ren·al·in
a·drift
a·droit
ad·sorb
ad·sor·bent
ad·sorp·tion
ad·u·late
·lat·ed ·lat·ing
ad·u·la·tion
a·dul·ter·ant
a·dul·ter·ate
·at·ed ·at·ing
a·dul·ter·a·tion
a·dul·ter·y
a·dult·hood
ad va·lo·rem
ad·vance
·vanced
·vanc·ing
ad·vance·ment
ad·van·tage
ad·van·ta·geous
ad·ven·ture
·tured ·tur·ing
ad·ven·tur·er
ad·ven·ture·some
ad·ven·tur·ous
ad·verb
ad·ver·bi·al
ad·ver·sar·y
·ies
ad·verse
(*opposed;* SEE averse)
ad·verse·ly
ad·ver·si·ty
·ties
ad·vert
ad·vert·ent
ad·ver·tise *or*
·tize
·tised *or* ·tized
·tis·ing *or* ·tiz·ing
ad·ver·tise·ment
or ·tize·ment
ad·vice *n.*
ad·vis·a·bil·i·ty
ad·vis·a·ble
ad·vis·a·bly
ad·vise *v.*
·vised ·vis·ing
ad·vis·ed·ly
ad·vise·ment
ad·vis·er *or*
·vi·sor
ad·vi·so·ry
ad·vo·ca·cy
ad·vo·cate
·cat·ed ·cat·ing
Ae·ge·an
ae·on
aer·ate
·at·ed ·at·ing
aer·a·tion
aer·a·tor
aer·i·al
aer·i·al·ist
aer·o·bat·ics
aer·o·sol
aer·o·space
Ae·sop
aes·thete
aes·thet·ic
aes·thet·i·cism
af·fa·bil·i·ty
af·fa·ble
af·fa·bly
af·fair
af·fect
(*to influence;* SEE effect)
af·fec·ta·tion
af·fect·ed
af·fec·tion
af·fec·tion·ate
af·fec·tive
(*of feelings;* SEE effective)
af·fi·ance
·anced ·anc·ing
af·fi·ant
af·fi·da·vit
af·fil·i·ate
·at·ed ·at·ing
af·fil·i·a·tion
af·fin·i·ty
af·firm
af·fir·ma·tion
af·firm·a·tive
af·firm·a·tive·ly
af·fix
·fixed *or* ·fixt
·fix·ing
af·flict
af·flic·tion
af·flu·ence
af·flu·ent
(*rich;* SEE effluent)
af·ford
af·fray
af·front
af·ghan
a·fi·cio·na·do
a·field
a·float
a·fore·men·tioned
a·fore·said
a·fore·thought
a·fore·time
a·fraid
Af·ri·can
af·ter·ef·fect
af·ter·im·age
af·ter·life
af·ter·math
af·ter·noon
af·ter·shock
af·ter·thought
af·ter·ward
a·gain
a·gainst
a·gape
ag·ate
age
aged, ag·ing *or*
age·ing
age·less

age·long
a·gen·cy
·cies
a·gen·da
a·gent
age-old
ag·gran·dize
·dized ·diz·ing
ag·gran·dize·ment
ag·gra·vate
·vat·ed ·vat·ing
ag·gra·va·tion
ag·gre·gate
·gat·ed ·gat·ing
ag·gre·ga·tion
ag·gres·sion
ag·gres·sive
ag·gres·sor
ag·grieve
·grieved
·griev·ing
a·ghast
ag·ile
ag·ile·ly
a·gil·i·ty
ag·i·tate
·tat·ed ·tat·ing
ag·i·ta·tion
ag·i·ta·tor
a·glow
ag·nos·tic
ag·nos·ti·cism
ag·o·nize
·nized ·niz·ing
ag·o·ny
·nies
ag·o·ra·pho·bi·a
a·grar·i·an
a·gree
·greed ·gree·ing
a·gree·a·bil·i·ty
a·gree·a·ble
a·gree·a·bly
a·gree·ment
ag·ri·busi·ness
ag·ri·cul·tur·al
ag·ri·cul·ture
ag·ri·cul·tur·ist
or ·tur·al·ist
a·gron·o·my

a·ground
a·head
aid (*help*)
aide (*assistant*)
aide-de-camp *or*
aid-de-camp
aides- *or* aids-
ail
ail·ing
aim·less
air
(*gases;* SEE heir)
air base
air·borne
air·bra·sive
air-con·di·tion
air-cool
air·craft
air express
air·field
air force
air frame
air gun
air·i·ly
air·i·ness
air·ing
air·lift
air·line
air·mail
air·man
·men
air·plane
air·port
air pressure
air pump
air raid
air rights
air·ship
air·sick
air·speed
air·tight
air·waves
air·y
air·i·er air·i·est
aisle
(*passage;* SEE isle)
a la carte
a·lac·ri·ty
a·larm

a·larm·ing
a·larm·ist
A·las·ka
al·ba·core
al·ba·tross
al·be·it
al·bum
Al·bu·quer·que
al·che·mist
al·che·my
al·co·hol
al·co·hol·ic
al·co·hol·ism
al·cove
al·der·man
·men
a·lert·ly
A·leu·tian
al·fres·co
al·gae
al·gae·cide
al·ge·bra
al·ge·bra·ic
a·li·as
al·i·bi
·bis
·bied ·bi·ing
al·ien
al·ien·ate
·at·ed ·at·ing
al·ien·a·tion
a·light
·light·ed *or* ·lit
·light·ing
a·lign *or* a·line
·ligned *or* ·lined
·lign·ing *or*
·lin·ing
a·lign·ment
or a·line·ment
a·like
al·i·men·ta·ry
(*nourishing;* SEE
elementary)
al·i·mo·ny
al·ka·li
·lies *or* ·lis
al·ka·line
al·ka·loid
all-A·mer·i·can

all-a·round
al·lay
·layed ·lay·ing
all-clear
al·le·ga·tion
al·lege
·leged ·leg·ing
al·leg·ed·ly
Al·le·ghe·ny
al·le·giance
al·le·gor·i·cal
al·le·go·rize
·rized ·riz·ing
al·le·go·ry
·ries
al·ler·gen
al·ler·gen·ic
al·ler·gic
al·ler·gist
al·ler·gy
·gies
al·le·vi·ate
·at·ed ·at·ing
al·le·vi·a·tion
al·ley
·leys
(*narrow lane;*
SEE ally)
al·li·ance
al·lied
all-im·por·tant
all-in·clu·sive
al·lit·er·ate
·at·ed ·at·ing
al·lit·er·a·tion
al·lo·cate
·cat·ed ·cat·ing
al·lo·ca·tion
al·lo·di·al
al·lot
·lot·ted ·lot·ting
al·lot·ment
al·lot·tee
all-out
all·o·ver
al·low
al·low·a·ble
al·low·ance
al·lowed
(*permitted,* SEE
aloud)

al·loy
all-pur·pose
all right
all-star
all·time
al·lude
·lud·ed ·lud·ing
(*refer to;* SEE elude)
al·lure
·lured ·lur·ing
al·lu·sion
(*mention;* SEE elusion, illusion)
al·lu·sive
(*mentioning;* SEE elusive, illusive)
al·lu·vi·al
al·ly′ *v.* al′ly *n.*
·lies
·lied ·ly·ing
(*join; partner;* SEE alley)
al·ma ma·ter
al·ma·nac
al·might·y
al·most
a·loft
a·long·shore
a·long·side
a·loof
a·loud
(*loudly,* SEE allowed)
al·pac·a
al·pha·bet
al·pha·bet·i·cal
al·pha·bet·ize
·ized ·iz·ing
al·pha·nu·mer·ic
al·read·y
al·tar
(*table for worship*)
al·ter
(*to change*)
al·ter·a·tion
al·ter·cate
·cat·ed ·cat·ing
al·ter·ca·tion
al·ter·nate
·nat·ed ·nat·ing
al·ter·na·tion
al·ter·na·tive
al·ter·na·tor
al·though
al·tim·e·ter
al·ti·tude
al·to·geth·er
al·tru·ism
al·tru·is·tic
a·lu·mi·num
a·lum·na *n. fem.*
·nae
a·lum·nus *n. masc.*
·ni
al·ways
a·mal·ga·mate
·mat·ed
·mat·ing
a·mal·ga·ma·tion
a·man·u·en·sis
·ses
am·a·teur
a·maze
·mazed
·maz·ing
a·maze·ment
am·bas·sa·dor
am·bas·sa·do·ri·al
am·ber
am·bi·ance
am·bi·dex·ter·i·ty
am·bi·dex·trous
am·bi·ent
am·bi·gu·i·ty
am·big·u·ous
am·bi·tion
am·bi·tious
am·biv·a·lence
am·ble
·bled ·bling
am·bu·lance
am·bu·late
·lat·ed ·lat·ing
am·bu·la·to·ry
am·bush
a·mel·io·rate
·rat·ed ·rat·ing
a·mel·io·ra·tion
a·mel·io·ra·tive
a·me·na·bil·i·ty
a·me·na·ble
a·mend
(*revise;* SEE emend)
a·mend·ment
a·men·i·ty
·ties
A·mer·i·can
A·mer·i·ca·na
A·mer·i·can·ism
A·mer·i·can·i·za·tion
A·mer·i·can·ize
·ized ·iz·ing
am·e·thyst
a·mi·a·bil·i·ty
a·mi·a·ble
a·mi·a·bly
am·i·ca·bil·i·ty
am·i·ca·ble
am·i·ca·bly
a·mi·cus cu·ri·ae
a·mid
a·mid·ships
a·midst
a·mi·no
Am·ish
am·i·ty
·ties
am·mo·nia
am·mu·ni·tion
am·ne·sia
am·nes·ty
·ties
·tied ·ty·ing
a·moe·ba
·bas *or* ·bae
a·mok
a·mong
a·mongst
a·mor·al
a·mor·al·i·ty
am·o·rous
a·mor·phous
am·or·ti·za·tion
am·or·tize
·tized ·tiz·ing
a·mount
a·mour
am·per·age
am·pere
am·per·sand
am·phi·the·a·ter
am·ple
am·pli·fi·ca·tion
am·pli·fi·er
am·pli·fy
·fied ·fy·ing
am·pli·tude
am·ply
am·pu·tate
·tat·ed ·tat·ing
am·pu·ta·tion
am·pu·tee
a·muse
·mused
·mus·ing
a·muse·ment
a·nach·ro·nism
a·nach·ro·nis·tic
a·nae·mi·a
a·nae·mic
an·aes·the·sia
an·aes·thet·ic
an·aes·the·tize
·tized ·tiz·ing
an·a·gram
an·al·ge·si·a
an·al·ge·sic
an·a·log computer
a·nal·o·gize
·gized ·giz·ing
a·nal·o·gous
a·nal·o·gy
·gies
a·nal·y·sis
·ses
an·a·lyst
(*one who analyzes;* SEE annalist)
an·a·lyt·i·cal
or an·a·lyt·ic
an·a·lyze
·lyzed ·lyz·ing
an·ar·chic
or ·chi·cal
an·ar·chism
an·ar·chist
an·ar·chis·tic
an·ar·chy
·chies
a·nath·e·ma
·mas

a·nath·e·ma·tize
·tized ·tiz·ing
an·a·tom·i·cal
or ·tom·ic
a·nat·o·mize
·mized ·miz·ing
a·nat·o·my
·mies
an·ces·tor
an·ces·tral
an·ces·tress
an·ces·try
·tries
an·chor
an·chor·age
an·cient
an·cil·lar·y
and·i·ron
an·ec·dot·al
an·ec·dote
(*story;* SEE antidote)
a·ne·mi·a
a·ne·mic
a·nem·o·ne
an·es·the·sia
an·es·the·si·ol·o·gy
an·es·thet·ic
an·es·the·tist
an·es·the·tize
·tized ·tiz·ing
an·gel
(*spirit;* SEE angle)
an·gel·ic
or ·gel·i·cal
an·ger
an·gi·na
an·gle
·gled ·gling
(*corner; scheme;* SEE angel)
an·gler
An·gli·can
An·gli·cism
An·gli·cize
·cized ·ciz·ing
An·glo-A·mer·i·can
An·glo·phile
An·glo-Sax·on
An·go·ra

an·gri·ly
an·gry
·gri·er ·gri·est
an·guish
an·gu·lar
an·gu·lar·i·ty
·ties
an·gu·la·tion
an·hy·drous
an·i·mal
an·i·mal·ism
an·i·mal·is·tic
an·i·mal·ize
·ized ·iz·ing
an·i·mate
·mat·ed ·mat·ing
an·i·ma·tor *or* ·mat·er
an·i·ma·tion
an·i·mism
an·i·mos·i·ty
·ties
an·i·mus
an·ise
an·i·sette
an·kle
an·nal·ist
(*a writer of annals;* SEE analyst)
an·nals
An·nap·o·lis
an·nex′ *v.*
an′nex *n.*
an·nex·a·tion
an·ni·hi·late
·lat·ed ·lat·ing
an·ni·hi·la·tion
an·ni·hi·la·tor
an·ni·ver·sa·ry
·ries
an·no Do·mi·ni
an·no·tate
·tat·ed ·tat·ing
an·no·ta·tion
an·nounce
·nounced
·nounc·ing
an·nounce·ment
an·nounc·er

an·noy
an·noy·ance
an·nu·al
an·nu·al·ly
an·nu·i·tant
an·nu·i·ty
·ties
an·nul
·nulled
·nul·ling
an·nul·ment
an·nun·ci·ate
·at·ed ·at·ing
(*announce;* SEE enunciate)
an·nun·ci·a·tor
an·ode
an·o·dize
·dized ·diz·ing
an·o·dyne
a·nom·a·lous
a·nom·a·ly
·lies
an·o·mie
an·o·nym·i·ty
a·non·y·mous
an·oth·er
an·swer
ant·ac·id
an·tag·o·nism
an·tag·o·nis·tic
an·tag·o·nize
·nized ·niz·ing
ant·al·ka·li
·lies *or* ·lis
ant·arc·tic
Ant·arc·ti·ca
an·te
·ted *or* ·teed
·te·ing
an·te- *prefix*
(*before;* SEE anti-)
an·te·bel·lum
an·te·cede
·ced·ed ·ced·ing
an·te·ced·ence
an·te·ced·ent
an·te·cham·ber
an·te·date
an·te·di·lu·vi·an

an·te me·ri·di·em
an·ten·na
·nae *or* ·nas
an·te·ri·or
an·te·room
an·them
an·thol·o·gist
an·thol·o·gy
·gies
an·thra·cite
an·thrax
·thra·ces
an·thro·pol·o·gist
an·thro·pol·o·gy
an·thro·po·mor·phic
an·ti- *prefix*
(*against;* SEE ante-)
an·ti·air·craft
an·ti·bac·te·ri·al
an·ti·bi·ot·ic
an·ti·bod·y
·ies
an·tic
·ticked ·tick·ing
an·tic·i·pant
an·tic·i·pate
·pat·ed ·pat·ing
an·tic·i·pa·tion
an·tic·i·pa·to·ry
an·ti·cli·mac·tic
an·ti·cli·max
an·ti·de·pres·sant
an·ti·dote
(*remedy;* SEE anecdote)
an·ti·freeze
an·ti·gen
an·ti·he·ro
an·ti·his·ta·mine
An·til·les
an·ti·mat·ter
an·ti·mo·ny
an·ti·par·ti·cle
an·ti·pas·to
an·ti·pa·thet·ic
an·tip·a·thy
·thies
an·ti·per·son·nel
an·ti·phon
an·tiph·o·nal

an·ti·quar·i·an
an·ti·quar·y
·ies
an·ti·quate
·quat·ed
·quat·ing
an·tique
·tiqued
·tiqu·ing
an·tiq·ui·ty
·ties
an·ti-Sem·ite
an·ti-Se·mit·ic
an·ti-Sem·i·tism
an·ti·sep·tic
an·ti·so·cial
an·tith·e·sis
·ses
an·ti·thet·i·cal
an·ti·thet·i·cal·ly
an·ti·tox·in
an·ti·trust
an·to·nym
anx·i·e·ty
·ties
anx·ious
an·y·bod·y
an·y·how
an·y·one
an·y·thing
an·y·way
an·y·where
A-OK or
A-O·kay
a·or·ta
·tas or ·tae
a·pace
a·part·heid
a·part·ment
ap·a·thet·ic
ap·a·thet·i·cal·ly
ap·a·thy
·thies
a·pe·ri·tif
ap·er·ture
a·pex
a·pex·es or
ap·i·ces
a·pha·si·a
aph·o·rism
aph·ro·dis·i·ac

a·pi·ar·y
·ies
a·piece
a·plomb
a·poc·a·lypse
a·poc·a·lyp·tic
a·poc·ry·phal
ap·o·gee
a·pol·o·get·ic
ap·o·lo·gi·a
a·pol·o·gize
·gized ·giz·ing
ap·o·logue
a·pol·o·gy
·gies
ap·o·plec·tic
ap·o·plex·y
a pos·te·ri·o·ri
a·pos·tro·phe
a·poth·e·car·y
·ies
a·poth·e·o·sis
·ses
Ap·pa·la·chi·an
ap·pall or ·pal
·palled
·pal·ling
ap·pa·ra·tus
·tus or ·tus·es
ap·par·el
·eled or ·elled
·el·ing or ·el·ling
ap·par·ent
ap·pa·ri·tion
ap·peal
ap·pear·ance
ap·peas·a·ble
ap·pease
·peased
·peas·ing
ap·pease·ment
ap·peas·er
ap·pel·lant
ap·pel·late
ap·pel·la·tion
ap·pend
ap·pend·age
ap·pend·ant or
·ent
ap·pen·dec·to·my
·mies

ap·pen·di·ci·tis
ap·pen·dix
·dix·es or ·di·ces
ap·per·cep·tion
ap·per·tain
ap·pe·tite
ap·pe·tiz·er
ap·pe·tiz·ing
ap·plaud
ap·plause
ap·pli·ance
ap·pli·ca·bil·i·ty
ap·pli·ca·ble
ap·pli·cant
ap·pli·ca·tion
ap·pli·ca·tor
ap·plied
ap·ply
·plied ·ply·ing
ap·point
ap·point·ee
ap·point·ive
ap·point·ment
ap·por·tion·ment
ap·po·site
ap·po·si·tion
ap·prais·a·ble
ap·prais·al
ap·praise
·praised
·prais·ing
(*estimate;* SEE apprise)
ap·prais·er
ap·pre·ci·a·ble
ap·pre·ci·ate
·at·ed ·at·ing
ap·pre·ci·a·tion
ap·pre·ci·a·tive
ap·pre·hend
ap·pre·hen·sion
ap·pre·hen·sive
ap·pren·tice
·ticed ·tic·ing
ap·prise or
·prize
·prised or ·prized
·pris·ing or
·priz·ing
(*inform;* SEE appraise)
ap·proach

ap·proach·a·ble
ap·pro·ba·tion
ap·pro·pri·ate
·at·ed ·at·ing
ap·pro·pri·ate·ly
ap·pro·pri·a·tion
ap·prov·a·ble
ap·prov·al
ap·prove
·proved
·prov·ing
ap·prox·i·mate
·mat·ed
·mat·ing
ap·prox·i·mate·ly
ap·prox·i·ma·tion
ap·pur·te·nance
A·pril
a pri·o·ri
ap·ro·pos
ap·ti·tude
apt·ly
aq·ua·lung
aq·ua·ma·rine
aq·ua·naut
aq·ua·plane
aq·ua·tint
aq·ue·duct
a·que·ous
aq·ui·line
A·ra·bi·an
Ar·a·bic
ar·a·ble
ar·bi·ter
ar·bi·tra·ble
ar·bi·trage
ar·bi·trag·eur
ar·bit·ra·ment
ar·bi·trar·i·ly
ar·bi·trar·i·ness
ar·bi·trar·y
ar·bi·trate
·trat·ed ·trat·ing
ar·bi·tra·tion
ar·bi·tra·tor
ar·bor
ar·bo·re·al
ar·bo·re·tum
·tums or ·ta

arc
arced *or* arcked
arc·ing *or* arck·ing
ar·cade
ar·chae·o·log·i·cal
ar·chae·ol·o·gy
ar·cha·ic
arch·bish·op
arch·dea·con
arch·di·o·cese
arch·duke
arched
arch·en·e·my
·mies
ar·che·o·log·i·cal
ar·che·ol·o·gy
arch·er·y
ar·che·type
ar·chi·pel·a·go
·goes *or* ·gos
ar·chi·tect
ar·chi·tec·ton·ics
ar·chi·tec·tur·al
ar·chi·tec·tur·al·ly
ar·chi·tec·ture
ar·chives
arch·way
arc·tic
ar·dent
ar·dor
ar·du·ous
a·re·na
aren't
Ar·gen·ti·na
ar·gon
ar·got
ar·gu·a·ble
ar·gu·a·bly
ar·gue
·gued ·gu·ing
ar·gu·ment
ar·gu·men·ta·tion
ar·gu·men·ta·tive
a·rid·i·ty
ar·id·ness
a·rise
·rose ·ris·en
·ris·ing
ar·is·toc·ra·cy
·cies
a·ris·to·crat
a·ris·to·crat·ic
a·ris·to·crat·i·cal·ly
Ar·is·to·te·li·an
Ar·is·tot·le
a·rith′me·tic′ *n.*
ar′ith·met′ic *adj.*
ar·ith·met·i·cal
ar·ith·me·ti·cian
Ar·i·zo·na
Ar·kan·sas
ar·ma·da
ar·ma·ment
ar·ma·ture
arm·chair
armed
ar·mi·stice
ar·mor
ar·mored
ar·mor-plat·ed
ar·mor·y
·ies
ar·my
·mies
a·ro·ma
ar·o·mat·ic
a·round
a·rous·al
a·rouse
·roused
·rous·ing
ar·peg·gio
·gios
ar·raign
ar·range
·ranged
·rang·ing
ar·range·ment
ar·rang·er
ar·rant
ar·ray
ar·ray·al
ar·rear·age
ar·rears
ar·rest
ar·riv·al
ar·rive
·rived ·riv·ing
ar·ro·gance
ar·ro·gant
ar·ro·gate
·gat·ed ·gat·ing
ar·ro·ga·tion
ar·row·head
ar·se·nal
ar·se·nic
ar·son
ar·son·ist
ar·te·fact
ar·te·ri·al
ar·te·ri·o·scle·ro·sis
ar·te·ri·o·scle·rot·ic
ar·ter·y
·ies
ar·te·sian
art·ful
art·ful·ly
ar·thrit·ic
ar·thri·tis
Ar·thu·ri·an
ar·ti·cle
ar·tic·u·late
·lat·ed
·lat·ing
ar·tic·u·late·ly
ar·tic·u·la·tion
ar·ti·fact
ar·ti·fice
ar·ti·fi·cial
ar·ti·fi·cial·ly
ar·ti·fi·ci·al·i·ty
·ties
ar·til·ler·y
ar·ti·san
art·ist
ar·tiste
ar·tis·tic
art·ist·ry
art·less
art·y
·i·er ·i·est
Ar·y·an
as·bes·tos
as·cend
as·cend·a·ble
as·cend·an·cy
as·cend·ant
as·cen·sion
as·cent
(*a rising;* SEE assent)
as·cer·tain
as·cet·ic
as·cet·i·cism
a·scor·bic
as·cot
as·crib·a·ble
as·cribe
·cribed
·crib·ing
as·crip·tion
a·sep·tic
a·sex·u·al
a·shamed
a·shore
A·sia
A·si·at·ic
as·i·nine
a·skance
a·skew
a·so·cial
as·pect
as·per·i·ty
as·perse
·persed ·pers·ing
as·per·sion
as·phalt
as·phyx·i·a
as·phyx·i·ate
·at·ed ·at·ing
as·phyx·i·a·tion
as·pir·ant
as·pi·rate
·rat·ed ·rat·ing
as·pi·ra·tion
as·pi·ra·tor
as·pire
·pired ·pir·ing
as·pi·rin
as·sail
as·sail·ant
as·sas·sin
as·sas·si·nate
·nat·ed ·nat·ing
as·sas·si·na·tion
as·sault

as·say
(*analyze;* SEE essay)
as·sem·blage
as·sem·ble
·bled ·bling
as·sem·bly
·blies
as·sem·bly·man
·men
as·sent
(*consent;* SEE ascent)
as·sert
as·ser·tion
as·ser·tive
as·sess
as·sess·ment
as·ses·sor
as·set
as·si·du·i·ty
as·sid·u·ous
as·sign
as·sign·a·ble
as·sig·na·tion
as·sign·ee
as·sign·ment
as·sim·i·la·ble
as·sim·i·late
·lat·ed ·lat·ing
as·sim·i·la·tion
as·sim·i·la·tive
as·sim·i·la·tor
as·sist
as·sist·ance
as·sist·ant
as·size
as·so·ci·ate
·at·ed ·at·ing
as·so·ci·a·tion
as·so·ci·a·tive
as·so·nance
as·so·nant
as·sort
as·sort·ed
as·sort·ment
as·suage
·suaged
·suag·ing
as·sua·sive
as·sum·a·ble
as·sume
·sumed
·sum·ing
as·sump·tion
as·sur·ance
as·sure
·sured ·sur·ing
as·sur·ed·ly
As·syr·i·a
as·ter·isk
as·ter·oid
asth·ma
asth·mat·ic
as·tig·mat·ic
a·stig·ma·tism
as·ton·ish
as·tound
a·stride
as·trin·gen·cy
as·trin·gent
as·tro·dome
as·trol·o·ger
as·tro·log·i·cal
as·trol·o·gy
as·tro·naut
as·tro·nau·ti·cal
as·tro·nau·tics
as·tron·o·mer
as·tro·nom·i·cal
or ·nom·ic
as·tron·o·my
as·tro·phys·i·cal
as·tro·phys·i·cist
as·tro·phys·ics
as·tute
a·sun·der
a·sy·lum
a·sym·met·ri·cal
or ·met·ric
a·sym·me·try
at·a·vism
at·a·vis·tic
at·el·ier
a·the·ism
a·the·ist
a·the·is·tic
ath·lete
ath·let·ic
At·lan·tic
at·las
at·mos·phere
at·mos·pher·ic
at·oll
at·om
a·tom·ic
a·tom·ics
at·om·ize
·ized ·iz·ing
at·om·iz·er
a·ton·al
a·tone
·toned ·ton·ing
a·tone·ment
a·tri·um
·tri·a *or* ·tri·ums
a·tro·cious
a·troc·i·ty
·ties
at·ro·phy
·phied ·phy·ing
at·tach
at·ta·ché
at·tach·ment
at·tack
at·tain
at·tain·a·ble
at·tain·der
at·tain·ment
at·taint
at·tar
at·tempt
at·tend
at·tend·ance
at·tend·ant
at·ten·tion
at·ten·tive
at·ten·u·ate
·at·ed ·at·ing
at·ten·u·a·tion
at·ten·u·a·tor
at·test
at·tes·ta·tion
at·tire
·tired ·tir·ing
at·ti·tude
at·ti·tu·di·nal
at·tor·ney
·neys
at·tract
at·trac·tion
at·trac·tive
at·trib·ut·a·ble
at′tri′bute *n.*
at·trib′ute *v.*
·ut·ed ·ut·ing
at·tri·bu·tion
at·trib·u·tive
at·tri·tion
at·tune
·tuned ·tun·ing
a·typ·i·cal
a·typ·i·cal·ly
auc·tion
auc·tion·eer
au·da·cious
au·dac·i·ty
·ties
au·di·ble
au·di·bly
au·di·ence
au·di·o
au·di·ol·o·gy
au·di·o-vis·u·al
au·di·phone
au·dit
au·di·tion
au·di·tor
au·di·to·ri·um
au·di·to·ry
aught
(*anything;* SEE
ought)
aug·ment
aug·men·ta·tion
aug·ment·a·tive
Au·gust
au jus
au na·tu·rel
au·ra
·ras *or* ·rae
au·ral
(*of the ear;* SEE
oral)
Au·re·o·my·cin
au re·voir
au·ric·u·lar
au·ro·ra bo·re·a·lis
aus·pi·ces
aus·pi·cious

aus·tere
aus·tere·ly
aus·ter·i·ty
·ties
Aus·tral·ia
au·then·tic
au·then·ti·cate
·cat·ed ·cat·ing
au·then·ti·ca·tion
au·then·tic·i·ty
au·thor
au·thor·i·tar·i·an
au·thor·i·ta·tive
au·thor·i·ty
·ties
au·thor·i·za·tion
au·thor·ize
·ized ·iz·ing
au·to
·tos
·toed ·to·ing
au·to·bi·o·graph·ic
or ·graph·i·cal
au·to·bi·og·ra·phy
·phies
au·toc·ra·cy
·cies
au·to·crat
au·to·crat·ic
au·to·graph
au·to·mat
au·to·mate
·mat·ed
·mat·ing
au·to·mat·ic
au·to·ma·tion
au·tom·a·tism
au·tom·a·ton
·tons *or* ·ta
au·to·mo·bile
au·to·mo·tive
au·to·nom·ic
au·ton·o·mous
au·ton·o·my
·mies
au·top·sy
·sies
au·to·sug·ges·tion
au·tumn
au·tum·nal

aux·il·ia·ry
·ries
a·vail·a·bil·i·ty
a·vail·a·ble
a·vail·a·bly
av·a·lanche
·lanched
·lanch·ing
a·vant-garde
av·a·rice
av·a·ri·cious
a·venge
·venged
·veng·ing
a·veng·er
av·e·nue
a·ver
·verred
·ver·ring
av·er·age
·aged ·ag·ing
a·verse
(*unwilling;* SEE
adverse)
a·ver·sion
a·vert
a·vi·ar·y
·ies
a·vi·a·tion
a·vi·a·tor
av·id·ly
av·o·ca·tion
a·void·a·ble
a·void·a·bly
a·void·ance
av·oir·du·pois
a·vow·al
a·vowed
a·vun·cu·lar
a·wait
a·wake
·woke *or*
·waked
·wak·ing
a·wak·en
a·ward
a·ware
awe·some
aw·ful
a·while
awk·ward

a·wry
ax *or* axe
ax·es
axed ax·ing
ax·i·om
ax·i·o·mat·ic
ax·is
ax·es
ax·le
Az·tec
az·ure

B

bab·bitt
bac·ca·lau·re·ate
bac·ca·rat
bac·cha·nal
bach·e·lor
ba·cil·lus
·li
back·ache
back·bite
·bit, ·bit·ten *or*
·bit, ·bit·ing
back·board
back·bone
back·break·ing
back·court
back·date
·dat·ed ·dat·ing
back·door
back·fire
·fired ·fir·ing
back·gam·mon
back·ground
back·hand
back·lash
back·list
back·log
·logged
·log·ging
back·rest
back·slide
·slid, ·slid *or*
·slid·den, ·slid·ing
back·space
·spaced
·spac·ing
back·track

back·up *or*
back-up
back·ward
back·wa·ter
bac·te·ri·a
(*sing.* bac·te·ri·um)
bac·te·ri·ol·o·gist
bac·te·ri·ol·o·gy
badge
badged badg·ing
badg·er
bad·i·nage
·naged ·nag·ing
baf·fle
·fled ·fling
bag
bagged bag·ging
bag·a·telle
ba·gel
bag·ful
·fuls
bag·gage
bag·gy
·gi·er ·gi·est
Ba·hai
Ba·ha·mas
bail
(*money;* SEE
bale)
bai·liff
bai·li·wick
bait·ed
(*lured;* SEE
bated)
bal·ance
·anced ·anc·ing
bal·ance·a·ble
bal·co·ny
·nies
bal·der·dash
bald·faced
bale
baled bal·ing
(*bundle;* SEE
bail)
bale·ful
balk·y
·i·er ·i·est
ball
bal·lad
bal·lad·eer

bal·last
ball bear·ing
bal·let
bal·lis·tic
bal·lot
ball·room
balm·y
·i·er ·i·est
bal·sa
bal·sam
Bal·tic
Bal·ti·more
bal·us·ter
bal·us·trade
bam·boo
bam·boo·zle
·zled ·zling
ba·nal
ba·nal·i·ty
·ties
band·age
·aged ·ag·ing
band-aid *or*
band·aid
ban·dit
band·mas·ter
band saw
band·stand
band·wag·on
ban·dy
·died
·dy·ing
bane·ful
ban·gle
bang-up
ban·ish
ban·is·ter
or ban·nis·ter
bank·book
bank note
bank·roll
bank·rupt
bank·rupt·cy
·cies
ban·ner
banns *or* bans
(*marriage notice*)
ban·quet
ban·tam
ban·tam·weight

ban·ter
bap·tism
bap·tis·mal
bap·tize
·tized
·tiz·ing
bar·bar·i·an
bar·bar·ic
bar·ba·rism
bar·bar·i·ty
·ties
bar·ba·rous
bar·ber
bar·ber·shop
bare
bared bar·ing
(*uncover;* SEE bear)
bare·back
bare·faced
bare·foot
bare·hand·ed
bare·head·ed
bare·leg·ged
bare·ly
bar·gain
barge
barged
barg·ing
bar·i·tone
bark·er
bar mitz·vah *or*
bar miz·vah
bar·na·cle
barn·storm
ba·rom·e·ter
bar·o·met·ric
bar·on
(*nobleman;* SEE
barren)
ba·roque
bar·racks
bar·rage
·raged ·rag·ing
barred
bar·rel
·reled *or* ·relled
·rel·ing *or*
·rel·ling
bar·ren
(*empty;* SEE baron)

bar·ri·cade
·cad·ed ·cad·ing
bar·ri·er
bar·ring
bar·ris·ter
bar·room
bar·row
bar·tend·er
bar·ter
bas·al
base
bas·es
based bas·ing
(*foundation; vile;*
SEE bass)
base·ball
base·board
base·burn·er
base·ly
base·ment
base·ness
bas·es
(*pl. of* base)
ba·ses
(*pl. of* basis)
bash·ful
bas·ic
ba·sil·i·ca
ba·sin
ba·sis
·ses
bas·ket
bas-re·lief
bass
(*singer;* SEE base)
bass
(*fish*)
bass horn
bas·soon
bass viol
bass·wood
bas·tille
bas·tion
batch
bate
bat·ed bat·ing
bat·ed
(*held in;* SEE baited)
bathe
bathed bath·ing
bath·er

bath·house
ba·thos
bath·y·sphere
ba·tik
ba·tiste
bat mitz·vah *or*
bat miz·vah
ba·ton
bat·tal·ion
bat·ten
bat·ter
bat·ter·y
·ies
bat·ting
bat·tle
·tled ·tling
bat·tle·field
bat·tle·ground
bat·tle·ment
bat·tle-scarred
bat·tle·ship
bau·ble
baud
bawd·y
·i·er ·i·est
bay·o·net
·net·ed *or* ·net·ted
·ne·ting
or ·net·ting
bay·ou
ba·zaar
(*market,* SEE
bizarre)
beach
(*shore;* SEE
beech)
beach·comb·er
beach·head
bea·con
bead·y
·i·er ·i·est
bea·gle
beak·er
bear
(*animal;* SEE
bare)
bear
bore, borne *or*
born,
bear·ing
(*carry;* SEE bare)

bear·a·ble
bear·a·bly
beard·ed
bear·er
bear·ish
beast·ly
·li·er ·li·est
beat
beat beat·en
beat·ing
be·a·tif·ic
be·at·i·fi·ca·tion
be·at·i·fy
·fied ·fy·ing
be·at·i·tude
beau
beaus *or* beaux
(*sweetheart;* SEE bow)
beau·ti·ful
beau·ti·fy
·fied ·fy·ing
beau·ty
·ties
bea·ver·board
be·calm
be·cause
beck·on
be·come
·came ·come
·com·ing
be·dev·il
·iled *or* ·illed
·il·ing *or* ·il·ling
bed·fast
bed·fel·low
bed·lam
Bed·ou·in
be·drag·gle
·gled ·gling
bed·rock
bed·room
beech
(*tree;* SEE beach)
Bee·tho·ven
bee·tle
be·fall
·fell ·fall·en
·fall·ing
be·fit
·fit·ted ·fit·ting

be·fog
·fogged
·fog·ging
be·fore·hand
be·friend
be·get
·got, ·got·ten *or*
·got, ·get·ting
beg·gar
be·gin
·gan ·gun
·gin·ning
be·gin·ner
be·gird
·girt *or* ·gird·ed,
·girt, ·gird·ing
be·gone
be·grudge
·grudged
·grudg·ing
be·guile
·guiled
·guil·ing
be·half
be·have
·haved ·hav·ing
be·hav·ior
be·he·moth
be·hest
be·hold
·held ·hold·ing
be·hoove
·hooved
·hoov·ing
beige
be·la·bor
be·lat·ed
be·lay
·layed ·lay·ing
belch
be·lea·guer
bel·fry
·fries
be·lie
·lied ·ly·ing
be·lief
be·liev·a·bil·i·ty
be·liev·a·ble
be·liev·a·bly
be·lieve
·lieved ·liev·ing

bell·boy
(*errand boy*)
bell buoy
(*signal bell*)
belles-let·tres
bel·li·cose
bel·li·cos·i·ty
bel·lig·er·ence
bel·lig·er·en·cy
bel·lig·er·ent
bell-like
bel·low
bell·weth·er
be·long
be·lov·ed
be·low
be·mire
·mired
·mir·ing
be·moan
be·neath
ben·e·dict
Ben·e·dic·tine
ben·e·dic·tion
ben·e·fac·tor
ben·e·fice
be·nef·i·cence
be·nef·i·cent
ben·e·fi·cial
ben·e·fi·ci·ar·y
·ar·ies
ben·e·fit
·fit·ed ·fit·ing
be·nev·o·lence
be·nev·o·lent
be·night·ed
be·nign
be·numb
ben·zene
(*in chemistry*)
ben·zine
(*cleaning fluid*)
be·queath
·queathed
·queath·ing
be·quest
be·rate
·rat·ed ·rat·ing

be·reave
·reaved *or* ·reft
·reav·ing
be·ret
Berke·ley
Ber·mu·da
ber·serk
berth
(*bed;* SEE birth)
ber·yl
be·ryl·li·um
be·seech
·sought *or*
·seeched
·seech·ing
be·set
·set ·set·ting
be·side
be·sides
be·siege
·sieged ·sieg·ing
be·smirch
Bes·se·mer
be·stow
best seller
be·tray·al
be·troth
be·troth·al
be·trothed
bet·ter
(*compar. of* good)
bet·tor *or* ·ter
(*one who bets*)
be·tween
bev·el
·eled *or* ·elled
·el·ing *or* ·el·ling
bev·er·age
bev·y
·ies
be·wail
be·ware
·wared ·war·ing
be·wil·dered
be·witch
be·yond
bi·an·nu·al
bi·as
·ased *or* ·assed
·as·ing *or* ·as·sing
Bi·ble

Bib·li·cal
bib·li·og·ra·phy
·phies
bib·li·o·phile
bi·car·bon·ate
bi·cen·te·nar·y
·ies
bi·cen·ten·ni·al
bi·ceps
·ceps *or* ·ceps·es
bick·er
bi·cus·pid
bi·cy·cle
·cled ·cling
bi·cy·clist
bid
bade *or* bid,
bid·den *or* bid,
bid·ding
bid·da·ble
bi·en·ni·al
bi·en·ni·al·ly
bi·fo·cals
bi·fur·cate
·cat·ed ·cat·ing
big·a·my
·mies
big·heart·ed
big·ot
big·ot·ed
big·ot·ry
·ries
bi·jou
·joux
bi·lat·er·al
bilge
bi·lin·gual
bil·ious
bill·board
bil·let
bil·let-doux
bil·lets-doux
bill·fold
bill·head
bil·liards
bill·ing
bil·lion
bil·lion·aire
bi·man·u·al
bi·month·ly

bi·na·ry
bind
bound bind·ing
bind·er
bind·er·y
·ies
binge
bin·oc·u·lars
bi·no·mi·al
bi·o·chem·ist
bi·o·chem·is·try
bi·og·ra·pher
bi·o·graph·i·cal
bi·og·ra·phy
·phies
bi·o·log·i·cal
bi·ol·o·gy
bi·o·phys·ics
bi·op·sy
·sies
bi·par·ti·san
bi·par·tite
bi·pro·pel·lant
bi·quar·ter·ly
bi·ra·cial
birth
(*being born;* SEE berth)
birth·day
birth·mark
birth·place
birth·rate
birth·right
bis·cuit
bi·sect
bi·sec·tion
bi·sec·tor
bish·op
bis·muth
bi·son
bisque
bis·tro
bite
bit, bit·ten *or*
bit, bit·ing
bit·ter
bi·tu·men
bi·tu·mi·nous
bi·va·lent
bi·valve

biv·ou·ac
·acked ·ack·ing
bi·week·ly
·lies
bi·year·ly
bi·zarre
(*odd;* SEE bazaar)
black·board
black·en
black·list
black·mail
black·out
blam·a·ble *or*
blame·a·ble
blame·wor·thy
blanc·mange
blan·dish
blan·ket
blare
blared blar·ing
bla·sé
blas·pheme
·phemed
·phem·ing
blas·phe·mous
blas·phe·my
·mies
blast·off *or*
blast-off
bla·tan·cy
·cies
bla·tant
blaze
blazed blaz·ing
bleach·ers
bleak·ly
blear·i·ness
blear·y
·i·er ·i·est
bleed
bled bleed·ing
blem·ish
blend
blend·ed *or* blent
blend·ing
blend·er
bless
blessed *or* blest
bless·ing
bless·ed·ness
blight

blind·fold
bliss·ful
blithe
blithe·some
blitz·krieg
bliz·zard
bloc
(*group*)
block
(*solid piece*)
block·ade
·ad·ed
·ad·ing
block·bust·ing
block·head
block·house
blood·less
blood·mo·bile
blood pressure
blood·shot
blood·stream
blood vessel
blood·y
·i·er ·i·est
·ied ·y·ing
blot
blot·ted blot·ting
blot·ter
blow
blew blown
blow·ing
blow·out
blow·torch
blow·up
bludg·eon
blue
blued, blu·ing *or*
blue·ing
blue-blood·ed
blue book
blue-chip
blue-col·lar
blue law
blue-pen·cil
·ciled *or* ·cilled
·cil·ing *or* ·cil·ling
blue·print
blue·stock·ing
bluff·er

blu·ing *or*
blue·ing
blun·der
blunt·ly
blur
blurred
blur·ring
blur·ri·ness
blur·ry
·ri·er ·ri·est
blus·ter
blus·ter·y
bo·a
boar
(*hog;* SEE bore)
board·er
board foot
board feet
board·ing·house
board·walk
boast·ful
boat·swain
bode
bod·ed bod·ing
bod·ied
bod·i·ly
bod·y
·ies
bod·y·guard
bog·gy
·gi·er ·gi·est
bo·gus
bois·ter·ous
bold·face
bold·faced
boll
boll weevil
bol·ster
bom·bard
bom·bar·dier
bom·bast
bom·bas·tic
bomb·proof
bomb·sight
bo·na fi·de
bo·nan·za
bond·age
bond·ed
bonds·man
·men

bone-dry
bon·fire
bon·go
·gos
bon·i·fi·ca·tion
bon·i·ness
bon mot
bons mots
bo·nus
bon vi·vant
bons vi·vants
bon voy·age
bon·y
·i·er ·i·est
book·bind·er
book·case
book club
book·end
book·ish
book·keep·er
book·let
book·mak·er
book·mark
book·mo·bile
book·sell·er
book·shelf
·shelves
book·store
book·worm
boom·er·ang
boon·docks
boon·dog·gle
·gled ·gling
boor·ish
boost·er
boot·black
boot·leg
·legged
·leg·ging
boot·strap
bo·rax
bor·der
bor·der·line
bore
(*dull person;*
SEE boar)
bore
bored bor·ing
bore·dom

born
(*brought into life*)
borne
(*participle of* bear)
bor·ough
(*town;* SEE burrow)
bor·row
boss·y
·i·er ·i·est
bo·tan·i·cal
bot·a·nist
bot·a·ny
botch
both·er·some
bot·tle·neck
bot·tom
bot·u·lism
bough
(*tree branch;* SEE bow)
bought
bouil·la·baisse
bouil·lon
(*broth;* SEE bullion)
boul·der
boul·e·vard
bound·a·ry
·ries
bound·less
boun·te·ous
boun·ti·ful
boun·ty
·ties
bour·bon
bour·geois
bour·geoi·sie
bourse
bou·tique
bow
(*curve;* SEE beau)
bow
(*of a ship;* SEE bough)
bowd·ler·ize
·ized ·iz·ing
bow·el
bow·er
bow·string
bow tie
box·car
box·er
box office

box·wood
boy·cott
brace
braced brac·ing
brack·et
brack·ish
brag
bragged
brag·ging
brag·gart
Brah·ma
braid
Braille
brain·child
brain·i·ness
brain·pow·er
brain·storm
brain·wash
brain wave
brain·y
·i·er ·i·est
branch·ing
brand-new
bran·dy
·dies
·died ·dy·ing
bras·siere
brass·i·ness
brass·ware
brass-wind *adj.*
brass winds
brass·y
·i·er ·i·est
bra·va·do
brave
braved brav·ing
brave·ly
brav·er·y
bra·vo
·vos
bra·zen
bra·zen·ness
Bra·zil
breach
(*a gap;* SEE
breech)
breadth
(*width;* SEE breath)
bread·win·ner

break·a·ble
break·age
break·down
break-e·ven
break·through
break·up
breast·work
breath
(*air;* SEE breadth)
breathe
breathed
breath·ing
breath·tak·ing
breech
(*rear;* SEE breach)
breed
bred breed·ing
breeze·way
breez·i·ly
breez·i·ness
breez·y
·i·er ·i·est
breth·ren
bre·vi·ar·y
·ies
brev·i·ty
brew·er·y
·ies
brib·a·ble
bribe
bribed brib·ing
brib·er·y
·ies
brick·lay·ing
brick·work
brick·yard
brid·al
(*wedding;* SEE bridle)
bridge
bridged
bridg·ing
bridge·a·ble
bridge·head
bridge·work
bri·dle
(*harness;* SEE bridal)
brief·case
bri·er *or* bri·ar
bri·gade
brig·a·dier

brig·and
brig·an·tine
bright·en
bril·liance
bril·liant
bring
brought
bring·ing
brink·man·ship
brisk·ly
bris·tle
·tled ·tling
Bris·tol board
Brit·ain
(*place*)
Brit·i·cism
Brit·on
(*person*)
broach
(*open;* SEE brooch)
broad·cast
·cast *or* ·cast·ed
·cast·ing
broad·cloth
broad·loom
broad·mind·ed
broad·side
bro·chure
bro·gan
brogue
broil·er
bro·ken-down
bro·ker
bro·ker·age
bro·mide
bro·mid·ic
bro·mine
bro·mo selt·zer
bron·chi·al
bron·chi·tis
brooch
(*pin;* SEE broach)
broth·er-in-law
broth·ers-in-law
brought
brou·ha·ha
brow·beat
·beat ·beat·en
·beat·ing

brown·out
brown·stone
browse
browsed
brows·ing
brush·work
brusque
brusque·ly
brusque·ness
bru·tal
bru·tal·i·ty
·ties
bru·tal·ize
·ized ·iz·ing
brut·ish
bu·bon·ic
buck·le
·led ·ling
buck-pass·er
buck·ram
bu·col·ic
Bud·dha
Bud·dhism
budge
budged budg·ing
budg·et
budg·et·ar·y
buff·er
buf·fet
bug·bear
build
built build·ing
build·up *or*
build-up
built-in
built-up
bul·bous
bulge
bulged
bulg·ing
bulk·i·ness
bulk·y
·i·er ·i·est
bull·doze
·dozed
·doz·ing
bull·doz·er
bul·let
bul·le·tin
bull·head·ed

bul·lion
(*gold;* SEE bouillon)
bull·ish
bull·ock
bull·pen
bull's-eye
bum·bling
bump·er
bump·kin
bump·tious
bump·y
·i·er ·i·est
bun·dle
·dled ·dling
bun·ga·low
bun·gle
·gled ·gling
Bun·sen burner
buoy
buoy·an·cy
buoy·ant
bur·den·some
bu·reau
·reaus *or* ·reaux
bu·reau·cra·cy
·cies
bu·reau·crat
bu·reau·crat·ic
bu·reau·crat·i·cal·ly
bur·geon
bur·glar
bur·gla·rize
·rized ·riz·ing
bur·gla·ry
·ries
Bur·gun·dy
bur·i·al
bur·lap
bur·lesque
·lesqued
·lesqu·ing
bur·ley (*tobacco*)
bur·ly
·li·er ·li·est
(*muscular*)
burn
burned *or* burnt
burn·ing
burn·a·ble

bur·nish
bur·noose
burn·out
bur·row
(*hole;* SEE
borough)
bur·sa
·sae *or* ·sas
bur·sar
bur·si·tis
burst
burst burst·ing
bush·el·bas·ket
bush·rang·er
bush·whack·er
bush·y
·i·er ·i·est
bus·i·ly
busi·ness
busi·ness·like
busi·ness·man
·men
busi·ness·wom·an
·wom·en
bus·kin
bus·man
·men
bus·tle
·tled ·tling
bus·y
·i·er ·i·est
·ied ·y·ing
bus·y·bod·y
·ies
bus·y·ness
butch·er·y
but·ler
butte
but·ton-down
but·ton·hole
·holed ·hol·ing
but·tress
buy·er
buy·ing
buz·zer
by·gone
by·law
by·line
by·pass
by·path
by·play
by·prod·uct *or*
by-prod·uct
by·road
by·stand·er
byte
by·way
by·word

C

ca·bal
·balled ·bal·ling
cab·i·net
ca·ble·gram
ca·boose
cab·ri·o·let
cache
cached cach·ing
ca·chet
ca·cog·ra·phy
ca·coph·o·nous
ca·coph·o·ny
ca·dav·er
ca·dav·er·ous
ca·dence
ca·det
cad·mi·um
ca·dre
Cae·sar·e·an
or ·i·an
ca·fé *or* ca·fe
caf·e·te·ri·a
caf·fe·ine *or* ·in
cais·son
ca·jole
·joled ·jol·ing
ca·lam·i·tous
ca·lam·i·ty
·ties
cal·ci·fi·ca·tion
cal·ci·fy
·fied ·fy·ing
cal·ci·um
cal·cu·la·ble
cal·cu·late
·lat·ed ·lat·ing
cal·cu·la·tion
cal·cu·la·tor
cal·cu·lus
·li *or* ·lus·es
cal·en·dar
(*table of dates*)
cal·en·der
(*roller*)
ca·les·cent
cal·i·ber *or* ·bre
cal·i·brate
·brat·ed ·brat·ing
cal·i·bra·tion
Cal·i·for·ni·a
cal·i·pers
ca·liph
cal·is·then·ics
call·board
cal·lig·ra·phy
cal·lous *adj.*
call-up
cal·lus *n.*
·lus·es
calm·ly
ca·lor·ic
cal·o·rie *or* ·ry
·ries
cal·o·rim·e·ter
cal·u·met
ca·lum·ni·ate
·at·ed ·at·ing
ca·lum·ni·ous
cal·um·ny
·nies
Cal·va·ry
(*Biblical place;*
SEE cavalry)
Cal·vin·ism
ca·ma·ra·de·rie
cam·ber
cam·bist
cam·bric
Cam·bridge
Cam·em·bert
cam·e·o
·os
cam·er·a
cam·er·a-shy
cam·ou·flage
·flaged ·flag·ing
cam·paign
cam·pus
Ca·naan
Can·a·da
Ca·na·di·an
ca·na·pé
(*food;* SEE
canopy)
ca·nard
ca·nas·ta
can·cel
·celed *or* ·celled
·cel·ing *or*
·cel·ling
can·cel·la·tion
can·cer
can·cer·ous
can·de·la·bra
·bras
can·des·cence
can·des·cent
can·did
can·di·da·cy
·cies
can·di·date
can·dle·light
can·dle·pow·er
can·dor
ca·nine
can·is·ter
can·na·bis
can·ni·ness
can·not
can·ny
·ni·er ·ni·est
can·on
(*law;* SEE
canyon)
ca·non·i·cal
can·on·ize
·ized ·iz·ing
can·o·py
·pies
(*hood;* SEE
canapé)
can·ta·loupe
or ·loup
can·tan·ker·ous
can·ter
can·ti·le·ver
can·ton
can·ton·ment

can·vas
(*cloth*)
can·vass
(*to solicit*)
can·yon *or* ca·ñon
(*valley;* SEE canon)
ca·pa·bil·i·ty
·ties
ca·pa·ble
ca·pa·bly
ca·pa·cious
ca·pac·i·ty
·ties
ca·per
cap·il·lar·y
·ies
cap·i·tal
(*city; chief;* SEE capitol)
cap·i·tal·ism
cap·i·tal·ist
cap·i·tal·is·tic
cap·i·tal·i·za·tion
cap·i·tal·ize
·ized ·iz·ing
cap·i·ta·tion
cap·i·tol
(*building;* SEE capital)
ca·pit·u·late
·lat·ed ·lat·ing
ca·pit·u·la·tion
ca·price
ca·pri·cious
cap·ri·ole
·oled ·ol·ing
cap·size
·sized ·siz·ing
cap·su·lar
cap·sule
·suled ·sul·ing
cap·sul·ize
·ized ·iz·ing
cap·tain
cap·tain·cy
·cies
cap·tion
cap·ti·vate
·vat·ed ·vat·ing
ca·rafe

car·at
(*weight;* SEE caret)
car·a·van
car·bine
car·bo·hy·drate
car·bol·ic
car·bon
car·bo·na·ceous
car·bon·ate
·at·ed ·at·ing
car·bon·a·tion
car·bon-date
-dat·ed -dat·ing
car·bon·ize
·ized ·iz·ing
car·bu·re·tor
car·cin·o·gen
car·ci·no·ma
card·board
card-car·ry·ing
car·di·ac
car·di·gan
car·di·nal
car·di·o·gram
car·di·o·graph
ca·reer
care·free
care·ful
care·less
car·et
(*insert mark;* SEE carat)
care·tak·er
car·fare
car·go
·goes *or* ·gos
Car·ib·be·an
car·i·ca·ture
·tured ·tur·ing
car·i·ca·tur·ist
car·ies
(*decay;* SEE carries)
car·il·lon
car·load
car·nage
car·nal
car·na·tion
car·net

car·ni·val
Car·o·li·nas
Car·o·lin·i·an
car·o·tene *or* ·tin
ca·rot·id
car·pen·ter
car·pen·try
car·pet
car·pet·bag·ger
car·pet·ing
carp·ing
car·port
car·ri·age
car·ri·er
car·ries
(*form of* carry; SEE caries)
car·ri·on
car·ry
·ried ·ry·ing
car·ry·all
car·ry·ing
car·ry·out
car·ry-o·ver
cart·age
carte blanche
cartes blanches
car·tel
car·ti·lage
car·to·gram
car·tog·ra·phy
car·ton
car·toon·ist
car·tridge
carve
carved carv·ing
car·wash
car·y·at·id
·ids *or* ·i·des
ca·sa·ba
or cas·sa·ba
cas·bah
cas·cade
·cad·ed ·cad·ing
cas·car·a
case
cased cas·ing
case·book
case·hard·ened
ca·se·in

case·load
case·mate
case·ment
case·work·er
cash-and-car·ry
cash·book
cash·ew
cash·ier
cash·mere
cas·ing
ca·si·no
·nos
cas·ket
cas·sa·va
cas·se·role
cash·ier
cas·sette
cas·sock
cast
cast cast·ing
caste
(*social class*)
cast·er
cas·ti·gate
·gat·ed
·gat·ing
cast-i·ron
cas·u·al
cas·u·al·ty
·ties
cas·u·ist
cas·u·is·tic
cas·u·ist·ry
cat·a·clysm
cat·a·comb
cat·a·lep·tic
cat·a·log *or*
·logue
·loged *or*
·logued
·log·ing *or*
·logu·ing
cat·a·log·er *or*
·logu·er
ca·tal·y·sis
·ses
cat·a·lyst
cat·a·pult
ca·tas·tro·phe
cat·a·stroph·ic

cat·a·to·ni·a
cat·e·gor·i·cal
cat·e·go·rize
 ·rized ·riz·ing
cat·e·go·ry
 ·ries
ca·ter
ca·ter·er
ca·thar·sis
ca·thar·tic
ca·the·dral
cath·ode
cath·o·lic
Ca·thol·i·cism
Cau·ca·sian
Cau·ca·soid
cau·cus
caul·dron
caulk
caus·a·ble
caus·al
cau·sal·i·ty
 ·ties
cau·sa·tion
caus·a·tive
cause
 caused caus·ing
cause·way
caus·tic
cau·ter·i·za·tion
cau·ter·ize
 ·ized ·iz·ing
cau·tion
cau·tion·ar·y
cau·tious
cav·al·cade
cav·a·lier
cav·al·ry
 ·ries
 (*troops;* SEE Calvary)
ca·ve·at emp·tor
cav·i·ar
cav·il
 ·iled *or* ·illed
 ·il·ing *or* ·il·ling
cav·i·ty
 ·ties
ca·vort
cay·enne

cease
 ceased ceas·ing
cease-fire
cease·less
cede
 ced·ed ced·ing
ceil·ing
cel·e·brant
cel·e·brate
 ·brat·ed ·brat·ing
cel·e·bra·tion
cel·e·bra·tor
ce·leb·ri·ty
 ·ties
cel·lo·phane
cel·lu·lar
cel·lu·loid
cel·lu·lose
Cel·o·tex
Cel·si·us
ce·ment
cem·e·ter·y
 ·ies
Ce·no·zo·ic
cen·ser
 (*incense box*)
cen·sor
 ·sored ·sor·ing
 (*prohibiter*)
cen·so·ri·al
cen·so·ri·ous
cen·sor·ship
cen·sur·a·ble
cen·sure
 ·sured ·sur·ing
 (*blame*)
cen·sus
cen·taur
cen·ta·vo
cen·te·nar·i·an
cen·te·nar·y
cen·ten·ni·al
cen·ter
cen·tered
cen·ti·grade
cen·ti·gram
cen·ti·li·ter
cen·time
cen·ti·me·ter
cen·ti·pede

cen·tral
cen·tral·i·za·tion
cen·tral·ize
 ·ized ·iz·ing
cen·trif·u·gal
cen·tri·fuge
cen·trist
cen·tu·ri·on
cen·tu·ry
 ·ries
cer·e·bel·lum
 ·lums *or* ·la
cer·e·bral
cer·e·brum
 ·brums *or* ·bra
cer·e·mo·ni·al
cer·e·mo·ni·al·ly
cer·e·mo·ni·ous
cer·e·mo·ny
 ·nies
cer·tain
cer·tain·ly
cer·tain·ty
 ·ties
cer·ti·fi·a·ble
cer·ti·fi·a·bly
cer·tif·i·cate
cer·ti·fi·ca·tion
cer·ti·fy
 ·fied ·fy·ing
cer·ti·tude
ce·ru·men
ces·sa·tion
ces·sion
 (*a giving up;* SEE session)
chair·man
 ·men
chair·wom·an
 ·wom·en
chal·lenge
 ·lenged ·leng·ing
chal·leng·er
chal·lis
cham·ber
cham·ber·lain
cham·bray
cham·ois
 ·ois
 ·oised ·ois·ing
cham·pagne (*wine*)

cham·paign
 (*open field*)
cham·pi·on
chance
 chanced
 chanc·ing
chan·cel
chan·cel·ler·y
 ·ies
chan·cel·lor
chan·cer·y
 ·ies
chanc·y
 ·i·er ·i·est
chan·de·lier
change·a·bil·i·ty
change·a·ble
change·ful
change·less
change·o·ver
change-up
chan·nel
 ·neled *or* ·nelled
 ·nel·ing *or*
 ·nel·ling
cha·os
cha·ot·ic
chap·ar·ral
chap·lain
chap·ter
char·ac·ter
char·ac·ter·is·tic
char·ac·ter·ize
 ·ized ·iz·ing
cha·rade
charge
 charged
 charg·ing
charge·a·ble
charg·er
char·i·ot
cha·ris·ma
char·is·mat·ic
char·i·ta·ble
char·i·ty
 ·ties
char·la·tan
char·ter
chasm

chas·sis
·sis
chas·tise
·tised ·tis·ing
chas·tise·ment
châ·teau
·teaux *or* ·teaus
chat·tel
chat·ty
·ti·er ·ti·est
chauf·fer
(*stove*)
chauf·feur
(*driver*)
chau·vin·ism
chau·vin·ist
chau·vin·is·tic
cheap
cheap·en
cheat·er
check·book
check·ered
check·list *or*
check list
check·out *or*
check out
check·point
check·room
check·up
cheer·ful
cheer·less
cheer·y
·i·er ·i·est
chem·i·cal
chem·ist
chem·is·try
·tries
chem·ur·gy
cher·ish
Cher·o·kee
che·root
cher·vil
chess·board
chev·i·ot
chev·ron
Chi·an·ti
chi·a·ro·scu·ro
·ros

chic
chic·quer
chic·quest
chi·can·er·y
chide
chid·ed *or* chid
or chid·den
chid·ing
chief·ly
chief·tain
child·hood
child·ish
child·like
chil·i
·ies
chill·i·ness
chill·y
·i·er ·i·est
chi·me·ra
chi·mer·i·cal
Chi·nese
chi·no
chi·rog·ra·phy
chi·rop·o·dist
chi·rop·o·dy
chi·ro·prac·tic
chi·ro·prac·tor
chis·el
·eled *or* ·elled
·el·ing *or* ·el·ling
chis·el·er *or*
chis·el·ler
chiv·al·rous
chiv·al·ry
chlo·ri·nate
·nat·ed ·nat·ing
chlo·ri·na·tion
chlo·rine
chlo·ro·form
chlo·ro·phyll
or ·phyl
choc·o·late
choice
choic·er choic·est
chol·er·a
chol·er·ic
cho·les·ter·ol
choose
chose cho·sen
choos·ing

cho·ral
(*of a chorus*)
cho·rale *or* ·ral
(*hymn tune*)
chord
(*music;* SEE cord)
cho·re·a
chor·e·og·ra·pher
chor·e·o·graph·ic
chor·e·o·graph·i·cal·ly
chor·e·og·ra·phy
chor·tle
·tled ·tling
cho·rus
cho·sen
Chris·tian
Chris·ti·an·i·ty
Christ·like
Christ·mas
chro·mat·ic
chro·ma·tin
chrome
chro·mic
chro·mi·um
chro·mo·some
chron·ic
chron·i·cle
·cled
·cling
chron·o·log·i·cal
chro·nol·o·gy
chro·nom·e·ter
chro·nom·e·try
chrys·a·lis
chrys·an·the·mum
churl·ish
churn
chut·ney
ci·bo·ri·um
·ri·a
ci·ca·da
·das *or* ·dae
cic·e·ly
Cic·er·o
cig·a·rette
or ·ret
cig·a·ril·lo
·los
Cin·cin·nat·i

cinc·ture
·tured ·tur·ing
cin·e·ma
cin·e·mat·o·graph
cin·e·rar·i·um
·rar·i·a
cin·er·a·tor
ci·pher
cir·ca
cir·cle
·cled ·cling
cir·clet
cir·cuit
cir·cu·i·tous
cir·cuit·ry
cir·cu·lar
cir·cu·lar·i·za·tion
cir·cu·lar·ize
·ized ·iz·ing
cir·cu·late
·lat·ed ·lat·ing
cir·cu·la·tion
cir·cu·la·to·ry
cir·cum·fer·ence
cir·cum·flex
cir·cum·lo·cu·tion
cir·cum·nav·i·gate
·gat·ed ·gat·ing
cir·cum·scribe
·scribed ·scrib·ing
cir·cum·scrip·tion
cir·cum·spect
cir·cum·spec·tion
cir·cum·stance
cir·cum·stan·tial
cir·cum·stan·ti·ate
·at·ed ·at·ing
cir·cum·vent
cir·cum·ven·tion
cir·rho·sis
cis·tern
cit·a·del
ci·ta·tion
cite
cit·ed cit·ing
(*mention;* SEE
sight, site)
cit·i·fied
cit·i·zen
cit·i·zen·ry

cit·i·zen·ship
cit·rate
cit·ric
cit·ron
cit·ron·el·la
cit·rous *adj.*
cit·rus *n.*
civ·ic
civ·il
ci·vil·ian
ci·vil·i·ty
·ties
civ·i·li·za·tion
civ·i·lize
·lized ·liz·ing
claim·ant
clair·voy·ance
clair·voy·ant
clam·or
clam·or·ous
clan·des·tine
clan·des·tine·ly
clan·nish
clans·man
claque
clar·et
clar·i·fi·ca·tion
clar·i·fi·er
clar·i·fy
·fied ·fy·ing
clar·i·net
clar·i·on
clar·i·ty
clas·sic
clas·si·cal
clas·si·cism
clas·si·cist
clas·si·fi·a·ble
clas·si·fi·ca·tion
clas·si·fi·er
clas·si·fy
·fied ·fy·ing
class·mate
class·room
clat·ter
clause
claus·tro·pho·bi·a
clav·i·cle
cla·vier
clean·hand·ed
clean·li·ness
clean·ly
·li·er ·li·est
clean·ness
cleanse
cleansed
cleans·ing
cleans·er
clean·up
clear·ance
clear·ing·house
clem·en·cy
clem·ent
clere·sto·ry
·ries
cler·ic
cler·i·cal
cler·i·cal·ism
clev·er
clew
cli·ché
cli·ent
cli·en·tele
cli·mac·ter·ic
cli·mac·tic
(*of a climax*)
cli·mate
cli·mat·ic (*of climate*)
cli·ma·tol·o·gy
cli·max
climb·er
clinch·er
cling
clung cling·ing
clin·ic
clin·i·cal
cli·ni·cian
clink·er
cli·nom·e·ter
clip·board
clip·per
clique
cloak·room
clock·wise
clock·work
cloi·son·né
clois·ter
close
closed clos·ing
close
clos·er clos·est
closed-end
close·ly
close·mouthed
clos·et
close-up
clo·sure
clot
clot·ted
clot·ting
cloth *n.*
clothe *v.*
clothed *or* clad
cloth·ing
cloth·ier
cloth·ing
cloud·y
·i·er ·i·est
cloy·ing·ly
clue
clued clu·ing
clum·si·ly
clum·si·ness
clum·sy
·si·er ·si·est
clus·ter
clut·ter
coach·man
co·ad·ju·tor
co·ag·u·la·ble
co·ag·u·late
·lat·ed ·lat·ing
co·ag·u·la·tion
co·a·lesce
·lesced ·lesc·ing
co·a·les·cence
co·a·les·cent
co·a·li·tion
coarse
(*common;* SEE course)
coarse·grained
coars·en
coarse·ness
coast·al
coast·er
coast guard
coast·line
co·au·thor
co·ax·i·al
coax·ing·ly
co·balt
co·caine
or ·cain
coc·cus
coc·ci
coc·cyx
coc·cy·ges
cock·ney
·neys
cock·pit
cock·sure
cock·tail
cod·dle
·dled ·dling
code
cod·ed cod·ing
co·de·fend·ant
co·deine
cod·i·cil
cod·i·fi·ca·tion
cod·i·fy
·fied ·fy·ing
co·ed·u·ca·tion
co·ef·fi·cient
co·erce
·erced ·erc·ing
co·er·cion
co·er·cive
co·e·val
co·ex·ist·ence
cof·fer
co·gen·cy
co·gent
cog·i·tate
·tat·ed ·tat·ing
cog·i·ta·tion
cog·ni·tion
cog·ni·tive
cog·ni·zance
cog·ni·zant
co·hab·it
co·hab·i·ta·tion
co·heir
co·her·ence
co·her·ent
co·he·sion

co·he·sive·ness
co·hort
coin·age
co·in·cide
·cid·ed ·cid·ing
co·in·ci·dence
co·in·ci·dent
co·in·ci·den·tal
co·le·op·ter·ous
col·i·se·um
co·li·tis
col·lab·o·rate
·rat·ed ·rat·ing
col·lab·o·ra·tion
col·lab·o·ra·tor
col·lage
col·lapse
·lapsed ·laps·ing
col·laps·i·bil·i·ty
col·laps·i·ble
col·late
·lat·ed ·lat·ing
col·lat·er·al
col·la·tion
col·la·tor
col·league
col·lect·a·ble
or ·i·ble
col·lec·tion
col·lec·tive
col·lec·tive·ly
col·lec·tiv·ism
col·lec·tiv·is·tic
col·lec·tiv·i·ty
col·lec·tiv·ize
·ized ·iz·ing
col·lec·tor
col·lege
col·le·gi·an
col·le·giate
col·lide
·lid·ed ·lid·ing
col·lin·e·ar
col·li·sion
col·lo·ca·tion
col·lo·qui·al
col·lo·qui·al·ism
col·lo·qui·um
·qui·a *or* ·qui·ums

col·lo·quy
·quies
col·lude
·lud·ed ·lud·ing
col·lu·sion
col·lu·sive
co-lo·cate
·cat·ed ·cat·ing
co-lo·ca·tion
colo·nel
(*officer;* SEE
kernel)
co·lo·ni·al
col·o·nist
col·o·ni·za·tion
col·o·nize
·nized ·niz·ing
col·on·nade
col·o·ny
·nies
col·o·phon
Col·o·rad·o
col·o·rant
col·or·a·tion
col·ored
col·or·fast
col·or·ful
col·or·less
co·los·sal
Col·os·se·um
co·los·sus
·los·si *or*
·los·sus·es
Co·lum·bi·a
col·umn
co·lum·nar
col·um·nist
co·ma
(*unconscious,* SEE comma)
com·a·tose
com·bat
·bat·ed *or*
·bat·ted
·bat·ing *or*
·bat·ting
com·bat·ant
com·bat·ive
com·bin·a·ble
com·bi·na·tion
com·bine
·bined ·bin·ing

com·bus·ti·bil·i·ty
com·bus·ti·ble
com·bus·ti·bly
com·bus·tion
com·bus·tor
come·back
co·mes·ti·ble
com·fit
com·fort
com·fort·a·ble
com·fort·a·bly
com·fort·er
com·ma
(*punctuation*
mark; SEE coma)
com·mand
com·man·dant
com·man·deer
com·mand·er
com·mand·ment
com·mem·o·rate
·rat·ed
·rat·ing
com·mem·o·ra·tion
com·mem·o·ra·tive
com·mence
·menced
·menc·ing
com·mence·ment
com·mend
com·mend·a·ble
com·mend·a·bly
com·men·da·tion
com·mend·a·to·ry
com·men·su·ra·ble
com·men·su·ra·bly
com·men·su·rate
com·ment
com·men·tar·y
·ies
com·men·tate
·tat·ed ·tat·ing
com·men·ta·tor
com·merce
com·mer·cial
com·mer·cial·ism
com·mer·cial·i·za·tion
com·mer·cial·ize
·ized ·iz·ing

com·min·gle
·gled ·gling
com·mis·er·ate
·at·ed
·at·ing
com·mis·er·a·tion
com·mis·sar
com·mis·sar·y
·ies
com·mis·sion
com·mis·sion·er
com·mit
·mit·ted
·mit·ting
com·mit·ment
com·mit·ta·ble
com·mit·tal
com·mit·tee
com·mit·tee·man
com·mod·i·ty
·ties
com·mo·dore
com·mon·al·ty
·ties
com·mon·er
com·mon·ness
com·mon·place
com·mon·weal
com·mon·wealth
com·mo·tion
com·mu·nal
com·mu·nal·ism
com·mune′ *v.*
·muned
·mun·ing
com′mune *n.*
com·mu·ni·ca·ble
com·mu·ni·cant
com·mu·ni·cate
·cat·ed
·cat·ing
com·mu·ni·ca·tion
com·mu·ni·ca·tive
com·mu·ni·ca·tor
com·mun·ion
com·mu·ni·qué
com·mu·nism
com·mu·nist
com·mu·nis·tic

com·mu·ni·ty
·ties
com·mu·nize
·nized ·niz·ing
com·mut·a·ble
com·mu·tate
·tat·ed ·tat·ing
com·mu·ta·tion
com·mu·ta·tive
com·mu·ta·tor
com·mute
·mut·ed
·mut·ing
com·mut·er
com·pact
com·pan·ion
com·pan·ion·a·ble
com·pa·ny
·nies
com·pa·ra·ble
com·pa·ra·bly
com·par·a·tive
com·par·a·tive·ly
com·pare
·pared ·par·ing
com·par·i·son
com·part·ment
com·part·men·tal·ize
·ized ·iz·ing
com·pass
com·pas·sion
com·pas·sion·ate
com·pat·i·bil·i·ty
com·pat·i·ble
com·pat·i·bly
com·pa·tri·ot
com·pel
·pelled ·pel·ling
com·pen·di·ous
com·pen·di·um
·ums *or* ·a
com·pen·sa·ble
com·pen·sate
·sat·ed ·sat·ing
com·pen·sa·tion
com·pen·sa·tive
com·pen·sa·tor
com·pen·sa·to·ry
com·pete
·pet·ed ·pet·ing

com·pe·tence
com·pe·ten·cy
com·pe·tent
com·pe·ti·tion
com·pet·i·tive
com·pet·i·tor
com·pi·la·tion
com·pile
·piled ·pil·ing
com·pil·er
com·pla·cence
com·pla·cen·cy
com·pla·cent
(*smug;* SEE complaisant)
com·plain
com·plain·ant
com·plaint
com·plai·sance
com·plai·sant
(*obliging;* SEE complacent)
com·ple·ment
(*completing part;* SEE compliment)
com·ple·men·ta·ry
com·plete
·plet·ed ·plet·ing
com·ple·tion
com·plex
com·plex·ion
com·plex·i·ty
·ties
com·pli·ance
com·pli·ant
com·pli·cate
·cat·ed ·cat·ing
com·pli·ca·tion
com·plic·i·ty
com·pli·er
com·pli·ment
(*praise;* SEE complement)
com·pli·men·ta·ry
com·pli·men·tar·i·ly
com·ply
·plied ·ply·ing
com·po·nent
com·port·ment
com·pose
·posed ·pos·ing

com·pos·er
com·pos·ite
com·po·si·tion
com·pos·i·tor
com·pos men·tis
com·po·sure
com·pound
com·pre·hend
com·pre·hen·si·ble
com·pre·hen·sion
com·pre·hen·sive
com·press
com·pressed
com·pres·si·ble
com·pres·sion
com·pres·sor
com·prise
·prised ·pris·ing
com·pro·mise
·mised ·mis·ing
comp·trol·ler
com·pul·sion
com·pul·sive
com·pul·so·ri·ly
com·pul·so·ri·ness
com·pul·so·ry
com·punc·tion
com·punc·tious
com·put·a·ble
com·pu·ta·tion
com·pute
·put·ed ·put·ing
com·put·er
com·put·er·i·za·tion
com·put·er·ize
·ized ·iz·ing
com·rade
con·cat·e·na·tion
con·cave
con·cav·i·ty
·ties
con·ceal
con·cede
·ced·ed ·ced·ing
con·ceit
con·ceit·ed
con·ceiv·a·bil·i·ty
con·ceiv·a·ble
con·ceiv·a·bly

con·ceive
·ceived ·ceiv·ing
con·cen·trate
·trat·ed ·trat·ing
con·cen·tra·tion
con·cen·tric
con·cept
con·cep·tion
con·cep·tu·al
con·cep·tu·al·i·za·tion
con·cep·tu·al·ize
·ized ·iz·ing
con·cern
con·cerned
con·cern·ing
con·cert
con·cert·ed
con·cer·to
·tos *or* ·ti
con·ces·sion
con·ces·sion·aire
con·ci·erge
con·cil·i·ar
con·cil·i·ate
·at·ed ·at·ing
con·cil·i·a·tion
con·cil·i·a·to·ry
con·cise
con·cise·ly
con·cise·ness
con·clave
con·clude
·clud·ed
·clud·ing
con·clu·sion
con·clu·sive
con·coct
con·coc·tion
con·com·i·tance
con·com·i·tant
con·cord
con·cord·ance
con·cor·dat
con·course
con·crete
con·cre·tion
con·cur
·curred ·cur·ring
con·cur·rence

con·cur·rent
con·cus·sion
con·demn
con·dem·na·ble
con·dem·na·tion
con·dem·na·to·ry
con·den·sa·ble
 or ·si·ble
con·den·sa·tion
con·dense
 ·densed
 ·dens·ing
con·dens·er
con·de·scend
con·de·scend·ing
con·de·scen·sion
con·di·tion
con·di·tion·al
con·do·la·to·ry
con·dole
 ·doled ·dol·ing
con·do·lence
con·do·min·i·um
 ·i·ums or ·i·a
con·do·na·tion
con·done
 ·doned ·don·ing
con·du·cive
con·duct
con·duct·ance
con·duct·i·ble
con·duc·tion
con·duc·tiv·i·ty
con·duc·tor
con·duit
con·fab·u·late
 ·lat·ed ·lat·ing
con·fed·er·a·cy
 ·cies
con·fed·er·ate
 ·at·ed ·at·ing
con·fed·er·a·tion
con·fer
 ·ferred ·fer·ring
con·fer·ee
con·fer·ence
con·fer·en·tial
con·fer·ment
con·fer·ral
con·fess
con·fes·sion
con·fes·sion·al
con·fes·sor
con·fi·dant *n.*
con·fide
 ·fid·ed ·fid·ing
con·fi·dence
con·fi·dent *adj.*
con·fi·den·tial
con·fi·den·tial·ly
con·fig·u·ra·tion
con·fin·a·ble or
 ·fine·a·ble
con·fine
 ·fined ·fin·ing
con·fine·ment
con·firm
con·fir·mand
con·fir·ma·tion
con·firm·a·to·ry
con·firmed
con·fis·cate
 ·cat·ed ·cat·ing
con·fis·ca·tion
con·fla·gra·tion
con·flict
con·flic·tion
con·flu·ence
con·form
con·form·a·ble
con·form·a·bly
con·form·ance
con·for·ma·tion
con·form·ist
con·form·i·ty
con·found·ed
con·front
con·fron·ta·tion
con·fuse
 ·fused ·fus·ing
con·fu·sion
con·fu·ta·tion
con·fute
 ·fut·ed ·fut·ing
con·geal
con·gen·ial
con·ge·ni·al·i·ty
con·gen·ial·ly
con·gen·i·tal
con·gen·i·tal·ly
con·gest
con·ges·tion
con·glom·er·ate
 ·at·ed ·at·ing
con·glom·er·a·tion
con·grat·u·late
 ·lat·ed ·lat·ing
con·grat·u·la·tion
con·grat·u·la·to·ry
con·gre·gate
 ·gat·ed ·gat·ing
con·gre·ga·tion
con·gres·sion·al
con·gress·man
con·gru·ence
con·gru·ent
con·gru·i·ty
con·gru·ous
con·ic
con·i·cal
con·i·cal·ly
con·jec·tur·al
con·jec·ture
 ·tured ·tur·ing
con·join
con·joint·ly
con·ju·gal
con·ju·gate
 ·gat·ed ·gat·ing
con·ju·ga·tion
con·junc·tion
con·junc·tive
con·junc·ture
con·jure
 ·jured ·jur·ing
con·jur·er or ·or
con·nect
Con·nect·i·cut
con·nec·tion
con·nec·tive
con·nec·tor
 or ·nect·er
con·niv·ance
con·nive
 ·nived ·niv·ing
con·nois·seur
con·no·ta·tion
con·no·ta·tive
con·note
 ·not·ed ·not·ing
con·nu·bi·al
con·quer
con·quer·or
con·quest
con·science
con·sci·en·tious
con·scious
con·script
con·se·crate
 ·crat·ed ·crat·ing
con·se·cra·tion
con·sec·u·tive
con·sen·sus
con·sent
con·se·quence
con·se·quen·tial
con·se·quent·ly
con·ser·van·cy
con·ser·va·tion
con·ser·va·tism
con·ser·va·tive
con·ser·va·tor
con·ser·va·to·ry
 ·ries
con·serve
 ·served
 ·serv·ing
con·sid·er
con·sid·er·a·ble
con·sid·er·a·bly
con·sid·er·ate
con·sid·er·a·tion
con·sid·ered
con·sign
con·sign·a·ble
con·sign·ee
con·sign·ment
con·sign·or
 or ·er
con·sist
con·sis·ten·cy
 ·cies
con·sis·tent
con·sol·a·ble
con·so·la·tion
con·sol·a·to·ry
con·sole
 ·soled ·sol·ing

con·sole
con·sol·i·date
·dat·ed ·dat·ing
con·sol·i·da·tion
con·sol·i·da·tor
con·som·mé
con·so·nance
con·so·nant
con·sort
con·sor·ti·um
·ti·a
con·spic·u·ous
con·spir·a·cy
·cies
con·spir·a·tor
con·spire
·spired ·spir·ing
con·sta·ble
con·stab·u·lar·y
·ies
con·stan·cy
con·stant
con·stel·la·tion
con·ster·na·tion
con·stit·u·en·cy
·cies
con·stit·u·ent
con·sti·tute
·tut·ed ·tut·ing
con·sti·tu·tion
con·sti·tu·tion·al
con·sti·tu·tion·al·i·ty
con·sti·tu·tion·al·ly
con·strain
con·straint
con·strict
con·stric·tion
con·stric·tor
con·stru·a·ble
con·struct
con·struc·tion
con·struc·tive
con·struc·tor *or*
·struct·er
con·strue
·strued ·stru·ing
con·sul
con·sul·ar
con·sul·ate
con·sult
con·sult·ant
con·sul·ta·tion
con·sul·ta·tive
con·sum·a·ble
con·sume
·sumed
·sum·ing
con·sum·er
con·sum·mate
·mat·ed ·mat·ing
con·sum·mate·ly
con·sum·ma·tion
con·sum·ma·tor
con·sump·tion
con·sump·tive
con·tact
con·ta·gion
con·ta·gious
con·tain·er
con·tain·ment
con·tam·i·nant
con·tam·i·nate
·nat·ed ·nat·ing
con·tam·i·na·tion
con·tam·i·na·tor
con·tem·plate
·plat·ed
·plat·ing
con·tem·pla·tion
con·tem·pla·tive
con·tem·pla·tor
con·tem·po·ra·ne·ous
con·tem·po·rar·y
con·tempt
con·tempt·i·bil·i·ty
con·tempt·i·ble
con·tempt·i·bly
con·temp·tu·ous
con·tend
con·tent
con·tent·ed·ly
con·ten·tion
con·ten·tious
con·tent·ment
con·test
con·test·a·ble
con·test·ant
con·text
con·tex·tu·al
con·ti·gu·i·ty
con·tig·u·ous
con·ti·nence
con·ti·nent
con·ti·nen·tal
con·tin·gen·cy
·cies
con·tin·gent
con·tin·u·a·ble
con·tin·u·al
con·tin·u·ance
con·tin·u·a·tion
con·tin·ue
·ued ·u·ing
con·ti·nu·i·ty
·ties
con·tin·u·ous
con·tin·u·ous·ly
con·tin·u·um
·u·a *or* ·u·ums
con·tort
con·tor·tion
con·tour
con·tra·band
con·tra·cep·tion
con·tra·cep·tive
con·tract
con·tract·i·bil·i·ty
con·tract·i·ble
con·trac·tile
con·trac·tion
con·trac·tor
con·trac·tu·al
con·tra·dict
con·tra·dic·tion
con·tra·dic·to·ry
con·tra·dis·tinc·tion
con·trar·i·ly
con·trar·i·ness
con·trar·i·wise
con·trar·y
con·trast
con·tra·vene
·vened ·ven·ing
con·tra·ven·tion
con·trib·ute
·ut·ed ·ut·ing
con·tri·bu·tion
con·trib·u·tor
con·trib·u·to·ry
con·trite
con·tri·tion
con·triv·a·ble
con·triv·ance
con·trive
·trived ·triv·ing
con·trol
·trolled
·trol·ling
con·trol·la·bil·i·ty
con·trol·la·ble
con·trol·ler
con·tro·ver·sial
con·tro·ver·sy
·sies
con·tro·vert
con·tro·vert·i·ble
con·tu·ma·cy
con·tuse
·tused ·tus·ing
con·tu·sion
co·nun·drum
con·ur·ba·tion
con·va·lesce
·lesced ·lesc·ing
con·va·les·cence
con·va·les·cent
con·vec·tion
con·vec·tive
con·vec·tor
con·vene
·vened ·ven·ing
con·ven·ience
con·ven·ient
con·vent
con·ven·tion
con·ven·tion·al
con·ven·tion·al·i·ty
·ties
con·ven·tion·al·ize
·ized ·iz·ing
con·ven·tion·eer
con·verge
·verged
·verg·ing
con·ver·gence
con·vers·a·ble
con·ver·sant
con·ver·sa·tion

con·ver·sa·tion·al
con·verse′
 ·versed ·vers·ing
con′verse
con·ver·sion
con·vert
con·vert·er
 or ·ver·tor
con·vert·i·ble
con·vex
con·vex·i·ty
con·vey
con·vey·ance
con·vey·or *or* ·er
con·vict
con·vic·tion
con·vince
 ·vinced
 ·vinc·ing
con·vin·ci·ble
con·viv·i·al
con·viv·i·al·i·ty
con·vo·ca·tion
con·voke
 ·voked ·vok·ing
con·vo·lut·ed
con·vo·lu·tion
con·voy
con·vulse
 ·vulsed
 ·vuls·ing
con·vul·sion
con·vul·sive
cool·ant
co-op
co·op·er·ate
 or co-op·
 ·at·ed ·at·ing
co·op·er·a·tion
 or co-op·
co·op·er·a·tive
 or co-op·
co-opt
co·or·di·nate
 or co-or·
 ·nat·ed ·nat·ing
co·or·di·na·tor
 or co-or·
co-own·er·ship
co·part·ner

cope
 coped cop·ing
cop·i·er
co·pi·lot
co·pi·ous
cop-out
cop·per
cop·y
 ·ies
 ·ied ·y·ing
cop·y·ist
cop·y·read·er
cop·y·right
cop·y·writ·er
cord
 (*heavy string;* SEE chord)
cord·age
cor·date
cor·dial
cor·di·al·i·ty
 ·ties
cor·don
cor·do·van
cor·du·roy
co·re·spond·ent
 (*in law;* SEE correspondent)
co·ri·an·der
Co·rin·thi·an
cor·nered
cor·ner·stone
cor·ner·wise
cor·net
cor·nu·co·pi·a
corn·y
 ·i·er ·i·est
cor·ol·lar·y
 ·ies
cor·o·nar·y
cor·o·na·tion
cor·o·ner
cor·o·net
cor·po·ral
cor·po·rate
cor·po·ra·tion
cor·po·ra·tive
cor·po·re·al
corps
 corps
 (*group of people*)

corpse
 (*dead body*)
corps·man
cor·pu·lence
cor·pu·lent
cor·pus
 cor·po·ra
cor·pus·cle
cor·ral
 ·ralled ·ral·ling
cor·rect
cor·rect·a·ble
cor·rec·tion
cor·rec·tive
cor·rec·tor
cor·re·late
 ·lat·ed ·lat·ing
cor·rel·a·tive
cor·re·spond
cor·re·spond·ence
cor·re·spond·ent
 (*writer;* SEE corespondent)
cor·ri·dor
cor·ri·gi·ble
cor·ri·gi·bly
cor·rob·o·rate
 ·rat·ed ·rat·ing
cor·rob·o·ra·tion
cor·rob·o·ra·tive
cor·rob·o·ra·tor
cor·rode
 ·rod·ed ·rod·ing
cor·rod·i·ble
cor·ro·sion
cor·ro·sive
cor·ru·gate
 ·gat·ed ·gat·ing
cor·ru·ga·tion
cor·rupt
cor·rupt·i·bil·i·ty
cor·rupt·i·ble
cor·rupt·i·bly
cor·rup·tion
cor·rup·tive
cor·tege *or* ·tège
cor·tex
 ·ti·ces
cor·ti·cal
cor·ti·sone

co·run·dum
cor·us·cate
 ·cat·ed ·cat·ing
cor·vette
co·sign
co·sign·er
co·sig·na·to·ry
 ·ries
cos·mic
cos·mol·o·gy
cos·mo·naut
cos·mo·pol·i·tan
cos·mos
co·spon·sor
cost·li·ness
cost·ly
 ·li·er ·li·est
cost-plus
cos·tume
 ·tumed ·tum·ing
cos·tum·er
co·te·rie
co·til·lion
cot·tage
cot·ton
coun·cil
 (*legislature;* SEE counsel)
coun·cil·man
coun·ci·lor
 or ·cil·lor
 (*council member;* SEE counselor)
coun·sel
 ·seled *or* ·selled
 ·sel·ing *or*
 ·sel·ling
 (*advice; advise;* SEE council)
coun·se·lor
 or ·sel·lor
 (*adviser;* SEE councilor)
count·down
coun·te·nance
count·er
 (*one that counts*)
coun·ter
 (*opposite*)
coun·ter·act
coun·ter·ac·tion

coun·ter·at·tack
coun·ter·bal·ance
coun·ter·claim
coun·ter·clock·wise
coun·ter·feit
coun·ter·foil
coun·ter·part
coun·ter·point
coun·ter·sign
coun·ter·weight
count·less
coun·tri·fied
coun·try
·tries
coun·try·side
coun·ty
·ties
coup de grâce
coup d'é·tat
coupe
cou·ple
·pled ·pling
cou·pon
cour·age
cou·ra·geous
cou·ri·er
course
coursed
cours·ing
(*way; run;* SEE coarse)
cour·te·ous
cour·te·sy
·sies
court·house
cour·ti·er
court·li·ness
court·ly
·li·er ·li·est
court-mar·tial
courts-mar·tial
·tialed *or* ·tialled
·tial·ing *or* ·tial·ling
cou·ture
cou·tu·rier
cov·e·nant
Cov·en·try
cov·er·age
cov·ered
cov·er·ing
cov·er·let
cov·ert
cov·er·up
cov·et·ous
cow·ard
cow·ard·ice
cow·ard·li·ness
cow·ard·ly
co-work·er
coy·ly
coy·o·te
cracked
crack·er
crack·ing
crack·le
·led ·ling
crack·up
craft·i·ly
craft·i·ness
craft·y
·i·er ·i·est
crag·gi·ness
crag·gy
·gi·er ·gi·est
cramped
crane
craned cran·ing
cra·ni·al
cra·ni·ol·o·gy
cra·ni·um
·ni·ums *or* ·ni·a
crank·case
crank·i·ness
crank·shaft
crank·y
·i·er ·i·est
cran·ny
·nies
crass·ly
crass·ness
cra·ter
crave
craved crav·ing
cra·ven
cream·er·y
·ies
cream·i·ness
cream·y
·i·er ·i·est
crease
creased
creas·ing
cre·ate
·at·ed ·at·ing
cre·a·tion
cre·a·tive
cre·a·tiv·i·ty
cre·a·tor
crea·ture
cre·dence
cre·den·tial
cred·i·bil·i·ty
cred·i·ble
cred·i·bly
cred·it
cred·it·a·bil·i·ty
cred·it·a·ble
cred·it·a·bly
cred·i·tor
cre·do
·dos
cre·du·li·ty
cred·u·lous
cre·mate
·mat·ed ·mat·ing
cre·ma·tion
cre·ma·to·ry
·ries
cre·o·sote
cres·cent
cre·tin
cre·vasse
crev·ice
cri·er
crim·i·nal
crim·i·nol·o·gy
crim·son
cringe
cringed
cring·ing
crin·kle
·kled ·kling
crip·ple
·pled ·pling
crip·pler
cri·sis
·ses
crisp·er
crisp·i·ness
crisp·y
·i·er ·i·est
criss·cross
cri·te·ri·on
·ri·a *or* ·ri·ons
crit·ic
crit·i·cal
crit·i·cism
crit·i·cize
·cized ·ciz·ing
cri·tique
crois·sant
cro·ny
·nies
crook·ed·ness
crop-dust·ing
cro·sier
cross·breed
·bred ·breed·ing
cross-check
cross-coun·try
cross·cur·rent
cross·cut
cross-ex·am·i·na·tion
cross-ex·am·ine
cross-eyed
cross-in·dex
cross·ing
cross·o·ver
cross·piece
cross-pur·pose
cross-re·fer
cross-ref·er·ence
cross·road
cross section
cross·walk
cross·wise
cross·word
crou·pi·er
crowd·ed
cru·cial
cru·cial·ly
cru·ci·ble
crude·ly
cru·di·ty
·ties
cru·el·ly
cru·el·ty
·ties

cruise
cruised cruis·ing
cruis·er
crum·ble
·bled ·bling
crum·bly
·bli·er ·bli·est
crumb·y
·i·er ·i·est
crum·ple
·pled ·pling
crunch·i·ness
crunch·y
·i·er ·i·est
cru·sade
crush·a·ble
crus·ta·cean
crust·ed
crust·i·ness
crust·y
·i·er ·i·est
crux
crux·es *or* cru·ces
cry
cries
cried cry·ing
cry·o·gen·ics
crypt
cryp·tic
cryp·ti·cal·ly
cryp·to·gram
cryp·to·gram·mic
cryp·to·graph·ic
cryp·to·graph·i·cal·ly
cryp·tog·ra·phy
crys·tal
crys·tal·line
crys·tal·liz·a·ble
crys·tal·li·za·tion
crys·tal·lize
·lized ·liz·ing
crys·tal·log·ra·phy
cube
cubed cub·ing
cu·bic
cu·bi·cal
(*cube-shaped*)
cu·bi·cal·ly
cu·bi·cle
(*compartment*)
cue
cued cu·ing
or cue·ing
(*signal;* SEE
queue)
cui·sine
cul-de-sac
cu·li·nar·y
cull
cul·mi·nate
·nat·ed ·nat·ing
cul·mi·na·tion
cul·pa·bil·i·ty
cul·pa·ble
cul·pa·bly
cul·prit
cult·ist
cul·ti·va·ble
cul·ti·vate
·vat·ed ·vat·ing
cul·ti·va·tion
cul·ti·va·tor
cul·tur·al
cul·ture
·tured ·tur·ing
cul·vert
cum·ber·some
cu·mu·late
·lat·ed ·lat·ing
cu·mu·la·tive
cu·mu·lous
cu·ne·i·form
cun·ning·ly
cu·po·la
cur·a·ble
cu·ra·çao
cu·rate
cur·a·tive
cu·ra·tor
cur·dle
·dled ·dling
cure
cured cur·ing
cure-all
cur·few
cu·rie
cu·ri·o
·os
cu·ri·os·i·ty
·ties
cu·ri·ous
curl·i·ness
curl·y
·i·er ·i·est
cur·mudg·eon
cur·rant
(*fruit*)
cur·ren·cy
·cies
cur·rent
(*a flowing*)
cur·ric·u·lar
cur·ric·u·lum
·u·la *or* ·u·lums
cur·ry
·ried ·ry·ing
curse
cursed *or* curst
curs·ing
cur·sive
cur·so·ri·ly
cur·so·ri·ness
cur·so·ry
cur·tail
curt·ness
cur·va·ture
cur·vi·lin·e·ar
curv·y
·i·er ·i·est
cush·ion
cus·pid
cus·to·di·al
cus·to·di·an
cus·to·dy
cus·tom
cus·tom·ar·i·ly
cus·tom·ar·y
cus·tom-built
cus·tom·er
cus·tom·house
cus·tom-made
cu·ta·ne·ous
cut·a·way
cut·back
cut·let
cut·off
cut·out
cut-rate
cut·ter
cut·throat
cy·a·nide
cy·ber·net·ics
cy·cla·mate
cy·cle
cy·cled cy·cling
cy·clic
cy·cli·cal
cy·clist
cy·clone
cy·clo·pe·di·a
cy·clo·tron
cyl·in·der
cy·lin·dri·cal
cyn·ic
cyn·i·cal
cyn·i·cal·ly
cyn·i·cism
cy·no·sure
cyst·ic
cyst·oid
cy·tol·o·gy
cy·to·plasm
czar
Czech·o·slo·va·ki·a

D

Da·cron
dac·tyl
da·guerre·o·type
dai·ly
·lies
dai·qui·ri
dair·y
·ies
da·is
dal·li·ance
dal·ly
·lied ·ly·ing
Dal·ma·tian
dam
dammed
dam·ming
(*barrier;* SEE
damn)
dam·age
·aged ·ag·ing
dam·age·a·ble

damn
damned
damn·ing
(*condemn;* SEE dam)
dam·na·ble
dam·na·bly
dam·na·tion
dam·na·to·ry
damp·en
damp·er
dam·sel
dance
danced
danc·ing
danc·er
dan·dle
·dled ·dling
dan·ger
dan·ger·ous
dan·gle
·gled ·gling
Dan·ish
dare
dared dar·ing
Dar·jee·ling
dark·en
dark·room
Dar·win·i·an
das·tard·li·ness
das·tard·ly
da·ta
(*sing.* da·tum)
date
dat·ed dat·ing
daugh·ter
daugh·ter-in-law
daugh·ters-in-law
daunt·less
dav·en·port
dav·it
daw·dle
·dled ·dling
day·book
day letter
day·light
day·long
day·time
day-to-day
day·work
daze
dazed daz·ing
daz·zle
·zled ·zling
D-day
dea·con
de·ac·ti·vate
dead·en
dead-end
dead·head
dead·line
dead·li·ness
dead·lock
dead·ly
·li·er ·li·est
dead·wood
deaf·en·ing·ly
deal
dealt deal·ing
deal·er-ship
dean·er·y
·ies
dearth
death·bed
death·blow
death·less
death·ly
death·trap
death·watch
de·ba·cle
de·bar
·barred ·bar·ring
de·bark
de·bar·ka·tion
de·base
·based ·bas·ing
de·bat·a·ble
de·bate
·bat·ed ·bat·ing
de·bauch
deb·au·chee
de·bauch·er·y
·ies
de·ben·ture
de·bil·i·tate
·tat·ed ·tat·ing
de·bil·i·ta·tion
de·bil·i·ty
·ties
deb·it
deb·o·nair
or ·naire
de·brief
de·bris
debt
debt·or
de·bug
de·bunk
de·but
deb·u·tante
dec·ade
dec·a·dence
dec·a·dent
dec·a·gram
dec·a·he·dron
·drons *or* ·dra
de·cal·ci·fy
·fied ·fy·ing
dec·a·li·ter
Dec·a·logue
or ·log
dec·a·me·ter
de·camp
de·cant
de·cant·er
de·cap·i·tate
·tat·ed ·tat·ing
de·cap·i·ta·tion
de·cath·lon
de·cay
de·cease
·ceased
·ceas·ing
de·ce·dent
de·ceit·ful
de·ceiv·a·ble
de·ceive
·ceived
·ceiv·ing
de·cel·er·ate
·at·ed ·at·ing
de·cel·er·a·tion
de·cel·er·a·tor
de·cel·er·on
De·cem·ber
de·cen·cy
·cies
de·cen·ni·al
de·cent
(*proper;* SEE descent, dissent)
de·cen·tral·i·za·tion
de·cen·tral·ize
·ized ·iz·ing
de·cep·tion
de·cep·tive·ly
dec·i·bel
de·cide
·cid·ed ·cid·ing
de·cid·ed·ly
de·cid·u·ous
dec·i·mal
dec·i·mal·ize
·ized ·iz·ing
dec·i·mal·ly
dec·i·mate
·mat·ed ·mat·ing
de·ci·pher
de·ci·sion
de·ci·sive
de·claim
dec·la·ma·tion
de·clam·a·to·ry
de·clar·a·ble
dec·la·ra·tion
de·clar·a·tive
de·clare
·clared
·clar·ing
de·clas·si·fy
·fied ·fy·ing
de·clen·sion
dec·li·na·tion
de·cline
·clined ·clin·ing
de·cliv·i·ty
·ties
de·code
de·cod·er
dé·col·le·tage
dé·col·le·té
de·com·pos·a·ble
de·com·pose
de·com·po·si·tion
de·com·pres·sion
de·con·gest·ant
de·con·tam·i·nate
de·con·trol
·trolled
·trol·ling
dé·cor *or* de·cor

dec·o·rate
·rat·ed
·rat·ing
dec·o·ra·tion
dec·o·ra·tive
dec·o·ra·tor
dec·o·rous
de·co·rum
de·cou·page
de·coy
de·crease
·creased
·creas·ing
de·cree
·creed ·cree·ing
de·crep·it
de·crep·i·tude
de·cre·scen·do
de·cres·cent
de·cri·al
de·cry
·cried ·cry·ing
de·crypt
de·cum·bent
ded·i·cate
·cat·ed ·cat·ing
ded·i·ca·tion
ded·i·ca·to·ry
de·duce
·duced ·duc·ing
de·duc·i·ble
de·duct
de·duct·i·ble
de·duc·tion
de·duc·tive
deed
de-em·pha·sis
de-em·pha·size
deep-chest·ed
deep-root·ed
deep-seat·ed
deep-set
de-es·ca·late
de-es·ca·la·tion
de·face
de fac·to
de·fal·cate
·cat·ed ·cat·ing
de·fal·ca·tion

def·a·ma·tion
de·fam·a·to·ry
de·fame
·famed
·fam·ing
de·fault
de·fea·sance
de·feat
de·feat·ist
def·e·cate
·cat·ed ·cat·ing
def·e·ca·tion
de·fect
de·fec·tion
de·fec·tive
de·fec·tor
de·fend
de·fend·ant
de·fense
de·fen·si·ble
de·fen·sive
de·fer
·ferred ·fer·ring
def·er·ence
def·er·en·tial
de·fer·ment
de·fer·ral
de·fi·ance
de·fi·ant
de·fi·cien·cy
·cies
de·fi·cient
def·i·cit
de·fi·er
de·file
·filed ·fil·ing
de·fin·a·ble
de·fine
·fined ·fin·ing
def·i·nite
def·i·ni·tion
de·fin·i·tive
de·flate
·flat·ed
·flat·ing
de·fla·tion
de·fla·tion·ar·y
de·fla·tor
de·flect
de·flec·tion

de·flec·tor
de·flow·er
de·fo·li·ate
·at·ed ·at·ing
de·for·ma·tion
de·formed
de·form·i·ty
·ties
de·fraud
de·fray
de·fray·al
de·funct
de·fuse
de·fy
·fied ·fy·ing
de·gen·er·a·cy
de·gen·er·ate
·at·ed ·at·ing
de·gen·er·a·tion
de·gen·er·a·tive
de·grad·a·ble
deg·ra·da·tion
de·grade
·grad·ed
·grad·ing
de·gree
de·hu·mid·i·fy
de·hy·drate
·drat·ed ·drat·ing
de·hy·dra·tion
de·hy·dra·tor
de·ic·er
de·i·fi·ca·tion
de·i·fy
·fied ·fy·ing
deign
de·ism
de·i·ty
·ties
de·ject·ed
de·jec·tion
de ju·re
Del·a·ware
de·lay
de·lec·ta·ble
del·e·gate
·gat·ed ·gat·ing
del·e·ga·tion
de·lete
·let·ed ·let·ing

del·e·te·ri·ous
de·le·tion
de·lib·er·ate
de·lib·er·ate·ly
de·lib·er·a·tion
del·i·ca·cy
·cies
del·i·cate
del·i·cate·ly
del·i·ca·tes·sen
de·li·cious
de·light·ful
de·light·ful·ly
de·lin·e·ate
·at·ed ·at·ing
de·lin·e·a·tion
de·lin·e·a·tor
de·lin·quen·cy
de·lin·quent
de·lir·i·ous
de·lir·i·um
de·liv·er·a·ble
de·liv·er·ance
de·liv·er·y
·ies
de·lude
·lud·ed ·lud·ing
del·uge
·uged ·ug·ing
de·lu·sion
de·lu·sive
de·luxe
delve
delved delv·ing
de·mag·net·ize
dem·a·gog·ic
dem·a·gogue
or ·gog
dem·a·gog·y
de·mand
de·mand·ing
de·mar·cate
·cat·ed ·cat·ing
de·mar·ca·tion
de·mean·or
de·men·tia
de·mer·it
de·mil·i·ta·rize
de·mise
dem·i·tasse

de·mo·bi·lize
de·moc·ra·cy
·cies
dem·o·crat·ic
de·moc·ra·ti·za·tion
de·moc·ra·tize
·tized ·tiz·ing
de·mog·ra·phy
de·mo·graph·ics
de·mol·ish
dem·o·li·tion
de·mon
de·mon·e·tize
·tized ·tiz·ing
de·mo·ni·ac
de·mon·ic
de·mon·stra·ble
dem·on·strate
·strat·ed ·strat·ing
dem·on·stra·tion
de·mon·stra·tive
dem·on·stra·tor
de·mor·al·ize
de·mote
·mot·ed ·mot·ing
de·mo·tion
de·mount
de·mur
·murred ·mur·ring
(to object)
de·mure
(coy)
de·mur·rage
de·mur·rer
de·na·tion·al·ize
de·nat·u·ral·ize
de·na·ture
·tured ·tur·ing
de·ni·a·ble
de·ni·al
de·nier′
(unit of measure)
de·ni′er
(one who denies)
den·im
den·i·zen
de·nom·i·nate
·nat·ed ·nat·ing
de·nom·i·na·tion
de·nom·i·na·tor

de·no·ta·tion
de·note
·not·ed ·not·ing
de·noue·ment
de·nounce
·nounced
·nounc·ing
dense
dens·er dens·est
dense·ly
den·si·ty
·ties
den·tal
den·tal·ly
den·tin
den·tist
den·tist·ry
den·ture
de·nude
·nud·ed ·nud·ing
de·nun·ci·a·tion
de·ny
·nied ·ny·ing
de·o·dor·ant
de·o·dor·ize
·ized ·iz·ing
de·o·dor·iz·er
de·part·ed
de·part·ment
de·part·men·tal
de·part·men·tal·ize
·ized ·iz·ing
de·par·ture
de·pend·a·bil·i·ty
de·pend·a·ble
de·pend·a·bly
de·pend·ence
de·pend·en·cy
·cies
de·pend·ent
de·per·son·al·ize
de·pict
de·pic·tion
de·pil·a·to·ry
·ries
de·plane
de·plete
·plet·ed ·plet·ing
de·ple·tion
de·plor·a·ble

de·plore
·plored
·plor·ing
de·ploy
de·pop·u·late
de·port·a·ble
de·por·ta·tion
de·port·ment
de·pose
de·pos·it
de·pos·i·tar·y
·ies
dep·o·si·tion
de·pos·i·tor
de·pos·i·to·ry
·ries
de·pot
dep·ra·va·tion
(a corrupting;
SEE deprivation)
de·prave
·praved
·prav·ing
de·prav·i·ty
·ties
dep·re·cate
·cat·ed ·cat·ing
dep·re·ca·tion
dep·re·ca·to·ry
de·pre·ci·a·ble
de·pre·ci·ate
·at·ed ·at·ing
de·pre·ci·a·tion
dep·re·da·tion
de·pres·sant
de·pressed
de·press·ing
de·pres·sion
dep·ri·va·tion
(a taking away;
SEE depravation)
de·prive
·prived ·priv·ing
depth
dep·u·ta·tion
dep·u·tize
·tized ·tiz·ing
dep·u·ty
·ties
de·rail

de·range
·ranged
·rang·ing
der·e·lict
der·e·lic·tion
de·ride
·rid·ed ·rid·ing
de ri·gueur
de·ri·sion
de·ri·sive
de·riv·a·ble
der·i·va·tion
de·riv·a·tive
de·rive
·rived ·riv·ing
der·ma·tol·o·gist
der·o·ga·tion
de·rog·a·to·ri·ly
de·rog·a·to·ry
der·rick
de·sal·i·na·tion
de·salt
des·cant
de·scend
de·scend·ant
de·scend·i·ble
de·scent
(going down; SEE
decent, dissent)
de·scrib·a·ble
de·scribe
·scribed
·scrib·ing
de·scrip·tion
de·scrip·tive
de·scry
·scried
·scry·ing
des·e·crate
·crat·ed ·crat·ing
des·e·cra·tion
de·seg·re·gate
·gat·ed ·gat·ing
de·seg·re·ga·tion
de·sen·si·tize
de·sen·si·tiz·er
de·sert′
(abandon; SEE
dessert)
des′ert
(dry area)

de·ser·tion
de·serts
(*reward, etc.*)
de·serve
·served
·serv·ing
de·serv·ed·ly
des·ic·cant
des·ic·cate
·cat·ed ·cat·ing
des·ic·ca·tion
de·sign
des·ig·nate
·nat·ed ·nat·ing
des·ig·na·tion
des·ig·na·tor
de·signed
de·sign·er
de·sir·a·bil·i·ty
de·sir·a·ble
de·sir·a·bly
de·sire
·sired ·sir·ing
de·sir·ous
de·sist
des·o·late
·lat·ed ·lat·ing
des·o·la·tion
de·spair
des·per·ate
(*hopeless;* SEE disparate)
des·per·a·tion
des·pi·ca·ble
de·spise
·spised
·spis·ing
de·spite
de·spoil
de·spo·li·a·tion
de·spond·en·cy
de·spond·ent
des·pot
des·pot·ic
des·pot·ism
des·sert
(*food;* SEE desert)
des·ti·na·tion
des·tine
·tined ·tin·ing
des·tin·y
·ies
des·ti·tute
des·ti·tu·tion
de·stroy·er
de·struct
de·struct·i·bil·i·ty
de·struct·i·ble
de·struc·tion
de·struc·tive
de·struc·tor
des·ul·to·ry
de·tach
de·tach·a·ble
de·tach·ment
de·tail
de·tain
de·tect
de·tect·a·ble
or ·i·ble
de·tec·tion
de·tec·tive
de·tec·tor
dé·tente
de·ten·tion
de·ter
·terred
·ter·ring
de·ter·gent
de·te·ri·o·rate
·rat·ed ·rat·ing
de·te·ri·o·ra·tion
de·ter·ment
de·ter·mi·na·ble
de·ter·mi·na·bly
de·ter·mi·nant
de·ter·mi·nate
de·ter·mi·na·tion
de·ter·mine
·mined ·min·ing
de·ter·min·ism
de·ter·rence
de·ter·rent
de·test
de·test·a·ble
de·test·a·bly
de·tes·ta·tion
de·throne
·throned
·thron·ing
det·o·nate
·nat·ed
·nat·ing
det·o·na·tion
det·o·na·tor
de·tour
de·tract
de·trac·tor
det·ri·ment
det·ri·men·tal
deuce
de·val·u·a·tion
de·val·ue
dev·as·tate
·tat·ed ·tat·ing
dev·as·ta·tion
de·vel·op·ment
de·vel·op·men·tal
de·vi·ant
de·vi·ate
·at·ed ·at·ing
de·vi·a·tion
de·vice
dev·il·ish
dev·il·ment
dev·il·try
·tries
de·vi·ous
de·vis·a·ble
(*that can be devised;* SEE divisible)
de·vise
·vised ·vis·ing
de·vis·ee
de·vis·or
de·vi·tal·ize
de·void
dev·o·lu·tion
de·volve
·volved
·volv·ing
de·vote
·vot·ed
·vot·ing
dev·o·tee
de·vo·tion
de·vour
de·vout
dex·ter·i·ty
dex·ter·ous
or dex·trous
dex·trose
di·a·be·tes
di·a·bet·ic
di·a·bol·ic
di·a·bol·i·cal
di·a·crit·i·cal
di·a·dem
di·ag·nos·a·ble
di·ag·nose
·nosed ·nos·ing
di·ag·no·sis
·no·ses
di·ag·nos·tic
di·ag·nos·ti·cian
di·ag·o·nal
di·a·gram·mat·ic
di·al
·aled *or* ·alled
·al·ing *or* al·ling
di·a·lect
di·a·lec·tal
di·a·lec·tic
di·a·lec·ti·cian
di·al·o·gist
di·a·logue *or* ·log
di·am·e·ter
di·a·met·ri·cal
di·a·mond
di·a·phragm
di·a·rist
di·ar·rhe·a
or ·rhoe·a
di·a·ry
·ries
di·a·ther·my
di·a·ton·ic
di·a·tribe
di·chot·o·mize
·mized ·miz·ing
di·chot·o·my
dick·er
Dic·ta·phone
dic·tate
·tat·ed ·tat·ing
dic·ta·tion
dic·ta·tor
dic·ta·to·ri·al

dic·tion·ar·y
·ies
Dic·to·graph
dic·tum
·tums *or* ·ta
di·dac·tic
die
dice (*cube*)
die
dies
died die·ing
(*mold; stamp*)
die
died dy·ing
(*stop living;* SEE dye)
die-hard
di·e·lec·tric
di·er·e·sis
·ses
die·sel
di·e·sis
·ses
di·e·tar·y
di·e·tet·ic
di·e·ti·tian
or ·cian
dif·fer·ence
dif·fer·ent
dif·fer·en·tial
dif·fer·en·ti·ate
·at·ed ·at·ing
dif·fer·en·ti·a·tion
dif·fi·cult
dif·fi·cul·ty
·ties
dif·fi·dence
dif·fi·dent
dif·fract
dif·frac·tion
dif·fuse
·fused ·fus·ing
dif·fus·i·ble
dif·fu·sion
dif·fu·sive
di·gest
di·gest·i·ble
di·ges·tive
dig·it
dig·it·al
dig·i·tal·is
dig·i·ti·grade
dig·ni·fy
·fied ·fy·ing
dig·ni·tar·y
·ies
dig·ni·ty
·ties
di·gress
di·gres·sion
di·lap·i·date
·dat·ed ·dat·ing
di·lat·a·ble
di·late
·lat·ed ·lat·ing
di·la·tion
dil·a·to·ry
di·lem·ma
dil·et·tante
·tantes *or* tan·ti
dil·et·tant·ish
dil·i·gence
dil·i·gent
dil·u·ent
di·lute
·lut·ed ·lut·ing
di·lu·tion
di·lu·vi·al
di·men·sion
di·min·ish
di·min·u·en·do
dim·i·nu·tion
di·min·u·tive
dine
dined din·ing
din·er
(*person eating;* SEE dinner)
din·ghy
·ghies
(*boat*)
din·gi·ness
din·gy
·gi·er ·gi·est
(*not bright*)
din·ner
(*meal;* SEE diner)
di·oc·e·san
di·o·cese
di·o·ra·ma
di·ox·ide
diph·the·ri·a
diph·thong
di·plo·ma
di·plo·ma·cy
·cies
dip·lo·mat
(*government representative*)
dip·lo·mate
(*doctor*)
dip·so·ma·ni·a
di·rect
di·rec·tion
di·rec·tive
di·rec·tor
di·rec·tor·ate
di·rec·to·ri·al
di·rec·to·ry
·ries
dire·ful
dirge
dir·i·gi·ble
dirt·i·ness
dirt·y
·i·er ·i·est
dis·a·bil·i·ty
·ties
dis·a·ble
·bled ·bling
dis·a·buse
·bused ·bus·ing
dis·ad·van·tage
dis·ad·van·ta·geous
dis·af·fect·ed
dis·ag·i·o
dis·a·gree
dis·a·gree·a·ble
dis·a·gree·a·bly
dis·a·gree·ment
dis·al·low
dis·ap·pear
dis·ap·pear·ance
dis·ap·point
dis·ap·pro·ba·tion
dis·ap·prov·al
dis·ap·prove
dis·ar·ma·ment
dis·arm·ing
dis·ar·range
dis·ar·ray
dis·as·sem·ble
dis·as·so·ci·ate
dis·as·ter
dis·as·trous
dis·a·vow
dis·a·vow·al
dis·band
dis·bar
dis·be·lief
dis·be·lieve
dis·be·liev·er
dis·burse
·bursed
·burs·ing
dis·burse·ment
disc
dis·card
dis·cern
dis·cern·i·ble
dis·cern·ment
dis·charge
dis·ci·ple
dis·ci·plin·a·ble
dis·ci·pli·nar·i·an
dis·ci·pli·nar·y
dis·ci·pline
·plined ·plin·ing
dis·claim
dis·claim·er
dis·close
dis·clo·sure
dis·cog·ra·phy
dis·coid
dis·col·or
dis·col·or·a·tion
dis·com·fit
dis·com·fi·ture
dis·com·fort
dis·com·pose
dis·com·po·sure
dis·con·cert
dis·con·nect
dis·con·so·late
dis·con·tent
dis·con·tin·u·ance
dis·con·tin·ue
dis·con·ti·nu·i·ty
dis·con·tin·u·ous
dis·cord
dis·cord·ant

dis·co·thèque
dis·count
dis·cour·age
·aged ·ag·ing
dis·cour·age·ment
dis·course
dis·cour·te·ous
dis·cour·te·sy
dis·cov·er
dis·cov·er·er
dis·cov·er·y
·ies
dis·cred·it
dis·creet
(*prudent;* SEE
discrete)
dis·crep·an·cy
·cies
dis·crete
(*separate;* SEE
discreet)
dis·cre·tion
dis·cre·tion·ar·y
dis·crim·i·nate
·nat·ed ·nat·ing
dis·crim·i·na·tion
dis·crim·i·na·to·ry
dis·cur·sive
dis·cuss
dis·cus·sion
dis·dain·ful
dis·ease
·eased ·eas·ing
dis·em·bark
dis·em·bod·y
dis·en·chant
dis·en·cum·ber
dis·en·gage
dis·en·tan·gle
dis·es·tab·lish
dis·fa·vor
dis·fig·ure
dis·fig·ure·ment
dis·fran·chise
·chised ·chis·ing
dis·gorge
dis·grace
·graced
·grac·ing
dis·grace·ful

dis·grun·tle
·tled ·tling
dis·guise
·guised
·guis·ing
dis·gust
dis·ha·bille
dis·har·mo·ny
dis·heart·en
di·shev·el
·eled *or* ·elled
·el·ing *or*
·el·ling
dis·hon·est
dis·hon·es·ty
dis·hon·or
dis·hon·or·a·ble
dis·il·lu·sion
dis·in·cli·na·tion
dis·in·cline
dis·in·fect
dis·in·fect·ant
dis·in·gen·u·ous
dis·in·her·it
dis·in·te·grate
·grat·ed
·grat·ing
dis·in·te·gra·tion
dis·in·ter
dis·in·ter·est·ed
dis·in·ter·me·di·a·tion
dis·join
dis·joint
dis·junc·tion
disk
dis·like
dis·lo·cate
dis·lo·ca·tion
dis·lodge
dis·loy·al
dis·loy·al·ty
dis·mal
dis·mal·ly
dis·man·tle
dis·may
dis·mem·ber
dis·miss
dis·miss·al
dis·mount

dis·o·be·di·ence
dis·o·be·di·ent
dis·o·bey
dis·or·der
dis·or·der·ly
dis·or·gan·i·za·tion
dis·or·gan·ize
dis·o·ri·ent
dis·own
dis·par·age
·aged ·ag·ing
dis·pa·rate
(*not alike;* SEE
desperate)
dis·par·i·ty
dis·pas·sion·ate
dis·patch
dis·patch·er
dis·pel
·pelled ·pel·ling
dis·pen·sa·bil·i·ty
dis·pen·sa·ble
dis·pen·sa·ry
·ries
dis·pen·sa·tion
dis·pense
·pensed ·pens·ing
dis·pen·ser
dis·per·sal
dis·perse
·persed ·pers·ing
dis·pers·i·ble
dis·per·sion
dis·pir·it·ed
dis·place
dis·place·ment
dis·play
dis·please
dis·pleas·ure
dis·port
dis·pos·a·ble
dis·pos·al
dis·pose
·posed ·pos·ing
dis·po·si·tion
dis·pos·sess
dis·proof
dis·pro·por·tion
dis·pro·por·tion·ate
dis·prove

dis·pu·ta·ble
dis·pu·tant
dis·pu·ta·tion
dis·pu·ta·tious
dis·pute
·put·ed ·put·ing
dis·qual·i·fi·ca·tion
dis·qual·i·fy
dis·qui·et
dis·qui·e·tude
dis·qui·si·tion
dis·re·gard
dis·re·pair
dis·rep·u·ta·ble
dis·rep·u·ta·bly
dis·re·pute
dis·re·spect·ful
dis·rupt
dis·rup·tion
dis·rup·tive
dis·sat·is·fac·tion
dis·sat·is·fy
·fied ·fy·ing
dis·sect
dis·sec·tion
dis·sec·tor
dis·sem·blance
dis·sem·ble
·bled ·bling
dis·sem·i·nate
·nat·ed
·nat·ing
dis·sem·i·na·tion
dis·sen·sion
dis·sent
(*disagree;* SEE
decent, descent)
dis·sen·tient
dis·sen·tious
dis·ser·ta·tion
dis·serv·ice
dis·sev·er
dis·si·dence
dis·si·dent
dis·sim·i·lar
dis·sim·i·lar·i·ty
dis·sim·i·la·tion
dis·sim·u·late
dis·si·pate
·pat·ed ·pat·ing

dis·si·pa·tion
dis·so·ci·ate
·at·ed ·at·ing
dis·so·ci·a·tion
dis·sol·u·ble
dis·so·lute
dis·so·lu·tion
dis·solv·a·ble
dis·solve
·solved ·solv·ing
dis·sol·vent
dis·so·nance
dis·so·nant
dis·suade
·suad·ed
·suad·ing
dis·sua·sion
dis·sym·me·try
dis·taff
dis·tance
dis·tant
dis·taste·ful
dis·tem·per
dis·tend
dis·ten·si·ble
dis·ten·tion *or*
dis·ten·sion
dis·till *or* ·til
·tilled ·till·ing
dis·til·late
dis·til·la·tion
dis·till·er
dis·till·er·y
·ies
dis·tinct
dis·tinc·tion
dis·tinc·tive
dis·tin·gué
dis·tin·guish
dis·tin·guish·a·ble
dis·tort
dis·tor·tion
dis·tract
dis·tract·i·ble
dis·trac·tion
dis·train
dis·trait
dis·traught
dis·tress
dis·trib·ut·a·ble
dis·trib·ute
·ut·ed ·ut·ing
dis·tri·bu·tion
dis·trib·u·tive
dis·trib·u·tor
dis·trict
dis·trust·ful
dis·turb
dis·turb·ance
dis·un·ion
dis·u·nite
dis·u·ni·ty
dis·use
ditch
dit·to
·tos
·toed ·to·ing
di·u·ret·ic
di·ur·nal
di·verge
·verged
·verg·ing
di·ver·gence
di·ver·gent
di·vers
(*sundry*)
di·verse
(*different*)
di·ver·si·fi·ca·tion
di·ver·si·form
di·ver·si·fy
·fied ·fy·ing
di·ver·sion
di·ver·sion·ar·y
di·ver·si·ty
di·vert
di·ver·tisse·ment
di·vest
di·vest·i·ture
di·vid·a·ble
di·vide
·vid·ed ·vid·ing
div·i·dend
div·i·na·tion
di·vine
·vined ·vin·ing
di·vin·i·ty
·ties
di·vis·i·bil·i·ty
di·vis·i·ble
(*that can be divided;*
SEE devisable)
di·vi·sion
di·vi·sor
di·vorce
·vorced ·vorc·ing
div·ot
di·vulge
·vulged
·vulg·ing
di·vul·gence
do·a·ble
dob·bin
do·cent
doc·ile
doc·ile·ly
do·cil·i·ty
dock
dock·age
dock·et
dock·yard
doc·tor
doc·tor·al
doc·tor·ate
doc·tri·naire
doc·tri·nal
doc·trine
doc·u·ment
doc·u·men·tal
doc·u·men·ta·ry
·ries
doc·u·men·ta·tion
dod·der·ing
do·er
does
does·n't
dog·ged·ly
dog·ger·el
dog·ma
·mas *or* ·ma·ta
dog·mat·ic
dog·ma·tism
dog·ma·tize
·tized ·tiz·ing
do-good·er
doi·ly
·lies
do-it-your·self
dol·ce
dol·drums
dole
doled dol·ing
dole·ful
dol·lar
dol·lop
dol·man
·mans (*robe*)
dol·men
(*tomb*)
do·lor·ous
dol·phin
dolt·ish
do·main
do·mes·tic
do·mes·ti·cate
·cat·ed ·cat·ing
do·mes·tic·i·ty
·ties
dom·i·cile
dom·i·nance
dom·i·nant
dom·i·nate
·nat·ed ·nat·ing
dom·i·na·tion
dom·i·neer·ing
do·min·i·cal
do·min·ion
dom·i·no
·noes *or* ·nos
do·nate
·nat·ed ·nat·ing
do·na·tion
do·nee
do·nor
Don Ju·an
don·ny·brook
do·nor
do-noth·ing
Don Qui·xo·te
don't
dooms·day
do-or-die
door·keep·er
door·knob
door·plate
door·stop
door-to-door
door·way

dor·man·cy
dor·mant
dor·mer
dor·mi·to·ry
·ries
dor·mouse
·mice
dor·sal
do·ry
·ries
dos·age
dos·si·er
dot·age
dot·ard
dote
dot·ed dot·ing
dou·ble
·bled ·bling
dou·ble-bar·reled
dou·ble-breast·ed
dou·ble-check
dou·ble-cross
dou·ble-deal·ing
dou·ble-deck·er
dou·ble-edged
dou·ble-en·ten·dre
dou·ble en·try
dou·ble-faced
dou·ble in·dem·ni·ty
dou·ble-park
dou·ble-space
dou·blet
dou·bly
doubt
doubt·ful
doubt·ful·ly
doubt·less
dough
dough·i·ness
douse
doused
dous·ing
dow·a·ger
dow·di·ness
dow·dy
·di·er ·di·est
dow·el
dow·er
down·beat
down·cast
down·fall
down·grade
down·heart·ed
down·hill
down·i·ness
down·right
down·state
down·time
down-to-earth
down·town
down·turn
down·ward
down·wind
down·y
·i·er ·i·est
dow·ry
·ries
dox·ol·o·gy
draft
draft·ee
draft·i·ness
drafts·man
draft·y
·i·er ·i·est
drag·net
drag·o·man
·mans *or* ·men
drag·on
drag·on·fly
·flies
dra·goon
drain·age
drain·pipe
dra·ma
dra·mat·ic
dra·mat·i·cal·ly
dram·a·tist
dram·a·ti·za·tion
dram·a·tize
·tized
·tiz·ing
dram·a·tur·gy
dras·tic
dras·ti·cal·ly
draughts·man
·men
draw
drew drawn
draw·ing
draw·back
draw·bridge
draw·ee
draw·er
drawl
drawn·work
draw·string
dray·age
dray·man
dread·ful
dread·nought
drear·i·ly
drear·i·ness
drear·y
·i·er ·i·est
dredge
dredged
dredg·ing
drenched
dri·er *or* dry·er
drill·mas·ter
drill press
drink
drank drunk
drink·ing
drink·a·ble
drip
dripped *or* dript
drip·ping
drip-dry
drive
drove driv·en
driv·ing
drive-in
driv·er
drive·way
droll·er·y
·ies
drol·ly
drom·e·dar·y
·ies
drone
droned dron·ing
droop·y
·i·er ·i·est
drop
dropped
drop·ping
drop-forge
-forged
-forg·ing
drop·let
drop·out
drop·per
dross
drought
or drouth
dro·ver
drown
drowse
drowsed
drows·ing
drow·si·ly
drow·si·ness
drow·sy
·si·er ·si·est
drudge
drudged
drudg·ing
drudg·er·y
drug
drugged
drug·ging
drug·gist
drug·store
drunk·ard
drunk·en·ness
drunk·o·me·ter
drupe·let
dry
dri·er dri·est
dried dry·ing
dry-clean
dry·er
dry·ly *or* dri·ly
dry·ness
du·al
(*of two;* SEE duel)
du·al·ism
du·al·is·tic
du·al·ly
du·al-pur·pose
du·bi·e·ty
du·bi·ous
du·cal
duc·at
duc·tile
duct·less
dudg·eon
due bill

du·el
·eled *or* ·elled
·el·ing *or*
·el·ling
(*fight;* SEE dual)
du·et
dul·cet
dul·ci·mer
dull·ard
dull·ness
dul·ly
(*in a dull manner*)
du·ly
(*as due*)
dumb·found *or*
dum·found
dump·i·ness
dump·y
·i·er ·i·est
dun
dunned
dun·ing
dun·der·head
dun·ga·ree
dun·geon
dun·nage
du·o
du·os *or* du·i
du·o·dec·i·mal
du·o·de·nal
du·o·logue
du·op·o·ly
du·o·tone
du·o·type
dupe
duped
dup·ing
du·plex
du·pli·cate
·cat·ed ·cat·ing
du·pli·ca·tion
du·pli·ca·tor
du·plic·i·ty
·ties
du·ra·bil·i·ty
du·ra·ble
du·ra·bly
dur·ance
du·ra·tion
du·ress
dur·ing
dust·y
·i·er ·i·est
du·te·ous
du·ti·a·ble
du·ti·ful
du·ti·ful·ly
du·ty
·ties
du·ty-free
dwell
dwelt *or* dwelled
dwell·ing
dwin·dle
·dled ·dling
dy·ad
dye
dyed dye·ing
(*color;* SEE die)
dyed-in-the-wool
dy·er
dye·stuff
dy·nam·ic
dy·na·mism
dy·na·mite
·mit·ed ·mit·ing
dy·na·mo
·mos
dy·na·mom·e·ter
dy·na·mo·tor
dy·nas·ty
·ties
dys·en·ter·y
dys·func·tion
dys·pep·si·a
dys·pep·tic
dys·tro·phy

E

ea·ger
ea·gle
ear·ly
·li·er ·li·est
ear·mark
earned
ear·nest
earn·ings
ear·phone
ear·ring
earth·en·ware
earth·i·ness
earth·ly
earth·quake
earth·shak·ing
earth·ward
earth·y
·i·er ·i·est
ease
eased eas·ing
ea·sel
ease·ment
eas·i·ly
eas·i·ness
east·er·ly
east·ern
east·ward
eas·y
·i·er ·i·est
eas·y·go·ing
eat
ate eat·en
eat·ing
eat·a·ble
eaves·drop
ebb tide
eb·on·y
e·bul·lient
e·bul·li·tion
ec·cen·tric
ec·cen·tric·i·ty
·ties
ec·cle·si·as·ti·cal
ech·e·lon
ech·o
·oes
é·clat
ec·lec·tic
ec·lec·ti·cism
e·clipse
·clipsed
·clips·ing
e·clip·tic
ec·o·log·i·cal
e·col·o·gist
e·col·o·gy
e·co·nom·ic
e·co·nom·i·cal
e·con·o·mist
e·con·o·mize
·mized ·miz·ing
e·con·o·my
·mies
e·co·sys·tem
e·co·tone
ec·ru
ec·sta·sy
·sies
ec·stat·ic
ec·u·men·i·cal
ec·ze·ma
ed·dy
·dies
e·de·ma
·mas *or* ·ma·ta
edge
edged edg·ing
edge·ways
edge·wise
edg·i·ness
edg·y
·i·er ·i·est
ed·i·bil·i·ty
ed·i·ble
e·dict
ed·i·fi·ca·tion
ed·i·fice
ed·i·fy
·fied ·fy·ing
e·di·tion
(*form of book;*
SEE addition)
ed·i·tor
ed·i·to·ri·al
ed·i·to·ri·al·ize
·ized ·iz·ing
ed·u·ca·bil·i·ty
ed·u·ca·ble
ed·u·cate
·cat·ed ·cat·ing
ed·u·ca·tion
ed·u·ca·tive
ed·u·ca·tor
e·duce
·duced ·duc·ing
e·duc·i·ble
ef·face
·faced ·fac·ing
ef·face·a·ble

ef·fect
(*result;* SEE affect)
ef·fec·tive
(*having effect;* SEE affective)
ef·fec·tu·al
ef·fec·tu·ate
·at·ed
·at·ing
ef·fer·ent
ef·fer·vesce
·vesced
·vesc·ing
ef·fer·ves·cence
ef·fete
ef·fi·ca·cious
ef·fi·ca·cy
ef·fi·cien·cy
ef·fi·cient
ef·fi·gy
·gies
ef·flo·res·cence
ef·flu·ence
ef·flu·ent
(*flowing;* SEE affluent)
ef·flu·vi·um
·vi·a *or* ·vi·ums
ef·fort
ef·fron·ter·y
·ies
ef·ful·gence
ef·fu·sion
ef·fu·sive
e·gal·i·tar·i·an
e·go
e·go·cen·tric
e·go·ism
e·go·ist
e·go·ma·ni·a
e·go·tism
e·go·tist
e·go·tis·tic
e·gre·gious
e·gress
e·gret
ei·det·ic
eight·een
eighth
eight·i·eth
eight·y
·ies
ei·ther
ei·ther-or
e·ject
e·jec·tion
e·jec·tor
eke
eked ek·ing
e·lab·o·rate
·rat·ed ·rat·ing
e·lab·o·rate·ly
e·lab·o·ra·tion
e·lapse
·lapsed
·laps·ing
e·las·tic
e·las·tic·i·ty
e·las·ti·cize
·cized ·ciz·ing
e·late
·lat·ed ·lat·ing
e·la·tion
eld·er·ly
eld·est
e·lec·tion
e·lec·tion·eer
e·lec·tive
e·lec·tor
e·lec·tor·al
e·lec·tor·ate
e·lec·tric
e·lec·tri·cal
e·lec·tri·cian
e·lec·tric·i·ty
e·lec·tri·fi·ca·tion
e·lec·tri·fy
·fied ·fy·ing
e·lec·tro·cute
·cut·ed ·cut·ing
e·lec·tro·cu·tion
e·lec·trode
e·lec·tro·lyte
e·lec·tro·mag·net
e·lec·trom·e·ter
e·lec·tro·mo·tive
e·lec·tron
e·lec·tron·ic
e·lec·tro·plate
e·lec·tro·scope
e·lec·tro·stat·ics
e·lec·tro·ther·a·py
e·lec·tro·type
el·ee·mos·y·nar·y
el·e·gance
el·e·gant
el·e·gi·ac
el·e·gy
·gies
el·e·ment
el·e·men·tal
el·e·men·ta·ri·ness
el·e·men·ta·ry
(*basic;* SEE alimentary)
El·eu·sin·i·an
el·e·vate
·vat·ed ·vat·ing
el·e·va·tion
el·e·va·tor
e·lev·enth
e·lic·it
(*draw forth;* SEE illicit)
e·lide
·lid·ed ·lid·ing
el·i·gi·bil·i·ty
el·i·gi·ble
el·i·gi·bly
e·lim·i·nate
·nat·ed ·nat·ing
e·lim·i·na·tion
e·li·sion
e·lite *or* é·lite
e·lix·ir
E·liz·a·be·than
el·lipse
el·lip·sis
·ses
el·lip·ti·cal
el·o·cu·tion
e·lon·gate
·gat·ed ·gat·ing
e·lon·ga·tion
e·lope
·loped ·lop·ing
el·o·quence
el·o·quent
else·where
e·lu·ci·date
·dat·ed ·dat·ing
e·lu·ci·da·tion
e·lude
·lud·ed ·lud·ing
(*escape;* SEE allude)
e·lu·sion
(*an escape;* SEE allusion, illusion)
e·lu·sive
(*hard to grasp;* SEE allusive, illusive)
e·ma·ci·ate
·at·ed ·at·ing
e·ma·ci·a·tion
em·a·nate
·nat·ed ·nat·ing
em·a·na·tion
e·man·ci·pate
·pat·ed ·pat·ing
e·man·ci·pa·tion
e·man·ci·pa·tor
em·bank·ment
em·bar·go
·goes
·goed ·go·ing
em·bark
em·bar·ka·tion
em·bar·rass
em·bar·rass·ment
em·bas·sy
·sies
em·bat·tle
·tled ·tling
em·bed
em·bel·lish
em·ber
em·bez·zle
·zled ·zling
em·bez·zler
em·bla·zon
em·blem
em·blem·at·ic
em·bod·i·ment
em·bod·y
·ied ·y·ing
em·bold·en
em·bo·lism
em·boss

em·bou·chure
em·brace
·braced
·brac·ing
em·brace·a·ble
em·bra·sure
em·broil
em·bry·o
·os
em·bry·on·ic
em·cee
·ceed
·cee·ing
e·mend
(*to correct;* SEE amend)
e·men·da·tion
em·er·ald
e·merge
·merged
·merg·ing
(*appear;* SEE immerge)
e·mer·gence
e·mer·gen·cy
·cies
e·mer·i·tus
em·er·y
e·met·ic
em·i·grant
em·i·grate
·grat·ed
·grat·ing
em·i·gra·tion
em·i·nence
em·i·nent
(*prominent;* SEE imminent)
em·is·sar·y
·ies
e·mis·sion
e·mit
·mit·ted
·mit·ting
e·mol·li·ent
e·mol·u·ment
e·mo·tion·al
e·mo·tion·al·ize
·ized
·iz·ing
em·path·ic
em·pa·thize
·thized ·thiz·ing
em·pa·thy
em·per·or
em·pha·sis
·ses
em·pha·size
·sized ·siz·ing
em·phat·ic
em·phy·se·ma
em·pire
em·pir·i·cal
em·pir·i·cism
em·place·ment
em·ploy
em·ploy·a·ble
em·ploy·ee
em·ploy·er
em·ploy·ment
em·po·ri·um
·ri·ums *or* ·ri·a
em·pow·er
em·press
emp·ti·ly
emp·ti·ness
emp·ty
·ti·er ·ti·est
·ties
·tied ·ty·ing
em·u·late
·lat·ed ·lat·ing
em·u·la·tion
em·u·lous
e·mul·si·fi·ca·tion
e·mul·si·fi·er
e·mul·si·fy
·fied ·fy·ing
e·mul·sion
en·a·ble
·bled ·bling
en·act·ment
en·am·ored
en·camp·ment
en·case
·cased ·cas·ing
en·caus·tic
en·ceph·a·li·tis
en·chant·ment
en·cir·cle
en·clave
en·close
·closed
·clos·ing
en·clo·sure
en·code
en·co·mi·ast
en·co·mi·um
·ums *or* ·a
en·com·pass
en·core
en·coun·ter
en·cour·age
·aged ·ag·ing
en·cour·age·ment
en·croach·ment
en·cum·ber
en·cum·brance
en·cyc·li·cal
en·cy·clo·pe·di·a
or ·pae·di·a
en·dan·ger
en·dear
en·dear·ment
en·deav·or
en·dem·ic
end·ing
end·less
end·most
en·do·crine
en·dog·a·my
en·do·me·tri·um
en·dorse
·dorsed
·dors·ing
en·dor·see
en·dorse·ment
en·dors·er
en·dow
en·dow·ment
end·pa·per
en·dur·a·ble
en·dur·a·bly
en·dur·ance
en·dure
·dured ·dur·ing
end·ways
en·e·my
·mies
en·er·get·ic
en·er·get·i·cal·ly
en·er·gize
·gized ·giz·ing
en·er·giz·er
en·er·gy
·gies
en·er·vate
·vat·ed ·vat·ing
en·fold
en·force
·forced
·forc·ing
en·force·a·ble
en·fran·chise
en·gage
·gaged ·gag·ing
en·gage·ment
en·gen·der
en·gine
en·gi·neer
Eng·lish
en·gorge
·gorged ·gorg·ing
en·grave
·graved
·grav·ing
en·grav·er
en·gross
en·gross·er
en·gulf
en·hance
·hanced
·hanc·ing
e·nig·ma
e·nig·mat·ic
en·join
en·joy·a·ble
en·joy·a·bly
en·joy·ment
en·kin·dle
·dled ·dling
en·large
·larged
·larg·ing
en·large·ment
en·larg·er
en·light·en
en·light·en·ment
en·list
en·list·ment
en·liv·en

en masse
en·mesh
en·mi·ty
·ties
en·no·ble
·bled ·bling
en·nui
e·nor·mi·ty
·ties
e·nor·mous
e·nough
en·plane
en·rage
en·rap·ture
·tured ·tur·ing
en·rich
en·roll *or* ·rol
·rolled ·roll·ing
en·roll·ee
en·roll·ment *or*
en·rol·ment
en route
en·sconce
·sconced
·sconc·ing
en·sem·ble
en·shrine
·shrined
·shrin·ing
en·sign
en·slave
en·snare
en·snarl
en·sue
·sued ·su·ing
en·sure
en·tail
en·tan·gle
en·tente
en·ter·prise
en·ter·pris·ing
en·ter·tain
en·thrall *or*
en·thral
·thralled
·thrall·ing
en·throne
en·thuse
·thused
·thus·ing
en·thu·si·asm
en·thu·si·as·tic
en·tice
·ticed ·tic·ing
en·tice·ment
en·tire
en·tire·ly
en·tire·ty
·ties
en·ti·tle
·tled ·tling
en·ti·ty
·ties
en·to·mol·o·gy
(*insect study;* SEE
etymology)
en·tou·rage
en·train
en′trance
en·trance′
·tranced
·tranc·ing
en·trant
en·trap
en·treat
en·treat·y
·ies
en·tree *or* ·trée
en·trench·ment
en·tre·pre·neur
en·trust
en·try
·tries
en·twine
e·nu·mer·ate
·at·ed ·at·ing
e·nu·mer·a·tion
e·nu·mer·a·tor
e·nun·ci·ate
·at·ed ·at·ing
(*pronounce;* SEE
annunciate)
e·nun·ci·a·tion
e·nun·ci·a·tor
en·vel′op *v.*
en′ve·lope′ *n.*
en·vi·a·ble
en·vi·a·bly
en·vi·ous
en·vi·ron·ment
en·vi·ron·men·tal
en·vi·rons
en·vis·age
·aged
·ag·ing
en·vi·sion
en·voy
en·vy
·vies
·vied ·vy·ing
en·zyme
e·o·lith·ic
e·on
ep·au·let *or*
·lette
e·phem·er·al
ep·ic
(*poem;* SEE
epoch)
ep·i·cen·ter
ep·i·cure
ep·i·cu·re·an
ep·i·dem·ic
ep·i·glot·tis
ep·i·gram
ep·i·gram·mat·ic
ep·i·graph
ep·i·graph·ic
ep·i·lep·sy
ep·i·lep·tic
ep·i·logue *or*
·log
E·piph·a·ny
e·pis·co·pal
E·pis·co·pa·li·an
ep·i·sode
ep·i·sod·ic
e·pis·tle
e·pis·to·lar·y
ep·i·taph
ep·i·thet
e·pit·o·me
e·pit·o·mize
·mized ·miz·ing
ep·och
(*period;* SEE epic)
ep·och·al
ep·o·nym
ep·ox·y
ep·si·lon
eq·ua·bil·i·ty
eq·ua·ble
eq·ua·bly
e·qual
·qualed *or*
·qualled
·qual·ing *or*
·qual·ling
e·qual·i·tar·i·an
e·qual·i·ty
·ties
e·qual·i·za·tion
e·qual·ize
·ized ·iz·ing
e·qual·ly
e·qua·nim·i·ty
e·quate
·quat·ed
·quat·ing
e·qua·tion
e·qua·tor
e·qua·to·ri·al
eq·uer·ry
·ries
e·ques·tri·an
e·qui·an·gu·lar
e·qui·dis·tant
e·qui·lat·er·al
e·quil·i·brant
e·quil·i·brate
·brat·ed ·brat·ing
e·qui·lib·ri·um
·ri·ums *or* ·ri·a
e·quine
e·qui·noc·tial
e·qui·nox
e·quip
·quipped
·quip·ping
eq·ui·page
e·quip·ment
e·qui·poise
e·qui·pol·lent
eq·ui·ta·ble
eq·ui·ta·bly
eq·ui·ty
·ties
e·quiv·a·lence
e·quiv·a·lent
e·quiv·o·cal
e·quiv·o·cate
·cat·ed ·cat·ing

e·quiv·o·ca·tion
e·quiv·o·ca·tor
e·ra
e·rad·i·ca·ble
e·rad·i·cate
·cat·ed ·cat·ing
e·rad·i·ca·tion
e·rad·i·ca·tor
e·ras·a·ble
e·rase
·rased ·ras·ing
e·ras·er
e·ra·sure
e·rect
e·rec·tile
e·rec·tion
e·rec·tor
erg
er·go
er·go·nom·ics
er·got
e·rode
·rod·ed ·rod·ing
e·rog·e·nous
e·ro·sion
e·ro·sive
e·rot·ic
e·rot·i·ca
e·rot·i·cism
e·ro·to·gen·ic
err
er·ran·cy
·cies
er·rand
er·rant
er·ra·ta
(*sing.* er·ra·tum)
er·rat·ic
er·ro·ne·ous
er·ror
er·satz
erst·while
e·ruct
e·ruc·tate
·tat·ed ·tat·ing
e·ruc·ta·tion
er·u·dite
er·u·di·tion
e·rupt
e·rupt·i·ble
e·rup·tion
e·rup·tive
e·ryth·ro·my·cin
es·ca·lade
·lad·ed ·lad·ing
es·ca·late
·lat·ed ·lat·ing
es·ca·la·tion
es·ca·la·tor
es·ca·pade
es·cape
·caped ·cap·ing
es·cape·ment
es·cap·ism
es·cap·ist
es·carp·ment
es·cheat
es·chew
es·cort
es·crow
es·cu·lent
es·cutch·eon
Es·ki·mo
·mos *or* ·mo
e·soph·a·gus
·a·gi
es·o·ter·ic
es·pal·ier
es·pe·cial
Es·pe·ran·to
es·pi·o·nage
es·pla·nade
es·pous·al
es·pouse
·poused
·pous·ing
es·pres·so
·sos
es·prit de corps
es·py
·pied ·py·ing
es·quire
es·say
(*try;* SEE assay)
es·say·ist
es·sence
es·sen·tial
es·sen·ti·al·i·ty
es·tab·lish
es·tab·lish·ment
es·tate
es·teem
es·thete
es·thet·ic
es·thet·i·cism
esti·ma·ble
es·ti·mate
·mat·ed ·mat·ing
es·ti·ma·tion
es·ti·ma·tor
es·ti·val
es·ti·vate
·vat·ed ·vat·ing
es·trange
·tranged
·trang·ing
es·trange·ment
es·tro·gen
es·trus
es·tu·ar·i·al
es·tu·ar·y
·ies
et cet·er·a
etch·ing
e·ter·nal
e·ter·ni·ty
·ties
e·ther
e·the·re·al
eth·i·cal
eth·ics
eth·nic
eth·no·cen·trism
eth·nog·ra·phy
eth·no·log·i·cal
eth·nol·o·gy
e·thos
eth·yl
e·ti·ol·o·gy
et·i·quette
é·tude
et·y·mo·log·i·cal
et·y·mol·o·gy
·gies
(*word study;* SEE entomology)
et·y·mon
Eu·cha·rist
eu·chre
eu·gen·ics
eu·lo·gize
·gized ·giz·ing
eu·lo·gy
·gies
eu·nuch
eu·phe·mism
eu·phe·mis·tic
eu·phe·mize
·mized ·miz·ing
eu·phon·ic
eu·pho·ni·ous
eu·pho·ni·um
eu·pho·ny
·nies
eu·pho·ri·a
eu·phor·ic
eu·phu·ism
eu·phu·is·tic
Eur·a·sian
Eu·ro·bond
Eu·ro·crat
Eu·ro·cur·ren·cy
Eu·ro·dol·lars
Eu·ro·pe·an
eu·ryth·mics
eu·ryth·my
Eu·sta·chi·an
eu·tha·na·si·a
e·vac·u·ate
·at·ed ·at·ing
e·vac·u·a·tion
e·vac·u·ee
e·vade
·vad·ed ·vad·ing
e·val·u·ate
·at·ed ·at·ing
e·val·u·a·tion
ev·a·nesce
·nesced ·nesc·ing
ev·a·nes·cence
ev·a·nes·cent
e·van·gel·i·cal
e·van·gel·ism
e·van·gel·ist
e·vap·o·rate
·rat·ed ·rat·ing
e·vap·o·ra·tion
e·va·sion
e·va·sive

e·ven·hand·ed
eve·ning
e·ven·ness
e·vent
e·ven-tem·pered
e·vent·ful
e·ven·tu·al
e·ven·tu·al·i·ty
·ties
e·ven·tu·ate
·at·ed ·at·ing
e·vert
ev·er·y·bod·y
ev·er·y·day
ev·er·y·one
ev·er·y·thing
ev·er·y·where
e·vict
e·vic·tion
ev·i·dence
·denced
·denc·ing
ev·i·dent
ev·i·den·tial
e·vil-mind·ed
e·vince
·vinced
·vinc·ing
e·vin·ci·ble
e·vis·cer·ate
·at·ed ·at·ing
e·vis·cer·a·tion
ev·o·ca·tion
e·voke
·voked ·vok·ing
ev·o·lu·tion
ev·o·lu·tion·ar·y
ev·o·lu·tion·ist
e·volve
·volved ·volv·ing
ex·ac·er·bate
·bat·ed ·bat·ing
ex·ac·er·ba·tion
ex·act
ex·act·ing
ex·ac·tion
ex·ac·ti·tude
ex·act·ly
ex·ag·ger·ate
·at·ed ·at·ing
ex·ag·ger·a·tion
ex·ag·ger·a·tor
ex·alt
ex·al·ta·tion
ex·am·i·na·tion
ex·am·ine
·ined ·in·ing
ex·am·in·er
ex·am·ple
ex·as·per·ate
·at·ed ·at·ing
ex·as·per·a·tion
ex·ca·vate
·vat·ed ·vat·ing
ex·ca·va·tion
ex·ca·va·tor
ex·ceed
(*surpass;* SEE accede)
ex·cel
·celled ·cel·ling
ex·cel·lence
ex·cel·len·cy
·cies
ex·cel·lent
ex·cel·si·or
ex·cept
(*omit;* SEE accept)
ex·cept·ed
(*left out;* SEE accepted)
ex·cep·tion
ex·cep·tion·a·ble
ex·cep·tion·al
ex·cerpt
ex·cess
(*surplus;* SEE access)
ex·ces·sive
ex·ces·sive·ly
ex·change
·changed
·chang·ing
ex·change·a·bil·i·ty
ex·change·a·ble
ex·cheq·uer
ex·cis·a·ble
ex′cise
ex·cise′
·cised ·cis·ing
ex·ci·sion
ex·cit·a·bil·i·ty
ex·cit·a·ble
ex·cit·a·bly
ex·ci·ta·tion
ex·cite
·cit·ed ·cit·ing
ex·cite·ment
ex·claim
ex·cla·ma·tion
ex·clam·a·to·ry
ex·clave
ex·clud·a·ble
ex·clude
·clud·ed
·clud·ing
ex·clu·sion
ex·clu·sive
ex·clu·siv·i·ty
ex·com·mu·ni·cate
·cat·ed ·cat·ing
ex·co·ri·ate
·at·ed ·at·ing
ex·co·ri·a·tion
ex·cru·ci·ate
·at·ed ·at·ing
ex·cul·pate
·pat·ed ·pat·ing
ex·cul·pa·tion
ex·cur·sion
ex·cus·a·ble
ex·cus·a·bly
ex·cuse
·cused ·cus·ing
ex·e·cra·ble
ex·e·crate
·crat·ed
·crat·ing
ex·e·cra·tion
ex·e·cute
·cut·ed ·cut·ing
ex·e·cu·tion
ex·e·cu·tion·er
ex·ec·u·tive
ex·ec·u·tor
ex·e·ge·sis
ex·em·plar
ex·em·pla·ry
ex·em·pli·fy
·fied ·fy·ing
ex·empt
ex·emp·tion
ex·er·cis·a·ble
ex·er·cise
·cised ·cis·ing
(*use;* SEE exorcise)
ex·ert
ex·er·tion
ex·ha·la·tion
ex·hale
·haled ·hal·ing
ex·haust
ex·haust·i·ble
ex·haus·tion
ex·haus·tive
ex·hib·it
ex·hi·bi·tion
ex·hi·bi·tion·ism
ex·hib·i·tor
ex·hil·a·rant
ex·hil·a·rate
·rat·ed ·rat·ing
ex·hil·a·ra·tion
ex·hort
ex·hor·ta·tion
ex·hu·ma·tion
ex·hume
·humed
·hum·ing
ex·i·gen·cy
·cies
ex·i·gent
ex·ile
ex·ist
ex·ist·ence
ex·ist·ent
ex·is·ten·tial
ex·is·ten·tial·ism
ex·it
ex·o·dus
ex of·fi·ci·o
ex·og·a·my
ex·on·er·ate
·at·ed ·at·ing
ex·on·er·a·tion
ex·o·ra·ble
ex·or·bi·tance
ex·or·bi·tant

ex·or·cise *or* ·cize
·cised *or* ·cized
·cis·ing *or* ·ciz·ing
(*expel;* SEE exercise)
ex·or·cism
ex·o·ter·ic
ex·ot·ic
ex·ot·i·ca
ex·pand
ex·panse
ex·pan·si·ble
ex·pan·sion
ex·pan·sive
ex·pa·ti·ate
·at·ed ·at·ing
ex·pa·ti·a·tion
ex·pa·tri·ate
·at·ed ·at·ing
ex·pa·tri·a·tion
ex·pect
ex·pect·an·cy
ex·pect·ant
ex·pec·ta·tion
ex·pec·to·rant
ex·pec·to·rate
·rat·ed ·rat·ing
ex·pec·to·ra·tion
ex·pe·di·ence
ex·pe·di·en·cy
·cies
ex·pe·di·ent
ex·pe·dite
·dit·ed ·dit·ing
ex·pe·dit·er
ex·pe·di·tion
ex·pe·di·tion·ar·y
ex·pe·di·tious
ex·pel
·pelled ·pel·ling
ex·pel·la·ble
ex·pend
ex·pend·a·bil·i·ty
ex·pend·a·ble
ex·pend·i·ture
ex·pense
ex·pen·sive
ex·pen·sive·ly

ex·pe·ri·ence
·enced ·enc·ing
ex·pe·ri·en·tial
ex·per·i·ment
ex·per·i·men·tal
ex·per·i·men·ta·tion
ex·pert
ex·pert·ise
ex·pi·a·ble
ex·pi·ate
·at·ed ·at·ing
ex·pi·a·tion
ex·pi·a·tor
ex·pi·ra·tion
ex·pir·a·to·ry
ex·pire
·pired ·pir·ing
ex·plain·a·ble
ex·pla·na·tion
ex·plan·a·to·ry
ex·ple·tive
ex·pli·ca·ble
ex·pli·cate
·cat·ed ·cat·ing
ex·pli·ca·tion
ex·plic·it
ex·plod·a·ble
ex·plode
·plod·ed
·plod·ing
ex·ploit
ex·ploi·ta·tion
ex·plo·ra·tion
ex·plor·a·to·ry
ex·plore
·plored
·plor·ing
ex·plor·er
ex·plo·sion
ex·plo·sive
ex·po·nent
ex·po·nen·tial
ex·port
ex·port·a·ble
ex·por·ta·tion
ex·pose
·posed ·pos·ing
ex·po·sé
ex·po·si·tion
ex·pos·i·tor

ex·pos·i·to·ry
ex post fac·to
ex·pos·tu·late
·lat·ed ·lat·ing
ex·pos·tu·la·tion
ex·pos·tu·la·tor
ex·po·sure
ex·pound
ex·press
ex·press·i·ble
ex·pres·sion
ex·pres·sion·ism
ex·pres·sion·is·tic
ex·pres·sive
ex·press·way
ex·pro·pri·ate
·at·ed ·at·ing
ex·pro·pri·a·tion
ex·pul·sion
ex·punge
·punged
·pung·ing
ex·pur·gate
·gat·ed ·gat·ing
ex·pur·ga·tion
ex·qui·site
ex·tant
(*existing;* SEE extent)
ex·tem·po·ra·ne·ous
ex·tem·po·re
ex·tem·po·rize
·rized ·riz·ing
ex·tend
ex·ten·si·ble
ex·ten·sion
ex·ten·sive
ex·tent
(*scope;* SEE extant)
ex·ten·u·ate
·at·ed ·at·ing
ex·ten·u·a·tion
ex·te·ri·or
ex·ter·mi·nate
·nat·ed ·nat·ing
ex·ter·mi·na·tion
ex·ter·mi·na·tor
ex·ter·nal
ex·ter·nal·ize
·ized ·iz·ing

ex·tinct
ex·tinc·tion
ex·tin·guish
ex·tir·pate
·pat·ed
·pat·ing
ex·tir·pa·tion
ex·tol *or* ·toll
·tolled
·tol·ling
ex·tort
ex·tor·tion
ex·tor·tion·ate
ex·tor·tion·er
ex·tor·tion·ist
ex·tra
ex·tract
ex·tract·a·ble
or ·i·ble
ex·trac·tion
ex·trac·tor
ex·tra·cur·ric·u·lar
ex·tra·dit·a·ble
ex·tra·dite
·dit·ed ·dit·ing
ex·tra·di·tion
ex·tra·le·gal
ex·tra·mar·i·tal
ex·tra·mu·ral
ex·tra·ne·ous
ex·traor·di·nar·i·ly
ex·traor·di·nar·y
ex·trap·o·late
·lat·ed ·lat·ing
ex·tra·sen·so·ry
ex·tra·ter·ri·to·ri·al
ex·trav·a·gance
ex·trav·a·gant
ex·trav·a·gan·za
ex·tra·ve·hic·u·lar
ex·treme
ex·treme·ly
ex·trem·ism
ex·trem·ist
ex·trem·i·ty
·ties
ex·tri·cate
·cat·ed ·cat·ing
ex·tri·ca·tion

ex·trin·sic
ex·tro·ver·sion
ex·tro·vert
ex·trude
·trud·ed
·trud·ing
ex·tru·sion
ex·u·ber·ance
ex·u·ber·ant
ex·u·da·tion
ex·ude
·ud·ed ·ud·ing
ex·ult
ex·ult·ant
ex·ul·ta·tion
ex·urb
ex·ur·ban·ite
ex·ur·bi·a
eye·glass
eye·let
(*hole,* SEE islet)
eye·lid
eye-o·pen·er
eye·piece
eye·shot
eye·sight
eye·sore
eye·strain
eye·wit·ness

F

fa·ble
·bled ·bling
fab·ric
fab·ri·cate
·cat·ed ·cat·ing
fab·ri·ca·tion
fab·ri·ca·tor
fab·u·lous
fa·çade *or* ·cade
face·plate
face-sav·ing
fac·et
fa·ce·tious
fa·cial
fac·ile
fa·cil·i·tate
·tat·ed ·tat·ing
fa·cil·i·ta·tion
fa·cil·i·ty
·ties
fac·sim·i·le
·led ·le·ing
fac·tion
fac·tious
fac·ti·tious
(*artificial;* SEE fictitious)
fac·tor
fac·to·ri·al
fac·to·ry
·ries
fac·to·tum
fac·tu·al
fac·ul·ty
·ties
fade
fad·ed fad·ing
fade-in
fade-out
Fahr·en·heit
fail-safe
fail·ure
faint
(*weak;* SEE feint)
fair·ground
fair·ly
fair-mind·ed
fair-spo·ken
fair-trade
fair·way
fair-weath·er
fait ac·com·pli
faith·ful
faith·less
fake
faked fak·ing
fak·er
(*fraud*)
fa·kir
(*Moslem beggar*)
fal·cate
fal·la·cious
fal·la·cy
·cies
fal·li·bil·i·ty
fal·li·ble
fal·li·bly
fall·ing-out
fall·off
fall·out
fal·low
false
fals·er fals·est
false·hood
fal·si·fi·ca·tion
fal·si·fi·er
fal·si·fy
·fied ·fy·ing
fal·si·ty
·ties
fal·ter
fa·mil·ial
fa·mil·iar
fa·mil·i·ar·i·ty
·ties
fa·mil·iar·i·za·tion
fa·mil·iar·ize
·ized ·iz·ing
fam·i·ly
·lies
fam·ine
fam·ish
fa·mous
fa·nat·ic
fa·nat·i·cism
fan·ci·ful
fan·cy
·cies
·ci·er ·ci·est
·cied ·cy·ing
fan·cy-free
fan·light
fan·ta·size
·sized ·siz·ing
fan·tas·tic
fan·ta·sy
·sies
·sied ·sy·ing
far
far·ther
far·thest
far·ad
farce
farced farc·ing
far·ci·cal
fare
fared far·ing
fare·well
far·fetched
far-flung
farm·hand
far-off
far-out
far-reach·ing
far·row
far·see·ing
far·sight·ed
far·ther
far·thing
fas·ci·cle
fas·ci·nate
·nat·ed ·nat·ing
fas·ci·na·tion
fas·ci·na·tor
fas·cism
fas·cist
fash·ion
fash·ion·a·ble
fash·ion·a·bly
fast·back
fas·ten
fas·ten·er
fas·ten·ing
fas·tid·i·ous
fat
fat·ter fat·test
fat·ted fat·ting
fa·tal
fa·tal·ism
fa·tal·ist
fa·tal·is·tic
fa·tal·is·ti·cal·ly
fa·tal·i·ty
·ties
fa·tal·ly
fate·ful
fa·ther·hood
fa·ther-in-law
fa·thers-in-law
fa·ther·land
fa·ther·less
fa·ther·li·ness
fa·ther·ly
fath·om
fath·om·a·ble
fath·om·less
fat·i·ga·ble

fa·tigue
·tigued
·tigu·ing
fat-sol·u·ble
fat·ten
fat·ti·ness
fat·ty
·ti·er ·ti·est
fa·tu·i·ty
·ties
fat·u·ous
fau·cet
fault·find·ing
fault·i·ness
fault·less
fault·y
·i·er ·i·est
fau·na
·nas *or* ·nae
faux pas
faux pas
fa·vor·a·ble
fa·vor·a·bly
fa·vored
fa·vor·ite
fa·vor·it·ism
faze
fazed faz·ing
(*disturb;* SEE phase)
fe·al·ty
fear·ful
fear·ful·ly
fear·less
fear·some
fea·si·bil·i·ty
fea·si·ble
fea·si·bly
feast
feat
feath·er·bed
feath·er·bed·ding
feath·er·brain
feath·ered
feath·er·weight
fea·ture
·tured ·tur·ing
fea·ture-length
feb·ri·fuge
fe·brile

Feb·ru·ar·y
feck·less
fe·cund
fe·cun·di·ty
fed·er·al
fed·er·al·ism
fed·er·al·i·za·tion
fed·er·al·ize
·ized ·iz·ing
fed·er·ate
·at·ed ·at·ing
fed·er·a·tion
fe·do·ra
fee·ble
·bler ·blest
feed·back
feel
felt feel·ing
fee-split·ting
feign
feint
(*pretense;* SEE faint)
fe·lic·i·tate
·tat·ed ·tat·ing
fe·lic·i·ta·tion
fe·lic·i·tous
fe·lic·i·ty
·ties
fe·line
fel·low·ship
fel·on
fe·lo·ni·ous
fel·o·ny
·nies
fe·male
fem·i·nine
fem·i·nin·i·ty
fem·i·nism
fem·i·nize
·nized ·niz·ing
fence
fenced fenc·ing
fend·er
fen·es·tra·tion
fen·nel
fer·ment
fer·men·ta·tion
fern
fe·ro·cious

fe·roc·i·ty
fer·ret
fer·ri·age
fer·ry·boat
fer·tile
fer·til·i·ty
fer·til·i·za·tion
fer·til·ize
·ized ·iz·ing
fer·til·iz·er
fer·vent
fer·vid
fer·vor
fes·tal
fes·ter
fes·ti·val
fes·tive
fes·tiv·i·ty
·ties
fes·toon
fe·tal
fetch·ing
fete *or* fête
fet·ed *or* fêt·ed
fet·ing *or* fêt·ing
fet·id
fet·lock
fet·ter
fet·tle
fet·tuc·ci·ne
feu·dal
feu·dal·ism
feu·dal·is·tic
fe·ver·ish
fi·an·cé *masc.*
fi·an·cée *fem.*
fi·as·co
·coes *or* ·cos
fi·at
fi·ber *or* ·bre
fi·ber·board
Fi·ber·glas
fi·bril·la·tion
fi·broid
fi·brous
fib·u·la
·lae *or* ·las
fick·le
fic·tion·al·ize
·ized ·iz·ing

fic·ti·tious
(*imaginary;* SEE factitious)
fid·dle
·dled ·dling
fi·del·i·ty
·ties
fidg·et
fidg·et·y
fi·du·ci·ar·y
·ies
field·er
field-strip
field-test
field·work
fiend·ish
fierce
fierc·er
fierc·est
fierce·ly
fi·er·y
·i·er ·i·est
fif·teen
fif·ti·eth
fif·ty
·ties
fight
fought
fight·ing
fig·ment
fig·u·ra·tion
fig·u·ra·tive
fig·ure
·ured ·ur·ing
fig·ure·head
fig·u·rine
fil·a·ment
fi·lar
file
filed fil·ing
fi·let mi·gnon
fil·i·al
fil·i·a·tion
fil·i·bus·ter
fil·i·gree
·greed
·gree·ing
fil·ings
Fil·i·pi·no
·nos
fil·let

fill-in
fill·ing
fil·lip
fil·ly
·lies
film·strip
film·y
·i·er ·i·est
fil·ter
fil·ter·a·ble
filth·i·ly
filth·i·ness
filth·y
·i·er ·i·est
fil·trate
·trat·ed
·trat·ing
fin·a·ble
fi·na·gle
·gled ·gling
fi·na·le
fi·nal·ist
fi·nal·i·ty
fi·nal·ize
·ized ·iz·ing
fi·nal·ly
fi·nance
·nanced
·nanc·ing
fi·nan·cial
fin·an·cier
find·er
fine-cut
fine-grained
fine·ly
fine·ness
fin·er·y
·ies
fi·nesse
·nessed
·ness·ing
fin·gered
fin·ger·print
fin·i·al
fin·i·cal
fin·ick·i·ness
fin·ick·y
fi·nis
fin·ish
fin·ished
fi·nite
fiord
fir
fire
fired fir·ing
fire·arm
fire·ball
fire escape
fire·place
fire·proof
fir·kin
fir·ma·ment
firm·ly
first-class
first·hand
first·ly
first-rate
firth
fis·cal
fis·cal·ly
fish·er·man
fish·er·y
·ies
fish·y
·i·er ·i·est
fis·sion
fis·sion·a·ble
fis·sure
·sured ·sur·ing
fist·i·cuffs
fis·tu·lous
fit
fit·ter fit·test
fit·ted fit·ting
fit·ful
fit·ful·ly
fit·ness
five·fold
fix·ate
·at·ed ·at·ing
fix·a·tion
fix·a·tive
fixed
fix·ed·ly
fix·ture
fiz·zle
·zled ·zling
fjord
flab·ber·gast
flab·bi·ness
flab·by
·bi·er ·bi·est
flac·cid
flac·cid·i·ty
fla·con
flag
flagged
flag·ging
flag·el·lant
flag·el·late
·lat·ed ·lat·ing
flag·el·la·tion
flag·pole
fla·gran·cy
fla·grant
flag·ship
flag·stone
flag-wav·ing
flail
flair
(*knack;* SEE flare)
flake
flaked flak·ing
flak·i·ness
flak·y
·i·er ·i·est
flam·boy·ance
flam·boy·ant
flame·proof
flam·ma·bil·i·ty
flam·ma·ble
flange
flanged
flang·ing
flank
flan·nel
flap
flapped
flap·ping
flare
flared flar·ing
(*blaze;* SEE flair)
flare-up
flash·back
flash·bulb
flash·card
flash·cube
flash·i·ly
flash·i·ness
flash·light
flash·y
·i·er ·i·est
flat
flat·ter flat·test
flat·ted flat·ting
flat·car
flat·i·ron
flat·ten
flat·ter
flat·ter·y
flat·u·lent
flat·ware
flat·work
flaunt
flau·tist
fla·vor·ful
fla·vor·ing
fla·vor·less
flaw·less
flax·en
fledg·ling
flee
fled flee·ing
fleet·ing
flesh·y
·i·er ·i·est
flex·i·bil·i·ty
flex·i·ble
flex·i·bly
flex·time
flick·er
fli·er *or* fly·er
flight·i·ness
flight·less
flight·y
·i·er ·i·est
flim·si·ly
flim·si·ness
flim·sy
·si·er ·si·est
flinch·ing·ly
fling
flung fling·ing
flint·y
·i·er ·i·est
flip
flipped
flip·ping
flip·pan·cy
·cies

flip·pant
flip·per
flir·ta·tion
flir·ta·tious
flit
 flit·ted flit·ting
float
float·er
float·ing
floc·cu·late
 ·lat·ed ·lat·ing
floc·cu·lent
flog
 flogged
 flog·ging
flood·gate
flood·light
 ·light·ed *or* ·lit
 ·light·ing
floor·walk·er
flop
 flopped
 flop·ping
flo·ra
 ·ras *or* ·rae
flo·ral
flo·res·cence
 (*blooming;* SEE fluorescence)
flo·res·cent
flo·ri·cul·ture
flor·id
Flor·i·da
flo·rid·i·ty
flor·in
flo·ta·tion
flo·til·la
flot·sam
flounce
 flounced
 flounc·ing
floun·der
flour·ish
flout
flow
flow·ered
flow·er·i·ness
fluc·tu·ate
 ·at·ed ·at·ing
flu·en·cy
flu·ent

fluf·fi·ness
fluf·fy
 ·fi·er ·fi·est
flu·id
flu·id·i·ty
flun·ky
 ·kies
flu·o·resce
 ·resced
 ·resc·ing
flu·o·res·cence
 (*light;* SEE florescence)
flu·o·res·cent
fluor·i·date
 ·dat·ed ·dat·ing
fluor·i·da·tion
fluor·i·nate
 ·nat·ed ·nat·ing
fluor·o·scope
flu·o·ros·co·py
flur·ry
 ·ries
 ·ried ·ry·ing
flus·ter
flu·vi·al
fly
 flies
 flew flown
 fly·ing
fly-by-night
fly·weight
fly·wheel
foam·i·ness
foam·y
 ·i·er ·i·est
fo·cal
fo·cal·ize
 ·ized ·iz·ing
fo·cus
 ·cus·es *or* ·ci
 ·cused *or* ·cussed
 ·cus·ing *or*
 ·cus·sing
fog·bound
fog·horn
foi·ble
foist
fold·a·way
fo·li·age
fo·li·ate
 ·at·ed ·at·ing
fo·li·a·tion

fo·li·o
 ·os
 ·oed ·o·ing
folk·lore
fol·li·cle
fol·low-through
fol·low-up
fol·ly
 ·lies
fo·ment
fo·men·ta·tion
fon·dant
fond·ness
font
food·stuff
fool·har·di·ness
fool·har·dy
fool·ish·ness
fool·proof
foot·age
foot·bridge
foot-can·dle
foot·note
foot·print
foot·race
foot·wear
foot·work
for·age
for·ay
for·bear
 ·bore ·borne
 ·bear·ing
 (*abstain;* SEE forebear)
for·bear·ance
for·bid
 ·bade *or* ·bad
 ·bid·den
 ·bid·ding
force
 forced forc·ing
force·ful
for·ci·ble
for·ci·bly
fore·arm
fore·bear
 (*ancestor;* SEE forbear)
fore·bode
 ·bod·ed ·bod·ing

fore·cast
 ·cast *or* ·cast·ed
 ·cast·ing
fore·close
fore·clo·sure
fore·fa·ther
fore·fin·ger
fore·foot
fore·go
 ·went ·gone
 ·go·ing
 (*precede;* SEE forgo)
fore·go·ing
fore·ground
fore·hand
fore·hand·ed
fore·head
for·eign
for·eign-born
for·eign·er
fore·knowl·edge
fore·leg
fore·lock
fore·man
fore·most
fore·named
fore·noon
fo·ren·sic
fo·ren·si·cal·ly
fore·or·dain
fore·quar·ter
fore·run·ner
fore·see
 ·saw ·seen
 ·see·ing
fore·see·a·ble
fore·se·er
fore·shad·ow
fore·short·en
fore·sight
for·est
fore·stall
for·est·a·tion
for·est·er
for·est·ry
fore·taste
fore·tell
 ·told ·tell·ing
fore·thought

for·ev·er
fore·warn
fore·wo·man
fore·word
(*preface;* SEE forward)
for·feit
for·fei·ture
forge
forged forg·ing
forg·er
for·ger·y
·ies
for·get
·got, ·got·ten or ·got,
·get·ting
for·get·ful
for·get-me-not
for·get·ta·ble
for·giv·a·ble
for·go
·went ·gone
·go·ing
(*do without;* SEE forego)
forked
fork·lift
for·lorn
for·mal
form·al·de·hyde
for·mal·i·ty
·ties
for·mal·i·za·tion
for·mal·ize
·ized ·iz·ing
for·mal·ly
for·mat
for·ma·tion
form·a·tive
for·mer
for·mer·ly
for·mi·da·ble
for·mi·da·bly
form·less
for·mu·la
·las or ·lae
for·mu·late
·lat·ed ·lat·ing
for·mu·la·tion
for·sake
·sook
·sak·en
·sak·ing
for·swear
·swore ·sworn
·swear·ing
fort
(*fortified place*)
forte
(*special skill*)
forth·com·ing
forth·right
forth·with
for·ti·eth
for·ti·fi·ca·tion
for·ti·fi·er
for·ti·fy
·fied ·fy·ing
for·ti·tude
for·tress
for·tu·i·tous
for·tu·i·ty
·ties
for·tu·nate
for·tune
for·ty
·ties
fo·rum
·rums or ·ra
for·ward
(*to the front;* SEE foreword)
fos·sil
fos·ter
foul
(*filthy;* SEE fowl)
fou·lard
foul·mouthed
foun·da·tion
foun′der *v.*
found′er *n.*
found·ry
·ries
foun·tain
foun·tain·head
four·fold
four-foot·ed
four-in-hand
four·some
four-star
four·teen
fourth
fourth-class
four-way
fowl
(*bird;* SEE foul)
fox·i·ly
fox·i·ness
fox·y
·i·er ·i·est
foy·er
fra·cas
frac·tion
frac·tious
frac·ture
·tured ·tur·ing
frag·ile
fra·gil·i·ty
frag·ment
frag·men·tar·y
fra·grance
fra·grant
frail·ty
·ties
frame
framed
fram·ing
frame-up
frame·work
franc
(*coin;* SEE frank)
fran·chise
·chised ·chis·ing
fran·gi·bil·i·ty
fran·gi·ble
frank
(*free;* SEE franc)
frank·furt·er
fran·tic
fra·ter·nal
fra·ter·nal·ly
fra·ter·ni·ty
·ties
frat·er·ni·za·tion
frat·er·nize
·nized ·niz·ing
frat·ri·cide
fraud
fraud·u·lence
fraud·u·lent
fraught
freak·ish
free
fre·er fre·est
freed free·ing
free·bie or ·by
·bies
free·dom
free-for-all
free-form
free·hand
free·hold
free-lance
free·load·er
free·man
free-spo·ken
free-stand·ing
free·stone
free·think·er
free·way
freez·a·ble
freeze
froze fro·zen
freez·ing
(*become ice;* SEE frieze)
freeze-dry
-dried -dry·ing
freight·age
freight·er
French cuff
French doors
fre·net·ic
fre·quen·cy
·cies
fre·quent
fres·co
·coes or ·cos
fresh·en
fresh·man
fret
fret·ted
fret·ting
fret·work
Freud·i·an
fri·a·bil·i·ty
fri·a·ble
fric·tion
Fri·day

friend·li·ness
friend·ly
·li·er
·li·est
friend·ship
frieze
(*in architecture;* SEE freeze)
frig·ate
fright·ened
fright·ful
frig·id
fri·gid·i·ty
fringe
fringed
fring·ing
frisk·i·ness
frisk·y
·i·er ·i·est
frit·ter
fri·vol·i·ty
·ties
friv·o·lous
frol·ic
·icked
·ick·ing
frol·ick·er
frol·ic·some
front·age
fron·tal
fron·tier
fron·tiers·man
front·let
frost·bite
·bit ·bit·ten
·bit·ing
frost·i·ly
frost·i·ness
frost·ing
frost·y
·i·er ·i·est
froth·i·ly
froth·i·ness
froth·y
·i·er ·i·est
fro·ward
frown
fruc·ti·fy
·fied ·fy·ing
fru·gal
fru·gal·i·ty
fru·gal·ly
fruit·ful
fruit·i·ness
fru·i·tion
fruit·less
fruit·wood
fruit·y
·i·er ·i·est
frus·trate
·trat·ed
·trat·ing
frus·tra·tion
frus·tum
·tums *or* ·ta
f-stop
fudge
fudged
fudg·ing
fu·el
·eled *or* ·elled
·el·ing *or* ·el·ling
fuel cell
fu·gi·tive
fugue
ful·crum
·crums *or* ·cra
ful·fill *or* ·fil
·filled ·fill·ing
ful·fill·ment
or ·fil·ment
full-blood·ed
full-blown
full-bod·ied
full-fash·ioned
full-fledged
full-length
full-scale
full-time
full·y
ful·mi·nate
·nat·ed ·nat·ing
ful·some
fum·ble
·bled ·bling
fume
fumed fum·ing
fu·mi·gant
fu·mi·gate
·gat·ed ·gat·ing
fu·mi·ga·tion
fu·mi·ga·tor
func·tion·al
func·tion·ar·y
·ar·ies
fun·da·men·tal
fun·da·men·tal·ism
fund-rais·er
fu·ner·al
fu·ne·re·al
fun·gi·cid·al
fun·gi·cide
fun·gous *adj.*
fun·gus *n.*
·gi *or* ·gus·es
fu·nic·u·lar
fun·nel
·neled *or* ·nelled
·nel·ing *or*
·nel·ling
fur·be·low
fur·bish
fu·ri·ous
fur·long
fur·lough
fur·nace
fur·nish·ings
fur·ni·ture
fu·ror
fur·ri·er
fur·ri·ness
fur·row
fur·ry
·ri·er ·ri·est
fur·ther
fur·ther·more
fur·ther·most
fur·thest
fur·tive
fu·ry
·ries
fuse
fused fus·ing
fu·se·lage
fu·si·bil·i·ty
fu·si·ble
fu·sil·lade
·lad·ed ·lad·ing
fu·sion
fus·tian
fust·y
·i·er ·i·est
fu·tile
fu·tile·ly
fu·til·i·ty
fu·ture
fu·tu·ri·ty
·ties

G

gab·ar·dine
gadg·et
gage
(*pledge;* SEE gauge)
gai·e·ty
gai·ly
gain·er
gain·ful
gain·ful·ly
gain·li·ness
gain·ly
·li·er ·li·est
gain·say
·said ·say·ing
gait
gai·ter
ga·la
gal·ax·y
·ies
gal·lant
gal·lant·ry
·ries
gal·ler·y
·ies
·ied ·y·ing
gal·ley
·leys
gall·ing
gal·li·vant
gal·lon
gal·lop
gal·lows
·lows·es *or*
·lows
gall·stone
ga·lore
gal·van·ic
gal·va·nism
gal·va·ni·za·tion

gal·va·nize
·nized ·niz·ing
gal·va·nom·e·ter
gam·bit
gam·ble
·bled ·bling
(*risk;* SEE
gambol)
gam·bler
gam·bol
·boled *or* ·bolled
·bol·ing *or*
·bol·ling
(*frolic;* SEE
gamble)
gam·brel
games·man·ship
gam·ma
gam·ut
gam·y
·i·er ·i·est
gan·gli·on
·gli·a *or* ·gli·ons
gant·let
gan·try
·tries
gap
gapped
gap·ping
gape
gaped gap·ing
gar·ble
·bled ·bling
gar·çon
·çons
gar·ish
gar·land
gar·ment
gar·ner
gar·net
gar·nish
gar·nish·ee
·eed ·ee·ing
gar·nish·ment
gar·ret
gar·ri·son
gar·rote
·rot·ed *or*
·rot·ted
·rot·ing *or*
·rot·ting
gar·ru·li·ty
gar·ru·lous
gas·e·ous
gas·ket
gas·light
gas·o·line *or*
·lene
gas·tric
gas·tro·nome
gas·tro·nom·i·cal
gas·tron·o·my
gate·way
gath·er·ing
gauche
gau·che·rie
gaud·i·ly
gaud·i·ness
gaud·y
·i·er ·i·est
gauge
gauged
gaug·ing
(*measure;* SEE
gage)
gauge·a·ble
gaunt
gaunt·let
gauze
gav·el
gear·box
gear·shift
gear·wheel
gel
gelled gel·ling
ge·lat·i·nize
·nized ·niz·ing
ge·lat·i·nous
gel·id
ge·lid·i·ty
gem·i·nate
·nat·ed
·nat·ing
Gem·i·ni
gen·darme
gen·der
ge·ne·a·log·i·cal
ge·ne·al·o·gy
·gies
gen·er·al
gen·er·al·i·ty
·ties
gen·er·al·i·za·tion
gen·er·al·ize
·ized ·iz·ing
gen·er·al·ly
gen·er·ate
·at·ed ·at·ing
gen·er·a·tion
gen·er·a·tor
ge·ner·ic
ge·ner·i·cal·ly
gen·er·os·i·ty
·ties
gen·er·ous
gen·e·sis
·ses
ge·net·ic
ge·net·i·cal·ly
ge·nial
ge·ni·al·i·ty
ge·nial·ly
ge·nius
gen·o·cide
gen·o·type
gen·re
gen·teel
Gen·tile
gen·til·i·ty
gen·tle
·tler ·tlest
gen·tly
gen·try
gen·u·flect
gen·u·ine
gen·u·ine·ly
ge·nus
gen·er·a
ge·o·cen·tric
ge·og·ra·pher
ge·o·graph·i·cal
ge·og·ra·phy
·phies
ge·o·log·ic
ge·o·log·i·cal·ly
ge·ol·o·gist
ge·ol·o·gy
·gies
ge·o·met·ric
ge·o·met·ri·cal·ly
ge·om·e·try
·tries
ge·o·phys·i·cal
ge·o·phys·i·cist
ge·o·phys·ics
ge·o·po·lit·i·cal
ge·o·pol·i·tics
Geor·gia
ge·o·stat·ics
ge·ot·ro·pism
ger·i·at·rics
ger·mane
ger·mi·cid·al
ger·mi·cide
ger·mi·nate
·nat·ed ·nat·ing
ger·mi·na·tion
ger·on·tol·o·gy
ger·ry·man·der
ger·und
Ge·stalt
ges·tate
·tat·ed ·tat·ing
ges·ta·tion
ges·tic·u·late
·lat·ed ·lat·ing
ges·tic·u·la·tion
ges·ture
·tured ·tur·ing
get-to·geth·er
gey·ser
ghast·li·ness
ghast·ly
·li·er ·li·est
ghet·to
·tos *or* ·toes
ghet·to·ize
·ized ·iz·ing
ghost·li·ness
ghost·ly
·li·er ·li·est
ghost·write
ghost·writ·er
ghoul·ish
gib·ber·ish
gibe
gibed gib·ing
(*taunt;* SEE jibe)
gib·let
gid·di·ly
gid·di·ness

gid·dy
·di·er ·di·est
gift·ed
gift-wrap
-wrapped
-wrap·ping
gi·gan·tic
gi·gan·ti·cal·ly
gi·gan·tism
gig·gle
·gled ·gling
gild
gild·ed *or* gilt
gild·ing
(*coat with gold;* SEE guild)
gilt
(*gold;* SEE guilt)
gilt-edged
gim·bals
gim·crack
gim·let
gim·mick
gin·ger
gird
gird·ed *or* girt
gird·ing
gird·er
gist
give·a·way
giz·zard
gla·cé
·céed ·cé·ing
gla·cial
gla·ci·ate
·at·ed ·at·ing
gla·cier
glad·some
glair
(*glaze;* SEE glare)
glam·or·ize
·ized ·iz·ing
glam·or·ous
glam·our *or* ·or
glance
glanced
glanc·ing
glan·du·lar
glare
glared glar·ing
(*strong light;* SEE glair)

glar·i·ness
glar·y
·i·er ·i·est
glass·ful
·fuls
glass·ine
glass·i·ness
glass·ware
glass·y
·i·er ·i·est
glau·co·ma
glaze
glazed glaz·ing
gla·zier
glean·ings
glee·ful
glib
glib·ber
glib·best
glib·ly
glide
glid·ed glid·ing
glid·er
glim·mer
glimpse
glimpsed
glimps·ing
glis·ten
glitch
glit·ter
glit·ter·y
gloam·ing
gloat
glob·al
globe-trot·ter
glob·u·lar
glob·ule
gloom·i·ly
gloom·i·ness
gloom·y
·i·er ·i·est
glo·ri·fi·ca·tion
glo·ri·fy
·fied ·fy·ing
glo·ri·ous
glo·ry
·ries
·ried ·ry·ing
glos·sa·ry
·ries
gloss·i·ness

gloss·y
·i·er ·i·est
·ies
glow·er
glow·ing·ly
glu·cose
glut
glut·ted
glut·ting
glu·ten
glu·ten·ous
(*having gluten*)
glu·ti·nous
(*gluey*)
glut·ton
glut·ton·ous
(*greedy*)
glut·ton·y
glyc·er·in *or* ·ine
gnarled
gnash
goad
go-a·head
go-be·tween
gob·let
god·li·ness
god·ly
·li·er
·li·est
go-get·ter
goi·ter *or* ·tre
gold·brick
gold·en
gold-filled
gold leaf
gold·smith
gon·do·la
gon·do·lier
good·bye *or* good-bye
·byes *or* -byes
good-for-noth·ing
good-heart·ed
good-hu·mored
good-look·ing
good·ly
·li·er ·li·est
good-na·tured
good night
good-sized
good-tem·pered

good·y
·ies
goose·neck
goose-step
gore
gored gor·ing
gorge
gorged
gorg·ing
gor·geous
gor·i·ness
gor·mand·ize
·ized ·iz·ing
gor·y
·i·er ·i·est
gouge
gouged
goug·ing
gou·lash
gourd
gour·mand
gour·met
gov·ern·ment
gov·ern·men·tal
gov·er·nor
grace·ful
grace·ful·ly
grace·less
gra·cious
gra·date
·dat·ed
·dat·ing
gra·da·tion
grade
grad·ed
grad·ing
grad·u·al
grad·u·ate
·at·ed ·at·ing
grad·u·a·tion
graf·fi·ti
(*sing.* graf·fi·to)
graft·er
gra·ham
grain·i·ness
grain·y
·i·er ·i·est
gram·mar
gram·mar·i·an
gram·mat·i·cal

gran·a·ry
·ries
gran·deur
gran·dil·o·quent
gran·di·ose
grand·stand
gran·ite
grant·ee
grant-in-aid
grants-in-aid
grant·or
gran·u·lar
gran·u·late
·lat·ed
·lat·ing
gran·ule
grape·vine
graph·ic
graph·i·cal·ly
graph·ite
graph·ol·o·gy
grap·nel
grap·ple
·pled ·pling
grap·pler
grasp·ing
grate
grat·ed
grat·ing
grate·ful
grate·ful·ly
grat·i·fi·ca·tion
grat·i·fy
·fied ·fy·ing
gra·tis
grat·i·tude
gra·tu·i·tous
gra·tu·i·ty
·ties
grav·el
·eled *or* ·elled
·el·ing *or* ·el·ling
grav·el·ly
grave·yard
grav·i·tate
·tat·ed ·tat·ing
grav·i·ta·tion
grav·i·ty
·ties

gra·vy
·vies
gray
gray-head·ed
graze
grazed graz·ing
grease
greased
greas·ing
greas·i·ness
greas·y
·i·er ·i·est
great·coat
greed·i·ly
greed·i·ness
greed·y
·i·er ·i·est
Greek-let·ter
green·back
green·er·y
green·gage
green·horn
gre·gar·i·ous
gre·nade
gren·a·dier
gren·a·dine
grey·hound *or*
gray·
grid·dle
·dled ·dling
grid·i·ron
grief-strick·en
griev·ance
grieve
grieved
griev·ing
griev·ous
grif·fin
grill·room
grim
grim·mer
grim·mest
gri·mace
·maced
·mac·ing
grime
grimed grim·ing
grim·i·ly
grim·i·ness
grim·y
·i·er ·i·est

grin
grinned grin·ning
grind
ground grind·ing
grind·stone
grip
gripped *or* gript
grip·ping
(*hold*)
gripe
griped grip·ing
(*distress*)
grippe
(*influenza*)
gris·li·ness
gris·ly
·li·er ·li·est
(*horrid*)
gris·tle
gris·tly
(*of gristle*)
grist·mill
grit
grit·ted grit·ting
grit·ti·ness
grit·ty
·ti·er ·ti·est
griz·zly bear
groan·ing
grog·gi·ly
grog·gi·ness
grog·gy
·gi·er ·gi·est
grom·met
grope
groped grop·ing
gros·grain
gross·ly
gross·ness
gro·tesque
gro·tesque·ly
grot·to
·toes *or* ·tos
ground·less
grounds·keep·er
ground·speed
ground·work
group
grout
grove

grov·el
·eled *or* ·elled
·el·ing *or* ·el·ling
grown-up
growth
grudge
grudged
grudg·ing
gru·el
gru·el·ing *or*
gru·el·ling
grue·some
grum·ble
·bled ·bling
grum·bler
grum·bly
grump·i·ness
grump·y
·i·er ·i·est
grun·ion
grunt
Gru·yère
guar·an·tee
·teed ·tee·ing
guar·an·tor
guar·an·ty
·ties
·tied ·ty·ing
guard·ed
guard·house
guard·i·an·ship
guard·rail
gu·ber·na·to·ri·al
Guern·sey
·seys
guess·work
guest
guid·a·ble
guid·ance
guide
guid·ed
guid·ing
guide·book
guide·line
guide·post
guild
(*union;* SEE gild)
guilds·man
guile·ful
guile·less

guilt
(*blame;* SEE gilt)
guilt·i·ly
guilt·i·ness
guilt·y
·i·er ·i·est
guise
gul·li·bil·i·ty
gul·li·ble
gul·li·bly
gum·mi·ness
gum·my
·mi·er ·mi·est
gun·fire
gun·ner·y
gun·play
gun·point
gush·er
gush·i·ness
gush·y
·i·er ·i·est
gus·set
gus·ta·to·ry
gus·to
gust·y
·i·er ·i·est
gut·tur·al
guz·zle
·zled ·zling
guz·zler
gym·na·si·um
·si·ums *or* ·si·a
gym·nast
gym·nas·tics
gyn·e·col·o·gist
gyn·e·col·o·gy
gyp
gypped gyp·ping
gyp·sum
Gyp·sy
·sies
gy·rate
·rat·ed ·rat·ing
gy·ra·tion
gy·ro·com·pass
gy·ro·scope
gy·ro·scop·ic
gy·ro·sta·bi·liz·er

H

ha·be·as cor·pus
hab·er·dash·er·y
·ies
ha·bil·i·tate
·tat·ed ·tat·ing
hab·it
hab·it·a·ble
hab·i·tat
hab·i·ta·tion
hab·it-form·ing
ha·bit·u·al
ha·bit·u·ate
·at·ed ·at·ing
hab·i·tude
ha·bit·u·é
hag·gle
·gled ·gling
hail·stone
hair·breadth
hair-rais·ing
hair·split·ting
hal·cy·on
hale
haled hal·ing
half
halves
half-hour
half-mast
half·tone
half·way
hall·mark
hal·lowed
hal·lu·ci·nate
·nat·ed ·nat·ing
hal·lu·ci·na·tion
hal·lu·ci·na·to·ry
hal·lu·ci·no·gen
hal·ter
halt·ing·ly
halve
halved halv·ing
hal·yard
ham·let
ham·per
ham·string
hand·bill
hand·book
hand·ful
·fuls
hand·gun
hand·i·cap
·capped ·cap·ping
hand·i·craft
hand·i·ly
hand·i·ness
hand·i·work
hand·ker·chief
·chiefs
han·dle
·dled ·dling
hand·ler
hand·made
hand·out
hand·picked
hand·shake
hand·some
hand-to-hand
hand·work
hand·writ·ing
hand·y
·i·er ·i·est
hang
hung hang·ing
(*suspend*)
hang
hanged hang·ing
(*put to death*)
hang·ar
(*aircraft shed*)
hang·er
(*garment holder*)
hang·er-on
hang·ers-on
han·som
Ha·nu·ka
hap·haz·ard
hap·less
hap·pen
hap·pen·stance
hap·pi·ly
hap·pi·ness
hap·py
·pi·er ·pi·est
ha·rangue
·rangued
·rangu·ing
har·ass
har·bin·ger
har·bor
hard·back
hard-bit·ten
hard-boiled
hard-bound
hard-core
hard-cov·er
hard·en
hard·goods
har·di·ly
har·di·ness
hard·ly
hard·pan
hard-shell
hard·ship
hard·top
hard·ware
hard·wood
har·dy
·di·er ·di·est
harm·ful
harm·less
har·mon·ic
har·mon·i·ca
har·mo·ni·ous
har·mo·nize
·nized
·niz·ing
har·mo·ny
har·ness
har·row
har·row·ing
har·ry
·ried ·ry·ing
harsh·ness
har·vest·er
has-been
has·sle
·sled ·sling
has·sock
haste
has·ten
hast·i·ly
hast·i·ness
hast·y
·i·er ·i·est
hat·band

hatch·er·y
·ies
hatch·et
hatch·ing
hatch·way
hate
hat·ed hat·ing
hate·a·ble
hate·ful
hat·rack
ha·tred
hat·ter
haugh·ti·ly
haugh·ti·ness
haugh·ty
·ti·er ·ti·est
haul·age
haunch
haunt·ed
haunt·ing
hau·teur
have
had hav·ing
have·lock
ha·ven
have-not
hav·oc
Ha·wai·i
haz·ard
haz·ard·ous
haze
hazed haz·ing
ha·zi·ly
ha·zi·ness
ha·zy
·zi·er ·zi·est
H-bomb
head·ache
head·first
head·i·ly
head·i·ness
head·land
head·less
head·light
head·line
head·long
head·man
head·mas·ter
head-on
head·phone
head·piece
head·quar·ters
head·rest
head·set
head start
head·strong
head·wa·ters
head·way
head wind
head·y
·i·er ·i·est
heal
(*cure;* SEE heel)
health·ful
health·i·ly
health·i·ness
health·y
·i·er ·i·est
hear·say
hearse
heart·beat
heart·burn
heart·en
heart·felt
hearth·stone
heart·i·ly
heart·i·ness
heart·less
heart-rend·ing
heart·warm·ing
heart·y
·i·er ·i·est
heat·ed·ly
heat·er
heath
hea·then
heath·er
heat·stroke
heave
heaved *or* hove
heav·ing
heav·en·ly
heav·i·ly
heav·i·ness
heav·y
·i·er ·i·est
heav·y-du·ty
heav·y-hand·ed
heav·y-heart·ed
heav·y·set
heav·y·weight
He·bra·ic
He·brew
heck·le
·led ·ling
hec·tic
hec·ti·cal·ly
hec·to·graph
hedge
hedged
hedg·ing
hedge·hop
he·do·nism
he·do·nis·tic
heed·ful
heed·less
heel
(*foot part;*
SEE heal)
heft·y
·i·er ·i·est
heif·er
height
height·en
hei·nous
heir
(*inheritor;* SEE
air)
heir·loom
hel·i·cal
hel·i·cop·ter
he·li·o·graph
he·li·o·trope
hel·i·port
he·li·um
he·lix
·lix·es *or* ·li·ces
helms·man
help·ful
help·ful·ly
help·less
he·ma·tol·o·gy
hem·i·sphere
hem·i·spher·i·cal
hem·line
he·mo·glo·bin
he·mo·phil·i·a
hem·or·rhage
·rhaged ·rhag·ing
hence·forth
he·pat·ic
hep·a·ti·tis
hep·ta·gon
her·ald
he·ral·dic
her·ald·ry
her·ba·ceous
her·bi·cide
her·bi·vore
her·biv·o·rous
here·a·bout
here·af·ter
here·by
he·red·i·tar·y
he·red·i·ty
·ties
here·in
here·in·af·ter
here's
her·e·sy
·sies
her·e·tic
he·ret·i·cal
here·to·fore
here·with
her·it·a·ble
her·it·age
her·met·i·cal·ly
he·ro·ic
her·o·in
(*narcotic*)
her·o·ine
(*female hero*)
her·o·ism
her·ring·bone
her·self
hes·i·tan·cy
·cies
hes·i·tant
hes·i·tate
·tat·ed ·tat·ing
hes·i·ta·tion
het·er·o·dox
het·er·o·dox·y
·ies
het·er·o·dyne
·dyned ·dyn·ing

het·er·o·ge·ne·i·ty
·ties
het·er·o·ge·ne·ous
het·er·o·nym
heu·ris·tic
hew
hewed, hewed *or* hewn, hew·ing
(*chop;* SEE hue)
hex·a·gon
hex·ag·o·nal
hex·a·he·dron
·drons *or* ·dra
hey·day
hi·a·tus
·tus·es *or* ·tus
hi·ber·nate
·nat·ed ·nat·ing
hi·ber·na·tion
hi·ber·na·tor
hi·bis·cus
hide
hid, hid·den *or* hid, hid·ing
hide·a·way
hide·bound
hid·e·ous
hide-out
hi·er·ar·chi·cal
hi·er·ar·chy
·chies
hi·er·o·glyph·ic
hi-fi
high·ball
high·brow
high-class
high·er-up
high-flown
high-grade
high·hand·ed
high-lev·el
high·light
high·ly
high-mind·ed
high-pitched
high-pow·ered
high-pres·sure
high-priced
high-rise

high-sound·ing
high-spir·it·ed
high-strung
high-ten·sion
high-test
high-toned
high·way
hi·jack
hi·lar·i·ous
hi·lar·i·ty
him·self
hind
hind·er, hind·most, *or* hind·er·most
hin·der
hin·drance
hind·sight
hinge
hinged hing·ing
hin·ter·land
hip·po·drome
hir·a·ble *or* hire·
hire
hired hir·ing
hire·ling
hiss·ing
his·ta·mine
his·tol·o·gy
his·to·ri·an
his·tor·i·cal
his·tor·i·cal·ly
his·to·ry
·ries
his·tri·on·ic
hit-and-run
hith·er·to
hoard
(*reserve;* SEE horde)
hoarse
hob·nail
hob·nob
·nobbed
·nob·bing
hoe
hoed hoe·ing
hoist
hold
held hold·ing

hold·out
hold·o·ver
hold·up
hole
holed
hol·ing
hole·y
(*with holes;* SEE holy, wholly)
hol·i·day
ho·li·ly
ho·li·ness
hol·low
hol·lo·ware
hol·ly
·lies
hol·o·caust
ho·log·ra·phy
ho·ly
·li·er ·li·est
·lies
(*sacred;* SEE holey, wholly)
hom·age
hom·burg
home·bod·y
home·bred
home-brew
home·com·ing
home-grown
home·land
home·less
home·li·ness
home·ly
·li·er ·li·est
(*plain;* SEE homey)
home·made
home·own·er
home·sick
home·stead
home·stretch
home·ward
home·work
home·y
hom·i·er
hom·i·est
(*cozy;* SEE homely)
home·y·ness
hom·i·ci·dal

hom·i·cide
hom·i·ly
·lies
hom·i·ny
ho·mo·ge·ne·i·ty
ho·mo·ge·ne·ous
ho·mog·e·nize
·nized ·niz·ing
hom·o·graph
ho·mol·o·gous
hom·o·nym
hom·o·phone
Ho·mo sa·pi·ens
hone
honed hon·ing
hon·est
hon·es·ty
hon·or·a·ble
hon·o·ra·ri·um
·ri·ums *or* ·ri·a
hon·or·ar·y
hon·or·if·ic
hood·ed
hood·lum
hoof·beat
hook·up
hope
hoped hop·ing
hope·ful
hope·ful·ly
hope·less
horde
hord·ed hord·ing
(*crowd;* SEE hoard)
ho·ri·zon
hor·i·zon·tal
hor·mo·nal
hor·mone
ho·rol·o·gy
hor·o·scope
hor·ren·dous
hor·ri·ble
hor·ri·bly
hor·rid
hor·ri·fy
·fied ·fy·ing
hor·ror

hors d'oeu·vre
·vres
horse·pow·er
horse·shoe
·shoed
·shoe·ing
hor·ta·to·ry
hor·ti·cul·ture
hor·ti·cul·tur·ist
hos·pice
hos·pi·ta·ble
hos·pi·ta·bly
hos·pi·tal
hos·pi·tal·i·ty
·ties
hos·pi·tal·i·za·tion
hos·pi·tal·ize
·ized ·iz·ing
hos·tage
hos·tel
(*inn;* SEE hostile)
hos·tel·ry
·ries
hos·tile
(*unfriendly;* SEE hostel)
hos·tile·ly
hos·til·i·ty
·ties
hos·tler
ho·tel
ho·tel·ier
hot-tem·pered
hound·ed
hour·glass
hour·ly
house
housed hous·ing
house·boat
house·ful
house·hold
house·keep·er
house·lights
house organ
house-rais·ing
house·warm·ing
hous·ing
hov·el
·eled *or* ·elled
·el·ing *or* ·el·ling
hov·er
how·ev·er
howl·ing
how·so·ev·er
how-to
hoy·den
hub·cap
huck·ster
hud·dle
·dled ·dling
hue
(*color;* SEE hew)
huff·i·ly
huff·i·ness
huff·y
·i·er ·i·est
hug
hugged hug·ging
huge·ness
hulk·ing
hum
hummed
hum·ming
hu·man
hu·mane
hu·man·ism
hu·man·is·tic
hu·man·is·ti·cal·ly
hu·man·i·tar·i·an
hu·man·i·ty
·ties
hu·man·ize
·ized ·iz·ing
hu·man·kind
hu·man·ly
hu·man·ness
hu·man·oid
hum·ble
·bler ·blest
·bled ·bling
hum·bly
hu·mid
hu·mid·i·fi·ca·tion
hu·mid·i·fi·er
hu·mid·i·fy
·fied ·fy·ing
hu·mid·i·ty
hu·mi·dor
hu·mil·i·ate
·at·ed ·at·ing
hu·mil·i·a·tion
hu·mil·i·ty
hu·mor
hu·mor·esque
hu·mor·ist
hu·mor·ous
hu·mus
hun·dred·fold
hun·dredth
hun·dred·weight
hun·ger
hun·gri·ly
hun·gri·ness
hun·gry
·gri·er ·gri·est
hur·dle
·dled ·dling
(*barrier;* SEE hurtle)
hurl·er
hur·rah
hur·ri·cane
hur·ried·ly
hur·ry
·ried ·ry·ing
hur·tle
·tled ·tling
(*rush;* SEE hurdle)
hus·band
hus·band·ry
husk·i·ly
husk·i·ness
hus·tle
·tled ·tling
hy·brid
hy·brid·ize
·ized ·iz·ing
hy·drant
hy·drate
·drat·ed ·drat·ing
hy·dra·tor
hy·drau·lic
hy·dro·chlo·ric
hy·dro·dy·nam·ics
hy·dro·e·lec·tric
hy·dro·gen·ate
·at·ed ·at·ing
hy·dro·gen·a·tion
hy·dro·ki·net·ics
hy·drol·o·gy
hy·drol·y·sis
hy·dro·lyt·ic
hy·dro·me·chan·ics
hy·drom·e·ter
hy·dro·naut
hy·dro·pho·bi·a
hy·dro·plane
hy·dro·pon·ics
hy·dro-ski
hy·dro·stat·ics
hy·dro·ther·a·py
hy·drous
hy·giene
hy·gi·en·ic
hy·gi·en·i·cal·ly
hy·gi·en·ist
hy·grom·e·ter
hy·gro·scope
hy·per·a·cid·i·ty
hy·per·ac·tive
hy·per·bo·la
(*curve*)
hy·per·bo·le
(*exaggeration*)
hy·per·bol·ic
hy·per·crit·i·cal
(*too critical;* SEE hypocritical)
hy·per·sen·si·tive
hy·per·son·ic
hy·per·ten·sion
hy·per·ven·ti·la·tion
hy·phen
hy·phen·ate
·at·ed ·at·ing
hy·phen·a·tion
hyp·no·sis
·ses
hyp·not·ic
hyp·not·i·cal·ly
hyp·no·tism
hyp·no·tiz·a·ble
hyp·no·tize
·tized ·tiz·ing
hy·po·chon·dri·a
hy·po·chon·dri·ac
hy·po·chon·dri·a·cal
hy·po·chon·dri·a·sis

hy·poc·ri·sy
·sies
hyp·o·crite
hyp·o·crit·i·cal
(*deceitful;* SEE hypercritical)
hy·po·der·mic
hy·pot·e·nuse
hy·poth·e·cate
·cat·ed ·cat·ing
hy·poth·e·sis
·ses
hy·poth·e·size
·sized ·siz·ing
hy·po·thet·i·cal

I

ice·berg
ice·bound
ice·break·er
ich·thy·ol·o·gy
i·ci·cle
i·ci·ly
i·ci·ness
ic·ing
i·con
i·con·ic
i·con·o·clast
i·cy
i·ci·er i·ci·est
I·da·ho
i·de·a
i·de·al
i·de·al·ism
i·de·al·ist
i·de·al·is·tic
i·de·al·i·za·tion
i·de·al·ize
·ized ·iz·ing
i·de·al·ly
i·de·ate
·at·ed ·at·ing
i·de·a·tion
i·dée fixe
i·den·ti·cal
i·den·ti·fi·a·ble
i·den·ti·fi·ca·tion
i·den·ti·fi·er
i·den·ti·fy
·fied ·fy·ing
i·den·ti·ty
·ties
id·e·o·gram
id·e·o·graph·ic
i·de·o·log·i·cal
i·de·ol·o·gist
i·de·ol·o·gize
·gized ·giz·ing
i·de·ol·o·gy
·gies
id·i·o·cy
id·i·om
id·i·o·mat·ic
id·i·o·syn·cra·sy
·sies
id·i·o·syn·crat·ic
i·dle
i·dled i·dling
(*not active;* SEE idol, idyll)
i·dle·ness
i·dler
i·dly
i·dol
(*image worshiped;* SEE idle, idyll)
i·dol·a·ter
i·dol·a·trous
i·dol·a·try
i·dol·ize
·ized ·iz·ing
i·dyll *or* i·dyl
(*pastoral poem;* SEE idle, idol)
i·dyl·lic
ig·ne·ous
ig·nit·a·ble
or ·i·ble
ig·nite
·nit·ed ·nit·ing
ig·ni·tion
ig·no·ble
ig·no·min·i·ous
ig·no·min·y
·ies
ig·no·ra·mus
ig·no·rance
ig·no·rant
ig·nore
·nored ·nor·ing
ill-ad·vised
ill-be·ing
ill-bod·ing
ill-bred
ill-con·sid·ered
ill-dis·posed
il·le·gal
il·le·gal·i·ty
·ties
il·le·gal·ly
il·leg·i·bil·i·ty
il·leg·i·ble
il·leg·i·bly
il·le·git·i·ma·cy
·cies
il·le·git·i·mate
il·le·git·i·mate·ly
ill-fat·ed
ill-fa·vored
ill-found·ed
ill-got·ten
ill-hu·mored
il·lib·er·al
il·lic·it
(*unlawful;* SEE elicit)
il·lim·it·a·ble
il·lim·it·a·bly
Il·li·nois
il·lit·er·a·cy
il·lit·er·ate
il·lit·er·ate·ly
ill-man·nered
ill-na·tured
ill·ness
il·log·i·cal
il·log·i·cal·ly
ill-sor·ted
ill-spent
ill-suit·ed
ill-tem·pered
ill-timed
il·lu·mi·nate
·nat·ed ·nat·ing
il·lu·mi·na·tion
il·lu·mi·na·tor
ill-us·age
ill-use
il·lu·sion
(*false idea;* SEE allusion, elusion)
il·lu·sive
(*deceptive;* SEE allusive, elusive)
il·lu·so·ri·ly
il·lu·so·ri·ness
il·lu·so·ry
il·lus·trate
·trat·ed ·trat·ing
il·lus·tra·tion
il·lus·tra·tive
il·lus·tra·tor
il·lus·tri·ous
im·age
·aged ·ag·ing
im·age·ry
·ries
i·mag·i·na·ble
i·mag·i·na·bly
i·mag·i·nar·i·ness
i·mag·i·nar·y
i·mag·i·na·tion
i·mag·i·na·tive
i·mag·ine
·ined ·in·ing
im·ag·ism
im·bal·ance
im·be·cile
im·be·cil·ic
im·be·cil·i·ty
·ties
im·bibe
·bibed ·bib·ing
im·bib·er
im·bro·glio
·glios
im·brue
·brued ·bru·ing
im·bue
·bued
·bu·ing
im·i·ta·ble
im·i·tate
·tat·ed ·tat·ing
im·i·ta·tion
im·i·ta·tive
im·i·ta·tor
im·mac·u·late

im·ma·nent
(*inherent;* SEE
imminent)
im·ma·te·ri·al
im·ma·ture
im·ma·tu·ri·ty
im·meas·ur·a·ble
im·me·di·a·cy
im·me·di·ate
im·me·di·ate·ly
im·me·mo·ri·al
im·mense
im·mense·ly
im·men·si·ty
im·merge
·merged
·merg·ing
(*plunge;* SEE
emerge)
im·mer·gence
im·merse
·mersed
·mers·ing
im·mers·i·ble
im·mer·sion
im·mi·grant
im·mi·grate
·grat·ed ·grat·ing
im·mi·gra·tion
im·mi·nence
im·mi·nent
(*impending;* SEE
eminent,
immanent)
im·mis·ci·ble
im·mit·i·ga·ble
im·mo·bile
im·mo·bil·i·ty
im·mo·bi·li·za·tion
im·mo·bi·lize
·lized ·liz·ing
im·mod·er·ate
im·mod·er·a·tion
im·mod·est
im·mod·es·ty
im·mor·al
im·mo·ral·i·ty
·ties
im·mor·tal
im·mor·tal·i·ty
im·mor·tal·i·za·tion
im·mor·tal·ize
·ized ·iz·ing
im·mov·a·bil·i·ty
im·mov·a·ble
im·mune
im·mu·ni·ty
·ties
im·mu·ni·za·tion
im·mu·nize
·nized ·niz·ing
im·mu·nol·o·gy
im·mure
·mured ·mur·ing
im·mu·ta·bil·i·ty
im·mu·ta·ble
im·mu·ta·bly
im·pact·ed
im·pac·tion
im·pair
im·pale
·paled ·pal·ing
im·pal·pa·bil·i·ty
im·pal·pa·ble
im·pan·el
·eled *or* ·elled
·el·ing *or* ·el·ling
im·part
im·part·a·ble
im·par·tial
im·par·ti·al·i·ty
im·part·i·ble
im·pas·sa·bil·i·ty
im·pass·a·ble
(*not passable;*
SEE impassible)
im·passe
im·pas·si·bil·i·ty
im·pas·si·ble
(*unfeeling;* SEE
impassable)
im·pas·sioned
im·pas·sive
im·pas·siv·i·ty
im·pa·tience
im·pa·tient
im·peach
im·peach·a·ble
im·pec·ca·bil·i·ty
im·pec·ca·ble
im·pec·ca·bly
im·pe·cu·ni·ous
im·ped·ance
im·pede
·ped·ed ·ped·ing
im·ped·i·ment
im·ped·i·men·ta
im·pel
·pelled ·pel·ling
im·pel·lent
im·pel·ler
im·pend
im·pend·ing
im·pen·e·tra·bil·i·ty
im·pen·e·tra·ble
im·pen·i·tence
im·pen·i·tent
im·per·a·tive
im·per·cep·ti·ble
im·per·cep·ti·bly
im·per·fect
im·per·fec·tion
im·per·fo·rate
im·pe·ri·al
im·pe·ri·al·ism
im·pe·ri·al·is·tic
im·pe·ri·al·ly
im·per·il
im·pe·ri·ous
im·per·ish·a·ble
im·per·ma·nent
im·per·me·a·ble
im·per·mis·si·ble
im·per·son·al
im·per·son·al·i·ty
im·per·son·al·ize
im·per·son·ate
·at·ed ·at·ing
im·per·son·a·tion
im·per·son·a·tor
im·per·ti·nence
im·per·ti·nent
im·per·turb·a·bil·i·ty
im·per·turb·a·ble
im·per·vi·ous
im·pet·u·os·i·ty
im·pet·u·ous
im·pe·tus
im·pi·e·ty
·ties
im·pinge
·pinged ·ping·ing
im·pinge·ment
im·pi·ous
imp·ish
im·pla·ca·ble
im·plant
im·plan·ta·tion
im·plau·si·ble
im·ple·ment
im·ple·men·tal
im·ple·men·ta·tion
im·pli·cate
·cat·ed
·ca·ting
im·pli·ca·tion
im·pli·ca·tive
im·plic·it
im·plode
·plod·ed ·plod·ing
im·plore
·plored ·plor·ing
im·plo·sion
im·ply
·plied ·ply·ing
im·po·lite
im·pol·i·tic
im·pon·der·a·ble
im·port
im·port·a·ble
im·por·tance
im·por·tant
im·por·ta·tion
im·port·er
im·por·tu·nate
im·por·tune
·tuned ·tun·ing
im·por·tu·ni·ty
·ties
im·pose
·posed ·pos·ing
im·po·si·tion
im·pos·si·bil·i·ty
·ties
im·pos·si·ble
im·post
im·pos·tor
(*deceiver*)
im·pos·ture
(*deception*)

im·po·tence
im·po·tent
im·pound
im·pov·er·ish
im·prac·ti·ca·bil·i·ty
im·prac·ti·ca·ble
im·prac·ti·cal
im·pre·cate
 ·cat·ed ·cat·ing
im·pre·ca·tion
im·pre·cise
im·preg·na·bil·i·ty
im·preg·na·ble
im·pre·sa·ri·o
 ·ri·os
im·pre·scrip·ti·ble
im·press
im·press·i·ble
im·pres·sion
im·pres·sion·a·ble
im·pres·sion·a·bly
im·pres·sion·ism
im·pres·sive
im·pres·sive·ly
im·pri·ma·tur
im·print
im·pris·on
im·prob·a·ble
im·promp·tu
im·prop·er
im·pro·pri·e·ty
 ·ties
im·prov·a·ble
im·prove
 ·proved ·prov·ing
im·prove·ment
im·prov·i·dent
im·prov·i·sa·tion
im·pro·vise
 ·vised ·vis·ing
im·pru·dence
im·pru·dent
im·pu·dence
im·pu·dent
im·pugn
im·pugn·a·ble
im·pulse
im·pul·sion
im·pul·sive
im·pul·sive·ly
im·pu·ni·ty
im·pure
im·pu·ri·ty
 ·ties
im·put·a·bil·i·ty
im·put·a·ble
im·pu·ta·tion
im·put·a·tive
im·pute
 ·put·ed ·put·ing
in·a·bil·i·ty
in ab·sen·tia
in·ac·ces·si·ble
in·ac·cu·ra·cy
 ·cies
in·ac·cu·rate
in·ac·tion
in·ac·ti·vate
 ·vat·ed ·vat·ing
in·ac·ti·va·tion
in·ac·tive
in·ac·tiv·i·ty
in·ad·e·qua·cy
 ·cies
in·ad·e·quate
in·ad·mis·si·ble
in·ad·vert·ence
in·ad·vert·ent
in·ad·vis·a·bil·i·ty
in·ad·vis·a·ble
in·al·ien·a·ble
in·al·ter·a·ble
in·ane
in·an·i·mate
in·an·i·ty
 ·ties
in·ap·pli·ca·ble
in·ap·pre·ci·a·ble
in·ap·proach·a·ble
in·ap·pro·pri·ate
in·apt
(*unsuitable;* SEE inept)
in·ar·tic·u·late
in·ar·tis·tic
in·as·much as
in·at·ten·tion
in·at·ten·tive
in·au·di·ble
in·au·gu·ral
in·au·gu·rate
 ·rat·ed ·rat·ing
in·aus·pi·cious
in·board
in·born
in·breed
 ·bred ·breed·ing
in·cal·cu·la·ble
in·cal·cu·la·bly
in·can·des·cence
in·can·des·cent
in·can·ta·tion
in·ca·pa·bil·i·ty
in·ca·pa·ble
in·ca·pac·i·tate
 ·tat·ed ·tat·ing
in·ca·pac·i·ta·tion
in·ca·pac·i·ty
in·car·cer·ate
 ·at·ed ·at·ing
in·car·cer·a·tion
in·car·nate
 ·nat·ed ·nat·ing
in·car·na·tion
in·cau·tious
in·cen·di·ar·y
 ·ies
in′cense
in·cense′
 ·censed ·cens·ing
in·cen·tive
in·cep·tion
in·cep·tive
in·cer·ti·tude
in·ces·sant
in·cho·ate
in·ci·dence
in·ci·dent
in·ci·den·tal
in·ci·den·tal·ly
in·cin·er·ate
 ·at·ed ·at·ing
in·cin·er·a·tor
in·cip·i·ence
in·cip·i·ent
in·cise
 ·cised ·cis·ing
in·ci·sion
in·ci·sive
in·cite
 ·cit·ed ·cit·ing
in·cit·er
in·ci·vil·i·ty
 ·ties
in·clem·en·cy
in·clem·ent
in·clin·a·ble
in·cli·na·tion
in·cline
 ·clined ·clin·ing
in·cli·nom·e·ter
in·clude
 ·clud·ed
 ·clud·ing
in·clu·sion
in·clu·sive
in·co·er·ci·ble
in·cog·ni·to
 ·tos
in·cog·ni·zance
in·cog·ni·zant
in·co·her·ence
in·co·her·ent
in·com·bus·ti·ble
in·come
in·com·ing
in·com·men·su·ra·ble
in·com·men·su·rate
in·com·mode
 ·mod·ed ·mod·ing
in·com·mo·di·ous
in·com·mu·ni·ca·ble
in·com·mu·ni·ca·do
in·com·pa·ra·ble
in·com·pat·i·bil·i·ty
 ·ties
in·com·pat·i·ble
in·com·pe·tence
in·com·pe·tent
in·com·plete
in·com·pre·hen·si·ble
in·com·press·i·ble
in·com·put·a·ble
in·con·ceiv·a·ble
in·con·clu·sive
in·con·dite
in·con·form·i·ty
in·con·gru·ent

in·con·gru·i·ty
·ties
in·con·gru·ous
in·con·se·quen·tial
in·con·sid·er·a·ble
in·con·sid·er·ate
in·con·sid·er·ate·ly
in·con·sid·er·a·tion
in·con·sis·ten·cy
·cies
in·con·sis·tent
in·con·sol·a·ble
in·con·spic·u·ous
in·con·stan·cy
in·con·stant
in·con·sum·a·ble
in·con·test·a·ble
in·con·trol·la·ble
in·con·tro·vert·i·ble
in·con·ven·ience
in·con·ven·ient
in·con·vert·i·ble
in·co·or·di·nate
in·cor·po·rate
·rat·ed ·rat·ing
in·cor·po·ra·tion
in·cor·po·ra·tor
in·cor·po·re·al
in·cor·rect
in·cor·ri·gi·bil·i·ty
in·cor·ri·gi·ble
in·cor·ri·gi·bly
in·cor·rupt
in·cor·rupt·i·ble
in·creas·a·ble
in·crease
·creased
·creas·ing
in·creas·ing·ly
in·cred·i·bil·i·ty
in·cred·i·ble
in·cred·i·bly
in·cre·du·li·ty
in·cred·u·lous
in·cre·ment
in·cre·men·tal
in·crim·i·nate
·nat·ed
·nat·ing
in·crim·i·na·tion
in·crim·i·na·to·ry
in·cul·cate
·cat·ed ·cat·ing
in·cul·ca·tion
in·culp·a·ble
in·cul·pa·tion
in·cum·ben·cy
·cies
in·cum·bent
in·cur
·curred
·cur·ring
in·cur·a·bil·i·ty
in·cur·a·ble
in·cur·a·bly
in·cu·ri·ous
in·cur·sion
in·debt·ed
in·debt·ed·ness
in·de·cen·cy
·cies
in·de·cent
in·de·ci·pher·a·ble
in·de·ci·sion
in·de·ci·sive
in·de·clin·a·ble
in·dec·o·rous
in·de·co·rum
in·deed
in·de·fat·i·ga·ble
in·de·fat·i·ga·bly
in·de·fea·si·ble
in·de·fect·i·ble
in·de·fen·si·ble
in·de·fin·a·ble
in·def·i·nite
in·del·i·ble
in·del·i·bly
in·del·i·ca·cy
·cies
in·del·i·cate
in·dem·ni·fi·ca·tion
in·dem·ni·fy
·fied ·fy·ing
in·dem·ni·ty
·ties
in·dent
in·den·ta·tion
in·den·ture
·tured
·tur·ing
in·de·pend·ence
in·de·pend·ent
in-depth
in·de·scrib·a·ble
in·de·scrib·a·bly
in·de·struct·i·ble
in·de·ter·mi·na·ble
in·de·ter·mi·na·cy
in·de·ter·mi·nate
in·de·ter·mi·na·tion
in·dex
·dex·es *or* ·di·ces
In·di·an·a
in·di·cate
·cat·ed ·cat·ing
in·di·ca·tion
in·dic·a·tive
in·di·ca·tor
in·dict
(*accuse formally;* SEE indite)
in·dict·a·ble
in·dict·ment
in·dif·fer·ence
in·dif·fer·ent
in·di·gence
in·dig·e·nous
in·di·gent
in·di·gest·i·ble
in·di·ges·tion
in·dig·nant
in·dig·na·tion
in·dig·ni·ty
·ties
in·di·rect
in·di·rec·tion
in·dis·cern·i·ble
in·dis·creet
(*lacking prudence*)
in·dis·crete
(*not separated*)
in·dis·cre·tion
(*indiscreet act*)
in·dis·crim·i·nate
in·dis·pen·sa·ble
in·dis·pose
in·dis·po·si·tion
in·dis·pu·ta·ble
in·dis·sol·u·ble
in·dis·tinct
in·dis·tinc·tive
in·dis·tin·guish·a·ble
in·dite
·dit·ed ·dit·ing
(*write;* SEE indict)
in·di·vid·u·al
in·di·vid·u·al·ism
in·di·vid·u·al·is·tic
in·di·vid·u·al·i·ty
in·di·vid·u·al·ize
·ized ·iz·ing
in·di·vid·u·al·ly
in·di·vid·u·ate
·at·ed ·at·ing
in·di·vis·i·bil·i·ty
in·di·vis·i·ble
in·doc·tri·nate
·nat·ed ·nat·ing
in·doc·tri·na·tion
in·doc·tri·na·tor
in·do·lence
in·do·lent
in·dom·i·ta·ble
in·dom·i·ta·bly
in·dorse
·dorsed
·dors·ing
in·du·bi·ta·ble
in·du·bi·ta·bly
in·duce
·duced ·duc·ing
in·duce·ment
in·duct
in·duct·ance
in·duct·ee
in·duc·tile
in·duc·tion
in·duc·tive
in·duc·tor
in·dulge
·dulged
·dulg·ing
in·dul·gence
in·dul·gent
in·du·rate
·rat·ed ·rat·ing
in·du·ra·tion

in·dus·tri·al
in·dus·tri·al·ism
in·dus·tri·al·ist
in·dus·tri·al·i·za·tion
in·dus·tri·al·ize
·ized ·iz·ing
in·dus·tri·ous
in·dus·try
·tries
in·e·bri·ate
·at·ed ·at·ing
in·e·bri·a·tion
in·e·bri·e·ty
in·ed·i·ble
in·ed·u·ca·ble
in·ef·fa·ble
in·ef·fa·bly
in·ef·face·a·ble
in·ef·fec·tive
in·ef·fec·tu·al
in·ef·fi·ca·cious
in·ef·fi·ca·cy
in·ef·fi·cien·cy
in·ef·fi·cient
in·el·e·gance
in·el·e·gant
in·el·i·gi·bil·i·ty
in·el·i·gi·ble
in·e·luc·ta·ble
in·e·lud·i·ble
in·ept
(*awkward;* SEE inapt)
in·ept·i·tude
in·e·qual·i·ty
·ties
in·eq·ui·ta·ble
in·eq·ui·ty
·ties
(*unfairness;* SEE iniquity)
in·e·rad·i·ca·ble
in·er·ra·ble
in·er·rant
in·ert
in·er·tia
in·es·cap·a·ble
in·es·cap·a·bly
in·es·sen·tial
in·es·ti·ma·ble

in·ev·i·ta·bil·i·ty
in·ev·i·ta·ble
in·ev·i·ta·bly
in·ex·act
in·ex·cus·a·ble
in·ex·haust·i·ble
in·ex·o·ra·ble
in·ex·pe·di·ent
in·ex·pen·sive
in·ex·pe·ri·ence
in·ex·pert
in·ex·pi·a·ble
in·ex·pli·ca·ble
in·ex·pli·ca·bly
in·ex·press·i·ble
in·ex·press·i·bly
in·ex·pres·sive
in·ex·ten·si·ble
in·ex·tin·guish·a·ble
in·ex·tri·ca·ble
in·ex·tri·ca·bly
in·fal·li·bil·i·ty
in·fal·li·ble
in·fal·li·bly
in·fa·mous
in·fa·my
·mies
in·fan·try
·tries
in·fan·try·man
in·fat·u·ate
·at·ed ·at·ing
in·fat·u·a·tion
in·fect
in·fec·tion
in·fec·tious
in·fec·tive
in·fec·tor
in·fe·lic·i·tous
in·fe·lic·i·ty
·ties
in·fer
·ferred ·fer·ing
in·fer·a·ble
in·fer·ence
in·fer·en·tial
in·fe·ri·or
in·fe·ri·or·i·ty
in·fer·nal

in·fer·no
·nos
in·fer·tile
in·fest
in·fi·del
in·fi·del·i·ty
·ties
in·field
in·fil·trate
·trat·ed ·trat·ing
in·fil·tra·tion
in·fil·tra·tor
in·fi·nite
in·fi·nite·ly
in·fin·i·tes·i·mal
in·fin·i·tive
in·fin·i·ty
·ties
in·firm
in·fir·ma·ry
·ries
in·fir·mi·ty
·ties
in·flame
·flamed
·flam·ing
in·flam·ma·ble
in·flam·ma·tion
in·flam·ma·to·ry
in·flat·a·ble
in·flate
·flat·ed
·flat·ing
in·fla·tion
in·fla·tion·ar·y
in·flec·tion
in·flex·i·ble
in·flex·i·bly
in·flict
in·flic·tion
in-flight
in·flow
in·flu·ence
·enced ·enc·ing
in·flu·en·tial
in·flu·en·za
in·flux
in·form
in·for·mal
in·for·mal·i·ty

in·form·ant
in·for·ma·tion
in·form·a·tive
in·form·er
in·frac·tion
in·fran·gi·ble
in·fra·red
in·fre·quent
in·fringe
in·fringe·ment
in·fu·ri·ate
·at·ed ·at·ing
in·fuse
·fused ·fus·ing
in·fu·sion
in·gen·ious
(*clever;* SEE ingenuous)
in·gé·nue
in·ge·nu·i·ty
in·gen·u·ous
(*frank;* SEE ingenious)
in·gest
in·ges·tion
in·glo·ri·ous
in·got
in·grained
in·grate
in·gra·ti·ate
·at·ed ·at·ing
in·grat·i·tude
in·gre·di·ent
in·gress
in-group
in·grown
in·hab·it
in·hab·it·a·ble
in·hab·it·ant
in·hal·ant
in·ha·la·tion
in·hale
·haled ·hal·ing
in·hal·er
in·har·mon·ic
in·har·mo·ni·ous
in·here
·hered ·her·ing
in·her·ence

in·her·ent
in·her·it
in·her·it·a·ble
in·her·it·ance
in·her·i·tor
in·hib·it
in·hi·bi·tion
in·hib·i·tive
in·hib·i·tor
in·hos·pi·ta·ble
in·hos·pi·tal·i·ty
in-house
in·hu·man
in·hu·mane
in·hu·man·i·ty
·ties
in·im·i·cal
in·im·i·ta·ble
in·iq·ui·tous
in·iq·ui·ty
·ties
(*wickedness;*
SEE inequity)
in·i·tial
·tialed *or* ·tialled
·tial·ing *or*
·tial·ling
in·i·tial·ly
in·i·ti·ate
·at·ed ·at·ing
in·i·ti·a·tion
in·i·ti·a·tive
in·i·ti·a·tor
in·ject
in·jec·tion
in·jec·tor
in·ju·di·cious
in·junc·tion
in·jure
·jured ·jur·ing
in·ju·ri·ous
in·ju·ry
·ries
in·jus·tice
ink·blot
ink·ling
in·laid
in·land
in-law
in·lay
·laid ·lay·ing
·lays
in·let
in·mate
in me·mo·ri·am
in·most
in·nards
in·nate
in·ner·most
in·ner·spring
in·ner·vate
·vat·ed ·vat·ing
in·ning
inn·keep·er
in·no·cence
in·no·cent
in·noc·u·ous
in·no·vate
·vat·ed ·vat·ing
in·no·va·tion
in·no·va·tive
in·no·va·tor
in·nu·en·do
·does *or* ·dos
in·nu·mer·a·ble
in·oc·u·late
·lat·ed ·lat·ing
in·oc·u·la·tion
in·of·fen·sive
in·op·er·a·ble
in·op·er·a·tive
in·op·por·tune
in·or·di·nate
in·or·gan·ic
in·pa·tient
in·put
in·quest
in·qui·e·tude
in·quire
·quired
·quir·ing
in·quir·y
·ies
in·qui·si·tion
in·quis·i·tive
in·quis·i·tor
in·road
in·sane
in·san·i·tar·y
in·san·i·ty
in·sa·ti·a·ble
in·scribe
·scribed
·scrib·ing
in·scrip·tion
in·scru·ta·bil·i·ty
in·scru·ta·ble
in·sect
in·sec·ti·cide
in·se·cure
in·se·cu·ri·ty
in·sen·sate
in·sen·si·bil·i·ty
in·sen·si·ble
in·sen·si·tive
in·sen·si·tiv·i·ty
in·sep·a·ra·ble
in·sert
in·ser·tion
in-ser·vice
in·side
in·sid·i·ous
in·sight
in·sig·ni·a
in·sig·nif·i·cance
in·sig·nif·i·cant
in·sin·cere
in·sin·cere·ly
in·sin·cer·i·ty
in·sin·u·ate
·at·ed ·at·ing
in·sin·u·a·tion
in·sip·id
in·si·pid·i·ty
in·sist
in·sist·ence
in·sist·ent
in·so·bri·e·ty
in·so·far
in·sole
in·so·lence
in·so·lent
in·sol·u·ble
in·sol·vent
in·som·ni·a
in·sou·ci·ance
in·sou·ci·ant
in·spect
in·spec·tion
in·spec·tor
in·spi·ra·tion
in·spire
·spired ·spir·ing
in·spir·it
in·sta·bil·i·ty
in·stall *or* ·stal
·stalled ·stall·ing
in·stal·la·tion
in·stall·ment
or ·stal·ment
in·stance
in·stant
in·stan·ta·ne·ous
in·stan·ter
in·state
·stat·ed ·stat·ing
in sta·tu quo
in·stead
in·step
in·sti·gate
·gat·ed ·gat·ing
in·sti·ga·tion
in·sti·ga·tor
in·still *or* ·stil
·stilled ·still·ing
in·stinct
in·stinc·tive
in·sti·tute
·tut·ed ·tut·ing
in·sti·tu·tion
in·sti·tu·tion·al·ize
·ized ·iz·ing
in·struct
in·struc·tion
in·struc·tive
in·struc·tor
in·stru·ment
in·stru·men·tal
in·stru·men·tal·i·ty
in·stru·men·ta·tion
in·sub·or·di·nate
in·sub·or·di·na·tion
in·sub·stan·tial
in·suf·fer·a·ble
in·suf·fi·cien·cy
·cies
in·suf·fi·cient

in·su·lar
in·su·late
·lat·ed ·lat·ing
in·su·la·tion
in·su·la·tor
in·su·lin
in·sult
in·su·per·a·ble
in·sup·port·a·ble
in·sup·press·i·ble
in·sur·a·bil·i·ty
in·sur·a·ble
in·sur·ance
in·sure
·sured
·sur·ing
in·sur·er
in·sur·gence
in·sur·gent
in·sur·mount·a·ble
in·sur·rec·tion
in·tact
in·tagl·io
·ios
in·take
in·tan·gi·ble
in·te·ger
in·te·gral
in·te·grate
·grat·ed ·grat·ing
in·te·gra·tion
in·teg·ri·ty
in·teg·u·ment
in·tel·lect
in·tel·lec·tu·al
in·tel·lec·tu·al·ize
·ized ·iz·ing
in·tel·lec·tu·al·ly
in·tel·li·gence
in·tel·li·gent
in·tel·li·gent·si·a
in·tel·li·gi·bil·i·ty
in·tel·li·gi·ble
in·tel·li·gi·bly
In·tel·sat
in·tem·per·ance
in·tem·per·ate
in·tend
in·tend·ant

in·tense
in·tense·ly
in·ten·si·fi·ca·tion
in·ten·si·fy
·fied ·fy·ing
in·ten·si·ty
in·ten·sive
in·tent
in·ten·tion
in·ten·tion·al
in·ten·tion·al·ly
in·ter
·terred ·ter·ring
in·ter·act
in·ter·ac·tion
in·ter·breed
·bred ·breed·ing
in·ter·cede
·ced·ed ·ced·ing
in·ter·cept
in·ter·cep·tion
in·ter·cep·tor
in·ter·ces·sion
in·ter·change
in·ter·change·a·ble
in·ter·com
in·ter·com·mu·ni·cate
in·ter·con·nect
in·ter·course
in·ter·de·nom·i·
na·tion·al
in·ter·de·part·men·tal
in·ter·de·pend·ence
in·ter·dict
in·ter·dis·ci·pli·nar·y
in·ter·est
in·ter·est·ed
in·ter·fere
·fered ·fer·ing
in·ter·fer·ence
in·ter·fer·on
in·ter·im
in·te·ri·or
in·ter·ject
in·ter·jec·tion
in·ter·lace
in·ter·lin·e·ar
in·ter·lin·ing
in·ter·lock

in·ter·lo·cu·tion
in·ter·loc·u·tor
in·ter·loc·u·to·ry
in·ter·lope
·loped ·lop·ing
in·ter·lop·er
in·ter·lude
in·ter·me·di·ar·y
·ar·ies
in·ter·me·di·ate
in·ter·ment
in·ter·mez·zo
·zos *or* ·zi
in·ter·mi·na·ble
in·ter·min·gle
in·ter·mis·sion
in·ter·mit·tent
in′tern
(doctor)
in·tern′
(detain)
in·ter·nal
in·ter·nal·ize
·ized ·iz·ing
in·ter·nal·ly
in·ter·na·tion·al
in·ter·ne·cine
in·tern·ee
in·ter·nist
in·tern·ment
in·tern·ship
in·ter·of·fice
in·ter·pen·e·trate
in·ter·per·son·al
in·ter·phone
in·ter·plan·e·tar·y
in·ter·play
in·ter·po·late
·lat·ed ·lat·ing
in·ter·po·la·tion
in·ter·pose
in·ter·pret
in·ter·pre·ta·tion
in·ter·pret·er
in·ter·ra·cial
in·ter·re·late
in·ter·re·la·tion
in·ter·ro·gate
·gat·ed ·gat·ing

in·ter·ro·ga·tion
in·ter·rog·a·tive
in·ter·ro·ga·tor
in·ter·rog·a·to·ry
in·ter·rupt
in·ter·rup·tion
in·ter·scho·las·tic
in·ter·sect
in·ter·sec·tion
in·ter·sperse
·spersed
·spers·ing
in·ter·sper·sion
in·ter·state
in·ter·stel·lar
in·ter·stice
·stic·es
in·ter·twine
in·ter·ur·ban
in·ter·val
in·ter·vene
·vened ·ven·ing
in·ter·ven·tion
in·ter·view
in·ter·view·er
in·ter·weave
·wove ·wov·en
·weav·ing
in·tes·tate
in·tes·tin·al
in·tes·tine
in·ti·ma·cy
·cies
in·ti·mate
in·ti·ma·tion
in·tim·i·date
·dat·ed ·dat·ing
in·tim·i·da·tion
in·tol·er·a·ble
in·tol·er·ance
in·tol·er·ant
in·to·na·tion
in·tone
in·tox·i·cant
in·tox·i·cate
·cat·ed ·cat·ing
in·tox·i·ca·tion
in·trac·ta·ble
in·tra·mu·ral
in·tra·mus·cu·lar

in·tran·si·gent
in·tran·si·tive
in·tra·state
in·tra·u·ter·ine
in·tra·ve·nous
in·trep·id
in·tre·pid·i·ty
in·tri·ca·cy
·cies
in·tri·cate
in·trigue
·trigued
·trigu·ing
in·trin·sic
in·tro·duce
·duced ·duc·ing
in·tro·duc·tion
in·tro·duc·to·ry
in·tro·spec·tion
in·tro·spec·tive
in·tro·ver·sion
in·tro·vert
in·trude
·trud·ed
·trud·ing
in·trud·er
in·tru·sion
in·tru·sive
in·tu·i·tion
in·tu·i·tive
in·un·date
·dat·ed ·dat·ing
in·un·da·tion
in·ure
·ured ·ur·ing
in·vade
·vad·ed ·vad·ing
in·vad·er
in′va·lid
in·val′id
in·val·i·date
·dat·ed ·dat·ing
in·val·i·da·tion
in·val·u·a·ble
in·val·u·a·bly
in·var·i·a·ble
in·var·i·a·bly
in·va·sion
in·vec·tive
in·veigh
in·vei·gle
·gled ·gling
in·vent
in·ven·tion
in·ven·tive
in·ven·tor
in·ven·to·ry
·ries
·ried ·ry·ing
in·verse
in·ver·sion
in·vert
in·ver·te·brate
in·vert·i·ble
in·vest
in·ves·ti·gate
·gat·ed ·gat·ing
in·ves·ti·ga·tion
in·ves·ti·ga·tor
in·ves·ti·ture
in·vest·ment
in·vet·er·ate
in·vi·a·ble
in·vid·i·ous
in·vig·or·ate
·at·ed ·at·ing
in·vin·ci·bil·i·ty
in·vin·ci·ble
in·vin·ci·bly
in·vi·o·la·ble
in·vi·o·late
in·vis·i·ble
in·vi·ta·tion
in·vite
·vit·ed ·vit·ing
in·vo·ca·tion
in·voice
·voiced ·voic·ing
in·voke
·voked ·vok·ing
in·vol·un·tar·i·ly
in·vol·un·tar·y
in·vo·lute
in·volve
·volved
·volv·ing
in·vul·ner·a·ble
in·ward
i·on
i·on·i·za·tion
i·on·ize
·ized ·iz·ing
i·on·o·sphere
i·o·ta
I·o·wa
ip·so fac·to
i·ras·ci·bil·i·ty
i·ras·ci·ble
i·rate
ire·ful·ly
ir·i·des·cence
ir·i·des·cent
irk·some
i·ron·bound
i·ron·clad
i·ron·i·cal
i·ron·i·cal·ly
i·ron·stone
i·ron·work
i·ro·ny
·nies
ir·ra·di·ate
ir·ra·di·a·tion
ir·ra·tion·al
ir·ra·tion·al·i·ty
ir·ra·tion·al·ly
ir·re·claim·a·ble
ir·rec·on·cil·a·ble
ir·re·cov·er·a·ble
ir·re·deem·a·ble
ir·re·duc·i·ble
ir·ref·u·ta·ble
ir·reg·u·lar
ir·reg·u·lar·i·ty
·ties
ir·rel·e·vant
ir·re·li·gious
ir·re·me·di·a·ble
ir·re·mis·si·ble
ir·re·mov·a·ble
ir·rep·a·ra·ble
ir·re·place·a·ble
ir·re·press·i·ble
ir·re·proach·a·ble
ir·re·sist·i·ble
ir·res·o·lute
ir·re·spec·tive
ir·re·spon·si·ble
ir·re·triev·a·ble
ir·rev·er·ence
ir·rev·er·ent
ir·re·vers·i·ble
ir·rev·o·ca·ble
ir·ri·ga·ble
ir·ri·gate
·gat·ed ·gat·ing
ir·ri·ga·tion
ir·ri·ta·bil·i·ty
ir·ri·ta·ble
ir·ri·ta·bly
ir·ri·tant
ir·ri·tate
·tat·ed ·tat·ing
ir·ri·ta·tion
ir·rupt
ir·rup·tion
is·land
isle
(*island;* SEE aisle)
is·let
(*small island;* SEE eyelet)
is·n't
i·so·bar
i·so·late
·lat·ed ·lat·ing
i·so·la·tion
i·so·la·tion·ist
i·so·mer
i·so·met·ric
i·so·met·ri·cal·ly
i·sos·ce·les
i·so·therm
i·so·tope
i·so·trop·ic
Is·ra·el
Is·rae·li
is·su·ance
is·sue
·sued ·su·ing
isth·mus
·mus·es *or* ·mi
i·tal·ic
i·tal·i·cize
·cized ·ciz·ing
i·tem·ize
·ized ·iz·ing

it·er·ate
 ·at·ed ·at·ing
it·er·a·tion
i·tin·er·ant
i·tin·er·ar·y
 ·ies
i·tin·er·ate
 ·at·ed ·at·ing
its
 (of it)
it's
 (it is)
it·self
I've

J

ja·bot
ja·cinth
jack·al
jack·et
jack·ham·mer
jack·knife
 ·knives
 ·knifed ·knif·ing
jack-of-all-trades
 jacks-
Jac·quard
jade
 jad·ed jad·ing
jag·ged
jag·uar
jai a·lai
jal·ou·sie
 (door; SEE
 jealousy)
jan·gle
 ·gled ·gling
jan·i·tor
Jan·u·ar·y
 ·ar·ies
ja·pan
 ·panned
 ·pan·ning
jar
 jarred jar·ring
jar·di·niere
jar·gon
jas·mine
jas·per
ja·to *or* JA·TO
jaun·dice
 ·diced ·dic·ing
Jay·cee
jay·walk·er
jazz·i·ness
jazz·y
 ·i·er ·i·est
jeal·ous
jeal·ous·y
 ·ies
 (envy; SEE jalousie)
jeans
jeer·ing·ly
jen·ny
 ·nies
jeop·ard·ize
 ·ized ·iz·ing
jeop·ard·y
je·quir·i·ty
 ·ties
jer·e·mi·ad
jerk·i·ly
Jer·sey
 ·seys
 (dairy cattle)
jer·sey
 ·seys
 (cloth; shirt)
jet
 jet·ted jet·ting
jet-black
jet·lin·er
jet·port
jet-pro·pelled
jet·sam
jet stream
jet·ti·son
jet·ty
 ·ties
 ·tied ·ty·ing
jew·el
 ·eled *or* ·elled
 ·el·ing *or* ·el·ling
jew·el·er *or*
 ·el·ler
jew·el·ry
Jew·ish
Jew·ry
 ·ries
jib
 jibbed jib·bing
jibe
 jibed jib·ing
 (nautical; agree;
 SEE gibe)
Jim-Crow
jin·gle
 ·gled ·gling
jin·go
 ·goes
jin·go·ism
jinx
jit·ney
 ·neys
jit·ter·y
job
 jobbed job·bing
job·ber
jock·ey
 ·eys
 ·eyed ·ey·ing
jo·cose
jo·cos·i·ty
 ·ties
joc·u·lar
joc·u·lar·i·ty
joc·und
jo·cun·di·ty
jog
 jogged jog·ging
jog·ger
jog·gle
 ·gled ·gling
join·er
joint·ly
joist
jol·li·ness
jol·li·ty
jol·ly
 ·li·er ·li·est
jon·quil
jos·tle
 ·tled ·tling
jot
 jot·ted jot·ting
jounce
 jounced
 jounc·ing
jour·nal
jour·nal·ese
jour·nal·ism
jour·nal·is·tic
jour·ney
 ·neys
 ·neyed ·ney·ing
jour·ney·man
joust
jo·vi·al
jo·vi·al·i·ty
jo·vi·al·ly
ju·bi·lant
ju·bi·la·tion
ju·bi·lee
Ju·da·i·ca
Ju·da·ism
judge
 judged judg·ing
judg·ment *or*
 judge·
ju·di·ca·to·ry
 ·ries
ju·di·cial
ju·di·ci·ar·y
 ·ies
ju·di·cious
ju·do
jug·ger·naut
juice
 juiced juic·ing
juic·er
juic·i·ness
juic·y
 ·i·er
 ·i·est
juke·box
ju·lep
ju·li·enne
Ju·ly
 ·lies
jum·ble
 ·bled
 ·bling
junc·tion
junc·ture
June
jun·gle
jun·ior
ju·ni·per
jun·ket
jun·ta
jun·to
 ·tos

ju·rid·i·cal
ju·rid·i·cal·ly
ju·ris·dic·tion
ju·ris·pru·dence
ju·rist
ju·ris·tic
ju·ror
ju·ry
·ries
ju·ry·man
jus·tice
jus·ti·fi·a·ble
jus·ti·fi·a·bly
jus·ti·fi·ca·tion
jus·ti·fy
·fied
·fy·ing
just·ly
jut
jut·ted
jut·ting
ju·ven·ile
jux·ta·pose
·posed
·pos·ing
jux·ta·po·si·tion

K

kai·ser
ka·lei·do·scope
ka·lei·do·scop·ic
kal·so·mine
Kan·sas
ka·o·lin
ka·pok
ka·put
kar·at
ka·ra·te
ka·sha
kay·ak
ke·bab
kedge
kedged kedg·ing
keen·ness
keep
kept keep·ing
keep·sake
ke·loid
kempt
ken·nel
·neled *or* ·nelled
·nel·ing *or*
·nel·ling
Ken·tuck·y
ker·a·tin
ker·mis *or* ·mess
ker·nel
(*grain;* SEE colonel)
ker·o·sene *or*
·sine
ke·tone
key
keys
keyed key·ing
(*lock;* SEE quay)
key·board
key club
key·hole
key·note
key punch
key·stone
key·way
kha·ki
kick·off
kid·ney
·neys
kill-joy
kiln
kil·o·gram
kil·o·li·ter
ki·lo·me·ter
kil·o·volt
kil·o·watt
kil·o·watt-hour
kil·ter
kin·dle
·dled ·dling
kind·ly
·li·er ·li·est
kin·dred
kin·e·mat·ics
kin·e·scope
ki·ne·sics
kin·es·thet·ic
ki·net·ic
kin·folk
king·dom
king·pin
king-size
kin·ship
kins·man
ki·osk
kitch·en·ware
kit·ty-cor·nered
klax·on
klep·to·ma·ni·ac
klieg light
knack
knack·wurst
knap·sack
knead
(*press;* SEE need)
knee
kneed knee·ing
knee·cap
knee·hole
kneel
knelt *or* kneeled
kneel·ing
knell
knick·er·bock·ers
knick·knack
knife
knives
knifed knif·ing
knife-edge
knight
(*rank;* SEE night)
knight·hood
knob·by
·bi·er ·bi·est
knock·a·bout
knock down
knock-kneed
knock·out
knoll
knot
knot·ted
knot·ting
knot·hole
knot·ty
·ti·er ·ti·est
know-how
know-it-all
knowl·edge
knowl·edge·a·ble
knowl·edge·a·bly
knuck·le
·led ·ling
knurled
Ko·ran
ko·sher
kow·tow
ku·dos
küm·mel
kum·quat

L

la·bel
·beled *or* ·belled
·bel·ing *or*
·bel·ling
la·bor
lab·o·ra·to·ry
·ries
la·bor·er
la·bo·ri·ous
la·bor-sav·ing
lab·y·rinth
lab·y·rin·thine
lac·er·ate
·at·ed ·at·ing
lac·er·a·tion
lach·ry·mose
lack·a·dai·si·cal
lack·ey
·eys
lack·lus·ter
la·con·ic
la·con·i·cal·ly
lac·quer
la·crosse
la·cu·na
·nas *or* ·nae
lad·der
lad·en
lad·ing
la·dle
·dled ·dling
lag
lagged lag·ging
la·ger
lag·gard
la·goon

lair
(*den;* SEE layer)
lais·sez faire
la·i·ty
lam·baste
·bast·ed ·bast·ing
lam·bent
lam·bre·quin
lame
(*crippled*)
la·mé
(*fabric*)
la·ment
lam·en·ta·ble
lam·en·ta·tion
lam·i·nate
·nat·ed ·nat·ing
lam·i·na·tion
lamp·black
lam·poon
lamp·post
lan·dau
land·fill
land·hold·er
land·ing
land·locked
land·lord
land·mark
land·own·er
land·scape
·scaped
·scap·ing
land·slide
lan·guage
lan·guid
lan·guish
lan·guor
lan·guor·ous
lank·i·ness
lank·ness
lank·y
·i·er ·i·est
lan·o·lin
lan·tern
lan·yard
lap
lapped lap·ping
la·pel
lap·i·dar·y
·ies
lap·in
lap·is laz·u·li
lapse
lapsed laps·ing
lar·ce·nous
lar·ce·ny
lard·er
large
larg·er larg·est
large·ly
large-scale
lar·gess *or* ·gesse
la·ryn·ge·al
lar·yn·gi·tis
lar·ynx
lar·ynx·es *or*
la·ryn·ges
las·civ·i·ous
lase
lased las·ing
(*emit laser light;* SEE laze)
la·ser
lash·ing
las·si·tude
last-ditch
last·ing
latch·key
latch·string
late
lat·er *or* lat·ter
lat·est *or* last
late·ly
la·ten·cy
la·tent
lat·er·al
la·tex
lat·i·ces *or*
la·tex·es
lath
(*wood strip*)
lathe
lathed lath·ing
(*machine*)
lath·er
lath·ing
lat·i·tude
lat·ter-day
laud·a·ble
laud·a·bly
laud·a·to·ry
laugh·a·ble
laugh·ing·stock
laugh·ter
lau·re·ate
lau·rel
lav·a·to·ry
·ries
lav·ish
law-a·bid·ing
law·break·er
law·ful
law·ful·ly
law·giv·er
law·less
law·mak·er
law·suit
law·yer
lax·i·ty
lay
laid lay·ing
(*put;* SEE lie)
lay·er
(*stratum;* SEE lair)
lay·man
lay·off
lay·out
lay·o·ver
laze
lazed laz·ing
(*loaf;* SEE lase)
la·zi·ly
la·zi·ness
la·zy
·zi·er ·zi·est
leach
(*filter;* SEE leech)
lead
led lead·ing
lead·en
lead·er·ship
lead-in
lead·off
league
leagued
leagu·ing
leagu·er
leak
(*escape;* SEE leek)
leak·age
leak·y
·i·er ·i·est
lean
leaned *or* leant
lean·ing
lean
(*thin;* SEE lien)
lean·ness
lean-to
·tos
leap
leaped *or* leapt
leap·ing
learn
learned *or* learnt
learn·ing
learn′ed *adj.*
leas·a·ble
lease
leased leas·ing
lease-back
lease·hold·er
least
leath·er
leath·er·y
leave
left leav·ing
(*let stay*)
leave
leaved leav·ing
(*bear leaves*)
leav·en·ing
leave-tak·ing
lech·er·ous
lec·i·thin
lec·tern
lec·ture
·tured ·tur·ing
ledge
ledg·er
leech
(*worm;* SEE leach)
leek
(*vegetable;* SEE leak)
leer·y
·i·er ·i·est
lee·ward
lee·way

left-hand·ed
left·ist
left·o·ver
left-wing·er
leg·a·cy
·cies
le·gal·ese
le·gal·i·ty
·ties
le·gal·i·za·tion
le·gal·ize
·ized ·iz·ing
le·gal·ly
le·ga·tion
leg·end
leg·end·ar·y
leg·er·de·main
leg·i·bil·i·ty
leg·i·ble
leg·i·bly
le·gion
leg·is·late
·lat·ed ·lat·ing
leg·is·la·tion
leg·is·la·tive
leg·is·la·tor
leg·is·la·ture
le·git·i·ma·cy
le·git·i·mate
le·git·i·mize
·mized ·miz·ing
lei·sure
lei·sure·ly
lend
lent lend·ing
length·en
length·i·ness
length·wise
length·y
·i·er ·i·est
le·ni·en·cy
le·ni·ent
lens
le·sion
les·see
less·en
(*make less*)
less·er
(*smaller*)
les·son
(*instruction*)
les·sor
(*one who leases*)
let
let let·ting
let·down
le·thal
le·thar·gic
le·thar·gi·cal·ly
leth·ar·gize
·gized ·giz·ing
leth·ar·gy
let·tered
let·ter·head
let·ter-per·fect
let·ter·press
let·up
lev·ee
·eed
·ee·ing
(*embankment;* SEE levy)
lev·el
·eled *or* ·elled
·el·ing *or* ·el·ling
lev·el·head·ed
lev·el·ly
lev·er·age
lev·i·a·ble
lev·i·er
lev·i·tate
·tat·ed ·tat·ing
lev·i·ta·tion
lev·i·ty
lev·y
·ies, ·ied ·y·ing
(*tax;* SEE levee)
lewd·ness
lex·i·cog·ra·pher
lex·i·con
li·a·bil·i·ty
·ties
li·a·ble
(*likely;* SEE libel)
li·ai·son
li·ar
(*one who tells lies;* SEE lyre)
li·ba·tion
li·bel
·beled *or* ·belled
·bel·ing *or* ·bel·ling
(*defame;* SEE liable)
li·bel·ous *or* ·bel·lous
lib·er·al
lib·er·al·i·ty
lib·er·al·ize
·ized ·iz·ing
lib·er·ate
·at·ed ·at·ing
lib·er·a·tion
lib·er·a·tor
lib·er·tar·i·an
lib·er·tine
lib·er·ty
·ties
li·bid·i·nous
li·bi·do
li·brar·i·an
li·brar·y
·ies
li·cense
·censed ·cens·ing
li·cen·tious
li·chen
lic·it
lie
lay lain ly·ing
(*to rest;* SEE lay)
lie
lied ly·ing
(*tell falsehood;* SEE lye)
li·en
(*claim;* SEE lean)
lieu
lieu·ten·an·cy
lieu·ten·ant
life
lives
life belt
life·blood
life·boat
life buoy
life-giv·ing
life·guard
life·less
life·like
life·line
life·long
life·sav·er
life-size
life·time
life·work
lift·off
lig·a·ment
lig·a·ture
·tured ·tur·ing
light
light·ed *or* lit
light·ing
light·en
·ened ·en·ing
(*make light or less heavy;* SEE lightning)
light·face
light·head·ed
light·heart·ed
light·house
light·ly
light·ning
(*flash of light;* SEE lighten)
light·weight
light-year
lig·ne·ous
lig·nite
lik·a·ble *or* like·
like
liked lik·ing
like·li·hood
like·ly
like-mind·ed
lik·en
like·ness
like·wise
limb
(*branch;* SEE limn)
lim·ber
lim·bo
lime
limed lim·ing
lime·light
lim·er·ick
lime·stone
lim·it·a·ble
lim·i·ta·tion

lim·it·ed
limn
(*draw;* SEE limb)
lim·ou·sine
lim·pid
limp·ness
lin·age *or* line·
(*number of lines;*
SEE lineage)
linch·pin
Lin·coln
lin·den
line
lined lin·ing
lin·e·age
(*ancestry;* SEE linage)
lin·e·al
lin·e·a·ment
(*feature;* SEE liniment)
lin·e·ar
line·man
lin·en
lin·er
lines·man
line·up
lin·ger
lin·go
·goes
lin·gual
lin·guist
lin·guis·tics
lin·i·ment
(*medication;*
SEE lineament)
lin·ing
link·age
li·no·le·um
lin·o·type
lin·seed
lip-read
-read -read·ing
lip-sync
liq·ue·fac·tion
liq·ue·fi·a·ble
liq·ue·fi·er
liq·ue·fy
·fied ·fy·ing
li·ques·cent
li·queur
liq·uid
liq·ui·date
·dat·ed ·dat·ing
liq·ui·da·tion
liq·ui·da·tor
liq·uor
lisle
lis·some *or* ·som
lis·ten
list·less
lit·a·ny
·nies
li·ter
lit·er·a·cy
lit·er·al
(*exact;* SEE littoral)
lit·er·al·ly
lit·er·ar·y
lit·er·ate
lit·er·a·ture
lithe·ly
lith·o·graph
li·thog·ra·pher
li·thog·ra·phy
lit·i·ga·ble
lit·i·gant
lit·i·gate
·gat·ed ·gat·ing
lit·i·ga·tion
lit·mus
li·to·tes
lit·ter
lit·tle
lit·tler *or* less *or*
less·er, lit·tlest
or least
lit·to·ral
(*shore;* SEE literal)
li·tur·gi·cal
lit·ur·gy
·gies
liv·a·ble *or* live·
live
lived liv·ing
live·li·hood
live·li·ness
live·long
live·ly
·li·er ·li·est
liv·en
liv·er·y
·ies
liv·id
load
(*burden;* SEE lode)
loaf
loaves
loaf·er
loan
(*something lent;*
SEE lone)
loath
(*unwilling*)
loathe
loathed loath·ing
(*detest*)
loath·some
lob
lobbed lob·bing
lob·by
·bies
·bied ·by·ing
lob·by·ist
lobe
lo·cal
lo·cale
lo·cal·ism
lo·cal·i·ty
·ties
lo·cal·ize
·ized ·iz·ing
lo·cal·ly
lo·cate
·cat·ed ·cat·ing
lo·ca·tion
lock·out
lock·smith
lo·co·mo·tion
lo·co·mo·tive
lo·cus
·ci
lo·cust
lo·cu·tion
lode
(*ore;* SEE load)
lode·stone
lodge
lodged lodg·ing
(*house;* SEE loge)
lodg·er
lodg·ment
loft·i·ly
loft·i·ness
loft·y
·i·er ·i·est
log
logged
log·ging
log·a·rithm
loge
(*theater box;*
SEE lodge)
log·ger·head
log·gi·a
·gi·as
log·ic
log·i·cal
log·i·cal·ly
lo·gi·cian
lo·gis·tics
log·o·gram
log·o·griph
log·or·rhe·a
lo·gy
·gi·er ·gi·est
loi·ter
lone
(*solitary;*
SEE loan)
lone·li·ness
lone·ly
·li·er ·li·est
lone·some
long-dis·tance
long-drawn
lon·gev·i·ty
long·hand
lon·gi·tude
lon·gi·tu·di·nal
long-lived
long-range
long-run
long·shore·man
long·stand·ing
long-suf·fer·ing
long-term
look·out
loop·hole
loose
loosed loos·ing
(*free;* SEE lose, loss)

loose-joint·ed
loose-leaf
loose·ly
loos·en
lop
lopped lop·ping
lope
loped lop·ing
lop·sid·ed
lo·qua·cious
lo·quac·i·ty
lor·do·sis
lor·ry
·ries
lose
lost los·ing
(*mislay;* SEE loose, loss)
los·er
loss
(*thing lost;* SEE loose, lose)
lo·tion
lot·ter·y
·ies
loud·speak·er
Lou·i·si·an·a
lounge
lounged
loung·ing
lout·ish
lou·ver
lov·a·ble *or* love·
love
loved lov·ing
love·li·ness
love·ly
·li·er ·li·est
lov·ing·kind·ness
low·boy
low·bred
low·brow
low-cost
low-down
low·er
low·er·class·man
low-grade
low-key
low-lev·el
low·li·ness
low·ly
·li·er ·li·est
low-mind·ed
low-pitched
low-spir·it·ed
lox
loy·al
loy·al·ly
loy·al·ty
·ties
loz·enge
lu·au
lu·bri·cant
lu·bri·cate
·cat·ed
·cat·ing
lu·bri·ca·tion
lu·bri·ca·tor
lu·cid
lu·cid·i·ty
luck·i·ly
luck·i·ness
luck·y
·i·er ·i·est
lu·cra·tive
lu·cre
lu·cu·bra·tion
lu·di·crous
lug·gage
lu·gu·bri·ous
luke·warm
lum·bar
(*of the loins*)
lum·ber (*timber*)
lum·ber·jack
lum·ber·yard
lu·men
·mi·na *or* ·mens
lu·mi·nar·y
·ies
lu·mi·nes·cent
lu·mi·nous
lump·i·ness
lump·y
·i·er ·i·est
lu·na·cy
lu·nar
lu·na·tic
lunch·eon
lunge
lunged
lung·ing
lu·pine
lure
lured lur·ing
lu·rid
lurk·ing
lus·cious
lush·ness
lus·ter
lust·i·ness
lus·trous
lust·y
·i·er ·i·est
lux·u·ri·ance
lux·u·ri·ant
lux·u·ri·ate
·at·ed ·at·ing
lux·u·ri·ous
lux·u·ry
·ries
ly·ce·um
lye
(*alkaline substance;* SEE lie)
ly·ing-in
lym·phat·ic
lynch·ing
lynx
ly·on·naise
lyre
(*harp;* SEE liar)
lyr·ic

M

mac·er·ate
·at·ed ·at·ing
mach·i·nate
·nat·ed ·nat·ing
mach·i·na·tion
ma·chine
·chined
·chin·ing
ma·chin·er·y
ma·chin·ist
mack·in·tosh
(*coat;* SEE McIntosh)
mac·ro·bi·ot·ics
mac·ro·cosm
mac·ro·e·co·nom·ics
ma·cron
mac·u·la
·lae
mad
mad·der
mad·dest
mad·am
mad·ame
mes·dames
mad·cap
mad·den·ing
ma·de·moi·selle
made-to-or·der
made-up
ma·dras
mad·ri·gal
mael·strom
ma·es·tro
·tros *or* ·tri
mag·a·zine
ma·gen·ta
mag·ic
ma·gi·cian
mag·is·te·ri·al
mag·is·trate
mag·na·nim·i·ty
mag·nan·i·mous
mag·nate
(*influential person*)
mag·ne·sia
mag·net
(*iron attractor*)
mag·net·ic
mag·net·ism
mag·net·ize
·ized ·iz·ing
mag·ne·to
·tos
mag·ni·fi·ca·tion
mag·nif·i·cence
mag·nif·i·cent
mag·ni·fi·er
mag·ni·fy
·fied ·fy·ing
mag·nil·o·quent
mag·ni·tude

mag·num
ma·hog·a·ny
mail·box
mail·man
maim
Maine
main·land
main·line
main·ly
main·spring
main·stream
main·tain
main·te·nance
maî·tre d'hô·tel
maize
(*corn;* SEE maze)
ma·jes·tic
ma·jes·ti·cal·ly
maj·es·ty
·ties
ma·jor
ma·jor-do·mo
·mos
ma·jor·i·ty
·ties
make
made mak·ing
make-be·lieve
make·shift
make·up
mal·a·dapt·ed
mal·ad·just·ed
mal·a·droit
mal·a·dy
·dies
ma·laise
mal·a·prop·ism
mal·ap·ro·pos
mal·con·tent
mal·e·dic·tion
mal·e·fac·tion
mal·e·fac·tor
ma·lef·i·cent
male·ness
ma·lev·o·lence
ma·lev·o·lent
mal·fea·sance
mal·for·ma·tion
mal·formed
mal·func·tion
mal·ice
ma·li·cious
ma·lign
ma·lig·nan·cy
ma·lig·nant
ma·lig·ni·ty
·ties
ma·lin·ger
ma·lin·ger·er
mall
(*promenade;* SEE maul)
mal·lard
mal·le·a·bil·i·ty
mal·le·a·ble
mal·let
mal·nu·tri·tion
mal·oc·clu·sion
mal·o·dor·ous
mal·prac·tice
malt·ose
mal·treat
mam·mon
mam·moth
man
men, manned
man·ning
man·a·cle
·cled ·cling
man·age
·aged ·ag·ing
man·age·a·ble
man·age·ment
man·ag·er
man·a·ge·ri·al
man·da·mus
man·da·rin
man·date
·dat·ed ·dat·ing
man·da·to·ry
man·di·ble
man·drel *or* ·dril
(*metal spindle*)
man·drill
(*baboon*)
ma·neu·ver
ma·neu·ver·a·ble
man·ga·nese
mange
man·ger
man·gi·ness
man·gle
·gled ·gling
man·gy
·gi·er ·gi·est
man·han·dle
Man·hat·tan
man·hole
man·hood
man-hour
ma·ni·a
ma·ni·ac
ma·ni·a·cal
man·ic
man·i·fest
man·i·fes·ta·tion
man·i·fes·to
·toes
man·i·fold
Ma·ni·la
ma·nip·u·late
·lat·ed ·lat·ing
ma·nip·u·la·tion
ma·nip·u·la·tive
ma·nip·u·la·tor
man·kind
man·li·ness
man·ly
·li·er ·li·est
man-made
man·ne·quin
man·ner
(*way;* SEE manor)
man·ner·ism
man·ner·ly
man·nish
man-of-war
men-of-war
ma·nom·e·ter
man·or
(*residence;*
SEE manner)
man·pow·er
man·sard
man·ser·vant
men·ser·vants
man·sion
man-sized
man·slaugh·ter
man·teau
·teaus
man·tel
(*fireplace fac-
ing;* SEE mantle)
man·tel·piece
man·til·la
man·tis
·tis·es *or* ·tes
man·tle
·tled ·tling
(*cloak;* SEE mantel)
man·tu·a
man·u·al
man·u·fac·to·ry
·ries
man·u·fac·ture
·tured ·tur·ing
man·u·fac·tur·er
man·u·script
man·y
more most
man·y-sid·ed
map
mapped
map·ping
mar
marred mar·ring
mar·a·thon
ma·raud
mar·ble
·bled ·bling
mar·ble·ize
·ized ·iz·ing
mar·ca·site
mar·cel
·celled ·cel·ling
March
mar·chion·ess
Mar·di gras
mar·gin
mar·gin·al
mar·gin·al·ly
ma·ri·jua·na *or*
·hua·na
ma·ri·na
mar·i·nade
·nad·ed ·nad·ing
mar·i·nate
·nat·ed ·nat·ing
ma·rine

mar·i·ner
mar·i·o·nette
mar·i·tal
(*of marriage;* SEE martial)
mar·i·time
mark·down
marked
mark·ed·ly
mar·ket·a·bil·i·ty
mar·ket·a·ble
mar·ket·place
marks·man
mark·up
mar·lin
(*fish*)
mar·line
(*cord*)
mar·mo·set
mar·mot
ma·roon
mar·quee
mar·quess
mar·que·try
mar·quis
mar·quise
mar·qui·sette
mar·riage
mar·riage·a·ble
mar·row
mar·row·bone
mar·ry
·ried ·ry·ing
mar·shal
·shaled *or* ·shalled
·shal·ing *or* ·shal·ling
mar·su·pi·al
mar·su·pi·um
·pi·a
mar·tial
(*military;* SEE marital)
Mar·tian
mar·ti·net
mar·ti·ni
·nis
mar·tyr
mar·tyr·dom
mar·tyr·ize
·ized ·iz·ing
mar·vel
·veled *or* ·velled
·vel·ing *or* ·vel·ling
mar·vel·ous
Marx·ism
Mar·y·land
mas·cot
mas·cu·line
mas·cu·lin·i·ty
ma·ser
mask
(*cover;* SEE masque)
masked
mas·och·ism
mas·och·is·tic
mas·och·is·ti·cal·ly
ma·son
Ma·son·ite
ma·son·ry
masque
(*masked ball;* SEE mask)
mas·quer·ade
·ad·ed ·ad·ing
Mas·sa·chu·setts
mas·sa·cre
·cred ·cring
mas·sage
·saged ·sag·ing
mas·seur
mas·seuse
mas·sive
mas·ter·ful
mas·ter·ly
mas·ter·mind
mas·ter·piece
mas·ter·y
·ies
mast·head
mas·ti·cate
·cat·ed ·cat·ing
mas·ti·ca·tion
mas·tiff
mas·to·don
mas·toid
mat
mat·ted
mat·ting
match·box
match·less
match·lock
match·mak·er
mate
mat·ed mat·ing
ma·te·ri·al
(*of matter;* SEE materiel)
ma·te·ri·al·ism
ma·te·ri·al·is·tic
ma·te·ri·al·ize
·ized ·iz·ing
ma·te·ri·al·ly
ma·te·ri·el
or ·té·ri·el
(*equipment;* SEE material)
math·e·mat·i·cal
math·e·ma·ti·cian
math·e·mat·ics
mat·i·nee
or ·i·née
ma·tri·arch
ma·tri·ar·chal
ma·tri·ar·chy
·chies
ma·tri·cide
ma·tric·u·lant
ma·tric·u·late
·lat·ed ·lat·ing
ma·tric·u·la·tion
mat·ri·mo·ni·al
mat·ri·mo·ny
ma·trix
·tri·ces *or* ·trix·es
ma·tron
mat·ter
mat·ter-of-fact
mat·tock
mat·u·rate
·rat·ed
·rat·ing
mat·u·ra·tion
ma·ture
·tured ·tur·ing
ma·ture·ly
ma·tu·ri·ty
maud·lin
maul
(*mallet; injure;* SEE mall)
maun·der
mau·so·le·um
·le·ums *or* ·le·a
mauve
mav·er·ick
mawk·ish
max·im
max·i·mal
max·i·mize
·mized ·miz·ing
max·i·mum
·mums *or* ·ma
May
may·be
May·day
may·hem
may·or
may·or·al·ty
·ties
maze
(*labyrinth;* SEE maize)
Mc·In·tosh
(*apple;* SEE mackintosh)
me·a cul·pa
mead·ow
mea·ger
meal·time
meal·y
·i·er ·i·est
meal·y-mouthed
mean *v.*
meant mean·ing
mean *adj., n.*
(*middle; low;* SEE mien)
me·an·der
mean·ing·ful
mean·ing·less
mean·ness
mean·time
mean·while
mea·sles
mea·sly
·sli·er ·sli·est
meas·ur·a·bil·i·ty

meas·ur·a·ble
meas·ur·a·bly
meas·ure
·ured ·ur·ing
meas·ure·less
meas·ure·ment
meas·ur·er
meat
(*flesh*, SEE meet, mete)
me·chan·ic
me·chan·i·cal
mech·a·ni·cian
me·chan·ics
mech·a·nism
mech·a·ni·za·tion
mech·a·nize
·nized ·niz·ing
med·al
(*award;* SEE meddle)
med·al·ist
me·dal·lion
med·dle
·dled ·dling
(*interfere;* SEE medal)
med·dler
med·dle·some
me·di·a
(*sing.* medium)
me·di·al
me·di·an
me·di·ate
·at·ed ·at·ing
me·di·a·tion
me·di·a·tor
med·i·cal
med·i·cate
·cat·ed ·cat·ing
med·i·ca·tion
me·dic·i·nal
med·i·cine
me·di·e·val
or ·ae·val
me·di·o·cre
me·di·oc·ri·ty
·ties
med·i·tate
·tat·ed ·tat·ing
med·i·ta·tion
med·i·ta·tor
Med·i·ter·ra·ne·an
me·di·um
·di·ums *or* ·di·a
meer·schaum
meet
met meet·ing
(*come upon;* SEE
meat, mete)
meg·a·lo·ma·ni·a
meg·a·lop·o·lis
meg·a·phone
meg·a·ton
mel·an·cho·li·a
mel·an·chol·ic
mel·an·chol·y
mé·lange
mel·a·nin
me·lee *or* mê·lée
mel·io·rate
·rat·ed ·rat·ing
mel·io·ra·tion
mel·lif·lu·ous
mel·low
me·lo·de·on
me·lod·ic
me·lo·di·ous
mel·o·dra·ma
mel·o·dra·mat·ic
mel·o·dy
·dies
melt·a·ble
mel·ton
mem·ber·ship
mem·brane
mem·bra·nous
me·men·to
·tos *or* ·toes
mem·oir
mem·o·ra·bil·i·a
mem·o·ra·ble
mem·o·ra·bly
mem·o·ran·dum
·dums *or* ·da
me·mo·ri·al
me·mo·ri·al·ize
·ized ·iz·ing
mem·o·ri·za·tion
mem·o·rize
·rized ·riz·ing
mem·o·ry
·ries
men·ace
·aced ·ac·ing
mé·nage *or* me·
me·nag·er·ie
men·da·cious
men·dac·i·ty
Men·de·li·an
men·di·cant
me·ni·al
men·in·gi·tis
me·nis·cus
·cus·es *or* ·ci
men·sur·a·ble
men·su·ra·tion
mens·wear
men·tal
men·tal·i·ty
men·thol
men·tho·lat·ed
men·tion
men·tor
men·u
·us
me·phit·ic
me·pro·ba·mate
mer·can·tile
mer·can·til·ism
mer·ce·nar·y
·nar·ies
mer·cer·ize
·ized
·iz·ing
mer·chan·dise
·dised
·dis·ing
mer·chan·dis·er
mer·chant
mer·ci·ful
mer·ci·ful·ly
mer·ci·less
mer·cu·ri·al
mer·cu·ry
mer·e·tri·cious
merge
merged
merg·ing
merg·er
me·rid·i·an
me·ri·no
·nos
mer·it
mer·i·to·ri·ous
mer·ri·ly
mer·ri·ment
mer·ri·ness
mer·ry
·ri·er ·ri·est
Mer·thi·o·late
me·sa
mé·sal·li·ance
mes·cal
mes·ca·line
mes·dames
mes·de·moi·selles
mesh·work
mes·mer·ism
mes·mer·ize
·ized ·iz·ing
mes·on
mes·sage
mes·sen·ger
mes·si·ah
mes·sieurs
mess·i·ness
mess·y
·i·er ·i·est
met·a·bol·ic
me·tab·o·lism
me·tab·o·lize
·lized ·liz·ing
met·al
·aled *or* ·alled
·al·ing *or* ·al·ling
(*mineral;* SEE
mettle)
me·tal·lic
met·al·lur·gi·cal
met·al·lur·gist
met·al·lur·gy
met·al·work
met·a·mor·phic
met·a·mor·phism
met·a·mor·phose
·phosed ·phos·ing
met·a·mor·pho·sis
·ses
met·a·phor
met·a·phor·i·cal
met·a·phor·i·cal·ly
met·a·phys·i·cal

met·a·phys·ics
met·a·tar·sal
mete
met·ed met·ing
(*allot;* SEE meat, meet)
me·te·or
me·te·or·ic
me·te·or·ite
me·te·or·oid
me·te·or·o·log·i·cal
me·te·or·ol·o·gist
me·te·or·ol·o·gy
me·ter
meth·a·done
meth·ane
meth·a·nol
meth·e·drine
meth·od
me·thod·i·cal
me·thod·i·cal·ly
Meth·od·ist
meth·od·ize
·ized ·iz·ing
meth·od·ol·o·gy
me·tic·u·lous
mé·tier
me·ton·y·my
met·ric
met·ri·cal
met·ro·nome
me·trop·o·lis
met·ro·pol·i·tan
met·tle
(*spirit;* SEE metal)
mez·za·nine
mez·zo·tint
mi·as·ma
·mas *or* ·ma·ta
mi·ca
Mich·i·gan
mi·cro·bar
mi·crobe
mi·cro·bic
mi·cro·com·put·er
mi·cro·cop·y
mi·cro·cosm
mi·cro·dot
mi·cro·e·co·nom·ics
mi·cro·fiche
mi·cro·film
mi·cro·groove
mi·crom·e·ter
mi·cro·or·gan·ism
mi·cro·phone
mi·cro·print
mi·cro·proc·es·sor
mi·cro·read·er
mi·cro·scope
mi·cro·scop·ic
mi·cro·wave
mid·air
mid·cult
mid·day
mid·dle
mid·dle-aged
mid·dle·brow
mid·dle-class
mid·dle·man
mid·dle-of-the-road
mid·dle·weight
mid·dling
mid·i·ron
mid·land
mid·night
mid·point
mid·ship·man
midst
mid·stream
mid·sum·mer
mid·term
mid-Vic·to·ri·an
mid·way
mid·week
Mid·west
Mid·west·ern·er
mid·win·ter
mid·year
mien
(*manner;* SEE mean)
miffed
might
might·i·ly
might·i·ness
might·y
·i·er ·i·est
mi·gnon
mi·graine
mi·grant
mi·grate
·grat·ed ·grat·ing
mi·gra·tion
mi·gra·to·ry
mil·dew
mild·ly
mile·age
mile·post
mile·stone
mi·lieu
mil·i·tan·cy
mil·i·tant
mil·i·tar·i·ly
mil·i·ta·rism
mil·i·ta·ris·tic
mil·i·ta·ri·za·tion
mil·i·ta·rize
·rized ·riz·ing
mil·i·tar·y
mil·i·tate
·tat·ed ·tat·ing
mi·li·tia
milk·i·ness
milk·man
milk·shake
milk·shed
milk·sop
milk·weed
milk·y
·i·er ·i·est
mill·age
mill·dam
milled
mil·len·ni·um
·ni·ums *or* ·ni·a
mill·er
mil·let
mil·liard
mil·li·bar
mil·li·gram
mil·li·li·ter
mil·li·me·ter
mil·line
mill·ing
mil·lion
mil·lion·aire
mil·lionth
mil·li·pede
mill·stone
mill·stream
mill wheel
mill·work
mill·wright
Mil·wau·kee
mime
mimed mim·ing
mim·e·o·graph
mim·er
mi·met·ic
mim·ic
·icked ·ick·ing
mim·ick·er
mim·ic·ry
mi·mo·sa
min·a·ret
min·a·to·ry
mind·ful
mind·less
mind reader
mine
mined min·ing
mine·lay·er
min·er
(*mine worker;* SEE minor)
min·er·al
min·er·al·i·za·tion
min·er·al·ize
·ized ·iz·ing
min·er·al·o·gist
min·er·al·o·gy
min·gle
·gled ·gling
min·i·a·ture
min·i·a·tur·i·za·tion
min·i·a·tur·ize
·ized ·iz·ing
min·i·bus
min·i·com·put·er
min·i·fi·ca·tion
min·i·fy
·fied ·fy·ing
min·im
min·i·mal
min·i·mal·ly
min·i·mize
·mized ·miz·ing

min·i·mum
·mums *or* ·ma
min·ion
min·is·ter
(*diplomat; clergy-man;* SEE minster)
min·is·te·ri·al
min·is·trant
min·is·tra·tion
min·is·try
·tries
min·i·track
min·i·ver
Min·ne·ap·o·lis
min·ne·sing·er
Min·ne·so·ta
mi·nor
(*lesser;* SEE miner)
mi·nor·i·ty
·ties
min·ster
(*church;* SEE minister)
mint·age
min·u·end
mi·nus
mi·nus·cule
min′ute *n.*
mi·nute′ *adj.*
mi·nute·ly
min·ute·man
mi·nu·ti·ae
(*sing.* mi·nu·ti·a)
minx
mir·a·cle
mi·rac·u·lous
mi·rage
mire
mired mir·ing
mir·ror
mirth·ful
mirth·less
mir·y
·i·er ·i·est
mis·ad·ven·ture
mis·ad·vise
mis·al·li·ance
mis·al·ly
mis·an·thrope
mis·an·throp·ic
mis·an·thro·py
mis·ap·pli·ca·tion
mis·ap·ply
mis·ap·pre·hend
mis·ap·pre·hen·sion
mis·ap·pro·pri·ate
mis·be·got·ten
mis·be·have
mis·be·hav·ior
mis·be·lief
mis·be·lieve
mis·cal·cu·late
mis·cal·cu·la·tion
mis·car·riage
mis·car·ry
mis·cast
mis·ce·ge·na·tion
mis·cel·la·ne·a
mis·cel·la·ne·ous
mis·cel·la·ny
·nies
mis·chance
mis·chief
mis·chief-mak·er
mis·chie·vous
mis·ci·bil·i·ty
mis·ci·ble
mis·con·ceive
mis·con·cep·tion
mis·con·duct
mis·con·struc·tion
mis·con·strue
mis·count
mis·cre·ant
mis·cue
mis·date
mis·deal
·dealt ·deal·ing
mis·deed
mis·de·mean·or
mis·di·rect
mi·ser
mis·er·a·ble
mis·er·a·bly
mi·ser·ly
mis·er·y
·ies
mis·es·ti·mate
mis·fea·sance
mis·file
mis·fire
mis·fit
mis·for·tune
mis·giv·ing
mis·gov·ern
mis·guid·ance
mis·guide
mis·han·dle
mis·hap
mis·in·form
mis·in·for·ma·tion
mis·in·ter·pret
mis·judge
mis·judg·ment
or ·judge·ment
mis·lay
·laid ·lay·ing
mis·lead
·led ·lead·ing
mis·man·age
mis·man·age·ment
mis·match
mis·mate
mis·no·mer
mi·sog·a·my
mi·sog·y·nist
mi·sog·y·ny
mis·place
mis·print
mis·pri·sion
mis·pro·nounce
mis·pro·nun·ci·a·tion
mis·quo·ta·tion
mis·quote
mis·read
·read ·read·ing
mis·rep·re·sent
mis·rep·re·sen·ta·tion
mis·rule
Miss
Miss·es
mis·sal
(*book;* SEE missile, missive)
mis·shape
mis·shap·en
mis·sile
(*weapon;* SEE missal, missive)
mis·sion
mis·sion·ar·y
Mis·sis·sip·pi
mis·sive
(*letter;* SEE missal, missile)
Mis·sour·i
mis·speak
·spoke
·spo·ken
·speak·ing
mis·spell
·spelled *or*
·spelt
·spell·ing
mis·spend
·spent
·spend·ing
mis·state
mis·state·ment
mis·step
mis·take
·took ·tak·en
·tak·ing
mist·i·ness
mis·tral
mis·treat·ment
mis·tress
mis·tri·al
mis·trust
mist·y
·i·er ·i·est
mis·un·der·stand
·stood
·stand·ing
mis·us·age
mis·use
mis·val·ue
mis·write
·wrote ·writ·ten
·writ·ing
mi·ter
mit·i·ga·ble
mit·i·gate
·gat·ed ·gat·ing
mit·i·ga·tion
mit·i·ga·tor
mi·tral

mix
mixed *or* mixt
mix·ing
mix·er
mix·ture
mix up
mne·mon·ic
moan·ing
mob
mobbed
mob·bing
mo·bile
mo·bil·i·ty
mo·bi·liz·a·ble
mo·bi·li·za·tion
mo·bi·lize
·lized ·liz·ing
mock·er·y
·ies
mock-up
mod·a·cryl·ic
mod·al
(*of a mode*)
mod·el
·eled *or* ·elled
·el·ing *or* ·el·ling
(*copy*)
mod·er·ate
·at·ed ·at·ing
mod·er·ate·ly
mod·er·a·tion
mod·er·a·tor
mod·ern
mod·ern·ism
mod·ern·is·tic
mo·der·ni·ty
mod·ern·i·za·tion
mod·ern·ize
·ized ·iz·ing
mod·ern·ness
mod·est
mod·es·ty
mod·i·cum
mod·i·fi·ca·tion
mod·i·fi·er
mod·i·fy
·fied ·fy·ing
mod·ish
mo·diste
mod·u·lar
mod·u·late
·lat·ed
·lat·ing
mod·u·la·tion
mod·u·la·tor
mod·ule
mo·dus o·pe·ran·di
mo·gul
moi·e·ty
·ties
moire
moi·ré
mois·ten
moist·ness
mois·ture
mois·tur·ize
·ized ·iz·ing
mo·lar
mold·board
mold·er
mold·i·ness
mold·ing
mold·y
·i·er ·i·est
mole
mo·lec·u·lar
mol·e·cule
mole·hill
mo·lest
mo·les·ta·tion
mol·li·fy
·fied ·fy·ing
molt
mol·ten
mo·lyb·de·num
mo·ment
mo·men·tar·i·ly
mo·men·tar·y
mo·men·tous
mo·men·tum
·tums *or* ·ta
mo·nan·drous
mon·arch
mo·nar·chal
mon·ar·chism
mon·ar·chy
·chies
mon·as·ter·y
·ies
mo·nas·tic
mo·nas·ti·cism
mon·au·ral
Mon·day
mon·e·tar·y
mon·e·tize
·tized ·tiz·ing
mon·ey
·eys *or* ·ies
mon·ey·bag
mon·ey-chang·er
mon·eyed
mon·ey·lend·er
mon·ey·mak·er
mon·ger
mo·ni·tion
mon·i·tor
mon·i·to·ry
·ries
monk's cloth
mon·o·chro·mat·ic
mon·o·chrome
mon·o·cle
mon·o·coque
mo·noc·u·lar
mon·o·dra·ma
mo·nog·a·mist
mo·nog·a·mous
mo·nog·a·my
mon·o·gram
·grammed
·gram·ming
mon·o·graph
mo·nog·y·ny
mon·o·lith
mon·o·logue
or ·log
mon·o·logu·ist *or*
mo·nol·o·gist
mon·o·ma·ni·a
mon·o·met·al·lism
mon·o·nu·cle·o·sis
mon·o·plane
mo·nop·o·list
mo·nop·o·lis·tic
mo·nop·o·li·za·tion
mo·nop·o·lize
·lized
·liz·ing
mo·nop·o·ly
·lies
mon·o·rail
mon·o·syl·lab·ic
mon·o·syl·la·ble
mon·o·the·ism
mon·o·the·is·tic
mon·o·tone
mo·not·o·nous
mo·not·o·ny
mon·o·type
mon·ox·ide
Mon·sei·gneur
Mes·sei·gneurs
mon·sieur
mes·sieurs
Mon·si·gnor
mon·stros·i·ty
·ties
mon·strous
mon·tage
·taged
·tag·ing
Mon·tan·a
month·ly
·lies
mon·u·ment
mon·u·men·tal
mood·i·ly
mood·i·ness
mood·y
·i·er ·i·est
moon·light
moon·light·ing
moon·lit
moon·rise
moon·set
moon·shot
moon·stone
moor·age
moor·ing
moot
(*debatable;*
SEE mute)
mop
mopped
mop·ping
mope
moped mop·ing
mop-up

mo·raine
mor·al
mo·rale
mor·al·ist
mor·al·is·tic
mor·al·is·ti·cal·ly
mo·ral·i·ty
mor·al·ize
·ized ·iz·ing
mor·al·ly
mo·rass
mor·a·to·ri·um
·ri·ums *or* ·ri·a
mor·bid
mor·bid·i·ty
more·o·ver
mo·res
mor·ga·nat·ic
morgue
mor·i·bund
mor·i·bun·di·ty
Mor·mon
mo·rose
mor·phine
mor·phol·o·gy
mor·sel
mor·tal
mor·tal·i·ty
mor·tal·ly
mor·tar
mor·tar·board
mort·gage
·gaged ·gag·ing
mort·ga·gee
mort·ga·gor
mor·ti·cian
mor·ti·fi·ca·tion
mor·ti·fy
·fied ·fy·ing
mor·tise
·tised ·tis·ing
mor·tu·ar·y
·ies
mo·sa·ic
·icked ·ick·ing
mosque
mos·qui·to
·toes *or* ·tos
moss·back
moss·i·ness
moss·y
·i·er ·i·est
most·ly
mo·tel
moth·er·hood
moth·er-in-law
moth·ers-in-law
moth·er·land
moth·er·li·ness
moth·er·ly
moth·er-of-pearl
moth·proof
mo·tif
mo·tile
mo·til·i·ty
mo·tion·less
mo·ti·vate
·vat·ed ·vat·ing
mo·ti·va·tion
mo·ti·va·tor
mo·tive
mot·ley
mo·tor·boat
mo·tor·bus
mo·tor·cade
mo·tor·cy·cle
mo·tor·drome
mo·tor·ist
mo·tor·ize
·ized ·iz·ing
mo·tor·man
mot·tle
·tled ·tling
mot·to
·toes *or* ·tos
mou·lage
mound
moun·tain
moun·tain·eer
moun·tain·ous
moun·te·bank
mourn·ful
mourn·ing
mousse
mousse·line de soie
mouth·ful
·fuls
mouth·part
mouth·piece
mouth-to-mouth
mouth·wash
mouth·wa·ter·ing
mov·a·ble
or move·
mov·a·bly
move
moved mov·ing
move·ment
mov·ie
mov·ie·go·er
mov·i·o·la
mow
mowed, mowed
or mown,
mow·ing
Mr.
Messrs.
Mrs.
Mmes.
mu·ci·lage
mu·ci·lag·i·nous
muck·rake
mu·cous *adj.*
mu·cus *n.*
mud·der
mud·di·ness
mud·dle
·dled ·dling
mud·dler
mud·dy
·di·er ·di·est
mud·sling·ing
Muen·ster
mu·ez·zin
muf·fle
·fled ·fling
muf·fler
muf·ti
mulch
mulct
mul·ish
mul·li·ga·taw·ny
mul·lion
mul·ti·col·ored
mul·ti·far·i·ous
mul·ti·form
mul·ti·lat·er·al
mul·ti·na·tion·al
mul·ti·ple
mul·ti·plex
mul·ti·pli·a·ble
mul·ti·pli·cand
mul·ti·pli·ca·tion
mul·ti·plic·i·ty
mul·ti·pli·er
mul·ti·ply
·plied ·ply·ing
mul·ti·tude
mul·ti·tu·di·nous
mul·ti·ver·si·ty
mum·ble
·bled ·bling
mum·bler
munch
mun·dane
mu·nic·i·pal
mu·nic·i·pal·i·ty
·ties
mu·nic·i·pal·ize
·ized ·iz·ing
mu·nif·i·cence
mu·nif·i·cent
mu·ni·tion
mu·ral
mur·der·er
mur·der·ous
murk·i·ly
murk·i·ness
murk·y
·i·er ·i·est
mur·mur
mur·mur·er
mus·ca·dine
mus·ca·tel
mus·cle
·cled ·cling
(*body part;* SEE mussel)
mus·cle-bound
mus·cu·lar
mus·cu·la·ture
muse
mused mus·ing
mu·sette
mu·se·um
mush·room
mu·sic
mu·si·cal *adj.*
mu·si·cale *n.*
mu·si·cian

mu·si·col·o·gist
mu·si·col·o·gy
mus·lin
mus·sel
(*shellfish;* SEE muscle)
mus·tache
or mous·
mus·ter
mus·ti·ness
mus·ty
·ti·er ·ti·est
mu·ta·bil·i·ty
mu·ta·ble
mu·tant
mu·tate
·tat·ed ·tat·ing
mu·ta·tion
mute
mut·ed mut·ing
(*silent;* SEE moot)
mu·ti·late
·lat·ed ·lat·ing
mu·ti·la·tion
mu·ti·neer
mu·ti·nous
mu·ti·ny
·nies
·nied ·ny·ing
mu·tu·al
mu·tu·al·i·ty
mu·tu·al·ly
muz·zle
·zled ·zling
my·e·li·tis
my·e·lo·gram
my·lar
my·o·pi·a
my·op·ic
myr·i·ad
myr·i·a·pod
myr·mi·don
my·self
mys·te·ri·ous
mys·ter·y
·ies
mys·tic
mys·ti·cal
mys·ti·cism
mys·ti·fi·ca·tion
mys·ti·fy
·fied ·fy·ing
mys·tique
myth·i·cal
myth·o·log·i·cal
my·thol·o·gy
·gies
myth·os

N

na·cre
na·cre·ous
na·dir
nail·head
nain·sook
na·ive *or* ·ïve
na·ive·té *or* ·ïve·
na·ked·ness
name·a·ble
or nam·
name-drop·per
name·less
name·ly
name·plate
name·sake
na·no·sec·ond
na·palm
naph·tha
naph·tha·lene
na·po·le·on
nar·cis·sism
nar·cis·sist
nar·cis·sis·tic
nar·cis·sus
nar·co·lep·sy
nar·co·sis
nar·cot·ic
nar·co·tism
nar·rate
·rat·ed ·rat·ing
nar·ra·tion
nar·ra·tive
nar·ra·tor
nar·row-mind·ed
na·sal
nas·cent
nas·ti·ly
nas·ti·ness
nas·ty
·ti·er ·ti·est
na·tal
na·tant
na·ta·to·ri·um
·ri·ums *or* ·ri·a
na·ta·to·ry
na·tion
na·tion·al
na·tion·al·ism
na·tion·al·is·ti·cal·ly
na·tion·al·i·ty
·ties
na·tion·al·i·za·tion
na·tion·al·ize
·ized ·iz·ing
na·tion·al·ly
na·tion·wide
na·tive
na·tive-born
na·tiv·i·ty
·ties
nat·ti·ly
nat·ty
·ti·er ·ti·est
nat·u·ral·ism
nat·u·ral·ist
nat·u·ral·is·tic
nat·u·ral·i·za·tion
nat·u·ral·ize
·ized ·iz·ing
nat·u·ral·ly
na·ture
naug·a·hyde
naught
nau·se·a
nau·se·ate
·at·ed ·at·ing
nau·seous
nau·ti·cal
nau·ti·lus
·lus·es *or* ·li
na·val
(*of a navy*)
nave
na·vel
(*umbilicus*)
nav·i·cert
nav·i·ga·ble
nav·i·gate
·gat·ed ·gat·ing
nav·i·ga·tion
nav·i·ga·tor
na·vy
·vies
near·by
near·ly
near·sight·ed
neat·ly
neat·ness
Ne·bras·ka
neb·u·la
·lae *or* ·las
neb·u·lar
neb·u·los·i·ty
neb·u·lous
nec·es·sar·i·ly
nec·es·sar·y
·ies
ne·ces·si·tate
·tat·ed ·tat·ing
ne·ces·si·tous
ne·ces·si·ty
·ties
neck·er·chief
neck·lace
neck·line
neck·tie
ne·crol·o·gy
·gies
nec·ro·man·cy
nee *or* née
need
(*require;* SEE knead)
need·ful
need·i·ness
nee·dle
·dled ·dling
nee·dler
need·less
need·n't
need·y
·i·er ·i·est
ne'er-do-well
ne·far·i·ous
ne·gate
·gat·ed ·gat·ing
ne·ga·tion

neg·a·tive
neg·a·tiv·ism
neg·lect
neg·lect·ful
neg·li·gence
neg·li·gent
neg·li·gi·ble
neg·li·gi·bly
ne·go·ti·a·bil·i·ty
ne·go·ti·a·ble
ne·go·ti·ate
 ·at·ed ·at·ing
ne·go·ti·a·tion
ne·go·ti·a·tor
Ne·gro
 ·groes
Ne·groid
neigh·bor
neigh·bor·hood
neigh·bor·li·ness
neigh·bor·ly
nei·ther
 (*not either;* SEE nether)
nem·a·tode
nem·e·sis
 ·ses
ne·o·clas·sic
ne·o·lith·ic
ne·ol·o·gism
ne·o·my·cin
ne·on
ne·o·phyte
neo·o·plasm
ne·o·prene
ne·pen·the
neph·ew
ne·phri·tis
nep·o·tism
nerve
 nerved nerv·ing
nerve-rack·ing
 or -wrack·
nerv·ous
nes·ci·ent
nes·tle
 ·tled ·tling
net
 net·ted net·ting
neth·er
 (*lower;* SEE neither)
net·tle
 ·tled ·tling
net·work
neu·ral
neu·ral·gia
neu·ras·the·ni·a
neu·ri·tis
neu·ro·log·i·cal
neu·rol·o·gist
neu·rol·o·gy
neu·ro·sis
 ·ses
neu·rot·ic
neu·ter
neu·tral
neu·tral·i·ty
neu·tral·i·za·tion
neu·tral·ize
 ·ized ·iz·ing
neu·tral·iz·er
neu·tri·no
neu·tron
Ne·vad·a
nev·er·more
nev·er·the·less
ne·vus
 ·vi
new·com·er
new·el
new·fan·gled
new-fash·ioned
New·found·land
New Hamp·shire
New Jer·sey
New Mex·i·co
news·boy
news·cast
news·deal·er
news·let·ter
news·man
news·pa·per
new·speak
news·print
news·reel
news·stand
news·wor·thy
New York
next-door
nex·us
 ·us·es *or* nex·us
ni·a·cin
Ni·ag·a·ra
nib·ble
 ·bled ·bling
nib·lick
nice
 nic·er nic·est
nice·ly
ni·ce·ty
 ·ties
niche
 (*recess*)
nick
 (*notch*)
nick·el
 ·eled *or* ·elled
 ·el·ing *or* ·el·ling
nick·el·o·de·on
nick·name
nic·o·tine
nic·ti·tate
 ·tat·ed ·tat·ing
niece
nig·gard·ly
night
 (*darkness;* SEE knight)
night·cap
night·club
night·fall
night·in·gale
night·long
night·ly
night·mare
night·shirt
night·time
ni·hil·ism
ni·hil·is·tic
nim·ble
 ·bler ·blest
nim·bly
nim·bus
 ·bi *or* ·bus·es
nine·fold
nine·pins
nine·teen
nine·ti·eth
nine·ty
 ·ties
ni·non
ninth
nip
 nipped nip·ping
nip·per
nip·pi·ness
nip·py
 ·pi·er ·pi·est
nir·va·na
ni·sei
 ·sei *or* ·seis
nit-pick·ing
ni·tro·gen
ni·tro·glyc·er·in
 or ·er·ine
nit·ty-grit·ty
no·bil·i·ty
no·ble
 ·bler ·blest
no·ble·man
no·blesse o·blige
no·bly
no·bod·y
 ·ies
noc·tur·nal
noc·tur·nal·ly
noc·turne
noc·u·ous
nod
 nod·ded nod·ding
nod·al
node
nod·u·lar
nod·ule
no·el *or* ·ël
noise
 noised nois·ing
noise·less
noise·mak·er
nois·i·ly
nois·i·ness
noi·some
nois·y
 ·i·er ·i·est
no·mad
no·mad·ic

nom de plume
 noms de plume
no·men·cla·ture
nom·i·nal
nom·i·nal·ly
nom·i·nate
 ·nat·ed ·nat·ing
nom·i·na·tion
nom·i·na·tive
nom·i·na·tor
nom·i·nee
non·a·ge·nar·i·an
non·as·sign·a·ble
non-book
nonce
non·cha·lance
non·cha·lant
non·com·bat·tant
non·com·mit·tal
non com·pos men·tis
non·con·form·ist
non·co·op·er·a·tion
non·cu·mu·la·tive
non·de·script
non·en·ti·ty
 ·ties
non·es·sen·tial
none·such
none·the·less
non·ex·ist·ent
non·fea·sance
non·ne·go·ti·a·ble
non·nu·cle·ar
no-non·sense
non·pa·reil
non·par·ti·san
non·plus
 ·plused *or*
 ·plussed
 ·plus·ing *or*
 ·plus·sing
non·prof·it
non·sched·uled
non·sec·tar·i·an
non·sense
non·sen·si·cal
non se·qui·tur
non-sked
non·skid
non·stop
non·sup·port
non·un·ion
non·vi·o·lence
noon·day
no one
noon·time
no-par
nor·mal
nor·mal·cy
nor·mal·i·ty
nor·mal·ize
 ·ized ·iz·ing
nor·mal·ly
north·bound
North Car·o·li·na
North Da·ko·ta
north·east
north·west
nose
 nosed nos·ing
nose·bleed
nose-dive
 -dived -div·ing
nose·piece
no-show
nos·tal·gia
nos·tal·gic
nos·tril
nos·tro
nos·trum
no·ta·ble
no·ta·bly
no·ta·ri·za·tion
no·ta·rize
 ·rized ·riz·ing
no·ta·ry pub·lic
 no·ta·ries pub·lic
 or no·ta·ry pub·lics
no·ta·tion
notched
note
 not·ed not·ing
note·book
note·wor·thy
noth·ing·ness
no·tice
 ·ticed ·tic·ing
no·tice·a·ble
no·tice·a·bly
no·ti·fi·a·ble
no·ti·fi·ca·tion
no·ti·fy
 ·fied ·fy·ing
no·tion
no·to·ri·e·ty
no·to·ri·ous
not·with·stand·ing
nought
nour·ish·ment
nou·veau riche
 nou·veaux riches
no·va
 ·vas *or* ·vae
no·va·tion
nov·el
nov·el·ette
nov·el·ist
no·vel·la
nov·el·ty
 ·ties
No·vem·ber
nov·ice
no·vi·ti·ate
now·a·days
no·where
no·wise
nox·ious
noz·zle
nu·ance
nub·by
 ·bi·er ·bi·est
nu·bile
nu·cle·ar
nu·cle·ate
 ·at·ed ·at·ing
nu·cle·on·ics
nu·cle·us
 ·cle·i *or*
 ·cle·us·es
nudge
 nudged nudg·ing
nu·ga·to·ry
nug·get
nui·sance
nul·li·fi·ca·tion
nul·li·fy
 ·fied ·fy·ing
num·ber
num·ber·less
numb·ly
numb·ness
nu·mer·a·ble
nu·mer·al
nu·mer·ate
 ·at·ed ·at·ing
nu·mer·a·tion
nu·mer·a·tor
nu·mer·i·cal
nu·mer·ol·o·gy
nu·mer·ous
nu·mis·mat·ic
nu·mis·ma·tist
nurse
 nursed nurs·ing
nur·ture
 ·tured ·tur·ing
nut·crack·er
nut·meat
nut·meg
nut·pick
nu·tri·a
nu·tri·ent
nu·tri·ment
nu·tri·tion
nu·tri·tious
nu·tri·tive
nut·shell
ny·lon
nymph

O

oar·lock
oars·man
o·a·sis
 ·ses
oath
ob·bli·ga·to
 ·tos *or* ·ti
ob·du·ra·cy
ob·du·rate
o·be·di·ence
o·be·di·ent
o·bei·sance
o·bei·sant
ob·e·lisk
o·bese

o·be·si·ty
o·bey
ob·fus·cate
·cat·ed ·cat·ing
ob·i·ter dic·tum
ob·i·ter dic·ta
o·bit·u·ar·y
·ies
ob·ject
ob·jec·tion
ob·jec·tion·a·ble
ob·jec·tion·a·bly
ob·jec·tive
ob·jec·tive·ly
ob·jec·tiv·i·ty
ob·jec·tor
ob·jet d'art
ob·jets d'art
ob·jur·gate
·gat·ed ·gat·ing
ob·jur·ga·tion
ob·la·tion
ob·li·gate
·gat·ed ·gat·ing
ob·li·ga·tion
ob·lig·a·to·ry
o·blige
o·bliged
o·blig·ing
ob·li·gee
ob·li·gor
ob·lique
ob·lique·ly
ob·liq·ui·ty
ob·lit·er·ate
·at·ed ·at·ing
ob·lit·er·a·tion
ob·lit·er·a·tor
ob·liv·i·on
ob·liv·i·ous
ob·long
ob·lo·quy
·quies
ob·nox·ious
ob·scene
ob·scen·i·ty
·ties
ob·scure
·scured ·scur·ing
ob·scure·ly
ob·scu·ri·ty
·ties
ob·se·quies
ob·se·qui·ous
ob·serv·a·ble
ob·serv·ance
ob·serv·ant
ob·ser·va·tion
ob·serv·a·to·ry
·ries
ob·serve
·served ·serv·ing
ob·serv·er
ob·sess
ob·ses·sion
ob·ses·sive
ob·sid·i·an
ob·so·lesce
·lesced ·lesc·ing
ob·so·les·cence
ob·so·les·cent
ob·so·lete
ob·sta·cle
ob·stet·ric
ob·stet·ri·cal
ob·ste·tri·cian
ob·sti·na·cy
·cies
ob·sti·nate
ob·sti·nate·ly
ob·strep·er·ous
ob·struct
ob·struc·tion
ob·struc·tion·ist
ob·struc·tive
ob·tain
ob·trude
·trud·ed
·trud·ing
ob·tru·sion
ob·tru·sive
ob·tru·sive·ly
ob·tuse
ob·verse
ob·vert
ob·vi·ate
·at·ed ·at·ing
ob·vi·ous
ob·vi·ous·ly
oc·ca·sion
oc·ca·sion·al
oc·ca·sion·al·ly
Oc·ci·dent
Oc·ci·den·tal
oc·cip·i·tal
oc·clude
·clud·ed
·clud·ing
oc·clu·sion
oc·cult
oc·cul·ta·tion
oc·cult·ism
oc·cu·pan·cy
·cies
oc·cu·pant
oc·cu·pa·tion
oc·cu·pa·tion·al·ly
oc·cu·py
·pied ·py·ing
oc·cur
·curred
·cur·ring
oc·cur·rence
o·cean
o·cean·go·ing
o·ce·an·ic
o·ce·a·nog·ra·phy
o·ce·an·ol·o·gy
o·cher *or* o·chre
o'·clock
oc·ta·gon
oc·tag·o·nal
oc·ta·he·dron
oc·tane
oc·tan·gu·lar
Oc·to·ber
oc·to·ge·nar·i·an
oc·tu·ple
oc·u·lar
oc·u·list
odd·i·ty
·ties
odd·ly
odds-on
o·di·ous
o·di·um
o·dom·e·ter
o·dor
o·dor·if·er·ous
o·dor·ous
Od·ys·sey
of·fal
off·beat
off-col·or
of·fend
of·fense
of·fen·sive
of·fer
of·fer·ing
off·hand
off·hand·ed·ly
of·fice
of·fice·hold·er
of·fi·cer
of·fi·cial·ese
of·fi·cial
of·fi·ci·ate
·at·ed ·at·ing
of·fi·ci·a·tion
of·fi·ci·a·tor
of·fi·cious
off·ing
off-key
off-lim·its
off-line
off·print
off·set
off·shoot
off·shore
off·side
off·spring
·spring *or*
·springs
off·stage
off-white
of·ten
of·ten·times
o·gle
o·gled o·gling
o·gre
o·gre·ish *or*
o·grish
O·hi·o
ohm·me·ter
oil·i·ness
oil·pa·per
oil·skin

oil·stone
oil·y
·i·er ·i·est
oint·ment
O·kla·ho·ma
old-fash·ioned
old-line
old-tim·er
old-world
ol·fac·tion
ol·fac·to·ry
·ries
ol·i·garch
ol·i·gar·chy
·chies
ol·i·gop·o·ly
·lies
O·lym·pic
om·buds·man
o·me·ga
o·men
om·i·nous
o·mis·si·ble
o·mis·sion
o·mit
o·mit·ted
o·mit·ting
om·ni·bus
om·ni·far·i·ous
om·nip·o·tence
om·nip·o·tent
om·ni·pres·ence
om·ni·pres·ent
om·ni·range
om·nis·cience
om·nis·cient
om·niv·o·rous
once-o·ver
on·com·ing
one·ness
on·er·ous
one·self
one-sid·ed
one-time
one-track
one-up
-upped
-up·ping
one-up·man·ship
one-way
on·go·ing
on·ion·skin
on-line
on·look·er
on·ly
on·o·mat·o·poe·ia
on·rush
on·set
on·shore
on·side
on·slaught
o·nus
on·ward
on·yx
oo·long
ooze
oozed ooz·ing
o·pac·i·ty
o·pal
o·pal·es·cent
o·paque
op. cit.
o·pen-and-shut
o·pen-end
o·pen-end·ed
o·pen·er
o·pen-eyed
o·pen·hand·ed
o·pen·ly
o·pen mind·ed
o·pen-mouthed
o·pen·ness
o·pen·work
op·er·a
op·er·a·ble
op·er·ate
·at·ed ·at·ing
op·er·at·ic
op·er·a·tion
op·er·a·tion·al
op·er·a·tion·al·ly
op·er·a·tive
op·er·a·tor
op·er·et·ta
oph·thal·mol·o·gist
oph·thal·mol·o·gy
oph·thal·mo·scope
o·pi·ate
o·pin·ion
o·pin·ion·at·ed
o·pin·ion·a·tive
o·pi·um
op·po·nent
op·por·tune
op·por·tun·ism
op·por·tun·ist
op·por·tu·ni·ty
·ties
op·pos·a·ble
op·pose
·posed ·pos·ing
op·pos·er
op·po·site
op·po·si·tion
op·press
op·pres·sion
op·pres·sive
op·pres·sive·ly
op·pres·sor
op·pro·bri·ous
op·pro·bri·um
op·tic
op·ti·cal
op·ti·cian
op·ti·mal
op·ti·mism
op·ti·mist
op·ti·mis·tic
op·ti·mis·ti·cal·ly
op·ti·mize
·mized
·miz·ing
op·ti·mum
·mums *or* ·ma
op·tion
op·tion·al
op·tion·al·ly
op·tion·ee
op·tion·er
op·tom·e·trist
op·tom·e·try
op·u·lence
op·u·lent
o·pus
op·er·a *or*
o·pus·es
or·a·cle
o·rac·u·lar
o·ral
(*of the mouth;*
SEE aural)
o·ral·ly
or·ange
or·ange·ade
o·ra·tion
or·a·tor
or·a·tor·i·cal
or·a·to·ri·o
·os
or·a·to·ry
·ries
or·bic·u·lar
or·bit
or·ches·tra
or·ches·tral
or·ches·trate
·trat·ed ·trat·ing
or·ches·tra·tion
or·dain
or·deal
or·der
or·der·li·ness
or·der·ly
·lies
or·di·nal
or·di·nance
(*law;* SEE
ordnance)
or·di·nar·i·ly
or·di·nar·y
·ies
or·di·nate
or·di·na·tion
ord·nance
(*artillery;* SEE
ordinance)
or·dure
Or·e·gon
or·gan
or·gan·ic
or·gan·i·cal·ly
or·gan·ism
or·gan·iz·a·ble
or·gan·i·za·tion
or·gan·ize
·ized ·iz·ing

or·gan·iz·er
O·ri·ent *n.*
o·ri·ent *v.*
O·ri·en·tal
o·ri·en·tate
·tat·ed ·tat·ing
o·ri·en·ta·tion
or·i·fice
or·i·gin
o·rig·i·nal
o·rig·i·nal·i·ty
o·rig·i·nal·ly
o·rig·i·nate
·nat·ed
·nat·ing
o·rig·i·na·tion
o·rig·i·na·tor
or·lon
or·na·ment
or·na·men·tal
or·na·men·ta·tion
or·nate
or·nate·ly
or·ni·thol·o·gy
o·ro·tund
or·phan·age
or·thi·con
or·tho·don·tics
or·tho·don·tist
or·tho·dox
or·tho·dox·y
·ies
or·thog·ra·phy
or·tho·pe·dics
or·tho·pe·dist
os·cil·late
·lat·ed ·lat·ing
(*fluctuate;* SEE osculate)
os·cil·la·tion
os·cil·la·tor
os·cil·lo·scope
os·cu·late
·lat·ed ·lat·ing
(*kiss;* SEE oscillate)
os·mo·sis
os·si·fy
·fied ·fy·ing
os·ten·si·ble
os·ten·si·bly
os·ten·sive
os·ten·sive·ly
os·ten·ta·tion
os·ten·ta·tious
os·te·o·path
os·te·op·a·thy
os·tra·cism
os·tra·cize
·cized ·ciz·ing
oth·er-di·rect·ed
oth·er·wise
o·ti·ose
ot·to·man
·mans
ought
(*be obliged;* SEE aught)
our·self
our·selves
oust·er
out-and-out
out·bid
·bid ·bid·ding
out·board
out·bound
out·build·ing
out·burst
out·cast
out·class
out·come
out·crop
out·cry
·cries
out·dat·ed
out·dis·tance
·tanced ·tanc·ing
out·do
·did ·done
·do·ing
out·door
out·doors
out·er·most
out·er space
out·er·wear
out·face
out·field·er
out·fit
out·fit·ter
out·flank
out·flow
out·go
·went ·gone
·go·ing
out·go
·goes
out·go·ing
out-group
out·grow
·grew ·grown
·grow·ing
out·growth
out·guess
out·ing
out·land·er
out·land·ish
out·last
out·law
out·lay
·laid ·lay·ing
out·let
out·li·er
out·line
out·live
out·look
out·ly·ing
out·ma·neu·ver
out·mod·ed
out·most
out·num·ber
out-of-date
out-of-doors
out-of-pock·et
out-of-the-way
out·pa·tient
out·post
out·pour·ing
out·put
out·rage
out·ra·geous
out·rank
out·reach
out·ride
·rode ·rid·den
·rid·ing
out·rid·er
out·rig·ger
out·right
out·run
·ran ·run
·run·ning
out·sell
·sold ·sell·ing
out·set
out·side
out·sid·er
out·sit
·sat ·sit·ting
out·size
out·skirts
out·smart
out·speak
·spoke ·spo·ken
·speak·ing
out·spo·ken·ness
out·stand·ing
out·sta·tion
out·stay
out·strip
out·talk
out·think
·thought
·think·ing
out·vote
out·ward
out·wear
·wore ·worn
·wear·ing
out·weigh
out·wit
·wit·ted
·wit·ting
out·work
o·val
o·va·tion
o·ver·age
o·ver·all
o·ver·alls
o·ver·awe
·awed ·aw·ing
o·ver·bal·ance
o·ver·bear
·bore ·borne
·bear·ing
o·ver·bid
·bid ·bid·ding
o·ver·bite
o·ver·board
o·ver·cap·i·tal·ize

o·ver·cast
o·ver·charge
o·ver·coat
o·ver·come
·came ·come
·com·ing
o·ver·com·pen·sate
o·ver·con·fi·dent
o·ver·crowd·ed
o·ver·do
·did ·done
·do·ing
o·ver·draft
o·ver·draw
·drew ·drawn
·draw·ing
o·ver·drive
o·ver·due
o·ver·flight
o·ver·flow
o·ver·glaze
o·ver·grow
·grew ·grown
·grow·ing
o·ver·hand
o·ver·hang
·hung
·hang·ing
o·ver·haul
o·ver·head
o·ver·hear
·heard
·hear·ing
o·ver·heat
o·ver·in·dul·gence
o·ver·is·sue
o·ver·joy
o·ver·lad·en
o·ver·lap
o·ver·lay
·laid ·lay·ing
o·ver·lie
·lay ·lain
·ly·ing
o·ver·load
o·ver·look
o·ver·ly
o·ver·nice
o·ver·night
o·ver·pass
o·ver·pay
·paid ·pay·ing
o·ver·pop·u·late
o·ver·pow·er
o·ver·pro·duce
o·ver·pro·tect
o·ver·rate
o·ver·reach
o·ver·ride
·rode ·rid·den
·rid·ing
o·ver·rule
o·ver·run
·ran ·run
·run·ning
o·ver·seas
o·ver·see
·saw ·seen
·see·ing
o·ver·se·er
o·ver·sell
·sold ·sell·ing
o·ver·shad·ow
o·ver·shoe
o·ver·sight
o·ver·sim·pli·fy
o·ver·size
o·ver·sleep
·slept ·sleep·ing
o·ver·spend
·spent ·spend·ing
o·ver·state
o·ver·stay
o·ver·step
o·ver·stock
o·ver·stuff
o·ver·sub·scribe
o·ver·sup·ply
o·vert
o·ver·take
·took ·tak·en
·tak·ing
o·ver·tax
o·ver-the-count·er
o·ver·throw
·threw ·thrown
·throw·ing
o·ver·time
o·ver·view
o·ver·whelm
o·ver·work
o·ver·write
·wrote ·writ·ten
·writ·ing
owe
owed ow·ing
own·er·ship
ox·i·da·tion
ox·i·dize
·dized ·diz·ing
ox·y·gen
ox·y·gen·ate
·at·ed ·at·ing
ox·y·gen·a·tion
o·zone

P

pace·mak·er
pa·cif·ic
pac·i·fi·ca·tion
pac·i·fi·er
pac·i·fism
pac·i·fy
·fied ·fy·ing
pack·age
·aged ·ag·ing
pack·et
pack·ing
pact
pad·dock
pad·lock
pae·an
(*song;* SEE peon)
pa·gan
page
paged pag·ing
pag·eant
pag·eant·ry
·ries
page·boy
pag·i·nate
·nat·ed ·nat·ing
pag·i·na·tion
pail
(*bucket;* SEE pale)
pain
(*hurt;* SEE pane)
pain·ful
pain·less
pains·tak·ing
pair
(*two;* SEE pare)
pal·an·quin
pal·at·a·ble
pal·at·a·bly
pal·a·tal
pal·ate
(*roof of mouth;* SEE palette, pallet)
pa·la·tial
pal·a·tine
pa·lav·er
pale
paled pal·ing
(*white;* SEE pail)
pale·ly
pa·le·o·lith·ic
pa·le·on·tol·o·gy
pal·ette
(*paint board;* SEE palate, pallet)
pal·ing
pal·i·sade
pall
palled pall·ing
pal·la·di·um
pall·bear·er
pal·let
(*tool; bed;* SEE palate, palette)
pal·li·ate
·at·ed ·at·ing
pal·li·a·tive
pal·lid
pall-mall
(*game;* SEE pell-mell)
pal·lor
pal·pa·ble
pal·pa·bly
pal·pate
·pat·ed ·pat·ing
pal·pi·tate
·tat·ed ·tat·ing
pal·pi·ta·tion
pal·sy
·sied ·sy·ing
pal·tri·ness
pal·try
·tri·er ·tri·est

pam·pas
pam·phlet
pam·phlet·eer
pan
panned pan·ning
pan·a·ce·a
pa·nache
Pan-A·mer·i·can
pan·a·tel·a
pan·chro·mat·ic
pan·cre·as
pan·cre·at·ic
pan·dem·ic
pan·de·mo·ni·um
pane
(*window;* SEE pain)
pan·e·gyr·ic
pan·e·gyr·i·cal
pan·el
·eled *or* ·elled
·el·ing *or* ·el·ling
pan·el·ist
pan·ic
·icked ·ick·ing
pan·ic·al·ly
pan·ick·y
pan·ic-strick·en
pan·o·ply
·plies
pan·o·ra·ma
pan·o·ram·ic
pan·o·ram·i·cal·ly
pan·the·ism
pan·the·is·tic
pan·the·on
pan·to·graph
pan·to·mime
·mimed
·mim·ing
pa·per·back
pa·per·bound
pa·per·weight
pa·per·y
pa·pier-mâ·ché
pa·py·rus
·ri *or* ·rus·es
par·a·ble
pa·rab·o·la
par·a·bol·ic
par·a·chute
·chut·ed
·chut·ing
par·a·chut·ist
pa·rade
·rad·ed ·rad·ing
par·a·digm
par·a·dise
par·a·dox
par·a·dox·i·cal
par·af·fin
par·a·gon
par·a·graph
par·al·lax
par·al·lel
·leled *or* ·lelled
·lel·ing *or* ·lel·ling
par·al·lel·ism
par·al·lel·o·gram
pa·ral·y·sis
par·a·lyt·ic
par·a·lyze
·lyzed ·lyz·ing
par·a·me·ci·um
·ci·a
par·a·med·ic
par·a·med·i·cal
pa·ram·e·ter
(*math. term;* SEE perimeter)
par·a·mount
par·a·mour
par·a·noi·a
par·a·noi·ac
par·a·noid
par·a·pet
par·a·pher·na·li·a
par·a·phrase
·phrased
·phras·ing
par·a·ple·gi·a
par·a·ple·gic
par·a·prax·is
·es
par·a·psy·chol·o·gy
par·a·site
par·a·sit·ic
par a·vion
par·cel
·celed *or* ·celled
·cel·ing *or* ·cel·ling
parch·ment
par·don·a·ble
par·don·a·bly
pare
pared par·ing
(*trim;* SEE pair)
par·ent
par·ent·age
pa·ren·tal
pa·ren·the·sis
·ses
pa·ren·the·size
·sized ·siz·ing
par·en·thet·i·cal
pa·re·sis
par·e·ve
par ex·cel·lence
par·he·li·on
·li·a
pa·ri·ah
pa·ri·e·tal
par·i·mu·tu·el
par·i·ty
·ties
par·ka
park·way
parl·ance
par·lay
(*bet*)
par·ley
(*confer*)
par·lia·ment
par·lia·men·tar·i·an
par·lia·men·ta·ry
par·lor
pa·ro·chi·al
par·o·dy
·dies
·died ·dy·ing
par·ox·ysm
par·ox·ys·mal
par·ri·ci·dal
par·ri·cide
par·ry
·ries
·ried ·ry·ing
par·sec
par·si·mo·ni·ous
par·si·mo·ny
par·take
·took ·tak·en
·tak·ing
par·terre
par·the·no·gen·e·sis
par·tial
par·ti·al·i·ty
par·tial·ly
par·ti·ble
par·tic·i·pant
par·tic·i·pate
·pat·ed ·pat·ing
par·tic·i·pa·tion
par·tic·i·pa·tor
par·ti·cip·i·al
par·ti·ci·ple
par·ti·cle
par·ti-col·ored
par·tic·u·lar
par·tic·u·lar·i·ty
·ties
par·tic·u·lar·ize
·ized ·iz·ing
par·tic·u·lar·ly
par·ti·san
par·ti·tion
part·ner
part·ner·ship
part-time
par·tu·ri·ent
par·tu·ri·tion
par·ty
·ties
par·ve·nu
·nus
pass·a·ble
pass·a·bly
pas·sage
pas·sage·way
pass·book
pas·sé
pas·sen·ger
pass·er-by
pass·ers-by
pas·sion
pas·sion·ate
pas·sive

pas·sive·ly
pas·siv·i·ty
pass·key
Pass·o·ver
pass·port
pass-through
pass·word
paste
past·ed past·ing
paste·board
pas·tel
pas·teur·i·za·tion
pas·teur·ize
·ized ·iz·ing
pas·time
pas·tor
pas·to·ral
pas·tor·ate
pas·ture
·tured ·tur·ing
patch·work
pat·ent
pat·ent·ee
pa·ter·nal
pa·ter·nal·is·tic
pa·ter·ni·ty
pa·thet·ic
path·o·gen·ic
path·o·log·i·cal
pa·thol·o·gy
·gies
pa·thos
pa·tience
pa·tient
pat·i·na
pa·tis·se·rie
pa·tri·arch
pa·tri·ar·chal
pa·tri·ar·chy
·chies
pa·tri·cian
pat·ri·cide
pat·ri·mo·ny
·nies
pa·tri·ot
pa·tri·ot·ic
pa·tri·ot·ism
pa·tron
pa·tron·age
pa·tron·ize
·ized ·iz·ing
pat·ro·nym·ic
pat·tern·mak·er
pau·ci·ty
paunch·i·ness
paunch·y
pau·per
pause
paused paus·ing
pave
paved pav·ing
pave·ment
pa·vil·ion
pawn·bro·ker
pay
paid pay·ing
pay·a·ble
pay·back
pay·check
pay·day
pay·ee
pay·load
pay·mas·ter
pay·ment
pay·off
pay·out
pay·roll
peace
peace·a·ble
peace·a·bly
peace·ful
peace·ful·ly
peace·mak·er
peace·time
peak
(highest point;
SEE peek, pique)
peaked
(pointed)
peak·ed
(thin and drawn)
pear-shaped
peas·ant
peas·ant·ry
pec·ca·dil·lo
·loes *or* ·los
pec·cant
peck
pec·tin
pec·to·ral
pec·u·late
·lat·ed ·lat·ing
pec·u·la·tion
pec·u·la·tor
pe·cul·iar
pe·cu·li·ar·i·ty
·ties
pe·cu·ni·ar·i·ly
pe·cu·ni·ar·y
ped·a·gog·ic
ped·a·gogue
or ·gog
ped·a·go·gy
ped·al
·aled *or* ·alled
·al·ing *or*
·al·ling
(foot lever; SEE
peddle)
ped·ant
pe·dan·tic
ped·ant·ry
·ries
ped·dle
·dled ·dling
(sell; SEE pedal)
ped·dler
ped·es·tal
pe·des·tri·an
pe·di·a·tri·cian
pe·di·at·rics
ped·i·cure
ped·i·gree
ped·i·greed
ped·i·ment
pe·dom·e·ter
peek
(sneak a look;
SEE peak, pique)
peer
peer group
peer·less
peeve
peeved peev·ing
pee·vish
peg·board
pe·jo·ra·tion
pe·jo·ra·tive
pe·koe
pel·let
pell-mell
(without order;
SEE pall-mall)
pel·lu·cid
pel·vic
pel·vis
pe·nal
pe·nal·i·za·tion
pe·nal·ize
·ized ·iz·ing
pen·al·ty
·ties
pen·ance
pen·chant
pen·cil
·ciled *or* ·cilled
·cil·ing *or*
·cil·ling
pend·ant *or*
·ent *n.*
pend·ent *or*
·ant *adj.*
pend·ing
pen·du·lum
pen·e·tra·bil·i·ty
pen·e·tra·ble
pen·e·tra·bly
pen·e·trate
·trat·ed ·trat·ing
pen·e·tra·tion
pen·e·trom·e·ter
pen·hold·er
pen·i·cil·lin
pen·in·su·la
pen·in·su·lar
pen·i·tence
pen·i·tent
pen·i·ten·tial
pen·i·ten·tia·ry
·ries
pen·knife
·knives
pen·man·ship
pen name
pen·nant
pen·non
Penn·syl·va·ni·a
pen·ny ante
pen·ny·weight
pen·ny-wise

pe·no·log·i·cal
pe·nol·o·gist
pe·nol·o·gy
pen·sion
pen·sion·ar·y
·ies
pen·sive
pen·sive·ly
pen·stock
pen·ta·gon
pen·tag·o·nal
pen·ta·he·dral
pen·ta·he·dron
·drons *or* ·dra
pen·tam·e·ter
Pen·ta·teuch
pen·tath·lon
Pen·te·cost
pent·house
pen·tom·ic
pent-up
pe·nult
pe·nul·ti·mate
pe·num·bra
·brae *or* ·bras
pe·nu·ri·ous
pen·u·ry
pe·on
(*laborer;* SEE paean)
pe·on·age
pep·lum
·lums *or* ·la
pep·sin
pep·tic
per·am·bu·late
·lat·ed ·lat·ing
per·am·bu·la·tion
per·am·bu·la·tor
per an·num
per cap·i·ta
per·ceiv·a·ble
per·ceiv·a·bly
per·ceive
·cieved ·ceiv·ing
per·cent *or*
per cent
per·cent·age
per·cen·tile
per·cept
per·cep·ti·ble
per·cep·ti·bly
per·cep·tion
per·cep·tive
per·cep·tive·ly
per·cep·tu·al
per·chance
per·cip·i·ent
per·cus·sion
per·cus·sive
per di·em
per·di·tion
per·du *or* ·due
per·dur·a·ble
per·e·gri·nate
·nat·ed ·nat·ing
per·e·gri·na·tion
per·emp·to·ri·ly
per·emp·to·ri·ness
per·emp·to·ry
per·en·ni·al
per·fect
per·fect·i·bil·i·ty
per·fect·i·ble
per·fec·tion
per·fec·tion·ism
per·fid·i·ous
per·fi·dy
·dies
per·fo·rate
·rat·ed ·rat·ing
per·fo·ra·tion
per·fo·ra·tor
per·force
per·form
per·form·ance
per·fume′
·fumed ·fum·ing
per′fume *n.*
per·fum·er
per·func·to·ri·ly
per·func·to·ry
per·haps
per·il
·iled *or* ·illed
·il·ing *or* ·il·ling
per·il·ous
pe·rim·e·ter
(*boundary;* SEE parameter)
pe·ri·od
pe·ri·od·ic
pe·ri·od·i·cal
pe·ri·o·dic·i·ty
per·i·pa·tet·ic
pe·riph·er·al
pe·riph·er·y
·ies
pe·riph·ra·sis
per·i·scope
per·ish
per·ish·a·bil·i·ty
per·ish·a·ble
per·i·stal·sis
per·i·to·ni·tis
per·jure
·jured ·jur·ing
per·jur·er
per·ju·ry
·ries
per·ma·frost
perm·al·loy
per·ma·nence
per·ma·nent
per·me·a·bil·i·ty
per·me·a·ble
per·me·ate
·at·ed ·at·ing
per·me·a·tion
per·mis·si·bil·i·ty
per·mis·si·ble
per·mis·si·bly
per·mis·sion
per·mis·sive
per·mis·sive·ly
per·mut·a·ble
per·mu·ta·tion
per·ni·cious
per·o·rate
·rat·ed ·rat·ing
per·o·ra·tion
per·ox·ide
·id·ed ·id·ing
per·pen·dic·u·lar
per·pe·trate
·trat·ed ·trat·ing
per·pe·tra·tion
per·pe·tra·tor
per·pet·u·al
per·pet·u·al·ly
per·pet·u·ate
·at·ed ·at·ing
per·pet·u·a·tion
per·pet·u·a·tor
per·pe·tu·i·ty
·ties
per·plex
per·plexed
per·plex·ed·ly
per·plex·i·ty
·ties
per·qui·site
(*privilege;* SEE prerequisite)
per se
per·se·cute
·cut·ed ·cut·ing
(*harass;* SEE prosecute)
per·se·cu·tion
per·se·cu·tor
per·se·ver·ance
per·se·vere
·vered ·ver·ing
per·sist
per·sist·ence
per·sist·ent
per·son
per·son·a·ble
per·son·age
per·so·na gra·ta
per·son·al
(*private;* SEE personnel)
per·son·al·i·ty
·ties
per·son·al·ize
·ized ·iz·ing
per·son·al·ly
per·so·na non gra·ta
per·son·ate
·at·ed ·at·ing
per·son·a·tion
per·son·a·tor
per·son·i·fi·ca·tion
per·son·i·fy
·fied ·fy·ing

per·son·nel
(*employees;* SEE personal)
per·spec·tive
(*view;* SEE prospective)
per·spi·ca·cious
per·spi·cac·i·ty
per·spi·cu·i·ty
per·spic·u·ous
per·spi·ra·tion
per·spir·a·to·ry
per·spire
·spired ·spir·ing
per·suad·a·ble
per·suade
·suad·ed
·suad·ing
per·sua·si·bil·i·ty
per·sua·sion
per·sua·sive
per·tain
per·ti·na·cious
per·ti·nac·i·ty
per·ti·nence
per·ti·nent
pert·ly
per·turb
per·tur·ba·tion
pe·rus·al
pe·ruse
·rused ·rus·ing
per·vade
·vad·ed ·vad·ing
per·va·sion
per·va·sive
per·verse
per·verse·ly
per·ver·sion
per·ver·si·ty
per·vert
per·vi·ous
pes·si·mism
pes·si·mist
pes·si·mis·tic
pes·ter
pes·ti·cide
pes·ti·lence
pes·ti·lent
pes·ti·len·tial
pe·tite
pe·ti·tion
pe·tit mal
pe·tri dish
pet·ri·fy
·fied ·fy·ing
pet·ro·la·tum
pe·tro·le·um
pet·ti·ness
pet·u·lance
pet·u·lant
pew·ter
pha·lanx
·lanx·es *or*
·lan·ges
phar·i·sa·ic
phar·i·see
phar·ma·ceu·ti·cal
phar·ma·cist
phar·ma·col·o·gy
phar·ma·co·pe·ia
phar·ma·cy
·cies
phar·ynx
·ynx·es *or*
pha·ryn·ges
phase
phased phas·ing
(*stage;* SEE faze)
phase-out
phe·nom·e·nal
phe·nom·e·nal·ly
phe·nom·e·non
·na *or* ·nons
phi·al
Phil·a·del·phi·a
phi·lan·der·er
phil·an·throp·ic
phi·lan·thro·pist
phi·lan·thro·py
·pies
phil·a·tel·ic
phi·lat·e·list
phi·lat·e·ly
phil·har·mon·ic
Phil·ip·pine
Phil·is·tine
phil·o·den·dron
phil·o·log·i·cal
phi·lol·o·gist
phi·lol·o·gy
phi·los·o·pher
phil·o·soph·ic
phi·los·o·phize
·phized
·phiz·ing
phi·los·o·phy
·phies
phle·bi·tis
phlegm
phleg·mat·ic
phlox
pho·bi·a
pho·bic
Phoe·nix
phone
phoned
phon·ing
pho·neme
pho·net·ic
pho·ne·ti·cian
phon·ics
pho·ni·ness
pho·no·graph
pho·nol·o·gy
pho·ny
·ni·er ·ni·est
·nies
phos·phate
phos·pho·res·cence
phos·pho·res·cent
pho·to·chron·o·graph
pho·to·cop·i·er
pho·to·cop·y
·ies
·ied ·y·ing
pho·to·e·lec·tric
pho·to·en·grave
·graved
·grav·ing
pho·to·flash
pho·to·gen·ic
pho·to·graph
pho·tog·ra·pher
pho·to·graph·ic
pho·tog·ra·phy
pho·to·gra·vure
pho·to·lith·o·graph
pho·to·li·thog·ra·phy
pho·to·map
pho·tom·e·ter
pho·to·met·ric
pho·tom·e·try
pho·to·mon·tage
pho·to·mu·ral
pho·to-off·set
pho·to·sen·si·tive
pho·to·stat
·stat·ed *or*
·stat·ted
·stat·ing *or*
·stat·ting
pho·to·stat·ic
pho·to·syn·the·sis
phras·al
phras·al·ly
phrase
phrased
phras·ing
phra·se·ol·o·gy
·gies
phre·net·ic
phre·nol·o·gy
phy·lac·ter·y
·ies
phy·lum
·la
phys·ic
·icked ·ick·ing
phys·i·cal
phys·i·cal·ly
phy·si·cian
phys·i·cist
phys·ics
phys·i·og·no·my
phys·i·og·ra·phy
phys·i·o·log·i·cal
phys·i·ol·o·gy
phys·i·o·ther·a·pist
phys·i·o·ther·a·py
phy·sique
pi·ca
pic·a·resque
Pic·ca·dil·ly
pick·et
pi·cot
·coted ·cot·ing
pic·to·graph
pic·to·ri·al

pic·to·ri·al·ly
pic·ture
·tured ·tur·ing
pic·tur·esque
piece-dyed
piece·meal
piece·rate
piece·work
pied·mont
pierce
pierced
pierc·ing
pi·geon·hole
·holed
·hol·ing
pig iron
pig·ment
pig·men·ta·tion
pi·laf *or* ·laff
pi·las·ter
pile
piled pil·ing
pi·le·ous
pile·up
pil·fer
pil·fer·age
pil·grim
pil·grim·age
pil·lage
·laged ·lag·ing
pil·lar
pill·box
pil·lion
pi·lot
pi·lot·house
Pil·sener *or*
Pil·sner
pin·ball
pince-nez
pin·cers
pinch-hit
-hit -hit·ting
pin·feath·er
ping-pong
pin·hole
pin·ion
pin·na·cle
·cled ·cling
pin·point
pin stripe
pi·o·neer
pi·ous
pipe
piped pip·ing
pipe·ful
·fuls
pipe·line
pi·quan·cy
pi·quant
pique
piqued piqu·ing
(*offend;* SEE peak, peek)
pi·qué *or* ·que
(*fabric*)
pi·ra·cy
pi·rate
·rat·ed ·rat·ing
pis·ca·to·ri·al
pis·ci·cul·ture
pis·til
(*part of plant*)
pis·tol
·toled *or* ·tolled
·tol·ing *or* ·tol·ling
(*firearm*)
pis·ton
pitch-black
pitch·blende
pitch-dark
pit·e·ous
pit·fall
pith·i·ness
pith·y
·i·er ·i·est
pit·i·a·ble
pit·i·ful
pit·i·less
pit·tance
Pitts·burgh
pit·y
·ies, ·ied ·y·ing
piv·ot
piv·ot·al
piz·za
piz·ze·ri·a
plac·a·bil·i·ty
plac·a·ble
plac·a·bly
plac·ard
pla·cate
·cat·ed ·cat·ing
place
placed plac·ing
pla·ce·bo
·bos *or* ·boes
place·ment
plac·er
plac·id
pla·cid·i·ty
plack·et
pla·gia·rism
pla·gia·rize
·rized ·riz·ing
pla·gia·ry
·ries
plague
plagued
plagu·ing
plain-spo·ken
plain·tiff
plain·tive
plain·tive·ly
plan·et
plan·e·tar·i·um
·i·ums *or* ·i·a
plan·e·tar·y
plan·et·oid
plank·ing
plank·ton
plan·ner
plan·tain
plan·ta·tion
plant·er
plaque
plas·ma
plas·ter
plas·ter·board
plas·ter·er
plas·tic
plas·ti·cine
plas·tic·i·ty
plas·ti·cize
·cized ·ciz·ing
pla·teau
·teaus *or*
·teaux
plate·ful
·fuls
plat·form
plat·i·num
plat·i·tude
plat·i·tu·di·nous
pla·ton·ic
pla·toon
plau·dit
plau·si·bil·i·ty
plau·si·ble
plau·si·bly
play·back
play-by-play
play-off
play·wright
pleas·ant
pleas·ant·ry
·ries
please
pleased
pleas·ing
pleas·ur·a·ble
pleas·ur·a·bly
pleas·ure
pleat
ple·be·ian
pleb·i·scite
pledge
pledged
pledg·ing
pledg·ee
ple·na·ry
plen·i·po·ten·ti·ar·y
·ies
plen·i·tude
plen·te·ous
plen·ti·ful
plen·ti·ful·ly
plen·ty
ple·num
·nums *or* ·na
pleth·o·ra
pleu·ral
(*of the pleura;*
SEE plural)
Plex·i·glas
pli·a·bil·i·ty
pli·a·ble
pli·an·cy
pli·ant
pli·ers
plight
plow·back
plow·share

plug
plugged
plug·ging
plum
(*fruit*)
plumb
(*lead weight*)
plumb·er
plumb·ing
plum·met
plun·der
plunge
plunged
plung·ing
plu·ral
(*more than one;* SEE pleural)
plu·ral·ism
plu·ral·is·tic
plu·ral·i·ty
·ties
plu·ral·ize
·ized ·iz·ing
plu·toc·ra·cy
·cies
plu·to·crat
plu·to·crat·ic
plu·to·ni·um
plu·vi·al
ply
plies
plied ply·ing
ply·wood
pneu·mat·ic
pock·et·knife
·knives
pock·et-size
po·di·a·trist
po·di·a·try
po·di·um
·di·a *or* ·di·ums
po·grom
poign·an·cy
poign·ant
point-blank
point·ed·ly
point·er
point·less
poise
poised pois·ing
poi·son·ous
po·lar
po·lar·i·ty
po·lar·i·za·tion
po·lar·ize
·ized ·iz·ing
po·lem·ic
po·lem·i·cist
pol·i·clin·ic
(*outpatient clinic;* SEE polyclinic)
pol·i·cy
·cies
pol·i·cy·hold·er
po·li·o·my·e·li·tis
pol·ish
po·lite·ly
po·lite·ness
pol·i·tic
·ticked ·tick·ing
po·lit·i·cal
pol·i·ti·cian
pol·i·tic·ly
po·lit·i·co
·cos
pol·i·tics
poll
pol·len
pol·li·nate
·nat·ed ·nat·ing
pol·li·na·tion
poll·ster
poll tax
pol·lu·tant
pol·lute
·lut·ed ·lut·ing
pol·lu·tion
pol·y·an·drous
pol·y·an·dry
pol·y·clin·ic
(*hospital;* SEE policlinic)
pol·y·es·ter
pol·y·eth·yl·ene
po·lyg·a·mous
po·lyg·a·my
pol·y·glot
pol·y·gon
pol·y·graph
pol·y·mer
pol·y·sty·rene
pol·y·syl·lab·ic
pol·y·syl·la·ble
pol·y·tech·nic
pol·y·the·ism
pol·y·un·sat·u·rat·ed
pom·ace
(*pulp;* SEE pumice)
po·ma·ceous
pom·mel
·meled *or* ·melled
·mel·ing *or* ·mel·ling
Pom·pei·i
pom·pos·i·ty
pom·pous
pon·cho
·chos
pon·der
pon·der·a·ble
pon·der·ous
pon·iard
pon·tiff
pon·tif·i·cal
pon·tif·i·cate
·cat·ed ·cat·ing
pon·toon
pool·room
pop·lar
(*tree;* SEE popular)
pop·lin
pop·u·lace
(*the masses;* SEE populous)
pop·u·lar
(*liked by many;* SEE poplar)
pop·u·lar·i·ty
pop·u·lar·i·za·tion
pop·u·lar·ize
·ized ·iz·ing
pop·u·late
·lat·ed ·lat·ing
pop·u·la·tion
pop·u·lous
(*full of people;* SEE populace)
por·ce·lain
por·cu·pine
pore
pored
por·ing
po·rous
por·phy·ry
·ries
port·a·bil·i·ty
port·a·ble
por·tage
·taged ·tag·ing
por·tal
por·tend
por·tent
por·ten·tous
por·ter·house
port·fo·li·o
·os
por·ti·co
·coes *or* ·cos
por·tion
port·li·ness
port·ly
·li·er ·li·est
por·trait
por·trai·ture
por·tray
por·tray·al
Por·tu·guese
po·si·tion
pos·i·tive
pos·i·tive·ly
pos·i·tiv·ism
pos·se
pos·sess
pos·sessed
pos·ses·sion
pos·ses·sive
pos·ses·sor
pos·si·bil·i·ty
·ties
pos·si·ble
pos·si·bly
post·age
post·box
post card
post·date
pos·te·ri·or
pos·ter·i·ty
post·grad·u·ate

post·haste
post·hu·mous
post·hyp·not·ic
pos·til·ion
post·man
post·mark
post·mas·ter
post me·ri·di·em
post-mor·tem
post·paid
post·pon·a·ble
post·pone
·poned ·pon·ing
post·pone·ment
post·script
pos·tu·late
·lat·ed ·lat·ing
pos·tu·la·tion
pos·tu·la·tor
pos·tur·al
pos·ture
·tured ·tur·ing
post·war
po·ta·ble
po·ta·tion
po·ten·cy
po·tent
po·ten·tate
po·ten·tial
po·ten·ti·al·i·ty
·ties
po·ten·tial·ly
po·tent·ly
po·tion
pot·latch
pot·pour·ri
pot·shot
pot·tage
poul·tice
pounce
pounced
pounc·ing
pound-fool·ish
pov·er·ty
pow·der·y
·i·er ·i·est
pow·er·ful
pow·er·ful·ly
pow·er·house
pow·er·less

prac·ti·ca·bil·i·ty
prac·ti·ca·ble
prac·ti·ca·bly
prac·ti·cal
prac·ti·cal·i·ty
·ties
prac·ti·cal·ly
prac·tice
·ticed ·tic·ing
prac·tic·er
prac·ti·cum
prac·ti·tion·er
prag·mat·ic
prag·ma·tism
prag·ma·tist
prai·rie
praise
praised
prais·ing
praise·wor·thy
pra·line
prance
pranced
pranc·ing
prank·ish
prate
prat·ed
prat·ing
prat·tle
·tled ·tling
pray
(*implore;* SEE prey)
preach·er
pre·am·ble
pre·ar·range
·ranged
·rang·ing
pre·ar·range·ment
pre·can·cel
pre·car·i·ous
pre·cau·tion
pre·cau·tion·ar·y
pre·cede
·ced·ed ·ced·ing
(*come before;* SEE proceed)
prec·e·dence
(*priority*)
prec·e·dent
(*example*)
pre-cen·sor

pre·cept
pre·cep·tor
pre·ces·sion
(*a going before;* SEE procession)
pre·ces·sion·al
pre·cinct
pre·ci·os·i·ty
pre·cious
prec·i·pice
pre·cip·i·tate
·tat·ed ·tat·ing
pre·cip·i·ta·tion
pre·cip·i·tous
pré·cis
·cis
(*abstract*)
pre·cise
(*definite*)
pre·cise·ly
pre·ci·sion
pre·clude
·clud·ed
·clud·ing
pre·clu·sion
pre·co·cious
pre·cog·ni·tion
pre·con·ceive
pre·con·cep·tion
pre·con·scious
pre·cur·sor
pre·cur·so·ry
pre·da·cious
pre·date
pred·a·tor
pred·a·to·ry
pre·de·cease
pred·e·ces·sor
pre·des·ti·na·tion
pre·des·tine
·tined ·tin·ing
pre·de·ter·mine
pred·i·ca·bil·i·ty
pred·i·ca·ble
pre·dic·a·ment
pred·i·cate
·cat·ed ·cat·ing
pred·i·ca·tion
pre·dict
pre·dict·a·ble

pre·dic·tion
pre·dic·tive
pre·dic·tor
pre·di·gest
pre·di·lec·tion
pre·dis·pose
pre·dis·po·si·tion
pre·dom·i·nant
pre·dom·i·nate
pre·em·i·nence
pre·em·i·nent
pre·empt
pre·emp·tion
pre·emp·tive
pre·emp·tor
pre·es·tab·lish
pre·ex·ist
pre·ex·ist·ence
pre·fab
pre·fab·ri·cate
pref·ace
·aced ·ac·ing
pref·a·to·ry
pre·fect
pre·fec·ture
pre·fer
·ferred ·fer·ring
pref·er·a·ble
pref·er·a·bly
pref·er·ence
pref·er·en·tial
pre·fer·ment
pre·fig·u·ra·tion
pre·fig·ur·a·tive
pre·fig·ure
pre·fix
pre·flight
preg·na·ble
pre·hen·sile
pre·his·tor·ic
pre·judge
pre·judg·ment *or* ·judge·
prej·u·dice
·diced ·dic·ing
prej·u·di·cial
pre·lim·i·nar·y
·ies
prel·ude

pre·ma·ture
pre·ma·ture·ly
pre·med·i·cal
pre·med·i·tate
pre·mier
(chief)
pre·mière
·mièred
·mièr·ing
(first showing)
prem·ise
·ised ·is·ing
pre·mi·um
pre·mo·ni·tion
pre·mon·i·to·ry
pre·oc·cu·pan·cy
pre·oc·cu·pa·tion
pre·oc·cu·py
·pied ·py·ing
pre·or·dain
pre·pack·age
pre·paid
prep·a·ra·tion
pre·par·a·tive
pre·par·a·to·ry
pre·pare
·pared ·par·ing
pre·par·ed·ness
pre·pay
·paid ·pay·ing
pre·pay·ment
pre·pon·der·ance
pre·pon·der·ant
pre·pon·der·ate
·at·ed ·at·ing
prep·o·si·tion
pre·pos·sess
pre·pos·sess·ing
pre·pos·ter·ous
pre·re·cord
pre·req·ui·site
(requirement; SEE perquisite)
pre·rog·a·tive
pre·sage
·saged ·sag·ing
Pres·by·te·ri·an
pre·school
pre·sci·ence
pre·sci·ent
pre·scribe
·scribed
·scrib·ing
(order; SEE proscribe)
pre·scrip·tion
pre·scrip·tive
pres·ence
pres·ent
pre·sent·a·ble
pre·sen·ta·tion
pres·ent-day
pre·sen·ti·ment
(premonition)
pre·sent·ment
(presentation)
pre·serv·a·ble
pres·er·va·tion
pre·serv·a·tive
pre·serve
·served
·serv·ing
pre·set
pre-shrunk
pre·side
·sid·ed ·sid·ing
pres·i·den·cy
·cies
pres·i·dent
pres·i·dent-e·lect
pres·i·den·tial
pre·sid·i·um
·i·a *or* ·i·ums
pre·sig·ni·fy
press box
press·ing
press·man
pres·sure
·sured ·sur·ing
pres·sur·ize
·ized ·iz·ing
press·work
pres·tige
pres·ti·gious
pre·stressed
pre·sum·a·ble
pre·sume
·sumed
·sum·ing
pre·sump·tion
pre·sump·tive
pre·sump·tu·ous
pre·sup·pose
pre·sup·po·si·tion
pre·tend
pre·tend·er
pre·tense
pre·ten·sion
pre·ten·tious
pre·text
pre·tri·al
pret·ti·fy
·fied ·fy·ing
pret·ti·ly
pret·ti·ness
pret·ty
·ti·er ·ti·est
·tied ·ty·ing
pre·vail
pre·vail·ing
prev·a·lence
prev·a·lent
pre·var·i·cate
·cat·ed ·cat·ing
pre·var·i·ca·tion
pre·var·i·ca·tor
pre·vent
pre·vent·a·ble *or*
·i·ble
pre·ven·tion
pre·ven·tive *or*
·vent·a·tive
pre·view
pre·vi·ous
pre·vi·sion
pre·war
prey
(victim; SEE pray)
price
priced pric·ing
price·less
priest·hood
priest·ly
·li·er ·li·est
pri·ma·cy
pri·ma fa·ci·e
pri·mal
pri·ma·ri·ly
pri·ma·ry
·ries
pri·mate
pri·me·val
prim·i·tive
prim·i·tive·ly
prim·i·tiv·ism
pri·mo·gen·i·tor
pri·mo·gen·i·ture
pri·mor·di·al
prin·ci·pal
(chief; SEE principle)
prin·ci·pal·i·ty
·ties
prin·ci·pal·ly
prin·ci·ple
(basic rule; SEE principal)
prin·ci·pled
print·a·ble
print·out
pri·or
pri·or·i·ty
·ties
pri·o·ry
·ries
pris·mat·ic
pris·tine
pri·va·cy
pri·vate
pri·va·teer
pri·va·tion
priv·i·lege
·leged ·leg·ing
priv·y
·ies
prize
prized priz·ing
prob·a·bil·i·ty
prob·a·ble
prob·a·bly
pro·bate
·bat·ed ·bat·ing
pro·ba·tion
pro·ba·tion·ar·y
pro·ba·tion·er
pro·ba·tive
probe
probed prob·ing
prob·i·ty
prob·lem

prob·lem·at·ic
pro·ce·dur·al
pro·ce·dure
pro·ceed
(*go on;* SEE precede)
pro·ceeds
proc·ess
pro·ces·sion
(*parade;* SEE precession)
proc·es·sor *or* proc·ess·er
pro·claim
proc·la·ma·tion
pro·cliv·i·ty
·ties
pro·cras·ti·nate
·nat·ed ·nat·ing
pro·cras·ti·na·tion
pro·cras·ti·na·tor
pro·cre·ant
pro·cre·ate
·at·ed ·at·ing
pro·cre·a·tor
proc·tol·o·gy
proc·tor
proc·to·scope
pro·cum·bent
pro·cur·a·ble
proc·u·ra·tor
pro·cure
·cured ·cur·ing
pro·cure·ment
prod
prod·ded
prod·ding
prod·i·gal
prod·i·gal·i·ty
pro·di·gious
prod·i·gy
·gies
(*genius;* SEE protégé)
pro·duce
·duced
·duc·ing
pro·duc·er
pro·duc·i·ble
prod·uct
pro·duc·tion
pro·duc·tive
pro·duc·tive·ly

pro·duc·tiv·i·ty
pro·fane
·faned ·fan·ing
pro·fane·ly
pro·fan·i·ty
·ties
pro·fess
pro·fessed
pro·fess·ed·ly
pro·fes·sion
pro·fes·sion·al·ly
pro·fes·sor
pro·fes·so·ri·al
pro·fes·so·ri·ate
prof·fer
pro·fi·cien·cy
pro·fi·cient
pro·file
·filed ·fil·ing
prof·it
(*gain;* SEE prophet)
prof·it·a·bil·i·ty
prof·it·a·ble
prof·it·a·bly
prof·i·teer
prof·li·ga·cy
prof·li·gate
pro for·ma
pro·found
pro·fun·di·ty
·ties
pro·fuse
pro·fuse·ly
pro·fu·sion
pro·gen·i·tor
prog·e·ny
·nies
prog·no·sis
·ses
prog·nos·tic
prog·nos·ti·cate
·cat·ed ·cat·ing
prog·nos·ti·ca·tion
prog·nos·ti·ca·tor
pro·gram
·grammed
or ·gramed
·gram·ming
or ·gram·ing

pro·gram·mat·ic
pro·gram·mer
or ·gram·er
prog·ress
pro·gres·sion
pro·gres·sive
pro·gres·siv·ism
pro·hib·it
pro·hi·bi·tion
pro·hib·i·tive
pro·hib·i·to·ry
proj·ect
pro·jec·tile
pro·jec·tion
pro·jec·tive
pro·jec·tor
pro·le·tar·i·an
pro·le·tar·i·at
pro·lif·er·ate
·at·ed ·at·ing
pro·lif·ic
pro·lix
pro·lix·i·ty
pro·loc·u·tor
pro·logue
pro·long
pro·lon·gate
·gat·ed ·gat·ing
pro·lon·ga·tion
prom·i·nence
prom·i·nent
prom·is·cu·i·ty
·ties
pro·mis·cu·ous
prom·ise
·ised ·is·ing
prom·is·so·ry
prom·on·to·ry
·ries
pro·mot·a·ble
pro·mote
·mot·ed ·mot·ing
pro·mot·er
pro·mo·tion
prompt·er
prompt·ly
prom·ul·gate
·gat·ed ·gat·ing
prom·ul·ga·tion

prom·ul·ga·tor
prone
pro·noun
pro·nounce
·nounced
·nounc·ing
pro·nounce·a·ble
pro·nounce·ment
pro·nun·ci·a·tion
proof·read
·read ·read·ing
prop·a·gan·da
prop·a·gan·dize
·dized ·diz·ing
prop·a·gate
·gat·ed ·gat·ing
prop·a·ga·tion
prop·a·ga·tor
pro·pane
pro·pel
·pelled ·pel·ling
pro·pel·lant *or* ·lent
pro·pel·ler
pro·pen·si·ty
·ties
prop·er·ly
prop·er·tied
prop·er·ty
·ties
proph·e·cy *n.*
·cies
proph·e·sy *v.*
·sied ·sy·ing
proph·et
(*predictor;* SEE profit)
pro·phet·ic
pro·phet·i·cal·ly
pro·phy·lac·tic
pro·phy·lax·is
·lax·es
pro·pin·qui·ty
pro·pi·ti·ate
·at·ed ·at·ing
pro·pi·ti·a·tion
pro·pi·ti·a·tor
pro·pi·ti·a·to·ry
pro·pi·tious
pro·po·nent
pro·por·tion

pro·por·tion·al
pro·por·tion·ate
pro·por·tion·ate·ly
pro·pos·al
pro·pose
·posed ·pos·ing
prop·o·si·tion
pro·pound
pro·pri·e·tar·y
·ies
pro·pri·e·tor
pro·pri·e·tor·ship
pro·pri·e·ty
·ties
pro·pul·sion
pro·pul·sive
pro ra·ta
pro·rat·a·ble
pro·rate
·rat·ed ·rat·ing
pro·ra·tion
pro·ro·ga·tion
pro·sa·ic
pro·sa·i·cal·ly
pro·sce·ni·um
·ni·ums *or* ·ni·a
pro·scribe
·scribed
·scrib·ing
(*forbid;* SEE
prescribe)
pro·scrip·tion
prose
pros·e·cut·a·ble
pros·e·cute
·cut·ed ·cut·ing
(*legal term;*
SEE persecute)
pros·e·cu·tion
pros·e·cu·tor
pros·e·lyte
·lyt·ed ·lyt·ing
pros·e·lyt·ism
pros·e·lyt·ize
·ized ·iz·ing
pros·o·dy
·dies
pros·pect
pro·spec·tive
(*expected;* SEE
perspective)
pros·pec·tor
pro·spec·tus
pros·per
pros·per·i·ty
pros·per·ous
pros·tate
(*gland;* SEE
prostrate)
pros·the·sis
·the·ses
pros·thet·ic
pros·trate
·trat·ed ·trat·ing
(*prone;* SEE
prostate)
pros·tra·tion
pro·tag·o·nist
pro·tect
pro·tec·tion
pro·tec·tive
pro·tec·tor
pro·tec·tor·ate
pro·té·gé
(*one helped by
another;* SEE
prodigy)
pro·tein
pro tem·po·re
pro·test
Prot·es·tant
prot·es·ta·tion
pro·test·er *or*
·tes·tor
pro·to·col
pro·to·plasm
pro·to·typ·al
pro·to·type
pro·tract
pro·tract·ed·ly
pro·tract·i·ble
pro·trac·tile
pro·trac·tion
pro·trac·tor
pro·trude
·trud·ed
·trud·ing
pro·tru·sion
pro·tru·sive
pro·tu·ber·ance
pro·tu·ber·ant
proud·ly
prov·a·bil·i·ty
prov·a·ble
prov·a·bly
prov·en·der
prov·erb
pro·ver·bi·al
pro·ver·bi·al·ly
pro·vide
·vid·ed ·vid·ing
prov·i·dence
prov·i·dent
prov·i·den·tial
pro·vid·er
prov·ince
pro·vin·cial
pro·vi·sion
pro·vi·sion·al
pro·vi·so
·sos *or* ·soes
pro·vi·so·ry
prov·o·ca·tion
pro·voc·a·tive
pro·voc·a·tive·ly
pro·voke
·voked ·vok·ing
pro·vost
prow·ess
prox·i·mal
prox·i·mate
prox·im·i·ty
prox·y
·ies
pru·dence
pru·dent
pru·den·tial
pru·dent·ly
prud·er·y
prud·ish
pru·ri·ence
pru·ri·ent
pseu·do
pseu·do·nym
pseu·do·nym·i·ty
pseu·don·y·mous
psy·che
psy·che·del·ic
psy·chi·at·ric
psy·chi·at·ri·cal·ly
psy·chi·a·trist
psy·chi·a·try
psy·chic
psy·cho·a·nal·y·sis
psy·cho·an·a·lyst
psy·cho·an·a·lyt·ic
psy·cho·an·a·lyze
·lyzed ·lyz·ing
psy·cho·dra·ma
psy·cho·dy·nam·ics
psy·cho·gen·ic
psy·cho·log·i·cal
psy·chol·o·gist
psy·chol·o·gize
·gized ·giz·ing
psy·chol·o·gy
psy·chom·e·try
psy·cho·neu·ro·sis
·ses
psy·cho·neu·rot·ic
psy·cho·path·ic
psy·cho·path·ol·o·gy
psy·cho·sis
·ses
psy·cho·so·mat·ic
psy·cho·ther·a·py
psy·chot·ic
pu·ber·ty
pu·bes·cence
pub·li·ca·tion
pub·li·cist
pub·lic·i·ty
pub·li·cize
·cized ·ciz·ing
pub·lic·ly
pub·lish
pu·er·ile
Puer·to Ri·co
pul·chri·tude
pul·chri·tu·di·nous
pull·out
pull·o·ver
pul·mo·nar·y
pul·mo·tor
pul·pit
pulp·wood
pulp·y
·i·er ·i·est

pul·sate
·sat·ed ·sat·ing
pul·sa·tion
pulse
pulsed puls·ing
pul·ver·iz·a·ble
pul·ver·i·za·tion
pul·ver·ize
·ized ·iz·ing
pum·ice
(*rock;* SEE pomace)
punch card
punc·til·i·ous
punc·tu·al
punc·tu·al·i·ty
punc·tu·al·ly
punc·tu·ate
·at·ed ·at·ing
punc·tu·a·tion
punc·tu·a·tor
punc·tur·a·ble
punc·ture
·tured ·tur·ing
pun·gen·cy
pun·gent
pun·ish
pun·ish·a·ble
pun·ish·ment
pu·ni·tive
pu·pil
pur·chas·a·ble
pur·chase
·chased
·chas·ing
pure·bred
pu·rée
·réed ·ré·ing
pure·ly
pur·ga·tion
pur·ga·tive
pur·ga·to·ry
purge
purged
purg·ing
pu·ri·fi·ca·tion
pu·ri·fi·er
pu·ri·fy
·fied ·fy·ing
pur·ism
pu·ri·tan
pu·ri·tan·i·cal
pu·ri·ty
pur·loin
pur·port
pur·pose
·posed ·pos·ing
pur·pose·ful
pur·pose·ful·ly
pur·pose·less
pur·pose·ly
purs·er
pur·su·ance
pur·sue
·sued ·su·ing
pur·suit
pu·ru·lence
pu·ru·lent
pur·vey
pur·vey·ance
pur·vey·or
pur·view
push·o·ver
pus·tu·lant
pus·tule
pu·ta·tive
pu·tre·fac·tion
pu·tre·fy
·fied ·fy·ing
pu·tres·cence
pu·tres·cent
pu·trid
put·tee
puz·zle
·zled ·zling
puz·zler
py·lon
py·or·rhe·a
pyr·a·mid
py·ram·i·dal
pyre
py·ret·ic
py·rog·ra·phy
py·ro·ma·ni·a
py·ro·ma·ni·ac
py·ro·tech·nics
Py·thag·o·ras
py·thon

Q

quad·ran·gle
quad·ran·gu·lar
quad·rant
quad·rate
·rat·ed ·rat·ing
quad·rat·ic
quad·ren·ni·al
quad·ri·lat·er·al
qua·drille
quad·ril·lion
quad·ru·ped
quad·ru·ple
·pled ·pling
quad·ru·plet
quad·ru·pli·cate
·cat·ed ·cat·ing
quake
quaked
quak·ing
qual·i·fi·ca·tion
qual·i·fi·er
qual·i·fy
·fied ·fy·ing
qual·i·ta·tive
qual·i·ty
·ties
qualm
quan·da·ry
·ries
quan·ti·ta·tive
quan·ti·ty
·ties
quan·tum
·ta
quar·an·tine
·tined ·tin·ing
quar·rel
·reled *or* ·relled
·rel·ing *or*
·rel·ling
quar·rel·some
quar·ry
·ries
·ried ·ry·ing
quart
quar·ter
quar·ter·ly
·lies
quar·ter·mas·ter
quar·tet *or* ·tette
quartz
qua·sar
quash
qua·si
qua·si con·tract
qua·ter·na·ry
·ries
quat·rain
qua·ver
quay
(*wharf;* SEE key)
quay·age
quea·si·ness
quea·sy
·si·er ·si·est
queen-size
queer
quell
quench·a·ble
quer·u·lous
que·ry
·ries
·ried ·ry·ing
quest
ques·tion
ques·tion·a·ble
ques·tion·naire
queue
queued
queu·ing
(*line;* SEE cue)
quib·ble
·bled ·bling
quick·en
quick-freeze
-froze -fro·zen
-freez·ing
quick·sil·ver
quick-tem·pered
quick-wit·ted
quid pro quo
qui·es·cence
qui·es·cent
qui·et (*still;* SEE quite)
qui·e·tude
qui·e·tus
quill

quilt·ing
quince
qui·nel·la
quin·quen·ni·al
quin·tes·sence
quin·tes·sen·tial
quin·tet
or ·tette
quin·til·lion
quin·tu·ple
·pled ·pling
quin·tu·plet
quin·tu·pli·cate
·cat·ed ·cat·ing
quip
quipped
quip·ping
quire
quirk
quis·ling
quit
quit *or* quit·ted
quit·ting
quit·claim
quite
(*fully;* SEE quiet)
quit·tance
quit·ter
quiv·er
quix·ot·ic
quiz
quiz·zes
quizzed
quiz·zing
quiz·zi·cal
quoit
quon·dam
Quon·set hut
quo·rum
quo·ta
quot·a·ble
quo·ta·tion
quote
quot·ed quot·ing
quo·tient

R

rab·bi
·bis *or* ·bies
rab·bin·i·cal
rab·ble
·bled ·bling
rab·id
ra·bies
race·horse
rac·er
race·way
ra·cial
ra·cial·ly
rac·i·ly
rac·i·ness
rac·ism
rack·et
rack·et·eer
rac·on·teur
rac·y
·i·er ·i·est
ra·dar
ra·di·al
ra·di·ance
ra·di·ant
ra·di·ate
·at·ed ·at·ing
ra·di·a·tion
ra·di·a·tor
rad·i·cal
rad·i·cal·ism
ra·di·o
·os, ·oed ·o·ing
ra·di·o·ac·tive
ra·di·o·gram
ra·di·o·graph
ra·di·og·ra·phy
ra·di·o·i·so·tope
ra·di·ol·o·gist
ra·di·ol·o·gy
ra·di·o·phone
ra·di·os·co·py
ra·di·o·tel·e·phone
ra·di·o·ther·a·py
ra·di·o·ther·my
ra·di·um
ra·di·us
·di·i *or* ·di·us·es
ra·dix
ra·di·ces *or*
ra·dix·es
ra·don
rage
raged rag·ing
rag·ged
rag·lan
rag·time
raid·er
rail·ing
rail·ler·y
·ies
rail·road
rail·way
rai·ment
rain check
rain·proof
rain·y
·i·er ·i·est
raise
raised
rais·ing
(*lift;* SEE raze)
rai·son d'être
ral·li·er
ral·ly
·lies
·lied ·ly·ing
ram·ble
·bled ·bling
ram·bler
ram·bunc·tious
ram·i·fi·ca·tion
ram·i·fy
·fied ·fy·ing
ramp
ram·page
·paged ·pag·ing
ram·pa·geous
ramp·ant
ram·part
ram·rod
ram·shack·le
ran·cid
ran·cor
ran·cor·ous
ran·dom
ran·dom·ize
·ized ·iz·ing
range
ranged
rang·ing
rang·i·ness
rang·y
·i·er ·i·est
ran·kle
·kled ·kling
ran·sack
ran·som
ra·pa·cious
ra·pac·i·ty
rap·id-fire
ra·pid·i·ty
rap·id·ly
ra·pi·er
rap·ine
rap·port
rap·proche·ment
rap·ture
rap·tur·ous
rare
rar·er
rar·est
rare·bit
rar·e·fy
·fied
·fy·ing
rare·ly
rar·i·ty
·ties
rash·er
rash·ness
rasp·i·ness
rasp·ing
rasp·y
·i·er ·i·est
rat·a·ble *or* rate·
ratch·et
rate
rat·ed rat·ing
rath·er
raths·kel·ler
rat·i·fi·ca·tion
rat·i·fi·er
rat·i·fy
·fied ·fy·ing
ra·tio
·tios
ra·ti·o·ci·nate
·nat·ed ·nat·ing
ra·tion·al
ra·tion·ale
ra·tion·al·ism

ra·tion·al·i·ty
ra·tion·al·i·za·tion
ra·tion·al·ize
·ized ·iz·ing
ra·tion·al·ly
rat·line *or* ·lin
rat·tan *or* ra·tan
rat·tle
·tled ·tling
rat·tle·brained
rat·tler
rau·cous
rav·age
·aged ·ag·ing
rave
raved rav·ing
rav·el
·eled *or* ·elled
·el·ing *or* ·el·ling
ra·ven
rav·e·nous
ra·vine
rav·ish
raw·boned
raw·hide
ray·on
raze
razed raz·ing
(*demolish;* SEE raise)
ra·zor
ra·zor·back
reach
re·act (*respond*)
re-act
(*act again*)
re·ac·tion
re·ac·tion·ar·y
·ies
re·ac·ti·vate
·vat·ed
·vat·ing
re·ac·tive·ly
re·ac·tor
read
read read·ing
read·a·bil·i·ty
read·a·ble
read·i·ly
read·i·ness
re·ad·just
read·out
read·y
·i·er ·i·est
·ied ·y·ing
read·y-made
re·a·gent
re·al
re·al·ism
re·al·ist
re·al·is·tic
re·al·is·ti·cal·ly
re·al·i·ty
·ties
(*real thing;* SEE realty)
re·al·iz·a·ble
re·al·i·za·tion
re·al·ize
·ized ·iz·ing
re·al-life
realm
Re·al·tor
re·al·ty
(*real estate;* SEE reality)
ream·er
re·an·i·mate
·mat·ed
·mat·ing
reap·er
re·ap·por·tion
rear guard
re·ar·ma·ment
re·ar·range
re·ar·range·ment
rear·ward
rea·son·a·ble
rea·son·a·bly
re·as·sur·ance
re·as·sure
·sured ·sur·ing
re·bate
·bat·ed ·bat·ing
reb′el *n.*
re·bel′ *v.*
·belled ·bel·ling
re·bel·lion
re·bel·lious
re·birth
re·bound
re·buff
(*blunt refusal*)
re-buff
(*buff again*)
re·buke
·buked
·buk·ing
re·but
·but·ted
·but·ting
re·but·tal
re·cal·ci·trant
re·call
re·cant
re·cap
·capped
·cap·ping
re·ca·pit·u·late
·lat·ed ·lat·ing
re·ca·pit·u·la·tion
re·cap·pa·ble
re·cap·ture
re·cede
·ced·ed ·ced·ing
re·ceipt
re·ceiv·a·ble
re·ceive
·ceived
·ceiv·ing
re·ceiv·er·ship
re·cen·sion
re·cent
re·cep·ta·cle
re·cep·tion
re·cep·tive
re·cep·tor
re·cess
re·ces·sion
re·ces·sive
re·charge·a·ble
re·cid·i·vism
rec·i·pe
re·cip·i·ent
re·cip·ro·cal
re·cip·ro·cal·ly
re·cip·ro·cate
·cat·ed ·cat·ing
re·cip·ro·ca·tion
re·cip·ro·ca·tor
rec·i·proc·i·ty
re·ci·sion
re·cit·al
rec·i·ta·tion
rec·i·ta·tive
re·cite
·cit·ed ·cit·ing
reck·less
reck·on·ing
re·claim
(*restore for use*)
re-claim
(*claim back*)
rec·la·ma·tion
re·cline
·clined ·clin·ing
rec·luse
re·clu·sion
rec·og·ni·tion
rec·og·niz·a·ble
re·cog·ni·zance
rec·og·nize
·nized ·niz·ing
re·coil′ (*draw back*)
re′-coil′
(*coil again*)
re·coil·less
rec′ol·lect′
(*remember*)
re′-col·lect′
(*collect again*)
rec·ol·lec·tion
rec·om·mend
rec·om·men·da·tion
re·com·mit
rec·om·pense
·pensed
·pens·ing
rec·on·cil·a·ble
rec·on·cile
·ciled ·cil·ing
rec·on·cil·i·a·tion
rec·on·dite
re·con·di·tion
re·con·nais·sance
rec·on·noi·ter
re·con·sid·er
re·con·struct
re·con·ver·sion
re·con·vert
re·cord′ *v.*

rec′ord *n.*
re·cord·er
re·count′
(*narrate*)
re′-count′
(*count again*)
re·coup
re·course
re·cov′er
(*get back*)
re′-cov′er
(*cover again*)
re·cov·er·y
·ies
rec·re·ant
rec′re·ate′
·at·ed ·at·ing
(*refresh*)
re′-cre·ate′
·at·ed ·at·ing
(*create anew*)
rec′re·a′tion
re′-cre·a′tion
re·crim·i·nate
·nat·ed ·nat·ing
re·crim·i·na·tion
re·cruit
rec·tan·gle
rec·tan·gu·lar
rec·ti·fi·a·ble
rec·ti·fi·ca·tion
rec·ti·fi·er
rec·ti·fy
·fied ·fy·ing
rec·ti·lin·e·ar
rec·ti·tude
re·cum·ben·cy
re·cum·bent
re·cu·per·ate
·at·ed ·at·ing
re·cu·per·a·tion
re·cur
·curred
·cur·ring
re·cur·rence
re·cur·rent
rec·u·sant
re·cy·cle
re·dact
re·dac·tion
re·dac·tor
re·deem·a·ble
re·demp·tion
re·de·ploy
re·de·vel·op·ment
re·di·rect
re·dis·trict
red-let·ter
red·lin·ing
re·do
·did ·done
·do·ing
red·o·lence
red·o·lent
re·dou·ble
re·doubt
re·doubt·a·ble
re·dound
red·out
re′dress′
(*remedy*)
re′-dress′
(*dress again*)
re·duce
·duced ·duc·ing
re·duc·i·ble
re·duc·tion
re·dun·dan·cy
·cies
re·dun·dant
re·du·pli·cate
re·du·pli·ca·tion
re·ech·o
reed·i·ness
re·ed·it
re·ed·u·cate
reed·y
·i·er ·i·est
re·e·lect
re·e·lec·tion
re·em·bark
re·em·bod·y
re·em·brace
re·e·merge
re·em·pha·sis
re·em·pha·size
re·em·ploy
re·en·act
re·en·dow
re·en·gage
re·en·list
re·en·ter
re·en·try
re·e·quip
re·es·tab·lish
re·e·val·u·ate
re·ex·am·ine
re·ex·change
re·ex·hib·it
re·ex·pe·ri·ence
re·ex·plain
re·ex·port
re·fec·tion
re·fer
·ferred
·fer·ring
ref·er·a·ble
ref·er·ee
·eed
·ee·ing
ref·er·ence
ref·er·en·dum
·dums *or* ·da
ref·er·ent
re·fer·ral
re·fill·a·ble
re·fi·nanc·ing
re·fine
·fined
·fin·ing
re·fine·ment
re·fin·er·y
·ies
re·fit
re·fla·tion
re·flect
re·flec·tion
re·flec·tive
re·flec·tor
re·flex
re·flex·ive
re·for·est·a·tion
re·form′
(*make better*)
re′-form′
(*form again*)
ref·or·ma·tion
re·form·a·to·ry
·ries
re·fract
re·frac·tion
re·frac·to·ry
re·frain
re·fran·gi·ble
re·fresh
re·fresh·ment
re·frig·er·ant
re·frig·er·ate
·at·ed ·at·ing
re·frig·er·a·tion
re·frig·er·a·tor
ref·uge
ref·u·gee
re·ful·gent
re·fund
re·fur·bish
re·fus·al
re·fuse′ *v.*
·fused
·fus·ing
ref′use *n.*
re·fut·a·ble
ref·u·ta·tion
re·fute
·fut·ed ·fut·ing
re·gain
re·gal *adj.*
re·gale *v.*
·galed
·gal·ing
re·ga·li·a
re·gal·i·ty
·ties
re·gard·ing
re·gard·less
re·gat·ta
re·gen·cy
·cies
re·gen·er·ate
·at·ed ·at·ing
re·gen·er·a·tion
re·gen·er·a·tive
re·gen·er·a·tor
re·gent
reg·i·cide
re·gime *or* ré·
reg·i·men
reg·i·ment
reg·i·men·tal
reg·i·men·ta·tion

re·gion·al
reg·is·ter
reg·is·trant
reg·is·trar
reg·is·tra·tion
reg·is·try
·tries
re·gress
re·gres·sion
re·gres·sive
re·gret
·gret·ted
·gret·ting
re·gret·ta·ble
re·gret·ful
re·gret·ful·ly
re·gret·ta·ble
re·gret·ta·bly
reg·u·lar
reg·u·lar·i·ty
·ties
reg·u·late
·lat·ed ·lat·ing
reg·u·la·tion
reg·u·la·tor
re·ha·bil·i·tate
·tat·ed ·tat·ing
re·gur·gi·ta·tion
re·ha·bil·i·tate
·tat·ed ·tat·ing
re·ha·bil·i·ta·tion
re·hears·al
re·hearse
·hearsed
·hears·ing
reign
(*rule;* SEE rein)
re·im·burs·a·ble
re·im·burse
·bursed
·burs·ing
rein
(*control;* SEE reign)
re·in·car·nate
·nat·ed ·nat·ing
re·in·car·na·tion
re·in·cur
re·in·force
·forced
·forc·ing

re·in·force·ment
re·in·state
·stat·ed
·stat·ing
re·in·sure
re·in·vest
re·it·er·ate
·at·ed ·at·ing
re·ject
re·jec·tion
re·joice
·joiced ·joic·ing
re·join·der
re·ju·ve·nate
·nat·ed ·nat·ing
re·lapse
·lapsed
·laps·ing
re·lat·a·ble
re·late
·lat·ed ·lat·ing
re·la·tion·ship
rel·a·tive
rel·a·tive·ly
rel·a·tiv·i·ty
re·lax
re·lax·ant
re·lax·a·tion
re′lay
·layed ·lay·ing
(*send by relay*)
re′-lay′
-laid -lay·ing
(*lay again*)
re·lease′
·leased
·leas·ing
(*set free*)
re′-lease′
(*lease again*)
rel·e·gate
·gat·ed ·gat·ing
rel·e·ga·tion
re·lent·less
rel·e·vance
rel·e·vant
re·li·a·bil·i·ty
re·li·a·ble
re·li·a·bly
re·li·ance
re·li·ant

rel·ic
re·lief
re·liev·a·ble
re·lieve
·lieved ·liev·ing
re·liev·er
re·li·gion
re·li·gious
re·lin·quish
re·luc·tance
re·luc·tant
re·ly
·lied ·ly·ing
re·main·der
re·make
·made
·mak·ing
re·mand
re·mark·a·ble
re·mark·a·bly
re·me·di·a·ble
re·me·di·al
rem·e·dy
·dies
·died ·dy·ing
re·mem·ber
re·mem·brance
re·mind·er
rem·i·nisce
·nisced
·nisc·ing
rem·i·nis·cence
rem·i·nis·cent
re·miss
re·mis·si·ble
re·mis·sion
re·mit
·mit·ted
·mit·ting
re·mit·ta·ble
re·mit·tance
re·mit·tent
rem·nant
re·mod·el
re·mon·strance
re·mon·strate
·strat·ed
·strat·ing
re·mon·stra·tion
re·mon·stra·tor

re·morse·ful
re·morse·less
re·mote
re·mote·ly
re·mov·a·ble
re·mov·al
re·move
·moved
·mov·ing
re·mu·ner·ate
·at·ed ·at·ing
re·mu·ner·a·tion
re·mu·ner·a·tive
re·mu·ner·a·tor
ren·ais·sance
re·nas·cent
rend
rent rend·ing
ren·der
ren·dez·vous
·vous
·voused
·vous·ing
rend
ren·der
ren·di·tion
ren·e·gade
re·nege
·neged ·neg·ing
re·new·a·ble
re·new·al
re·nounce
·nounced
·nounc·ing
ren·o·vate
·vat·ed ·vat·ing
ren·o·va·tion
re·nown
re·nowned
rent·al
rent-free
re·nun·ci·a·tion
re·or·der
re·or·gan·i·za·tion
re·or·gan·ize
·ized ·iz·ing
rep·a·ra·ble
rep·a·ra·tion
rep·ar·tee
re·past

re·pa·tri·ate
·at·ed ·at·ing
re·pa·tri·a·tion
re·pay′
·paid ·pay·ing
(*pay back*)
re′-pay′
-paid -pay·ing
(*pay again*)
re·peal
re·peat
re·pel
·pelled ·pel·ling
re·pel·lent
re·pent
re·pent·ance
re·pent·ant
re·per·cus·sion
rep·er·toire
rep·er·to·ry
·ries
rep′e·ti′tion
(*a repeating*)
re′-pe·ti′tion
(*petition again*)
rep·e·ti·tious
re·pet·i·tive
re·phrase
re·place
re·place·a·ble
re·place·ment
re·plen·ish
re·plete
re·ple·tion
rep·li·ca
re·ply
·plies
·plied ·ply·ing
re·port·ed·ly
re·port·er
re·pose′
·posed ·pos·ing
(*rest*)
re′-pose′
(*pose again*)
re·pos·i·to·ry
·ries
re·pos·sess
re·pos·ses·sion
rep·re·hend
rep·re·hen·si·ble
rep·re·hen·sion
rep′re·sent′
(*stand for*)
re′-pre·sent′
(*present again*)
rep·re·sen·ta·tion
rep·re·sent·a·tive
re·press′
(*restrain*)
re′-press′
(*press again*)
re·pressed
re·press·i·ble
re·pres·sion
re·prieve
·prieved
·priev·ing
rep·ri·mand
re·print
re·pris·al
re·proach
re·proach·ful
rep·ro·bate
·bat·ed ·bat·ing
re·proc·essed
re·pro·duce
re·pro·duc·i·ble
re·pro·duc·tion
re·pro·duc·tive
re·pro·graph·ics
re·proof
re·prove′
·proved
·prov·ing
(*rebuke*)
re′-prove′
(*prove again*)
re·pub·lic
re·pub·li·can
re·pu·di·ate
·at·ed ·at·ing
re·pu·di·a·tion
re·pug·nance
re·pug·nant
re·pulse
·pulsed
·puls·ing
re·pul·sion
re·pul·sive
re·pur·chase
rep·u·ta·bil·i·ty
rep·u·ta·ble
rep·u·ta·bly
rep·u·ta·tion
re·pute
·put·ed ·put·ing
re·quest
Re·qui·em
re·quire
·quired
·quir·ing
re·quire·ment
req·ui·site
req·ui·si·tion
re·quit·al
re·quite
·quit·ed
·quit·ing
re·route
re·sal·a·ble
re·sale
re·scind
re·scind·a·ble
re·scis·sion
res·cu·a·ble
res·cue
·cued ·cu·ing
res·cu·er
re·search
re·sem·blance
re·sem·ble
·bled ·bling
re·sent′
(*feel a hurt*)
re′-sent′
(*sent again*)
re·sent·ful
re·sent·ment
res·er·va·tion
re·serve′
·served
·serv·ing
(*set aside*)
re′-serve′
(*serve again*)
re·serv·ed·ly
re·serv·ist
res·er·voir
re·set
·set ·set·ting
re·ship·ment
re·side
·sid·ed ·sid·ing
res·i·dence
res·i·den·cy
·cies
res·i·dent
res·i·den·tial
re·sid·u·al
re·sid·u·ar·y
res·i·due
re·sign′
(*give up*)
re′-sign′
(*sign again*)
res·ig·na·tion
re·sil·i·ence
re·sil·i·ent
res·in
res·in·ous
re·sist
re·sist·ance
re·sist·ant
re·sist·er
(*one who resists*)
re·sist·i·ble
re·sis·tor
(*electrical device*)
re·sole
·soled ·sol·ing
res·o·lute
res·o·lu·tion
re·solv·a·ble
re·solve′
·solved
·solv·ing
(*break into parts*)
re′-solve′
(*solve again*)
re·sol·vent
res·o·nance
res·o·nant
res·o·na·tor
re·sort′
(*go for help*)
re′-sort′
(*sort again*)
re·sound′ (*echo*)
re′-sound′
(*sound again*)
re·source

re·source·ful
re·spect·a·bil·i·ty
re·spect·a·ble
re·spect·ful
re·spect·ful·ly
re·spec·tive
re·spec·tive·ly
res·pi·ra·tion
res·pi·ra·tor
res·pi·ra·to·ry
re·spire
·spired
·spir·ing
res·pite
·pit·ed ·pit·ing
re·splend·ence
re·splend·ent
re·spond
re·spond·ent
re·sponse
re·spon·si·bil·i·ty
·ties
re·spon·si·ble
re·spon·si·bly
re·spon·sive
re·state
·stat·ed ·stat·ing
res·tau·rant
res·tau·ra·teur
rest·ful
res·ti·tu·tion
res·tive
rest·less
res·to·ra·tion
re·stor·a·tive
re·store
·stored ·stor·ing
re·strain′
(*hold back*)
re′-strain′
(*strain again*)
re·straint
re·strict
re·stric·tion
re·stric·tive
re·struc·ture
re·sult
re·sult·ant
re·sum·a·ble
re·sume *v.*
·sumed
·sum·ing
ré·su·mé *n.*
re·sump·tion
re·sur·face
re·sur·gence
re·sur·gent
res·ur·rect
res·ur·rec·tion
re·sus·ci·tate
·tat·ed ·tat·ing
re·sus·ci·ta·tion
re·sus·ci·ta·tor
re·tail
re·tain
re·tain·er
re·take
·took ·tak·en
·tak·ing
re·tal·i·ate
·at·ed ·at·ing
re·tal·i·a·tion
re·tal·i·a·to·ry
re·tard
re·tard·ant
re·tard·ate
re·tar·da·tion
re·ten·tion
re·ten·tive
re·ten·tiv·i·ty
ret·i·cence
ret·i·cent
re·tic·u·lar
re·tic·u·late
·lat·ed ·lat·ing
ret·i·cule
ret·i·na
·nas *or* ·nae
ret·i·nue
re·tire
·tired ·tir·ing
re·tir·ee
re·tire·ment
re·tool
re·tort
re·touch
re·trace′
(*go back over*)
re′-trace′
(*trace again*)
re·trace·a·ble
re·tract
re·tract·a·ble
re·trac·tile
re·trac·tion
re·trac·tor
re·tread *v.*
·tread·ed
·tread·ing
re·tread *n.*
re·treat′
(*go back*)
re′-treat′
(*treat again*)
re·trench
ret·ri·bu·tion
re·triev·a·ble
re·triev·al
re·trieve
·trieved
·triev·ing
re·triev·er
ret·ro·ac·tive
ret·ro·ces·sion
ret·ro·fit
ret·ro·grade
·grad·ed
·grad·ing
ret·ro·gress
ret·ro·gres·sion
ret·ro·spect
ret·ro·spec·tion
re·turn
re·turn·a·ble
re·turn·ee
re·un·ion
re·u·nite
re·us·a·ble
re·use
re·val·u·a·tion
re·vamp
re·veal
rev·el
·eled *or* ·elled
·el·ing *or* ·el·ling
rev·e·la·tion
rev·el·ry
re·venge
·venged
·veng·ing
re·venge·ful
re·veng·er
rev·e·nue
re·ver·ber·ant
re·ver·ber·ate
·at·ed ·at·ing
re·ver·ber·a·tion
re·ver·ber·a·tor
re·vere
·vered
·ver·ing
rev·er·ence
rev·er·end
rev·er·ent
rev·er·en·tial
rev·er·ie
re·ver·sal
re·verse
·versed
·vers·ing
re·vers·i·ble
re·vers·i·bly
re·ver·sion
re·ver·sion·ar·y
re·vert
re·view
re·view·al
re·view·er
re·vile
·viled ·vil·ing
re·vise
·vised ·vis·ing
re·vi·sion
re·vi·so·ry
re·vi·tal·ize
re·viv·a·ble
re·viv·al
re·vive
·vived ·viv·ing
re·viv·i·fy
rev·o·ca·ble
rev·o·ca·bly
rev·o·ca·tion
re·voke
·voked ·vok·ing
re·volt
re·volt·ing

rev·o·lu·tion
rev·o·lu·tion·ar·y
 ·ies
rev·o·lu·tion·ize
 ·ized ·iz·ing
re·volv·a·ble
re·volve
 ·volved
 ·volv·ing
re·volv·er
re·vue
re·vul·sion
re·ward
re·wind
 ·wound
 ·wind·ing
re·write
 ·wrote ·writ·ten
 ·writ·ing
rhe·o·stat
rhet·o·ric
rhe·tor·i·cal
rhe·tor·i·cal·ly
rhet·o·ri·cian
Rhode Island
rhom·boid
rhom·bus
 ·bus·es *or* ·bi
rhyme
 rhymed
 rhym·ing
rhythm
rhyth·mic
rhyth·mi·cal·ly
rib·ald
rib·ald·ry
ri·bo·fla·vin
rich·ness
ric·o·chet
 ·cheted *or*
 ·chet·ted
 ·chet·ing *or*
 ·chet·ting
rid·a·ble *or* ride·
rid·dance
rid·dle
 ·dled ·dling
ride
 rode rid·den
 rid·ing
rid·er
rid·er·less
ridge
 ridged
 ridg·ing
rid·i·cule
 ·culed ·cul·ing
ri·dic·u·lous
rife
right
 (*correct;* SEE rite, write)
right-an·gled
right·eous
right·ful·ly
right-hand·ed
right·ist
rig·id
ri·gid·i·ty
rig·ma·role
rig·or
rig·or mor·tis
rig·or·ous
rile
 riled ril·ing
rim
 rimmed
 rim·ming
ring·er
ring·lead·er
ring·mas·ter
ring·side
ri·ot·ous
ri·par·i·an
rip·en
ripe·ness
ri·poste *or*
 ·post
rip·per
rip·ple
 ·pled ·pling
rip·saw
rip·tide
rise
 rose ris·en
 ris·ing
ris·er
ris·i·bil·i·ty
 ·ties
ris·i·ble
risk·i·ly
risk·i·ness
risk·y
 ·i·er ·i·est
ris·qué
ris·sole
rite
 (*ceremonial act;*
 SEE right, write)
rit·u·al
rit·u·al·is·tic
rit·u·al·ly
ri·val
 ·valed *or* ·valled
 ·val·ing *or*
 ·val·ling
ri·val·ry
 ·ries
riv·et
riv·et·er
riv·u·let
roach
road·a·bil·i·ty
road·side
road·ster
road·work
roam·er
roan
roar·ing
roast·er
rob
 robbed rob·bing
rob·ber
rob·ber·y
 ·ies
robe
 robed rob·ing
ro·bot
ro·bust
rock·er
rock·et
rock·et·ry
rock·i·ness
rock·y
 ·i·er ·i·est
ro·de·o
 ·os
roe
roent·gen
rogue
 rogued rogu·ing
ro·guer·y
 ·ies
ro·guish
roil
 (*stir up;* SEE royal)
roist·er·er
roist·er·ous
role *or* rôle
 (*actor's part*)
roll
 (*revolve*)
roll·a·way
roll·back
roll call
roll·er
roll·o·ver
roll-top
rood
 (*cross;* SEE rude)
roof·er
rook
rook·er·y
 ·ies
rook·ie
room·er
 (*lodger;* SEE
 rumor)
room·ful
 ·fuls
room·i·ness
room·mate
room·y
 ·i·er ·i·est
root·er
root·less
root·let
rope
 roped rop·ing
Roque·fort
ro·sa·ry
 ·ries
ro·se·ate
rose·bud
rose·bush
rose-col·ored
rose·wood
Rosh Ha·sha·na
ros·in
ros·ter
ros·trum
 ·trums *or* ·tra

ro·ta·ry
·ries
ro·tat·a·ble
ro·tate
·tat·ed ·tat·ing
ro·ta·tion
ro·ta·tor
rote
(*routine;* SEE wrote)
ro·tis·ser·ie
ro·to·gra·vure
ro·tor
rot·ten
ro·tund
ro·tun·da
ro·tun·di·ty
rou·é
rough
(*not smooth;* SEE ruff)
rough·age
rough·cast
·cast ·cast·ing
rough-dry
-dried -dry·ing
rough·en
rough-hew
-hewed, -hewed *or* -hewn, -hew·ing
rough·ly
rough·shod
rou·lade
rou·leau
·leaux *or* ·leaus
rou·lette
round·a·bout
round·house
round·up
rouse
roused rous·ing
roust·a·bout
rout
(*noisy mob; dig up; defeat*)
route
rout·ed rout·ing
(*course*)
rou·tine
rove
roved rov·ing
row·el
·eled *or* ·elled
·el·ing *or* ·el·ling
roy·al
(*regal;* SEE roil)
roy·al·ist
roy·al·ly
roy·al·ty
·ties
rub·ble
rub·down
ru·bi·cund
ru·bric
ruche
ruch·ing
ruck·sack
rud·der
rud·di·ness
rud·dy
·di·er ·di·est
rude
(*crude;* SEE rood)
rude·ly
ru·di·ment
ru·di·men·ta·ry
rue
rued ru·ing
rue·ful
ruff
(*collar;* SEE rough)
ruf·fi·an
ruf·fle
·fled ·fling
rug·ged
ru·in·a·tion
ru·in·ous
rule
ruled rul·ing
rul·er
rum·ble
·bled ·bling
ru·mi·nant
ru·mi·nate
·nat·ed
·nat·ing
ru·mi·na·tor
rum·mage
·maged
·mag·ing
ru·mor
(*hearsay;* SEE roomer)
rum·ple
·pled ·pling
run·a·bout
run·a·way
run-down
run-in
run·ner-up
run·ners-up
run·off
run-on
run·way
rup·ture
·tured ·tur·ing
ru·ral
ru·ral·ly
ruse
rush
rus·tic
rus·ti·cal·ly
rus·ti·cate
·cat·ed ·cat·ing
rust·i·ness
rust·le
·tled ·tling
rus·tler
rust·proof
rust·y
·i·er ·i·est
ruth·less

S

Sab·bath
sab·bat·i·cal
sa·ber *or* ·bre
sa·ble
sa·bot
sab·o·tage
·taged ·tag·ing
sab·o·teur
sac
(*pouch;* SEE sack)
sac·cha·rin *n.*
sac·cha·rine *adj.*
sac·er·do·tal
sa·chet
sack
(*bag;* SEE sac)
sack·cloth
sack·ful
·fuls
sack·ing
sac·ra·ment
sac·ra·men·tal
sa·cred
sac·ri·fice
·ficed ·fic·ing
sac·ri·fi·cial
sac·ri·lege
sac·ri·le·gious
sac·ris·tan
sac·ris·ty
·ties
sac·ro·il·i·ac
sac·ro·sanct
sad·den
sad·dle
·dled ·dling
sad·ism
sad·ist
sa·dis·tic
sa·dis·ti·cal·ly
sa·fa·ri
·ris
safe
saf·er saf·est
safe-con·duct
safe-de·pos·it
safe·guard
safe·keep·ing
safe·ty
·ties
saf·fron
sag
sagged sag·ging
sa·ga
sa·ga·cious
sa·gac·i·ty
sage
sag·er sag·est
sage·brush
sag·gy
·gi·er ·gi·est
sail·er
(*boat*)

sail·or
(*person; hat*)
sal·a·ble *or* sale·
sa·la·cious
sal·ad
sal·a·ried
sal·a·ry
·ries
sales·clerk
sales·man
sales·man·ship
sales·peo·ple
sales·per·son
sales·wom·an
sa·lient
sa·line
sa·lin·i·ty
sa·li·va
sal·i·var·y
sal·i·vate
·vat·ed ·vat·ing
sal·low
salm·on
sal·mo·nel·la
·lae *or* ·la *or* ·las
sa·lon
sal·si·fy
salt·pe·ter
salt·wa·ter
sa·lu·bri·ous
sal·u·tar·y
sal·u·ta·tion
sa·lu·ta·to·ri·an
sa·lu·ta·to·ry
·ries
sa·lute
·lut·ed ·lut·ing
sal·vage
·vaged ·vag·ing
sal·vage·a·ble
sal·va·tion
salve
salved salv·ing
sal·ver
sal·vo
·vos *or* ·voes
Sa·mar·i·tan
same·ness
sam·o·var
sam·ple
·pled ·pling
sam·pler
sanc·ti·fi·ca·tion
sanc·ti·fy
·fied ·fy·ing
sanc·ti·mo·ni·ous
sanc·ti·mo·ny
sanc·tion
sanc·ti·ty
sanc·tu·ar·y
·ies
sanc·tum
·tums *or* ·ta
sand·blast
sand·hog
sand·lot
sand·man
sand·pa·per
sand·stone
sane·ly
sang-froid
san·gui·nar·y
san·guine
san·i·tar·i·um
·i·ums *or* ·i·a
san·i·tar·y
san·i·ta·tion
san·i·tize
·tized ·tiz·ing
san·i·ty
sa·pi·ent
sap·ling
sap·phire
sa·ran
sar·casm
sar·cas·tic
sar·cas·ti·cal·ly
sar·co·ma
·mas *or* ·ma·ta
sar·coph·a·gus
·a·gi
sar·dine
sar·don·ic
sar·don·i·cal·ly
sar·do·nyx
sar·to·ri·al
sa·tan·ic
sa·tan·i·cal·ly
satch·el
sate
sat·ed sat·ing
sa·teen
sat·el·lite
sa·tia·ble
sa·ti·ate
·at·ed ·at·ing
sa·ti·a·tion
sa·ti·e·ty
sa·tin
sat·in·wood
sat·in·y
sat·ire
sa·tir·i·cal
sat·i·rist
sat·i·rize
·rized ·riz·ing
sat·is·fac·tion
sat·is·fac·to·ri·ly
sat·is·fac·to·ry
sat·is·fy
·fied ·fy·ing
sa·to·ri
sa·trap
sat·su·ma
sat·u·ra·ble
sat·u·rate
·rat·ed ·rat·ing
sat·u·ra·tion
Sat·ur·day
sat·ur·nine
sat·yr
sau·ci·ness
sau·cy
·ci·er ·ci·est
sau·er·bra·ten
sau·er·kraut
sau·na
saun·ter
sau·sage
sau·té
·téed ·té·ing
sau·terne
sav·a·ble *or* save·
sav·age
sav·age·ly
sav·age·ry
sa·van·na
sa·vant
save
saved sav·ing
sav·ior
sa·voir-faire
sa·vor
sa·vor·i·ness
sa·vor·y
·i·er ·i·est
sa·voy
saw·horse
saw·mill
say-so
scab
scabbed scab·bing
scab·bard
scab·bi·ness
scab·by
·bi·er ·bi·est
scaf·fold
scal·a·ble
scald
scale
scaled scal·ing
sca·lene
scal·pel
scalp·er
scal·y
·i·er ·i·est
scam·per
scan
scanned
scan·ning
scan·dal
scan·dal·ize
·ized ·iz·ing
scan·dal·ous
scan·na·ble
scan·ner
scan·sion
scant·i·ly
scant·i·ness
scant·ness
scant·y
·i·er ·i·est
scape·goat
scap·u·la
·lae *or* ·las
scap·u·lar
scar
scarred
scar·ring

scar·ab
scarce·ly
scar·ci·ty
 ·ties
scare
 scared scar·ing
scarf
 scarfs *or* scarves
 (*long cloth*)
scarf
 scarfs
 (*joint; cut*)
scar·i·fi·ca·tion
scar·i·fy
 ·fied ·fy·ing
scar·i·ness
scar·let
scarp
scar·y
 ·i·er ·i·est
scat
 scat·ted
 scat·ting
scathe
 scathed
 scath·ing
scat·ter
scat·ter·brain
scav·enge
 ·enged ·eng·ing
scav·eng·er
sce·nar·i·o
 ·os
scene
sce·ner·y
 ·ies
sce·nic
scent (*odor;* SEE sent)
sched·ule
 ·uled ·ul·ing
sche·ma
 ·ma·ta
sche·mat·ic
sche·mat·i·cal·ly
scheme
 schemed
 schem·ing
schism
schis·mat·ic
schiz·oid
schiz·o·phre·ni·a
schiz·o·phren·ic
schol·ar·ly
schol·ar·ship
scho·las·tic
scho·las·ti·cal·ly
scho·las·ti·cism
school·house
school·room
school·teach·er
school·work
schoon·er
schwa
sci·at·i·ca
sci·ence
sci·en·tif·ic
sci·en·tif·i·cal·ly
sci·en·tist
scin·til·late
 ·lat·ed ·lat·ing
scin·til·la·tor
sci·on
scis·sors
scle·ro·sis
scoff
scold·ing
sconce
scone
scoop·ful
 ·fuls
scope
scorch·ing
score
 scored scor·ing
score·less
scorn·ful
scot-free
scoun·drel
scour
scourge
 scourged
 scourg·ing
scowl
scrab·ble
 ·bled ·bling
scrag·gly
 ·gli·er ·gli·est
scrag·gy
 ·gi·er ·gi·est
scram·ble
 ·bled ·bling
scrap
 scrapped
 scrap·ping
scrap·book
scrape
 scraped
 scrap·ing
scrap·heap
scrap·ple
scrawl
scraw·ny
 ·ni·er ·ni·est
screen·play
screw·driv·er
scrib·ble
 ·bled ·bling
scrib·bler
scribe
 scribed scrib·ing
scrim·mage
 ·maged ·mag·ing
scrimp·i·ness
scrimp·y
 ·i·er ·i·est
scrip
 (*certificate*)
script
 (*manuscript*)
scrip·tur·al
scroll·work
scrub
 scrubbed
 scrub·bing
scrub·by
 ·bi·er ·bi·est
scrunch
scru·ple
 ·pled ·pling
scru·pu·lous
scru·ta·ble
scru·ti·nize
 ·nized ·niz·ing
scru·ti·ny
scu·ba
scuf·fle
 ·fled ·fling
scull
 (*oar; boat;* SEE
 skull)
sculpt
sculp·tor
sculp·tur·al
sculp·ture
 ·tured ·tur·ing
scur·ril·i·ty
 ·ties
scur·ril·ous
scur·ry
 ·ried ·ry·ing
scur·vy
 ·vi·er ·vi·est
scut·tle
 ·tled ·tling
scythe
 scythed
 scyth·ing
sea·board
sea·borne
sea·coast
sea·far·er
sea·food
sea·go·ing
seal·ant
sea level
seal·skin
seam
sea·man
seam·less
seam·stress
seam·y
 ·i·er ·i·est
sé·ance
sea·plane
sea·port
sear
search·light
sea·shell
sea·shore
sea·sick·ness
sea·side
sea·son
sea·son·a·ble
sea·son·al
seat belt
sea·ward
sea·weed
sea·wor·thy
se·ba·ceous
se·cant
se·cede
 ·ced·ed
 ·ced·ing

se·ces·sion
se·clude
·clud·ed
·clud·ing
se·clu·sion
se·clu·sive
sec·ond
sec·ond·ar·i·ly
sec·ond·ar·y
sec·ond-class
sec·ond-guess
sec·ond-hand
sec·ond rate
se·cre·cy
se·cret
sec·re·tar·i·al
sec·re·tar·i·at
sec·re·tar·y
·ies
se·crete
·cret·ed ·cret·ing
se·cre·tion
se·cre·tive
se·cre·to·ry
sect
sec·tar·i·an
sec·tion·al
sec·tion·al·ize
·ized ·iz·ing
sec·tor
sec·u·lar
sec·u·lar·ize
·ized ·iz·ing
se·cun·dum
se·cur·a·ble
se·cure
·cured ·cur·ing
se·cure·ly
se·cu·ri·ty
·ties
se·dan
se·date
·dat·ed ·dat·ing
se·date·ly
se·da·tion
sed·a·tive
sed·en·tar·y
sed·i·ment
sed·i·men·ta·ry
sed·i·men·ta·tion
se·di·tion
se·di·tious
se·duce
·duced ·duc·ing
se·duc·i·ble
se·duc·tion
se·duc·tive
se·du·li·ty
sed·u·lous
seed·bed
seed·i·ness
seed·y
·i·er ·i·est
seek
sought seek·ing
seem·ing·ly
seem·li·ness
seem·ly
·li·er ·li·est
seep·age
seer·suck·er
seethe
seethed
seeth·ing
seg·ment
seg·men·tal
seg·men·ta·tion
seg·re·gate
·gat·ed ·gat·ing
seg·re·ga·tion
seg·re·ga·tion·ist
sei·del
seis·mic
seis·mi·cal·ly
seis·mo·graph
seis·mog·ra·pher
seis·mol·o·gist
seis·mol·o·gy
seize
seized seiz·ing
sei·zure
sel·dom
se·lect
se·lect·ee
se·lec·tion
se·lec·tive
se·lec·tiv·i·ty
se·lec·tor
self
selves
self-ad·dressed
self-ap·point·ed
self-cen·tered
self-con·fi·dence
self-con·scious
self-con·tained
self-de·fense
self-dis·ci·pline
self-driv·en
self-ed·u·cat·ed
self-em·ployed
self-es·teem
self-ev·i·dent
self-ex·plan·a·to·ry
self-ex·pres·sion
self-im·age
self-im·por·tant
self-im·posed
self-im·prove·ment
self-in·duced
self-in·dul·gence
self-in·flict·ed
self-in·sured
self-in·ter·est
self·ish
self·less
self-load·ing
self-made
self-mail·er
self-por·trait
self-pos·sessed
self-pres·er·va·tion
self-reg·u·lat·ing
self-re·li·ance
self-re·proach
self-re·spect
self-re·straint
self-right·eous
self-ris·ing
self-sac·ri·fice
self·same
self-sat·is·fied
self-seal·ing
self-serv·ice
self-start·er
self-styled
self-suf·fi·cient
self-sup·port
self-taught
self-tor·ture
self-willed
self-wind·ing
sell
sold sell·ing
sell-off
sell·out
sel·vage *or*
·vedge
se·man·tic
sem·a·phore
·phored
·phor·ing
sem·blance
se·mes·ter
sem·i·an·nu·al
sem·i·au·to·mat·ic
sem·i·cir·cle
sem·i·co·lon
sem·i·con·duc·tor
sem·i·con·scious
sem·i·de·tached
sem·i·fi·nal
sem·i·for·mal
sem·i·month·ly
sem·i·nal
sem·i·nar
sem·i·nar·y
·ies
sem·i·of·fi·cial
sem·i·pre·cious
sem·i·pri·vate
sem·i·pro·fes·sion·al
sem·i·rig·id
sem·i·skilled
sem·i·sol·id
Sem·ite
Se·mit·ic
sem·i·trail·er
sem·i·trop·i·cal
sem·i·week·ly
sem·i·year·ly
sem·o·li·na
sen·ate
sen·a·tor
sen·a·to·ri·al
send
sent send·ing

send-off
se·nes·cent
se·nile
se·nil·i·ty
sen·ior
sen·ior·i·ty
sen·sa·tion
sen·sa·tion·al·ly
sense
 sensed sens·ing
sense·less
sen·si·bil·i·ty
 ·ties
sen·si·ble
sen·si·bly
sen·si·tive
sen·si·tiv·i·ty
sen·si·ti·za·tion
sen·si·tize
 ·tized ·tiz·ing
sen·so·ry
sen·su·al
sen·su·al·i·ty
sen·su·ous
sent
 (*transmitted;* SEE scent)
sen·tence
 ·tenced ·tenc·ing
sen·ten·tious
sen·tient
sen·ti·ment
sen·ti·men·tal
sen·ti·men·tal·i·ty
sen·ti·men·tal·ize
 ·ized ·iz·ing
sen·ti·nel
 ·neled *or* ·nelled
 ·nel·ing *or*
 ·nel·ling
sen·try
 ·tries
sep·a·ra·ble
sep·a·rate
 ·rat·ed ·rat·ing
sep·a·ra·tion
sep·a·ra·tism
sep·a·ra·tor
se·pi·a
Sep·tem·ber
sep·tet *or*
 ·tette
sep·tic
sep·tu·a·ge·nar·i·an
sep·ul·cher
se·pul·chral
se·quel
se·quence
se·quen·tial
se·ques·ter
ser·e·nade
 ·nad·ed ·nad·ing
ser·en·dip·i·ty
se·rene
se·ren·i·ty
serf
serge (*fabric;* SEE surge)
ser·geant
se·ri·al
se·ri·al·ize
 ·ized ·iz·ing
se·ries
 ·ries
ser·if
se·ri·ous
se·ri·ous-mind·ed
ser·mon
se·rous
ser·pent
ser·pen·tine
ser·rate
 ·rat·ed ·rat·ing
se·rum
 ·rums *or* ·ra
ser·vant
serve
 served serv·ing
serv·ice
 ·iced ·ic·ing
serv·ice·a·bil·i·ty
serv·ice·a·ble
serv·ice·a·bly
serv·ice·man
ser·vile
ser·vil·i·ty
ser·vi·tude
ses·qui·cen·ten·ni·al
ses·sion
 (*meeting;* SEE cession)
set
 set set·ting
set·back
set-in
set·off
set·screw
set·tle
 ·tled ·tling
set·tle·ment
set·tler
set-to
 -tos
sev·en·teen
sev·enth
sev·en·ti·eth
sev·en·ty
 ·ties
sev·er
sev·er·al
sev·er·al·ly
sev·er·ance
se·vere
se·vere·ly
se·ver·i·ty
 ·ties
sew·age
sew·er
sew·er·age
sex·a·ge·nar·i·an
sex·i·ness
sex·less
sex·tant
sex·tet *or*
 ·tette
sex·ton
sex·tu·ple
 ·pled ·pling
sex·tu·plet
sex·u·al
sex·u·al·i·ty
sex·u·al·ly
shab·bi·ly
shab·bi·ness
shab·by
 ·bi·er ·bi·est
shack·le
 ·led ·ling
shade
 shad·ed
 shad·ing
shad·i·ness
shad·ow
shad·ow·y
shad·y
 ·i·er ·i·est
shaft
shak·a·ble *or*
 shake·a·ble
shake
 shook shak·en
 shak·ing
Shake·speare
Shake·spear·e·an
 or ·i·an
shake-up
shak·i·ly
shak·i·ness
shak·y
 ·i·er ·i·est
shal·low
sham
 shammed
 sham·ming
sham·ble
 ·bled ·bling
shame
 shamed
 sham·ing
shame·faced
shame·ful
shame·ful·ly
shame·less
shape
 shaped shap·ing
shape·less
shape·li·ness
shape·ly
 ·li·er ·li·est
share
 shared shar·ing
share·crop·per
share·hold·er
shark·skin
sharp·en·er
sharp-eyed
sharp·shoot·er
sharp-sight·ed
sharp-tongued
sharp-wit·ted
shat·ter

shat·ter·proof
shave
shaved, shaved
or shav·en,
shav·ing
shear
sheared, sheared
or shorn,
shear·ing
(*cut;* SEE sheer)
shears
sheath
(*a case; dress*)
sheathe
sheathed
sheath·ing
(*put into a sheath*)
shed
shed shed·ding
sheen
sheep·ish·ly
sheep·skin
sheep·walk
sheer
(*thin; steep;* SEE shear)
sheet·ing
sheik *or* sheikh
shelf
shelves
shell
shel·lac *or* ·lack
·lacked ·lack·ing
shell·fish
shell-like
shell·proof
shel·ter
shelve
shelved
shelv·ing
shep·herd
sher·bet
sher·iff
sher·ry
·ries
shib·bo·leth
shield
shift·i·ly
shift·i·ness
shift·less
shift·y
·i·er ·i·est
shil·le·lagh *or*
shil·la·lah
shim
shimmed
shim·ming
shim·mer·y
shim·my
·mies
·mied ·my·ing
shin
shinned
shin·ning
shine
shone *or* shined
shin·ing
shin·gle
·gled ·gling
shin·i·ness
shin·y
·i·er ·i·est
ship
shipped
ship·ping
ship·board
ship·mate
ship·ment
ship·own·er
ship·pa·ble
ship·per
ship·shape
ship·wreck
ship·wright
ship·yard
shirt·waist
shiv·er
shoal
shock·ing
shock·proof
shod·di·ly
shod·di·ness
shod·dy
·di·er ·di·est
shoe·horn
shoe·lace
shoe·mak·er
sho·er
shoe·shine
shoe·string
shoe tree
shoot
shot shoot·ing
shop
shopped
shop·ping
shop·keep·er
shop·lift·er
shop·per
shop·talk
shop·worn
shore·line
shor·ing
short·age
short·change
short-cir·cuit
short·com·ing
short·cut
short·en
short·en·ing
short·hand
short-hand·ed
short-lived
short-range
short·sight·ed
short·stop
short-tem·pered
short term
short·wave
short-wind·ed
should
shoul·der
should·n't
shov·el
·eled *or* ·elled
·el·ing *or* ·el·ling
shov·el·ful
·fuls
show
showed, shown
or showed,
show·ing
show·boat
show·case
show·down
show·er
show·i·ly
show·i·ness
show·man
show·piece
show·place
show·room
show·y
·i·er ·i·est
shrap·nel
shred
shred·ded *or*
shred
shred·ding
shrewd
shriek
shrill·ness
shrine
shrink
shrank *or* shrunk,
shrunk *or*
shrunk·en,
shrink·ing
shrink·age
shriv·el
·eled *or* ·elled
·el·ing *or* ·el·ling
shroud
shrub·ber·y
shrug
shrugged
shrug·ging
shud·der
shuf·fle
·fled ·fling
shun
shunned
shun·ning
shunt
shut
shut
shut·ting
shut·down
shut-in
shut-off
shut·out
shut·ter
shut·tle
·tled ·tling
sib·i·lance
sib·i·lant
sib·ling
sick·en
sick·le
sick·li·ness
sick·ly
·li·er ·li·est

side
 sid·ed sid·ing
side·board
side·burns
side·car
side·light
side·line
side·long
side·show
side·swipe
side·track
side·walk
side·ways
side·wise
sid·ing
si·dle
 ·dled ·dling
siege
si·en·na
si·er·ra
si·es·ta
sieve
 sieved siev·ing
sift·er
sigh
sight
 (*view;* SEE cite, site)
sight·less
sight·ly
 ·li·er ·li·est
sight·see·ing
sight·se·er
sign
 (*signal;* SEE sine)
sig·nal
 ·naled *or* ·nalled
 ·nal·ing *or* ·nal·ling
sig·nal·ize
 ·ized ·iz·ing
sig·nal·ly
sig·na·to·ry
 ·ries
sig·na·ture
sign·board
sig·net
sig·nif·i·cance
sig·nif·i·cant
sig·ni·fi·ca·tion
sig·ni·fy
 ·fied ·fy·ing
sign·post
si·lence
 ·lenced ·lenc·ing
si·lenc·er
si·lent
si·lex
sil·hou·ette
 ·et·ted ·et·ting
sil·i·ca
sil·i·cate
si·li·ceous
sil·i·cone
sil·i·co·sis
silk·en
silk·i·ness
silk-screen
silk·y
 ·i·er ·i·est
si·lo
 ·los, ·loed ·lo·ing
sil·ver
silver plate
sil·ver·smith
sil·ver·ware
sil·ver·y
sim·i·an
sim·i·lar
sim·i·lar·i·ty
 ·ties
sim·i·le
si·mil·i·tude
sim·per
sim·ple
 ·pler ·plest
sim·ple·ton
sim·plic·i·ty
 ·ties
sim·pli·fi·ca·tion
sim·pli·fi·er
sim·pli·fy
 ·fied ·fy·ing
sim·ply
sim·u·lant
sim·u·late
 ·lat·ed ·lat·ing
sim·u·la·tion
sim·u·la·tor
si·mul·cast
 ·cast *or* ·cast·ed
 ·cast·ing
si·mul·ta·ne·ous
sin·cere
 ·cer·er ·cer·est
sin·cere·ly
sin·cer·i·ty
sine
 (*ratio;* SEE sign)
si·ne qua non
si·ne·cure
sin·ew·y
singe
 singed
 singe·ing
sin·gle
 ·gled ·gling
sin·gle-breast·ed
sin·gle-hand·ed
sin·gle-pay·ment
sin·gle-space
sin·gle·ton
sin·gly
sin·gu·lar
sin·gu·lar·i·ty
sin·gu·lar·ize
 ·ized ·iz·ing
sin·is·ter
sink
 sank *or* sunk,
 sunk sink·ing
sin·ner
sin·u·ous
si·nus
si·nus·i·tis
si·phon
si·ren
sir·loin
si·roc·co
 ·cos
si·sal
sis·ter·hood
sis·ter-in-law
 sis·ters-in-law
sis·ter·li·ness
sis·ter·ly
sit-down
site
 (*place;* SEE cite, sight)
sit-in
sit·u·ate
 ·at·ed ·at·ing
sit·u·a·tion
sit-up *or* sit·up
six·fold
six·teenth
sixth
six·ti·eth
six·ty
 ·ties
siz·a·ble *or* size·
size
 sized siz·ing
siz·zle
 ·zled ·zling
skate
 skat·ed
 skat·ing
skein
skel·e·ton
skep·tic
skep·ti·cal
skep·ti·cal·ly
skep·ti·cism
sketch·book
sketch·y
 ·i·er ·i·est
skew·er
ski
 skis *or* ski
 skied ski·ing
skid
 skid·ded
 skid·ding
ski·er
skil·let
skill·ful
skim
 skimmed
 skim·ming
skimp·i·ly
skimp·i·ness
skimp·y
 ·i·er ·i·est
skin-deep
skin·flint
skin·ni·ness
skin·ny
 ·ni·er ·ni·est

skip
skipped
skip·ping
skip·per
skir·mish
skit·tish
skulk
skull (*head;* SEE scull)
skull·cap
sky
skies
sky·cap
sky-dive
-dived -div·ing
sky-high
sky·light
sky·line
sky·scrap·er
sky·ward
sky·ways
slack·en
slack·er
slake
slaked slak·ing
sla·lom
slam
slammed
slam·ming
slan·der
slan·der·ous
slant·wise
slap
slapped
slap·ping
slap·dash
slash
slate
slat·ed slat·ing
slat·tern
slaugh·ter
slave
slaved slav·ing
slav·er
slav·er·y
slav·ish·ly
slay
slew slain
slay·ing
(*kill;* SEE sleigh)
slea·zi·ness
slea·zy
·zi·er ·zi·est
sled
sled·ded
sled·ding
sledge
sledged
sledg·ing
sleek·ly
sleep
slept sleep·ing
sleep·i·ly
sleep·i·ness
sleep·less
sleep·walk·ing
sleep·y
·i·er ·i·est
sleet
sleeve·less
sleigh
(*snow vehicle;* SEE slay)
sleight
(*skill;* SEE slight)
slen·der
slen·der·ize
·ized ·iz·ing
sleuth
slice
sliced slic·ing
slick·er
slide
slid slid·ing
slide rule
slight
(*frail;* SEE sleight)
slim
slim·mer
slim·mest
slimmed
slim·ming
slim·i·ness
slim·ness
slim·y
·i·er ·i·est
sling
slung sling·ing
slip
slipped slip·ping
slip-on
slip·page
slip·per·i·ness
slip·per·y
·i·er ·i·est
slip·shod
slip·stream
slip-up
slit
slit slit·ting
slith·er
sliv·er
slob·ber
slog
slogged
slog·ging
slo·gan
sloop
slop
slopped
slop·ping
slope
sloped slop·ing
slop·pi·ly
slop·pi·ness
slop·py
·pi·er ·pi·est
slosh
slot
slot·ted slot·ting
sloth·ful
slough
slov·en·li·ness
slov·en·ly
·li·er ·li·est
slow-wit·ted
sludge
slug
slugged
slug·ging
slug·gish
sluice
sluiced sluic·ing
slum
slummed
slum·ming
slum·ber
slump
slur
slurred
slur·ring
slush·y
·i·er ·i·est
sly
sli·er *or* sly·er
sli·est *or* sly·est
sly·ly *or* sli·ly
smack
small-mind·ed
small·pox
small-scale
smash·up
smat·ter·ing
smear·y
·i·er ·i·est
smell
smelled *or* smelt
smell·ing
smell·i·ness
smell·y
·i·er ·i·est
smidg·en
smirch
smirk
smog
smog·gy
·gi·er ·gi·est
smok·a·ble *or*
smoke·a·ble
smoke screen
smoke·stack
smok·y
·i·er ·i·est
smol·der
smooth
smooth-shav·en
smooth-spo·ken
smoth·er
smudge
smudged
smudg·ing
smudg·i·ness
smudg·y
·i·er ·i·est
smug
smug·ger
smug·gest
smug·gle
·gled ·gling
snaf·fle
·fled ·fling
sna·fu

snag
 snagged
 snag·ging
snail-paced
snap
 snapped
 snap·ping
snap·pish
snap·shot
snare
 snared snar·ing
snatch
sneak·i·ly
sneak·i·ness
sneak·y
 ·i·er ·i·est
sneer·ing·ly
sneeze
 sneezed
 sneez·ing
snick·er
snif·fle
 ·fled ·fling
snif·ter
snip
 snipped
 snip·ping
snipe
 sniped snip·ing
sniv·el
 ·eled *or* ·elled
 ·el·ing *or*
 ·el·ling
snob·ber·y
snob·bish
snore
 snored snor·ing
snor·kel
snout
snow·bound
snow·drift
snow·fall
snow·flake
snow line
snow·mo·bile
 ·biled ·bil·ing
snow·plow
snow·storm
snow·y
 ·i·er ·i·est
snub
 snubbed
 snub·bing
snug
 snug·ger
 snug·gest
snug·gle
 ·gled ·gling
soap·box
soap·y
 ·i·er ·i·est
soar
 (*fly;* SEE sore)
sob
 sobbed
 sob·bing
so·ber-mind·ed
so·bri·e·ty
so·bri·quet
so-called
soc·cer
so·cia·bil·i·ty
so·cia·ble
so·cia·bly
so·cial
so·cial·ism
so·cial·ite
so·cial·i·za·tion
so·cial·ize
 ·ized ·iz·ing
so·ci·e·tal
so·ci·e·tal·ly
so·ci·e·ty
 ·ties
so·ci·o·cul·tu·ral
so·ci·o·e·co·nom·ic
so·ci·o·gram
so·ci·o·log·i·cal
so·ci·ol·o·gist
so·ci·ol·o·gy
so·ci·o·path
so·ci·o·po·lit·i·cal
sock·et
sod
 sod·ded sod·ding
so·dal·i·ty
 ·ties
sod·den·ness
soft·ball
soft-boiled
soft-cov·er
sof·ten·er
soft·heart·ed
soft-shell
soft-spo·ken
soft·ware
sog·gi·ness
sog·gy
 ·gi·er ·gi·est
soil
so·journ
sol·ace
 ·aced ·ac·ing
so·lar
so·lar·i·um
 ·lar·i·a
sol·der
 (*metal alloy*)
sol·dier
 (*person in an army*)
sole
 soled sol·ing
 (*bottom surface;*
 only; SEE soul)
sol·e·cism
sole·ly
sol·emn
so·lem·ni·fy
 ·fied ·fy·ing
so·lem·ni·ty
 ·ties
so·lic·it
so·lic·i·ta·tion
so·lic·i·tor
so·lic·i·tous
so·lic·i·tude
sol·id
sol·i·dar·i·ty
so·lid·i·fi·ca·tion
so·lid·i·fy
 ·fied ·fy·ing
sol·id-state
so·lil·o·quize
 ·quized
 ·quiz·ing
so·lil·o·quy
 ·quies
sol·i·taire
sol·i·tar·y
sol·i·tude
so·lo
 ·los
so·lo·ist
sol·stice
sol·u·bil·i·ty
sol·u·ble
sol·ute
so·lu·tion
solv·a·bil·i·ty
solv·a·ble
solve
 solved
 solv·ing
sol·ven·cy
sol·vent
som·ber
some·bod·y
some·day
some·how
some·one
some·thing
some·time
some·times
some·what
some·where
som·no·lent
so·nar
so·na·ta
song·ster
son·ic
son-in-law
 sons-in-law
son·net
so·nor·i·ty
so·no·rous
soon·er
soothe
 soothed
 sooth·ing
soot·i·ness
soot·y
 ·i·er ·iest
soph·ism
soph·ist
so·phis·ti·cal
so·phis·ti·cate
 ·cat·ed ·cat·ing
so·phis·ti·ca·tion
soph·is·try
 ·tries

soph·o·more
soph·o·mor·ic
sop·o·rif·ic
so·pra·no
·nos *or* ·ni
sor·did
sore
(*painful;* SEE soar)
sore·ly
sor·ghum
so·ror·i·ty
·ties
sor·rel
sor·ri·ly
sor·ri·ness
sor·row
sor·row·ful
sor·ry
·ri·er ·ri·est
sor·tie
sou·brette
souf·flé
soul
(*spirit;* SEE sole)
soul·ful
soul-search·ing
sound·proof
soup·çon
source·book
sour·dough
sour·ness
South Car·o·li·na
South Da·ko·ta
south·east
south·west
sou·ve·nir
sov·er·eign
sov·er·eign·ty
·ties
so·vi·et
soy·bean
space
spaced spac·ing
space·craft
·craft
space·flight
space·man
space·port
space·ship
space·suit
space·walk
spa·cious
spack·le
·led ·ling
spade·work
span
spanned
span·ning
span·sule
spar
sparred
spar·ring
spare
spared spar·ing
spar·kle
·kled ·kling
spar·kler
sparse·ly
spasm
spas·mod·ic
spas·tic
spa·tial
spat·ter
spawn
spay
speak
spoke spo·ken
speak·ing
speak·er
spear·head
spear·mint
spe·cial
spe·cial·ist
spe·cial·ize
·ized ·iz·ing
spe·cial·ly
spe·cial·ty
·ties
spe·cie
(*coin money*)
spe·cies
·cies
(*kind*)
spec·i·fi·a·ble
spe·cif·ic
spe·cif·i·cal·ly
spec·i·fi·ca·tion
spec·i·fy
·fied ·fy·ing
spec·i·men
spe·cious
speck·le
·led ·ling
spec·ta·cle
spec·ta·cled
spec·tac·u·lar
spec·ta·tor
spec·ter
spec·tral
spec·tro·scope
spec·tros·co·py
spec·trum
·tra *or* ·trums
spec·u·late
·lat·ed ·lat·ing
spec·u·la·tion
spec·u·la·tive
spec·u·la·tor
speech·less
speed·boat
speed·i·ly
speed·om·e·ter
speed·up
speed·y
·i·er ·i·est
spell
spelled *or* spelt
spell·ing
(*name the letters*)
spell
spelled spell·ing
(*work in place of*)
spell·bind
·bound ·bind·ing
spell·down
spend
spent spend·ing
spend·thrift
spew
sphere
spher·i·cal
sphinx
sphinx·es *or* sphin·ges
spice
spiced spic·ing
spic·i·ness
spic·y
·i·er ·i·est
spi·er
spike
spiked spik·ing
spill
spilled *or* spilt
spill·ing
spin
spun spin·ning
spi·nal
spin·dle
·dled ·dling
spin·dly
·dli·er ·dli·est
spin·drift
spine·less
spin·ner
spin·off
spin·ster
spin·y
·i·er ·i·est
spi·ral
·raled *or* ·ralled
·ral·ing *or* ·ral·ling
spir·it·less
spir·it·u·al
spir·it·u·ous
spite
spit·ed
spit·ing
spite·ful
spit·fire
spit·tle
spitz
splash·down
splat·ter
spleen·ful
splen·did
splen·dor
splice
spliced
splic·ing
splin·ter
split
split split·ting
split-lev·el
split-up
splurge
splurged
splurg·ing

spoil
spoiled *or* spoilt
spoil·ing
spoil·age
spoke
spoked
spok·ing
spokes·man
spo·li·a·tion
sponge
sponged
spong·ing
spon·gi·ness
spon·gy
·gi·er ·gi·est
spon·sor
spon·ta·ne·i·ty
·ties
spon·ta·ne·ous
spoon·er·ism
spoon-feed
-fed -feed·ing
spoon·ful
·fuls
spo·rad·ic
sport·ing
spor·tive
sports·man
sports·wear
spot
spot·ted
spot·ting
spot-check
spot·light
sprain
sprawl
spray
spread
spread
spread·ing
spright·li·ness
spright·ly
·li·er ·li·est
spring
sprang *or*
sprung, sprung,
spring·ing
spring·board
spring·i·ness
spring·time
spring·y
·i·er ·i·est

sprin·kle
·kled
·kling
sprin·kler
sprint·er
spritz
sprock·et
sprout
spruce
spruc·er
spruc·est
spruced
spruc·ing
spry
spri·er *or* spry·er
spri·est *or*
spry·est
spry·ly
spry·ness
spur
spurred
spur·ring
spu·ri·ous
spurn
spurt
sput·nik
sput·ter
spy
spies
spied
spy·ing
spy·glass
squab·ble
·bled ·bling
squab·bler
squad·ron
squal·id
squall
squal·or
squan·der
square
squared
squar·ing
squar·ish
squash·i·ness
squash·y
·i·er ·i·est
squat
squat·ted
squat·ting
squat·ter
squawk

squeak·i·ly
squeak·y
·i·er ·i·est
squeal·er
squeam·ish
squeez·a·ble
squeeze
squeezed
squeez·ing
squelch
squint-eyed
squire
squired
squir·ing
squirm·y
·i·er ·i·est
squirt
stab
stabbed
stab·bing
sta·bil·i·ty
sta·bi·li·za·tion
sta·bi·lize
·lized ·liz·ing
sta·bi·liz·er
sta·ble
·bled ·bling
stac·ca·to
·tos
stack·up
sta·di·um
·di·a *or* ·di·ums
staff
staffs *or* staves
(*stick; music*)
staff
(*people*)
stage
staged
stag·ing
stage·craft
stage·hand
stage-struck
stag·fla·tion
stag·ger
stag·nan·cy
stag·nant
stag·nate
·nat·ed ·nat·ing
stag·na·tion

stag·y
·i·er ·i·est
staid
stain·less
stake
staked
stak·ing
stake·hold·er
stake·out
sta·lac·tite
sta·lag·mite
stale
stal·er stal·est
staled stal·ing
stale·mate
·mat·ed ·mat·ing
stalk·ing-horse
stall
stal·lion
stal·wart
stam·i·na
stam·mer
stam·pede
·ped·ed ·ped·ing
stance
stan·chion
stand
stood stand·ing
stand·ard
stand·ard-bear·er
stand·ard·i·za·tion
stand·ard·ize
·ized ·iz·ing
stand·by
·bys
stand·ee
stand-in
stand·ing
stand·off
stand·pat
stand·point
stand·still
stand-up
stan·za
sta·ple
·pled ·pling
sta·pler
star
starred
star·ring
star·board

starch·i·ness
starch·y
·i·er ·i·est
star·dom
stare
stared
star·ing
star·gaze
·gazed ·gaz·ing
star·light
star·lit
star·ry
·ri·er ·ri·est
star-span·gled
start·er
star·tle
·tled ·tling
star·va·tion
starve
starved
starv·ing
starve·ling
stat·a·ble
state
stat·ed
stat·ing
State·hood
state·li·ness
state·ly
·li·er ·li·est
state·ment
state·room
states·man
state-wide
stat·ic
stat·i·cal·ly
sta·tion
sta·tion·ar·y
(not moving)
sta·tion·er
sta·tion·er·y
(writing paper)
sta·tis·tic
sta·tis·ti·cal
stat·is·ti·cian
stat·u·ar·y
·ies
stat·ue
stat·u·esque
stat·u·ette

stat·ure
sta·tus
sta·tus quo
stat·ute
stat·u·to·ry
staunch
stave
staved *or* stove
stav·ing
stead·fast
stead·i·ly
stead·i·ness
stead·y
·i·er ·i·est
·ied ·y·ing
steal
stole stol·en
steal·ing
stealth·i·ly
stealth·y
·i·er ·i·est
steam·boat
steam·er
steam·roll·er
steam·ship
steam shovel
steam·y
·i·er ·i·est
steel mill
steel·work·er
steel·yard
stee·ple
stee·ple·chase
stee·ple·jack
stein
stel·lar
stem
stemmed
stem·ming
stem-wind·ing
sten·cil
·ciled *or* cilled
·cil·ing *or*
·cil·ling
ste·nog·ra·pher
sten·o·graph·ic
ste·nog·ra·phy
sten·o·type
sten·o·typ·ist
sten·o·typ·y
sten·to·ri·an

step
stepped
step·ping
step·broth·er
step·child
·chil·dren
step·daugh·ter
step-down
step·fa·ther
step·lad·der
step·moth·er
step·par·ent
steppe
(treeless plain)
stepped-up
step·ping·stone
step·sis·ter
step·son
step-up
ster·e·o
ster·e·o·phon·ic
ster·e·o·scope
ster·e·o·scop·ic
ster·e·o·type
·typed ·typ·ing
ster·e·o·typ·ic
ster·ile
ste·ril·i·ty
ster·i·li·za·tion
ster·i·lize
·lized ·liz·ing
ster·ling
stern·ness
stet
stet·ted
stet·ting
steth·o·scope
ste·ve·dore
stew·ard
stick
stuck stick·ing
stick·i·ness
stick·le
·led ·ling
stick·ler
stick·pin
stick·y
·i·er ·i·est
stiff·en

sti·fle
·fled ·fling
stig·ma
·mas *or* ·ma·ta
stig·ma·tize
·tized ·tiz·ing
stile
(steps; SEE style)
sti·let·to
·tos *or* ·toes
still·born
still life
still·y
stilt·ed
stim·u·lant
stim·u·late
·lat·ed ·lat·ing
stim·u·la·tion
stim·u·la·tive
stim·u·lus
·li
sting
stung sting·ing
stin·gi·ly
stin·gi·ness
stin·gy
·gi·er ·gi·est
stink
stank *or* stunk,
stunk stink·ing
stint·ing·ly
sti·pend
sti·pen·di·ar·y
·ar·ies
stip·ple
·pled ·pling
stip·u·late
·lat·ed ·lat·ing
stip·u·la·tion
stip·u·la·tor
stir
stirred stir·ring
stitch
stock·ade
·ad·ed ·ad·ing
stock·bro·ker
stock·hold·er
stock·i·ness
stock·pile
stock·room
stock still

stock·y
·i·er ·i·est
stock·yard
stodg·i·ness
stodg·y
·i·er ·i·est
sto·ic
sto·i·cal
sto·i·cism
stoke
stoked stok·ing
stok·er
stole
stol·en
(*pp. of* steal)
stol·id
stol·len
(*sweet bread*)
stom·ach
stom·ach·ache
stone·cut·ter
stone·ma·son
stone·ware
stone·work
ston·i·ly
ston·y
·i·er ·i·est
stoop
stop·gap
stop·light
stop·o·ver
stop·page
stop·per
stop·watch
stor·a·ble
stor·age
store
stored stor·ing
store·house
store·keep·er
store·room
storm door
storm·i·ly
storm·i·ness
storm·y
·i·er ·i·est
sto·ry
·ries
·ried ·ry·ing
stout·heart·ed

stove·pipe
stow·a·way
strad·dle
·dled ·dling
strafe
strafed
straf·ing
strag·gle
·gled ·gling
strag·gler
straight
(*not bent;*
SEE strait)
straight·a·way
straight·edge
straight·ened
(*made straight;*
SEE straitened)
straight-faced
straight·for·ward
strain·er
strait
(*waterway;* SEE
straight)
strait·ened
(*limited;* SEE
straightened)
strait·jack·et
strait-laced
strange
strang·er
strang·est
strange·ly
stran·ger
stran·gle
·gled ·gling
stran·gle·hold
stran·gu·late
·lat·ed ·lat·ing
stran·gu·la·tion
strap
strapped
strap·ping
strat·a·gem
stra·te·gic
stra·te·gi·cal·ly
strat·e·gist
strat·e·gy
·gies
strat·i·fi·ca·tion
strat·i·fy
·fied ·fy·ing

strat·o·sphere
stra·tum
·ta *or* ·tums
stra·tus
·ti
stray
streak·i·ness
streak·y
·i·er ·i·est
stream·line
·lined ·lin·ing
street·car
strength·en
stren·u·ous
stretch·er
stretch·i·ness
stretch·y
·i·er ·i·est
strew
strewed, strewed
or strewn,
strew·ing
stri·ate
·at·ed ·at·ing
stri·a·tion
strict·ly
stric·ture
stride
strode strid·den
strid·ing
stri·dent
strid·u·late
·lat·ed ·lat·ing
strife
strike
struck, struck *or*
strick·en,
strik·ing
strike·break·er
string
strung
string·ing
strin·gen·cy
·cies
strin·gent
strip
stripped
strip·ping
stripe
striped
strip·ing
strip·ling

strive
strove *or* strived,
striv·en *or*
strived, striv·ing
strobe
stroke
stroked
strok·ing
stroll·er
strong-arm
strong·box
strong·hold
strong-mind·ed
strong-willed
strop
stropped
strop·ping
struc·tur·al
struc·ture
·tured
·tur·ing
strug·gle
·gled ·gling
strum
strummed
strum·ming
strut
strut·ted
strut·ting
stub
stubbed
stub·bing
stub·ble
stub·bly
·bli·er ·bli·est
stub·born
stub·by
·bi·er ·bi·est
stuc·co
·coes *or* ·cos
·coed ·co·ing
stud·book
stu·dent
stud·horse
stu·di·o
·os
stu·di·ous
stud·y
·ies, ·ied ·y·ing
stuff·i·ness
stuff·y
·i·er ·i·est

stul·ti·fy
·fied ·fy·ing
stum·ble
·bled ·bling
stun
stunned
stun·ning
stu·pe·fac·tion
stu·pe·fy
·fied ·fy·ing
stu·pen·dous
stu·pid
stu·pid·i·ty
·ties
stu·por
stur·di·ly
stur·di·ness
stur·dy
·di·er ·di·est
stur·geon
stut·ter
stut·ter·er
style
styled styl·ing
(*mode;* SEE stile)
style·book
styl·ish
styl·ist
sty·lis·tic
styl·i·za·tion
styl·ize
·ized ·iz·ing
sty·lus
·lus·es *or* ·li
sty·mie
·mied ·mie·ing
sty·rene
Sty·ro·foam
su·a·ble
suave
sub·as·sem·bly
sub·base·ment
sub·com·mit·tee
sub·con·scious
sub·con·tract
sub·cul·ture
sub·cu·ta·ne·ous
sub·di·vide
sub·di·vi·sion
sub·due
·dued ·du·ing
sub·ject
sub·jec·tive
sub·jec·tiv·i·ty
sub·join·der
sub·ju·gate
·gated ·gat·ing
sub·ju·ga·tion
sub·ju·ga·tor
sub·junc·tive
sub·lease
sub·les·see
sub·les·sor
sub·let
·let ·let·ting
sub·li·mate
·mat·ed ·mat·ing
sub·li·ma·tion
sub·lime
·limed ·lim·ing
sub·lim·i·nal
sub·lim·i·ty
sub·mar·gin·al
sub·ma·rine
sub·merge
sub·mer·gence
sub·mer·gi·ble
sub·merse
·mersed
·mers·ing
sub·mers·i·ble
sub·mer·sion
sub·mis·sion
sub·mis·sive
sub·mit
·mit·ted ·mit·ting
sub·nor·mal
sub·nor·mal·i·ty
sub·or·di·nate
·nat·ed ·nat·ing
sub·or·di·na·tion
sub·or·na·tion
sub·plot
sub·poe·na
·naed ·na·ing
sub ro·sa
sub·scribe
·scribed
·scrib·ing
sub·script
sub·scrip·tion
sub·se·quent
sub·ser·vi·ent
sub·side
·sid·ed ·sid·ing
sub·sid·i·ar·y
·ies
sub·si·di·za·tion
sub·si·dize
·dized ·diz·ing
sub·si·dy
·dies
sub·sist·ence
sub·stance
sub·stand·ard
sub·stan·tial
sub·stan·tial·ly
sub·stan·ti·ate
·at·ed ·at·ing
sub·stan·ti·a·tion
sub·stan·ti·val
sub·stan·tive
sub·sta·tion
sub·sti·tut·a·ble
sub·sti·tute
·tut·ed ·tut·ing
sub·sti·tu·tion
sub·stra·tum
·ta *or* ·tums
sub·struc·tur·al
sub·struc·ture
sub·ten·ant
sub·ter·fuge
sub·ter·ra·ne·an
sub·ti·tle
sub·tle
·tler ·tlest
sub·tle·ty
·ties
sub·tly
sub·tract
sub·trac·tion
sub·tra·hend
sub·trop·i·cal
sub·urb
sub·ur·ban
sub·ur·ban·ite
sub·ur·bi·a
sub·ver·sion
sub·ver·sive
sub·vert
sub·way
suc·ceed
suc·cess
suc·cess·ful
suc·cess·ful·ly
suc·ces·sion
suc·ces·sive
suc·ces·sor
suc·cinct
suc·cor
suc·cu·lence
suc·cu·lent
suc·cumb
su·crose
suc·tion
sud·den·ly
sud·den·ness
su·dor·if·ic
sue
sued su·ing
suede *or* suède
su·et
suf·fer
suf·fer·ance
suf·fer·ing
suf·fice
·ficed ·fic·ing
suf·fi·cien·cy
suf·fi·cient
suf·fix
suf·fo·cate
·cat·ed
·cat·ing
suf·fo·ca·tion
suf·frage
suf·fra·gist
suf·fuse
·fused ·fus·ing
suf·fu·sion
sug·ar-cured
sug·ar·y
sug·gest
sug·gest·i·ble
sug·ges·tion
sug·ges·tive
su·i·ci·dal
su·i·cide

suit
(*set;* SEE suite)
suit·a·bil·i·ty
suit·a·ble
suit·a·bly
suit·case
suite
(*rooms; furniture;* SEE suit, sweet)
su·i ge·ne·ris
suit·or
sul·fa
sul·fur
sulk·y
·i·er ·i·est
sul·len
sul·ly
·lied ·ly·ing
sul·try
·tri·er ·tri·est
sum
summed
sum·ming
sum·mar·i·ly
sum·ma·rize
·rized ·riz·ing
sum·ma·ry
·ries
sum·ma·tion
sum·mit
sum·mon
sum·mons
·mons·es
sump·tu·ar·y
sump·tu·ous
sun·burn
sun·burst
sun-cured
Sun·day
sun·di·al
sun·down
sun·dries
sun·dry
sunk·en
sun·light
sun·lit
sun·proof
sun·rise
sun·set
sun·shade
sun·shine
sun·spot
sun·stroke
sun·tan
su·perb
su·per·car·go
·goes *or* ·gos
su·per·charge
su·per·cil·i·ous
su·per·e·go
su·per·fi·cial
su·per·fi·ci·al·i·ty
·ties
su·per·fi·cial·ly
su·per·flu·i·ty
·ties
su·per·flu·ous
su·per·hu·man
su·per·im·pose
su·per·in·duce
su·per·in·tend·ent
su·pe·ri·or
su·pe·ri·or·i·ty
su·per·la·tive
su·per·sede
·sed·ed ·sed·ing
su·per·son·ic
su·per·sti·tion
su·per·sti·tious
su·per·struc·ture
su·per·vise
·vised
·vis·ing
su·per·vi·sion
su·per·vi·sor
su·per·vi·so·ry
su·pine
sup·plant
sup·ple
sup·ple·ly
sup·ple·ment
sup·ple·men·tal
sup·ple·men·ta·ry
sup·ple·men·ta·tion
sup·pli·ant
sup·pli·cant
sup·pli·cate
·cat·ed ·cat·ing
sup·pli·ca·tion
sup·pli·er
sup·ply
·plies
·plied ·ply·ing
sup·port
sup·port·ive
sup·pose
·posed ·pos·ing
sup·pos·ed·ly
sup·po·si·tion
sup·pos·i·to·ry
·ries
sup·press
sup·press·i·ble
sup·pres·sion
sup·pres·sor
su·prem·a·cist
su·prem·a·cy
su·preme·ly
sur·charge
sure·ly
sur·e·ty
·ties
sur·face
·faced ·fac·ing
sur·feit
surge
surged surg·ing
(*sudden rush;* SEE serge)
sur·geon
sur·ger·y
·ies
sur·gi·cal
sur·gi·cal·ly
sur·i·ty
sur·li·ness
sur·ly
·li·er ·li·est
sur·mise
·mised ·mis·ing
sur·mount
sur·name
·named
·nam·ing
sur·pass
sur·plus
sur·prise
·prised
·pris·ing
sur·pris·ing·ly
sur·re·al
sur·re·al·ism
sur·ren·der
sur·rep·ti·tious
sur·ro·gate
·gat·ed ·gat·ing
sur·round
sur·tax
sur·veil·lance
sur·vey
·veys
sur·vey·or
sur·viv·a·ble
sur·viv·al
sur·vive
·vived ·viv·ing
sur·vi·vor
sur·vi·vor·ship
sus·cep·ti·bil·i·ty
sus·cep·ti·ble
sus·pect
sus·pend
sus·pense
sus·pen·sion
sus·pen·so·ry
sus·pi·cion
sus·pi·cious
sus·tain
sus·tain·a·ble
sus·te·nance
swap
swapped
swap·ping
swarm
swarth·y
·i·er ·i·est
swat
swat·ted
swat·ting
swath *n.*
(*strip*)
swathe *v., n.*
swathed
swath·ing
(*bandage*)
swear
swore
sworn
swear·ing

sweat
sweat *or*
sweat·ed,
sweat·ing
sweat·er
sweat shirt
sweat·shop
sweep
swept sweep·ing
sweep·stakes
·stakes
sweet
(like sugar;
SEE suite)
sweet·heart
swell
swelled, swelled
or swol·len,
swell·ing
swel·ter
swept·back
swerve
swerved
swerv·ing
swift·ness
swim
swam swum
swim·ming
swim·ming·ly
swin·dle
·dled ·dling
swing
swung
swing·ing
swipe
swiped
swip·ing
swirl
switch·board
switch·man
swiv·el
·eled *or* ·elled
·el·ing *or* ·el·ling
swol·len
syb·a·rite
syc·a·more
syc·o·phant
syc·o·phan·tic
syl·lab·ic
syl·lab·i·fi·ca·tion
syl·lab·i·fy
·fied ·fy·ing

syl·la·ble
syl·la·bus
·bus·es *or* ·bi
syl·lo·gism
sylph
syl·van
sym·bi·ot·ic
sym·bol
sym·bol·ic
sym·bol·ism
sym·bol·is·tic
sym·bol·ize
·ized ·iz·ing
sym·met·ri·cal
sym·me·try
·tries
sym·pa·thet·ic
sym·pa·thize
·thized ·thiz·ing
sym·pa·thy
·thies
sym·phon·ic
sym·pho·ny
·nies
sym·po·si·um
·ums *or* ·a
symp·tom
symp·to·mat·ic
syn·a·gogue
syn·chro·mesh
syn·chro·nism
syn·chro·ni·za·tion
syn·chro·nize
·nized ·niz·ing
syn·chro·nous
syn·chro·tron
syn·co·pate
·pat·ed ·pat·ing
syn·co·pa·tion
syn·co·pe
syn·cre·tize
·tized ·tiz·ing
syn·di·cal·ism
syn·di·cate
·cat·ed ·cat·ing
syn·drome
syn·od
syn·od·i·cal
syn·o·nym
syn·on·y·mous

syn·on·y·my
·mies
syn·op·sis
·ses
syn·op·size
·sized ·siz·ing
syn·op·tic
syn·tac·tic
syn·tac·ti·cal·ly
syn·tax
syn·the·sis
·ses
syn·the·size
·sized ·siz·ing
syn·thet·ic
syn·thet·i·cal·ly
syph·i·lis
syph·i·lit·ic
sy·ringe
·ringed ·ring·ing
sys·tem
sys·tem·at·ic
sys·tem·at·i·cal·ly
sys·tem·a·tize
·tized ·tiz·ing
sys·tem·ic

T

tab·ard
ta·ble
·bled ·bling
tab·leau
·leaux *or* ·leaus
ta·ble d'hôte
ta·ble-hop
ta·ble·spoon·ful
·fuls
tab·let
tab·loid
ta·boo *or* ·bu
·boos *or* ·bus
·booed *or* ·bued
·boo·ing *or*
·bu·ing
tab·u·lar
tab·u·late
·lat·ed ·lat·ing
tab·u·la·tion
tab·u·la·tor

ta·chom·e·ter
tac·it
tac·i·turn
tac·i·tur·ni·ty
tack·i·ness
tack·le
·led ·ling
tack·y
·i·er ·i·est
tact·ful
tact·ful·ly
tac·ti·cal
tac·ti·cian
tac·tics
tac·tile
tact·less
tac·tu·al
tail·gate
·gat·ed ·gat·ing
tail·less
tail·light
tai·lor
tai·lor-made
tail·spin
tail wind
taint·ed
tak·a·ble *or* take·
take
took tak·en
tak·ing
take·off
take·out
take·o·ver
tal·ent·ed
tal·is·man
·mans
talk·a·tive
talk·y
tal·low
tal·ly
·lies, ·lied
·ly·ing
Tal·mud
tal·on
tam·a·ble *or*
tame·
tam·bour
tam·bou·rine
tame
tamed tam·ing

tamp′er *n.*
tam′per *v.*
tam·per·er
tam·pi·on
tan·dem
tan·gent
tan·gen·tial
tan·gi·ble
tan·gi·bly
tan·gle
 ·gled ·gling
tang·y
 ·i·er ·i·est
tank·age
tank·ard
tank·er
tank·ful
 ·fuls
tan·ner·y
 ·ies
tan·nic
tan·nin
tan·ta·lize
 ·lized ·liz·ing
tan·ta·mount
tan·trum
tape
 taped tap·ing
tape deck
ta·per
tape-re·cord
tape recorder
tap·es·try
 ·tries
tap·room
tap·root
tar
 tarred
 tar·ring
tar·di·ness
tar·dy
 ·di·er ·di·est
tar·get
tar·iff
tar·nish
tar·ot
tar·pau·lin
tar·pon
tar·ra·gon
tar·ry
 ·ried ·ry·ing
tar·tan
tar·tar
tart·ly
task force
task·mas·ter
tas·sel
 ·seled *or* ·selled
 ·sel·ing *or*
 ·sel·ling
taste
 tast·ed tast·ing
taste·ful
taste·ful·ly
taste·less
tast·er
tast·i·ness
tast·y
 ·i·er ·i·est
tat·tered
tat·ter·sall
tat·tle
 ·tled ·tling
tat·too
 ·toos
 ·tooed ·too·ing
taught
 (*trained;* SEE taut)
taunt
taupe
taut
 (*tight;* SEE taught)
tau·tol·o·gy
 ·gies
tav·ern
taw·dry
 ·dri·er ·dri·est
taw·ny
 ·ni·er ·ni·est
tax·a·bil·i·ty
tax·a·ble
tax·a·tion
tax-de·duct·i·ble
tax-ex·empt
tax·i
 ·is, ·ied
 ·i·ing *or* ·y·ing
tax·i·cab
tax·i·der·my
tax·i·me·ter
tax·on·o·my
tax·pay·er
teach
 taught teach·ing
teach·a·ble
teach·er
tea·cup·ful
 ·fuls
teak
team
 (*group;* SEE teem)
team·mate
team·ster
team·work
tear
 tore torn
 tear·ing
 (*rip*)
tear
 teared tear·ing
 (*eye fluid*)
tear·drop
tear·ful
tear·i·ness
tear·y
 ·i·er ·i·est
tease
 teased teas·ing
tea·sel
 ·seled *or* ·selled
 ·sel·ing *or*
 ·sel·ling
tea·spoon·ful
 ·fuls
tea·time
tech·nic
tech·ni·cal
tech·ni·cal·i·ty
 ·ties
tech·ni·cal·ly
tech·ni·cian
tech·ni·col·or
tech·nique
tech·noc·ra·cy
tech·nog·ra·phy
tech·no·log·i·cal
tech·nol·o·gy
te·di·ous
te·di·um
teem
 (*abound;* SEE team)
teen-age
tee·to·tal·er
tee·to·tal·ism
Tef·lon
teg·u·ment
Tel·au·to·graph
tel·e·cast
 ·cast *or* ·cast·ed
 ·cast·ing
tel·e·com·mu·
 ni·ca·tion
tel·e·course
tel·e·gen·ic
tel·e·gram
tel·e·graph
te·leg·ra·pher
tel·e·graph·ic
te·leg·ra·phy
tel·e·ki·ne·sis
tel·e·me·ter
te·le·o·log·i·cal
te·le·ol·o·gy
tel·e·path·ic
te·lep·a·thy
tel·e·phone
 ·phoned
 ·phon·ing
tel·e·phon·ic
te·leph·o·ny
tel·e·pho·to
tel·e·pho·to·graph
tel·e·pho·tog·ra·phy
tel·e·play
tel·e·prompt·er
tel·e·scope
 ·scoped ·scop·ing
tel·e·scop·ic
tel·e·thon
Tel·e·type
 ·typed ·typ·ing
tel·e·type·writ·er
tel·e·view·er
tel·e·vise
 ·vised ·vis·ing
tel·e·vi·sion
tell·er
tell·tale

Tel·star
te·mer·i·ty
tem·per
tem·per·a
tem·per·a·ment
tem·per·a·men·tal
tem·per·ance
tem·per·ate
tem·per·a·ture
tem·pered
tem·pest
tem·pes·tu·ous
tem·plate *or* ·plet
tem·ple
tem·po
·pos *or* ·pi
tem·po·ral
tem·po·rar·i·ly
tem·po·rar·i·ness
tem·po·rar·y
tem·po·rize
·rized ·riz·ing
temp·ta·tion
tempt·er
tempt·ing
ten·a·ble
te·na·cious
te·nac·i·ty
ten·an·cy
·cies
ten·ant
ten·ant·a·ble
ten·ant·ry
·ries
tend·en·cy
·cies
ten·der
(soft; offer)
tend·er
(one who tends)
ten·der·ize
·ized ·iz·ing
ten·don
ten·dril
ten·e·ment
ten·et
ten·fold
Ten·nes·see
ten·on
tense
tens·er tens·est
tensed tens·ing
tense·ly
tense·ness
ten·sile
ten·sil·i·ty
ten·sion
ten·ta·cle
ten·ta·tive
ten·ta·tive·ly
ten·ter
ten·ter·hook
tenth
ten·u·ous
ten·ure
ten·u·ri·al
tep·id
te·pid·i·ty
ter·cen·te·nar·y
·ies
ter·mi·na·ble
ter·mi·na·bly
ter·mi·nal
ter·mi·nate
·nat·ed ·nat·ing
ter·mi·na·tion
ter·mi·nol·o·gy
ter·mi·nus
·ni *or* ·nus·es
ter·na·ry
ter·race
·raced ·rac·ing
ter·ra cot·ta
ter·ra fir·ma
ter·rain
ter·ra·pin
ter·rar·i·um
·i·ums *or* ·i·a
ter·raz·zo
ter·res·tri·al
ter·ri·ble
ter·ri·bly
ter·ri·er
ter·rif·ic
ter·ri·fy
·fied ·fy·ing
ter·ri·to·ri·al
ter·ri·to·ri·al·i·ty
ter·ri·to·ry
·ries
ter·ror
ter·ror·ism
ter·ror·ist
ter·ror·is·tic
ter·ror·i·za·tion
ter·ror·ize
·ized
·iz·ing
terse
ters·er
ters·est
terse·ness
ter·ti·ar·y
test·a·ble
tes·ta·ment
tes·tate
tes·ta·tor
tes·ti·fi·er
tes·ti·fy
·fied
·fy·ing
tes·ti·ly
tes·ti·mo·ni·al
tes·ti·mo·ny
·nies
tet·a·nus
tête-à-tête
teth·er
tet·ra·cy·cline
tet·ra·he·dron
·drons *or* ·dra
te·tral·o·gy
·gies
Tex·as
text·book
tex·tile
tex·tu·al
tex·tur·al
tex·ture
than *conj., prep.*
thanks·giv·ing
thatch
the·a·ter *or* ·tre
the·at·ri·cal
theft
the·ism
the·is·tic
the·mat·ic
theme
them·selves
then
(at that time)
thence·forth
the·oc·ra·cy
·cies
the·o·lo·gian
the·o·log·i·cal
the·ol·o·gy
·gies
the·o·rem
the·o·ret·i·cal
the·o·ret·i·cal·ly
the·o·re·ti·cian
the·o·rize
·rized ·riz·ing
the·o·ry
·ries
the·os·o·phy
·phies
ther·a·peu·tic
ther·a·pist
ther·a·py
·pies
there
there·af·ter
there·by
there·for
(for it)
there·fore
(for that reason)
there·in
there·in·to
there·to·fore
there·with
ther·mal
therm·i·on·ics
ther·mo·dy·nam·ics
ther·mom·e·ter
ther·mo·nu·cle·ar
ther·mo·pile
ther·mo·plas·tic
ther·mos
ther·mo·stat
the·sau·rus
·ri *or* ·rus·es
the·sis
·ses
thi·a·mine

thick·en·ing
thick·et
thick·ness
thick·set
thick-skinned
thing
think
 thought
 think·ing
thin-skinned
third-class
third-rate
thirst·y
 ·i·er ·i·est
thir·teenth
thir·ti·eth
thir·ty
 ·ties
thong
tho·rac·ic
tho·rax
 ·rax·es *or* ·ra·ces
tho·ri·um
thorn·y
 ·i·er ·i·est
thor·ough
thor·ough·bred
thor·ough·fare
thor·ough·go·ing
though
thought
thought·ful·ly
thought·ful·ness
thought·less
thou·sand·fold
thrash
thread·bare
threat·en
three-deck·er
three-di·men·sion·al
three·fold
three-ply
three-quar·ter
three·score
three·some
three-way
thren·o·dy
 ·dies
thresh·er
thresh·old
threw
 (*pt. of* throw;
 SEE through)
thrift·y
 ·i·er ·i·est
thrill·er
thrive
 thrived *or* throve,
 thrived *or*
 thriv·en,
 thriv·ing
throat·y
 ·i·er ·i·est
throb
 throbbed
 throb·bing
throm·bo·sis
throne
 throned
 thron·ing
throng
throt·tle
 ·tled
 ·tling
through
 (*from end to end*
 of; SEE threw)
through·out
throw
 threw thrown
 throw·ing
throw·a·way
throw·back
thrust
 thrust
 thrust·ing
thud
 thud·ded
 thud·ding
thumb·nail
thumb·tack
thump
thun·der·cloud
thun·der·head
thun·der·ous
thun·der·storm
thun·der·struck
Thurs·day
thus
thwart
thy·mus
thy·roid
tib·i·a
tick·er tape
tick·et
tick·ing
tick·le
 ·led ·ling
tick·ler
tick·lish
tid·al
tide·land
tide·mark
tide·wa·ter
ti·di·ly
ti·di·ness
ti·dings
ti·dy
 ·di·er ·di·est
 ·died ·dy·ing
tie
 tied ty·ing
tie·back
tie-in
tie tack
tie-up
tight·en
tight·fist·ed
tight·fit·ting
tight-lipped
tile
 tiled til·ing
till·a·ble
tilt-top
tim·bale
tim·ber
 (*wood*)
tim·ber·line
tim·bre
 (*quality of sound*)
time
 timed tim·ing
time·card
time clock
time-con·sum·ing
time-hon·ored
time·keep·er
time·less
time·li·ness
time·ly
 ·li·er ·li·est
time·out
time·piece
tim·er
time·sav·ing
time·ta·ble
time-test·ed
time·worn
time zone
ti·mid·i·ty
tim·id·ly
tim·or·ous
tinc·ture
 ·tured ·tur·ing
tin·der·box
tin·foil
tinge
 tinged, tinge·ing
 or ting·ing
tin·gle
 ·gled ·gling
ti·ni·ness
tin·ker
tin·ker·er
tin·ni·ness
tin·ny
 ·ni·er ·ni·est
tin-plate
 ·plat·ed ·plat·ing
tin·sel
 ·seled *or* ·selled
 ·sel·ing *or*
 ·sel·ling
tin·smith
tin·tin·nab·u·la·tion
tin·type
tin·ware
tip-off
tip·pet
tip·ple
 ·pled ·pling
tip·top
ti·rade
tire
 tired tir·ing
tired·ly
tire·less
tire·some
tis·sue
ti·tan

tithe
 tithed tith·ing
ti·tian
tit·il·late
 ·lat·ed ·lat·ing
tit·il·la·tion
ti·tle
 ·tled ·tling
ti·tle·hold·er
tit·u·lar
toad·y·ism
toast·mas·ter
to·bac·co
 ·cos
to·bac·co·nist
toc·sin
 (*alarm;* SEE toxin)
to·day
tod·dy
 ·dies
to-do
toe·hold
toe-in
tof·fee *or* ·fy
to·ga
 ·gas *or* ·gae
to·geth·er
tog·gle
 ·gled ·gling
toi·let
toi·let·ry
 ·ries
toil·some
toil·worn
to·ken
to·ken·ism
tole
tol·er·a·ble
tol·er·a·bly
tol·er·ance
tol·er·ant
tol·er·ate
 ·at·ed ·at·ing
tol·er·a·tion
tol·er·a·tor
toll·booth
toll bridge
toll call
toll·gate
toll·keep·er
toll road
tomb·stone
to·mor·row
ton
ton·al
to·nal·i·ty
 ·ties
tone
 toned ton·ing
tone-deaf
tongs
tongue
 tongued
 tongu·ing
ton·ic
to·night
ton·nage
ton·neau
 ·neaus *or*
 ·neaux
ton·so·ri·al
ton·sure
 ·sured ·sur·ing
ton·tine
tool·mak·er
tooth·ache
tooth·brush
tooth·paste
tooth·pick
top·coat
top-drawer
top-dress·ing
top-flight
top-heavy
to·pi·ar·y
top·ic
top·i·cal
top-lev·el
top·most
top-notch
to·pog·ra·pher
top·o·graph·i·cal
to·pog·ra·phy
 (*surface features;*
 SEE typography)
top·ple
 ·pled ·pling
top·sail
top-se·cret
top·soil
toque
torch·bear·er
tor·ment
tor·men·tor
tor·na·do
 ·does *or* ·dos
tor·pe·do
 ·does
tor·pid
tor·pid·i·ty
tor·por
torque
tor·rent
tor·ren·tial
tor·rid
tor·rid·i·ty
tor·sion
tor·so
 ·sos *or* ·si
tort
 (*wrongful act*)
torte
 (*cake*)
tor·tu·ous
 (*winding*)
tor·ture
 ·tured ·tur·ing
tor·tur·ous
 (*agonizing*)
toss·up
to·tal
 ·taled *or* ·talled
 ·tal·ing *or* ·tal·ling
to·tal·i·tar·i·an
to·tal·i·ty
to·tal·i·za·tor
to·tal·ly
tote
 tot·ed tot·ing
touch·back
touch·down
tou·ché
touch·stone
touch-type
touch-typ·ist
touch·y
 ·i·er ·i·est
tough·en
tough-mind·ed
tour de force
 tours de force
tour·ism
tour·ist
tour·ma·line
tour·na·ment
tour·ney
 ·neys
tour·ni·quet
tow·age
to·ward
tow·er·ing
tow·head
tow·line
town·ship
towns·peo·ple
tow·path
tow·rope
tox·e·mi·a
tox·ic
tox·i·cant
tox·i·col·o·gy
tox·in
 (*poison;* SEE tocsin)
trace
 traced trac·ing
trace·a·ble
trac·er
trac·er·y
 ·ies
tra·che·a
 ·ae *or* ·as
track (*trace*)
tract
 (*land; leaflet*)
trac·ta·ble
trac·tile
trac·tion
trac·tor
trad·a·ble *or*
 trade·a·ble
trade
 trad·ed trad·ing
trade-in
trade-last
trade·mark
trade name
trades·man
trades·peo·ple
trade wind
tra·di·ti·o
tra·di·tion

tra·di·tion·al
tra·duce
·duced ·duc·ing
traf·fic
·ficked ·fick·ing
traf·fick·er
trag·e·dy
·dies
trag·ic
trag·i·cal·ly
trail·er
train·ee
trait
trai·tor
trai·tor·ous
tra·jec·to·ry
·ries
tram·mel
·meled *or* ·melled
·mel·ing *or*
·mel·ling
tram·ple
·pled ·pling
tram·po·line
trance
tranced
tranc·ing
tran·quil
·quil·er *or*
·quil·ler
·quil·est *or*
·quil·lest
tran·quil·ize
or ·quil·lize
·ized *or* ·lized
·iz·ing *or* ·liz·ing
tran·quil·iz·er *or*
·quil·liz·er
tran·quil·li·ty *or*
·quil·i·ty
tran·quil·ly
trans·act
trans·ac·tion
trans·ac·tor
trans·at·lan·tic
trans·ceiv·er
tran·scend
tran·scend·ent
tran·scen·den·tal
trans·con·ti·nen·tal
tran·scribe
·scribed ·scrib·ing
tran·script
tran·scrip·tion
tran·sept
trans·fer
·ferred
·fer·ring
trans·fer·a·ble
or ·fer·ra·ble
trans·fer·al
or ·fer·ral
trans·fer·ee
trans·fer·ence
trans·fer·rer
trans·fig·u·ra·tion
trans·fig·ure
trans·fix
trans·form
trans·for·ma·tion
trans·form·er
trans·fuse
trans·fus·i·ble
trans·fu·sion
trans·gress
trans·gres·sion
trans·gres·sor
tran·sient
tran·sis·tor
tran·sis·tor·ize
·ized ·iz·ing
trans·it
tran·si·tion
tran·si·tion·al·ly
tran·si·tive
tran·si·to·ry
trans·lat·a·ble
trans·late
·lat·ed ·lat·ing
trans·la·tion
trans·la·tor
trans·lit·er·ate
·at·ed ·at·ing
trans·lit·er·a·tion
trans·lu·cence
trans·lu·cent
trans·mi·grate
·grat·ed ·grat·ing
trans·mi·gra·tion
trans·mis·si·ble
trans·mis·sion
trans·mit
·mit·ted
·mit·ting
trans·mit·tal
trans·mit·tance
trans·mit·ter
trans·mut·a·ble
trans·mu·ta·tion
trans·mute
·mut·ed
·mut·ing
trans·o·ce·an·ic
trans·pa·cif·ic
trans·par·en·cy
·cies
trans·par·ent
tran·spire
·spired ·spir·ing
trans·plant
tran·spon·der
trans·port
trans·por·ta·tion
trans·pos·a·ble
trans·pose
·posed ·pos·ing
trans·po·si·tion
trans·ship
·shipped
·ship·ping
tran·sub·stan·ti·ate
trans·val·ue
trans·ver·sal
trans·verse
trans·verse·ly
trap·door
trap·per
trap·pings
trap·shoot·ing
trau·ma
·mas *or* ·ma·ta
trau·mat·ic
trau·mat·i·cal·ly
trav·ail
(*hard work*)
trav·el
·eled *or* ·elled
·el·ing *or* ·el·ling
(*journey*)
trav·el·er *or*
·el·ler
trav·e·logue *or*
·log
trav·ers·a·ble
trav·ers·al
trav·erse
·ersed ·ers·ing
trav·es·ty
·ties
·tied ·ty·ing
trawl·er
treach·er·ous
treach·er·y
·ies
trea·cle
tread
trod, trod·den *or*
trod, tread·ing
trea·dle
·dled ·dling
tread·mill
trea·son
trea·son·ous
treas·ure
·ured ·ur·ing
treas·ur·er
treas·ur·y
·ies
treat·a·ble
trea·tise
treat·ment
trea·ty
·ties
tre·ble
·bled ·bling
tree·top
tre·foil
trek
trekked
trek·king
trel·lis
trem·ble
·bled ·bling
tre·men·dous
trem·or
trem·u·lous
trench·ant
trend
tre·men·dous
trep·i·da·tion
tres·pass
tres·tle

tri·a·ble
tri·ad
tri·al
tri·an·gle
tri·an·gu·lar
trib·al
trib·al·ism
tribes·man
trib·u·la·tion
tri·bu·nal
trib·une
trib·u·tar·y
·ies
trib·ute
tri·cen·ten·ni·al
tri·ceps
·cep·ses *or* ·ceps
tri·chot·o·my
tri·chro·mat·ic
trick·er·y
trick·le
·led ·ling
trick·ster
trick·y
·i·er ·i·est
tri·col·or
tri·cot
tri·di·men·sion·al
tri·en·ni·al
tri·en·ni·um
·ums *or* ·a
tri·er
tri·fle
·fled ·fling
tri·fo·cal
trig·o·no·met·ric
trig·o·nom·e·try
tri·lat·er·al
tri·lin·gual
tril·lion
tril·li·um
tril·o·gy
·gies
tri·mes·ter
tri·month·ly
trin·i·ty
·ties
trin·ket
tri·no·mi·al

tri·o
·os
tri·par·tite
trip·ham·mer
tri·ple
·pled ·pling
tri·ple-space
tri·plet
trip·li·cate
·cat·ed ·cat·ing
tri·ply
tri·pod
trip·tych
tri·sect
trite
trit·er trit·est
trite·ly
trit·u·rate
·rat·ed ·rat·ing
tri·umph
tri·um·phal
tri·um·phant
tri·um·vi·rate
triv·et
triv·i·a
triv·i·al
triv·i·al·i·ty
·ties
triv·i·al·ly
tri·week·ly
·lies
trod·den
trof·fer
trog·lo·dyte
troop
(*of soldiers;* SEE troupe)
troop·ship
tro·phy
·phies
trop·ic
trop·i·cal
tro·pism
trop·o·sphere
trou·ble
·bled ·bling
trou·ble·mak·er
trou·ble-shoot·er
trou·ble·some
trough

trounce
trounced
trounc·ing
troupe
trouped
troup·ing
(*of actors;* SEE troop)
troup·er
trou·sers
trous·seau
·seaux *or* ·seaus
trout
trow·el
·eled *or* ·elled
·el·ing *or* ·el·ling
tru·an·cy
·cies
tru·ant
truce
truc·u·lence
truc·u·lent
trudge
trudged
trudg·ing
true blue
true-life
tru·ism
tru·ly
trump
trumped-up
trump·er·y
·ies
trun·cate
·cat·ed
·cat·ing
trun·ca·tion
trun·cheon
trun·dle
·dled ·dling
trunk line
trus·tee
·teed
·tee·ing
(*manager;* SEE trusty)
trus·tee·ship
trust·ful
trust·ful·ly
trust·i·ness
trust·wor·thy

trust·y
·ies, ·i·er ·i·est
(*relied upon;* SEE trustee)
truth·ful
truth·ful·ly
truth·ful·ness
try
tries
tried try·ing
try·out
tube
tubed tub·ing
tu·ber
tu·ber·cle
tu·ber·cu·lar
tu·ber·cu·lo·sis
tu·ber·cu·lous
tu·ber·ous
tu·bu·lar
tuck·er
Tues·day
tuft·ed
tug·boat
tu·i·tion
tulle
tum·ble
·bled ·bling
tum·bler
tum·brel
tu·mes·cence
tu·mes·cent
tu·mor
tu·mor·ous
tu·mult
tu·mul·tu·ous
tun·a·ble
or tune·
tun·dra
tune
tuned
tun·ing
tune·ful
tune·less
tun·er
tune·up *or*
tune-up
tung·sten
tu·nic

tun·nel
·neled *or* ·nelled
·nel·ing *or*
·nel·ling
tur·bid
tur·bine
tur·bo·jet
tur·bo·prop
tur·bu·lence
tur·bu·lent
tu·reen
tur·gid
tur·mer·ic
tur·moil
turn·a·bout
turn·a·round
turn·down
turn·key
·keys
turn·off
turn·out
turn·o·ver
turn·pike
turn·stile
turn·ta·ble
tur·pen·tine
tur·pi·tude
tur·quoise
tur·ret
tur·tle·neck
tus·sle
·sled
·sling
tu·te·lage
tu·te·lar·y
tu·tor
tu·to·ri·al
tux·e·do
·dos
twang
tweak
tweed
tweed·y
·i·er ·i·est
tweeze
tweezed
tweez·ing
twelfth
twen·ti·eth

twen·ty
·ties
twice-told
twi·light
twill
twine
twined twin·ing
twin-en·gined
twinge
twinged
twing·ing
twirl·er
twist·er
twitch
two-by-four
two-edged
two-faced
two·fold
two-hand·ed
two-piece
two-ply
two-sid·ed
two·some
two-way
ty·coon
tym·pan·ic
typ·a·ble *or* type·
typ·al
type
typed typ·ing
type·bar
type·cast
·cast ·cast·ing
(*in acting*)
type-cast
-cast -cast·ing
(*in printing*)
type·script
type·set
·set ·set·ting
type·set·ter
type·write
·wrote ·writ·ten
·writ·ing
type·writ·er
ty·phoid
ty·phoon
ty·phus
typ·i·cal
typ·i·cal·ly

typ·i·fy
·fied ·fy·ing
typ·ist
ty·pog·ra·pher
ty·po·graph·i·cal
ty·pog·ra·phy
(*setting of type;*
SEE topography)
ty·pol·o·gy
ty·ran·ni·cal
tyr·an·nize
·nized ·niz·ing
tyr·an·nous
tyr·an·ny
·nies
ty·rant

U

u·biq·ui·tous
u·biq·ui·ty
ul·cer
ul·cer·ate
·at·ed ·at·ing
ul·cer·ous
ul·te·ri·or
ul·ti·mate
ul·ti·mate·ly
ul·ti·ma·tum
·tums *or* ·ta
ul·tra
ul·tra·con·serv·a·tive
ul·tra·ma·rine
ul·tra·mi·cro·scope
ul·tra·mod·ern
ul·tra·na·tion·al·ism
ul·tra·son·ic
ul·tra·sound
ul·tra·vi·o·let
um·ber
um·brage
um·pire
·pired ·pir·ing
un·a·bridged
un·ac·count·a·ble
un·ac·count·ed-for
un·ac·cus·tomed
un·af·fect·ed

un-A·mer·i·can
u·na·nim·i·ty
u·nan·i·mous
un·apt
un·armed
un·as·sum·ing
un·at·tached
un·au·thor·ized
un·a·void·a·ble
un·a·ware
un·a·wares
un·bal·anced
un·bear·a·ble
un·beat·a·ble
un·be·com·ing
un·be·known
un·be·lief
un·be·liev·a·ble
un·be·liev·er
un·bend
·bent *or*
·bend·ed
·bend·ing
un·bi·ased *or*
·assed
un·bound·ed
un·bri·dled
un·bro·ken
un·called-for
un·can·ni·ly
un·can·ni·ness
un·can·ny
un·cer·e·mo·ni·ous
un·cer·tain
un·cer·tain·ty
·ties
un·char·i·ta·ble
un·chris·tian
un·civ·il
un·civ·i·lized
un·clad
un·claimed
un·class·i·fied
un·col·lect·ed
un·com·fort·a·ble
un·com·pro·mis·ing
un·con·cerned
un·con·di·tion·al
un·con·scion·a·ble

un·con·scious
un·con·sti·tu·tion·al
un·de·cid·ed
un·de·ni·a·ble
un·der·buy
·bought
·buy·ing
un·der·car·riage
un·der·class·man
un·der·cov·er
un·der·cur·rent
un·der·cut
un·der·de·vel·oped
un·der·do
·did ·done
·do·ing
un·der·em·ployed
un·der·es·ti·mate
un·der·fired
un·der·glaze
un·der·go
·went ·gone
·go·ing
un·der·grad·u·ate
un·der·ground
un·der·growth
un·der·hand
un·der·hand·ed
un·der·lay
·laid ·lay·ing
un·der·lease
un·der·les·see
un·der·let
un·der·lie
·lay ·lain
·ly·ing
un·der·line
un·der·ling
un·der·lin·ing
un·der·mine
un·der·neath
un·der·nour·ish
un·der·pass
un·der·pay
·paid
·pay·ing
un·der·pin·ning
un·der·play
un·der·priv·i·leged
un·der·proof
un·der·rate
un·der·score
un·der·sec·re·tar·y
·ies
un·der·sell
·sold ·sell·ing
un·der·shot
un·der·side
un·der·signed
un·der·sized
un·der·staffed
un·der·stand
·stood ·stand·ing
un·der·stand·a·ble
un·der·stand·a·bly
un·der·state·ment
un·der·stud·y
·ies, ·ied ·y·ing
un·der·take
·took ·tak·en
·tak·ing
un·der·tak·ing
un·der·tone
un·der·val·ue
un·der·weight
un·der·write
·wrote ·writ·ten
·writ·ing
un·dis·closed
un·dis·trib·ut·ed
un·di·vid·ed
un·do
·did ·done
·do·ing
un·doubt·ed·ly
un·due
un·du·lant
un·du·late
·lat·ed ·lat·ing
un·du·ly
un·dy·ing
un·earned
un·earth
un·eas·i·ness
un·eas·y
un·em·ploy·a·ble
un·em·ploy·ment
un·en·cum·bered
un·en·force·a·ble
un·e·qualed
or ·qualled
un·e·quiv·o·cal·ly
un·err·ing
un·es·sen·tial
un·e·ven·ness
un·e·vent·ful·ly
un·ex·cep·tion·a·ble
un·ex·cep·tion·al
un·ex·pect·ed
un·fair
un·faith·ful
un·fa·mil·iar
un·feel·ing
un·for·get·ta·ble
un·for·tu·nate
un·found·ed
un·hand
un·heard-of
un·hoped-for
u·ni·fi·a·ble
u·ni·fi·ca·tion
u·ni·fi·er
u·ni·form
u·ni·form·i·ty
u·ni·fy
·fied ·fy·ing
u·ni·lat·er·al
un·im·peach·a·ble
un·in·hib·it·ed
un·in·tel·li·gi·ble
un·in·ter·est·ed
un·ion
un·ion·ize
·ized ·iz·ing
u·nique
u·ni·son
un·is·sued
u·nit
u·nite
·nit·ed ·nit·ing
u·ni·ty
·ties
u·ni·ver·sal
u·ni·ver·sal·i·ty
uni·ver·sal·ly
u·ni·verse
u·ni·ver·si·ty
·ties
un·known
un·law·ful
un·let·tered
un·like·li·hood
un·like·ly
un·lim·it·ed
un·list·ed
un·looked-for
un·man·age·a·ble
un·men·tion·a·ble
un·mer·ci·ful
un·mis·tak·a·ble
un·mit·i·gat·ed
un·nat·u·ral
un·nec·es·sar·i·ly
un·nec·es·sar·y
un·nerve
·nerved
·nerv·ing
un·num·bered
un·oc·cu·pied
un·or·gan·ized
un·paid
un·paid-for
un·par·al·leled
un·pleas·ant
un·prec·e·dent·ed
un·prej·u·diced
un·prin·ci·pled
un·prof·it·a·ble
un·qual·i·fied
un·ques·tion·a·bly
un·re·al·is·tic
un·re·al·ized
un·rea·son·a·ble
un·re·cov·ered
un·re·gen·er·ate
un·rest
un·rul·i·ness
un·rul·y
·i·er
·i·est
un·said
un·sa·vor·i·ness
un·sa·vor·y
un·scathed
un·scru·pu·lous
un·seat
un·se·cured

un·seem·ly
un·sight·li·ness
un·sight·ly
un·speak·a·ble
un·stead·y
un·tan·gle
·gled ·gling
un·ten·a·ble
un·think·a·ble
un·thought-of
un·tie
·tied ·ty·ing *or* ·tie·ing
un·til
un·time·ly
un·told
un·touch·a·ble
un·to·ward
un·truth·ful
un·tu·tored
un·u·su·al
un·veil·ing
un·want·ed
(*not wanted;* SEE unwonted)
un·war·y
un·whole·some
un·wield·i·ness
un·wield·y
un·wit·ting·ly
un·wont·ed
(*not usual;* SEE unwanted)
un·wor·thy
un·writ·ten
up-and-com·ing
up-and-down
up·beat
up·bring·ing
up·date
up·end
up·grade
up·heav·al
up·hold
·held ·hold·ing
up·keep
up·on
up·per-case
-cased -cas·ing
up·per·class·man
up·per·most
up·right
up·ris·ing
up·roar
up·roar·i·ous
up·root
up·set
·set ·set·ting
up·shot
up·stand·ing
up·start
up·state
up·swing
up·take
up-tight *or* up·tight
up-to-date
up·town
up·turn
up·ward
u·ra·ni·um
ur·ban
(*of the city*)
ur·bane
(*socially poised*)
ur·ban·i·ty
·ties
ur·ban·i·za·tion
ur·ban·ize
·ized ·iz·ing
urge
urged urg·ing
ur·gen·cy
·cies
ur·gent
u·ro·log·i·cal
u·rol·o·gy
u·ros·co·py
us·a·ble *or* use·
us·age
us·ance
us·er
ush·er
u·su·al
u·su·al·ly
u·su·fruct
u·su·fruc·tu·ar·y
u·su·rer
u·su·ri·ous
u·surp
u·sur·pa·tion
u·su·ry
·ries
U·tah
u·til·i·tar·i·an
u·til·i·ty
·ties
u·ti·liz·a·ble
u·ti·li·za·tion
u·ti·lize
·lized ·liz·ing
ut·most
ut·ter·ance
U-turn
ux·o·ri·ous

V

va·can·cy
·cies
va·cant
va·cate
·cat·ed ·cat·ing
va·ca·tion
vac·ci·nate
·nat·ed ·nat·ing
vac·ci·na·tion
vac·cine
vac·il·late
·lat·ed ·lat·ing
vac·il·la·tion
vac·il·la·tor
va·cu·i·ty
·ties
vac·u·ous
vac·u·um
·ums *or* ·a
va·gar·y
·ies
va·gran·cy
·cies
va·grant
vague
vague·ly
vain
(*futile; conceited;* SEE vane, vein)
vain·glo·ri·ous
vain·glo·ry
val·ance
(*drapery;* SEE valence)
val·e·dic·tion
val·e·dic·to·ri·an
val·e·dic·to·ry
·ries
va·lence
(*term in chemistry;* SEE valance)
val·et
val·iant
val·id
val·i·date
·dat·ed ·dat·ing
val·i·da·tion
va·lid·i·ty
va·lise
val·or
val·or·i·za·tion
val·u·a·ble
val·u·a·tion
val·ue
·ued ·u·ing
val·ue·less
valve
val·vu·lar
van·dal
van·dal·ism
van·dal·ize
·ized ·iz·ing
vane
(*blade;* SEE vain, vein)
van·guard
van·ish
van·i·ty
·ties
van·quish
van·tage
vap·id
va·por
va·por·i·za·tion
va·por·ize
·ized ·iz·ing
va·por·iz·er
va·por·ous
var·i·a·ble
var·i·a·bly
var·i·ance

var·i·ant
var·i·a·tion
var·i·col·ored
var·ied
var·i·e·gate
 ·gat·ed
 ·gat·ing
var·i·e·ga·tion
va·ri·e·tal
va·ri·e·ty
 ·ties
var·i·o·rum
var·i·ous
var·si·ty
 ·ties
var·y
 ·ied ·y·ing
 (*change;* SEE very)
vas·cu·lar
vas·sal
vast·ness
vat-dyed
vault
vault·ing
vaunt
vec·tor
vec·to·ri·al
veer
ve·he·mence
ve·he·ment
ve·hi·cle
ve·hic·u·lar
veil
vein
 (*blood vessel; streak;* SEE vain, vane)
vel·lum
ve·loc·i·pede
ve·loc·i·ty
 ·ties
ve·lour *or*
 ·lours
ve·lure
vel·vet
ve·nal
 (*corrupt;* SEE venial)
ve·nal·i·ty
 ·ties
vend·ee
ven·det·ta
ven·dor *or*
 vend·er
ve·neer
ven·er·a·ble
ven·er·ate
 ·at·ed ·at·ing
ven·er·a·tion
venge·ance
venge·ful
ve·ni·al
 (*pardonable;* SEE venal)
ven·i·son
ven·om·ous
ve·nous
ven·ti·late
 ·lat·ed ·lat·ing
ven·ti·la·tion
ven·ti·la·tor
ven·tri·cle
ven·ture
 ·tured ·tur·ing
ven·ture·some
ven·tur·ous
ven·ue
ve·ra·cious
 (*truthful;* SEE voracious)
ve·rac·i·ty
ver·bal
ver·bal·i·za·tion
ver·bal·ize
 ·ized ·iz·ing
ver·bal·ly
ver·ba·tim
ver·be·na
ver·bi·age
ver·bose
ver·bos·i·ty
ver·dant
ver·dict
ver·di·gris
ver·dure
verge
 verged verg·ing
ver·i·fi·a·ble
ver·i·fi·ca·tion
ver·i·fy
 ·fied ·fy·ing
ver·i·ly
ver·i·si·mil·i·tude
ver·i·ta·ble
ver·i·ta·bly
ver·i·ty
 ·ties
ver·mi·cel·li
ver·mi·cide
ver·mic·u·lar
ver·mic·u·lite
ver·mi·form
ver·mi·fuge
ver·mil·ion
Ver·mont
ver·mouth
ver·nac·u·lar
ver·nal
ver·ni·er
ver·sa·tile
ver·sa·tile·ly
ver·sa·til·i·ty
versed
ver·si·fi·ca·tion
ver·si·fy
 ·fied ·fy·ing
ver·sion
ver·sus
ver·tex
 ·tex·es *or* ·ti·ces
ver·ti·cal
ver·tig·i·nous
ver·ti·go
verve
ver·y
 ·i·er ·i·est
 (*complete; exceedingly;* SEE vary)
ves·i·cant
ves·i·cate
 ·cat·ed ·cat·ing
ves·i·cle
ves·per
vest·ed
ves·ti·bule
ves·tige
ves·tig·i·al
vest·ment
vest pock·et
vet·er·an
ve·to
 ·toes
 ·toed
 ·to·ing
vex·a·tion
vex·a·tious
vi·a
vi·a·bil·i·ty
vi·a·ble
vi·a·duct
vi·al
 (*bottle;* SEE vile)
vi·and
vi·brant
vi·brate
 ·brat·ed
 ·brat·ing
vi·bra·tion
vi·bra·to
 ·tos
vic·ar
vic·ar·age
vi·car·i·al
vi·car·i·ous
vice
 (*evil conduct; flaw;* SEE vise)
vice-chair·man
vice-chan·cel·lor
vice-con·sul
vice-pres·i·dent
vice·roy
vi·ce ver·sa
vi·chy·ssoise
vi·cin·i·ty
 ·ties
vi·cious
vi·cis·si·tude
vic·tim
vic·tim·ize
 ·ized ·iz·ing
vic·tor
vic·to·ri·a
vic·to·ri·ous
vic·to·ry
 ·ries
vi·cu·ña
vid·e·o
vid·i·con

vie
 vied
 vy·ing
view·point
vig·il
vig·i·lance
vig·i·lant
vig·i·lan·te
vi·gnette
vig·or
vig·or·ous
vile
 (*evil; offensive;* SEE vial)
vile·ly
vil·i·fi·ca·tion
vil·i·fy
 ·fied ·fy·ing
vil·lain
 (*scoundrel;* SEE villein)
vil·lain·ous
vil·lain·y
 ·ies
vil·lein
 (*serf;* SEE villain)
vin·ai·grette
vin·ci·ble
vin·di·cate
 ·cat·ed ·cat·ing
vin·di·ca·tion
vin·di·ca·tive
vin·di·ca·tor
vin·dic·tive
vine·yard
vin·i·cul·ture
vi·nous
vin·tage
vint·ner
vi·nyl
vi·o·la·ble
vi·o·late
 ·lat·ed ·lat·ing
vi·o·la·tion
vi·o·la·tor
vi·o·lence
vi·o·lent
vi·ra·go
 ·goes *or* ·gos
vi·ral
Vir·gin·ia
vir·gule
vi·rol·o·gy
vir·tu
vir·tu·al
vir·tu·al·ly
vir·tue
vir·tu·os·i·ty
vir·tu·o·so
 ·sos *or* ·si
vir·tu·ous
vir·u·lence
vir·u·lent
vi·rus
vi·sa
vis·age
vis-à-vis
vis·cer·a
vis·cid
vis·cos·i·ty
vis·cous
vise
 vised vis·ing
 (*clamp;* SEE vice)
vis·i·bil·i·ty
vis·i·ble
vis·i·bly
vi·sion
vi·sion·ar·y
 ·ies
vis·it·ant
vis·it·a·tion
vis·i·tor
vi·sor
vis·ta
vis·u·al
vis·u·al·ize
 ·ized ·iz·ing
vi·ta
 ·tae
vi·tal
vi·tal·i·ty
 ·ties
vi·tal·ize
 ·ized ·iz·ing
vi·ta·min
vi·ti·a·ble
vi·ti·ate
 ·at·ed ·at·ing
vi·ti·a·tion
vi·ti·a·tor
vit·re·ous
vit·ri·fy
 ·fied
 ·fy·ing
vit·ri·ol
vit·ri·ol·ic
vi·tu·per·ate
 ·at·ed ·at·ing
vi·tu·per·a·tion
vi·va·cious
vi·vac·i·ty
vi·va vo·ce
viv·id
viv·i·fy
 ·fied ·fy·ing
viv·i·sect
viv·i·sec·tion
vix·en
vo·cab·u·lar·y
 ·ies
vo·cal·ist
vo·cal·ize
 ·ized ·iz·ing
vo·ca·tion
vo·cif·er·ate
 ·at·ed ·at·ing
vo·cif·er·ous
vo·cod·er
vod·ka
vogue
voice·less
voice·print
void·a·ble
vol·a·tile
vol·a·til·i·ty
vol·can·ic
vol·ca·no
 ·noes *or* ·nos
vol·i·tant
vo·li·tion
vol·ley
 ·leys
 ·leyed
 ·ley·ing
volt·age
vol·ta·ic
vol·tam·e·ter
volt·me·ter
vol·u·bil·i·ty
vol·u·ble
vol·u·bly
vol·ume
vo·lu·mi·nous
vol·un·tar·i·ly
vol·un·tar·y
vol·un·teer
vo·lute
vo·lu·tion
vo·ra·cious
 (*greedy;* SEE veracious)
vo·rac·i·ty
vor·tex
 ·tex·es *or* ·ti·ces
vos·tro
vot·a·ble *or* vote·
vo·ta·ry
 ·ries
vo·tive
vouch·er
vouch·safe
 ·safed ·saf·ing
vow·el
vox po·pu·li
voy·age
 ·aged ·ag·ing
voy·ag·er
vo·yeur
vul·can·i·za·tion
vul·can·ize
 ·ized ·iz·ing
vul·gar
vul·gar·i·an
vul·gar·ism
vul·gar·i·ty
 ·ties
vul·gar·ize
 ·ized ·iz·ing
vul·ner·a·bil·i·ty
vul·ner·a·ble
vul·ner·a·bly
vul·ture
vul·tur·ous
vy·ing

W

wade
wad·ed
wad·ing
wa·fer
waft
wag
wagged
wag·ging
wage
waged wag·ing
wa·ger
wag·ger·y
·ies
wail
(*cry;* SEE wale)
wain·scot
·scot·ed *or*
·scot·ted
·scot·ing *or*
·scot·ting
wain·wright
waist·band
waist·coat
waist-high
waist·line
wait·er
waive
waived waiv·ing
(*give up;* SEE wave)
waiv·er
(*a relinquishing;* SEE waver)
wake
woke *or* waked,
waked *or* wok·en,
wak·ing
wake·ful
wak·en
wale
waled wal·ing
(*ridge;* SEE wail)
walk·a·way
walk·ie-talk·ie
walk-in
walk-on
walk·out
walk-through
walk-up
walk·way
wall board
wal·let
wall·eyed
wal·low
wall-to-wall
wan
wan·ner
wan·nest
wan·der
(*stray;* SEE wonder)
wan·der·lust
wane
waned
wan·ing
wan·gle
·gled ·gling
want·ing
wan·ton
war
warred
war·ring
ward
war·den
ward·robe
ward·room
ware·house
·housed
·hous·ing
war·fare
war·head
war·i·ly
war·i·ness
war·like
warm·blood·ed
warmed-o·ver
warm·heart·ed
war·mon·ger
warmth
warm-up
warn·ing
warp
warped
war·plane
war·rant
war·ran·tee
war·ran·tor
war·ran·ty
·ties
war·ren
war·ri·or
war·time
war·y
·i·er ·i·est
wash·a·ble
wash-and-wear
washed-out
washed-up
wash·er
Wash·ing·ton
wash·out
wash·room
was·n't
wasp·ish
was·sail
wast·age
waste
wast·ed
wast·ing
waste·bas·ket
waste·ful
waste·land
waste·pa·per
wast·rel
watch·band
watch·case
watch·ful
watch·man
watch·tow·er
watch·word
wa·ter·col·or
wa·ter-cooled
water cooler
wa·ter·course
wa·ter·cy·cle
wa·tered
wa·ter·fall
wa·ter·front
water hole
wa·ter·less
wa·ter·line
wa·ter·logged
wa·ter·mark
water pipe
water power
wa·ter·proof
wa·ter-re·pel·lent
wa·ter-re·sist·ant
wa·ter·shed
wa·ter·side
wa·ter-soak
wa·ter-sol·u·ble
wa·ter·spout
wa·ter·tight
water tower
wa·ter·way
water wheel
water wings
wa·ter·works
wa·ter·worn
wa·ter·y
watt·age
watt-hour
wave
waved wav·ing
(*curving motion;* SEE waive)
wave·length
wav'er
(*one that waves;* SEE waiver)
wa'ver
(*falter;* SEE waiver)
wax
wax·en
wax·i·ness
wax·work
wax·y
·i·er ·i·est
way
(*route; manner;* SEE weigh, whey)
way·bill
way·far·er
way·far·ing
way·lay
·laid
·lay·ing
way·side
way·ward
weak·en
weak·ling
weak·ly
·li·er ·li·est
weak-mind·ed

weak·ness
weal (*ridge; welfare;* SEE wheel)
wealth·i·ness
wealth·y
·i·er ·i·est
weap·on
wear
wore worn
wear·ing
wear·a·ble
wea·ri·ly
wea·ri·ness
wea·ri·some
wea·ry
·ri·er ·ri·est
·ried ·ry·ing
weath·er
(*atmospheric conditions;* SEE whether)
weath·er-beat·en
weath·er-bound
weath·er·man
weath·er·proof
weath·er·strip
·stripped
·strip·ping
weather vane
weave
wove, wov·en *or* wove, weav·ing
(*interlace*)
weave
weaved
weav·ing
(*move in and out as in traffic*)
weav·er
wedge
wedged
wedg·ing
Wednes·day
week·day
week·end *or* week-end
week·ly
·lies
wee·vil
weigh
weighed
weigh·ing
(*measure weight of;* SEE way, whey)

weight·i·ness
weight·less
weight·y
·i·er ·i·est
weird
wel·come
·comed ·com·ing
weld·er
wel·fare
well-ad·vised
well-ap·point·ed
well-bal·anced
well-be·haved
well-be·ing
well·born
well-bred
well-chos·en
well-con·tent
well-dis·posed
well·do·ing
well-done
well-fa·vored
well-fed
well-found·ed
well-groomed
well-ground·ed
well-han·dled
well·head
well-in·formed
well-in·ten·tioned
well-known
well-made
well-man·nered
well-mean·ing
well-meant
well-off
well-or·dered
well-pre·served
well-read
well-round·ed
well-spo·ken
well·spring
well-thought-of
well-timed
well-to-do
well-turned
well-wish·er
well-worn

we'll
welt·er
welt·er·weight
wes·kit
west·er·ly
·lies
west·ern·er
west·ern·ize
·ized ·iz·ing
west-north·west
west-south·west
West Vir·gin·ia
west·ward
wet·back
wet·ta·ble
wharf
wharves *or* wharfs
wharf·age
wharf·in·ger
what·ev·er
what·not
what·so·ev·er
wheat
whee·dle
·dled
·dling
wheel
(*disk for turning;* SEE weal)
wheel·bar·row
wheel·base
wheel·chair
wheel·house
wheel·wright
when
whence
when·ev·er
where
where·a·bouts
where·as
where·by
where·fore
where·in
where·of
where·up·on
wher·ev·er
where·with
where·with·al

whet
whet·ted
whet·ting
wheth·er
(*if;* SEE weather)
whet·stone
whey
(*thin part of milk;* SEE way, weigh)
which·ev·er
whiff
while
whiled whil·ing
(*time;* SEE wile)
whim
whim·si·cal
whim·sy
·sies
whine
whined whin·ing
(*cry;* SEE wine)
whin·i·ness
whin·ny
·nies
·nied ·ny·ing
(*neigh*)
whin·y
·i·er ·i·est
(*complaining*)
whip
whipped
whip·ping
whip·cord
whip·lash
whip·saw
whirl
whirl·pool
whirl·wind
whis·key
·keys *or* ·kies
whis·per
whis·tle
·tled ·tling
whis·tler
white
whit·ed whit·ing
white·cap
white-col·lar
white-haired
white-hot
whit·en·er
white·ness

whit·en·ing
white·wash
whith·er
(*where;* SEE wither)
whit·ing
whit·tle
·tled
·tling
whiz *or* whizz
whizzed
whiz·zing
who·ev·er
whole·heart·ed
whole·sale
·saled
·sal·ing
whole·sal·er
whole·some
whol·ly
(*completely;* SEE holey, holy)
whom·ev·er
whom·so·ev·er
who·so·ev·er
why
wick·ed
wick·er·work
wick·et
wide-an·gle
wide-a·wake
wide-eyed
wid·en
wide-o·pen
wide·spread
widg·et
wid·ow
width
wield
wield·y
·i·er ·i·est
wild·cat
·cat·ted ·cat·ting
wil·der·ness
wild-eyed
wild·fire
wild·life
wile
wiled wil·ing
(*trick;* SEE while)
wil·i·ness
will·ful *or* wil·
will·ing·ness
wil·low·y
will·pow·er
wil·y
·i·er ·i·est
win
won win·ning
wind
wound wind·ing
wind·blown
wind-borne
wind·break·er
wind·burn
wind·fall
wind·i·ness
wind·lass
(*winch*)
wind·less
(*without wind*)
wind·mill
win·dow
win·dow·pane
wind·row
wind·shield
wind·storm
wind-swept
wind·up
wind·ward
wind·y
·i·er ·i·est
wine
wined win·ing
(*drink;* SEE whine)
wine-col·ored
wine·glass
wine·grow·er
win·er·y
·ies
wine·skin
wing chair
wing·span
wing·spread
win·ner
win·some
win·ter
win·ter·green
win·ter·ize
·ized ·iz·ing
win·ter·time
win·try
·tri·er ·tri·est
wipe
wiped wip·ing
wire
wired wir·ing
wire·draw
·drew ·drawn
·draw·ing
wire·less
Wire·pho·to
wire·tap
wir·i·ness
wir·y
·i·er ·i·est
Wis·con·sin
wis·dom
wise
wis·er wis·est
wise·ly
wish·bone
wish·ful
with·draw
·drew ·drawn
·draw·ing
with·draw·al
with·er
(*wilt;* SEE whither)
with·hold
·held ·hold·ing
with·in
with·out
with·stand
·stood ·stand·ing
wit·less
wit·ness
wit·ti·cism
wit·ti·ness
wit·ty
·ti·er ·ti·est
woe·ful
wolf
wolves
wolf·hound
wom·an
wom·en
wom·an·hood
wom·an·kind
wom·an·li·ness
wom·an·ly
wom·en·folk
won·der
(*marvel;* SEE wander)
won·der·ful
won·der·land
won·der·work
won·drous
wood·carv·ing
wood·craft
wood·cut
wood·ed
wood·land
wood·peck·er
wood·pile
wood pulp
wood·shed
woods·man
wood·sy
·si·er ·si·est
wood·wind
wood·work
wood·y
·i·er ·i·est
wool·en
wool·gath·er·ing
wool·grow·er
wool·lies *or* wool·ies
wool·li·ness *or* wool·i·ness
wool·ly *or* wool·y
·li·er *or* ·i·er
·li·est *or* ·i·est
Worces·ter·shire
word·age
word·book
word·i·ly
word·i·ness
word·less
word-of-mouth
word·play
word·y
·i·er ·i·est
work
worked *or* wrought
work·ing
work·a·ble

work·a·day
work·a·hol·ic
work·bench
work·book
work·day
work·house
work·ing·man
work·load
work·man·like
work·man·ship
work·out
work·room
work·shop
work·ta·ble
work·week
world·li·ness
world·ly
·li·er ·li·est
world·ly-wise
world-shak·ing
world-wea·ry
world·wide
worm·wood
worn-out
wor·ri·er
wor·ri·ment
wor·ri·some
wor·ry
·ries
·ried ·ry·ing
worse
wors·en
wor·ship
·shiped *or* ·shipped
·ship·ing *or* ·ship·ping
wor·ship·er *or* wor·ship·per
wor·ship·ful
worst
wor·sted
wor·thi·ly
wor·thi·ness
worth·less
worth·while
wor·thy
·thi·er ·thi·est
wound
wrack
wraith
wran·gle
·gled ·gling
wran·gler
wrap
wrapped *or* wrapt
wrap·ping
wrap·a·round
wrap·per
wrath·ful
wreak
wreath *n.*
wreathe *v.*
wreathed
wreath·ing
wreck·age
wreck·er
wrench
wres·tle
·tled ·tling
wres·tler
wretch
wretch·ed
wring
wrung wring·ing
wrin·kle
·kled ·kling
wrin·kly
·kli·er ·kli·est
wrist·band
wrist·let
wrist pin
wrist·watch
writ
write
wrote writ·ten
writ·ing
(*inscribe;* SEE right, rite)
write-down
write-in
write-off
writ·er
write-up
writhe
writhed
writh·ing
wrong·do·er
wrong·do·ing
wrong·ful
wrote
(*pt. of* write; SEE rote)
wrought
wrought-up
wrung
wry
wried wry·ing
wri·er wri·est
wry·ly
Wy·o·ming

X

x
x-ed *or* x'd
x-ing *or* x'ing
xen·o·pho·bi·a
xe·ro·graph·ic
xe·rog·ra·phy
xe·roph·i·lous
Xe·rox
Xmas
X-ray *or* X ray

Y

yacht
yachts·man
Yan·kee
yard·age
yard·arm
yard·mas·ter
yard·stick
yarn-dyed
yawl
year·book
year-end
year·ling
year·long
year·ly
yearn
year-round
yeast
yel·low
yeo·man
yes·ter·day
yes·ter·year
Yid·dish
yield
yip·pie
yo·ga
yo·gi
·gis
yo·gurt
yoke
yoked yok·ing
(*harness*)
yolk
(*of an egg*)
Yom Kip·pur
yon·der
young·ster
your
(*poss. of* you)
you're
(*you are*)
yours
your·self
·selves
youth·ful
you've
yowl
yo-yo

Z

za·ni·ness
za·ny
·nies, ·ni·er ·ni·est
zeal
zeal·ot
zeal·ous
Zeit·geist
Zen
ze·nith
ze·o·lite
ze·o·lit·ic
zeph·yr
zep·pe·lin
ze·ro
·ros *or* ·roes
·roed ·ro·ing
zest·ful·ly

zest·ful·ness
zinc
zincked *or* zinced
zinck·ing *or*
zinc·ing
zin·ni·a
Zi·on·ism
zip
zipped zip·ping
ZIP Code
zip·per
zir·con
zith·er
zo·di·ac
zo·di·a·cal
zom·bie
zon·al
zone
zoned zon·ing
zo·o·ge·og·ra·phy
zo·o·log·i·cal
zo·ol·o·gist
zo·ol·o·gy
zoom lens
zoy·si·a
zy·gote
zy·mol·o·gy
zy·mur·gy

PART II
GLOSSARY OF BUSINESS TERMS

Guide to the Glossary of Business Terms

This glossary includes terms from all areas of general business, as well as those specific to accounting and bookkeeping, banking and finance, electronic data processing, government regulations, insurance, manufacturing, distribution, merchandising, real estate, wholesale and retail sales, and relevant areas of the law. The terms were selected for their importance and frequency of use in modern business offices.

Inflected forms for nouns and verbs are shown if they are irregular or if some spelling difficulty exists: **moratorium** (*n., pl.* **-toriums** or **-toria**) and **subpoena** (*v.,* **-naed, -naing**). All terms, including single words, hyphenated and unhyphenated compounds, proper nouns, and abbreviations, are listed in alphabetical order. The spellings given are those known or judged to be the most frequently used. Derived entries are run-in after the base word when these entries are considered useful. For example, **deduction** (*n.*) appears under the main entry **deduct** (*v.*). Abbreviations and acronyms are entered after those terms from which they are derived. For example, **CD** appears under **certificate of deposit** and **LIFO** is listed under **Last In, First Out.** A more complete listing of business abbreviations and acronyms is contained in the reference section "Abbreviations and Acronyms" on page 315.

A

abandon (*v.*) to give up title or claim to real estate, usually because of financial necessity. —**abandonment** (*n.*)

abeyance (*n.*) the suspension of title to real estate until correct ownership is established.

abstract of title a document tracing the history of the ownership of a piece of land, upon which the present owner's title is based.

acceleration clause a clause in a contract, such as a bank loan document, that speeds up the requirement for payment or other terms if a breach of contract or another stated condition occurs.

access (*v.*) to obtain data from or place data into computer storage.

accession (*n.*) the addition of real estate or other property to a person's holdings through the passing of title.

access time the amount of time it takes a computer to find stored data and deliver it or to perform a directed manipulation of data.

account (*n.*) a record of financial data on items relating to a business's assets, liabilities, income, expenses, and net worth.

accountant (*n.*) a person who is trained in recording, inspecting, analyzing, and reporting on financial records and accounts.

accounting (*n.*) 1. the systematic recording, analyzing, and reporting of the financial data of a business based on standards widely accepted in commerce. 2. the principles and practices of accounting.

accounting cycle 1. the period of time during which a business routinely performs a complete set of accounting procedures. 2. a complete set of accounting procedures, from the balancing of all accounts, the recording of new transactions, and the rebalancing of accounts to the preparation of financial statements.

accounts payable the bookkeeping records of transactions on which a business owes payment.

accounts receivable the bookkeeping records of transactions on which a business is owed payment.

accrual (*n.*) 1. the act or process of accruing. 2. something accruing or accrued; amount accrued.

accrue (*v.*) to grow or accumulate, such as the assets or liabilities of a business.

acquisition (*n.*) the obtaining of an interest in or ownership of property or a business.

acquittance (*n.*) 1. a discharge from or settlement of a debt or other obligation. 2. in law, a written statement confirming this discharge or settlement, such as a receipt in full.

acronym (*n.*) a word formed by combining most or all of the first letters or syllables of a compound term, such as *ERISA* for *E*(mployee) *R*(etirement) *I*(ncome) *S*(ecurity) *A*(ct) and *Amex* for *Am*(erican) (Stock) *Ex*(change).

actionable (*adj.*) subject to or providing grounds for a lawsuit.

actuary (*n., pl.* **-ries**) a person whose work is analyzing insurance risks in order to calculate insurance premiums, rates, and dividends.

addendum (*n., pl.* **-denda**) an addition to a written work, such as a contract or a report.

adjuster (*n.*) a person who evaluates claims and determines settlement of damages under insurance policies. Also, **adjustor.**

ad valorem tax 1. a tax or duty based on a fixed percentage of the value of real estate or merchandise. 2. a customs levy on imports based on a percentage of their value.

advance (*n.*) a payment for work not yet performed or for goods not yet received.

affiant (*n.*) a person who swears to an affidavit.

affidavit (*n.*) a written statement sworn to before an authorized official, such as a judge.

affiliate (*n.*) a company associated with or owned by another, usually larger, company.

affirmative action a corporate policy or program for correcting the effects of racial or sexual discrimination in employment by recruiting, employing, and promoting members of groups previously discriminated against.

agenda (*n.*) a list of things to be done, especially a list of topics to be discussed or acted upon at a meeting.

agio (*n., pl.* **-os**) a fee paid for the exchange of one nation's money for another's or for the exchange of devalued or depreciated money for money of full value.

agreement (*n.*) an understanding reached by two or more parties, such as a contract, treaty, or policy.

agribusiness (*n.*) a large commercial business that specializes in agricultural products or services.

air rights the legal right to use the air space above a piece of land or a building, usually to build a structure.

allocate (*v.*) in accounting, to assign an item of cost or revenue to one or more time periods, operations, activities, or products, according to cost responsibilities and benefits received.

allocation (*n.*) money set aside for a specific purpose within a business's formal budget.

allonge (*n.*) a paper attached to a document, such as a promissory note, to provide room for endorsements because the original document has insufficient space for them.

allotment (*n.*) in accounting, the apportionment of anticipated revenues into different classes of expenditures.

alphanumeric (*adj.*) in data processing, pertaining to both alphabetical and numerical symbols. Also, **alphabetic-numeric** and **alphameric.**

amalgamation (*n.*) a merger of two or more corporate entities.

amendment (*n.*) a formal change in or revision of the text of a contract, law, or regulation.

American Federation of Labor–Congress of Industrial Organizations a federation of labor unions in the United States and Canada that was formed by the merger of the American Federation of Labor with the Congress of Industrial Organizations in 1955. *Abbrev.:* **AFL-CIO**

amicus curiae *Latin.* literally, "friend of the court." One who advises or offers arguments to the court regarding a suit to which he or she is not a party. An individual, group, or institution may act as an amicus curiae.

amortize (*v.*) 1. to retire a debt by periodic payments. 2. in accounting, to write off a portion or all of the cost of an asset over its tax-deductible life. **—amortization** (*n.*)

annex (*v.*) to add to real estate already owned, usually by purchase of adjacent lots. **—annexation** (*n.*)

annual report a publication issued by a corporation that discloses its financial data for the most recent fiscal year, including earnings per share of stock, par value of stock, and total profit or loss for the period.

annuity (*n., pl.* **-ties**) 1. a fixed sum of money paid or received at regular intervals. 2. an investment, usually made with an insurance company, whereby a guaranteed annual return is paid during the investor's lifetime or for a contracted number of years.

antitrust (*adj.*) relating to the regulation of or opposition to monopolies, trusts, or other business combinations or practices that cause unlawful restraint of trade.

appraise (*v.*) to give an expert valuation of real estate or other property. **—appraisal** (*n.*)

appraiser (*n.*) a person who makes an appraisal.

appreciate (*v.*) to increase in value, as real estate, shares of stock, or goods. **—appreciation** (*n.*)

apprentice (*n.*) a person who is learning a skilled trade, such as carpentry or plumbing, under specified conditions and for a certain period of time, often in accordance with labor union rules.

appropriation (*n.*) an amount of money budgeted for a specified use during a given fiscal year.

appurtenance (*n.*) any subordinate right accompanying other rights that come with the ownership of a piece of real estate, such as a right of way.

arbitrage (*n.*) the simultaneous purchase and sale of stocks, bonds, or bills of exchange in different markets in order to profit from price differences.

arbitrageur (*n.*) an arbitrage dealer.

arbitrate (*v.*) to judge and settle a labor dispute after hearing both sides of an issue in collective bargaining negotiations.

arbitration (*n.*) the hearing and settlement of differences between management and labor in collective bargaining negotiations by a person chosen by both sides.

arbitrator (*n.*) a person, often qualified by a state labor department, who hears and settles disputes in collective bargaining negotiations through the process of arbitration.

arrears (*n. pl.*) 1. debts that are due but unpaid. 2. **in arrears** behind in payment of a debt or debts.

assess (*v.*) to set the value of something, often real estate, for taxation purposes.

assessment (*n.*) 1. the amount of tax imposed on real estate based on a percentage of or its full appraised market value, often expressed in mills per thousand dollars of value. 2. a fee levied on stockholders or association members as a means of raising money, usually for group operating expenses. 3. a special tax levied on real estate owners by a municipal authority for repairs to or improvement of community property under its control, such as sidewalks or street lighting.

assessor (*n.*) a person who sets the value of something, often real estate, for tax purposes.

asset (*n.*) property, money, or any other tangible or intangible item of value owned by a business or person. Opposite of LIABILITY.

assignment (*n.*) the transfer of a right to or ownership of property or an interest in a business.

attach (*v.*) to seize property by means of a court writ, usually because of the owner's failure to meet a financial obligation. **—attachment** (*n.*)

attrition (*n.*) the reduction of a work force through the death, resignation, or retirement of workers.

auction (*n.*) a public sale of repossessed property, such as automobiles and real estate, to the highest of competing bidders.

audit (*v.*) to examine and verify officially the financial accounts of a business. (*n.*) 1. a formal examination and verification of the financial accounts and records of a business. 2. a final statement, prepared by an auditor, of the financial accounts and records of a business.

auditor (*n.*) a person who is authorized to examine and verify a business's financial accounts and records.

automated clearinghouse a regional financial clearinghouse, governed by the Federal Reserve System, that employs electronic account verification and information-posting.

automated teller machine a computerized machine used in retail banking that customers use to perform such transactions as deposits to or withdrawals from their accounts. *Abbrev.:* **ATM**

B

backlog (*n.*) 1. a reserve supply of merchandise. 2. an accumulation of unfinished work, such as orders to be filled.

bad debt in accounting, a receivable that has proved to be uncollectible.

balance (*n.*) 1. in bookkeeping, the difference between the debit and credit sides of an account. 2. the amount of funds remaining in a bank account after a deposit or withdrawal.

balance due 1. the amount still owed after a payment is made on a debt. 2. in bookkeeping, the amount needed to equalize the debit and credit sides of an account.

balance of payments a record of all economic transactions between one country and another country or countries in a given period, including exports and imports, debt payments, and grants.

balance of trade the difference in value between a country's imports and exports.

balance sheet an itemized statement showing the financial condition of a business at a given date by summarizing its assets, liabilities, and net worth.

balloon note a loan contract requiring periodic payments over a specified term that are not large enough to pay off the entire loan. At the end of the term, the remaining principal and interest are due in one payment.

bank (*n.*) a bank may be defined by its function, method of organization, or relationship to another bank.

See: central bank
commercial bank
correspondent bank
country bank
Federal Reserve Bank
independent bank
mutual savings bank
national bank
private bank
savings bank
state bank

bank acceptance a draft or a bill of exchange drawn on a bank and acknowledged as valid by that bank.

bank account money deposited in a bank to the credit of, and subject to withdrawal by, the depositor.

bank call a periodic demand upon a bank by a supervising authority, such as the Comptroller of Currency of the

United States for national banks or the state banking commissioner for state banks, for a sworn statement of a bank's financial condition as of a particular date.

bank draft a check drawn by a bank against its account in another bank.

bankers' blanket bond insurance offered to banking institutions to protect them against fraud, theft by employees, burglary, and similar insurable losses.

bank note a promissory note issued by a bank that serves as currency and is payable to the bearer on demand.

bank rate the discount rate set by a country's national bank.

bankrupt (*n.*) a person declared legally unable to pay his or her debts. (*adj.*) in a condition of financial ruin.

bankruptcy (*n.*) the state of being bankrupt.

bank statement 1. the periodic statement of assets, liabilities, and net worth of a bank. 2. the periodic statement of a customer's account by a bank.

bar code magnetically coded lines printed on consumer products that can be read by electronic scanning equipment. The coded lines represent the product's price and other information, such as its manufacturer, stock number, and product category.

barrister (*n.*) in England, a member of the legal profession qualified to present and plead cases in court.

barter (*v.*) to trade goods or services for other goods or services without exchanging money. (*n.*) the act or practice of bartering.

base pay standard wages paid for a job, exclusive of any overtime pay or bonuses.

BASIC see BEGINNER'S ALL-PURPOSE SYMBOLIC INSTRUCTION CODE.

basic stock merchandise in such constant demand that the manufacturer or vendor must keep continual inventory of it.

basic yield the annual return produced by an investment that carries no risk of default.

batch processing a method of processing data in which jobs are performed in separate groups by a computer.

baud (*n.*) in data processing, a unit of transmission speed.

bear (*n.*) a person who expects that stock market prices will decline and who sells in anticipation of such an event. Opposite of BULL.

bearer bond a bond that is not registered to a particular owner and pays its interest and principal to anyone who holds it.

Beginner's All-purpose Symbolic Instruction Code a computer language that uses English words and algebra. *Acronym:* **BASIC**

bench mark in data processing, a standard or set of specifications used in judging the quality of a particular computer or computer program.

beneficiary (*n.*) a person or an organization named to receive the income or other proceeds from a will, trust, or insurance policy.

bequeath (*v.*) to give or leave property to a person or organization by a last will and testament.

bequest (*n.*) 1. the act of bequeathing. 2. anything that is bequeathed.

bid (*v.*) to offer a certain price for something. (*n.*) an offer of a price for something.

Big Board a popular term for the New York Stock Exchange.

Big Eight a popular term for the eight largest public accounting firms in the United States.

bill of exchange a written order given by one person to another to pay to a designated person a certain sum of money at a specified time.

bill of lading a written contract issued by a common carrier that acknowledges the receipt of goods to be shipped and sets forth the terms of their shipment.

bill of sale a written document confirming that the ownership of something has been transferred by sale.

binary system a number system in which each number is expressed in powers of two by using only the digits 0 and 1. Often used as a number system in computer science.

binder (*n.*) a temporary contract made by two parties pending completion of a final contract. In real estate, a binder often involves the exchange of money.

bit (*n.*) the smallest unit of computer information, equal to one digit of the binary number system used by computers (from *bi*[nary] [digi]*t*). See BYTE.

blacklist (*n.*) a list of persons who are disapproved of, refused employment, and generally discriminated against. (*v.*) to place on a blacklist.

blackmail (*n.*) the act of forcing a person to surrender money or other things of value by threatening to expose damaging information. (*v.*) to force or attempt to force a person to surrender money by threats of exposure.

black market a place for or method of selling goods in violation of official controls, especially rationing.

blanket agreement a collective bargaining agreement based on negotiations that are industry wide or that cover an industry in a large geographical area.

blanket bond a bond secured by all the assets of a business.

blanket mortgage a mortgage that includes all of a person's or a business's property as security for a loan.

blanket order a preseason order for a product made to meet expected buyer demand.

blanket policy an insurance policy that covers several properties, shipments, or locations under a single policy item.

blind entry a bookkeeping entry that lists the credit and debit amounts to accounts but leaves out other data that is essential for an accurate accounting record.

block-busting (*n.*) the unethical real estate practice of selling or renting to people of a different race or religion from the current residents of a neighborhood in order to exploit prejudice and create fear of declining property values, causing residents to sell quickly and at reduced prices.

blue-chip stock the stock of a well-established corporation that has a good earnings record and is valued for its stable price.

blue-collar (*adj.*) relating to industrial or maintenance workers, in contrast to white-collar office and professional workers. See WHITE-COLLAR.

blue law any state or local law that prohibits business activity on Sunday.

blueprint (*n.*) a photographic reproduction in white on a blue background, used chiefly for architects' plans and mechanical drawings.

blue-sky law a law that regulates the sale and trading of securities for the protection of the public from fraud.

board of directors a group of people elected by the stockholders of a corporation to create policy and to operate the corporation.

boilerplate (*n.*) 1. the standardized text used in contracts. 2. any standardized text reused in a number of documents, often stored on floppy diskettes for use in word-processing systems.

bona fide *Latin.* made or done in good faith.

bond (*n.*) 1. a certificate of debt, issued by a corporation or government, that promises to repay a specified sum of money at a fixed future date. 2. an insurance agreement guaranteeing against loss caused by a third party.
See: bankers' blanket bond
bearer bond
blanket bond
callable bond
convertible bond
debenture bond
deferred bond
indemnity bond
mortgage bond
registered bond
surety bond

bond broker a person who sells bonds, debentures, and other debt securities.

bond discount the amount by which the selling price of a bond is less than its face value.

bonded (*adj.*) 1. secured or guaranteed by an insurance bond or pledge of property. 2. stored in a bonded warehouse.

bonded warehouse a warehouse approved by the U.S. Treasury Department for storage of goods without payment of excise or customs duties until the goods leave the warehouse.

bondholder (*n.*) an owner of a bond issued by a corporation or government.

bond indenture a contract that describes a bond's interest rate, maturity date, and other vital terms under which the bond is issued.

bonding company a business that sells surety bonds and other insurance bonds.

bond premium the difference between the selling price of a bond and its face value.

bond rating the quality of a bond as an investment, as appraised and rated by a recognized bond-rating service.

bonification (*n.*) the refund of taxes paid and later found not to be due.

bookkeeper (*n.*) a person whose work is keeping systematic records of business accounts or transactions.

bookkeeping (*n.*) the work of keeping systematic records of business accounts or transactions.

book of original entry the journal in which all accounting transactions are first recorded; a daybook or journal.

book value 1. the worth of assets as carried on the books of a business but not necessarily what these could bring on the open market. 2. in the securities industry, a determination of the value of a share of common stock made by totaling all assets of a company, deducting all debts and other liabilities, and dividing the result by the number of shares of common stock outstanding.

bottom line 1. the net income line on a financial statement after taxes, which describes the net profit or net loss of a business. 2. the final result of an analysis, as of profits and losses, or the pros and cons of a policy or management issue.

bottom out (*v.*) (of stock market prices) to drop to a low level and remain there for a time before rising, thereby establishing a new low base for growth.

Bourse (*n.*) 1. the stock exchange in Paris and certain other European cities. 2. **bourse** any stock or commodity exchange.

boycott (*v.*) 1. to join together in refusing to deal with or participate in. 2. to refuse to buy, sell, or use a product or service. (*n.*) the act of boycotting.

branch banking a banking system in which a bank establishes more than one office through which to conduct business.

brand name the name used to identify a supplier's goods or services and to distinguish them from others, usually registered with the U.S. Office of Trademarks and Patents.

breach of contract the failure to fulfill the terms of a contract.

break-even point the point at which the revenue generated by a product or service equals the complete cost of producing and marketing that product or service; the point at which revenue equals expenses.

broker (*n.*) a person who arranges for the purchase or sale of stocks, bonds, commodities, or other properties; negotiates contracts; or handles other business affairs for a client and receives a commission or fee for services, especially in the securities, insurance, and real estate industries.

brokerage (*n.*) 1. the business activity or office of a broker. 2. the fee or commission charged by a broker.

broker's loan a loan made by a bank to a stockbroker, secured by the collateral of the stock exchange of which the broker is a member.

broker's market a condition of the stock market that occurs when investors are generally inactive while brokers are trading heavily with their own accounts.

broker's ticket a written statement of all buy and sell orders executed by a stockbroker.

budget (*n.*) 1. a detailed estimate of the expected revenues and the expected expenses of a business during a specified period of time, often a quarter year or a full year. 2. the amount of money needed or allotted for a particular purpose. (*v.*) to plan for in a budget; plan according to a budget.

budget deficit a condition in which expenses exceed revenues.

budget surplus a condition in which revenues exceed expenses.

buffer (*n.*) a computer storage unit that compensates for the difference in the rate of data flow during data transfer from one computer to another.

bulk mail second-, third-, or fourth-class mail, including parcel post and direct mail circulars.

bull (*n.*) a person who expects that stockmarket prices will rise and who buys in anticipation of such an event Opposite of BEAR.

bullion (*n.*) gold or silver in the form of bars or ingots.

bureaucracy (*n.*) 1. a government or business organized in bureaus or departments managed by employees who follow set procedures. 2. a written statement of the regulations and procedures of an organization. 3. the excessive multiplication of and concentration of power in administrative bureaus. 4. governmental or business red tape, resulting from strict adherence to routines and procedures.

bureaucrat (*n.*) 1. an employee in a bureaucracy. 2. an employee who rigidly follows routines and procedures.

business (*n.*) 1. the buying and selling of products and services. 2. an organization that buys, produces, and sells products and services.

business day 1. any day on which business is conducted, usually a day from Monday through Friday. 2. in many states, a day on which banks and stock markets are open.

buyer (*n.*) a person whose work is to purchase merchandise for resale in a retail business.

buyer's market a market in which the buyers tend to set the prices and terms of a sale, usually because the supply of a product or service is greater than the demand for it.

buy long to buy securities and pay their full price in order to sell them at a profit when prices rise.

buy on margin to buy securities without paying the full price at the time of purchase; to buy securities with a down payment.

buy out (*v.*) 1. to buy all the stock, assets, and interests of an ongoing business. 2. to buy all of a person's stock, rights, and interest in a partnership or other business.

bylaw (*n.*) any of the rules adopted by a business or other organization to regulate its internal affairs.

byte (*n.*) a sequence of bits, usually eight, that computers use as a basic unit of information. See BIT.

C

call (*n.*) 1. a demand by a business or brokerage house for payment on the purchase of stocks and bonds. 2. an agreement by which a buyer secures the right to purchase a fixed amount of stock at a certain price for a specified period of time. See PUT. **call in** (*v.*) 1. to collect money due on debts. 2. to withdraw currency from circulation.

callable bond a bond that may be redeemed by the issuing institution before its maturity date.

cambist (*n.*) 1. a dealer in foreign currencies and exchange rates. 2. a manual for computing foreign currency exchange rates.

capital (*n.*) 1. the total value of money or property owned or used by a business; net worth. 2. wealth that is available for the purpose of producing new wealth. 3. the fixed and liquid assets of a business.

capital account an account showing the total capital invested in the fixed assets of a business by its owners.

capital asset an asset held by a business that is intended for use over a long period of time.

capital budget a formal estimate of the anticipated sale or purchase of major items for a business, in addition to those items covered in the normal operating budget.

capital cost allowance an Internal Revenue Service term for property depreciation.

capital formation the creation or expansion of capital through interest earned on savings accounts or dividends on investments.

capital gain the profit resulting from the sale of capital investments, such as stocks and real estate, at a price higher than was paid.

capital goods fixed assets; tangible goods, such as raw materials, used in the production of other goods, such as consumer goods.

capital investment money invested in the fixed assets of a business.

capitalism (*n.*) an economic system based on the private ownership of the means of production and distribution.

capitalist (*n.*) 1. a person who has capital; an owner of wealth used in business. 2. a supporter of capitalism.

capitalization (*n.*) 1. the process of converting something into capital. 2. the total capital funds of a business, represented by stocks, bonds, debentures, and so on.

capitalize (*v.*) 1. to finance or provide capital for a business venture. 2. to convert to capital.

capital liability a fixed liability that is created in order to acquire fixed assets or for funding purposes.

capital loss a loss resulting from the sale of capital investments, such as stocks and real estate, at a price lower than was paid.

capital stock the total number of authorized shares of stock issued by a business; all the shares representing ownership of a business.

capital turnover the rate at which the assets of a business are converted into cash.

captive market purchasers who have little latitude in their choice of a vendor of goods or services.

carnet (*n.*) a customs certificate that permits the passage of goods or people across national boundaries.

carrier see COMMON CARRIER.

carry (*v.*) to provide temporary financial assistance to an insolvent debtor in the hope of future repayment.

carry back (*v.*) in the computation of federal income taxes, to average out gains and losses over a period of more than one year.

carry forward (*v.*) to transfer a bookkeeping item from one column, page, or category to another.

carrying charge 1. the interest or other fee added to the cost of purchases made on an installment payment plan. 2. a service charge paid to a broker for securities that are bought on margin.

carte blanche complete discretionary freedom, as in the disbursement of money for the transaction of business.

cartel (*n.*) an international syndicate or trust of commercial enterprises formed to gain control over prices and production; monopoly.

cash (*n.*) money that circulates as currency. (*v.*) to convert a check, money order, or other negotiable instrument into currency.

cash audit in accounting, an examination to determine whether all cash transactions for a specified period have been documented.

cash flow the pattern of a business's receipts and expenditures, resulting in the availability or nonavailability of cash.

cashier (*n.*) a person in charge of the receipt and disbursement of money for a business.

cashier's check a negotiable instrument drawn by a bank on its own funds and signed by its cashier.

cash position the ratio of a business's cash to its total assets, after deducting current liabilities.

cash reserve the portion of an organization's cash or liquid assets set aside for a special purpose or an emergency expenditure.

cash surrender value the amount an insurance company will pay upon the cancellation of a policy.

casualty insurance accident insurance that protects the insured against personal injury and property damage.

cathode-ray tube display a computer terminal display, resembling a television screen, used in data- and word-processing systems. Also called VIDEO DISPLAY TERMINAL. *Abbrev.:* **CRT**

cats and dogs *Colloq.* highly speculative securities.

caveat emptor *Latin.* let the buyer beware; a term indicating that buyers purchase products at their own risk.

cease-and-desist order a court decree directing the halt of an unfair or illegal practice.

central bank a bank that holds the bulk of monetary reserves for a country. The Federal Reserve Bank is the central bank for the United States. Its responsibilities include setting national banking policy, coordinating national credit policy, controlling gold reserves, and assisting in check collection for other banks.

central processing unit the part of a computer that controls all its operations. Frequently called the "brains" of a computer. *Abbrev.:* **CPU**

certificate of deposit 1. a type of bank deposit account that earns interest and operates over a fixed period of time. 2. a bank document acknowledging receipt of money into a certificate-of-deposit account. *Abbrev.:* **CD**

certificate of incorporation a document issued by a state that approves the formation of a corporation.

certificate of indebtedness a government-issued note representing a loan to a business.

certificate of no defense a document, issued by a mortgagor (usually a bank) and signed by a mortgage buyer, that identifies the full amount of the mortgage debt.

certificate of occupancy a document issued by a municipal authority stating that a building complies with current building codes and may be occupied.

certificate of origin a shipping document that specifies the place where merchandise was manufactured.

certificate of release a document signed by a lender attesting that a mortgage has been paid in full.

certificate of title a document stating that the seller of a piece of real estate has clear and complete title to it.

certified check a check whose payment is guaranteed by the bank upon which it is drawn.

certified mail uninsured first-class mail requiring the receiver to sign a form as proof of delivery.

certified public accountant a person certified by the state as having met the requirements to act as a public accountant. *Abbrev.:* **CPA**

chamber of commerce an association of business people organized to promote the commercial and industrial interests of a community.

charge account a credit arrangement that allows a purchaser to defer payment on goods or services until a later date.

charter (*n.*) 1. the lease or hire of a carrier, such as a ship, truck, airplane, and so on. (*v.*) to lease or hire such a carrier. 2. a document granting a bank the right to do business and defining the conditions under which it may operate. (*v.*) to grant a charter to.

chattel (*n.*) articles of movable personal property such as furniture and livestock, as distinguished from real property such as land and buildings.

chattel mortgage a mortgage on personal property, used mainly for the purchase of consumer goods.

check clearance the return of a check for final payment to the bank on which it is drawn.

checking account a bank account against which the depositor can draw checks that are payable on demand.

chief executive officer the highest-ranking officer in a corporation, usually the president or chairman of the board. *Abbrev.:* **CEO**

citation (*n.*) 1. a summons to appear before a court of law. 2. in law, a formal reference to a court case.

civil action litigation involving alleged violation of civil, as opposed to criminal, law.

claim (*n.*) a demand for payment, reimbursement, or compensation under the law or under the terms of a contract.

class action suit a legal action brought by a person on behalf of himself or herself and the other members of a group, all of whom have the same grounds for action.

classified stock corporate stock that is divided into different groups, such as Class A and Class B, typically on the basis of the holder's voting rights.

clearinghouse 1. in finance, an establishment maintained by banks for settling mutual claims and accounts among its members. 2. any central facility for the accumulation or exchange of information in a certain area.

closed corporation a corporation whose stock is owned by a small number of people and is not for sale on the open market.

closed-end investment company an investment firm that makes a fixed number of shares available to the public and is not obligated to redeem them.

closed shop a business or factory in which only members of a certain union are hired.

closing (*n.*) a real estate proceeding in which property is officially sold and title is turned over to the new owner.

closing costs fees involved in the sale of real estate such as title fees, loan fees, and appraisal fees.

closing price the price at which the final sale of the day is transacted at an organized market such as a stock exchange.

cloud on the title an outstanding claim on a piece of real estate that affects its title.

code of ethics standards of proper behavior established by an industry or profession and voluntarily adopted by its members.

codicil (*n.*) a supplement to a will that changes, explains, or adds to something in it and takes precedence over anything in the will that is inconsistent with it.

co-insurance (*n.*) 1. a form of property insurance in which the insured shares losses with the insurer according to a predetermined formula. 2. joint insurance underwritten by two or more insurers.

collaborate (*v.*) to work together with another or others. **—collaboration** (*n.*)

collate (*v.*) to combine items from two or more sets into one set having a specified order.

collateral (*n.*) personal property or real estate pledged as security for a loan.

colleague (*n.*) a business or professional associate; fellow member of the same profession or business group.

collection agency a business that collects debts for its clients.

collective agreement a contract between one or more unions and the employer or employers involved.

collective bargaining negotiation between union representatives and employers to establish terms of employment.

collision insurance insurance protecting the insured against damage to specified vehicles as a result of collisions.

collusion (*n.*) a secret understanding between two or more parties to engage in unfair or unlawful business practices.

command (*n.*) a direction to an information-processing system to perform a specified operation.

commerce (*n.*) the buying and selling of goods and services, especially when done on a large scale between cities, states, or countries; trade.

commercial acre the part of an acre that is available for building structures after the space for streets, sidewalks, and other common-use areas has been deducted. Also called **net acre.**

commercial bank a bank whose primary function is the acceptance of demand deposits used as checking accounts. Commercial banks also finance the production, distribution, and sale of goods through short-term loans.

commercial credit 1. credit extended by a bank to a business. 2. credit used by manufacturers, jobbers, retailers, wholesalers, and other commercial enterprises for the production and distribution of goods.

commercialism (*n.*) the methods, principles, and practices of commerce.

commercial paper any negotiable instrument used in business, such as a check, draft, or bill of exchange.

commercial property 1. real estate used for business purposes. 2. property located within a district zoned for commercial use.

commission (*n.*) a fee for services or work done, often based on a percentage of the total amount of business transacted.

commission house a brokerage firm whose employees execute buy-and-sell orders as members of stock exchanges and commodities exchanges.

commodities exchange an exchange or board of trade organized to trade in commodities.

commodity (*n., pl.* **-ties**) 1. any item of commerce. 2. **commodities** basic goods or staple products, as of agriculture.

Commodity Futures Trading Commission a U.S. agency that regulates the commodities exchanges. *Abbrev.:* **CFTC**

commodity paper a note, draft, or bill of exchange secured by warehouse receipts covering commodities.

commodity prices quotes for approved commodities contracts.

common carrier a person or company in the business of transporting persons, goods, or information for a fee, having uniform rates and being available to the public.

common law the body of law based on custom, usage, and court decisions. Distinguished from STATUTORY

LAW, which is enacted through legislation.

Common Market see EUROPEAN ECONOMIC COMMUNITY.

common stock securities representing an ownership interest in a corporation; carrying voting rights and paying dividends only after those due to holders of preferred stock have been paid.

community property property that is owned jointly by a husband and a wife.

compensation (*n.*) payment for labor or services performed, losses sustained, or damages done.

compound interest interest computed on the sum of the principal and accrued interest.

comptroller (*n.*) an alternate spelling of **controller.** See CONTROLLER.

computer (*n.*) an electronic machine that, by means of stored instructions and information, rapidly performs complex logical and mathematical calculations.

conciliation (*n.*) the process of resolving a labor dispute through compromise or voluntary agreement rather than arbitration.

condemn (*v.*) 1. to declare officially that a building is unfit for use or occupation. 2. to expropriate private property for public use under the government's right of eminent domain. —**condemnation** (*n.*)

conditional sale a transaction in which the seller reserves title to goods or property sold until the full purchase price is paid.

condominium (*n.*) an apartment complex in which the individual living units are owned by their tenants.

conference call a telephone link of three or more parties, often including visual as well as vocal communication.

configuration (*n.*) a group of interconnected information-processing machines that are programmed to operate as a single system.

confiscate (*v.*) to seize private property by governmental authority, usually as a penalty. —**confiscation** (*n.*)

conglomerate (*n.*) a corporation that is composed of multiple, widely diversified companies.

conservator (*n.*) 1. a person appointed by a court to manage the estate of someone who has been adjudged incompetent. 2. a person appointed to liquidate a firm that has gone out of business.

consign (*v.*) to transfer or assign property from one person or business to another.

consignee (*n.*) a person to whom or a business to which property is consigned.

consignment (*n.*) 1. the act of consigning. 2. a shipment of goods to an agent for safekeeping or sale. 3. **on consignment** shipped to the retailer with the understanding that there will be no payment until the goods are sold.

consignor (*n.*) a person or business that consigns merchandise or property. Also, **consigner.**

console (*n.*) a keyboard input station of an electronic information-processing system.

consortium (*n.*) 1. an association; partnership. 2. an international coalition of banks, businesses, or individuals formed to raise and invest money for a specific purpose.

construction warranty a promise by a building contractor that a new home is free from structural, electrical, and plumbing defects; required in many states before a certificate of occupancy can be issued.

consultant (*n.*) a person who provides professional or technical advice to a business, usually on a contractual basis.

consumer goods goods produced for personal consumption, such as food and clothing, rather than goods used for the production of other goods.

consumer price index a collective record, usually compiled monthly, of the current price of consumer goods. *Abbrev.:* **CPI**

contingency fund money reserved for unanticipated expenses.

contract (*n.*) a legally binding document of agreement.

controller (*n.*) an officer, as in a bank or corporation, in charge of the bookkeeping, accounting, and auditing procedures and reports. Also spelled **comptroller.**

controlling interest the ownership by an organization or person of a large enough percentage of corporate common stock, usually 51 percent, to decisively influence corporate policy through voting rights.

conversion (*n.*) 1. an unlawful transfer or appropriation of property. 2. the changeover of a residential building from tenant-occupied to owner-occupied, such as to a condominium or a cooperative apartment building. 3. the exchange of one type of security or currency for another.

convertible bond a bond that gives its owner the right to exchange it for shares of the issuing corporation's stock at a particular time and at a specified price.

conveyance (*n.*) 1. the transfer of ownership of real estate. 2. a document by which the transfer is officially executed.

cooperative (*n.*) an enterprise entirely owned and operated by its members, who share in its profits and liabilities.

cooperative apartment building a building with two or more apartment units in which the right to occupy a unit is secured by the purchase of stock in the corporation that owns the building.

copyright (*n.*) the exclusive legal right to the production, publication, or sale of a literary or artistic work for a specified period of time. (*v.*) to protect by copyright.

corner (*n.*) the acquisition of a stock or commodity on a scale large enough to give the buyer control over its market price. (*v.*) to acquire enough of a stock or commodity to control its market price.

corporate dissolution the termination of a business's charter of incorporation by vote of the stockholders, by consolidation, or by order of state authorities.

corporate stock equity shares in a corporation, including common, preferred, and classified stocks. 2. in municipal financing, the term used for long-term bonds.

corporation (*n.*) a state-chartered organization that exists as a legal entity independent of the individuals who establish, own, or manage it. A corporation has the rights and liabilities of an individual, including the right to buy and sell property and to enter into contracts.

corpus 1. the principal, as distinguished from the income or interest, of a trust, estate, or fund.

correspondent bank a bank that accepts deposits and collects items for a smaller bank in the same region.

cost accounting the branch of accounting that deals with the classification, recording, allocation, and summarization of cost factors in the affairs of a business.

cost-of-living increase an automatic pay raise based on a rise in the consumer price index.

countersign (*v.*) to add a signature to a previously signed check, contract, or other document to confirm or authenticate it.

country bank a national or state bank that is not located in an area having a Federal Reserve branch bank and that generally has less than $10 million in assets.

covenant (*n.*) 1. an agreement or promise of legal validity written into a contract. 2. a contract.

credit (*n.*) 1. an amount of money in a bank account that may be drawn against. 2. the ability to make deferred payment on purchases. 3. in accounting, an entry on the right-hand side of a ledger. 4. a bookkeeping balance in favor of the account holder. (*v.*) in accounting, to enter an amount paid against a debt or paid into a bank account.

credit bureau an agency that is a clearinghouse for information on the credit rating of individuals or organizations.

credit card a card entitling its bearer to make purchases or obtain services on credit from certain establishments, such as restaurants and hotels.

credit investigation an inquiry into information on a credit application to determine the worth of the applicant's credit.

credit line the maximum amount in a credit account against which the account holder may draw.

creditor (*n.*) a person who gives credit or to whom money is owed.

credit rating a stated appraisal of credit based on a review of the person's or business's credit history.

credit union a cooperative savings and loan association that is able to make loans to its members at lower than prevailing interest rates.

cumulative dividend a dividend that must be paid to the holders of a class of preferred stock before dividends can be paid to holders of common stock.

cumulative stock preferred stock on which unpaid dividends continue to accumulate.

currency (*n.*) coins and paper money in circulation.

cursor (*n.*) an electrical indicator that shows the position at which information being keyed into a computer or word processor will appear on its display screen.

custodial account a bank account held in guardianship for someone else, usually a minor.

custodian (*n.*) a person who has custody of property owned by someone else, such as a bank account or a trust fund.

customs (*n., pl.*) 1. taxes or duties levied on imports or exports. 2. a government agency responsible for collecting applicable taxes or duties on imported or exported goods.

cycle billing a periodic billing system that matches days of the month to letters of the alphabet, so that all debtors whose surnames begin with a certain letter are billed on a particular day of the month.

D

damages (*n.*) money claimed or awarded in a civil lawsuit as compensation for injury or loss.

data (*n. pl., sing.* **-tum**) 1. information organized and represented in a formal manner, usually for processing by a computer. 2. a set of facts and figures from which conclusions are drawn.

data bank an organized file of information, usually stored in a computer.

data base an organized collection of information stored in a computer in such a way that it can easily be retrieved, expanded, and updated.

data capture the collecting of data in a form that can be used directly by a computer.

data center a data-processing installation that serves a business and its employees.

data processing the use of computers to sort, record, analyze, or process facts and figures. *Abbrev.:* **DP**

date of issue 1. the beginning of the term for which bonds or notes in a series bear interest. 2. the date written on an insurance policy, in contrast to its execution or delivery date.

daybook (*n.*) in bookkeeping, a book in which business transactions are recorded chronologically.

day loan a one-day loan granted for a broker's convenience and used for the purchase of stock.

day order a brokerage order to buy or sell securities that expires at the end of the trading day on which it was placed if the order cannot be executed by then.

days of grace extra days, usually three, allowed to make a payment of a debt after the day it was originally due.

deadlock (*n.*) a stalemate in negotiations that results from the unwillingness of both parties to compromise.

debenture (*n.*) 1. any certificate that acknowledges a debt owed by the signer. 2. a certificate of indebtedness, such as a corporate or government bond, that is not secured by collateral but issued against the general credit of the institution. 3. a customs certificate that entitles an importer to a refund of excess duties already paid.

debenture bond a bond, representing a business's funded debt, that is backed only by the business's credit and not secured by a mortgage or pledge.

debit (*n.*) in accounting, an entry on the left hand side of a ledger that increases an asset or expense account and decreases a liability, revenue, or owner's equity account. (*v.*) 1. in accounting, to enter an amount on the left side of the ledger. 2. to charge against an account.

debit card a magnetically coded plastic card issued by a bank for use in guaranteeing checks, withdrawing cash from automated teller machines, and making purchases through point-of-sale systems.

debt (*n.*) money, materials, or service owed by one party to another.

debt capital money borrowed to finance a business's operation.

debt ceiling the maximum amount of money that the federal government can borrow, as set by Congress.

debtee (*n.*) a person to whom a debt is owed; creditor.

debt limit the maximum amount that a state or local government can borrow.

debtor (*n.*) a person who owes a debt.

debtor relief provisions of the National Bankruptcy Act that allow an insolvent business to reorganize and obtain access to refinancing in order to pay off its debts.

debt service in accounting, the amount of interest that a debtor pays within a given period, usually a year.

debug (*v.*) to find and correct errors in the programming of a computer.

declaration of trust a written declaration acknowledging that a person who holds title to property is holding it in trust for, or use by, another person, who is the actual owner.

declare (*v.*) 1. to make a formal statement of total income for tax purposes. 2. to authorize the payment of a dividend on stock. 3. to list goods that require payment of customs duties. **—declaration** (*n.*)

declared value the value of merchandise stated by the owner, usually for insurance purposes, when it is delivered to a carrier for shipment.

declining-balance depreciation a depreciation method that charges larger amounts of depreciation expense in earlier years and smaller amounts in later years of an asset's life.

decreasing term insurance a type of insurance policy for which the insured pays the same premium every year while the insurance value declines over the period of coverage.

deduct (*v.*) to subtract an expense from income on a tax return.

deductible (*adj.*) legally allowed to be deducted from taxable income. (*n.*) an agreed upon sum that the insured will pay for loss of or damage to insured property, after which the insurance company will pay the balance. **—deduction** (*n.*).

deed (*n.*) a document conveying title to real estate. (*v.*) to transfer title to real estate by deed.

deed of release a deed that releases property from a mortgage or other lien after payment of a debt.

deed of surrender a deed transferring real estate to someone else for a contracted period after which it returns to the grantor.

de facto *Latin.* in fact. Existing in actuality, but not legally. See DE JURE.

de facto corporation a corporation that operates without a charter from the state.

default (*v.*) to fail to fulfill a financial or legal obligation. (*n.*) the failure to fulfill such an obligation.

defective title a title to real estate that may be subject to a claim by another party.

defendant (*n.*) person or organization being sued or accused in a court of law. Opposite of PLAINTIFF.

defense (*n.*) 1. the arguments of defendants or their lawyers in court. 2. the defendant and his or her lawyers collectively.

defer (*v.*) to put off payment to a future time.

deferral (*n.*) an accounting technique for postponing the official recognition of revenue earned or expenses paid.

deferred annuity an annuity on which payments do not begin until after a specified time.

deferred bond a bond on which payment may be postponed.

deferred credit in banking, a credit delayed in posting to an account, usually because the deposit was made after business hours and will not be posted until the next business day.

deferred expense in accounting, an expense that is paid now but is written off on the books over a period of time. Also called **deferred charge.**

deferred payment payment, such as for a mortgage, postponed to a future date through a special allowance.

deferred revenue in accounting, revenue that has been received within one accounting period but will not be earned until a later period. Also called **deferred income.**

deferred stock securities on which dividends are not paid until after a specified date or after an anticipated event takes place.

deferred tax the tax owed on present income that need not be paid until a later time, usually resulting from a business's use of a different depreciation schedule for tax and financial reporting purposes.

deficit (*n.*) 1. an excess of expenses over income in a given period. 2. the amount by which actual expenses in a given period exceed the expenses planned for in the budget.

deficit spending a government policy of borrowing in order to spend more money than is raised by taxes. Also called **deficit financing.**

deflation (*n.*) a decline in the general level of prices resulting from a reduction in the amount of money circulating in the economy.

defraud (*v.*) to deprive by fraud of something rightfully due another; cheat; swindle.

defray (*v.*) to pay costs or expenses.

de jure *Latin.* by right; according to law. See DE FACTO.

delegate (*v.*) to entrust someone with the authority and responsibility to accomplish a task.

delinquency (*n.*) the failure to pay a debt when it is due.

delinquent (*adj.*) overdue in payment of a debt.

demand (*n.*) *Economics.* the willingness and ability of consumers to buy goods and services.

demand deposit money in a bank account on which checks can be written or funds withdrawn without advance notice to the bank.

demand loan a loan that must be repaid whenever the lender demands it, rather than at a specified time.

demonetization (*n.*) 1. the withdrawal of a specified currency from circulation. 2. the act of depriving a currency of its standard value.

demote (*v.*) to reduce an employee's status by a lowering of job classification, salary, or title. —**demotion** (*n.*)

demurrage (*n.*) 1. the delaying of a ship, freight car, or other common carrier by the shipper's failure to load or unload cargo within a specified time. 2. the carrier's extra charge for the delay caused by the shipper.

dependent (*n.*) 1. a person who is supported financially by someone else. 2. a person supported by someone else for whom the supporter can claim a tax deduction.

deposit (*v.*) 1. to put money into a bank account. 2. to give a partial payment as security on a larger debt. (*n.*) 1. money placed in a bank account. 2. money or items given as partial payment or security; down payment.

deposit account a bank account from which funds cannot be withdrawn until the bank is given the required notice.

deposition (*n.*) a written statement made under oath and used as testimony in a court trial.

deposit loan a loan that a bank grants by crediting funds to a depositor's account.

depositor (*n.*) a person who deposits money in a bank account.

depreciable life the estimated length of time during which an asset can be depreciated for tax purposes.

depreciate (*v.*) to decrease in value, as real estate, shares of stock, or other assets. —**depreciation** (*n.*)

depreciated cost the original cost of an asset minus its accumulated depreciation.

depreciation allowance the amount that can be claimed for depreciation of an asset on a tax return.

depreciation rate the rate at which an asset's value decreases.

depression (*n.*) an economic condition marked by reduced business activity, high unemployment, and low wages and prices.

devaluation (*n.*) the lowering of the value of a currency in relation to the currencies of other countries.

devise (*n.*) 1. a gift, usually of real estate, made through a will. 2. a will bequeathing real estate. (*v.*) to transmit ownership of real estate through a will.

devisee (*n.*) a person to whom real estate is given by a will.

devisor (*n.*) a person who gives real estate by a will.

devolution (*n.*) the transfer of title to real estate by hereditary succession from one generation to the next.

diminishing returns a reduction in productivity that occurs at a certain point and in proportion to the increased amount of capital and labor invested in a given project or operation.

direct cost any cost of a product or service that contributes directly to the production of product or service. Also called **direct expense.**

direct financing capital raised without an underwriting.

direct liability a debtor's obligation to repay a loan from a creditor.

direct mail a marketing technique that involves mailing letters, catalogs, and other promotional material directly to potential customers.

direct offering the public offering of a stock or bond by the issuing corporation rather than through an investment dealer or securities broker.

direct sales a marketing technique in which a manufacturer sells a product directly to a retailer or customer without the services of a wholesaler.

disagio (*n., pl.* **-os**) a fee for the exchanging of a depreciated foreign currency.

disbursement (*n.*) 1. the payment in cash toward the full or partial fulfillment of a financial obligation. 2. any payment in cash. 3. any expenditure.

disc (*n.*) alternate spelling of **disk.**

disclaimer (*n.*) a denial of liability under certain specified conditions, often a part of product warranties and equipment contracts.

disclosure (*n.*) 1. the act of revealing financial information for use by investors and other interested parties. 2. the obligation of public corporations to reveal financial information to investors, as under the Securities Exchange Act of 1934. 3. the obligation of financial institutions to reveal information on credit terms to borrowers under truth-in-lending regulations.

discount (*v.*) to sell an item or service for less than its normal or listed price. (*n.*) 1. a reduction in the price of an item or service. 2. the amount by which a preferred stock sells below its par value. 3. the amount by which a bond sells below its face value.

discount broker a person or business who advances money on securities and discounts bills of exchange and promissory notes.

discount house a retail business that sells large quantities of goods at prices below those of other retail businesses.

discount rate interest charged in advance for the discounting of notes, bills, and other negotiable paper.

discretionary income income left for spending or saving after all necessary living expenses are paid.

dishonor (*v.*) to refuse to accept or pay a check or other note.

disintermediation (*n.*) the removal of money from interest-bearing bank accounts for investment at higher rates of return in stocks or bonds.

disk (*n.*) a circular plate for storing magnetically encoded computer data. Also spelled **disc**.

disk memory a random-access computer memory stored on disks.

disk pack a set of magnetic disks used in a computer's processing unit.

disposable income income left after payment of taxes and available for spending or saving.

dispossess (*v.*) to remove a tenant from occupancy or possession of real estate by legal action.

distrain (*v.*) to seize property as security for a debt.

distress for rent the seizure of a tenant's belongings in payment for rent.

distress sale a sale forced by any one of several adverse conditions affecting the seller, such as damage to merchandise or financial difficulties.

distress warrant an order authorizing the seizure of personal property and its sale at public auction, the proceeds of which go to pay overdue taxes.

distribution (*n.*) 1. a system for getting goods into the hands of consumers. 2. the dividing up of something among many people or interests.

distribution costs costs that result directly from the distribution and sale of a product, such as shipping expenses.

distributor (*n.*) a business that distributes goods to consumer markets for a manufacturer.

divest (*v.*) 1. to deprive of rights, authority, or property. 2. to free oneself of interest in and responsibility for a business. **—divestiture** (*n.*)

dividend (*n.*) a portion of a corporation's profits distributed to its shareholders, usually on a quarterly basis.

dock (*v.*) to deduct part of an employee's wages for lateness, breakage, or infringement of other rules.

document (*n.*) anything written or printed in order to record information.

documentation (*n.*) the use of written information to support facts or claims.

documentary stamp a revenue seal issued as payment of a fee on such actions as deed filings.

domicile (*n.*) a legal residence; a person's permanent home.

dominion (*n.*) 1. complete control of right of ownership. 2. in the transfer of property, the process by which the former owner surrenders power over the property and passes it to the new owner.

donate (*v.*) to give as a gift, as to charity. **—donation** (*n.*)

donated stock outstanding capital stock given to the issuing corporation by its stockholders for resale at a price not subject to legal restrictions.

donee (*n.*) a person who receives a gift.

donor (*n.*) 1. a person who gives a gift. 2. a person who sets up a voluntary trust.

dormant account a bank account that has had little or no deposit or withdrawal activity for a long time.

double-entry bookkeeping a standard method of bookkeeping in which each transaction is recorded as both a debit and a credit. See SINGLE-ENTRY BOOKKEEPING.

double indemnity a clause in an insurance policy that provides for the payment of twice the face value of the policy under certain specified conditions, as in the case of accidental death.

double time twice the regular rate of pay, usually earned by employees who work on Sundays or holidays.

Dow-Jones averages an average of stock prices on the New York Stock Exchange, as computed by Dow Jones & Co., based on the opening, closing, high, and low average prices of a representative group of stocks on a particular day.

down payment a partial payment that gives the purchaser possession of merchandise or real estate, subject to full payment in the future.

downtime (*n.*) a period during which machinery is out of operation, usually for repair; often used in reference to computer systems.

draft (*n.*) a written order, such as a check, directing a bank or other financial institution to make payment to a third party.

drawee (*n.*) a bank or other financial institution that, upon receiving the drawer's draft, makes payment to a third party.

drawer (*n.*) a person who draws an order for the payment of money.

drop-ship (*v.*) to send merchandise directly from the manufacturer to the retailer. **—drop-shipment** (*n.*)

drop-shipper (*n.*) a jobber who takes orders from buyers and forwards them to manufacturers, who then ship directly to those buyers.

due bill a signed document acknowledging a debt that is payable in goods and services.

dump (*v.*) 1. to sell goods in foreign markets at low prices, often below the cost of manufacture, in order to eliminate surplus or undercut competitors in those markets. 2. in the United States, to sell imported goods at low prices, often below the cost of manufacture.

dun (*v.*) to demand repeatedly and forcefully the payment of a debt.

duty (*n.*) a customs tax on imported and exported goods.

duty-free (*adj.*) free of or exempt from customs taxes.

E

early retirement the voluntary departure of an employee from a business before he or she reaches the age or number of years of service required to receive full pension benefits.

earned income the income received for goods and services delivered.

earned surplus income retained as profit.

earnest money money paid to the owner of real estate by a prospective purchaser as evidence of a serious intent to buy.

earnings *(n., pl.)* the income received by a business for the services or products it provides.

earnings per share the net income from common stock over a given period of time divided by the number of shares outstanding. *Abbrev.:* **EPS**

easement *(n.)* the right of a property owner or tenant to use land owned by someone else for a right of way, as for access to water or electrical lines.

economic goods manufactured goods that take on an additional value because of the scarcity of some of the materials needed to produce them.

economic growth a per capita increase in real income over a given period of time.

economic indicators data used to analyze and forecast business conditions, such as the consumer price index, the prime lending rate, and the Dow-Jones averages.

economic life the period of time during which a fixed asset can yield a profit.

economics *(n.)* the social science that is concerned with the production, distribution, and consumption of wealth, goods, and services and with the related problems of finance, taxation, labor, and so on.

economic sanctions the imposition of an embargo, boycott, or other trade restriction, usually by several countries on another country, in an attempt to force the sanctioned country into conformity with international law.

economy *(n.)* 1. the state of a nation's finances. 2. the careful management of wealth and resources to achieve thrift and avoid waste.

economy of scale the condition in which the average cost of production declines as output is increased.

edge corporation a foreign banking organization formed in compliance with the Federal Reserve Act and authorized to finance foreign trade.

effective date the date on which a contract, insurance policy, or other agreement goes into effect.

effective tax rate the average tax rate arrived at by dividing the total tax payable by the income on which the tax was calculated.

electronic funds transfer system a computerized system that processes financial transactions between member banks through the use of electronically transmitted messages. *Abbrev.:* **EFTS**

eligible investment an income-producing investment considered by the Federal Reserve Board to be a sound repository for savings bank deposits.

embargo *(n., pl.* **-goes***)* 1. a restriction imposed upon commerce by law, especially upon the import, export, or sale of certain goods. 2. an order by a government restraining or prohibiting merchant ships from entering or leaving its ports.

embezzle *(v.)* to misappropriate or steal something entrusted to one's care, especially money or stocks and bonds. **—embezzlement** *(n.)*

eminent domain the right of certain governmental bodies to acquire private property for public use with provision for just compensation to the owner.

employ (*v.*) 1. to engage the services of someone for wages, salary, or other compensation; hire.

employee (*n.*) one who is employed by a person or business for wages, salary, or other compensation.

employee profit sharing a company-sponsored fund made up of a given percentage of annual profits for distribution to eligible employees in proportion to their earnings.

employee stock ownership plan an employee-sponsored program that permits eligible employees to acquire stock in the corporation for which they work. *Abbrev.:* **ESOP**

employer (*n.*) a person or business that employs one or more persons for wages, salary, or other compensation.

employment (*n.*) 1. act of employing; being employed. 2. work in which one engages or is employed; job; occupation.

employment agency a business licensed to recruit qualified applicants for available positions and to find suitable positions for applicants seeking employment.

encroachment (*n.*) in real estate, the intrusion of some structure such as a building or a fence upon another's property.

encumbrance (*n.*) a claim against title to real estate or personal property.

endorse (*v.*) 1. to write one's signature on the back of a check or draft as evidence of its legal transfer or validity. 2. to give support to a political candidate.

endorsee (*n.*) a person to whom a check or draft is transferred.

endorsement (*n.*) 1. the writing of a signature on the back of a check or draft as evidence of its legal transfer. 2. an amendment or addition to a contract or legislative bill. 3. a rider to an insurance policy.

endorser (*n.*) a person who endorses.

endow (*v.*) to give money, real estate, or personal property as a source of income for the support of a college or other nonprofit institution. **—endowment** (*n.*)

engross (*v.*) to buy up a large enough quantity of a product to corner the market and control the price. **—engrosser** (*n.*)

en route *French.* on the way.

entail (*v.*) 1. to limit the inheritance of property to a specific line or type of heir. 2. to bring about or require as a necessary consequence of; necessitate. (*n.*) 1. that which is entailed, such as an estate. 2. a necessary order, such as the order of descent, for an entailed inheritance.

enterprise (*n.*) any business undertaking that involves risk.

entrepreneur (*n.*) a person who organizes, manages, and assumes the financial risks of a business enterprise.

entry (*n.*, *pl.* **-tries**) 1. one unit of information that has been or is being input on a computer terminal. 2. the recording of data in an account or account book. 3. a. the registration of a ship or its cargo at a customhouse. b. the documents involved in registration. c. the movement of goods through customs.

equal-opportunity (*adj.*) not practicing discrimination in employment because of race, color, sex, religion, or country of national origin.

equitable mortgage an unofficial document, clearly intended as a mortgage, that does not legally constitute a mortgage but is enforceable in a court of equity.

equitable ownership ownership of real estate by a person who does not have legal title, such as a beneficiary under a deed of trust. Also called **equitable title.**

equity (*n.*) 1. the value of an ownership interest in real estate or other assets after all debts and mortgages are paid. 2. the value placed on income that is distributed among owners. 3. the set of legal principles used by a court of equity to deal with matters for which there are no adequate or fair remedies under common law or civil law. 4. the claim or right recognized by a court of equity.

equity capital 1. the investments in a business made by the stockholders. 2. the net worth of a business equal to the total investments minus the total liabilities.

equity financing the sale of capital stock by a corporation.

equity of redemption the right of a mortgagor to reclaim property by paying the mortgage debt in full after the mortgagee has foreclosed on the property.

equity securities any issue of common or preferred stock.

equity transaction any transaction that results in an increase or decrease of a firm's net worth.

equity turnover the ratio measuring the relationship between sales and the common stock holders' equity in a corporation.

ergonomics (*n.*) the study of the relationship of people to their work, especially with regard to matching the needs of workers to the equipment they use and the jobs they do, for the purpose of increasing productivity.

escalation clause a contract clause that specifies conditions under which upward adjustment of prices may be permitted or faster debt repayment may be made.

escape clause a contract clause that stipulates conditions under which parties may withdraw from the agreement or modify their performance.

escheat (*n.*) the reversion of property to the government when a person dies intestate, and either has no legal heirs or the legal heirs fail to establish a claim to the property. (*v.*) to cause to revert by escheat.

escrow (*n.*) 1. a document, as a deed or bond or money or other property deposited with a third party to be returned only upon fulfillment of certain conditions. 2. **in escrow** held by a third party pending the fulfillment of certain conditions.

escrow account a liability account managed by an escrow agent in which all funds given in escrow are deposited.

escrow closing a real estate closing at which title instruments are not transferred, but placed in escrow.

estate (*n.*) 1. all property and assets owned by a person at the time of his or her death. 2. the right to, title to, or interest in any property, as opposed to the property itself.

estate at will a tenancy for an indefinite time, the duration of which is mutually agreed upon by owner and tenant.

estate tax a tax levied by a government on the estate of a deceased person before the estate is turned over to the heirs; as distinguished from the inheritance tax levied on the heirs' individual inheritances.

et al. (from *Latin*) and others.

Eurobond a bond released for sale in Europe by a non-European company.

Eurocurrency money from various countries deposited in European banks for use in the European financial market. Also called **Euromoney.**

Eurodollar (*n.*) a U.S. dollar that is deposited in a European bank and that is used as a medium of exchange in Europe, often in short-term financing.

European Economic Community an economic union established in Europe to abolish or mitigate trade barriers between members, which include Belgium, Denmark, France, Great Britain, Greece, Ireland, Italy, Luxembourg, the Netherlands, and West Germany. Also called **Common Market, European Common Market, Euromarket, Euromart.** *Abbrev.*: **EEC**

even lots stock shares sold in units of 100 or multiples thereof.

evict (*v.*) to expel a tenant from rented premises for nonpayment of rent or violation of a lease. —**eviction** (*n.*)

eviction notice a legal notice to a tenant to vacate premises.

excess insurance an insurance policy or bond that covers the insured party for losses or damages in excess of a specified amount, as distinguished from PRIMARY INSURANCE.

excess loan a bank loan, made to one customer, that is for more than the amount specified as a legal maximum.

excess profits tax a tax levied on profits that are greater than the law declares proper.

exchange (*v.*) 1. to trade one thing for another of equal value, as in trading the currency of one country for the equivalent amount of another country's currency. 2. to return merchandise for credit or for an equivalent item. (*n.*) 1. a place or organization where securities are traded. 2. the trade of one item for another of equal value, as in the trade of one country's currency for an equivalent amount of another country's currency. 3. a central location or system where telephone lines interconnect to provide local communication.

exchange acquisition a method of filling orders to buy blocks of stock on the trading floor of an exchange.

exchange distribution a method of selling off large amounts of stock on the trading floor of an exchange.

exchange rate the relative values of different countries' currencies with respect to each other, used to determine how much of one currency is equivalent to a given amount of another currency.

excise tax (*n.*) a tax levied on the manufacture, sale, or consumption of certain commodities in a country, such as tobacco, liquor, and gasoline. 2. a fee paid for the right to engage in certain businesses, trades, or sports.

exclusion (*n.*) the provision in an insurance policy for specific circumstances, hazards, or property that the policy does not cover.

exclusion allowance that portion of an annuity payment that is not taxable as income, determined by dividing the recipient's annuity investment by his or her life expectancy.

exclusive distribution a manufacturer's promise to a dealer not to distribute products to another dealer in the same area.

exclusive listing a contract in which the Realtor is given the sole right to market a piece of real estate that is listed for sale.

execute (*v.*) to enter an instruction or utilize a processing function on a computer system. —**execution** (*n.*)

execution time the period during which an instruction is decoded and performed by a computer. Also called **executive phase** or **execution cycle.**

executive (*adj.*) 1. of, relating to, or suitable for the management of affairs, as in business or industry. 2. concerned with the administration and enforcement of laws or the affairs of government. (*n.*) 1. a person who directs or manages affairs, as of a corporation. 2. the branch of government responsible for administering and enforcing the laws and for managing the affairs of a nation; the person or persons constituting this branch of government.

executor (*n.*) a person appointed under the terms of a will to carry out its provisions.

executrix (*n., pl.* **-trixes** or **-trices**) a woman executor.

exempt (*v.*) to free from taxes, requirements, or regulations that apply to others. —**exemption** (*n.*)

ex officio *Latin.* by virtue of a person's office or position.

expense (*n.*) the cost of goods or services used by a business to create its revenue, as opposed to a cost from which the business expects no financial return. See OPERATING EXPENSE.

expense account 1. an arrangement between a company and an employee whereby the company pays all expenses incurred in the performance of the employee's duties. 2. a record of such expenses. 3. an accounting record of costs incurred in order to produce revenue.

expense budget an amount that is allocated to pay for the cost of producing revenue.

expiration date the date on which an agreement, contract, or obligation terminates.

expire (*v.*) to come to an end, as a lease, contract, insurance policy, or a term of office. —**expiration** (*n.*)

export (*v.*) to carry or send commodities to other countries for sale or trade. (*n.*) 1. that which is exported. 2. the act of exporting. —**exporter** (*n.*)

ex post facto *Latin.* made or done after something but having retroactive effect, as a law or regulation.

expropriate (*v.*) to take private property from a person or business, especially for public use by right of eminent domain. 2. to deprive (a person) of ownership or possession. —**expropriation** (*n.*)

extended coverage endorsement a rider that extends insurance coverage beyond that provided by the standard policy.

extension (*n.*) an allowance of more time in which to pay a debt.

external audit a review of a business's accounts carried out by an auditor who is not a member of the business's permanent staff.

external financing operating revenue raised through loans or stock sales.

extort (*v.*) to obtain something, especially money or valuables, by threats, force, or abuse of authority. —**extortion** (*n.*)

extortionist (*n.*) a person who extorts.

F

face value the value printed or written on a negotiable instrument such as a currency note or bond.

facsimile (*n.*) 1. an exact copy or reproduction. 2. the sending and reproduction of written or graphic materials by electronic means. *Slang:* **fax**

factor (*n.*) 1. a person who conducts business for another. 2. a finance company that buys the rights to debts owed to a business.

factorage (*n.*) the commission that is charged by a factor.

factoring (*n.*) the act of doing business as or with a factor.

fair market value the value an item would have in a completely unrestricted market, as opposed to an estimated or artificially manipulated value.

feasibility study an investigation of the probable success of a business venture before it is undertaken.

featherbedding (*n.*) labor union tactics that require an employer to hire unnecessary personnel.

Federal Deposit Insurance Corporation a federal agency that supervises commercial banking and insures the deposits of member banks and their depositors. *Abbrev.:* **FDIC**

Federal Reserve Bank one of the 12 regional banks operating under the Federal Reserve Act of 1913.

Federal Reserve Board the seven-member governing body of the Federal Reserve System.

Federal Reserve note paper currency issued by a Federal Reserve Bank.

Federal Reserve System the central banking system of the United States, controlled by the federal government through the Federal Reserve Board and operated through a system of 12 Federal Reserve Banks, which are privately owned by commercial banks and which regulate the member banks in their respective districts. It was established in 1913 by the Federal Reserve Act to stabilize the economy by regulating the flow of currency and credit in accordance with business practices. *Slang:* **Fed**

Federal Savings and Loan Insurance Corporation a federal agency that insures deposits in member savings and loan associations. *Abbrev.:* **FSLIC**

Federal Trade Commission the federal agency that oversees trade practices in interstate commerce. *Abbrev.:* **FTC**

fee simple outright ownership of real estate with unrestricted rights of disposition. Also called **fee simple absolute.**

felony (*n.*) a serious crime, usually punishable by a minimum penalty of a year in prison. See MISDEMEANOR.

fiat (*n.*) an authoritative order, decree, or sanction.

fiat money paper currency that is issued by a government, but not backed by reserves of gold or silver.

fidelity insurance insurance that protects a business against losses resulting from wrongdoing by employees.

fiduciary (*adj.*) relating to or designating a person who holds something in trust for another; of a trustee. (*n.*) a trustee.

field auditor an internal auditor from the home office of a business who examines the records of branch offices.

finance (*n.*) 1. the theory and management of monetary affairs of individuals, businesses, or governments, including such matters as credit, banking, and investments. 2. **finances** monetary, credit, and capital resources of an individual or organization. (*v.*) to provide capital for the formation or operation of a business.

finance company any company other than a bank that lends money to consumers and businesses.

finance cost the interest rate paid on money borrowed to finance a business or to make a purchase.

financial institution a business that uses depositors' money as loans or investments in order to earn more money, such as banks, insurance companies, credit unions, and pension funds.

financial intermediary a business in which the deposits of savers are used as sources of funds for borrowers.

financial statement a summary report of a business's resources and liabilities, usually prepared at regular intervals.

financier (*n.*) 1. a person who provides financing for new businesses. 2. a person engaged in large-scale financial matters.

finder (*n.*) a person who, for a fee, effects a business transaction between others, especially in real estate.

finder's fee money paid to a person who, as a profession, effects business transactions between others.

finished goods products fully manufactured and ready for sale.

fire insurance insurance protection against losses caused by fire.

fire sale a sale, at lowered prices, of goods damaged in a fire.

First In, First Out a method of inventory accounting based on the assumption that items bought first will be sold or used first. *Acronym:* **FIFO**

first mortgage a mortgage that takes precedence over all other claims against the same property, except for those claims given priority by law, such as real estate taxes.

first mortgage bond a corporate bond that is secured by a first mortgage on the issuer's property.

fiscal (*adj.*) relating to money matters; financial.

fiscal policy government policy regarding the disposition of receipts, including taxes, and expenditures, including the federal budget.

fiscal year a business's accounting year, which can be any consecutive 12-month period.

fixed annuity an annuity contract providing for fixed payments to an annuitant at regular intervals.

fixed asset a tangible asset necessary to the operation of a business, such as land, equipment, or buildings. A fixed asset is held for use rather than sale. Also called **permanent asset.**

fixed capital money invested in material assets necessary for carrying on a business, such as buildings, equipment, and vehicles.

fixed charges financial obligations that must be met on specified dates, such as taxes, rent, mortgage payments, and debt service.

fixed cost an indirect expense, such as an insurance premium, that does not necessarily change when the volume of production or activity in a business changes. Fixed costs tend to remain relatively stable regardless of fluctuations in production or sales.

fixed income income that does not fluctuate over periods of time, such as interest on bonds, annuity receipts, and preferred stock premiums.

fixed liability a liability, such as a bond issue, that will not mature in less than a year; a long-term liability.

flagship (*n.*) a store or office that contains the executive offices of a business and is the main site of the business's operations.

flat rate 1. a percentage of interest on a loan that stays in effect throughout the duration of the obligation. 2. a set fee established for the performance of a service, no matter how much work is involved.

flextime (*n.*) a flexible time schedule that allows employees to set their own starting and finishing times for a work day within a range of established hours. Also called **flexitime.**

float (*n.*) funds that are tied up in checks or other negotiable instruments that have not been cashed, processed, or collected. (*v.*) 1. to put a bond or stock issue on the market for sale. 2. to obtain or negotiate a loan.

floating debt a short-term debt that has no specific date established for repayment and bears no fixed interest rate but is tied to the prime rate. Interest rates for floating debts are often expressed as a number of percentage points above the prime rate.

floor trader a person employed by a member firm of an exchange who trades stocks, bonds, or commodities on the exchange floor on behalf of the firm's clients.

floorwalker a person employed by a large retail store to supervise sales and services not usually handled by the regular sales staff.

floppy disk see DISK.

foreclose (*v.*) legally to deprive a mortgagor of the right to redeem a property on which payments have not been kept up.

foreclosure (*n.*) the legal process by which a mortgagor is deprived of the right to redeem property.

foreclosure sale the sale of real estate for repayment of a mortgage on which the mortgage holder has foreclosed.

foreign corporation a corporation doing business outside the state or country in which it is chartered.

foreign exchange a transaction exchanging currency of one country for that of another country.

foreign exchange rate the value of one country's currency as expressed in the currency of another country.

forfeit (*v.*) to lose ownership or rights as a penalty for some offense, error, or omission.

forger (*n.*) a person who commits forgery.

forgery (*n., pl.* **-geries**) 1. the fraudulent copying or altering of something, especially printed material and negotiable instruments. 2. an item that is forged.

form letter a letter designed to be duplicated and sent to many people.

Fortune 500 the 500 largest corporations in the United States, as ranked by *Fortune* magazine.

fractional lot a grouping of stock amounting to fewer than 100 shares.

franchise (*n.*) 1. an authorization granted to a businessman or businesswoman by a corporation to sell a product or service produced by the corporation. 2. the geographic area for which such authorization is given.

franchised dealer a retail business owner who sells goods or services under a franchise agreement with the manufacturer.

franchise tax a charge levied by a state or local government for the right to operate a monopoly business such as a bus line or public utility.

fraud (*n.*) 1. deliberate deception intended to deprive a person or organization of rights or property. 2. one who commits such deception.

free enterprise an economic system that allows private industry to operate under freely competitive circumstances and with minimal government control.

freehold (*n.*) the holding of a piece of real estate for life, usually with the right to pass it on through inheritance.

free-lance (*adj.*) pertaining to or acting as a free lance. (*v.*) to work as a free lance.

free lance (*n.*) a worker who provides services on a project basis rather than as a regular employee, especially a writer or artist. Also **free-lancer.**

free on board delivered aboard a common carrier by the seller without a delivery charge to the buyer. *Abbrev.:* **FOB**

free trade 1. international commerce that is free from governmental restrictions, such as tariffs or quotas.

freeze (*v.*) 1. officially to prevent the collection, use, or liquidation of funds as by government order. 2. to fix a price or wage at a certain level for a period of time. (*n.*) the keeping of wages and prices at a certain level over a period of time.

free zone a geographical area that is free from import, export, and excise taxes.

freight absorption shipping expenses paid by a manufacturer and not passed along to the buyer of the merchandise shipped.

fringe benefit a payment to an employee other than wages or salary, such as health or life insurance, a paid vacation, or maternity or sick leave.

frontage (*n.*) 1. the length of the front boundary line of a property. 2. the number of feet from the front of a lot or building to the property boundary.

frozen account a bank account on which activity has been suspended by a court order.

frozen asset 1. an asset that cannot be sold or used by its owner because of pending or current litigation. 2. an asset that cannot be sold within a short period of time without incurring a loss.

full coverage insurance in which losses are reimbursed at their full insured value.

fund (*v.*) 1. to provide money for. 2. to retire a short-term debt. (*n.*) 1. money or assets set aside for a specific purpose. 2. an available supply of allocated money.

funded debt a corporation's long-term, usually secured, financial obligation.

furlough (*v.*) to lay off workers temporarily.

future estate an estate scheduled for possession at a later time, such as land that will go to a wife after a husband's death.

futures (*n. pl.*) contracts for the purchase or sale of commodities for future delivery.

G

gain (*n.*) a monetary profit or other benefit or advantage.

garnish (*v.*) legally to withhold a person's wages or other property for payment of a debt.

garnishee (*n.*) a person served with a garnishment.

garnishment (*n.*) a court order directing the withholding of all or part of a person's wages or other property, and payment of such to the court or to the creditor until a debt is paid.

general contractor a person or business responsible for an entire construction project. A general contractor may hire subsidiary contractors to perform some or all of the work.

general ledger a bookkeeping record of all accounts with entries and balances that show assets, liabilities, expenses, and each component of ownership equity.

general mortgage a mortgage on all of a debtor's property, not restricted to one parcel. Also called **blanket mortgage.**

general mortgage bond a bond that is secured by a general mortgage on a business's property.

general obligation bond a municipal, county, or state bond backed by the credit of its issuer.

general partner a business partner who is responsible for the liabilities of the partnership up to the full extent of his or her own assets. See LIMITED PARTNER.

general strike a strike involving most of the workers in an industry or in an entire area or country.

general warranty deed a deed that includes a promise by the seller to defend the title of the real estate conveyed by the deed against all claims.

gift (*n.*) a property transfer made without payment in return.

gift causa mortis a gift given by a person before his or her death, and in anticipation of it, for the purpose of saving heirs the inheritance tax.

gift deed a deed for property transferred without payment.

gift tax a graduated tax levied by some states and the federal government, which is paid by the donor of a gift.

glamour stock a corporation's stock that attracts investors and sells at a high price because it is expected to increase at a substantial rate.

global search a procedure performed by a computer in which it searches the data base for a word or phrase, lists the occurrences, and when so instructed, makes a requested change in the data.

glut (*n.*) an oversupply of a commodity. (*v.*) to oversupply the market with a commodity.

gold standard a monetary system that defines the basic currency unit in terms of a specific amount of gold and that uses gold to back the currency.

goods in process partially finished manufactured products made from raw materials.

good will (*n.*) an intangible asset of a business that results from the good relations it has established with the public.

grace period a specific period of time past the due date for payment of a bill, during which it can be paid without the payer being considered in default.

graduated lease a long-term lease that provides for increases or decreases based upon future determinations or periodic appraisals. Also called **graded lease.**

graduated tax a tax whose rate increases or decreases along with the taxpayer's income or the value of his or her property.

graft (*n.*) an advantage or profit gained by dishonest means, especially through political influence or position.

grandfather clause a contract clause that permits existing conditions, rights, or privileges to continue, despite subsequent changes in legal requirements.

grand jury a jury summoned to hear accusations in criminal cases and to determine if the evidence is sufficient for the accused to be brought to trial.

grant (*n.*) in a deed, the clause that transfers title to real estate. (*v.*) in a deed, to transfer title to real estate.

grantee (*n.*) a person or organization to whom a grant is made.

grantor (*n.*) a person or organization who makes a grant.

grievance period the period each year when owners may register objections to real estate assessments made by local tax authorities.

gross (*n.*) 1. a total amount before anything has been deducted from it, as income. 2. a quantity of 12 dozen.

gross income total revenues before any expenses have been deducted.

gross national product the total value of goods and services produced in a country within a specified period, usually one year. *Abbrev.*: **GNP**

gross profit the difference between the amount derived from sales and the cost of goods or services sold. Also called **gross margin.**

gross revenue the total income gained from goods sold or services performed, before any expenses are deducted. Also called **gross sales.**

gross weight the weight of packaged goods including both the contents and the packaging.

ground lease a lease for the use of a piece of undeveloped land or for land exclusive of the buildings on it.

group insurance insurance, usually taken out by employers or associations, on the lives or health of employees or members at rates below individual policy rates.

guarantee (*n.*) 1. a pledge that a product is as represented and that it will be replaced or repaired if it is not, or an assurance that a service will be performed in the manner stated.

guaranteed income mortgage a purchase-money mortgage on income-producing real estate that includes a guarantee by the seller who holds the mortgage of a minimum cash flow or operating income.

guaranteed loan a loan or mortgage guaranteed to be paid by a third party if the borrower defaults.

guaranteed sale a commitment by a real estate broker to buy a specified piece of real estate if he or she does not find a buyer within a given amount of time.

guarantor (*n.*) a person or business who makes or gives a guaranty or guarantee.

guaranty (*n., pl.* **-ties**) an agreement to be responsible for the debts or obligations of another party in the event of that party's default.

guardian (*n.*) a person chosen by a court to care for the person and property rights of a minor or other individual who is considered incapable of managing his or her affairs.

guardian deed a deed conveying the property of a minor or an incompetent to a guardian.

guardianship (*n.*) the condition or authority of being a guardian.

H

hard copy a document written, typed, or printed on paper, as opposed to one kept in a computer file or on microfilm.

hard goods durable consumer products, such as small appliances, tools, and utensils.

hard hat 1. a protective helmet worn by miners, workers on construction sites, and so on. 2. *Colloq.* a worker who wears such a hat.

hardware (*n.*) the physical equipment that makes up and is used in a computer system or other information-processing system.

hazard insurance insurance protection against losses resulting from damage by fire, flood, windstorm, or other natural hazards.

heavy market a high volume of selling on the stock market without a corresponding volume of buying.

hedge (*n.*) a financial transaction that forestalls any profit or loss arising from price fluctuations.

heir (*n.*) 1. a person who receives or is entitled to receive another person's property through the legal right of inheritance. 2. a person legally appointed to inherit property in the event that no surviving heir is named in a will.

hereditament (*n.*) any property that is capable of being inherited.

hidden asset a business asset whose value is not easily ascertainable by examining a balance sheet.

hierarchy (*n., pl.* **-chies**) a vertical organizational ranking system in which each rank is subordinate to all those above it.

high finance *Colloq.* complex financial transactions.

historical cost accounting the most widely used accounting procedure, which records only costs and revenues realized at the time of transactions, without regard for replacement costs or fluctuations in value.

holdback (*n.*) a portion of monies owed to a general contractor that is withheld as security that the job will be done satisfactorily.

holdback provision a clause in a loan agreement for new construction, which allows the lender to fund only a portion of the loan until the building reaches a specified rent level or cash flow level.

hold-harmless agreement a contract in which one person's liability for damages is assumed by another, so that the person originally liable is not held responsible.

holding company a corporation whose primary business is the acquisition and management of subsidiary companies, in which it usually owns the majority of stock.

holdover tenant a tenant who remains in leased premises after the lease expires.

holographic will a will written in a person's own handwriting.

homeowner's insurance insurance against loss of or damage to a dwelling, against injury to its inhabitants and visitors, and against loss of or damage to their property.

homestead (*v.*) to settle on and claim land. (*n.*) any house and adjacent buildings, and the land on which they stand.

homesteading (*n.*) the process by which abandoned or foreclosed real estate is turned over, for a nominal fee, to a person who promises to rehabilitate it and live in it for a specified time before acquiring title.

homestead right the right to uninterrupted use of real estate as a family home, clear of creditors' claims.

honorarium (*n., pl.* **-ariums** or **-aria**) a fee, often nominal, paid to a professional person for a special task, such as a speech, performed in keeping with his or her profession.

horizontal consistency the uniformity of accounting procedures from period to period, as determined by an audit.

host computer 1. the computer that controls the operations of all other computers in a multiple-unit data communications system. 2. a computer used to prepare programs for use in other computers.

housing starts newly constructed single- and multiple-family housing units.

human resource accounting an assessment of the importance of skilled and loyal employees to a business's earnings outlook.

hypothecate (*v.*) to pledge something as security for a loan or other debt without transferring its ownership. **—hypothecation** (*n.*)

hypothecated asset an asset that is mortgaged to secure a debt.

I

illegal strike a strike in violation of a law, court injunction, or union contract. See WILDCAT STRIKE.

impasse (*n.*) a point in negotiation, as for a union contract, from which no further progress is possible; deadlock.

import (*v.*) to receive products or goods from another country, especially for purposes of sale. (*n.*) products or goods imported.

import duty any tax on imported goods.

import quota a government limitation on the quantity of a particular product that may be imported.

impound (*v.*) to seize goods by court order and hold them in protective custody.

imprest cash a small amount of cash kept on hand by a business for miscellaneous expenses; petty cash. Also called **imprest fund.**

in arrears see ARREARS.

income (*n.*) money received by a person or business from the sale of goods, services, or property, return on investments; and so on during a specified period of time.

income averaging a method for taxpayers to minimize taxes on a suddenly increased income by averaging current high income with lower incomes of previous years.

income debenture a bond that pays interest contingent upon the earnings of the issuing business. Also called **income bond.**

income/expense ratio see OPERATING RATIO.

income property real estate that produces income or is purchased for the sake of producing income.

income tax a tax on the yearly income or profits of individuals and businesses.

incorporate (*v.*) to form a corporation by charter from a state. **—incorporation** (*n.*)

increment (*n.*) an increase in the value of an investment or in income.

incremental (*adj.*) of or relating to the additional investment needed for a project or additional revenue resulting from a project.

indemnify (*v.*) 1. to repay for damage or loss. 2. to insure against future damage or loss. **—indemnification** (*n.*)

indemnity (*n., pl.* **-ties**) 1. in securities trading, an option to buy or sell a specified quantity of stock at a stated price within a given time. 2. repayment for damage or loss. 3. insurance against future damage or loss.

indemnity bond an insurance bond that protects an employer against loss resulting from the acts of employees or from other unforeseeable circumstances.

indenture (*n.*) an agreement between a borrowing business or corporation and a trustee, usually a bank, under which debentures or bonds are issued, setting forth the maturity date, interest rate, and other terms.

independent bank a local bank that has no branches outside of the community where it is established.

indirect cost a cost that is not readily identifiable with the production of specific goods or services but which can be applied to production activity in general. Overhead and wages are examples of indirect costs.

Individual Retirement Account an individual pension account in which a person may deposit 15 percent of income up to $2000 yearly and deduct this amount from taxable income. The funds may not be withdrawn until the account holder reaches age 59. Principal and interest on the account are tax-free until that time. *Abbrev.:* **IRA**

indorse (*v.*) 1. in banking, to endorse. 2. to transfer title to real estate by writing one's name on the back of a negotiable instrument. **—indorsement** (*n.*)

industrial (*adj.*) of, relating to, or produced by industry. (*n.*) the stock of an industrial corporation.

industrialist (*n.*) a person who owns or controls an industrial business.

industrial revenue bond a municipal bond used to attract industry to an area by providing capital for building industrial plants.

industry (*n., pl.* **-tries**) 1. manufacturing businesses as a whole. 2. a particular branch of business, trade, or manufacture, as the tourist or automobile industry.

inflation (*n.*) an increase in the amount of currency in circulation, which results in a rise in the general level of prices and a decline in the buying power of money.

inflation accounting a bookkeeping technique that reveals the effects of inflation on a business's assets and profits.

information processing see DATA PROCESSING.

information retrieval the procedures for recovering stored data, usually from a computer system.

infrastructure (*n.*) the way in which various sectors of a nation's economy, such as communication and transportation, relate to each other.

inheritance tax a tax on property received by inheritance.

injunction (*n.*) a court order that prohibits an action or directs that an action be performed.

in kind describing the replacement of lost or damaged property or goods with similar property or goods, or repayment for a service rendered by the performance of a similar service.

input (*n.*) information entered into a computer system. (*v.*) to enter information into a computer system.

in re *Latin.* concerning; in the matter of.

insolvency (*n.*) the inability to pay debts when they fall due. **—insolvent** (*adj.*)

installment (*n.*) a single payment of a debt made at regular intervals until the debt is retired.

installment buying the buying of goods or services by making a small down payment followed by periodic payments until the total price is paid.

installment lending the lending of money to be repaid in a series of periodic payments over a specified period.

instant vesting a policy that allows employees to change jobs within an industry without losing pension rights.

institutional investor a financial business, such as a bank, credit union, insurance company, pension fund, or mutual fund, that invests large sums in securities.

insufficient funds a term used by banks to indicate that a depositor does not have enough money in an account to cover a check drawn on that account.

insurable interest an ownership interest, as in real estate or personal property, that is large enough to qualify for insurance protection against loss or liability.

insurance (*n.*) the protection against loss by means of a contract with an insurance company that guarantees to pay specified sums for specified losses. The insured pays a fixed fee to the insurance company for such protection.

See: blanket policy
casualty insurance
double indemnity
extended coverage endorsement
fidelity insurance
fire insurance
full coverage
group insurance
hazard insurance
homeowner's insurance
joint life insurance
leasehold insurance
liability insurance
life insurance
malpractice insurance
no-fault insurance
reinsurance
straight-life insurance
term insurance
title insurance

insurance agent a person who sells insurance policies for an insurance company.

insurance broker a person who sells insurance, but who is independent of any insurance company and seeks to find for his client the best policy among those being offered.

insurance premium a fixed sum paid to an insurance company for insurance protection.

insurance trust a trust made up of insurance policy contracts.

insure (*v.*) to protect a person, business, or property against risk or loss by means of insurance.

insured (*n.*) a person whose life, business, or property is covered by an insurance policy.

insurer (*n.*) a person or company that insures against losses.

interest (*n.*) 1. a fee paid for the use of borrowed money. 2. a legal right, claim, or share in real estate, personal property, or a business.

interest rate the amount of money charged by a creditor for the use of borrowed money, calculated as a percentage of the total loan.

interest warrant an order drawn by a corporation directing its bank to pay interest to a bondholder.

interface (*n.*) a connection between one part of a computer system and another, such as the point at which the printer connects to the central processing unit. (*v.*) to connect two parts of a computer system.

interim audit a preliminary audit done before the end of an accounting cycle to give the business an estimate of its performance to date.

interline (*v.*) to transfer equipment carrying freight from one carrier to another.

intermediate carrier a transportation company that carries freight between two points on a route, neither of which is the point of origin or destination.

intermediary (*n., pl.* **-ries**) 1. a middleman. 2. a person who attempts to make two opposing parties agree or compromise.

internal audit an audit carried out by a business's own accounting staff.

Internal Revenue Service the U.S. Treasury Department agency responsible for collecting federal income taxes and administering the tax laws. *Abbrev.:* **IRS**

interstate (*adj.*) between or among states.

interstate commerce any commerce that involves more than one state and crosses state boundaries.

Interstate Commerce Commission the federal agency responsible for regulating commerce that crosses state boundaries. *Abbrev.:* **ICC**

intestate (*adj.*) without having made a will. (*n.*) a person who dies without having made a will. See TESTATE.

in the black operating at a profit.

in the red operating at a loss.

in transit en route between the point of origin and the point of destination.

intrastate commerce any commerce that is conducted entirely within the boundaries of one state.

intrinsic value an asset's inherent value that does not depend on the marketplace, in contrast to the market value of the asset.

invalid (*adj.*) without basis or authority.

invalidate (*v.*) to nullify or void a contract, permit, or license. **—invalidation** (*n.*)

inventory (*n., pl.* **-ries**) 1. the assets of a business. 2. a descriptive list of the articles in stock at a given time. 3. the stock on hand or the products carried by a business.

inventory control a method of accounting for articles in stock by both bookkeeping and physical methods.

inventory turnover rate the rate at which inventory is fully replaced within a given period of time, such as a year. Also called **stockturn rate.**

inverse demand a condition in which the demand for a product or commodity rises as its price rises.

invest (*v.*) to put money into stock, real estate, or other property for the purpose of producing income. **—investment** (*n.*) **—investor** (*n.*)

investment counselor a person who advises individual or corporate clients about making and managing investments.

investment property a piece of real estate acquired for producing profit.

investment trust a trust whose main purpose is to generate income by making investments.

invoice (*n.*) an itemized bill of sale.

irrevocable trust a trust that cannot be changed or ended by its creator.

issue (*v.*) to offer a group of securities for sale on the open market. (*n.*) a group of identical securities offered for sale on the open market by a corporation. **—issuer** (*n.*)

itemize (*v.*) to list each item specifically, as in a tax return or invoice. **—itemization** (*n.*)

itinerary (*n., pl.* **-aries**) a list of people and places to be visited on a sales route or a business trip.

J

job action an employee protest against work conditions that may take the form of a work slowdown, a strike, or mass absenteeism.

jobber a person who buys products from a manufacturer and sells them to a retailer or who deals in job lots.

job classification the evaluation of the skills required for the performance of a job in order to establish an appropriate salary range for it.

job cost system an accounting method by which the total cost of a job is determined from the cumulative costs of each production stage.

job description an outline of the tasks and responsibilities required of a person in a particular job.

job lot a quantity of mixed, unsorted, or possibly defective goods sold at a reduced price.

job order a document authorizing work on a specified project.

job security 1. an assurance from an employer that an employee will be retained in his or her job. 2. a contract that protects an employee's tenure in his or her job.

joint account a bank account that is held by two or more people, each of whom has access to the account individually.

joint agreement 1. a contract between management and labor involving several organizations. 2. an agreement involving several groups or individuals.

joint contract an agreement made by two or more people or businesses promising to fulfill a specified obligation to another person or business.

joint executors two or more people who together ensure that the terms of a will are carried out.

joint liability the legal responsibility for an obligation or debt shared by two or more parties.

joint life insurance a policy covering the lives of two or more people, payable to the beneficiary upon the death of the first.

jointly and severally in law, a term denoting that each and all of the parties to an agreement can be held responsible for the actions and liabilities of any member or members of the group, within the limits of the agreement and to the extent of the members' respective shares.

joint note a document acknowledging a debt, signed by two or more people who share responsibility for repayment.

joint ownership the possession of a business or of a piece of property by two or more parties.

joint return an income tax statement filed by a husband and wife.

joint tenancy the right and title of two or more parties to hold equal interest in specified premises or land.

jointure (*n.*) the property given to a woman by her husband at the time of marriage for her use after her husband's death.

joint venture a form of partnership entered into by two or more parties to carry out one specified project, such as a real estate sale or a securities underwriting.

joint will a single document providing for the disposition of property owned separately or together by two or more people, after the death of one or more of them.

journal (*n.*) an account book in which the original records of transactions are entered.

journeyman (*n., pl.* **-men**) a tradesman or craftsman who has completed an apprenticeship but is not yet eligible to become a master and therefore works for a master tradesman.

judgment (*n.*) 1. the determination of a court of law regarding the validity of a claim. 2. an order, decree, or penalty handed down by a court of law.

judgment creditor a person or business whose claim against an alleged debtor has been upheld by a court of law.

judgment debt a money obligation or liability claimed by the creditor against a debtor and validated by a court decision.

judgment debtor a person or business ordered by a court of law to pay money that is owed to another party.

judicial partition a legal proceeding in which a co-owner of real estate or other property gives up his or her interest in it.

judicial sale the sale of property, ordered and supervised by a court of law, the proceeds of which are used to pay a legal debt.

junket (*n.*) a pleasure trip or excursion, as one taken by a governmental official or business executive, paid for by public or organizational funds and made ostensibly for purposes of official business.

jurat (*n.*) a memorandum in an affidavit stating when, where, and before whom the document was sworn.

juratory (*adj.*) comprising or having the force of a legal oath.

jurisdiction (*n.*) 1. the power or right to exercise authority. 2. the judicial or territorial limits within which authority may be exercised. 3. the authority of a court to try a specified range of cases.

jurisdictional (*adj.*) pertaining to jurisdiction.

jurisdictional dispute 1. a conflict between two or more unions over which should concern itself with a particular job, or should operate within a particular geographical area. 2. a conflict between any parties concerning their authority to act or make decisions in a particular case.

jurisdictional strike a strike resulting from conflict over the limits of authority of rival unions.

K

keyboard (*n.*) an arrangement of keys, similar to those on a typewriter, that are used to enter data and instructions into a computer, word processor, adding machine, or other such machine. (*v.*) to feed data and instructions into a computer by using a keyboard.

keyboard entry a method of entering data using a keyboard.

kickback (*v.*) 1. to make a forced return of part of one's wages to one's employer. 2. to make an illegal and secret rebate to a buyer or a buyer's agent in return for receiving an order. (*n.*) 1. a forced return of wages to an employer. 2. an illegal rebate to a buyer or buyer's agent.

killing (*n.*) *Colloq.* an exceptionally large profit on an investment.

kite (*v.*) to issue a check for an amount that exceeds a bank account balance.

kiting (*n.*) the act of fraudulently padding a bank account balance by transferring a check between two accounts and recording only the deposit.

L

labor dispute a controversy regarding terms, tenure, or conditions of employment.

labor force 1. the total number of people willing and able to work. 2. the total number of people employed by a business.

labor pool the source of personnel from which prospective employees are recruited.

labor union an organization of workers formed for the purpose of engaging in collective bargaining to improve members' wages, benefits, and working conditions.

landlord (*n.*) the owner of land or buildings who leases the use of his property to others.

landlord's warrant a court-approved warrant that is obtained by a landlord and permits him or her to seize a tenant's personal property until past-due rent payments are paid.

land trust a trust composed of titles to real estate.

Last In, First Out 1. a method of inventory valuation that bases current valuations on the price of the most recent shipment of a given item. 2. in banking, withdrawals, as from a savings account, are made from the money most recently deposited. *Acronym:* **LIFO**

last will and testament the final will made by a person, superseding all previous ones.

late charge an additional fee charged to a borrower who does not make a regular installment payment by a certain day of the month.

layaway (*n.*) a payment method in which a store will hold goods for a customer who pays a deposit, the balance being due when the customer picks up the goods.

lay off (*v.*) to suspend employment temporarily because of a cut-back in production or a change in budget allocation. (*n.*) a suspension of employment. —**layoff** (*n.*)

lead time the interval between the time an order is placed and the time it is delivered, or the time between the conception of a project and its actual execution.

lease (*n.*) a contract permitting the use or occupancy of real estate for a specified period of time at a specified rental fee. (*v.*) to grant a lease.

leaseback (*n.*) an arrangement by which the seller of real estate remains as a tenant after completing the sale and delivering the deed.

leasehold (*n.*) 1. tenure by lease. 2. real estate held under a lease. —**leaseholder** (*n.*)

leasehold insurance an insurance policy that protects the landlord against the leaseholder's default in rental payments for the remainder of the lease.

leasehold mortgage a mortgage secured by a leasehold interest in real estate.

lease-purchase agreement a contract that allows an established portion of a leaseholder's rent to be applied to the purchase of the leased property.

leave of absence a period of time off from work, usually without loss of seniority, that is granted with the assumption that the employee will return to the job.

ledger (*n.*) the bookkeeping record that shows the totals of all accounts, and in which a separate account is created for every type of transaction.

legacy (*n., pl.* **-cies**) personal property bequeathed in a will.

legal reserve the amount that a bank or insurance company is legally required to maintain to meet withdrawal demands and claims.

legal tender coin and currency of a country that, by law, must be accepted in payment of all debts in that country.

lend (*v.*) to give up money or something else of value for a period of time without giving up ownership of it and with the expectation of having it returned. **—lender** (*n.*)

lessee (*n.*) a person or organization that rents from an owner; tenant who holds a lease.

lessor (*n.*) an owner who rents property to others; landlord who conveys a lease to a tenant.

letterhead (*n.*) a sheet of stationery on which is printed the name and address of a person or business.

letter of credit a document, issued by a bank on behalf of a buyer, guaranteeing payment to a seller.

levy (*v.,* **-vied, -vying**) to impose a tax on or demand additional capital from. (*n., pl.* **-vies**) a tax assessment or demand for additional capital.

liability (*n., pl.* **-ties**) 1. a debt owed by a business or the funds a bank owes to its depositors. Opposite of ASSET. 2. a legal obligation.

liability insurance insurance against loss resulting from injury or damage.

liable (*adj.*) 1. being subject to a particular risk, expense, or penalty that is likely to happen or be met with. 2. legally responsible for something.

libel (*v.*) to write, print, or publish false and malicious statements defaming a person or intending to harm the person's good name or reputation. (*n.*) a false or malicious statement. Distinguished from SLANDER.

license (*n.*) a permit granted or issued to a person or business to carry on an activity that could not be performed without such authorization. (*v.*) to grant or issue a license. **—licenser** (*n.*)

licensee (*n.*) a person or business to whom a license is granted.

lien (*n.*) a legal claim against the property of a person or business for payment of a debt.

lienee (*n.*) a person or business against whose property a lien is charged.

lienor (*n.*) the holder of a lien.

life estate an interest in real estate or personal property that is limited to the lifetime of the owner.

life insurance a form of insurance that pays a specific sum to a designated beneficiary upon the death of the person who is insured.

life tenant 1. a beneficiary who has possession of real estate during his or her lifetime. 2. an interest in real estate that is limited to the lifetime of the owner; life estate.

limited guarantee a product guarantee with certain restrictions or limitations as allowed by law.

limited liability the legal exemption of stockholders from the debts of the corporation or limited partnership over the amount each has invested.

limited partner a business partner whose liability for the business's debts is limited to a specific amount. See GENERAL PARTNER.

line executive an executive who has the authority to make policy decisions and order others to perform tasks. See STAFF EXECUTIVE.

line of credit 1. the maximum amount of money a lender allows a person or business to borrow. 2. the maximum dollar amount of goods a business can purchase from a vendor on open account.

line printer a computer device that prints a line of characters all at once as a unit.

liquid (*adj.*) cash or the capability of being readily converted to cash.

liquid asset cash or an asset that can be readily converted to cash such as a government bond.

liquidate (*v.*) 1. to convert assets to cash. 2. to discharge, pay off, or settle accounts by applying the assets to the debts. **—liquidation** (*n.*)

liquidating dividend a final dividend declared at the closing of a corporation, which is distributed among the stockholders.

liquidating partner a partner who is appointed to settle all accounts for a partnership that is going out of business.

liquidator (*n.*) a person legally in charge of liquidating a business.

liquidity (*n.*) 1. the solvency of a business, especially as it relates to the ability to convert assets quickly into cash. 2. the power of the market to absorb a reasonable amount of buying or selling of a particular security at reasonable price fluctuations.

list (*v.*) 1. to write a series of items designating quantities for data-processing input or output. 2. to enter corporate stock on the roster of those traded on an exchange. 3. to authorize a real estate broker to advertise property for sale or rent.

listing (*n.*) 1. an agreement between an owner of real estate and a broker whereby the broker agrees to sell or rent a property in return for a commission. 2. the admission of a corporation's securities to trading status on an exchange.

list price the published retail price that may be reduced at the discretion of the retail store.

litigate (*v.*) to contest in a lawsuit. **—litigation** (*n.*)

living trust a voluntary trust created from the specified assets of a living person.

loan (*n.*) a sum of money lent to a borrower, which must be repaid with interest.

loan application a questionnaire provided by a lender to be filled out by a prospective borrower, the information from which helps the lender to decide whether or not to grant the loan.

loan shark a person who lends money, often to poor credit risks, at rates of interest well above the legal limit.

loan value the amount a lender will lend with property as collateral, or the amount that can be borrowed against a life insurance policy.

long-term capital gain the profit made from the sale of capital assets that have been held for more than 12 months.

long-term debt a liability that becomes due more than one year after it is incurred.

loss (*n.*) 1. any decrease in quality, quantity, or value of property. 2. the excess of the cost of an asset over the price received upon its sale. Opposite of PROFIT.

loss leader a product offered for sale at a loss in order to draw customers into the store in the hope that they will also buy other items on which a profit will be made.

loss ratio a ratio of losses incurred, by an insurance company, to premiums earned.

loss reserve the fund an insurance firm maintains for payment of incurred losses.

lot (*n.*) 1. the goods or services that make up a single transaction. 2. a parcel of land. 3. a quantity of stock shares, usually 100.

M

machine language the coded instructions that need no translation to be read or acted upon by a computer.

machine-readable (*adj.*) able to be used directly by a computer.

macroeconomics (*n.*) the branch of economics that deals with an economy as a whole or with large factors in an economy, such as total consumption, gross national product, and the like.

mail order a method of selling goods in which orders, payments, and shipments are all made by mail.

main frame the central processing unit of a computer.

majority stockholders the stockholders who have a controlling interest in a corporation because they own more than 50 percent of the voting stock. See MINORITY STOCKHOLDERS.

malfeasance (*n.*) the performance of an unlawful act, especially by a public official. See MISFEASANCE.

malpractice (*n.*) 1. injurious treatment or blameful neglect of a patient by a doctor or surgeon. 2. improper practice or misconduct by any person in an official or professional position.

malpractice insurance an insurance policy that protects professional people from claims for damages brought about by alleged improper performance of their services.

management (*n.*) 1. the person or persons who direct or control a business. 2. such persons collectively, especially in relation to workers or unions.

management by objectives a method by which managers and subordinate employees work together to establish goals for a specified period, meeting from time to time to assess their progress in achieving these goals.

management consultant a person who is hired by a business to study its management and to recommend improvements in it.

manager (*n.*) a person who is responsible for the supervision or direction of other people, a department, or a business.

margin (*n.*) 1. the difference between the market value of collateral securing a loan and the amount of the loan itself. 2. the amount paid by a customer when securities are bought using a broker's credit with the securities serving as collateral. 3. the difference between the cost of goods sold and the total sales income.

margin account a client's account at a brokerage firm that is maintained so the broker can buy stock on the client's demand without the client having to pay in full before the purchase is transacted.

margin call 1. a demand placed upon a customer by his or her broker to put up additional money or securities with the broker in order to maintain the minimum required balance in a margin account. 2. a demand by a bank for additional collateral or partial payment of a loan when the loan is secured by securities and the value of those securities has declined.

margin of safety 1. the balance of income remaining after the payment of fixed charges. 2. the amount by which sales are greater than the break-even point, which provides a cushion against a decline in sales or other unexpected event. 3. the difference between the value of a bond issue and the market value of the collateral securing the issue.

markdown (*n.*) 1. a reduction in a previously established selling price. 2. a revaluation of stocks following their decline in market quotations.

market (*n.*) 1. the people who have the money, ability, and desire to purchase a product or service. 2. a geographic area where there is a demand for a product or service. 3. an estimated or actual demand for a product or service. (*v.*) to offer for sale.

marketable title a property title that is free of defects and legally is acceptable.

marketing (*n.*) the total activities required to move goods or services from the manufacturer to the consumer, such as distribution, advertising, product planning, transportation, and so on.

market order an order to buy or sell securities at the best price obtainable when the order is made.

market price 1. the price of a security, brought about by supply and demand. 2. the most recently reported price of a security.

market research a study that seeks to determine the size and nature of a market for goods or services.

market share the percentage of a market controlled by a business or a product.

market value the current value of real estate, goods, securities, and other properties as established by sales on the open market.

markup (*n.*) 1. the difference, in dollars or percentage, between the cost of an item and its selling price. 2. the increase in the value of an asset, such as a security, which reflects growth in market value.

mass production the production of goods in quantity, involving the use of machinery, interchangeable parts, and short, repetitive assembly procedures.

maturity date the date on which a debt becomes due for payment or on which an obligation or contract expires.

maturity value the money to be paid when a debt or other contractual obligation becomes due.

mediate (*v.*) to bring together the parties in a labor dispute. —**mediator** (*n.*)

mediation (*n.*) the efforts of a third party to bring together the parties in a labor dispute in order to effect a compromise.

memorandum (*n., pl.* **-dums** or **-da**) 1. a short written note that serves as a reminder to a person to do something. 2. a record of events or observations that is retained for future use. 3. an informal written communication, often from one office or department to another. 4. a statement made by the consignor listing the goods and terms of a returnable consignment.

memory (*n.*) in data processing, the storage area or device that holds information, including computer programs and the data upon which the programs act.

mercantile (*adj.*) of or relating to merchants or trade; engaged in trade.

merchandise (*n.*) purchased goods held for resale. (*v.*) to plan or promote the sale of goods.

merchandising (*n.*) all activities connected with the buying and selling of a product, such as promotion, advertising, pricing, and display.

merge (*v.*) 1. to combine two or more items, businesses, positions, or other things into one. 2. in computer terminology, to combine two or more sequentially ordered lists into one list.

merger (*n.*) the union of corporations by which one corporation continues to retain its identity while absorbing all the rights, privileges, franchises, and properties of another corporation or corporations.

metered mail any mail on which the postage is printed by a meter approved for the purpose by the U.S. Postal Service.

microcomputer (*n.*) a very small computer that contains a microprocessor combined with complementary devices such as memory units, a cathode-ray tube display, and so on.

microeconomics (*n.*) that branch of economics that studies the fiscal behavior of individual units in the economy, such as a family, a business, or a corporation.

microfiche (*n.*) a small sheet of microfilm on which can be recorded a number of pages of copy.

microfilm (*n.*) film on which documents, printed pages, and other such material are photographed in reduced size for ease of storage.

microprocessor (*n.*) a tiny silicon chip processing unit used in computers.

mill[1] (*n.*) a factory or plant, especially one in which the grinding of grain takes place.

mill[2] one-tenth of 1 cent ($0.001), used in calculating tax rates.

minicomputer (*n.*) a small computer that has a greater capacity for data processing and memory storage than a microcomputer. A minicomputer contains several microprocessors, whereas a microcomputer contains only one microprocessor. See MICROCOMPUTER and MICROPROCESSOR.

minimum wage the least amount of money that may be paid to workers as established by law or by union contract, usually on an hourly or daily basis.

minority interest the part of a subsidiary company's net worth connected with shares that are not owned by the controlling company or by other members of a combined group.

minority stockholders the stockholders who do not have a controlling interest in a corporation because they own less than 50 percent of the voting stock. See MAJORITY STOCKHOLDERS.

mint (*v.*) to coin money. (*n.*) the place where money is coined under government authority or by a government itself.

mint ratio the ratio in a bimetal money system between the prices of gold and silver as established by the government.

minutes (*n.*) a record of the proceedings of a meeting.

misdemeanor (*n.*) a criminal offense that is less serious than a felony and that is usually punished by a fine or a short term of imprisonment.

misfeasance (*n.*) the improper or illegal performance of a lawful act in which there is an infringement of the rights of another or others. See MALFEASANCE.

mistrial (*n.*) a trial that is declared void because of an error in the proceedings, lack of jurisdiction, or the inability of the jury to reach a verdict.

modus operandi *Latin.* method of operation; manner of working.

monetary policy a policy of the Federal Reserve System that attempts to regulate the money supply and the availability of credit in private markets in order to influence the level of national economic activity.

monetary standard the basis on which a nation's currency is issued.

money market the market for short-term, high-grade assets.

money market fund an investment offering made up of money market negotiable instruments that allows participants to invest and withdraw cash on a short-term basis while earning prevailing high-grade investment interest rates.

money order a negotiable instrument, similar to a check, that is purchased at a bank, post office, or other place of issue and is used primarily by people who do not maintain their own checking accounts.

money supply the total amount of currency in circulation in a country.

monopoly (*n.*) the exclusive control of a commodity or service in a particular market, or sufficient control to fix prices and eliminate competition.

moonlight (*v.*) to hold another job, especially at night, in addition to a regular one.

moratorium (*n., pl.* **-toriums** or **-toria**) 1. a legal authorization to delay the payment of money due. 2. the time during which such an authorization is in effect.

mortgage (*n.*) 1. a written conveyance of title to real estate as security of a debt with the proviso that the conveyance ends upon final payment of the debt. 2. any property that is pledged as security for payment of a debt. (*v.*) to pledge property by a mortgage.

See: blanket mortgage
chattel mortgage
equitable mortgage
first mortgage
general mortgage
guaranteed income mortgage
leasehold mortgage
open-end mortgage
package mortgage
participation mortgage
purchase-money mortgage
seasoned mortgage
second mortgage
standby mortgage
variable payment mortgage
wraparound mortgage

mortgage banker a banker or a financial institution that specializes in mortgage financing.

mortgage bond a bond that is secured by a mortgage on the real estate and other property of the issuing corporation.

mortgage broker a person who charges a fee for bringing together borrowers and lenders and for preparing any necessary documents.

mortgagee (*n.*) the person or institution to whom mortgaged property is pledged.

mortgage lien a debt secured by a mortgage that serves as a lien on the real estate involved after the mortgage is recorded.

mortgage note a note that offers a mortgage as proof of an indebtedness and states the way in which the mortgage is to be paid. The note is for the actual amount of the debt and makes the mortgagor personally liable for repayment.

mortgagor (*n.*) a person or institution that mortgages property.

multinational corporation a corporation that has investments and does business in a number of countries.

multiple listing a real estate property listing available to all brokers.

municipal bond a bond, issued by a city, town, or other municipality, that is usually free of tax on the interest paid.

mutual fund a business that invests the money of investors, as well as its own money, in the securities of other businesses.

mutual savings bank a savings bank that has no capital stock and that operates under law for the benefit of its depositors, who share in the net profits.

N

nanosecond (*n.*) one billionth of a second, a time measurement used to describe the speed of computer operations.

national bank a commercial bank that is chartered by the federal government and is a member of the Federal Reserve System and the Federal Deposit Insurance Corporation.

nationalize (*v.*) to transfer the control of a private business or industry to the national government of a country. **—nationalization** (*n.*)

naturalization (*n.*) the granting of citizenship to a foreign-born person.

negligent (*adj.*) failing to take adequate care or precaution in a situation, which may leave a person or organization liable for resulting damage. **—negligence** (*n.*)

negotiable instrument a document, such as a security, bond, or deed, whose ownership can be transferred from one person to another.

negotiate (*v.*) to bargain in order to reach a satisfactory solution to a dispute. **—negotiation** (*n.*)

negotiator (*n.*) a person who bargains in order to settle a dispute.

nepotism (*n.*) the granting of a job on the basis of a person's family relationship to the employer.

net (*n.*) the amount remaining after all deductions are made. (*adj.*) remaining after expenses have been deducted from the gross amount. (*v.*) **netted, netting** to earn or produce as a final profit.

net acre see COMMERCIAL ACRE.

net income the income that remains after costs, taxes, and other expenses have been deducted.

net lease a lease that requires the tenant to pay all operating expenses as well as the rent.

net loss a loss that occurs if the expenses of an operation exceed its income.

net profit the amount that remains after the expenses of an operation have been deducted from gross revenues.

net sales the amount of sales after discounts, returns, and allowances have been deducted.

net weight the weight of an item exclusive of its packaging.

network (*n.*) an interconnected communications system that transmits the same information to many different recipients.

net worth the value of the assets of a business or an individual after all liabilities have been deducted.

ninety-nine-year lease the longest lease allowable by law in many states.

no-fault insurance an insurance policy, usually for automobiles, that does not require the determination of fault for claims to be paid and that limits the right of the injured party to sue.

nonassignable contract a contract whose rights or obligations cannot be transferred to another party.

nonconforming use the use of real estate in a way that does not conform to zoning regulations, usually because the property was occupied before the regulations took effect.

noncumulative dividend a dividend that is payable only during the period when it is due and not at any time thereafter.

noncumulative stock a preferred stock whose dividends remain unpaid and do not accumulate if they are omitted in any particular year.

nonfeasance (*n.*) the failure to perform a legal duty. See MISFEASANCE.

noninterest-bearing note a note on which the issuer does not pay interest.

nonnegotiable instrument a financial document, such as a registered bond or savings account passbook, that cannot be transferred to another person by endorsement.

nonnegotiable title a title to real estate that cannot be transferred to another person by endorsement.

nonperformance (*n.*) the failure to fulfill part of an agreement, which can serve as the basis for a lawsuit.

nonprofit corporation a corporation organized to provide a social service rather than to make a profit, and which is given special tax status. Also called **not-for-profit corporation.**

nostro account an account maintained by a domestic bank with a bank in a foreign country. See VOSTRO ACCOUNT.

notarize (*v.*) to attest to the authenticity of a signature on a legal document, as by a notary public.

notary public a person appointed by a state to verify signatures and authenticate legal documents.

note (*n.*) a document acknowledging a debt and promising repayment.

novation (*n.*) the substitution of a new debt or contract for an old one by the agreement of both parties involved.

null and void without legal force; not binding; invalid.

O

obligation (*n.*) 1. any enforceable debt. 2. an agreement obliging one person to perform a service or duty for another.

obligation bond (*n.*) a bond authorized by a mortgagor that is larger than the amount of the mortgage.

obligee (*n.*) a person to whom another person is bound by a contract.

obligor (*n.*) a person who binds himself or herself to another person by a contract.

occupancy (*n.*) 1. an occupying, or taking possession, as of a dwelling. 2. the period during which a dwelling is occupied. 3. in law, the establishment of ownership by taking possession of a previously unowned thing or place.

occupancy rate (*n.*) the ratio of occupants to the number of available dwellings in a building or area.

occupancy tax (*n.*) a tax imposed on occupants who rent rather than own the property they occupy.

occupant (*n.*) 1. a person who occupies a dwelling or post. 2. a person who acquires title to something by right of occupancy.

occupational disease (*n.*) an illness frequently contracted by workers in a particular occupation.

occupational hazard (*n.*) the risk of illness or injury that is inherent in a certain occupation.

odd lot a quantity of less than 100 shares of a stock in a transaction.

offer (*v.*) to express willingness to buy or sell something at a stated price.

offering (*n.*) in finance, an issue of securities to be sold either publicly or privately.

off-line (*adj.*) designating a unit of data-processing equipment that is not under the direct control of its central computer. Opposite of ON-LINE.

offset (*v.*) 1. to equalize by balancing out or compensating for something. 2. in banking, to seize a debtor's deposits as compensation for a loan in default.

ombudsman (*n.*) a public official appointed to investigate complaints lodged by citizens against the government, especially where individual rights allegedly are being violated.

on consignment describing an arrangement whereby an owner turns over goods to a seller and defers collection of payment until the goods have been sold.

on demand of or concerning a bill of exchange that is payable upon presentation to the person or organization owing money on it.

on-line (*adj.*) designating a unit of data-processing equipment that is under the direct control of its central processor. Opposite of OFF-LINE.

on-line real-time designating a data-processing operation in which results are monitored during the same time that the computer is receiving input data.

on order designating goods that are paid for but not yet received.

open account 1. credit extended to a buyer as part of a sales transaction. 2. **to sell on open account** to extend credit.

open-end (*adj.*) designating the capital structure of a corporation whose securities are not transferable but are redeemable at the discretion of the securities holder.

open-end agreement 1. any agreement of indefinite duration. 2. a union contract having no date of expiration.

open-end contract an agreement calling for the performance of services during a specified time period but at no fixed date.

open-end mortgage a mortgage that allows the borrower to reborrow mon-eys paid on the principal, up to the original amount.

opening balance the amount of funds in a financial account at the beginning of an accounting period.

open listing a listing that makes property available to more than one broker.

open stock replacement items kept in stock to fill out sets of goods such as silverware and china.

operating expense any expense incurred as a result of the normal operations of a business or other organization.

operating ratio the proportion of a business's total operating costs to its total income.

operational audit an investigation of a business's operating policies and practices to determine their overall efficiency.

optical character recognition the machine identification of numbers and characters on printed or typed material through the use of light-sensitive devices. *Abbrev.:* **OCR**

optical reader a device that converts written or printed symbols into computer data; used to read encoded portions of checks, utility bills, and other documents and speed their processing.

option (*n.*) the right to buy or sell something at a future date for a price stipulated at the granting of the option.

optionee (*n.*) a person having an option on something; prospective buyer or tenant.

optioner (*n.*) a person granting an option; seller; landlord.

ordinary income an Internal Revenue Service term for income that does not qualify as capital gains.

organizational chart a chart that identifies positions of authority within an organization and their interrelationships.

organized labor the part of a labor force that is unionized.

original cost all costs accruing to the acquisition and implementation of a fixed asset such as a factory.

original entry the first record of a transaction in an account book or set of books.

origination fee money charged for initiating and processing a mortgage loan.

out-of-pocket expense an expense incurred by one person on behalf of another person or an organization and not yet reimbursed.

output (*n.*) 1. information produced by a computer or other data-processing system. 2. the quantity of services or goods produced in any way.

outside director a member of a corporation's governing board who is not an employee of the corporation.

overage (*n.*) a surplus; an excess of goods. Opposite of SHORTAGE.

overcapitalization (*n.*) losses resulting from overcapitalizing.

overcapitalize (*v.*) to furnish an unprofitably large amount of capital for the operation of a business.

overdraft (*n.*) a withdrawal of money from a bank account exceeding the amount credited to the drawer.

overdraw (*v.*) to create an overdraft.

overdue (*adj.*) past the due date of a loan, installment payment, or other obligation.

overextend (*v.*) to extend beyond one's ability to meet commitments or obligations, as in borrowing beyond one's capacity to repay.

overhead (*n.*) the continuing costs of operating a business, such as taxes, rent, maintenance, and so on.

override (*n.*) a commission paid to a manager in the form of a salary increase.

over-the-counter (*adj.*) referring to the sale of securities that are unlisted, or sold directly to buyers rather than on the floor of a stock exchange.

overtime (*n.*) 1. time worked beyond the normal daily or weekly working hours. 2. pay received for such work.

owner-operator (*n.*) a person who manages the business he or she owns.

P

package mortgage a home mortgage that covers appliances and other such household items.

paid-in capital the capital acquired by a business from the sale of stock to stockholders.

paid-in surplus the amount of capital contributed by stockholders that is credited to an account other than that authorized by the terms of the business's incorporation.

paper profit a profit that is predicted but as yet unrealized.

par (*n.*) the nominal or face value of stocks, bonds, or other negotiable instruments, without consideration of premiums or discounts.

parent company a business that owns or manages subsidiaries or other properties.

par item an item that can be collected at its face value upon presentation.

parity (*n., pl.* **-ties**) the equality of purchase power of one currency with another, as indicated by their exchange value in gold or silver.

Parkinson's Law any one of several statements expressed as economic law, such as that work invariably expands to fill the time allotted to it, and expenditures always climb to reach income.

par list a list issued by the Federal Reserve System of cities and towns in which banks will remit checks and other items at par.

participating stock type of preferred stock that pays a dividend not less than that paid by common stock.

participation loan a large loan in which each of two or more banks lend a portion of the total amount.

participation mortgage a mortgage in which the creditor receives repayment plus a percentage of the profits from ownership.

partner (*n.*) one of the parties in a partnership.

partnership (*n.*) two or more parties sharing in the risks and profits of a business.

partnership dissolution the termination of a business according to the wishes of the partners, by the death or incapacity of a partner, or by legal action.

party (*n., pl.* **-ties**) an individual or group directly participating in a legal or business matter.

party at interest an individual or group with a vested interest in a business venture.

par value the face value of a share of stock or other negotiable instrument.

passbook (*n.*) a booklet issued by a bank to a depositor to show the record of all credits and withdrawals in a savings account.

passbook loan a loan, secured against the balance of a savings account for which the borrower's passbook is held as collateral.

past-due item any note of indebtedness for which a scheduled reimbursement has not been received.

patent (*n.*) a government license that grants a first inventor exclusive rights to manufacture, sell, and benefit from the invention for a specified period of time, usually 17 years.

patent monopoly a business that has secured a patent giving it exclusive rights to manufacture, sell, and benefit from its invention.

patent pending the U.S. Patent Office's term indicating that an international search is being conducted to verify an invention as new and patentable under the law.

pawn (*v.*) to deposit an item of value as security for a loan.

pawnbroker (*n.*) a person licensed to lend money at a legally specified rate of interest upon the security of valuable personal items that the borrower may reclaim when the loan is repaid.

payback period the time necessary for the cash inflow from a project to equal the amount of money invested.

payee (*n.*) the party to whom a check, note, or other negotiable instrument is payable.

payer (*n.*) the party responsible for paying an amount owed, as evidenced by a check, note, or other negotiable instrument.

payout (*n.*) after-tax earnings paid to stockholders in the form of dividends.

payout ratio the ratio within a specific accounting period of a business's payout to its total earnings.

payroll (*n.*) 1. a list of employees to be paid, with the amounts to which each is entitled. 2. the total amount of money to be paid to employees.

payroll deduction amount withheld from an employee's gross pay for such nontax items as savings bonds and health insurance.

payroll tax a tax levied on a business's payroll, as for the amount of an employer's contribution to social security.

peak season the period of time in which an item or service is in greatest demand by customers.

peculation (*n.*) the stealing or misuse of money, property, or especially, public funds by the person to whose care they have been entrusted.

penetration pricing the low pricing of an item in order to enter a market quickly.

penny stock a low-priced stock, usually selling at less than a dollar per share.

pension (*n.*) 1. a benefit paid regularly to a retired employee. 2. the system under which payroll deductions are made and benefits are paid to retirees. 3. assets set aside for the payment of pensions.

pension plan a company-sponsored program for the payment of pensions or annuities to qualified employees upon their retirement.

per annum *Latin.* annually.

per capita *Latin.* for each person.

percentile (*n.*) any one of 100 groups into which a series of individuals is divided according to equal frequency.

per diem *Latin.* for each day.

performance report a comparison of actual results against those forecast in a particular budget.

peripherals (*n. pl.*) auxiliary units of computer equipment controlled by a central processing unit.

perjury (*n., pl.* **-ries**) the willful telling of a lie while under oath.

perpetual inventory a daily record of stock for maintaining up-to-date information on inventory.

perpetuity (*n., pl.* **-ties**) a period of time theoretically without limitation, but often limited to a specific legal period, as is a pension or annuity.

perquisite (*n.*) any additional profit or benefit received apart from a regular salary, especially something expected as a result of one's position or employment, such as the use of a company car. Also, *slang:* **perk.**

per se *Latin.* by or in itself.

personal check a check drawn by an individual on a personal rather than a corporate account.

personal loan a loan, usually under $1000, obtained by an individual borrower.

personal property all movable possessions; property other than real estate. Also called **personalty.**

Peter Principle the theory that each employee in a business tends to be promoted until he or she reaches a level of incompetence.

petrodollars (*n., pl.*) *Colloq.* the money earned by oil-exporting nations, especially in the Middle East.

petty cash a fund of money made available to cover minor incidental expenses.

philanthropy (*n., pl.* **-pies**) a gift or endowment, and often the administration thereof, devoted to charity or humanitarian institutions. **—philanthropist** (*n.*)

Phillips Curve a procedure in statistics whereby the relationship between unemployment and inflation is plotted curvilinearly on a graph.

photocopier (*n.*) a machine for photographically reproducing printed or other graphic material, usually in black and white.

photocopy (*n., pl.* **-copies**) a reproduction of printed or other graphic material made by a photocopier. (*v.,* **-copied, -copying**) to make a photocopy of.

piece rate a means of compensation whereby an employee is paid for the number of items produced or processed rather than by the amount of time spent.

plaintiff (*n.*) the party that initiates an action in a court of law. See DEFENDANT.

planned obsolescence the incorporation of changes into a product to make an earlier model of it out-of-date, or the intentional designing of a product to have a short physical life.

planning and zoning commission a municipal body that regulates land use.

plenary session a meeting of a body attended by all qualifying members.

plow back to reinvest a portion of a business's earnings in the same business rather than to declare dividends.

points (*n. pl.*) a charge assessed by a bank or creditor to increase the yield of a mortgage to maintain competitiveness with other investments.

policy (*n., pl.* **-cies**) 1. a written agreement between an insurance company and the insured party. 2. a method of action maintained by a business.

policyholder (*n.*) the person insured by a policy or having control of a policy.

policy loan a loan, usually at low interest, secured against the cash value of a holder's insurance policy.

poll tax a tax levied equally on all parties required to pay it, regardless of assets.

port authority a municipal body established to regulate transportation facilities of a port, especially those affecting the loading and unloading of cargo.

portfolio (*n., pl.* **-lios**) all the securities held by an individual or institution.

post (*v.*) in bookkeeping, to transfer an amount from source documents to an original entry record, such as a journal, or from original entry records to a subsidiary record or ledger.

postdate (*v.*) to put a future date on a check or other document in order to postpone its payment or negotiation.

postmark (*n.*) an official mark placed on mail to cancel postage stamps and record time and place of mailing.

power of attorney a legal document empowering another party to act in the first party's behalf, either in a specified or unspecified manner.

preemptive right the option of a stockholder to purchase new issues of stock on a basis proportionate to his or her current holdings.

preferred creditor a creditor whose claim against a party legally takes precedence over those of other creditors.

preferred stock stock on which dividends must be paid before they can be paid on common stock.

premises (*n. pl.*) a plot of land and the buildings on it.

premium (*n.*) an amount in excess of the par, or face, value of a security.

prepay (*v.,* **-paid, -paying**) to pay in advance of receipt of goods, or in advance of due date.

prepayment (*n.*) the payment of a debt before it becomes due. In many installment loans, prepayment results in a reduction in interest costs.

prepayment penalty a penalty levied on the mortgagor for paying the obligation before its due date.

prepayment privilege a clause in a mortgage or other contract allowing repayment in whole or in part in advance of the due date.

prepayment yield the sum realized in reduced interest-costs that may be gained by prepaying a debt.

present value the current monetary value of some future funds, computed by taking into account all benefits or liabilities that may result from an investment.

prestige pricing increasing the price of a product to establish an image of quality.

pretax income gross income before taxes.

price (*n.*) the amount of money for which goods or services are bought or sold. (*v.*) to set a price on goods or services before offering for sale.

price control regulation of prices to curb cost-of-living increases.

price-earnings ratio the market price of a common stock divided by the annual earnings per share. *Abbrev.:* **P/E ratio**

price fixing 1. the setting of a retail price on a trademarked brand by a manufacturer. 2. the collusive setting of prices by manufacturers of competing products.

price level a relative position in a scale of prices, calculated by comparing current prices of labor, materials, and so on with prices at a particular point in the past.

price stabilization the maintaining of prices at a specified level.

price support an artificial means for maintaining a market price above a minimum level, such as governmental subsidies offered to certain growers, producers, or distributors.

price war a consistent, systematic reduction of the price of a specific product or service by two or more competitors. See RATE WAR.

primary account a first account of external transactions.

primary insurance an insurance policy or bond that covers the insured party for losses or damages up to but not beyond a specified amount, as opposed to excess insurance.

prime rate the lowest rate of interest available, usually reserved by banks for their preferred customers.

principal (*n.*) 1. a person who has another act as an agent for him or her in a transaction with a third party. 2. the sum on which interest is charged or earned.

private bank a bank that is organized under the laws of and chartered by a state and is subject to examinations by the state banking authorities, and that is often established as a partnership or a sole proprietorship.

private enterprise see FREE ENTERPRISE.

probate (*v.*) to prove in court that a document is a person's genuine last will and testament. (*n.*) the process of proving that a person's last will and testament is genuine.

proceeds (*n. pl.*) in accounting, the total amount realized from any single business transaction.

product (*n.*) a manufactured item or a service sold to consumers.

product development the process of generating and developing new ideas that result in products that improve or replace existing products on the market.

production (*n.*) the process of manufacturing a finished product. 2. the total output of a manufactured product.

product liability the responsibility of a manufacturer or seller for injury or damage caused by a product, usually through some defect in the product.

production capacity the largest quantity of goods that can be produced in a specific time period, using available equipment.

profit (*n.*) the income remaining after costs of production and other overhead have been subtracted, usually measured over a specific period of time. (*v.*) to gain financially through business transactions.

profitability (*n.*) the capacity of a business to earn a profit.

profit and loss statement an income statement for a set period, recording such items as sales, expenses, gross profit, and net profit. *Abbrev.:* **P. and L. statement**

profit center any section of a business that yields specific revenues.

profiteer (*n.*) a person seeking excessive profit, usually through the promotion of goods during a shortage.

profit margin the ratio of gross or net profit to number of sales.

profit sharing a program through which an employer offers employees bonuses based on business profits.

program (*v.*, **-grammed, -gramming**) to give a computer a series of instructions in a computer language that the computer can act upon.

programmer (*n.*) a person who conceives, writes, or inputs computer software.

programming (*n.*) the action of entering software into a computer's memory.

programming language the form of communication used between a programmer and a computer.

progressive tax a tax in which the tax rate rises as the tax base increases.

promissory note a written promise by one party to pay a sum to another at a specific future date.

promotion (*n.*) advertising, publicity, and other product exposure aimed at increasing consumer demand.

property (*n.*, *pl.* **-ties**) the exclusive right of a person to exercise control over an economic entity. Tangible property, such as jewelry, has physical structure; intangible property, such as a patent, has no physical structure.

property tax tax on the ownership of real estate, levied as a percentage of total value.

proprietary company a business that owns other businesses. Also called **parent company** or **holding company.**

proprietary interest net worth; assets after liabilities.

proprietary product a product under protection of a copyright, patent, or trademark.

proprietor (*n.*) the sole owner of a business or proprietorship.

proprietorship (*n.*) an unincorporated business owned by one person.

prorate (*v.*) to divide, distribute, or assess proportionately among members of a certain group, such as heirs or stockholders.

proration (*n.*) the equal or proportionate division of taxes.

prosecute (*v.*) to institute or conduct legal proceedings against a party in a court of law. —**prosecutor** (*n.*)

prosecution (*n.*) 1. the act or process of instituting and conducting proceedings in a court of law. 2. a person or persons instituting and conducting such proceedings.

prospectus (*n.*) a detailed printed statement describing a proposed enterprise or undertaking, issued by a business to prospective investors or buyers.

prototype (*n.*) an early or original model of a product or plan, proposed for development into a final model.

proxy (*n.*, *pl.* **proxies**) a person authorized to act for another, especially a person authorized to vote in place of a stockholder.

proxy statement a brief description of a stock given to prospective holders of a stock.

public carrier a common carrier or transportation line offering transport to anyone for a fee. See COMMON CARRIER.

public corporation a corporation whose stocks are owned mostly by the public.

public domain 1. the condition of those creative works and inventions that, not being protected by copyright or patent, can be used by anyone. 2. all land owned by the federal government for use by the public.

public relations the enhancement of a business's or organization's public image by gaining positive attention, usually through methods other than advertising.

public sector that part of an economy consisting of government-owned institutions.

public utility a privately owned corporation providing such services to the public as electricity, gas, telephone, or water.

purchase and leaseback an arrangement whereby an investor buys property from an owner-occupant who then continues to occupy the property under a long-term lease.

purchase-money mortgage a mortgage given by the buyer to the seller as part of the purchase agreement, and in lieu of an unpaid balance of the purchase price.

purchase order a form ordering goods or services and authorizing their delivery at a particular price.

purchasing agent an independent broker who acts as a business's agent in purchasing.

purchasing power the value of a currency considered in terms of its ability to buy items.

put (*n.*) an option to sell a certain stock at a specific price within a specified period of time. See CALL and PUTS AND CALLS.

puts and calls options allowing the buying or selling of a fixed amount of certain stocks at a set price within a specified period of time.

pyramid scheme 1. in the securities industry, the purchasing or selling of increasing size lots of stocks in a rising or falling market, using profits from previous transactions as collateral. 2. a business-opportunity fraud, often promoted through advertising that offers large profits for little personal investment.

pyramid selling a method of selling in which a core group recruits regional organizers who then recruit subdistributors who recruit salespersons who ultimately sell the product.

Q

qualified endorsement an endorsement releasing an endorser of a document from any responsibility if the terms of the document are not met or if the document is not accepted.

qualified statement a note by an auditor stating a disagreement with part of a report or pointing out a limitation of the audit.

qualifying share a share in a corporation that qualifies the holder to be a director of the corporation.

quality control the process of maintaining a standard level of quality in goods and services through inspection and correction of defects before the products or services reach the market.

quantity discount a reduction in price given for buying a product in large amounts.

quarter (*n.*) one fourth of a year; three months.

quarterly (*adj.*) at three-month intervals. (*adv.*) four times each year.

quasi contract an implied obligation that is not formally stated but is imposed by law to prevent injustice.

quasi-public corporation a privately owned incorporated business in which the public interest is also involved.

quayage (*n.*) a fee charged for use of a landing ship, wharf, or pier when loading or unloading cargo from ships.

queue (*n.*) 1. a line in which people or tasks wait for service or processing. 2. the system in data processing by which the processor assigns priority to the jobs to be performed.

quick asset an asset that can be converted into cash quickly with little or no loss of value.

quick ratio the ratio of a business's quick assets to its liabilities, showing the ability of the business to pay its debts quickly.

quid pro quo *Latin.* something for something; a mutual consideration or exchange of favors.

quiet enjoyment the legal right to own and use property without interference.

quiet title action a legal claim to establish or deny a person's claim to ownership of real estate.

quitclaim (*n.*) the legal release of a person's claim to rights or ownership.

quitclaim deed a document releasing the signer's claim to rights or ownership of property, usually without guarantees concerning all other claims.

quittance (*n.*) discharge from a debt or other obligation.

quorum (*n.*) the minimum number of members who must be present for a meeting to be able to conduct its business.

quota (*n.*) 1. the amount of production expected from each employee. 2. a fixed proportion of a total amount, as of imports or exports.

quota rule a union regulation that sets the number of employees to be hired for a given job within that union's jurisdiction.

quotation (*n.*) the current price quoted or published for goods, securities, or commodities.

quote (*v.*) to provide a current price for, as goods, securities, or commodities. (*n.*) quotation.

R

rally (*v.*, **-lied, -lying**) of stock prices, to show recovery of original strength after a decline. (*n.*, *pl.* **-lies**) of stock prices, the act of rallying.

random access memory a computer memory available to the user for writing programs and storing data. *Abbrev.:* **RAM**

random sample a group of items selected by chance to be representative of the whole.

rate of exchange the price at which one currency can be bought with another currency.

rate of inflation the percentage of increase in the amount of money in circulation, usually computed on an annual basis, indicating a decrease in the money's purchasing power.

rate of return the percentage of an invested sum that is earned by an investor annually.

rate setting 1. the setting of price limits on goods and services by a government. 2. the establishment of rates according to an agreement between an employer and employees.

rate war extreme competition between businesses, resulting in a reduction of prices to below cost, usually with the aim of bankrupting a competitor. See PRICE WAR.

ration (*n.*) a fixed portion, share, or allowance. (*v.*) to restrict to fixed portions; distribute in fixed portions.

rationing (*n.*) a method for restricting purchases or use of a product during periods of short supply.

raw materials goods used in the manufacture of products.

re (*prep.*) *Latin.* concerning; as regards.

read-only memory a computer memory that allows data to be accessed by the user but not modified in any way. *Abbrev.:* **ROM**

real cost expense expressed in physical units of measurement, such as tons or bushels.

real estate land and any structures or natural growth on it; real property.

real estate tax see PROPERTY TAX.

real income the total purchasing power of an individual or other entity.

realize (*v.*) to convert assets or property into cash. **—realization** (*n.*)

realized appreciation a gain in value reflected in assets.

real property land, including all structures and natural growth on it.

real time the time used by a computer to solve a problem and report an answer.

Realtor (*n.*) a real estate agent who is a member of the National Association of Realtors.

realty (*n.*) real estate; real property.

ream (*n.*) a quantity of paper, usually 500 sheets.

rebate (*n.*) the return to a customer of part of the amount paid for goods or services. (*v.*) to return (part of an amount paid for goods or services).

recall (*v.*) 1. to take back a distributed product for repair or other adjustment. 2. to call laid-off employees back to work.

recapture (*v.*) to earn through dividends the same amount of money that was invested.

recapture rate a rate of interest calculated to ensure the return of an original investment.

receipt (*n.*) a written record acknowledging the delivery of goods or services.

receiver (*n.*) a person appointed by a court of law to take charge of the property or business of another during litigation.

receivership (*n.*) 1. the state of being administered by a receiver. 2. the duties of a receiver.

recession (*n.*) a temporary period of economic decline in production and employment.

reciprocal trade agreement an agreement between two governments resulting in mutual adjustment of import duties.

reciprocity (*n.*) 1. a tariff agreement by which two governments promise to match any decrease in import taxes made by the other. 2. in real estate, the recognition of the license of one state in another.

reconcile (*v.*) to solve a discrepancy between two accounts.

reconciliation (*n.*) the process of bringing into agreement a bank's record and an individual's record of the same account.

recoup (*v.*) to recover an expenditure, as through sales or services.

recovery value net income estimated from the realization of an asset.

recycle (*v.*) to convert waste into usable material.

redemption (*n.*) the settlement of a debt on or before maturity.

redlining (*n.*) the practice of refusing to lend money or grant mortgages and insurance in a neighborhood considered a high-risk area financially. Some states have passed laws against this practice.

referee (*n.*) a court officer assigned to oversee the actions of a receiver or debtor.

referendum (*n., pl.* **-dums** or **-da**) 1. the submission of a law, either proposed or already in effect, to the direct vote of the people. 2. the submission of a contract to a vote by the rank-and-file members of a union.

refinance (*v.*) to renegotiate an existing loan or mortgage to obtain additional capital.

refinancing (*n.*) the renegotiation of an existing loan or mortgage to obtain new capital, usually at a different rate of interest.

refund (*n.*) a sum returned to a customer because of overcollection. (*v.*) to repay (an overcollected amount) to a customer by returning cash or issuing a credit.

registered bond a bond that is registered with the issuing institution in the owner's name and that can be transferred only when endorsed by the owner.

registered mail United States mail whose progress is recorded at each stage of handling to ensure special care in delivery.

registered representative a person employed by a member of a stock exchange to act as a broker for customers of the exchange.

registrar (*n.*) 1. a trust company in charge of recording stock transfers. 2. a person in charge of a corporation's records of shareholders and bondholders.

regressive tax a tax that decreases in rate as the amount taxed increases.

reinsurance (*n.*) the transferral by an insurance company of all or part of an insurance risk to one or more other insurance companies.

reinsure (*v.*) to lessen an insurance risk by spreading it among several companies.

reinvest (*v.*) to use the dividends or profits from the sale of a security to buy more of that security or of another security. **—reinvestment** (*n.*)

release clause a mortgage clause allowing a specific sum of money to be paid for the release of a proportionate part of the property from mortgage.

remand (*v.*) to send (a case) back to a lower, often original, court for further proceedings, sometimes accompanied by instructions.

remit (*v.*) to send money in payment for items or services received.

remittance (*n.*) 1. a transfer of payment. 2. the money sent.

remote access the ability of a distant station to communicate with a central data-processing facility.

remunerate (*v.*) to pay for services. **—remuneration** (*n.*)

rent controls legislation affecting the maximum rent that can be charged on certain types of real estate.

reorganization (*n.*) the legal redesigning of the corporate structure of a business, as in a merger or effort to avoid bankruptcy.

repatriation of capital the removing of one's capital from investments in a foreign country and returning it to one's home country.

replacement cost the estimated present cost of replacing existing structures or machines with ones of similar function.

repossess (*v.*) to take back consumer goods from a buyer who has failed to make payments on an installment plan. **—repossession** (*n.*)

reprographics (*n.*) the process or business of making reproductions or copies of documents.

repurchase agreement an agreement between a buyer and a seller that the seller will buy back a security or other property from the buyer at the end of a specified period of time.

requisition (*n.*) a formal written request for supplies or other equipment. (*v.*) to request formally in writing.

rescind (*v.*) to revoke or cancel (an agreement or part of an agreement).

rescission (*n.*) the act of rescinding.

research and development the process of creating or improving products or services with knowledge gained through study, experimentation, and technological advances. *Abbrev.:* **R & D**

reserve (*n.*) funds removed from net earnings and set aside, usually for protection against unexpected losses.

reserve account that portion of a business's excess of earnings not distributed to stockholders, but held for a future purpose.

residual (*n.*) 1. that amount left after something has been subtracted. 2. in advertising, a fee paid to a performer for a rerun of a filmed or taped performance in which he or she participated.

restitution (*n.*) 1. the return to a rightful owner of something that had been illegally taken away. 2. the payment of money to someone who has suffered a loss.

restraining order a court order demanding the maintenance of the existing state of affairs until all parties have been heard and a decision rendered.

restraint of trade any activity, such as price fixing, that interferes with free competition or the movement of goods.

résumé (*n.*) a summary of a job applicant's education, previous job experience, qualifications, and skills.

retail (*adj.*) involved in the sale of goods directly to consumers.

retailer (*n.*) a person or business that sells goods directly to consumers.

retailing (*n.*) all operations within a business involved in selling merchandise directly to consumers.

retained earnings the accumulated income of a business after expenses and the distribution of dividends to stockholders.

retainer (*n.*) a fee paid to a lawyer or other professional for the right to engage his or her services whenever necessary over a specified period of time.

retroactive pay increase an increase in current wages that applies also to work done previously at a lower wage.

return on investment net annual income divided by average amount of investment during a given year. *Abbrev.:* **ROI**

revaluation (*n.*) the upward valuation of a nation's currency that was previously devalued.

revenue (*n.*) the sum of all forms of a business's income.

revenue sharing the returning of tax revenues by a higher level of government to a lower level.

revenue stamp an adhesive stamp issued by federal or state governments and affixed to certain negotiable instruments to prove that payment of appropriate transfer taxes has been made.

reversion (*n.*) the return of real estate to a grantor after the terms of the grant have lapsed.

revolving credit an arrangement allowing a buyer to charge purchases against an account within a certain credit limit each month.

revolving loan a loan that automatically renews upon maturity.

rider (*n.*) 1. an addition or amendment to a contract. 2. a clause, usually unrelated, attached to a bill before consideration for passage.

right of survivorship a right giving ownership of jointly owned property to the surviving joint owner.

right of way a right of passage or easement granted by an owner of real estate to another to pass over the land or place on it a road, power lines, underground pipes, or the like.

right-to-work laws laws prohibiting union-employer agreements requiring all employees to become union members.

riparian right the right of a landowner to the water on, under, or adjacent to his or her property, and to the use of its banks or bed.

risk (*n.*) 1. in insurance, the degree of possible loss. 2. a person or thing that is insured. 3. a thing that is insured against, such as a fire or flood.

risk capital business capital gained from sale of stock plus retained earnings; capital to be reinvested in a business. Also called **equity capital.**

risk management the management of assets so as to enhance their stability and earning power while reducing the risk of their accidental loss.

risk rating an evaluation of relative risks to determine the soundness of a business proposition.

rollback (*n.*) a reduction of advanced or inflated prices to a former level. **roll back** (*v.*) to reduce inflated prices to a former level.

rollover (*n.*) the reinvestment of funds so as to defer payment of taxes.

royalty (*n., pl.* **-ties**) a payment made for the use of another's work or property for financial gain.

S

safe-deposit box a metal box rented from and stored in the vault of a bank for the protection of valuables.

safe rate the interest rate on government bonds, savings accounts, and other insured investments.

sale and leaseback the sale of an asset through which the seller gains a long-term lease to the asset.

sales presentation the process of presenting, explaining, and describing a product or service to a prospective customer.

sales tax a tax paid by the consumer at the time of purchase of goods or services.

salvage value the value of an item after it has fully depreciated. Also called **scrap value.**

savings and loan association a government-chartered financial institution that sells shares, invests deposits primarily in home mortgages, and pays dividends to its member investors. *Abbrev.*: **S & L**

savings bank a bank that accepts deposits and pays interest on them, using the deposited funds to invest in long-term bonds, mortgages, and other eligible investments.

savings bond a bond issued by the U.S. Treasury for the purpose of encouraging thrift and financing wars.

savings certificate a debt security offered by a chartered bank for a specific period of time at an established interest rate.

scab (*n.*) a person who is not a union member and who works for lower wages or takes over the job of a striking worker.

scale order an order to buy or sell a specified number of securities at specific market variations.

scaling (*n.*) the buying, trading, or selling of a specified number of securities at specific market variations.

scarcity value the increased value of a commodity brought about by its short supply or by increased demand.

scare buying excessive purchasing to accumulate a large supply, brought on by fear of a future shortage.

scheduled maintenance a prescribed plan for maintaining equipment on an established schedule. The term often is used in connection with maintenance plans for computer systems.

scienter (*n.*) awareness of one's own misrepresentation or fraud.

scrap value see SALVAGE VALUE.

search warrant an order, signed by a judge, authorizing police to search a named person, work premises, residence, or some other place for specified items that could provide evidence of the commission of a crime.

seasonal discount a reduction in the price of products or services purchased out of season.

seasonal employee a worker employed for a limited time for work related to seasons of the year, such as the Christmas season in retailing.

seasoned mortgage a mortgage whose payments have been made regularly over a long time span, establishing a satisfactory pattern of payment by the borrower.

seasoned security a security with a sound record of paying dividends, earning interest, and selling at stable prices.

seat on the exchange in the securities industry, a term denoting that a brokerage firm is a member of a stock exchange.

secondary offering the sale of a large block of stock shares by stockholders themselves, usually on the floor of an exchange.

secondary strike a strike against an employer for conducting business with a company whose employees are on strike.

second-class mail newspapers and magazines that qualify for a low postal rate and fast delivery.

second mortgage an additional mortgage on a piece of real estate secured against the owner's remaining equity.

seconds (*n.*) merchandise containing defects that is priced lower than first-quality merchandise and often is sold in discount stores.

secured creditor a creditor that holds the rights to pledged assets of a borrower until the debt is paid.

secured loan a loan secured by pledged assets in the event of the borrower's default. Also called **secured liability.**

Securities and Exchange Commission an agency established by the Federal Securities Exchange Act of 1934 to regulate the nation's stock exchanges. *Abbrev.:* **SEC**

security (*n., pl.* **-ties**) 1. property pledged as collateral for repayment of a loan or fulfillment of a contract. 2. in insurance, protection against risk. 3. a stock or bond: *usually used in plural.*

4. a person who agrees to be financially responsible for another person.

security agreement an agreement between a seller and a buyer specifying the seller's interest in the items sold.

security deposit funds deposited by a tenant with a landlord, generally to ensure the reparation of any damage to the premises or to ensure against future failure to pay the rent.

security interest a creditor's interest in a borrower's property that secures a debt or other obligation; lien.

seed money the funds necessary to begin a new business venture.

self-employed (*adj.*) employed in one's own business or profession rather than earning a salary from an employer.

self-insured (*adj.*) protecting oneself against losses by setting aside personal assets or funds as insurance rather than paying for an insurance policy.

self-liquidating (*adj.*) of a financial project that, from its own operation, generates the funds to repay the original investment.

self-liquidating loan a short-term commercial loan based on the sale proceeds of products or liens upon properties.

seller's market a market in which prices are high because demand is greater than the supply of a product.

sell short (*v.*) to sell securities that are not yet fully paid for with the expectation of a drop in market price, which will enable the seller to pay a lower price for them and make a profit on their sale.

seniority (*n.*) an employee's greater right to job security or tenure because of his or her lengthy period of service.

serial number a number, usually unique in a series, assigned to one of multiple items, as an automobile engine, for the purpose of identification.

service charge 1. a charge levied by a financial institution for the handling of a transaction. 2. a charge in addition to the standard fee for a service. 3. a fee charged by a bank for maintaining an account.

setback (*n.*) the distance required by zoning regulations between a building and a curb or other boundary. 2. a partial or temporary loss or reversal.

settlement (*n.*) 1. the payment of a debt. 2. the act of giving money or property to a person or organization as resolution of a claim, as in a divorce. 3. the conveyance of money or property, often through trustees, to benefit another person. 4. the amount of property included in a settlement. 5. the paying of any bills to a bank or stock exchange.

severalty (*n., pl.* **-ties**) property that is owned by one person.

severalty ownership the ownership of property by one person.

severance pay a supplemental sum of money paid to an employee upon the employer's termination of his or her employment.

severance tax a tax on the removal of natural products, such as minerals, from land or water.

shading (*n.*) in retailing, a slight reduction in price or small alteration in the terms of a sale.

share (*n.*) a unit of ownership, or stock, in a corporation. 2. one of the equal portions into which the capital of a corporation is divided.

shareholder (*n.*) a person who owns one or more units of stock in a corporation. Also called **stockholder.**

share of market the portion of an industry's total sales captured by a single business, measured in a percentage or ratio.

sheriff's deed a court-ordered document drawn to satisfy a legal judgment by conveying title of ownership, usually of a debtor's property to a creditor.

sheriff's sale a court-ordered sale of property, usually to pay a debt.

shoplift (*v.*) to steal merchandise from a store. —**shoplifter** (*n.*)

shop steward a member of a labor union elected to represent employees in dealings with management.

short sale a sale of borrowed stock that will be returned to the lender when the stock is bought back.

short-term capital gain a gain from the sale of an asset that has been owned for less than six months.

short-term capital loss a loss from the sale of an asset that has been owned for less than six months.

short-term debt a financial obligation scheduled for repayment within one year.

shutdown (*n.*) a temporary suspension of production, as in a factory.

shutout (*n.*) the locking out of employees by employers as part of a job action.

sick leave a contractually agreed upon number of days per year for which an employer will pay employees for absence due to illness.

sick pay compensation paid to an employee while he or she is out of work because of illness.

sign-off (*n.*) the final instructions that terminate communication with a computer system.

sign-on (*n.*) the opening instructions that begin communication with a computer system.

silent partner a partner in a business who provides capital but does not take an active part in management or operation of the business.

silver certificate a certificate issued by the U.S. government, formerly circulated as currency, guaranteed redeemable, on demand, in silver.

simple interest interest earned on a principal sum and not on any interest accrued by that principal.

sinecure (*n.*) a position of little responsibility or work, especially one with a good salary.

single-entry bookkeeping a bookkeeping method, seldom used now, in which each entry is made in the ledger only once, not balancing debit and credit sides of an account. See DOUBLE-ENTRY BOOKKEEPING.

single-payment loan a loan on which the total amount is due on one specified date.

sinking fund a corporation's reserves of cash or other assets that are accumulated to redeem debts or capital stock whenever necessary.

sit-down strike a labor strike during which employees remain on the site of their employment but do not work.

site audit an examination of an organization's accounts, conducted on its premises.

skilled labor personnel who are capable of performing specialized labor as a result of training and expertise.

slander (*n.*) the criminal utterance of a false and malicious statement that is damaging to the reputation or well-being of a person or organization. Distinguished from LIBEL. (*v.*) to utter false and malicious statements about; injure by spreading slander against.

slave computer a second computer performing identical functions as, and acting as a backup to, a master computer.

sliding scale a scale of prices or other costs adjusted according to the change of one or more factors.

Small Business Administration an independent federal agency established in 1953 to assist small businesses with loans and management advice. *Abbrev.:* **SBA**

smart money money invested by security traders who are in a position to take advantage of information not available to other investors.

Social Security payments made under the Federal Old Age Benefits Law of 1936 and subsequent amendments to it, providing old age, unemployment, and disability benefits for various unemployed and dependent individuals. It is financed largely through mandatory employee and employer contributions in the form of salary deductions.

soft currency that part of a nation's currency governed by exchange procedures that limit its convertibility into gold or other currencies.

software (*n.*) all programs, routines, instructions, and other data entered into a computer.

solvency (*n.*) the ability to pay debts fully and on time.

solvent (*adj.*) able to meet all financial obligations, as a business whose assets exceed its liabilities.

source document a form containing data to be processed by a computer.

source program a computer program in machine language used by the computer to direct equipment or to translate machine language to human language.

special delivery the prepaid delivery of mail by special messenger that takes priority over first-class mail.

special handling a priority service for handling fourth-class or parcel-post mail.

special offering a block of stock available for sale that requires special attention because of its size and potential market.

special warranty deed a deed that includes a warranty agreement in which the seller agrees to defend the title only from claims against him or herself or the seller's heirs, but not against previous owners.

specification (*n.*) a written statement detailing exact and precise conditions, such as terms of a contract or a plan for building construction.

specific tax a tax on a commodity levied per unit.

speculate (*v.*) to invest in high-risk securities and commodities. —**speculation** (*n.*)

speculator (*n.*) an investor who takes financial risks in hope of making a large profit.

split-rate interest interest on a mortgage that offers one rate for the land and another for buildings.

split shift a workday that is divided into two or more shifts so that employees are available during peak hours.

spool the mounting for a magnetic computer tape.

spot cash ready cash available for making purchases.

spot contract a contract for an immediate payment, usually used in commodities transactions.

spot delivery immediate delivery.

spot market a market in which commodities are sold for immediate cash delivery.

spot price the price of a commodity in a spot market.

spot zoning land use permitted for a specific location that does not conform with the zoning regulations of the surrounding area.

squatter (*n.*) a person who illegally occupies public or unoccupied land or buildings.

staff executive an executive who has the responsibility to plan, recommend, advise, and assist in the management of a company or department, but who has no authority to order the performance of activities. See LINE EXECUTIVE.

stagflation (*n.*) an economic condition marked by an inflation in prices and a simultaneous decline in capital investment.

stamp tax a tax on legal documents or products that require revenue stamps to witness payment, such as title deeds, stock certificates, liquor, and tobacco.

standard deduction a sum specified by the Internal Revenue Service for a taxpayer to deduct from taxable income rather than itemize deductions.

Standard Metropolitan Statistical Area a county or group of counties containing a city populated by 50,000 or more persons, as defined by the U.S. Bureau of the Census.

standard of living a nation's wealth determined by its per capita output.

standby commitment a lender's agreement to make funds available on specific terms at a future date for a previously paid fee.

standby fee the fee charged by a lender for a standby commitment.

standby mortgage a mortgage requiring interest payments on a fixed schedule, but repayment of the principal upon maturity.

standby order a customer's authorization to a bank to regularly pay out a specified amount from his or her account.

start-up cost the cost of implementing a project; cost incurred before any gain can be realized.

state bank any commercial bank that is organized according to the laws of the state in which it operates and that is chartered by the state.

statistical accounting the use of probability theories and statistical sampling methods in accounting and auditing.

status quo *Latin.* the existing state of affairs.

statute of limitations a law limiting the time in which legal action can be taken, such as the collection of bills or the prosecution of a person for a crime.

statutory audit an audit conducted under the provisions of law.

statutory law law that is established and enacted by a legislative body. Distinguished from COMMON LAW.

stenography (*n.*) shorthand dictation and transcription.

step (*n.*) a single instruction in a computer routine in the execution of a program.

stipend (*n.*) payment for services; salary or wage.

stipulation (*n.*) a term, condition, or limitation in a contract or agreement.

stock (*n.*) 1. goods or merchandise supplied or stored for sale. 2. a share of ownership in a corporation, paying dividends or profit shares.

See: basic stock
blue-chip stock
capital stock
classified stock
common stock
cumulative stock
deferred stock
donated stock
glamour stock
noncumulative stock
participating stock
par value stock
penny stock
preferred stock
treasury stock
unissued stock
voting stock
yo-yo stock

stockbroker (*n.*) a person or business that buys, sells, and trades securities.

stock certificate a document identifying ownership of one or more shares of stock.

stock exchange a market regulated by the federal government for the trading of stocks and bonds.

stockholder (*n.*) a person who owns shares of stock in a corporation. Also called **shareholder.**

stock option an option to buy or sell a certain number of shares of stock for a specific price within a specified time period.

stock split the generating of new stock in a corporation by dividing each share into more than one share, keeping the total value equal by proportionately reducing each share's selling price.

stock transfer the cancellation of one stock certificate to reissue another certificate for the same stock in a different name, recording the change of ownership in the corporation's stock-transfer records.

stock transfer tax a federal or state tax on the sale, transfer, or loan of stocks.

stock warrant a certificate issued by a corporation entitling the owner of the certificate to buy a specific amount of capital stock in the corporation at a fixed price during a given time period.

stop loss an agreement guaranteeing that a reinsuring company will pay the reinsured company for losses that exceed a specified amount.

stop-loss order an order to a stock broker to sell securities after the price has dropped to a specific level.

stop order an order to a stockbroker specifying a price at which to buy or sell stock.

stop payment an account holder's order to a bank not to honor a check written by the account holder.

stop price the price specified in a stop order at which the broker is directed to buy or sell.

straight investment a preferred stock or bond that an investor buys because it offers a limited but steady income, rather than because it may increase in value.

straight-life insurance a life insurance policy for a specific amount, on which the insured pays premiums throughout his or her lifetime and which matures and becomes payable to the beneficiary at the insured's death or at a specified date. Also called **ordinary-life insurance** and **whole-life insurance.**

straight-line depreciation a depreciation method that charges the same amount of depreciation expense each year throughout an asset's life.

straight time the rate of pay an employee receives for working during a normal work schedule, as prescribed by law or by union contract.

street broker an over-the-counter broker, as distinguished from a broker who is a member of an exchange.

street certificate a stock certificate registered in the name of the dealer who bought it for a customer, rather than in the name of the actual customer-owner. Also called **street name.**

strike (*n.*) the refusal of most or all of the workers in a company or an industry to do the work for which they were hired in order to receive certain demands, such as higher pay or better working conditions. (*v.*) to refuse to do the work for which one was hired in order to get management to agree to certain demands.

strikebreaker (*n.*) a person who continues to work during a strike, takes the place of a worker on strike, or supplies workers to take the place of strikers.

strike fund the portion of union dues held in reserve to pay for such expenses as benefits, union literature, or picket signs during a strike.

strike notice a formal notice to an employer that a union has rejected a company's latest offer and is about to go on strike.

strike pay money paid to union members by the union to help compensate for the loss of income during a strike.

strike vote a vote by union members to decide whether union management will call a strike.

struck work any goods produced for a company during a strike by the company's employees either by strikebreakers or by another company that is not on strike.

subcontract (*v.*) to hire out all or part of the work on a contracted project to another person or company. (*n.*) the work given out to another person or company.

subcontractor (*n.*) a person or company to whom work is hired out.

subdivide (*v.*) to divide a large piece of land into building lots.

subdivision (*n.*) 1. a large piece of land that has been divided into building lots. 2. one of the portions of land resulting from subdividing.

sublease (*v.*) to lease all or part of the premises a person or business holds as a tenant; to underlease premises. (*n.*) an agreement by which a tenant leases all or part of the premises he or she holds as a tenant; an underlease.

sublessee (*n.*) a party to whom premises are subleased.

sublessor (*n.*) a party who grants a sublease.

sublet (*v.*) to grant or obtain a sublease for premises.

subordinated debt a debt that has a lower priority for repayment than other debts.

subordinated debenture a debenture bond that is specified as lower in priority than other specified securities.

subordinated interest an interest in property that is lower in priority than another interest in the same property, such as a second mortgage, which can be paid after a first mortgage is paid.

subordination (*n.*) a practice in bankruptcy law that ranks the priority of creditor claims.

subordination clause an agreement specifying that one debt has lower priority for repayment than another debt.

subpoena (*n.*) a legal document requiring a person or a specific piece of evidence to be in a court of law at a specified time. (*v.*, **-naed, -naing**) to summon to a court of law by presenting with a subpoena.

subrogate (*v.*) to substitute one creditor for another so that the substituted creditor may exercise certain rights, privileges, or claims of the original creditor. —**subrogation** (*n.*)

subrogee (*n.*) a creditor who is substituted for an original creditor.

subrogor (*n.*) a creditor for whom a subrogee is substituted.

subsidiary (*n.*, *pl.* **-ries**) any business that has more than 50 percent of its voting stock owned by another business, but that operates under its own name and often under its own management.

subsidize (*v.*) to support financially a person or a business without expectation of goods, services, or payments in return.

subsidy (*n.*) the financial support of a person or a business, for which the payer receives no goods, services, or payments in return.

substantiate (*v.*) to prove a claim by providing documents or witnesses that establish its validity.

subtenant (*n.*) a person or business who leases property from another tenant; sublessee; undertenant.

succession (*n.*) the legal transfer of rights, responsibilities, and property to the heirs of a deceased person.

succession tax a tax on the privilege of receiving property from another person through a will, by title transfer, or by descent.

successor (*n.*) a person who receives the rights, obligations, and property of another person through a will, by title transfer, or by descent.

sue (*v.*) to bring a civil legal action in a court of law.

suit (*n.*) 1. an action in a court of law to recover a right or claim. 2. any action intended to obtain a legal decision.

summons (*n.*) a written order to appear in court in order to respond as a defendant to a charge. A summons notifies a defendant of a legal action and warns that it will be decided against the defendant if he or she does not appear.

sunk cost a cost that results from a decision made in the past that cannot be reversed in the present.

supply (*n.*) *Economics.* the quantity of goods available for sale at a certain price at a given time.

supply and demand *Economics.* a classic economic theory that describes the relationship among the supply of goods and services, their prices, and the demand for them. Increased demand for a product or service tends to raise its price, which encourages manufacturers or suppliers to increase its supply, whereas decreased demand lowers prices and leads to a decreased supply.

surcharge (*n.*) an extra charge or tax added to the standard amount, fare, or fee.

surety (*n.*) a person who agrees to be responsible for the fulfillment of another person's contract or the payment of another person's debt.

surety bond a guarantee given by a bonding company to pay another person's debt, usually in the event of default or failure to perform a contracted-for service within a particular period of time.

surety company a company that, for a fee, agrees to become responsible for the fulfillment of a contract or the payment of a debt for another person.

surplus (*n.*) in accounting, an excess of earnings not distributed to shareholders and held in reserve for a future need.

surrender (*v.*) in real estate, to voluntarily give up rights, claims, or title, usually by contractual agreement.

surrender value the amount of money that an insurance company will pay a policyholder in exchange for the surrender of a policy, based on the number of premiums paid.

surtax (*n.*) 1. an extra tax charged to corporations that have a taxable income greater than some specified amount. 2. any extra tax added to any normal income tax.

survivorship (*n.*) the right of a joint owner or interest holder to receive the share in a business or interest in property of a co-owner or joint interest holder who dies.

suspension (*n.*) the disciplinary layoff of an employee without pay.

swing shift 1. a system of rotating workers among work shifts in a factory in order to allow continuous 24-hour-a-day operation. 2. a work shift from about 4 P.M. to midnight.

sympathy strike a strike called by a group of workers solely to demonstrate support for a strike by another group of workers.

syndicate (*n.*) 1. a group of investors who participate in a joint venture, especially one requiring a large amount of capital, and who share in all profits and losses from the business in proportion to their investment. 2. a group of investment bankers and brokers who join together to distribute a new issue of a corporation's securities. (*v.*) to form a syndicate. —**syndication** (*n.*)

systems analyst a person who works with current and potential users of a computer system to implement their particular data-processing needs.

systems management the design and management of a business as a complete system, involving such elements as human interaction, utilization of tools and equipment, and the business's goals.

T

tacit agreement an unspoken agreement, often the result of failure to disagree with another's suggestion or action.

takedown (*n.*) the act of disassembling a machine or mechanical system.

take-home pay wages or salary left after taxes are deducted.

takeover bid a bid to buy the outstanding shares of a corporation in order to gain control of that corporation.

tandem increase a pay raise given to certain employees of a factory, usually office workers, as a result of a raise negotiated by production workers.

tangible asset a physical, material asset of a business, such as cash, land, buildings, or equipment.

tape drive a device that reads and records magnetic tape for computer data storage.

target pricing a method of setting prices so as to make a targeted amount of profit.

tariff (*n.*) 1. a system of taxes on goods imported and exported. 2. a tax on an import or export.

tax (*n.*) a fee charged by a government against individuals and businesses for the support of that government. (*v.*) to charge a fee against individuals and businesses for the support of government.

tax abatement a reduction or refund of tax that was improperly levied or is no longer required by the government.

taxable income income on which tax must be paid, after all legal deductions and exemptions have been claimed.

tax assessor an official who determines the value of wealth and property rights for tax purposes.

tax base 1. the portion of income, or of the value of a product or service, on which taxes are levied. 2. the portion of an item's value that can be taxed.

tax collector an official who is responsible for the collection of taxes in a given area.

tax evasion illegal attempts to avoid paying taxes, often by underreporting income.

tax exemption a legal right not to pay taxes.

tax rate a percentage that describes the amount of tax charged per unit of the tax base, as a 10 percent rate that charges $10 of tax on $100 of income.

tax roll a government list of all real estate, including the name of each owner, the value of each parcel, and the amount of tax due.

tax sale a public sale of land seized by the government as a penalty for nonpayment of taxes.

tax shelter a means of legally avoiding taxes on a portion of income; a tax deduction created without a decrease in cash flow.

telecommunications (*n., pl.*) communications by radio, telephone, telegraph, or television; electronic communication over a distance.

telecommunications system an electronic system, such as television broadcasting, telex, or microwave transmission, for communicating over a distance.

teller (*n.*) 1. a bank clerk who pays out and receives money. 2. a person who counts votes at a stockholders' meeting.

teller's check a bank check signed by a teller or tellers.

tenancy at will a condition in which a tenant resides on real estate with the owner's permission but without a lease.

tenancy by the entirety an estate owned jointly by a husband and wife so that, upon the death of one, the survivor receives the total estate.

tenancy in common the ownership of real estate by two or more persons so that each has a separate interest that passes, at death, to an heir or devisee and not to one of the surviving co-owners.

tenancy in sufferance a situation in which a tenant continues to occupy real estate after the owner has denied him or her permission to do so.

tenant (*n.*) a person or business that occupies real estate owned by another. —**tenancy** (*n.*)

tender (*n.*) an offer to purchase something under specified conditions, including price and time.

tenure (*n.*) 1. the act or right of holding or possessing something, as property, a title, or office. 2. the length of time during which something is held. 3. status assuring an employee, such as a teacher or civil servant, of holding his or her position permanently, which is acquired after specified requirements are fulfilled.

terminal (*n.*) a keyboard, equipped with a printer or television screen, that is used for communication with a computer.

term insurance insurance that offers protection only for a stated period of time.

terms of sale the specific conditions under which a sale is made, including the amount of time given the buyer to pay the vendor's invoice, any discounts offered, and other details.

testament (*n.*) a will; a person's declaration of intent for the disposition of his or her property after death.

testate (*adv.*) describing the dying of a person who has made a legally valid will. See INTESTATE.

testator (*n.*) a deceased person who has made a will.

testatrix (*n., pl.* **-trices**) a woman testator.

testify (*v.,* **-fied, -fying**) to give evidence or make a declaration under oath in a court of law.

testimonial a statement by a satisfied customer praising a product or service, used in advertising and promotion.

test marketing a test of public acceptance of a new product through trial distribution in a small market.

third-class mail printed material, usually circulars and advertising, of less than 24 pages.

third-party transaction a business deal that involves a buyer, a seller, and a source of consumer credit.

thrift institution a savings bank or savings and loan association.

time and a half one and a half times the normal rate of pay, usually paid to employees working overtime.

time-and-motion study a study of the time and movements required to complete a specific task, intended to increase worker efficiency.

time deposit a deposit of money that receives interest from the day of deposit if the money remains in the account for at least 30 days.

time-sharing (*n.*) a data-processing technique that allows many users to work with one computer at the same time. The computer divides each user's job into stages and rotates among the jobs, completing one stage of each job at a time.

title (*n.*) evidence of rightful ownership.

title defect a fact or condition that offers a challenge to rightful ownership.

title guaranty a guarantee of clear title to real estate issued by a title guaranty company that has researched the legal status of a parcel of real estate.

title insurance insurance issued by a title guaranty company that protects a property owner against the discovery of a defect in his or her title; insurance that backs up a title guaranty.

title search the searching of records for evidence of defects, such as unpaid taxes or mortgages, in a real estate title.

tokenism (*n.*) an attempt to appease pressure groups or government affirmative action demands by hiring a few minority group members, usually for unimportant jobs.

toll (*n.*) a charge for permission to use a public facility or service, such as a highway or bridge.

tonnage (*n.*) the number of tons of cargo handled.

tort (*n.*) in law, a wrongful act committed by one person against another or against another's property.

tracer (*n.*) a request to trace a shipment in order to locate it or alter it.

trade association a nonprofit organization that serves the interests of members who usually work in closely related industries.

trade discount a discount offered only to "the trade," that is, to buyers within an industry.

trade-in the exchange of an old product for a new one, with the difference in value made up in cash.

trademark (*n.*) a distinctive word or symbol used to identify a product or company and registered with the U.S. Office of Trademarks and Patents.

trade union 1. a labor union in which the members are workers engaged in a particular trade or craft. 2. any labor union.

traditio (*n.*) the transfer and delivery of the possession of property by an owner.

traffic (*n.*) 1. the number of potential customers entering a retail store within a given period. 2. the amount of business done by a transportation or communications company. 3. trade, in general.

transaction (*n.*) any agreement between two or more parties that establishes a legal obligation; business deal.

transcribe (*v.*) to write or type material from shorthand notes or recorded dictation. —**transcription** (*n.*)

transfer agent a person who keeps records of a corporation's stocks and bonds and who is responsible for the issuing and transfer of shares to stockholders.

transfer of title the change of title to property from a former owner to a new one.

transfer price the price charged by one part of an organization for the sale of goods or services to another part of the same organization.

traveler's checks (or **cheques**) special checks that are designed for use by travelers and tourists, and are internationally accepted.

Treasury bill a short-term security issued weekly by the Treasury Department for sale to the public, and which matures in three to six months. *Abbrev.*: **T-bill**

Treasury bond a long-term security, issued by the Treasury Department for sale to the public, that has a maturity longer than five years.

Treasury certificate a short-term security, issued by the Treasury Department for sale to the public, that matures in one year.

Treasury note a long-term security, issued by the Treasury Department for sale to the public, that matures in one to five years.

treasury share one of the authorized but unused shares of a corporation.

treasury stock previously issued stock that a corporation has reacquired from its stockholders and that may be resold or canceled.

trespass (*v.*) to enter wrongfully and without permission onto another person's property.

trial balance a record of all the accounts in the ledger, used to check their accuracy before preparing the final balance sheet and income statement.

trickle-down (*n.*) an effort of the federal government to stimulate growth by distributing federal funds to businesses and other organizations, in hopes that increased prosperity will benefit everyone in the economy, in contrast to stimulating growth by direct payments to individuals (welfare, for example).

trigger-price system a federal system for identifying inferior-grade steel "dumped" in U.S. markets. Steel sold below minimum prices automatically triggers a Treasury Department investigation.

troy weight a system of weights for measuring silver and gold in which 1 troy pound is equal to 12 ounces.

trust (*n.*) an arrangement by which one person or corporation holds the title to property for the benefit of another person or persons.

trust company a company, such as a bank, whose main function is the management of property, such as money, securities, or real estate, entrusted to it by others. Trust companies are usually state-supervised and usually engage in all commercial banking activities.

trustee (*n.*) a person who, by agreement, holds title to property for another's benefit.

trustee in bankruptcy a person appointed by a court of law or by creditors to manage a bankrupt estate in the best interests of all parties.

trusteeship (*n.*) 1. the position or function of a trustee. 2. the suspension of the officers of a local union by the international union, after which the international union takes over management of the local.

trust fund money, securities, property, or the like held by a trustee.

Truth-in-Lending Act federal legislation passed in 1968 that requires lenders to disclose truthfully the terms of a loan, including the annual interest rate and the total dollar cost.

turnkey (*n.*) a ready-to-use computer system with equipment and programs designed to meet the needs of particular customers.

turnover (*n.*) 1. the rate at which employees enter and leave jobs with a particular company. 2. in retail sales, the number of times an inventory is sold and replaced within a given period; the flow of merchandise. 3. in securities trading, the volume of business in a particular stock or an entire stock exchange.

tycoon (*n.*) a person who has acquired a huge fortune and great influence in industry or commerce.

U

unauthorized strike a job action that is not authorized by the union having jurisdiction in the company or area.

unclaimed balance the balance in a bank account that has not been active for a period of time designated by the bank or by law.

uncollected funds deposits to a bank account of checks and drafts that have not yet been collected by the bank.

undercapitalize (*v.*) to provide insufficient funds for a new business to be able to carry out its operations. **—undercapitalization** (*n.*)

underlease (*v.*) to sublet a property. (*n.*) a sublease.

underlessee (*n.*) a subtenant.

underlet (*v.*, **-let, -letting**) to lease real estate for less than its actual value.

undersell (*v.*, **-sold, -selling**) to sell goods at a price that is lower than a competitor's price.

undersigned (*adj.*) having a signature or signatures at the end of a document; signed. (*n.*) **the undersigned** the person or persons who have signed at the end of a document such as a contract.

under-the-rule (*adj.*) describing an action by officers of a stock exchange, in which a transaction is completed on behalf of a delinquent member of the exchange who is charged for any loss that occurs as a result of the transaction.

under-the-table (*adj.*) of or pertaining to an unethical or illegal business transaction, conducted in secrecy and off the books. Also called **under-the-counter.**

underwrite (*v.*, **-wrote, -written, -writing**) 1. to guarantee the purchase of stocks or bonds or agree to buy securities at a fixed price. 2. to agree to insure.

underwriter (*n.*) 1. a person or institution that assumes a risk for a fee. 2. a person in the insurance business who is responsible for accepting risks and for deciding how much insurance the company will provide. 3. a person or business that agrees to underwrite a stock or securities issue.

undisclosed principal a party in a business transaction whose identity remains a secret and who is represented by a broker.

undistributed profits net income that is not distributed to the shareholders or owners of a business. Also called **undivided profits.**

undivided interest a joint investment or joint ownership that does not specify which parts belong to which owners.

undivided profits see UNDISTRIBUTED PROFITS.

unearned discount in accounting, interest in the form of a discount that is received but not yet earned.

unearned income any income received before the work is performed, or from sources that do not involve an individual's personal efforts.

unearned increment an increase in the value of real estate that is not due to any effort on the owner's part, but rather is due to changing social conditions.

unemployment insurance a system by which certain taxes paid by employers are used to compensate out-of-work individuals for a limited period of time.

unencumbered property real estate with no mortgages or debts against it, and with no claims against its title.

unenforceable contract an unwritten contract or agreement, often in the sale of real estate, that cannot be legally enforced.

unfair competition a selling tactic that takes unfair advantage of a competing business, such as using false advertising.

unfair labor practice an illegal action on the part of either an employer or a union, as determined by the National Labor Relations Board.

Uniform Commercial Code a set of laws intended to provide consistency among different states' laws, covering such things as sales, bills of lading, or negotiable instruments. *Abbrev.:* **UCC**

unilateral contract a contract that calls for complete fulfillment of the terms by one party before the other party must fulfill its obligations.

union (*n.*) see LABOR UNION.

union shop a factory or business that requires all new employees to pay union dues and, usually, to join the union.

unissued stock the stock that is not issued or outstanding in a corporation, although it is authorized by the corporation's charter and must be listed in any financial statement.

unit billing the itemization of all purchases made by a customer on one bill.

unit pricing a method of price listing based on standard measurements, such as cents per ounce, allowing easy comparison of size and price between competing products.

unity of title the common ownership of, and title to, a piece of property through joint ownership.

unlisted securities any stocks that are traded over the counter because they are not listed with a stock exchange.

unpaid balance the amount of a loan that is not yet paid, or the difference between a down payment and the purchase price of an item.

unpaid dividend a dividend declared by a corporation but not yet distributed to its shareholders.

unrealized profits the profits of a corporation that are real only on paper until the corporation's securities are sold.

unsecured loan a loan for which the lender does not require the borrower to provide collateral, but relies upon the borrower's credit history.

usance (*n.*) 1. a period of time allowed for payment of a foreign debt. 2. an amount of interest or income.

useful life the period of time during which an asset retains its value.

usufruct (*n.*) the right to interest earned on property or an investment, but not the right to the property or investment itself. (*v.*) to hold something in usufruct.

usufructary (*n., pl.* **-ries**) an agent who has the right to interest earned on a piece of property or an investment, but does not have the right to the property or investment itself. (*adj.*) having the right to interest earned on property or an investment without having the right to the property or investment itself.

usurer (*n.*) a person who charges an exorbitant rate of interest on loaned money beyond the legal maximum interest rate.

usury (*n.*) the practice of charging an exorbitant rate of interest on loaned money beyond the legal maximum interest rate.

utility program a computer program that performs a routine task.

V

validate (*v.*) to make binding or give legal force to documents, actions, and transactions. **—validation** (*n.*)

valorize (*v.*) to establish or control the market price of a commodity by governmental intervention. **—valorization** (*n.*)

valuable consideration a legal term describing anything of value given or performed by another that makes a contract binding.

valuation (*n.*) an appraisal of real estate or other property.

value added that portion of the worth of a finished product developed in a company through manufacturing and marketing.

value-added tax a tax, levied at each stage of a product's manufacture and distribution as the value of the item theoretically increases, that ultimately has the impact of a sales tax on the consumer.

value date the date on which a bank deposit becomes available for withdrawal.

variable annuity an annuity providing for a lifetime or other specified time payments that fluctuate with the performance of an investment portfolio. See ANNUITY.

variable interest rate an interest rate that fluctuates depending on the economic indicators to which it is tied.

variable payment mortgage a mortgage on which the monthly payments change based on conditions outlined in the mortgage contract.

variance (*n.*) 1. any discrepancy between two sets of figures or facts. 2. the difference between expectations and results. 3. permission to depart from zoning regulations or building codes.

vendee (*n.*) a person who purchases or agrees to purchase something; a buyer.

vendor (*n.*) a person or business from whom goods are purchased; a seller.

venture capital 1. business capital available from the sale of new stock. 2. reinvested funds from stockholders. 3. funds invested in businesses that cannot get money from the usual sources such as bank loans and stock issues.

venue (*n.*) the proper locality for filing a lawsuit, or the area over which a court of law presides.

verbatim (*adj., adv.*) word for word; in exactly the same words.

verdict (*n.*) the decision of a judge or jury in a legal case.

vertically integrated a term describing a business that performs all stages of production required to produce a finished item.

vest (*v.*) to place authority, power, or rights in the control of a person, such as to vest an employee in a pension plan for which he or she is eligible under company rules.

vested interest something in which a person or group has a fixed interest as by right or law.

vesting (*n.*) the right of an employee in a retirement plan to keep all or part of the annuities that the employer has contributed on his or her behalf.

veto (*v.*) 1. to prevent a bill from becoming law. 2. to prohibit or not consent to. (*n.*) 1. an order prohibiting some proposed action. 2. the right or power to reject a measure passed by another governmental body, as the President's power to veto bills passed by the Congress.

video display terminal see CATHODE-RAY TUBE DISPLAY. *Abbrev.:* **VDT**

vital statistics data concerning birth, death, marriage, and so on.

voiceprint (*n.*) the graphic representation of a person's voice on a device, which is used to determine whether a voice being heard live belongs to the person identified on the sound print.

voice recognition a computer technique that allows an information-processing system to be activated by oral commands.

void (*v.*) to make invalid or ineffective. (*adj.*) 1. not legally valid. 2. ineffective or without force.

volume discount a discount extended to buyers who purchase products in large quantities. See QUANTITY DISCOUNT.

voluntary arbitration a method of settling a labor dispute by which both sides freely choose to abide by the decision of an impartial third party.

voluntary lien a claim against property placed with the consent of its owner, such as a lien against a house used as collateral for a loan.

voluntary trust a trust in which a person or other legal entity voluntarily transfers property to a trustee for a specified purpose.

vostro account an account maintained with a domestic bank by a foreign bank. See NOSTRO ACCOUNT.

vote by proxy a person's vote, as at a stockholders' meeting, that is cast by someone else who is legally authorized to do so.

voting stock a type of corporate stock that gives the holder the right to vote at meetings of the corporation. Common stock usually carries one vote per share. Preferred stock often carries the right to vote if dividends on the preferred stock are in default for a specified length of time.

voting trust an agreement whereby the stockholders of a corporation temporarily turn over their voting rights to a trustee or a small group of people.

vouch (*v.*) to give evidence for or to guarantee.

voucher (*n.*) 1. a statement that serves as evidence of payment or the correctness of an account. 2. a person who gives evidence for or who guarantees, as to the authenticity of a document.

voucher check a type of check to which is attached a voucher that gives the issuer a record of the amount paid and allows the recipient of the check to record the payment properly.

voucher system an accounting system in which liabilities are recorded as soon as they are incurred and checks issued only in payment of approved expenditures for which a written authorizing voucher is prepared.

W

wage (*n.*) see WAGES.

wage and hour laws the federal and state regulations governing the legal minimum hourly pay and the maximum number of hours that a person may work.

wage and price controls the anti-inflationary regulations issued by the federal government from time to time that limit the percentage amount of wage and salary increases and also limit price increases on goods.

wages (*n.*) an employee's fixed rate of pay based on some unit such as an hour, a day, or a piece of work.

wage stabilization a government program to keep wages at existing levels in a geographic area or a specific industry.

waiting period 1. a span of time specified in certain insurance policies before payment will begin. 2. the time between filing a claim for unemployment compensation or workmen's compensation and the start of such payments. 3. the period of time, usually 20 days, following the registration of a securities issue with the Securities and Exchange Commission before it can be sold to the public.

waive (*v.*) to forgo or relinquish voluntarily, as in the giving up of a claim or right.

waiver (*n.*) 1. a voluntary relinquishment of a legal right or claim against another's property. 2. an exemption to zoning standards that allows a petitioner to develop or improve real estate in a way not otherwise allowed by zoning ordinances.

waiver of premium a provision in an insurance policy that, under certain specified conditions, provides for the policy to remain in force without further payment of premiums.

walkout (*n.*) a strike that starts after employees have already begun work.

Wall Street *Colloq.* the popular name for the New York City business and financial center.

warehouse (*v.*) to place goods in a warehouse for storage, often in a government warehouse, until duties are paid. (*n.*) a building where goods are stored prior to distribution.

warehouse loan a loan made against warehouse receipts as evidence of goods stored in a warehouse.

warehouse receipt a negotiable or nonnegotiable instrument that lists the goods or commodities stored in a warehouse.

warrant (*n.*) 1. a written order in the name of a state signed by a judge, directing that an arrest or a search be made. 2. a certificate that gives the holder the right to purchase securities at stated prices with or without a given time limit. 3. a short-term municipal debt of up to six months that is part of a floating debt issued in anticipation of receiving revenues from taxes.

warrantee (*n.*) a person to whom a warranty is given.

warrantor (*n.*) a person who gives a warranty.

warranty (*n.*) 1. a written statement that another statement in a contract is now true or will later be true. 2. a promise given by a seller to a buyer that the product or property being sold is as represented, usually with provision for repair or replacement if it is not. 3. a statement in an insurance policy concerning the condition of the insured that, if not true, will void the policy.

warranty deed a deed that guarantees a good title, free of debt, to the purchaser of real estate, and that also guarantees that the seller will defend the title against any claims.

wash sale an illegal, staged sale in which the seller buys from himself in order to establish activity and a market price in the goods, commodities, or securities the seller wishes to lure the public into buying.

waybill (*n.*) a document, made out by a carrier, identifying a shipment; showing what is being shipped, the routing, the weights, and the shipping rates; and providing the carrier with an internal record.

wetback (*n.*) a derogatory term for Mexican agricultural workers who enter the United States without a visa and accept work, usually at substandard wages.

white-collar (*adj.*) the term used for office and professional personnel, as opposed to production or maintenance workers. See BLUE-COLLAR.

white-collar crime nonviolent crime, such as theft, embezzlement, and fraud committed by professionals and business executives in the course of their work.

whole-life insurance see STRAIGHT-LIFE INSURANCE.

wholesale (*n.*) the sale of goods, usually in large quantities, to retailers for resale.

wholesaler (*n.*) a person or business that buys and sells goods to retailers.

wholesale price index a measurement of the average price change in some 2200 commodities at the primary market level compared with the average in selected base years.

widow's exemption a privilege extended to a debtor's surviving spouse to keep a certain amount of property free from liability in order to prevent its seizure for payment of the deceased's debt.

wildcat strike an illegal strike by workers, staged without their union's approval.

will (*n.*) a written, signed, and witnessed document directing the disposition of a person's property after death.

withdraw (*v.*) to remove funds from a bank account by means of check or draft. —**withdrawal** (*n.*)

withholding tax the federal taxes and any state or city income taxes that are deducted from an employee's pay and sent directly to the taxing authority.

without prejudice of a statement, given with the understanding that it cannot be taken as an admission of liability or used as evidence.

witness (*n.*) 1. a person who testifies in court or at a hearing. 2. a person who attests that another person has signed a document and who is on record as having observed the action. (*v.*) to give evidence; testify.

working capital the capital immediately available for the operation of a business; the excess of current assets over current liabilities.

working control the ownership of 51 percent of a corporation's voting stock, which is necessary to control the business, although in practice effective control can often be exercised with less than 51 percent of the stock.

working papers a legal document authorizing an adolescent to be gainfully employed.

work in progress goods or contracts that are in a partially finished state at a particular time.

workmen's compensation insurance payments provided by law to wage earners who are injured or disabled on the job.

work rules the rules regulating on-the-job working conditions, usually part of a union contract, which are designed to protect employees from arbitrary employer action and to secure satisfactory working conditions and health standards.

wraparound mortgage a second mortgage, usually given on real estate with an older first mortgage whose interest rate is low, under which the lender assumes the balance of the first mortgage and provides additional financing at a higher rate of interest.

writ (*n.*) a court order requiring an officer of the court to perform some act or enjoining a person to do or to refrain from doing something.

write-down (*n.*) an accounting procedure in which the value of an asset has been reduced to adjust for capital lost as a result of the decline in the asset's worth.

write-off (*n.*) in accounting, an asset that has been rendered worthless and, thus, is charged off as a loss.

write-up (*n.*) in accounting, any increase in the book value of an asset that does not result from added costs, or any adjustment in the book value of an asset to correspond to an appraisal value.

X

xerography (*n.*) a widely used process for copying images on paper, in which electrically charged plates are used to print copies.

Y

year-end (*n.*) the close of a business's fiscal year. (*adj.*) made at the end of a year, as a report.

yield (*v.*) to produce a profit from an investment. (*n.*) the annual cash dividend on an investment or the annual earnings per share of stock, often expressed as a percentage.

yield to maturity the annual rate of return on an investment that is held to maturity, expressed as a percentage.

yo-yo stock a high-priced specialty stock whose price fluctuates often and widely.

Z

zero-base budgeting a technique for preparing a new budget in which each item is evaluated on its own merit, without regard to amounts allocated to it by previous budgets, and which begins with the premise that zero dollars could be allocated to any item.

zone delivery pricing a system of freight pricing in which all customers in the same area are charged at the same rate for a delivery.

zoning (*n.*) the establishment by municipal or county government of land areas that are restricted to commercial, industrial, or residential use.

zoning ordinance a law that restricts the use of land and buildings within certain areas to specific purposes determined by a zoning board.

PART III
REFERENCE SECTIONS

Reference Sections Contents

GLOSSARY OF USAGE

Standard English usage is based on the language of educated speakers and writers, but such usage varies in its degree of formality according to the individual situation. Formal English is characterized by longer sentences, more difficult vocabulary, and fewer contractions than are found in the more conversational style of informal English. The term *colloquial,* included in some of the following entries, describes usage that is standard and "generally characteristic of conversation and informal writing" *(Webster's New World Dictionary of the American Language,* Second College Edition).

In written business English the current trend is to avoid both the stiffness of very formal English and the casualness of very informal usage. Written business English should be clear and concise, reflecting care and precision in word choice. As a general rule, avoid the use of colloquialisms in business writing; using them in conversation is a matter of individual taste and judgment.

The following list of words and phrases should clarify the most common usage problems.

a, an The indefinite articles *a* and *an* denote one among other persons or things. The choice between them is determined by the *sound* of the following word.

A is placed before a word beginning with a consonant sound and before a long *u,* a sounded *h,* or an *o* pronounced like a *w*: a broker, a wonderful invention, a unique experience, a handful, a one-way street.

An is placed before a vowel sound: an appointment, an F.O.B. shipment, an heir, an honor, an understanding.

about Distinguish between *at* (precise) and *about* (approximate). Do not use *at about.*

INCORRECT: I will meet you *at about* 6:30.

APPROXIMATE: I will meet you *about* 6:30.

PRECISE: I will meet you *at* 6:30.

above The use of *above* as an adjective meaning "placed, found, or mentioned earlier" is acceptable. The use of *above* as an adverb to express that same meaning is preferred.

ACCEPTABLE: the above description

PREFERRED: the description given above

OR

the preceding description

accept, except *Accept* means "to receive willingly or formally; to approve."

I cannot *accept* any excuse for that behavior.

Except, as a verb, means "to omit; to exclude." *Except* as a preposition means "with the exception of."

She *excepted* that essay from the contest.

I will be able to finish everything *except* the filing.

adapt, adopt *Adapt* means "to change so as to make suitable."

We *adapted* the building to our current needs.

Miss Barnes *adapts* very well to new situations.

Adopt means "to take as one's own."

The board *adopted* the committee's suggestions.

adverse, averse *Adverse* means "opposed; unfavorable; harmful."

It is difficult to write under such *adverse* conditions.

Averse means "not willing; reluctant."

I am *averse* to continuing this discussion.

advice, advise, inform *Advice* is a noun meaning "opinion given as to what to do or how to handle a situation; counsel."

I would appreciate your *advice* in this matter.

Advise is a verb meaning "to give advice or an opinion; to recommend."

He *advised* me to reconsider my decision.

Inform means "to give knowledge of something; to tell; to acquaint with a fact."

My lawyer *informed* me that several sections of our contract are unclear.

affect, effect *Affect* is a verb meaning "to influence or to make a pretense of."

The weather *affects* his mood.

She *affected* a sophisticated air.

Noun use: *Affect* is a technical term in psychology referring to emotion or emotional response.

Her *affect* was clearly inappropriate.

As a verb, *effect* means "to bring about; to produce."

> The board is *effecting* changes in its bonus plan.
>
> His closer attention to detail has *effected* an improvement in his work.

Effect is also a noun meaning "consequence or result."

> We discussed the *effect* of the recent strike on company morale.

alike *Alike* is correctly used as an adjective to mean "like one another; similar; showing resemblance" or as an adverb to mean "in the same manner; similarly." Do not use the expression *both alike.*

> INCORRECT: They *both* think *alike* about politics.
>
> CORRECT: They think *alike* about politics.

all of Do not use "of" unless a pronoun follows.

> *All* the committee members will be present.
>
> Be sure to invite *all of* them.

all ready, already *All ready* means "completely prepared to act or be used immediately."

> This material is *all ready* for mailing.
>
> We were *all ready* to offer our assistance.

Already is an adverb meaning "previously; before a specified time."

> I have *already* completed the survey you requested.

all right Do not use *alright,* an incorrect spelling of *all right.*

all together, altogether Do not confuse *altogether,* meaning "entirely; completely," with *all together,* meaning "collectively; everyone in one group or place."

> It was an *altogether* satisfactory experience.
>
> I would like to meet with you and your staff *all together.*

all ways, always Do not confuse *always,* meaning "at all times; forever; with no exception," with *all ways,* meaning "every manner or method."

> She is *always* the first to arrive.
>
> I have examined *all ways* of approaching that problem.

almost, most Use *almost* rather than *most* to modify *all, any,* and the indefinite pronouns *anybody, anyone, anything, everybody, everyone, everything, nobody, no one,* and *nothing.* *(See* most, *page 238.)*

> We have called *almost* all the board members.
>
> *Almost* everyone was present at last night's meeting.

although, whereas, while *Although,* meaning "in spite of the fact that," should be used when the adverbial clause it introduces expresses concession: an idea that is opposed but not contradictory to the idea in the main clause.

> *Although* we have a sufficient supply of paper on hand, we shall accept this shipment.

Use *whereas* when the adverbial clause it introduces is one of contrast.

Iron rusts, *whereas* steel resists corrosion.

While introduces an adverbial clause that relates to time.

Mr. Croft will supervise the department *while* Mr. Harris is away.

among, between In general, use *among* when referring to more than two and *between* when referring to two.

A heated discussion went on *between* the director and his assistant.

The five of us discussed his offer *among* ourselves before the meeting.

Between is used for more than two when each member of the group is relating *individually* to each of the others.

The negotiations resulted in an arms agreement *between* the three nations.

Avoid using *amongst.*

amount, number Use *amount* when referring to a singular word. Use *number* when referring to a plural word.

I was surprised at the *amount* of paperwork.

The *number* of papers he has to review is overwhelming.

anyone, everyone, someone Write as one word:

Anyone when *anybody* could be substituted.

Everyone when *everybody* could be substituted.

Someone when *somebody* could be substituted.

anyplace Colloquial for the word *anywhere,* which means "in, at, or to any place."

COLLOQUIAL: He is willing to travel *anyplace* the job requires.

WRITTEN BUSINESS ENGLISH: He is willing to travel *anywhere* the job requires.

any time Always write as two words.

any way, anyway *Any way,* consisting of the adjective *any* and the noun *way,* means "no matter what means or method."

I will help you in *any way* I can.

Use *anyway* as an adverb to mean "nevertheless."

He is extremely busy but will attend the convention *anyway.*

anywhere Always write as one word.

anxious, eager To be *anxious* is to look forward to something with uneasiness and worry.

She is *anxious* to receive the results of the examination.

To be *eager* is to look forward to something with enthusiasm.

We are *eager* to hear the details of your promotion.

apt to, liable to, likely to *Apt to* expresses habitual tendency

Miss Fisher is *apt to* leave the use of punctuation up to her secretary.

Liable to expresses risk.

The pavement is icy, and the car is *liable to* skid.

Likely to expresses probability.

Their report is *likely to* be true.

as Do not confuse with *that* or *whether*.

INCORRECT: I do not know *as* you are invited.

CORRECT: I do not know *whether* you are invited.

as . . . as, so . . . as The connectives *as . . . as* in adverbial clauses of comparison are used in both affirmative and negative statements.

This letter is *as* long *as* that one.

This letter is not *as* long *as* that one.

So . . . as is used only in negative statements.

This letter is not *so* long *as* that one.

as, like *As* is correctly used as a conjunction meaning "in the same manner that; at the same time that; because."

She writes *as* she talks— bluntly.

As is also used as a preposition meaning "in the function, role, or sense of."

As a supervisor she is demanding but fair.

Like is a preposition meaning "similar to; in a manner characteristic of."

It will be hard to find someone *like* Peter for that job.

She sounds just *like* you on the telephone.

The use of *like* as a conjunction is restricted to colloquial English.

COLLOQUIAL: Nobody works *like* she does.

WRITTEN BUSINESS ENGLISH: Nobody works *as* she does.

Never use *like* as a substitute for *as if* or *as though*.

INCORRECT: She acted *like* she hadn't heard the news.

CORRECT: She acted *as if* (or *as though*) she hadn't heard the news.

bad, badly *Bad* is correctly used as an adjective after a linking verb to describe the subject.

I *feel bad* (sad) about what happened.

Badly is correctly used as an adverb after an action verb.

She *reacted badly* to the announcement.

Do not use *badly* to mean *urgently, very much, greatly,* or *extremely* or to modify words denoting "to want" and "to need."

> The office *urgently needs* reorganization.
>
> Sally *wants very much* to take a December vacation.

balance The word *balance,* in the sense in which it is often misused, is a financial term referring to the amount remaining on the credit or debit side of an account. Do not use *balance* when you mean *rest* or *remainder.*

> He has a large *balance* in his checking account.
>
> The *rest* of the books are still in the storeroom.
>
> She left the *remainder* of her meal untouched.

because of, due to To introduce an adverbial prepositional phrase, use *because of.*

> *Because of* the hazardous weather conditions, he canceled his trip.

Used most frequently after a form of the verb *be, due to* means "caused by; resulting from."

> The accident was *due to* hazardous weather conditions.

The use of *due to* as a synonym for *because of* is colloquial.

being as, being that Do not use either of these incorrect expressions as substitutes for *because.*

> INCORRECT: Being as he will be in Chicago, he will be unable to attend.
>
> CORRECT: Because he will be in Chicago, he will be unable to attend.

beside, besides Do not confuse *beside,* meaning "at the side of; next to," with *besides,* meaning "in addition to."

> She sat *beside* me at yesterday's conference.
>
> *Besides* the budget we have the election to consider.

between See *among, between.*

between you and me Never use the pronoun *I* after the preposition *between.*

biannual This adjective means "occurring twice a year at no particular time intervals."

Biennial means "occurring every two years."

Semiannual means "occurring twice a year at six-month intervals."

Bimonthly means "occurring every two months."

Semimonthly means "occurring twice a month."

bring, take Use *bring* when the action is directed toward the speaker or toward the place where the speaker is.

> *Bring* it *here* this afternoon.
>
> He *brought* this machine *to me* at my office yesterday.

Use *take* when the action is directed away from the speaker.

Please *take* these to Chicago with you.

She *took* that book back to the library yesterday.

(See also *come, go.*)

but . . . however Use one or the other but not both.

INCORRECT: The atmosphere was depressing, *but* the food was good, *however*.

CORRECT: The atmosphere was depressing, *but* the food was good.

The atmosphere was depressing; *however*, the food was good.

can, could, may, might *Can* and *could* express ability or freedom to act or be acted upon and possibility of existence. *Could* also expresses conditional or past ability.

ABILITY TO ACT: *Can* you meet that deadline?

ABILITY TO BE ACTED UPON: The papers *can be sent* to the office.

POSSIBILITY: The caller *could* be he.

CONDITIONAL ABILITY: If you have the time, he *could install* the equipment today.

PAST ABILITY: When Mr. Carle was younger, he *could* speak several foreign languages.

May expresses permission and possibility.

Might expresses possibility but implies doubt or a remote possibility.

PERMISSION: *May* I use your name as a reference?

POSSIBILITY: We *may* be able to increase our use of noncommercial timber.

POSSIBILITY WITH DOUBT: You *might* be able to reach him at home this evening.

The substitution of *can* for *may* is colloquial English.

COLLOQUIAL: *Can* I tell him to request an advance?

WRITTEN BUSINESS ENGLISH: *May* I tell him to request an advance?

cannot Always write as one word.

She *cannot* attend tomorrow's luncheon.

can't hardly, can't scarcely See *double negatives.*

can't (cannot) help but After *can't* (*cannot*) use either *help* or *but,* but not both.

INCORRECT: I *can't help but* wonder why he called.

CORRECT: I *can't help* wondering why he called.

I *cannot but* wonder why he called.

capital, capitol The word *Capitol* refers to the building in Washington, D.C., in which the United States Congress meets. Without a capital letter, *capitol* refers to the building in which a state legislature meets.

The adjective *capital* usually means "involving or punishable by death" or "of or having to do with wealth." It also indicates "the form of an alphabetical letter used to begin a sentence or a proper noun."

He doesn't believe in *capital* punishment.

They made a *capital* investment of $85,000.

Every sentence begins with a *capital* letter.

The noun *capital* usually refers to one of the following:

A city that is the official seat of government of a state or nation or the hub of an industry

Madison is the *capital* of Wisconsin.

New York City is the financial *capital* of the United States.

Wealth—money or property.

If I had sufficient *capital,* I would invest in that business.

come and In written business communications use *come to.*

COLLOQUIAL: *Come and* meet the president.

WRITTEN BUSINESS ENGLISH: *Come to* meet the president.

come, go *Come* indicates motion toward the speaker; *go* indicates motion away from the speaker.

If you *come* to my office at 6 P.M., I will *go* out to dinner with you.

(See also *bring, take.*)

complement, compliment *Complement,* used as a noun or a verb, denotes a balance or harmonious completion.

Bold headings will be a good *complement* to the fine print of the text.

Those designs will certainly *complement* our layout.

Compliment, used as a noun or a verb, means "to praise; something said in praise."

I want to *compliment* you on the fine job you did for us.

Compliments means "courteous greetings; respects."

Please accept the enclosed material with our *compliments.*

consensus The word *consensus* means "an opinion held by all or most." It is therefore redundant to write "consensus of opinion."

continually, continuously Do not confuse *continually* ("occurring at frequent intervals") with *continuously* ("occurring without interruption").

She is *continually* inventing excuses for her absences.

He talked *continuously* for over an hour.

could of After *could, ought to, might,* use the verb *have.* The use of the preposition *of* after these words is incorrect.

They *ought to have* finished the repairs by now.

council, counsel *Council* refers to "a group of people called together for consultation, discussion, or advice."

> The City *Council* will meet at 8 P.M.

Counsel means "advice; to advise."

> I am going to seek *counsel* from my lawyer before I proceed.

data The word *data* is plural.

> These *data* are surprising, and I would like to discuss them with you.

The use of a singular verb with *data* is now acceptable in standard English. The singular form, *datum,* is rarely used today.

deem Use a less stilted word, such as *think, consider,* or *believe.*

disburse, disperse *Disburse* means "to pay out; to expend."

> They are willing to *disburse* every cent they have to make this project succeed.

Disperse means "to scatter in all directions; to spread about, to distribute widely."

> After the meeting the crowd *dispersed* quickly and quietly.

disinterested, uninterested Do not confuse *disinterested* ("impartial, unbiased") with *uninterested* ("not interested; indifferent").

> We need a *disinterested* person as mediator.
>
> She seemed *uninterested* in the results of the survey.

double negatives Only one negative word should be used to express a single negative idea. With such negative words as *barely, hardly, scarcely,* and *but* (meaning *only*), the use of *not* is incorrect.

> We *can hardly* refuse to hear his point of view.
>
> As Mr. Colby told you, we *can take but* one more carload of coal.

due to See *because of, due to.*

each other, one another Use *each other* when referring to two persons or things. Use *one another* when referring to more than two.

> Mr. Harris and Mr. Jones are helping *each other* with their budgets.
>
> If all six of us help *one another,* we should finish before 5 P.M.

eager See *anxious, eager.*

effect See *affect, effect.*

emigrate, immigrate *Emigrate* means "to go out of one country or region to settle in another."

> When they *emigrated* from Russia, they left everything behind but the clothes they were wearing.

Immigrate means "to come into a new country or region, usually to settle there."

> This country was founded by people who *immigrated* here to escape religious persecution.

eminent, immanent, imminent *Eminent* means "high; lofty; renowned; distinguished."

He is an *eminent* author and lecturer.

Immanent means "living, remaining, or operating within; inherent."

Humor is an *immanent* part of his writing.

Imminent means "likely to happen without delay."

They said that a severe snowstorm is *imminent.*

ensure, insure *Ensure* means "to make sure or certain; to make safe; to protect." (*Insure* may be used in this context as well.)

Careful proofreading *ensures* accuracy.

Insure means "to contract to be paid or to pay money in the case of loss or damage."

We will *insure* all the new equipment.

equally as Do not use together.

INCORRECT: She plays *equally as well.*

CORRECT: She plays *as well as he.*
She plays *just as well as he.*
They play *equally well.*

etc. (abbreviation of the Latin *et cetera,* meaning "and the rest") The expressions *and others, and so forth,* or *and so on* are preferable in writing to the abbreviation *etc.* Use a comma before and after these expressions unless end punctuation eliminates the need for the second comma.

Never use *etc.* or one of its equivalents after examples introduced by *such as,* which indicates the selection of a few out of many, or in any context where the reader cannot easily fill in what is omitted.

He named every state in alphabetical order: Alabama, Alaska, *and so forth.*

every day, everyday Use *everyday* as an adjective.

an *everyday* occurrence

one's *everyday* clothes

Otherwise, write as two words.

I eat an apple *every day* of my life.

everyone See *anyone, everyone, someone.*

except See *accept, except.*

farther, further *Farther* and *farthest* refer to measurable distance.

Electric cars run even *farther* without battery recharging.

His office is the *farthest* from the hospital.

Further and *furthest* denote figurative distance in degree, quality, or time.

That report requires *further* study.

Public recognition was the *furthest* thing from his mind.

fewer, less, lesser *Fewer* answers the question How many? and modifies a plural noun.

> *Fewer* persons attended the meeting than we expected.

Less answers the question How much? and refers to quantity in mass or bulk. It modifies a singular noun.

> Last year we expended *less* money for repairs than we did the year before.

Lesser is used in reference to value or importance.

> The *lesser* sum is the correct one.

first When the word *first* introduces the first item of a run-on enumeration, use *second* and *third,* not *secondly* and *thirdly,* to introduce subsequent items.

> *First,* outline the problem. *Second,* list the possible solutions.

formally, formerly *Formally* means "in a formal manner."

> We were asked to dress *formally* for dinner.

Formerly means "at an earlier time; in the past."

> She was *formerly* the director of personnel with a large marine insurance company.

former, latter *Former* and *latter,* respectively, refer to the first and the second of two persons or things mentioned.

> Carol Smith and John Noble have decided to join us. The *former* will arrive on May 1; the *latter* will arrive on May 8.

go See *come, go.*

good, well *Good* is an adjective and is correctly used after a linking verb. *Good* is never used to modify a verb.

> The repertory plays this year were quite *good.*
>
> The benefits seem *good,* and the salary is excellent.
>
> I feel *good* about our investment.

Well is correctly used . . .

As an adverb meaning satisfactorily or skillfully

> The repairs are proceeding very *well.*
>
> I was amazed at how *well* she typed.

As an adjective meaning in good health or suitable.

> She has looked and felt *well* for the past three months.
>
> It is just as *well* that we didn't schedule our meeting until next month.

hardly See *double negatives.*

healthful, healthy *Healthful* means "beneficial to one's health"; *healthy* means "enjoying good health."

> Her diet is a *healthful* one.
>
> You're looking *healthy.*

if, whether *If* is correctly used to introduce an adverbial clause of condition.

He will attend the meeting *if* it is held in Miami.

Use *whether* to introduce a noun clause; do not use *if*.

Mr. Beck will tell us today *whether* he can attend the meeting.

In colloquial usage *if* and *whether* are often used interchangeably.

COLLOQUIAL: Ask him *if* he knows her.

WRITTEN BUSINESS ENGLISH: Ask him *whether* he knows her.

immanent, imminent See *eminent, immanent, imminent.*

immigrate See *emigrate, immigrate.*

imply, infer *Imply* means "to suggest something without specifically stating it." A speaker or writer implies.

He *implied* by what he said that the cost was prohibitive.

Infer means "to come to a conclusion; to interpret; to judge from evidence." A listener or reader *infers.*

From what he said, we *infer* that an announcement is imminent.

in, in to, into *In* describes the location of a thing or person within a certain space.

Mr. Bates is *in* his office.

The group will spend two weeks traveling *in* Italy.

In to is composed of the adverb *in* and the infinitive *to.*

He stopped *in to* tell us about his promotion.

Into denotes motion from outside to within or a change in form.

Mr. Wells has gone *into* Mr. Ellis's office.

The proposal will be divided *into* three parts.

in regard to Use *in regard to, with regard to,* or *as regards.* Do not use *in regards to.*

inform See *advice, advise, inform.*

insure See *ensure, insure.*

irregardless Do not use. The correct word is *regardless.*

it *It* is correctly used in reference to time and weather.

It is almost nine o'clock.

I wonder whether *it* is raining.

It is sometimes used as an expletive, a word that occupies the position of the subject but has no meaning of its own.

It is a pleasure to serve on your committee.

Because the use of the expletive delays the meaningful part of the sentence, expletives are used sparingly in business writing.

> *To serve on your committee* is a pleasure.

its, it's *Its* is a possessive pronoun.

> The cat is licking *its* dish clean.

It's is a contraction of *it is* or *it has*.

> *It's* time to reconsider our decision.
>
> *It's* been several weeks since her call.

kind of, sort of, type of *Kind, sort,* and *type* are singular nouns and are correctly modified by *this* or *that*.

> That *kind* of policy is favored by young executives.

Kinds, sorts, and *types* are plural nouns and are correctly modified by *these* or *those*.

> We no longer manufacture those *kinds*.

Do not use *kind of* and *sort of* to replace such adverbs as *somewhat* and *rather*.

> Mr. Wells's schedule is *rather* crowded this week.
>
> We are *somewhat* late in mailing our new price lists.

Do not use the articles *a* or *an* after *kind of* and *sort of*.

> INCORRECT: That *kind of* a paint is not practical.
>
> CORRECT: That *kind of* paint is not practical.

last, late, latest *Late,* adjective or adverb, refers to time.

> We didn't finish these figures until *late* last night.

Last and *latest* are superlative forms of *late*. *Last* refers to the final item in a series. *Latest* means "the most recent."

> *Country Squire* is the author's *latest* novel, and it is also the *last* one he intends to write.

latter See *former, latter*.

lay, lie *Lay* (*lay, laid, laid, laying*) is a transitive verb meaning "to put or place." It always has a receiver.

> Mr. Baldwin *lays* great stress on accuracy.
>
> They are *laying* the foundation today.
>
> The cornerstone was *laid* in 1980.
>
> The pipeline will have been *laid* by November 1.

Lie (*lie, lay, lain, lying*) is an intransitive verb meaning "to rest or recline."

> Responsibility for promotion will *lie* with Mr. Burns's office.
>
> The mail is *lying* on your desk.
>
> Yesterday the catalog *lay* on Mr. Ryan's desk.
>
> The manuscript *had lain* unnoticed on top of the files.

leave, let *Leave* means "to depart; to abandon"; *let* means "to allow."

Will you *let* me go if I *leave* these documents with you?

lend, loan *Lend,* not *loan,* is the preferred verb form; use *loan* as a noun.

If you *will lend* me the money, I will repay the *loan* with interest in six months.

less, lesser See *fewer, less, lesser.*

like See *as, like.*

***ly* adverbs** Separate two or more adverbs ending in *ly.*

AVOID: We are *usually particularly* rushed during December.

CORRECT: *Usually* we are *particularly* rushed during December.

may, might See *can, could, may, might.*

meantime Use *meanwhile* or *in the meantime.*

media *Media* is the plural form of *medium* and therefore requires a plural verb.

Other *media* are being considered for the ad campaign.

more important, more importantly Use *more important* (a short form of "what is more important is that"), not *more importantly,* to introduce a thought.

More important, the deadline has been moved back from June 1 to March 1.

most *Most,* the superlative form of *more,* is correctly used before an adjective or adverb to mean "to the highest degree" when more than two items are compared.

Miss Welch was the *most* cordial of all the receptionists.

The actors are seen *most* clearly from these seats.

Most is also correctly used as an adjective or as an indefinite pronoun.

Most letterheads are conservative in appearance.

Most of the mail has been sorted.

Do not use *most* to modify an adjective when no comparison is intended. Instead, use an adverb such as *greatly, very,* or *exceedingly.*

INCORRECT: Miss Welch was *most* cordial.

CORRECT: Miss Welch was *very* cordial.

most See *almost, most.*

one another See *each other, one another.*

opposite As a noun *opposite* is followed by *of.* Otherwise, it is followed by *from* or *to* or is not used with a preposition.

Mr. Poole's temperament is the *opposite of* hers.

Mr. Poole's temperament is *opposite to* hers.

Your desk will be *opposite* the window.

party In general, except in legal usage, avoid using *party* as a substitute for *person*.

personal, personnel *Personal* means "private; individual; belonging to oneself."

> I requested a *personal* interview with the president.

Personnel refers to employees.

> Please direct that memorandum to all company *personnel*.

precede, proceed *Precede* means "to be, come, or go before in time, place, order, or importance."

> He spoke last but gave us more information than any of the speakers who *preceded* him.

Proceed means "to advance or go on, especially after stopping."

> Turn right; then *proceed* down the hall until you reach my office.

principal, principle As a noun, *principal* means "chief; head; presiding officer, specifically of a school; main performer."

> We have discussed the schedule change with the *principal*.

Used in a financial sense, it refers to the amount of a debt or investment minus the interest.

> Mrs. Bently was able to use her interest as income without touching her *principal*.

As an adjective *principal* means "first in rank, authority, or importance."

> Miss Kantor was the *principal* speaker at this morning's meeting.

Principle means "the source or origin of something; a fundamental truth, law, doctrine, or motivating force."

> The *principle* behind his actions is a simple one: You must spend money to make money.

prior to Use *before*, which is less stilted than *prior to*.

proved, proven Use *proved* as a verb; use *proven* as an adjective.

> We *proved* that success was possible.
>
> We have a *proven* formula for success.

provided, providing *Provided* or *provided that*, equivalent to *if*, introduces an adverbial clause of condition.

> You can make a substantial saving *provided that* you pay your bills within the discount period.

Providing is a participle and means "giving or offering."

> Redwood enclosures, *providing* privacy and attractive fencing, are widely used in the suburbs.

raise, rise *Raise* (*raising*, *raised*) is a transitive verb meaning "to lift; to cause to rise in level or amount; to bring up for consideration; to collect; to rear or grow."

> Manufacturers are *raising* the price of automotive parts.
>
> The issue of an employment freeze was *raised* by the committee.
>
> We must *raise* $10,000 to pay the mortgage.
>
> *Raising* corn may be especially lucrative this year.

Rise (*rising, rose, risen*) is an intransitive verb meaning "to move or to extend upward."

> Prices often *rise* at this time of year.
>
> The price of the stock *rose* twelve points.

Re:, In re: Avoid these Latin terms meaning *regarding, concerning,* or *about* in written business English.

real, sure, really, surely *Real* and *sure* are adjectives. *Really* and *surely* are adverbs. If *certainly* or *very* can be inserted correctly, use *really* or *surely.*

> INCORRECT: Your exhibit at the show was *real* impressive.
>
> CORRECT: Your exhibit at the show was *really* impressive.

reason is that Use *that,* not *because,* to introduce a noun clause after *the reason is.*

> INCORRECT: *The reason* I suggested Sheila Blake *is because* she has had more experience in that field.
>
> CORRECT: *The reason* I suggested Sheila Blake *is that* she has had more experience in that field.

respectfully, respectively *Respectfully* means "in a respectful manner; with deference."

> He treats his employees fairly and *respectfully.*

Respectively means "in regard to each (of two or more) in the order named."

> Ann and Tom were elected president and vice-president, *respectively.*

retroactive Use *retroactive to,* not *retroactive from.*

> The new increases will be *retroactive to* July 1.

said Except in legal usage do not use expressions such as "*said* client" when you mean "*this* client" or "the client *mentioned above.*"

scarcely See *double negatives.*

set, sit *Set* is usually a transitive verb meaning "to put or place something in position; to establish."

> She *sets* her marginal stops before she begins to type.
>
> Last week she *set* a new record for speed and accuracy.

Set is used intransitively in sentences like these:

> The sun is *setting.*
>
> We can't begin until the cement has *set.*

Sit is an intransitive verb meaning "to rest; to assume a sitting position." A person *sits* or *seats* himself voluntarily; a thing *sits* where it has been placed.

> The caller is *sitting* in the reception room.
>
> Your package has *sat* on the table ever since you placed it there.

shall, should, will, would *Shall* and *should* were once considered the only correct verb forms to express the future and conditional tenses, respectively, when *I* or *we* was the subject. Today, except in very formal speech and writing, *will* and *would* are used to express the future and conditional tenses, respectively, with all three persons.

> VERY FORMAL: I *shall (should)* be glad to review the final copy.
>
> LESS FORMAL: I *will (would)* be glad to review the final copy.

Shall in all three persons signifies control by some authority.

> The bylaws state that he as chairman *shall* preside.
>
> Mr. Barnes is determined that his son *shall* assume more of the management responsibilities.

Would and *should* also imply a conditional circumstance or uncertainty.

> I *would* provide office space for you if you *should* decide to take the job.

Would expresses past action as well.

> When we were students, we *would* take advantage of the reduced rates on buses, planes, and trains during the holidays.
>
> Mr. Johnson *would* always take the shuttle when he went to Washington, D.C.

Will and *would* denote willingness, promise, and intention.

> We *will* gladly accommodate you.

Should can also express moral obligation.

> Everyone *should* comply with the terms of the agreement.

so In writing, avoid the use of *so* to connect clauses.

> AVOID: We will complete the budget, so we should be able to submit it by Thursday morning.
>
> CORRECT: We will complete the budget today and should, therefore, be able to submit it by Thursday morning.
>
> CORRECT: Since we will complete the budget today, we should be able to submit it by Thursday.

some time, sometime, sometimes *Some time,* written as two words, consists of an adjective and a noun, and means "an amount of time."

> He spent *some time* working on the plan.
>
> For *some time* we have been considering major renovations.
>
> *Some time* ago we quoted them a price on our steel files.

Sometime is an adverb and means "at an unspecified time."

Please come to see the demonstration *sometime.*

Sometimes is an adverb and means "occasionally; now and then."

Sometimes another salesman takes an order.

somewhere *Somewhere* is preferable to *someplace.*

someone See *anyone, everyone, someone.*

stationary, stationery *Stationary* means "fixed in position; unchanging in condition or value."

The interest rate has remained *stationary* for the last six weeks.

Stationery refers to writing materials, especially paper and envelopes used for letters.

Office *stationery* should be plain but of good quality.

sure, surely See *real, sure, really, surely.*

take See *bring, take.*

than, then *Than* is a conjunction used to introduce the second element in a comparison.

Our profits were higher *than* we had expected them to be.

Then is an adverb meaning "at that time; soon afterward; next in order; in that case."

We will complete a rough estimate of costs involved and *then* meet with our clients.

that, which, who In general, *that* is used as a connective when the adjective clause following is essential, providing information necessary to the meaning or identification of the noun or the pronoun that it modifies.

We need a duplicator *that* is small but *that* will produce legible copies.

The duplicator *that* produces legible copies is the one we want.

That usually refers to things, although it is sometimes used in an impersonal reference to people.

Is the dictionary *that* you selected thumb-indexed?

The candidate *that* wins this election will need the full support of the party.

Which is used when the adjective clause is nonessential, unnecessary to the identification of the noun or pronoun that it modifies.

Duplicator 236, *which* is small and *which* produces legible copies, is our choice.

EXCEPTION: When a sentence contains a noun clause or an adverbial clause beginning with *that,* an essential adjective clause should begin with *which.*

We said *that* the duplicator *which* we need must be small.

We are glad *that* the duplicator *which* Mr. Branton ordered is portable.

Which usually refers to things but may also refer to a collective noun, a group of persons acting as a unit.

> The Harcourt Building, *which* is on Maple Street, has been sold.
>
> The Maxwell Company, *which* has an office in this building, is a brokerage firm.

Who refers to persons.

> Mr. Bell is the man *who* founded our company.

their, there, they're *Their* is a possessive adjective indicating "of, belonging to, made, or done by them."

> They gave us *their* statistics this afternoon.

There is an adverb meaning "at or in that place."

> I will try to be *there* by 3 P.M.

There may also be used as an expletive, a word that occupies the position of the subject but has no meaning of its own. Because the true subject is delayed and appears after the verb in such a sentence, avoid the use of expletives (*it* and *there*) in written business English.

> AVOID: *There* are several letters on your desk. (*Letters* is the true subject.)
>
> CORRECT: Several letters are on your desk.

They're is the contraction of *they are.*

> *They're* sending us their revised figures tomorrow.

therein, thereon Avoid such overly formal words in ordinary business communications.

uninterested See *disinterested, uninterested.*

well See *good, well.*

whereas See *although, whereas, while.*

whether See *if, whether.*

while See *although, whereas, while.*

who, whom Use *who* as the subject of a verb or as the complement of a linking verb.

> *Who* answered the telephone?
>
> She is the secretary *who answered* the telephone.
>
> I don't know *who* she is.

Use *whom* . . .

As the direct object of a verb

> Miss Granger is the secretary *whom* we employed. (We employed *her.*)
>
> *Whom* did you call? (You did call *her.*)

As the object of a preposition

She is the secretary to *whom* I gave the letter. (I gave the letter *to her.*)

To *whom* did you give the letter? (You did give the letter *to her.*)

As the subject of an infinitive

She is a person *whom* we believe to be very capable. (We believe *her to be* very capable.)

Whom did you ask to do that job? (You did ask *her to do* that job.)

As the complement of an infinitive.

He is the one *whom* we wish to interview. (We wish *to interview him.*)

Whom do you wish to interview? (You do wish to interview *him.*)

NOTE: In choosing between *who* or *whom,* put the sentence or clause to which *who* or *whom* belongs in subject-verb-complement order. Substitute *he* or *him* (*she* or *her*) for *who* or *whom.* If *he* (*she*) is correct, use *who.* If *him* (*her*) is correct, use *whom.*

who's, whose *Who's* is the contraction for *who is* and *who has.*

We don't know *who's* been recommended for that position.

Whose is the possessive form of *who.*

Whose are these?

She is the applicant *whose* résumé I discussed with you yesterday.

Whose may be used as a substitute for *of which the* to avoid awkwardness.

We rented an office *whose* windows overlooked Park Avenue.

will, would See *shall, should, will, would.*

you're, your *You're* is the contraction for *you are.*

Please call me by Friday to let me know whether *you're* willing to undertake this project.

Your is a possessive adjective.

I would appreciate knowing *your* opinion of the enclosed material.

EASILY CONFUSED WORDS

The words in the following list are often used incorrectly because they look or sound alike. NOTE: Some of the most frequently confused words are further discussed in the "Glossary of Usage," page 225.

accede	to attain to duties or an office; to consent
exceed	to go beyond; to outdo or surpass
accent	(*v.*) to stress; (*n.*) the way words are pronounced; a mark of pronunciation
ascent	(*n.*) the act of rising; a climb
assent	(*v.*) to agree to something; (*n.*) agreement
accept	(*v.*) to approve; to receive
except	(*v.*) to leave out; (*prep.*) excluding something
access	(*n.*) a means of entry; the right to enter
excess	(*n.*) beyond the usual amount; (*adj.*) extra
acclamation	strong approval
acclimatization	the process of adjusting to a different climate
ad	(*n.*) a shortened form of the word *advertisement*
add	(*n.*) to combine numbers; to calculate a total
adapt	(*v.*) to adjust to something
adept	(*adj.*) skilled; (*n.*) an expert
adopt	(*v.*) to take in, choose, or use as one's own, as in *adopt an idea*
adherence	attachment or devotion to something
adherents	supporters or followers
adopt	see *adapt*
adverse	opposed; unfavorable
averse	unwilling; reluctant
advice	(*n.*) an opinion that is offered
advise	(*v.*) to offer an opinion; to give counsel
affect	to influence events
effect	the result of an event
almost	(*adv.*) nearly but not completely
most	(*adj.*) the superlative form of many: many, more, *most*
all ready	everything or everyone is completely prepared
already	(*adv.*) before a given time
all right	correct; safe; adequate for a purpose (two words: *all* and *right*)
all together	everything or everyone in a group

altogether	(*adv.*) completely
allude	to refer to something indirectly
elude	to escape or evade
allusion	an indirect reference
illusion	a false concept or perception
all ways	by every means
always	(*adv.*) all the time
altar	(*n.*) a place of worship
alter	(*v.*) to make a change
ante	(*n.*) an amount paid in advance as a share in a business venture
anti-	prefix meaning *against*
antecedence	(*n.*) the condition of being before; precedence
antecedent	(*adj.*) occurring first in time or space; (*n.*) something that precedes something else
any one	just one person or thing
anyone	(*pron.*) any person; anybody
any way	(*adv.*) by whatever method
anyway	informal: in any case
apportion	(*v.*) to divide and distribute
portion	(*n.*) a part of something
proportion	(*n.*) the relationship between parts of a thing
appraise	to estimate; to evaluate
apprise	(also, *apprize*) to inform; to notify
arraign	to bring to court; to accuse legally
arrange	to put in order; to prepare
arrant	(*adj.*) plainly; clearly
errand	(*n.*) a short trip made for a specific purpose
errant	(*adj.*) wandering; straying
ascent	see *accent*
assay	(*n.*) a test; (*v.*) to evaluate something
essay	(*n.*) a short written analysis; an attempt; (*v.*) to attempt something
assent	see *accent*
assure	to guarantee; to give confidence to someone
ensure	to make certain; to make safe; to protect
insure	to make a contract to protect against loss or damage
attendance	the act of attending something; the number of people who attend
attendants	people who attend or serve others

bases	plural of *base* (a supporting structure); plural of *basis*
basis	a foundation, often of an idea, as in "the *basis* of my opinion . . ."
berth	a ship's anchorage; a built-in bed
birth	the process of being born or of having a baby
beside	(*prep.*) by the side of; next to
besides	(*adv.*) in addition to
biannual	twice each year
biennial	once every two years
birth	see *berth*
board	(*n.*) a group having administrative authority; a piece of wood
bored	(*v.*) to be wearied by something; to have drilled into or through something
boarder	a person who rents living quarters
border	the edge of a thing
borough	a self-governing town
burrow	a hole in the ground
breach	(*v.*) to break a contract; to break through a barrier
breech	(*n.*) the lower end of a thing
canvas	(*n.*) rough cloth
canvass	(*v.*) to solicit thoroughly
capital	(*n.*) a city that is a seat of state or national government; money or property; (*adj.*) punishable by death
capitol	(*n.*) the building in which a state legislature meets
Capitol	(*n.*) the building in which the United States Congress meets
carton	a box
cartoon	a comic drawing
casual	informal
causal	related to the cause of an event
cede	(*v.*) to give up rights or title to something
seed	(*n.*) the embryo of a plant; the beginning or origin of something
censor	an official empowered to inspect and to remove portions of publications, films, letters, and so forth thought to be objectionable
censure	strong disapproval
sensor	a device that reacts to physical events
census	a population count
senses	physical receptors for perception: "sight is one of the five *senses*"; mental capacity
cent	(*n.*) a penny (1/100 of a dollar)

scent	(*n.*) a smell; (*v.*) to smell
sent	(*v.*) having caused someone or something to go (past tense and past participle of *send*)
cession	yielding of rights
session	a meeting; a period of activity
choose	to select
chose	the past tense of *choose*
cite	(*v.*) to summon to a court of law; to quote directly from a work
sight	(*n.*) something seen; (*v.*) to observe; to take aim
site	(*n.*) a place
close	(*v.*) to shut (*adj.*) stuffy; shut; tight in space
clothes	(*n.*) apparel
cloth	fabric made of natural or synthetic fibers
clothe	to dress or provide with clothing
coarse	rough; of inferior quality
course	a path to follow; a direction; progress through time or space
collision	a crash
collusion	a secret deal or partnership
complacence	contentment; smugness
complaisance	a willingness to please
complement	(*v.*) to make complete; (*n.*) a thing that completes something else
compliment	(*v.*) to praise; (*n.*) an expression of respect or admiration
compose	(*v.*) to put together; to arrange
comprise	(*v.*) to include; to consist of
compromise	(*v.*) to settle a dispute by having both sides make concessions; (*n.*) the settlement of a dispute
comprehensible	able to be understood
comprehensive	all-inclusive
comptroller	a financial officer
controller	one who is in control; also, a variant of *comptroller*
concert	(*v.*) to arrange or plan together; (*n.*) mutual agreement; a musical program
consort	(*v.*) to associate with; to join with; (*n.*) a partner
confidant	(*n. masc.*) a trusted friend
confidante	(*n. fem.*)
confident	(*adj.*) sure of oneself
conscience	(*n.*) a knowledge of right and wrong
conscientious	(*adj.*) scrupulous; precise

conscious	(*adj.*) awake; self-aware
consul	(*n.*) a foreign official
council	(*n.*) a group formed for a specific purpose, often to give advice
counsel	(*n.*) advice; (*v.*) to advise
consular	(*adj.*) of a consul
councilor	(*n.*) a member of a council
counselor	(also, *counsellor*) (*n.*) an adviser, especially a legal adviser
continual	occurring over and over again
continuous	continuing without interruption
correspon-dence	letters written or received; similarity or agreement between two things
correspon-dents	people with whom one exchanges letters; writers hired by the various news media to write news articles
credible	believable
creditable	deserving of praise
credulous	believing too easily
currant	(*n.*) a berry
current	(*adj.*) relating to the present time; flow of water or electricity
decent	(*adj.*) proper or fair
descent	(*n.*) the act of going downward
dissent	(*v.*) to disagree or reject
decree	an official order
degree	a step in a process; an academic award
deference	courteous regard or yielding
difference	the condition or quality that makes a thing unlike others
delusion	a false idea or belief
elusion	an escape or evasion
depositary	a trustee; also, a variant of *depository*
depository	a safe place
deposition	removal from office; legal testimony; something deposited
disposition	arrangement or settlement; a person's temperament
depraved	morally corrupt
deprived	lacking essential things
deprecate	to express disapproval; to belittle
depreciate	to reduce in value
descent	see *decent*
desert	(*v.*) to abandon; (*n.*) a dry, sandy area; (plural) *deserts:* earned reward or punishment, as in *just deserts*
dessert	(*n.*) a course at the end of a meal, usually sweet food

desperate	extreme; drastic; without hope
disparate	very different
detract	to take away from
distract	to divert the attention
device	(*n.*) a mechanical contrivance; a plan; a design
devise	(*v.*) to work out a plan
dew	(*n.*) moisture
do	(*v.*) to act
due	(*adj.*) owed; owing to
difference	see *deference*
disapprove	to hold an unfavorable opinion of something or someone
disprove	to show that something is false
disassemble	to take something apart
dissemble	to pretend or disguise
disassociate	to sever a connection
dissociate	to part company; to break a social tie
disburse	to pay out money
disperse	to scatter widely
discomfit	(*v.*) to frustrate; to make someone uneasy
discomfort	(*n.*) an uneasy feeling; (*v.*) to cause distress
discreet	careful in behavior and conversation
discrete	in separate pieces

disinterested	impartial; objective
uninter-ested	indifferent; not concerned
disparate	see *desperate*
disperse	see *disburse*
disposition	see *deposition*
dissent	see *decent*
distract	see *detract*
do	see *dew*
draft	(*n.*) an early or incomplete plan or version; a current of air; (*v.*) to choose, as "*draft* a candidate"; to make a preliminary sketch
draught	British variation of *draft*
dual	(*adj.*) double
duel	(*n.*) a contest
due	see *dew*
effect	see *affect*
elicit	(*v.*) to evoke; to draw out of
illicit	(*adj.*) illegal
eligible	qualified; suitable
illegible	difficult to read
elude	see *allude*
elusion	see *delusion*
elusive	hard to grasp
illusive	unreal; illusory
emanate	(*v.*) to flow out of
eminent	(*adj.*) distinguished; well-known
immanent	(*adj.*) living within something; inherent

imminent	(*adj.*) likely to happen immediately
emerge	to become visible; to rise from
immerse	to plunge into so as to be completely covered
emersion	emergence; coming out of
immersion	total submerging
emigrant	one who moves out of a country
immigrant	one who arrives in a country
emigrate	to leave one's country
immigrate	to take up residence in a new country
eminent	see *emanate*
ensure	see *assure*
envelop	(*v.*) to wrap up; to surround
envelope	(*n.*) a paper wrapper, as for a letter
equable	steady; unvarying
equitable	fair
erasable	able to be removed
irascible	quick to anger
errand	see *arrant*
errant	see *arrant*
especially	to a high degree; unusually
specially	particularly; for a special purpose
essay	see *assay*
every day	each specific day
everyday	daily; ordinary

every one	each individual person or thing
everyone	(*pron.*) all the people
exceed	see *accede*
except	see *accept*
exceptionable	open to objection
exceptional	above the ordinary
excess	see *access*
expand	to enlarge; to spread out
expend	to spend; to use up
expatiate	to be expansive; to elaborate
expiate	to make amends; to pay a penalty
explicit	clearly stated; definite
implicit	suggested; not plainly expressed
extant	(*adj.*) still in existence
extent	(*n.*) the range of a thing
facetious	joking
factious	causing disagreements
factitious	forced; artificial
fictitious	imaginary; false
facilitate	to make easy
felicitate	to offer congratulations
facility	skill; ease
felicity	happiness
farther	(*adj.*) more distant in space (comparative form of *far*)
further	(*adj.*) to a greater degree (comparative of *far*); (*v.*) to promote

fictitious	see *factious*
finale	(*n.*) the end
finally	(*adv.*) at last
fineness	delicacy
finesse	tact; diplomacy; skill
flair	natural talent or aptitude; style
flare	a sudden blaze of light; a device for lighting or marking an area
flaunt	to display in a gaudy manner
flout	to show scorn or contempt
flounder	(*n.*) a flat fish; (*v.*) to move or speak awkwardly
founder	(*n.*) one who establishes something; (*v.*) to run aground or fall
forego	to go before
forgo	to do without
foreword	(*n.*) an introduction
forward	(*adj.*) in front of; (*adv.*) to the front; (*v.*) to send ahead
formally	in a formal way
formerly	at an earlier time
forth	(*adv.*) forward; onward
fourth	(*adj.*) number four in a series
founder	see *flounder*
gibe	(*v.*) to jeer (at); (*n.*) a taunt
jibe	(*v.*) to be in agreement with
guarantee	a promise that something is as it is represented to be
guaranty	alternate spelling of *guarantee*
hear	(*v.*) to perceive sounds with the ears; to listen
here	(*adv.*) in this place; at this point
higher	(*adj.*) the comparative form of high: high, *higher*, highest
hire	(*v.*) to employ someone
hole	a cavity; a pit; a burrow
whole	complete
holey	(*adj.*) full of holes
holy	(*adj.*) sacred
wholly	(*adv.*) entirely; completely
illegible	see *eligible*
illicit	see *elicit*
illusion	see *allusion*
illusive	see *elusive*
imitate	(*v.*) to copy
intimate	(*adj.*) most personal; (*n.*) a very close friend; (*v.*) to make known
immanent	see *emanate*
immigrant	see *emigrant*
immigrate	see *emigrate*
immersion	see *emersion*
imminent	see *emanate*
implicit	see *explicit*
in	(*prep.*) contained inside; within

into	(*prep.*) from the outside to the inside
in to	(*adv.* and *prep.*) toward the inside, as in "go *in to* see them"
inapt	not suitable
inept	lacking skill
incidence	the degree or number of occurrence(s)
incidents	a group of events
incinerate	to burn up
insinuate	to suggest indirectly; to imply
incite	(*v.*) to urge into action
insight	(*n.*) clear understanding
indentation	a dent; a slight hollow
indention	amount of space in from a margin
indict	to charge with a crime
indite	to put in writing
indigenous	native to an area
indigent	in need; destitute
indignant	angry; scornful
inept	see *inapt*
ingenious	clever; original
ingenuous	open or candid; artless; without guile
insight	see *incite*
insinuate	see *incinerate*
insoluble	cannot be dissolved (in a liquid)
insolvable	that cannot be solved (a problem)
insolvent	without money; bankrupt
insure	see *assure*
intense	(*adj.*) very strong; extreme
intents	(*n.*) goals; purposes
inter-	a prefix meaning *between* or *among*, as in *interstate:* between or among states
intra-	a prefix meaning *within*, as in *intrastate:* within one state
invade	to enter using force
inveigh	to make a violent verbal attack
irascible	see *erasable*
it's	the contraction of *it is* or *it has*
its	the possessive form of the pronoun *it*
jibe	see *gibe*
lead	(*v.*) to show the way; (*n.*) a metal
led	(*v.*) the past tense of *lead*
lean	(*v.*) to slant or bend (against); (*adj.*) very thin; without fat
lien	(*n.*) a legal claim
leased	(*v.*) rented
least	(*adj.*) the smallest; superlative form of *little:* little, less, *least*
led	see *lead*
legislator	a lawmaker
legislature	a group of lawmakers

lessee (*n.*) one who rents through a lease

lesser (*adj.*) smaller; comparative form (alternate) of *little:* little, *lesser,* least

lessor (*n.*) a landlord; one who owns a lease

lessen (*v.*) to make less; to minimize

lesson (*n.*) something to be learned

liable (*adj.*) legally responsible; likely to happen

libel (*n.*) a false and malicious written statement

lien see *lean*

literal (*adj.*) word for word; the exact meaning

literally (*adv.*) exactly; in fact

literate (*adj.*) able to read and write; well-educated

loan (*v.*) to let someone borrow something; (*n.*) money loaned

lone (*adj.*) solitary; alone

local (*adj.*) related to a specific place

locale (*n.*) a place

loose (*adj.*) not tied; free

lose (*v.*) to misplace; to fail to win

manner a method; behavior

manor a large house

material (*adj.*) of matter; important; (*n.*) what a thing is made of

materiel (*n.*) things necessary to any work, especially war supplies

may be is possible that

maybe (*adv.*) perhaps

mean (*v.*) intend; (*adj.*) nasty; stingy; (*n.*) the mathematical average

mien (*n.*) manner; appearance

migrant (*n.*) one who moves from place to place

migrate (*v.*) to move from one place to another

militate to work against

mitigate to make milder

missal the official book of the Roman Catholic Mass

missile an object that is thrown; a projectile

most see *almost*

no body without a body

nobody (*pron.*) not any person

no one not any person

none (*n.*) nothing; not any

official (*adj.*) having authority; (*n.*) a person in a position of authority

officious (*adj.*) meddlesome; overbearing; highhanded

ordinance a command; a law

ordnance weapons; military hardware

overdo	(*v.*) to do too much; to exaggerate
overdue	(*adj.*) past the time for payment; delayed
parameter	a constant with values that vary according to its application
perimeter	a boundary
patience	(*n.*) willingness to wait
patient	(*adj.*) able to wait or endure
patients	(*n.*) people receiving medical care
peak	(*n.*) the top; the maximum
peek	(*v.*) to sneak a look
pique	(*n.*) hurt feelings
perfect	(*adj.*) without flaws; (*v.*) to make more nearly perfect
prefect	(*n.*) a highly placed official
perquisite	(*n.*) an additional privilege
prerequisite	(*adj.*) required first; (*n.*) a requirement
persecute	to oppress
prosecute	to pursue, especially in a legal proceeding
personal	(*adj.*) private; (*n.*) a type of news item
personnel	(*n.*) employees; staff members
perspective	(*n.*) a point of view
prospective	(*adj.*) expected; looking to the future
peruse	to read carefully
pursue	to chase; to continue
pique	see *peek*
plaintiff	(*n.*) a person who sues someone else
plaintive	(*adj.*) sad; mournful
portend	(*v.*) to give warning
portent	(*n.*) a warning event
pretend	(*v.*) to make believe
portion	see *apportion*
practicable	possible; usable
practical	workable; concerned with everyday matters
precede	to come before
proceed	to go ahead
precedence	coming before; a higher rank
precedents	things that happened earlier and now serve as examples
preposition	a part of speech that relates one thing to another
proposition	an offer
prescribe	to set rules; to advise
proscribe	to forbid; to outlaw
presentiment	a foreboding feeling
*present-*ment	the exhibition or proposal of something
principal	(*adj.*) first in rank; (*n.*) a sum of money; a school official
principle	(*n.*) a standard or rule
profit	to gain

prophet	a religious teacher
prophecy	(*n.*) a prediction
prophesy	(*v.*) to make a prediction
proportion	see *apportion*
propose	(*v.*) to suggest
purpose	(*n.*) an intention or goal
pursue	see *peruse*
quiet	(*adj.*) silent; calm
quite	(*adv.*) positively
read	(*v.*) to understand written words
reed	(*n.*) a hollow grassy stem
real	(*adj.*) actual; existent
reel	(*v.*) to stagger; (*n.*) fishing tackle
recent	(*adj.*) in the near past
resent	(*v.*) to be indignant
reference	the directing of attention
reverence	awe; respect
rend	to tear or rip apart
render	to give; to represent
resent	see *recent*
respectably	in a manner worthy of respect
respectfully	in a manner showing respect
respective	relating individually to two or more
respectively	in the order that is given
review	(*v.*) to take another look at; to look back at
revue	(*n.*) a musical show
scent	see *cent*
seed	see *cede*
sees	(*v.* the present-tense, third-person of *see*) perceives visually
seize	to take suddenly by force
senses	see *census*
sensor	see *censor*
sent	see *cent*
session	see *cession*
sight	see *cite*
site	see *cite*
some one	just one person
someone	(*n.*) some person
sometime	at an unspecified time
sometimes	occasionally; once in a while
spacious	large; having much space
specious	seemingly correct but actually false
specially	see *especially*
stationary	(*adj.*) remaining still; fixed
stationery	(*n.*) writing paper
there	(*adv.*) at that place
their	(*pron.*) belonging to them
they're	contraction of *they are*

there for — in place for a purpose
therefore — (*adv.*) as a result; it follows that

to — (*prep.*) toward
too — (*adv.*) in addition
two — (*adj.*) a cardinal number

topographical — (*adj.*) relating to the shape of a surface
topography — (*n.*) the shape of a surface
typograph-ical — (*adj.*) relating to the art of arranging type for printing
typography — (*n.*) the art of arranging type for printing

tortuous — crooked; winding; not straightforward
torturous — painful

track — a series of marks
tract — a religious or political essay; an expanse of land

typographical — see *topographical*

typography — see *topographical*

undo — (*v.*) to release; to open
undue — (*adj.*) not appropriate; excessive

uninterested — see *disinterested*

urban — characteristic of a city
urbane — smoothly polite; polished in manner

veracity — truthfulness; honesty
voracity — great greed

waive — to give up the rights to something
wave — to signal by moving a hand or arm

waiver — (*n.*) a written statement giving up certain rights
waver — (*v.*) to hesitate

ware — (*n.*) something to be sold
wear — (*v.*) to have on, as in "*wear* a hat"; to grind down
where — (*adv.*) at what place?

weather — (*n.*) general atmospheric conditions, such as clouds, rain, or temperature
whether — (*conj.*) in whichever case; in either case; if; used to introduce alternatives, as in "Call *whether* it's early or late."

were — (*v.*) past tense of *be*
we're — contraction of *we are*

whole — see *hole*

wholly — see *holey*

who's — the contraction of *who is* or *who has*
whose — the possessive form of the pronouns *who* and *whom*

your — the possessive form of the pronoun *you*
you're — the contraction of *you are*

CORRECT PREPOSITIONS

abhorrence	
of	She made clear her *abhorrence of* the layoffs.
abhorrent	
to	Carelessness is *abhorrent to* me.
ability	
at an activity	He showed *ability at* long-range planning.
with a thing	Her *ability with* the computer is amazing.
abstain	
from	The chairman *abstained from* voting.
abstract	
from (to remove; to form a general idea from)	He *abstracted* two conclusions *from* the long report.
accede	
to	Management *acceded to* the union's demands.
accommodate	
to (to adapt)	She will *accommodate to* the problems of business travel.
with (to help by supplying something)	We *accommodated* the treasurer *with* a budget forecast.
accompany	
by a person	They were *accompanied by* a lawyer.
with a thing	She *accompanied* her report *with* a slide show.
accord (*n.*)	
between two parties	Everyone hailed the *accord between* the former competitors.
in (an agreement)	The partners have reached an *accord in* their business plans.
of two or more things	The committee reached an *accord of* opinions.
with something else	This rule is in *accord with* the bylaws.
accord (*v.*)	
to (to give)	She was glad to *accord* bonuses *to* her staff.
accordance	
with	We are in *accordance with* the sales manager's decision.
accordant	
to or *with*	He was offered a salary *accordant to* (*with*) his experience.
accountable	
for (responsible for)	A manager is *accountable for* an employee's mistakes.
to a person or group	Ms. Jenkins is *accountable* only *to* the president.

acquaintance

among more than two	She has many *acquaintances among* the firm's directors.
between two	How close is the *acquaintance between* you and the district manager?
of a person	She made the *acquaintance of* our district sales representative.
with a thing	I have some *acquaintance with* the textile industry.

acquiesce

in	He was forced to *acquiesce in* the decision.

acquit

of a charge	They were *acquitted of* any involvement in the theft.
with (to act with positive result)	She *acquitted* herself *with* honor in the sales meeting.

adapt

for a purpose	The mechanic *adapted* the copier *for* heavy use.
from a previous version	This proposal is *adapted from* my earlier report.
to a condition	The staff *adapted to* longer hours.

adept

at or *in*	She was *adept at* (*in*) fund raising.

adequate

for a purpose	A three-person staff is *adequate for* the research project.
to a need	Our present phone system is *adequate to* our volume of calls.

adhere

to	We will *adhere to* the original plan.

adverse

to	The board was not *adverse to* our suggestion.

advise

of or *concerning*	Frank *advises* his staff members *of* (*concerning*) new developments.

affiliate

with a person or group	He is *affiliated with* Johnston Industries.

affinity

between people	We noticed the *affinity between* Tom and Doris.
with a group or setting	They felt an *affinity with* the organization.

amplify

by something added	They will *amplify* their oral report *by* a slide presentation.
on or *upon* the foregoing	He *amplified* later *on* his introductory remarks.

analogous
to — Her sales presentation is *analogous to* a Broadway show.

analogy
between two things — The *analogy between* the two departments' problems is striking.
with something — He always sees an *analogy with* past history in present situations.

angry
at or *about* a situation — He was *angry at* (*about*) the lack of progress.
with a person — She was *angry with* her assistant

annoyed
by a condition — The executives were *annoyed by* the delay.
at or *with* a person or group — She was *annoyed at* (*with*) the new advertising manager.

answer
for (accept the consequences of) — She must *answer for* her previous decisions.
to (be judged by) — The president must *answer to* the board of directors.

apply
for something — He will *apply for* the data-processing job.
to a person or group — She *applied to* the personnel department.

apropos
of (in regard to) — *Apropos of* your report, the committee thought it was very thorough.

arrive
at a specific place — We *arrived at* the airport in plenty of time.
in a country or city — They will *arrive in* Chicago tomorrow.
upon (in the phrase "arrive upon the scene") — Security guards *arrived upon* the scene.

assent
to — The manager *assented to* our proposal.

assist
at a place — Maggie *assisted at* the sales conference.
in an action — She *assisted in* landing the big sale.
with a project — She later *assisted with* the drafting of the company's contracts.

attend
to (to work on) — He must *attend to* his weekly report.

attest
to — The auditor *attests to* the financial soundness of the company.

authority
for (the source of) — Who is your *authority for* those facts?

on a subject	Mr. Jansen is an *authority on* mergers.
over an area or group	Ms. Phelps has *authority over* bookkeeping.
basis	
for an activity	The report provided the *basis for* their recent discussion.
of (foundation)	Proven facts are always the *basis of* her sound opinions.
bid	
on (to place a bid)	She *bid on* the construction job.
for (to bid actively against others)	He *bid for* the tractor at the auction.
break (*n.*)	
in	There was a *break in* the discussion.
break (*v.*)	
into an action	The Japanese workers *broke into* the company song.
up (to end)	The meeting *broke up* at lunchtime.
with precedent	This company must *break with* a century of industry tradition.
call	
for (to pick up for an appointment)	He will *call for* you at noon.
on (to visit)	The sales agent plans to *call on* all her former customers.
capable	
of	She is *capable of* greater effort.
capacity	
of (upper limit)	The computer memory has a *capacity of* two million bytes.
for volume or effort	Last week tested his *capacity for* stress.
to (authority)	The treasurer has the *capacity to* sign company checks.
capitalize	
at (amass capital for a business)	The business was *capitalized at* $500,000.
on (use as an opportunity)	We *capitalized on* the sluggish sales efforts of our competitors.
center	
on (not *around*)	The meeting *centered on* the need for better communication.
characteristic	
of	Extreme caution is *characteristic of* him.

characterized	
by	Last year was *characterized by* increased sales.
choose	
among three or more alternatives	The committee *chose among* a dozen options.
between two alternatives	The supervisor had to *choose between* two qualified candidates for the job.
coincident	
with (at the same time)	The company increased production *coincident with* improving its sales.
compare	
to something general	*Compared to* his previous work, he did an outstanding job.
with something specific	She *compared* her salary *with* her earnings of the previous year.
compete	
for something	The executives *compete for* the bonus.
with others	We *compete with* two other manufacturers.
comply	
with	He will *comply with* the terms of the recent agreement.
concern (*v.*)	
about a person or situation	She is *concerned about* the owner's health.
in an affair	He is also *concerned in* the merger.
with (to deal with)	Her firm *concerns* itself *with* public relations.
concern (*n.*)	
in (a financial interest)	They have a *concern in* three other companies.
for a person or group	He shows *concern for* his staff.
concur	
in an action or decision	Personnel *concurs in* our decision.
with others	The president *concurs with* the committee.
confer	
on or *upon* (to grant)	He *conferred* his half of the business *on* (*upon*) his partner.
with (meet and discuss)	I must *confer with* the staff before reaching a decision.
confide	
in (to tell secrets)	I am able to *confide in* one of my co-workers.
to (to entrust)	He *confided* his will *to* his lawyer.
conform	
to or *with*	The extra designs *conform to* (*with*) the architect's original plan.
consist	
in something abstract	Success *consists in* doing something you enjoy for a living.

of something specific	Our proposal *consists of* a description, a budget, and a revenue projection.
consistent	
in (within a set of actions or statements)	She is not *consistent in* her job performance.
with (in relation to a set)	Her performance today is not *consistent with* her performance last week.
contingent	
on or *upon*	The bank will transfer the deed to us *contingent on (upon)* payment of the loan.
contrast (*v.*)	
with	*Contrast* this month's travel expenses *with* travel expenses last month.
contrast (*n.*)	
between two things	We noted the *contrast between* the two firms.
to or *with* (a striking difference)	This check arrived early, in *contrast to* (*with*) the late check last quarter.
convenient	
for a purpose or use	This room is *convenient for* meetings.
to (near a place)	The office is *convenient to* the bus depot.
conversant	
with	She is not *conversant with* the contract.
correspond	
to (relate to)	The actual budget does not *correspond to* the estimate at all.
with (to write)	I *correspond with* Sharon once a month.
deal	
in (buy or sell)	What produce does he *deal in*?
with (work with or use)	We *deal with* a number of lumber companies.
defect	
in an object	The secretary discovered a *defect in* the floppy disk.
of an abstract quality	Greg has serious *defects of* judgment.
demanding	
of	The executive is very *demanding of* everyone on her staff.
depend	
on or *upon*	He *depends* a great deal *on* (*upon*) his secretary.
dependent	
on	We are *dependent on* his good business sense.
deprive	
of	High interest rates will *deprive* the company *of* ready cash.

derogatory	
to	His thoughtless remarks were *derogatory to* women.
desire	
for	Tod has a strong *desire for* success.
desirous	
of	The company is *desirous of* more credit.
desist	
from	A judge ordered the firm to *desist from* dumping wastes in the river.
destructive	
of something general	Poor management is *destructive of* morale.
to something specific	Overuse can be highly *destructive to* a small copier.
detract	
from	A single shoddy product can *detract from* the company's image.
deviate	
from	Do not *deviate from* proper style in a business letter.
devoid	
of	The stock market reports this week have been *devoid of* good news.
differ	
about or *on* an issue	We *differ about* (*on*) the way to do the job.
from a person or thing	My calculations *differ from* yours.
with a person	I *differ with* my co-workers concerning certain values.
different	
from (not *than*)	The final product is *different from* what I had been expecting.
disappointed	
in a person, hope, or result	She was *disappointed in* Larry.
by or *with* a thing	We are *disappointed by (with)* the low production figures.
disassociate	
from	He tried to *disassociate* himself *from* his former associates' mistakes.
discourage	
from	We *discouraged* him *from* a risky investment.
discrepancy	
between two things	There is a *discrepancy between* the two sets of blueprints.
in a single thing	There is a *discrepancy in* the paragraph.

disdain
for — We had *disdain for* their shady tactics.

dispense
with — Let us *dispense with* formality.

dissension
among more than two — There was polite *dissension among* the representatives of the Maryland delegation.
between two — The *dissension between* the two executives remained friendly.
with one — She was soon in *dissension with* the majority of the committee.
in a group — He sensed the *dissension in* the ranks.

dissent
from — He *dissented from* the final decision of the company's board.

dissimilar
to — This product is *dissimilar to* competing brands.

distaste
for — He expressed *distaste for* the cafeteria food.

distinguished
by (made noticeable by) — Marie is *distinguished by* her perfectionism.
from (set apart from) — Colorful packaging *distinguishes* our product *from* similar ones.

divert
by (entertain) — We were *diverted by* the entertaining show.
from (turn aside) — She *diverted* money *from* the budget for her own use.
to (to turn aside to) — He *diverted* the company plane *to* Bermuda for the weekend.

divest
of — They *divested* the company *of* unwanted assets.

divide
among more than two — He *divided* the work *among* the department's fourteen secretaries.
between two — She *divided* the job *between* two typists.
into — We *divided* the report *into* six sections.

eligible
for (with a noun) — Sandra became *eligible for* the company's pension plan.
to (with a verb) — Gene is *eligible to* receive a promotion.

employ
at a wage or place — He was *employed at* $20,000 per year.
in a field or department — She was *employed in* the media department.
for a specific task or period of time — They *employed* temporary typists *for* a week.

empty	
of	The photocopier is *empty of* paper.
enter	
by means of	We can *enter by* the main doors of the office.
in a record	*Enter* the total sales *in* the ledger.
into an endeavor	You may want to *enter into* business after your graduation.
entrust	
to a person	The financial records were *entrusted to* her.
with a thing	They *entrusted* her *with* the records.
estimate	
at	They *estimated* their expenses *at* $15,000.
evidence	
of	They presented *evidence of* a change in consumer buying habits.
exception	
to	There is an *exception to* most rules in business.
excerpt	
from (never *of*)	She read aloud an *excerpt from* a leading business magazine.
exclusive	
of (not including)	The wife inherited her husband's estate, *exclusive of* bequests for the children.
expect	
from a person or thing	He *expected* a call *from* the insurance company.
of a person	She *expected* loyalty *of* her employees.
expert	
in or *at* a subject or an activity	He was an *expert in* (*at*) contract law.
with a tool or material	The designer is an *expert with* an airbrush.
extract	
from	He *extracted* the truth *from* the confused and contradictory reports.
familiar	
to a person	The company headquarters is *familiar to* most local residents.
with a task, subject, or thing	My new boss is not *familiar with* his job yet.
favorable	
for (describes a condition)	The market is *favorable for* the introduction of a new product.
to (describes a person's attitude)	She was *favorable to* my suggestion.
forbid	
to (never *from*)	Company rules *forbid* us *to* give out information about our clients.

foreign	
to	His ideas were *foreign to* my way of thinking.
grateful	
for a gift or service	He was *grateful for* our help with the job.
to a person	He was *grateful to* us for our help.
guard	
against (to protect from general danger)	Safety helmets *guard against* head injuries.
from (to protect a specific person or group from danger)	An insurance company *guards* the firm *from* damage claims.
hinder	
from	A weak economy *hinders* the salespeople *from* meeting their quotas.
hindrance	
to	Plain stubbornness is the main *hindrance to* a settlement.
hint	
at	He did not *hint at* any financial problems.
identical	
with or *to*	This room is *identical with* (*to*) my office.
impatient	
at an action or problem	They became *impatient at* the long delay in payment.
with a person	He is often *impatient with* his partner.
improvement	
in a person or thing	Our customers like the *improvement in* service.
upon a previous condition	This new typewriter is an *improvement upon* that old model.
inconsistent	
with	Her words are *inconsistent with* her actions.
independent	
of	Joan's job makes her almost *independent of* supervision.
index	
of	He studied the *index of* leading indicators.
infer	
from	He *inferred* the real story *from* his partner's double talk.
inferior	
to	Our present office machines are *inferior to* the new systems.

influence (*v.*)	
by an action	He was *influenced by* his boss's relaxed style.
for a purpose	She tried to *influence* him *for* his own good.
influence (*n.*)	
of a person or condition	Tom is under the *influence of* a good manager.
over a person or situation	The shop steward has *influence over* the other union members.
upon a person	The leader exerted *influence upon* the delegates.
initiate	
into	He *initiated* the new employee *into* company procedures.
inquire	
into causes or conditions	The vice-president *inquired into* the delays at the warehouse.
of a person	He *inquired of* Ms. Watson's secretary.
inseparable	
from	One problem is *inseparable from* the other.
intention	
of (usually in negative form)	He had no *intention of* selling.
to (with a verb)	She told him of her *intention to* take a leave of absence.
interfere	
in an activity	He often *interferes in* my work.
with a person	She asked Frank not to *interfere with* Diego.
intermediary	
between two persons or groups	He acted as an *intermediary between* labor and management.
in a disagreement	He works part time as an *intermediary in* labor negotiations.
intervene	
between two persons or groups	The skillful manager *intervened between* the feuding employees.
in a situation	The president *intervened in* the quarrel.
introduce	
to a person or thing	I *introduced* Sandy *to* the new southern district sales representative.
into a vessel, an object, or a situation	The consultant *introduced* a new viewpoint *into* the discussion.
invest	
in a market or enterprise	She *invested* her bonus *in* IBM stock.
with authority	The vice-president is *invested with* power to sign contracts.
jealous	
of	He was *jealous of* her success.

justified

in — She believed that she was *justified in* ordering the cutbacks.

labor

at a task — He *labored at* finishing the report.

for or *in* a cause — He *labored for* the advancement of civil rights.

under a person or condition — She *labored under* an impossible deadline.

lacking

in — She is *lacking in* ordinary politeness.

liable

for (responsible for) — The company is *liable for* any damages.

to (prosecution) — She is *liable to* her employer for the diverted funds.

mediate

between two parties — We *mediated between* management and the striking employees.

among more than two — The consultant *mediates among* the many different viewpoints.

necessity

for (with a noun) — She questioned the *necessity for* an immediate decision.

of (with a gerund) — She quickly questioned the *necessity of* deciding immediately.

to (with a verb) — She questioned the *necessity to* decide these important issues immediately.

need

for — Janet explained her *need for* a bigger staff.

of (in the phrase "in need of") — The office is *in need of* redecorating.

oblivious

of or *to* — She was *oblivious of* (*to*) the consequences.

opportunity

for (with a noun) — The company offers many *opportunities for* advancement.

of (with a gerund) — He took the *opportunity of* visiting the plant.

to (with a verb) — She enjoyed the *opportunity to* travel at the company's expense.

originate

from a previous version — Modern computers *originated from* mechanical calculating machines.

in a person's mind — The plan *originated in* Arthur's clever mind.

with a person or group — The idea for the company picnic *originated with* an employee.

part	
from a person	She refused to *part from* her secretary.
with a thing	He hated to *part with* his corner office.
participate	
in	Everyone can *participate in* the profit-sharing plan.
possibility	
of	There is little *possibility of* a drop in price.
precedent	
for or *of*	He cited a *precedent for* his decision.
precluded	
from	The firm is *precluded from* doing business in another state.
preparatory	
to	The owner chose a successor *preparatory to* retiring.
prerequisite	
of or *for*	A degree in computer programming is a *prerequisite of* (*for*) this job.
prior	
to	The sales representative reviewed her notes *prior to* the meeting.
proficient	
at a specific activity	She is *proficient at* selling by phone.
in a subject or field	He is *proficient in* finance.
prohibit	
from	Business ethics *prohibit* us *from* discussing our client's affairs.
purchase	
of	Vince approved the *purchase of* materials.
reason (*v.*)	
with a person	He was able to *reason with* his angry client.
reason (*n.*)	
for (explanation of)	He gave several *reasons for* his choice.
receptive	
to	Customers were *receptive to* the new service.
regard	
for a person or personal matter	He expressed his *regard for* her fine work.
to (in the phrase "in [or] with regard to")	They discussed problems *in regard to* her proposal.
regardless	
of	They went ahead *regardless of* expense.

renege
on — Their backer *reneged on* the deal.

repugnant
to — The offer was *repugnant to* them.

respect
to (in the phrase "with respect to") — She advised the company with *respect to* their investments.

retroactive
to — The agreement is *retroactive to* January 1.

secure
by (to obtain) — They will *secure* the contract *by* any means.
by or *with* (to guarantee payment) — The loan is *secured by* (*with*) a mortgage on the building.

sensitive
to — The president is *sensitive to* the firm's image.

separate
from — The special deal was *separate from* the contract.

stock
in (purchase of shares) — We bought *stock in* the corporation.
of (in the phrase "to take stock of") — She took *stock of* her chances for advancement.

subject
to — This contract is *subject to* state laws.

superior
to — Our produce is *superior to* all others.

tally
up (to check or add) — He *tallied up* the day's receipts.
with (to agree with) — Your estimate does not *tally with* mine.

tantamount
to (virtually equals) — Their offer is *tantamount to* a takeover bid.

unequal
in a quality or amount — The two candidates are *unequal in* experience.
to a task — He was *unequal to* his job as director.

unmindful
of — The supervisor was *unmindful of* the problems.

unpopular
with — She is *unpopular with* her superiors.

variance
with (in the phrase "at variance with") — The company's discriminatory business practices are at *variance with* state law.

vest	
in a person	Authority is *vested in* the president.
with an ability	The president is *vested with* authority to act for the corporation.
wait	
for something or someone	We *waited for* the repair technician.
on (to serve)	The woman *waited on* six tables at once.
write	
on a material	He *wrote* his report *on* the proper form.
off a debt or loss	The bank *wrote off* their loan of $12,000.
to (to move information in a computer)	She *wrote* the data *to* a floppy disk.

SPELLING RULES

The spelling of words in English is highly irregular. While there are some spelling rules for English, the rules have many exceptions. The following general rules may, however, be useful in spelling unfamiliar words.

GENERAL RULES

Words That Contain *ie* or *ei*

The general rule is "*i* before *e* except after *c*, or when sounded like a long *a* as in *neighbor* and *weigh*."

achieve	yield	reprieve	thief
freight	ceiling	receive	eight

EXCEPTION: Use *e* before *i* in some words when *ei* is pronounced as long *e*.

either seize weird neither leisure

EXCEPTION: Use *e* before *i* in some words when *ei* is pronounced as a long or short *i*.

height (long *i*)	Fahrenheit (long *i*)
foreign (short *i*)	counterfeit (short *i*)

EXCEPTION: Use *i* before *e* after *c* in syllables that are pronounced "shent" or "shens."

efficient conscience sufficient

Words That End With *sede, ceed,* or *cede*

All three suffixes have the same "seed" pronunciation but are spelled differently.

Only one word ends with *sede: supersede.*
Only three words end with *ceed.*

exceed proceed succeed

All other "seed" words are spelled *cede.*

accede	intercede	antecede
concede	recede	secede

Words That End With *ize, ise,* or *yze*

Many verbs end with *ize.*

realize	criticize	economize
apologize	summarize	emphasize

Many other words end with *ise.*

supervise	enterprise	compromise
advertise	franchise	merchandise

A few words end with *yze.*

catalyze analyze paralyze

COMBINING WORDS

When suffixes are added to words, or when two words are combined, spelling often becomes a problem. The following rules are an aid to avoiding spelling problems when combining words. When in doubt, always use a dictionary.

Doubling the Final Consonant

Double the final consonant of a one-syllable word that ends with a single consonant (swi*m*) preceded by a single vowel (sw*i*m) when adding a suffix that begins with a vowel or the suffix *y.*

trip/tripped skin/skinny

ship/shipper bag/baggage

EXCEPTIONS:

saw/sawing tax/taxed

tow/towing bus/buses

Double the final consonant of a word of more than one syllable that is accented on the final syllable and ends with a single consonant (begi*n*) preceded by a single vowel (beg*i*n) when adding a suffix that begins with a vowel.

occur/occurring omit/omitted

excel/excellent defer/deferral

EXCEPTION: If the accent shifts from the last syllable to the first syllable when the suffix is added, the final consonant is not doubled.

defer deferred deference

prefer preferred preference

When the Final Consonant Is Not Doubled

Do not double the final consonant of a one-syllable word that ends with a single consonant (shi*p*) preceded by a single vowel (sh*i*p) when adding a suffix that begins with a consonant (shipment).

bad/badly glad/gladness slip/slipshod

Do not double the final consonant of a word of more than one syllable that ends with a single consonant (profi*t*) preceded by a single vowel (prof*i*t) when adding a suffix that begins with a vowel if the word is not accented on the last syllable.

benefit/benefited cancel/canceling

total/totaled travel/traveler

EXCEPTIONS:

program/programmed	kidnap/kidnapping

Do not double the final consonant of a word that ends in a single consonant preceded by more than one vowel.

read/reader	succeed/succeeded
deceit/deceitful	cloud/cloudy

EXCEPTION: equip/equipped

Do not double the final consonant of words that end with more than one consonant.

tact/tactful	mark/marking
fact/factor	confirm/confirmation

Words That End With a Silent *e*

Words that end with a silent *e* usually drop the *e* when adding a suffix that begins with a vowel.

argue/arguing	write/writing
sale/salable	value/valuable

The final *e* is retained in some words that would be confusing or unclear without it.

dye/dyeing	singe/singeing
eye/eyeing	agree/agreeing

Words that end with *ce* or *ge* usually retain the *e* when adding suffixes that begin with *a*, *o*, or *u*.

enforceable	manageable (*but* managing)
knowledgeable	embraceable (*but* embracing)

Words that end with a silent *e* usually retain the *e* when adding a suffix that begins with a consonant.

manage/management	hope/hopeful
encourage/encouragement	sincere/sincerely

EXCEPTIONS:

argue/argument	due/duly
judge/judgment	true/truly

Words that end with *ie* change the *ie* to *y* when adding *ing*.

lie/lying	die/dying	tie/tying

Combining Consonants

When combining prefixes, suffixes, and words that have the combining letters in common, retain both letters.

di*ss*atisfied   mi*ss*pell   boo*kk*eeper

EXCEPTION: eighteen (*not* eigh*tt*een)

Words That End With *ant, ance* or *ent, ence*

Nouns that end with *ant* and *ance* are usually formed from verbs that end with vowels.

defy/defiant   endure/endurance
rely/reliant   issue/issuance

Nouns that end with *ent* and *ence* are usually formed from verbs that end with consonants.

exist/existence   persist/persistent
concur/concurrent   refer/reference

Words That End With *y*

Words that end with *y* preceded by a consonant change the *y* to *i* unless the suffix already begins with *i*.

vary/variance   try/trying
heavy/heaviness   carry/carrying

Words that end with *y* preceded by a vowel usually retain the *y* when adding a suffix.

enjoy/enjoyment   deploy/deployment
employ/employer   portray/portrayal

EXCEPTIONS:

pay/paid   say/said   day/daily

Words That End With *ic*

Verbs that end with *ic* usually add a *k* when joined to a suffix that begins with *e, i,* or *y.*

mimic/mimicked/mimicking   panic/panicked/panicky

Verbs that end with *ic* do not add a *k* when joined to a suffix that begins with *a, o, u,* or a consonant.

mimic/mimicry   frolic/frolicsome

FREQUENTLY MISSPELLED WORDS

The following list includes words in frequent use that are often misspelled. The spellings shown are the preferred spellings given in *Webster's New World Dictionary*. To check for spellings that are acceptable but not preferred, consult the Speller/Divider on pages 1 to 135 or *Webster's New World Dictionary*.

A

ab·bre·vi·ate
ab·sence
ab·sen·tee·ism
ab·sorb
ab·sorp·tion
a·bun·dance
ac·cede
ac·cel·er·a·tion
ac·cept
ac·cess
ac·com·mo·date
ac·com·mo·da·tion
ac·com·pa·ny·ing
ac·com·plish
ac·cord·ing
ac·cru·al
ac·cu·mu·late
ac·cu·rate
ac·cus·tom
a·chieve·ment
ac·knowl·edge
ac·knowl·edge·a·ble
ac·knowl·edg·ment
ac·quaint·ance
ac·qui·esce
ac·qui·es·cence
ac·quire
ac·qui·si·tion
ac·quit
  ac·quit·ted
  ac·quit·ting
ac·quit·tal
a·cross
ac·tu·ar·i·al
ac·tu·ar·y
a·dapt
a·dapt·a·ble
ad·den·dum
  PL. *ad·den·da*
ad·ept
ad·her·ent
ad·ja·cent
ad·min·is·tra·tive
ad·min·is·tra·tor
ad·mit·tance
a·dopt
ad·van·ta·geous
ad·ver·tise
ad·ver·tise·ment
ad·ver·tis·ing
ad·vice
ad·vis·a·ble
ad·vise
af·fect *(influence)*
af·fi·da·vit
a·gen·cy
a·gen·dum
  PL. *a·gen·da*
ag·gra·vate
ag·gra·va·tion
a·gree·a·ble
aisle
al·leged
al·le·giance
al·lo·cate
al·lot *(apportion)*
  al·lot·ted
  al·lot·ting
al·lot·ment
al·low·a·ble
all right *(correct)*
al·lu·sion
al·to·geth·er
a·ma·teur
am·bi·gu·i·ty
am·big·u·ous
a·mend·ment
a·mong
am·or·tize
a·nal·y·sis
  PL. *a·nal·y·ses*
an·a·lyst
an·a·lyt·i·cal
an·a·lyze
  an·a·lyz·ing
an·nu·al
an·nu·i·ty
a·non·y·mous
an·swer
an·tag·o·nize
an·te·ced·ence
an·te·date
anx·i·e·ty
anx·ious
a·pex
  PL. *a·pex·es*
a·pol·o·gize
a·pol·o·gy
  PL. *a·pol·o·gies*
a·pos·tro·phe
ap·pa·ra·tus
  PL. *ap·pa·ra·tus*
ap·par·ent·ly
ap·pear·ance
ap·pli·ca·ble
ap·plied
ap·point·ment
ap·prais·al
ap·pre·ci·a·ble

ap·proach
ap·pro·pri·ate
ap·prox·i·mate
ap·ro·pos
ar·bi·trar·y
ar·gu·ment
a·ris·ing
ar·range·ment
as·cend
as·cer·tain
as·sess·ment
as·sist·ance
as·so·ci·a·tion
as·sump·tion
as·sure
at·ta·ché
at·tend·ance
at·tor·ney
au·di·ble
au·di·ence
aus·pices
au·thor·ize
au·to·ma·tion
au·tom·a·ton
  PL. *au·tom·a·tons*
aux·il·ia·ry
a·vail·a·ble
awk·ward

B

bach·e·lor
bank·rupt·cy
  PL. *bank·rupt·cies*
bar·gain
bas·i·cal·ly
ba·sis
  PL. *ba·ses*
be·fore
be·gin·ning
be·liev·ing
ben·e·fi·cial
ben·e·fi·ci·ar·y
ben·e·fit
bi·an·nu·al
bi·as
  PL. *bi·as·es*
  bi·ased
  bi·as·ing
blam·a·ble
book·keep·er
bound·a·ry
  PL. *bound·a·ries*
bro·chure
budg·et·ar·y
bu·reau
  PL. *bu·reaus*
bu·reau·cra·cy
bur·sar
busi·ness
busi·ness·like
busi·ness·man

C

cal·cu·la·ble
cal·cu·la·tor
cal·en·dar
cam·paign
can·cel
  can·celed
  can·cel·ing
can·cel·la·tion
cap·i·tal *(money; city; upper-case letter)*
Cap·i·tol *(building)*
ca·reer
care·ful
car·goes
car·ry·ing
cas·u·al·ty
cat·a·log
cat·e·go·ry
cede
cen·sus
cer·tain
cer·ti·fy
chal·lenge
change·a·ble
chang·ing
chan·nel
  chan·neled
  chan·nel·ing
char·ac·ter·is·tic
charge·a·ble
charg·ing
chauf·feur
choose
  choos·ing
chose
  cho·sen
chron·o·log·i·cal
cite *(summon; quote)*
cli·en·tele
cod·i·cil
co·her·ent
co·in·ci·dence
col·late
col·lat·er·al
col·la·tor
col·lect·i·ble
col·umn
co·lum·nar
com·fort·a·ble
com·fort·a·bly
com·ing
com·mis·sar·y
com·mis·sion
com·mit
  com·mit·ted
  com·mit·ting
com·mit·ment
com·mit·tee
com·mu·ni·ca·tion
com·pa·nies
com·pa·ra·ble
com·par·a·tive
com·par·i·son
com·pel
  com·pelled
  com·pel·ling
com·pe·tence
com·pe·tent
com·pe·ti·tion
com·pet·i·tive

com·pet·i·tor
com·pla·cence
com·ple·ment
(*completes whole*)
com·ple·men·ta·ry
com·pli·ment (*praise*)
com·pli·men·ta·ry
com·pre·hen·sion
com·pul·so·ry
com·put·er
con·ceal
con·cede
con·ceiv·a·ble
con·ceive
con·cern
con·cur
con·curred
con·cur·ring
con·cur·rence
con·cur·rent
con·demn
con·dense
con·fer
con·ferred
con·fer·ring
con·fer·ence
con·fi·dant (*masculine*)
con·fi·dante (*feminine*)
con·fi·dent
con·fi·den·tial
con·grat·u·late
con·grat·u·la·tions
con·science
con·sci·en·tious
con·scious
con·sen·sus
con·se·quent
con·sid·er·a·ble
con·sign·ee
con·sis·tent
con·spic·u·ous
con·sult·ant
con·tem·po·rar·y
con·tin·gen·cy
con·tin·gent
con·tin·u·ance
con·tin·u·ous
con·tin·u·um
con·trib·ute
con·trol
con·trolled
con·trol·ling
con·trol·ler
con·tro·ver·sy
con·ven·ience
con·ven·ient
con·vert·er
con·vey·ance
co·op·er·ate
cor·po·ra·tion
cor·re·spond·ence
coun·cil (*group*)
coun·sel (*advice, advise*)
coun·se·lor
coun·ter·feit
cou·pon
cour·te·ous
cre·den·tials
cred·it·a·ble
cri·sis
PL. *cri·ses*
cri·te·ri·on
PL. *cri·te·ri·a*
crit·i·cism
crit·i·cize
cur·ric·u·lum
PL. *cur·ric·u·la*

D

da·tum
PL. *da·ta*
dealt
debt·or
de·ceive
de·cide
de·ci·sion
de·duct·i·ble
de·fend·ant
de·fer
de·ferred
de·fer·ring
de·fi·cien·cy
de·fi·cient
def·i·cit
def·i·nite
def·i·nite·ly
def·i·ni·tion
de·funct
de·moc·ra·cy
de·pend·ence
de·pend·en·cy
de·pend·ent
de·pos·i·tor
de·scend·ant
de·scent
de·scribe
de·scrip·tion
de·sir·a·ble
de·spair
des·per·ate
de·ter·min·ing
det·ri·ment
det·ri·men·tal
de·vel·op
de·vel·op·ment
de·vice
de·vise
di·ag·no·sis
PL. *di·ag·no·ses*
dic·tum
PL. *dic·tums*
dif·fer·ence
dif·fer·en·tial
di·lem·ma
di·min·ish
di·rec·tor
dis·a·gree
dis·ap·pear
dis·ap·point
dis·as·trous
dis·burse (*pay out*)

dis·burse·ment
dis·cern·i·ble
dis·ci·pline
dis·crep·an·cy
dis·il·lu·sion
dis·miss·al
dis·perse *(scatter)*
dis·sat·is·fac·tion
dis·sat·is·fied
dis·sim·i·lar
dis·tin·guish
dis·tor·tion
dis·trib·u·tor
di·vide
dom·i·nant
du·pli·ca·tor
du·ra·ble
dur·ing
du·ti·a·ble

E

ear·li·est
ease·ment
e·co·nom·ic
e·co·nom·i·cal
e·di·tion
ef·fect *(result)*
ef·fi·cien·cy
ef·fi·cient
e·gress
eighth
ei·ther
el·i·gi·ble
e·lim·i·nate
em·a·nate *(issue from)*
em·bar·rass
em·bar·rass·ment
em·i·nent *(important)*
em·pha·sis
  PL. *em·pha·ses*
em·pha·size
  em·pha·sized
  em·pha·siz·ing
em·ploy·ee
en·close
en·cum·brance
en·cy·clo·pe·di·a
en·dorse·ment
en·force·a·ble
en·sem·ble
en·thu·si·asm
en·thu·si·as·tic
en·tre·pre·neur
e·nu·mer·ate
en·vel·op *(cover completely)*
en·vel·ope *(container for letters)*
en·vi·ron·ment
e·qual
  e·qualed
  e·qual·ing
e·qual·ize
e·qual·ly
e·quip
  e·quipped
  e·quip·ping
e·quip·ment
eq·ui·ta·ble
e·quiv·a·lent
e·rad·i·cate
e·rad·i·ca·tor
er·ra·tum
  PL. *er·ra·ta*
er·ro·ne·ous
es·crow
es·pe·cial·ly
es·sen·tial
es·ti·mate
e·val·u·ate
e·ven·tu·al·ly
ev·er·y·bod·y
ex·ag·ger·ate
  ex·ag·ger·at·ed
  ex·ag·ger·at·ing
ex·ag·ger·a·tion
ex·ceed
ex·cel·lent
ex·cept
ex·cep·tion·al·ly
ex·cerpt
ex·cess
ex·ces·sive
ex·cite·ment
ex·cus·a·ble
ex·e·cut·or
ex·er·cise
ex·haust
ex·haust·i·ble
ex·haus·tion
ex·hib·it
ex·hib·it·or
ex·hil·a·rate
ex·ist·ence
ex·or·bi·tant
ex·pe·di·ent
ex·pend·i·ture
ex·pe·ri·ence
ex·pla·na·tion
ex·port·a·ble
ex·traor·di·nar·y
ex·trav·a·gant
ex·treme·ly

F

fa·cil·i·tate
fa·cil·i·ty
  PL. *fa·cil·i·ties*
fac·sim·i·le
fal·la·cy
fa·mil·iar
fa·mil·iar·ize
fas·ci·nate
  fas·ci·nat·ing
fa·vor·a·ble
fa·vor·ite
fea·si·ble
fi·nal·ly
fi·nan·cial
fi·nan·cial·ly
fin·an·cier
flex·i·ble

flu·o·res·cent
fo·cus
  PL. *fo·cus·es*
for·ci·ble
fore·cast
fore·clo·sure
for·eign
fore·see
fore·word
for·feit
for·fei·ture
for·get·ta·ble
for·mal·ly
for·mer·ly
for·mu·la
  PL. *for·mu·las*
for·ty
for·ward
four·teen
fourth
frag·ile
fran·chise
fraud·u·lent
freight
fre·quen·cy
ful·fill
ful·fill·ment
fu·tu·ri·ty

G

gain·ful
gar·nish·ee
gauge
gen·er·al·ize
gen·er·al·ly
ge·nius
gen·u·ine
gen·u·ine·ly
gov·ern·ment
gram·mar
grate·ful
gra·tu·i·tous
griev·ance
griev·ous
guar·an·tee
  guar·an·teed
  guar·an·tee·ing
guar·an·tor
guard·i·an
guess·work
guid·ance

H

hand·i·capped
har·ass
haz·ard·ous
height
here·to·fore
hes·i·tant
hin·drance
hur·ried·ly
hy·poc·ri·sy
hy·poth·e·cate
hy·poth·e·sis
  PL. *hy·poth·e·ses*

I

i·den·ti·cal
il·le·gal
il·leg·i·ble
il·lit·er·ate
il·lu·sion
i·mag·i·nar·y
i·mag·i·na·tion
im·ma·nent *(within)*
im·me·di·ate·ly
im·mense
im·mi·nent *(impending)*
im·pel
  im·pelled
  im·pel·ling
im·per·a·tive
im·per·cep·ti·ble
im·por·tant
im·pos·si·ble
im·promp·tu
in·ad·e·quate
in·ad·vert·ent
in·ad·vis·a·ble
in·as·much
in·ca·pa·ble
in·ci·den·tal·ly
in·com·pe·tent
in·con·ceiv·a·ble
in·con·test·a·ble
in·con·ven·ience
in·con·ven·ient
in·cred·i·ble
in·cur
  in·curred
  in·cur·ring
in·debt·ed·ness
in·de·fen·si·ble
in·def·i·nite
in·def·i·nite·ly
in·dem·ni·ty
in·de·scrib·a·ble
in·dict·ment
in·dis·crim·i·nate
in·dis·pen·sa·ble
in·di·vid·u·al
in·duce·ment
in·dus·tri·al
in·ev·i·ta·ble
in·fer
  in·ferred
  in·fer·ring
in·fi·nite
in·flu·ence
in·gen·ious
in·i·tial
in·i·ti·ate
in·i·ti·a·tive
in·noc·u·ous
in·no·va·tion
in·oc·u·late
in·sep·a·ra·ble
in·sight
in·sist·ence
in·stall·ment
in·sur·a·ble
in·tel·lec·tu·al

in·tel·li·gence
in·ten·tion·al·ly
in·ter·cede
in·ter·est·ing
in·ter·fere
in·ter·pre·ta·tion
in·ter·pret·er
in·ter·rupt
in·ter·sperse
in·ter·view
in·tri·cate
in·val·i·date
in·val·u·a·ble
in·var·i·a·ble
in·vei·gle
in·ves·ti·ga·tor
in·voic·ing
ir·re·duc·i·ble
ir·rel·e·vant
ir·rep·a·ra·ble
ir·re·sist·i·ble
ir·ri·ta·ble
i·tem·ize
i·tin·er·ar·y
its *(possessive pronoun)*
it's *(it is)*

J

jeop·ard·ize
judg·ment
jus·ti·fi·a·ble
jus·ti·fy

K

knowl·edge
knowl·edge·a·ble

L

la·bel
  la·beled
  la·bel·ing
lab·o·ra·to·ry
lan·guage
law·suit
leg·i·ble
le·git·i·mate
lei·sure
lei·sure·ly
length·en·ing
let·ter·head
li·a·ble
li·ai·son
li·bel
li·brar·i·an
li·cense
li·en
lieu·ten·ant
lik·a·ble
like·li·hood
lim·ou·sine
lin·e·ar
liq·ue·fy
lit·er·al·ly
lit·er·a·ture
lit·i·ga·tion
live·li·hood
lock·out
loose
lose
lu·cra·tive
lunch·eon

M

ma·chin·er·y
mag·nif·i·cent
mail·a·ble
main·te·nance
make·shift
man·age·a·ble
man·ag·ing
man·a·ge·ri·al
man·da·to·ry
ma·neu·ver
ma·nip·u·la·tion
man·u·fac·tur·er
man·u·fac·tur·ing
mar·ket·a·ble
ma·trix
  PL. *ma·tri·ces*
max·i·mize
max·i·mum
mean·time
mean·while
meas·ur·a·ble
meas·ure·ment
mech·a·nism
me·di·a·tor
me·di·o·cre
me·men·to
  PL. *me·men·tos*
mem·o·ran·dum
  PL. *mem·o·ran·dums*
mem·o·rize
mer·can·tile
mer·chan·dise *(goods; promote)*
merg·er
met·ro·pol·i·tan
mile·age
mim·e·o·graph
min·i·a·ture
min·i·mize
min·i·mum
mi·nu·ti·a
  PL. *mi·nu·ti·ae*
mis·ap·pre·hen·sion
mis·cel·la·ne·ous
mis·spell
mis·state
mis·us·age
mod·er·ate
mod·ern·ize
mod·i·fy
  mod·i·fied
  mod·i·fy·ing
mo·nop·o·lize
mo·not·o·nous
more·o·ver
mort·gage
mort·ga·gee
mort·gag·ing

mort·ga·gor
mov·a·ble
mu·nic·i·pal

N

nat·u·ral·ly
nec·es·sar·i·ly
nec·es·sar·y
ne·ces·si·tate
neg·a·tive
neg·li·gence
neg·li·gent
neg·li·gi·ble
ne·go·ti·a·ble
ne·go·ti·ate
ne·go·ti·a·tor
nei·ther
neu·tral·i·ty
neu·tral·ize
nev·er·the·less
nine·teen
nine·ty
ninth
nom·i·nal
non·stop
non·un·ion
north·east
north·ern
north·west
no·ta·rize
no·ta·ry
note·book
no·tice·a·ble
no·tic·ing
no·ti·fy
  no·ti·fied
  no·ti·fy·ing
now·a·days
nu·mer·ous

O

ob·jec·tion·a·ble
ob·lig·a·to·ry
o·blige
ob·so·les·cence
ob·so·les·cent
ob·so·lete
ob·sta·cle
ob·tain·a·ble
oc·ca·sion
oc·ca·sion·al·ly
oc·cu·pant
oc·cur
  oc·curred
  oc·cur·ring
oc·cur·rence
of·fense
of·fered
o·mis·sion
o·mit
  o·mit·ted
  o·mit·ting
one·self
op·er·ate
op·er·a·tor
o·pin·ion
op·por·tu·ni·ty
op·ti·mism
op·ti·mis·tic
or·di·nance
or·gan·i·za·tion
or·gan·ize
o·rig·i·nal
os·cil·la·tion
o·ver·charge
o·ver·draw
o·ver·due
o·ver·head
o·ver·time
o·ver·whelm·ing
o·ver·work
ox·i·dize

P

paid
pam·phlet
pan·ic
pan·ick·y
par·al·lel
  par·al·leled
  par·al·lel·ing
par·a·lyze
par·don·a·ble
pa·ren·the·sis
  PL. *pa·ren·the·ses*
par·i·ty
par·tial
par·ti·al·i·ty
par·tial·ly
par·tic·i·pant
par·tic·u·lar·ly
pas·time
pat·ent·a·ble
pat·ent·ee
pa·tience
pa·tron·ize
pay·a·ble
pay·ee
pay·roll
pe·cu·li·ar·i·ties
pe·nal·ize
per an·num
per cap·i·ta
per·ceive
per·cent
per·cent·age
per·cep·ti·ble
per di·em
per·ma·nence
per·ma·nent
per·mis·si·ble
per·mit
  per·mit·ted
  per·mit·ting
per·se·ver·ance
per·se·vere
per·sist·ence
per·sist·ent
per·son·al
per·son·nel
per·suade

per·sua·sion
per·sua·sive
per·ti·nent
pet·ro·le·um
phar·ma·ceu·ti·cal
phe·nom·e·nal
phe·nom·e·non
  PL. *phe·nom·e·na*
phys·i·cal
phys·i·o·log·i·cal
piece·work
plau·si·ble
por·trayed
pos·ses·sion
post·age
post·mark
prac·ti·ca·ble
prac·ti·cal
prac·ti·cal·ly
pre·cede
  pre·ced·ing
prec·e·dence
pre·ced·ent
pre·cip·i·tate
pre·cise
pre·ci·sion
pre·fer
  pre·ferred
  pre·fer·ring
pref·er·a·ble
pref·er·ence
prej·u·dice
pre·lim·i·nar·y
pre·paid
prep·a·ra·tion
pre·req·ui·site
pre·rog·a·tive
pres·ence
pres·tige
pre·sump·tu·ous
prev·a·lent
pre·ven·tive
pre·vi·ous
prin·ci·pal *(main; money)*
prin·ci·ple *(rule)*
priv·i·lege
prob·a·ble
prob·a·bly
pro·ce·dure
pro·ceed
pro·fes·sion
pro·fes·sor
pro·fi·cient
prof·it·a·ble
prog·no·sis
pro·gram
  pro·grammed
  pro·gram·ming
pro·hi·bi·tion
prom·i·nent
pro·nun·ci·a·tion
pro ra·ta
pro·rate
pros·e·cute
pro·tec·tor·ate
psy·cho·log·i·cal
pub·lic·ly
punc·tu·at·ed
pur·sue

Q

quad·ru·pli·cate
quan·da·ry
quan·ti·ty
ques·tion·a·ble
ques·tion·naire
queue
  queued
  queu·ing

R

rat·i·fi·ca·tion
read·i·ly
re·al·ize
rea·son·a·ble
re·cede
re·ceipt
re·ceiv·a·ble
re·ceive
re·cip·i·ent
re·cip·ro·cal
rec·og·nize
rec·om·mend
rec·on·cile
rec·on·cil·i·a·tion
re·con·nais·sance
re·course
re·cruit
rec·ti·fy
re·cur
  re·curred
  re·cur·ring
re·cur·rence
re·fer
  re·ferred
  re·fer·ring
ref·er·ence
ref·er·en·dum
  PL. *ref·er·en·dums*
re·gard
re·gret·ta·ble
re·im·burse
re·it·er·ate
rel·e·vant
re·lieve
re·luc·tant
re·mit·tance
re·new·a·ble
re·nowned
rep·e·ti·tion
re·pet·i·tive
re·place·a·ble
rep·re·sent·a·tive
rep·u·ta·tion
req·ui·si·tion
re·scind
re·sist·ance
re·spon·si·ble
res·tau·rant
ré·su·mé
re·tail·er
re·triev·al

re·trieve
ret·ro·ac·tive
re·turn·a·ble

S

sal·a·ble
sal·a·ry
sat·is·fac·tion
scar·ci·ty
sched·ule
scru·ti·nize
sec·re·tar·y
seize
sei·zure
sen·ior·i·ty
sense
sen·si·ble
sen·tence
sep·a·rate
sep·a·ra·tion
serv·ice·a·ble
sev·er·al
siege
sig·nif·i·cance
sim·i·lar
si·mul·ta·ne·ous
sin·cere·ly
site *(locale)*
sit·u·a·tion
siz·a·ble
so·lic·it
spe·cial·ize
spe·cie
spe·cif·ic
spe·cif·i·cal·ly
spec·i·men
spon·sor
sta·bi·liz·er
stand·ard·ize
sta·tion·ar·y *(immobile)*
sta·tion·er·y *(paper)*
sta·tis·ti·cal
stat·is·ti·cian
sta·tis·tics
stat·ute
stat·u·to·ry
stopped
  stop·ping
straight·en
strat·e·gy
stren·u·ous
strict·ly
stud·ied
  stud·y·ing
sub·poe·na
sub·stan·ti·ate
sub·tle
sub·tle·ty
sub·tly
suc·ceed
suc·cess
suc·cess·ful
suc·ces·sor
sud·den·ness
suf·fi·cient
su·ing
sum·ma·rize
sum·ma·ry
su·per·in·tend·ent
su·per·sede
sup·ple·ment
sur·mise
sur·prise
sur·veil·lance
sus·cep·ti·ble
syl·la·ble
sym·met·ri·cal
sym·po·si·um
  PL. *sym·po·si·ums*
syn·er·gism
syn·on·y·mous
syn·op·sis
  PL. *syn·op·ses*

T

tar·iff
tax·a·ble
tech·ni·cal
tech·ni·cian
tech·nique
tech·nol·o·gy
tem·per·a·ment
tem·per·a·ture
tem·po·rar·i·ly
ten·a·ble
ten·ant
ten·e·ment
tes·ti·mo·ni·al
there·fore
there·in
the·sis
  PL. *the·ses*
thor·ough
thor·ough·ly
though
thought
thresh·old
through
time·ta·ble
ti·tle
to·taled
  to·tal·ing
trace·a·ble
trans·fer
  trans·ferred
  trans·fer·ring
trans·fer·ence
trans·it
trav·el
  trav·eled
  trav·el·ing
treas·ur·er
tre·men·dous
trip·li·cate
tru·ly
try
  PL. *tries*
  tried
  try·ing
turn·o·ver
twelfth
twen·ti·eth

U

ul·ti·ma·tum
u·nan·i·mous
un·a·void·a·ble
un·bi·ased
un·de·ni·a·ble
un·der·sell
un·der·write
un·de·sir·a·ble
un·doubt·ed·ly
un·du·ly
un·eas·i·ness
un·for·get·ta·ble
un·ion·ize
u·nique
un·man·age·a·ble
un·nec·es·sar·i·ly
un·nec·es·sar·y
un·par·al·leled
un·til
un·wield·y
us·a·ble
us·age
u·su·ry
u·ti·lize

V

va·cant
val·i·date
val·u·a·ble
val·u·a·tion
va·ri·e·ties
ve·hi·cle
ven·ti·late
ver·i·fy
  ver·i·fied
  ver·i·fy·ing
vice-pres·i·dent
vi·ce ver·sa
vi·cin·i·ty
view
vig·or·ous
vis·i·ble
vol·ume
vol·un·tar·y

W

waive
waiv·er
ware·house
war·ran·ty
week·day
week·end
wharf
where·as
wheth·er
who·ev·er
whole·sale
whol·ly
who's *(who is; who has)*
whose *(belonging to whom?)*
wield
with·draw·al
with·hold·ing
with·out
wit·nessed
work·a·ble
writ·ing
wrought

Y

yield
your *(possessive)*
you're *(you are)*

AMERICAN AND BRITISH SPELLINGS

American and British spelling is identical throughout the English language, with the exception of the word groups listed below.

Words Ending With *er* or *re*

American	British
caliber	calibre
center	centre
somber	sombre
theater or theatre	theatre

NOTE: *Meter* is used in the United States and *metre* in Britain when referring to the metric system. However, *meter* is the accepted spelling in both countries when referring to any measuring device (e.g., *altimeter, speedometer*).

Words Ending With *ense* or *ence*

American	British
defense	defence
license (*n.*)	licence (*n.*)
license (*v.*)	license (*v.*)
offense	offence
pretense	pretence

Words Ending With *ize* or *ise*

The ending *ise* is generally preferred in Britain, but many British publications use *ize*. *Aggrandize, amortize,* and *recognize* are usually spelled in Britain with the *ize* ending.

American	British
advertise	advertise
chastise	chastise
criticize	criticise
exorcise	exorcise
mechanize	mechanise
memorize	memorise
normalize	normalise

Words Ending With *or* or *our*

Although *or* is the usual word ending in the United States, *glamour* is still spelled with the *our* ending.

American	British
behavior	behaviour
color	colour
harbor	harbour
honor	honour
labor	labour

NOTE: In Britain, the *u* before an *r* preceding a suffix is sometimes retained (as in humourless) and sometimes dropped (as in coloration).

Words Ending With *yze* or *yse*

American	British
analyze	analyse
electrolyze	electrolyse
paralyze	paralyse

Words Containing *ol* or *oul*

American	British
mold	mould
molt	moult
smolder	smoulder

NOTE: In Britain, *molten* never takes the letter *u*.

Other Spelling Differences

American	British
check *(n.)*	cheque *(n.)*
connection	connexion
curb	kerb
pajamas	pyjamas
vise (the tool)	vice (the tool)

COMPOUND WORDS

A compound word is a word made up of two or more shorter words. Compounds can appear as nouns, adjectives, verbs, and other parts of speech.

Compounds are often spelled differently, depending on the context in which they are used. Consult a dictionary when necessary to make sure of the spelling of compound words.

There are three kinds of compounds: closed, hyphenated, and open. A closed compound is a single word; a hyphenated compound contains two or more elements joined by a hyphen; an open compound consists of two separate words joined only by usage. The guidelines below will explain how to use the three kinds of compounds correctly.

There is one general rule to keep in mind concerning compound words: If a compound is not listed in the dictionary, then it is spelled as an open compound, as in the following examples:

fellow employee   parent organization   telephone call

COMPOUND WORDS AS NOUNS

Many compound nouns originate from verb phrases. These compound nouns are generally closed or hyphenated.

Verb Phrase	Noun
Planes *take off* regularly.	Many passengers dislike *takeoff.*
The thieves *break in.*	We suffered a *break-in.*

NOTE: Do not confuse the use of these identical root words as compound nouns with their use as verb phrases. When used as nouns, they are solid or hyphenated; when used as verb phrases, they are separate words.

Compound nouns that end with the word *in* are usually hyphenated.

break-in   drive-in   shut-in   stand-in

Compound nouns that end in *up, out,* or *off* are either closed or hyphenated. Consult a dictionary as needed.

backup	hang-up	markup	write-up
blackout	fade-out	cookout	timeout
layoff	play-off	standoff	showoff

Hyphenate a compound word that stands as a noun but does not contain a noun.

the have-nots	do-it-yourselfer	hand-me-downs
a know-it-all	the well-to-do	go-between

Compound nouns ending in *ing*, such as *profit sharing*, are generally open. These words are often not listed in the dictionary.

decision making	tape recording	truck driving
problem solving	word processing	time sharing

BUT

bookkeeping	housekeeping	flag-waving

Hyphenate compound nouns composed of a pair of nouns that describe a person or thing having two functions.

writer-editor   producer-director   dinner-dance

Civil and military titles are generally written as open compounds.

Chief Justice Burger	Special Assistant Ross
Lieutenant Commander Bean	Deputy Mayor Sanchez

All titles containing the prefix *vice* were once hyphenated, but the hyphen is slowly being eliminated by contemporary usage.

Vice-President Bush   BUT   Vice Admiral Davenport

The use of compound nouns containing the word *man* or *men* is rapidly changing because of the expanding role of women in public and business life. It is no longer appropriate to use words like *businessman, congressman*, and *salesman* in business communications unless referring to a particular individual who is male.

In Place of	**Use**
businessmen	executives, managers, business people
congressman	member of Congress, representative
salesmen	sales representatives, sales force
foreman	supervisor
mailmen	mail carriers
man-hours	worker-hours

One solution to the problem of generic titles, such as *chairman*, is to substitute the word *person* for *man*. Individual taste will dictate whether or not this solution is appropriate.

chairperson   spokesperson   salesperson

Beware of a biased use of such words as *doctor, lawyer*, and *secretary*. These words apply equally to women and men. Do not use a term like *women doctors* or *male secretary* unless there is a reason to differentiate, for example, when describing a group of women who are also doctors.

> The newsletter addresses the particular problems that *women doctors* face in a largely male profession.

COMPOUND WORDS AS VERBS

Compound verbs are usually closed or hyphenated.

to double-space	to hand-feed
to air-condition	to downgrade
to spot-check	to tape-record
to dry-clean	to blue-pencil

Do not mistake a compound verb for a verb-adverb combination. Verb-adverb combinations include such compounds as *lock out, break up, write off,* and *make up* and are open compounds.

COMPOUND WORDS AS ADJECTIVES

Compound words used as adjectives are difficult to spell because they change form as they change their grammatical function. A phrase such as *out of date* is not hyphenated in the sentence *This ledger is out of date,* but it is hyphenated in the sentence *He worked on the out-of-date ledger.*

Compound adjectives are generally hyphenated to make their meaning and function clear to the reader. The hyphens in *out-of-date* serve to connect the elements of the compound and to make clear that it is a compound word expressing a single thought.

Always Hyphenated

Some compound adjectives are always hyphenated. These compounds are hyphenated whether they precede a noun or follow it.

Nouns and participles These compound adjectives combine a noun with a present or past participle.

interest-bearing	computer-controlled	factory-sealed
motor-driven	time-consuming	labor-saving

NOTE: A few of these combinations, because of long and frequent use, have come to be written as closed compounds: *handmade, handwritten, timesaving.*

Adjectives and participles These compound adjectives combine an adjective with a participle. The comparative and superlative forms of these compounds are also hyphenated.

fast-talking	foul-smelling	high-ranking
best-sounding	faster-acting	softest-spoken
high-priced	old-fashioned	double-spaced
quickest-witted	shorter-term	longer-range

Sometimes Hyphenated

A much larger group of compounds are hyphenated only when they are used as adjectives.

Adjectives and nouns Hyphenate this combination when it appears as an adjective before a noun or as a predicate adjective. Do not hyphenate it when it is acting as another part of speech. The comparative and superlative forms of these compounds are also hyphenated.

These are our *long-term* goals. *(adjective)*
Their commitment is *long-term. (predicate adjective)*
He invests for the *long term. (object of preposition)*

That store sells the *finest-quality* products. *(adjective)*
These products are *finest-quality. (predicate adjective)*
The material is of the *finest quality. (object of preposition)*

She has a *part-time* job. *(adjective)*
Her job is only *part-time. (predicate adjective)*
She works only *part time. (adverb phrase)*

Adverbs and participles Hyphenate this combination when it appears as an adjective before a noun. This combination does not appear as a predicate adjective. The hyphen is retained in the comparative and superlative forms.

She is a *well-known* troubleshooter. *(adjective)*
Her expertise *is* well *known. (passive verb modified by an adverb)*

This is a *better-known* brand. *(adjective)*
Our brand *is* better *known. (passive verb modified by an adverb)*

NOTE: Do not hyphenate an adverb-participle combination if the adverb ends in *ly*, as in *poorly staffed office* or *highly paid employee.*

In some adverb-participle combinations, the participle does not make sense if it stands alone, as in the phrase *a well-behaved child* (there is no such thing as *a behaved child*). In these combinations, retain the hyphen no matter where the compound appears.

clear-cut case   The case is *clear-cut.*

Participles and adverbs Hyphenate this combination when it appears as an adjective *before* a noun. This combination does not appear as a predicate adjective.

a *wound-up* feeling		The meeting left him feeling *wound up.*
unheard-of actions	BUT	Her actions were *unheard of.*

burned-out buildings	The hard day left him feeling *burned out.*

Numbers and nouns Hyphenate this combination when it appears as an adjective before a noun or as a predicate adjective. Do not hyphenate it when it is acting as another part of speech.

They signed a *14-year* contract. *(adjective)*

The contract is *14-year.* *(predicate adjective)*

The contract is in force for *14 years.* *(object of preposition)*

Phrases as compounds Many phrases are routinely used as compound adjectives. They are hyphenated when used as adjectives before a noun. They do not appear as predicate adjectives and are not hyphenated when they appear as other parts of speech.

an *out-of-town* executive		He is from *out of town.*
a *nine-year-old* building	BUT	The building is *nine years old.*
a *$20,000-a-year* job		The job pays *$20,000 a year.*
out-of-pocket expenses		He paid the bills *out of pocket.*

Never Hyphenated

The compound adjectives in this group are well-known compounds that do not require a hyphen to make them clear, or are not true compounds at all.

Adverbs and adjectives These combinations often resemble compound words. They are not compounds, however, because adverbs normally modify adjectives, and they are not hyphenated.

a very exciting story	a less complex situation
a rather strange event	a most dangerous plan

Adjectives and adjectives These combinations often resemble compound words but seldom are. When two independent adjectives modify the same noun, they are not hyphenated.

a respected tax attorney   a new business consultant

an exciting and stressful morning

NOTE: Occasionally, two adjectives are joined to form a compound word, as in the words *gray-green, red-hot,* and a *hard-and-fast* rule. Notice that while *gray-green* is hyphenated, *grayish green* is not, because *grayish* modifies *green.*

Compound nouns When familiar compound nouns are used as adjectives, they do not need a hyphen to make their meaning clear.

income tax return	*life insurance* policy
real estate agent	*social security* tax

Proper names Do not hyphenate a proper name even when it is used as an adjective.

the *North American* population   a *Western Union* clerk
a *Wall Street* firm

NOTE: Use a hyphen when combining two different proper names to express a single idea.

the *Japanese-American* population   the *Atlanta-Boston* train

SUSPENDED HYPHENS

It is sometimes necessary to write a series of compound adjectives that all have one element in common. In such a case, suspended hyphens are used to avoid unnecessary repetition.

5-, 10-, and 15-year mortgages
8½- by 11-inch paper
long- and short-term investments

PREFIXES AND SUFFIXES

Words with prefixes and suffixes are not compound words and are generally not hyphenated. In a few cases, however, prefixes and suffixes are set off by hyphens for the sake of clarity.

When the prefix ends with *a* or *i* and the base word begins with the same letter, use a hyphen to separate them.

ultra-atomic   semi-informed   anti-intellectual

However, when a prefix ends with *e* or *o* and the base word begins with the same letter, do not use a hyphen. Note the exceptions to this rule.

cooperate   reemploy   preemptive

BUT

co-op   co-owner   de-emphasize   de-escalate

The prefix *self* is followed by a hyphen.

self-assured   self-employed   self-interest

The hyphen is omitted when *self* is used as a base word.

selfless   selfish   selfhood

The prefix *re* is not followed by a hyphen, except in words that must be distinguished from other words with the same spelling but different meanings.

I heard his *remark*.   BUT   She *re-marked* the form.
He will *reform* his ways.   He asked the group to *re-form* later.

The prefix *ex* is followed by a hyphen when it is attached to a noun but not when it is part of a Latin phrase.

ex-wife ex-officer ex-employee *ex cathedra*

When any prefix is added to a base word that begins with a capital letter, the prefix is followed by a hyphen.

trans-Alaskan pre-Civil War pro-American

Family terms that use the prefix *great* or the suffix *in-law* are hyphenated, but family terms that use *step* and *grand* are closed.

great-uncle mother-in-law grandmother stepfather

PLURAL NOUNS

Most ordinary nouns form their plurals by adding an *s* or an *es*. Most nouns do not change the spelling of their singular form before the *s* or *es* is added; however, other nouns require that one or two letters of the singular form be changed. Some nouns change their spellings entirely, and a few nouns have plural forms that are the same as their singular forms. The rules and examples that follow can be of assistance in choosing the correct form for plural nouns.

GENERAL RULES

Most nouns add *s* to their singular forms to make their plural forms.

chair	BECOMES	chairs
house		houses
idea		ideas
pen		pens
table		tables

Nouns that end in *s* or *ss* form their plurals by adding *es*. Nouns that end in *ch, sh, x,* or *z* also add *es* to form their plurals.

glass	BECOMES	glasses
lunch		lunches
sash		sashes
tax		taxes

NOTE: Nouns that end in silent *s* have the same singular and plural forms.

chassis	REMAINS	chassis
faux pas		faux pas

Some nouns that end in *o* add an *s;* other nouns that end in *o* add an *es.*

If the *o* is preceded by a vowel, add an *s* to form the plural.

patio	BECOMES	patios
stereo		stereos

If the *o* ends a word relating to music, add an *s* to form the plural, no matter what letter precedes the *o*.

alto	BECOMES	altos
folio		folios
piano		pianos

If the *o* is preceded by a consonant, check a dictionary. Some nouns add an *s*, some nouns add an *es*, and some nouns add either one—they have two plural forms. When there are alternate spellings, the preferred spelling appears first.

echo	BECOMES	echoes
halo		halos or haloes
potato		potatoes

silo		silos
volcano		volcanoes or volcanos

Some nouns that end in *y* add an *s;* others change their spelling and add an *es* to form their plurals.

If the *y* is preceded by a vowel, add an *s* to form the plural.

delay	BECOMES	delays
toy		toys
valley		valleys
BUT		
soliloquy		soliloquies

If the *y* is preceded by a consonant, change the *y* to an *i* and add an *es* to form the plural.

copy	BECOMES	copies
library		libraries
quantity		quantities

If a noun ends in *f, fe,* or *ff,* check a dictionary. Some nouns ending in *f, fe,* or *ff* add an *s* to form their plurals, some change the *f* to a *v* and add *es,* and others can do either—they have two plural forms. Preferred spellings appear first.

chief	BECOMES	chiefs
elf		elves
life		lives
safe		safes
sheriff		sheriffs
staff		staffs
wharf		wharves or wharfs

Some nouns have one form for both singular and plural uses.

One group of nouns can be either singular or plural; their spellings remain the same.

deer	REMAINS	deer
politics		politics
salmon		salmon
wheat		wheat

Another group is always singular. Their spellings remain the same and the nouns always take singular verbs.

economics	REMAINS	economics
music		music
news		news

A third group is always plural. Their spellings remain the same and the nouns always take plural verbs.

credentials	REMAINS	credentials
proceeds		proceeds

scales	scales
thanks	thanks

Some nouns change their spellings when they form their plurals. Irregular plural forms change the pronunciation of the base word as well as the spelling.

axis	BECOMES	axes
datum		data
focus		focuses or foci
goose		geese
mouse		mice
woman		women

A few irregular plurals add *ren* or *en* to the noun.

child	BECOMES	children
ox		oxen

NOTE: Some words ending in *man* simply add an *s* to form their plurals.

German	BECOMES	Germans
ottoman		ottomans
talisman		talismans

COMPOUND NOUNS

One-word compound nouns (closed compound nouns) form their plurals by making the final part of the word plural. Form the plurals of these words according to the standard rules for forming plurals.

bookshelf	BECOMES	bookshelves
coffeecup		coffeecups
hallway		hallways
photocopy		photocopies
toothbrush		toothbrushes
typewriter		typewriters
	BUT	
passerby		passersby

Compound nouns ending in *ful* usually add *s* to the end of the word when they form their plurals.

basketful	BECOMES	basketfuls
cupful		cupfuls
pailful		pailfuls

Multiword compound nouns (open or hyphenated compound nouns) form their plurals by making the most important word plural. Form the plurals of these compounds according to the rules for forming the plurals of noncompound nouns.

bill of lading	BECOMES	bills of lading
project chairman		project chairmen

son-in-law	sons-in-law
treasurer-elect	treasurers-elect
vice-president	vice-presidents

If a multiword compound does not contain a noun as one of its parts, make the last word in the compound plural. Form the plural according to the rules for forming plurals of noncompound nouns.

drive-in	BECOMES	drive-ins
free-for-all		free-for-alls
forget-me-not		forget-me-nots
takeoff		takeoffs

NOUNS OF FOREIGN ORIGIN

Many foreign nouns have become a part of the English language. Some of these nouns have retained their original plural endings; others have had their plural forms Anglicized. Check a dictionary to be certain of the preferred spellings for the plurals of foreign nouns.

medium media

BUT

memorandum memorandums

PROPER NAMES

Form the plurals of proper names by adding an *s* or an *es* according to the rules for forming common noun plurals.

J. and J. Palmer	BECOMES	the Palmers
L. and D. Ellis		the Ellises
A. and M. Walsh		the Walshes

If the addition of an extra syllable would make pronunciation of the name awkward, add only an *s* or add nothing at all.

P. and R. Rogers	REMAINS	the Rogers (not Rogerses)
W. and C. Smith	BECOMES	the Smiths (not Smithes)

Names ending in *y* or *f* do not change their spellings, nor do names that would have irregular plurals. Their plurals are always formed by adding *s*.

H. and O. Lyman	BECOMES	the Lymans (not Lymen)
B. and B. Wolf		the Wolfs (not Wolves)
E. and T. Berry		Berrys (not Berries)

If a name is hyphenated or contains several parts, make the last part plural.

S. and F. Gilby-Long	BECOMES	the Gilby-Longs (not Gilbies-Long)
M. and K. de la Rama		the de la Ramas (not de las Rama)

The same rules apply when forming plurals of first names or of names belonging to places or organizations.

NOTE: The Allegheny Mountains and the Rocky Mountains become the Alleghenies and the Rockies.

If a name ends in *Jr.*, *Sr.*, or a number (such as *2nd* or *III*), you may choose either formal or informal usage. In the formal usage, make the surname plural. In the informal usage, make the *Jr.*, *Sr.*, or numbers plural. Do not use both.

Informal	**Formal**
the Hampton, Jrs.	the Hamptons, Jr.
the Mendoza, IIIs	the Mendozas, III

To form the plurals of personal titles, use the spellings below.

Mr.	BECOMES	Messrs.
Mrs. (or Mme.)		Mmes.
Ms.		Mses. or Mss.
Miss		Misses

When forming plurals of names preceded by titles, either part may be made plural. Making the title plural is formal usage; making the name plural is informal usage. Choose one or the other, but not both, depending upon the circumstances. If the formal usage is awkward, use the informal style.

Informal	**Formal**
the Mr. Hansons	the Messrs. Hanson
Mrs. Soren and Mrs. Gray	Mmes. Soren and Gray

ABBREVIATED NOUNS

Form the plurals of most abbreviations of common nouns by adding an *s*.

dept.	BECOMES	depts.
univ.		univs.
yr.		yrs.

The plural forms of abbreviations for weights and measures are usually the same as the singular forms. The abbreviations for a few units of measurement form their plurals by adding an *s*, although the trend in contemporary usage is to drop the *s*.

ft (foot)	REMAINS	ft
gal (gallon)		gal
lb (pound)		lb or lbs
oz (ounce)		oz
yd (yard)		yd or yds
kg (kilogram)		kg
cc (cubic centimeter)		cc
mm (millimeter)		mm

EXCEPTION: Some single-letter abbreviations form their plurals by doubling the letter.

p. (page)	BECOMES	pp. (pages)
f. (following one)		ff. (following several)

Form the plurals of lower-case letters by adding an apostrophe and an *s*.

abc	BECOMES	abc's
c.o.d.		c.o.d.'s

Form the plurals of capital letters and capitalized abbreviations by adding *s*. An exception to this rule occurs when an apostrophe is needed to make the meaning clear.

BA	BECOMES	BAs
I		I's (not Is)
Lt.		Lt.s
M.D.		M.D.s

NUMBERS

Numbers expressed as figures (numerals) form their plurals by adding an *s*. Numbers expressed as words form their plurals according to the rules for forming plurals of common nouns.

20	BECOMES	20s
1930		1930s
fifty		fifties
hundred		hundreds

Other parts of speech that are used as nouns form their plurals by adding *s* or *es*. Use an apostrophe and an *s* only if the plural would be confusing without the apostrophe. If the word already has an apostrophe, use only *s*.

didn't	BECOMES	didn'ts
pro or con		pros or cons
this or that		this's or that's
up and down		ups and downs

POSSESSIVE NOUNS

Singular nouns usually show possession by adding an apostrophe and an *s*, while plural nouns usually add only the apostrophe to show possession. Exceptions to these two rules occur primarily when pronunciation would be awkward or when a noun has an irregular plural form.

Singular nouns Singular nouns that do not end in *s* add an apostrophe and an *s* to form their possessives.

the assistant's telephone

this company's products

the soprano's performance

the staff's competence

If a singular noun ends in an *s*, an *ss*, a *ch*, an *sh*, an *x*, or a *z*, either an apostrophe and an *s* or only an apostrophe may be added.

Add an apostrophe and an *s* if an extra syllable can be pronounced easily.

the boss's new office

Mr. Garsh's letters

Ms. March's promotion

Add only an apostrophe if an extra syllable is awkward to pronounce.

Mr. Molineaux' report (not Molineaux's)

Mrs. Gonzalez' appointment (not Gonzalez's)

NOTE: Ancient or classical names that end in *s* take only an apostrophe.

Jesus' teachings

Mars' sword

Plural nouns Regular plural nouns add only an apostrophe to make their plural possessive forms.

the nurses' watches

the secretaries' telephones

the states' legislatures

the Willises' company

If a noun has an irregular plural, the plural possessive form is made by adding an apostrophe and an *s*.

all the data's references

six geese's nests

the men's clubs

NOTE: Avoid errors when using the plural possessive forms of nouns by making the plural form of the noun first. Then make the plural form possessive.

Singular	**Plural**	**Plural Possessive**
baby	babies	babies'
Mr. Hartz	the Hartzes	the Hartzes'
minute	minutes	minutes'

Inanimate objects Generally, nouns that refer to inanimate objects should not be made possessive. Avoid making such nouns possessive by rephrasing the sentence, using *of* in place of the possessive form. Often, the possessive form of a singular noun is not really necessary.

the doors of the bus the tray of the copier

the bus doors the copier tray

NOT NOT

the bus's doors the copier's tray

the branches of the trees

NOT

the trees' branches

NOTE: In a few idiomatic expressions, the object of the preposition *of* is made possessive.

They are neighbors of Don's. (not of Don)

She is a friend of mine. (not of me)

If an inanimate noun refers to time or to a measurement, it is acceptable to make the noun possessive. Inanimate nouns that are personified also may take a possessive form.

a building's gloom a mile's distance

the week's news an hour's work

the sun's fierce heat the decade's events

several months' time the leaves' whispers

Compound nouns To make compound nouns possessive, add an apostrophe and an *s* or only an apostrophe to the last part of the noun. Follow the rules for making noncompound nouns possessive. This applies both to singular and to plural compound nouns.

the editor in chief's plan the bus driver's route

the editors in chief's plans the bus drivers' routes

his granddaughter's letters

his granddaughters' letters

NOTE: If the sentence construction is awkward when the plural possessive form is used, rephrase the sentence.

The editors in chief's plans were accepted.

The plans of the editors in chief were accepted.

Elided words A few possessive nouns are commonly used without the word they modify. In such cases the word modified by the possessive is understood. Form the possessive as if the word (in brackets below) it modified were actually written.

He went to his lawyer's [office] today.

Meet me by the receptionist's [desk].

When using possessive nouns without the words they modify, be sure to make the sentence construction parallel.

This year's gains are better than last year's.

NOT

The gains this year are better than last year's.

Personal pronouns Personal pronouns have separate possessive forms. They do not use an apostrophe and an *s* to form their possessives.

my book	our files
your desk	your offices
her calendar	their notices
his telephone	its tail

NOTE: Distinguish between possessive forms of personal pronouns and contractions that are made from personal pronouns.

your	you're (you are)
their	they're (they are)

Indefinite pronouns Singular indefinite pronouns use an apostrophe and an *s* to make their possessive forms. Plural indefinite pronouns use only an apostrophe to make their possessive forms.

anyone's guess	many others' pens
one another's pens	everybody's coffeepot

If an indefinite pronoun is followed by *else,* add an apostrophe and an *s* to *else,* not to the indefinite pronoun.

anyone else's	NOT	anyone's else
somebody else's		somebody's else

Is it possessive or descriptive? At times it is difficult to distinguish between possessive phrases and descriptive phrases. To determine whether a phrase is possessive or not, substitute a phrase using *of* or *by*. If the new phrase can be substituted and still retain the sense and meaning of the original, the original phrase is possessive.

The *cashier's desk* is here.

SUBSTITUTE:

The *desk of the cashier* is here. (The original meaning is retained; *cashier's* is correct as a possessive.)

Buy me some *brokers forms,* please.

SUBSTITUTE:

Buy me some *forms of brokers,* please. (The original meaning is lost; *brokers* is merely descriptive, not possessive.)

Possessives that modify other possessives are awkward to say and confusing to read. It is best to change the sentence construction to avoid consecutive possessives.

AWKWARD: Where is the stockbroker's company's report?

PREFERRED: Where is the report of the stockbroker's company?

Appositives Possessive forms that are part of appositive phrases are usually awkward also. Again, it is best to change the sentence construction to avoid the possessive appositive. Where this is not possible, add an apostrophe and an *s* or only an apostrophe to the appositive phrase, not to the noun being modified by the appositive. In such cases, drop the second comma (which would follow the appositive).

AWKWARD: Send it to Ms. Peters', the editor, office.

PREFERRED: Send it to the office of Ms. Peters, the editor.

Send it to Ms. Peters, the editor's office.

Gerunds When a noun precedes a gerund, the noun must be possessive. (A gerund is a verb form ending in *ing* that is used as a noun.)

The clerk's *leaving* early made us angry.

The doctors' *meeting* with us is at two.

The director's *being* ill concerns all of us.

Abbreviations Form the possessive of a singular abbreviation by adding an apostrophe and an *s*. Form the possessive of a plural abbreviation by adding an apostrophe.

the AMA's annual report

several YMCAs' facilities

the Ph.D.s' seminars

Preference When making the name of a person or an organization possessive, *always* follow the preference of the person or organization, even if that preference is grammatically questionable or incorrect.

Macy's Gimbels

Joint possession Form the possessive of a person's name by adding an apostrophe and an *s*. If two or more people own something jointly, only the last name in the series is possessive. If two or more people own things separately, both names take a possessive form. If one of the parties is represented by a pronoun, each party takes a possessive form.

Judy's gallery	Judy's and Ken's galleries
Judy and Ken's daughter	Judy's and his daughter

Holidays Holidays generally take an apostrophe and an *s*.

New Year's Day

Father's Day

EXCEPTIONS: Veterans Day and April Fools' Day

PREFIXES AND SUFFIXES

Many prefixes and suffixes have similar spellings or pronunciations but different meanings. Use the lists that follow to determine the correct meaning of words containing these common prefixes and suffixes. Use a dictionary when in doubt.

Prefix	Definition	Example
ante	before	She *antedated* the check to June 7.
anti	against	Shy people may seem *antisocial.*
auto	self, by oneself	Please *autograph* a picture for me.
bi	two	We receive paychecks *biweekly.*
bio	life	He enjoys reading *biographies.*
co (col, con, com)	with, together	They *congregated* in the plaza.
counter	against	The negotiator made a *counteroffer.*
dis	not	The files seemed *disorganized.*
en	put into, make	We *enlarged* our store this year.
equi	equal	The two roads are *equidistant* from us.
ex	formerly, out, beyond	His *ex-partner* is on vacation.
fore	front	The *foreground* of the photo was blurred.
hyper	above, more	He suffers from *hypertension.*
hypo	below, less	This *hypothesis* seems reasonable.
in (il, im, ir)	not	Their report was *incomplete.*
inter	between	The two parts are *interchangeable.*
intra (intro)	within, into	That law deals with *intrastate* truckers.
mal	bad, ill, wrong	The computer *malfunctioned* today.
micro	very small	Use a *microscope* to see bacteria.
mid	middle	At *midnight* the shift changes.
mini	small	*Minibuses* run through our neighborhood.
mis (miso)	bad, wrong	The project was *misdirected.*
multi	many	This problem is *multifaceted.*
non	not	Your comments were *nonspecific.*
omni	all	*Omnidirectional* radios are useful.
para	beside	She enjoys her *paralegal* work.
per	through, completely	The seal must be carefully *perforated.*
post	after	Please don't *postdate* your checks.

pre	before	Lunch was *prearranged* for them.
pro	forward, in behalf of	We made *provision* for extra people.
re	back, again	His firm will *rebuild* the offices.
retro	backward	Make the salary increase *retroactive.*
sub	below	They often *subcontract* work to us.
tele	at a distance	*Telephones* are everywhere today.
trans	across	A shipper *transports* many things.
tri	three	It will be a *tristate* conference.
ultra	beyond, extreme	Their decor is *ultramodern.*
un	not	We enjoyed an *uninterrupted* day.
uni	one	The quality is *uniformly* good.

Suffix	**Definition**	**Example**
able (ible)	capable of	His attitude was a *sensible* one.
ance (ence)	state or condition of	Their *insistence* was annoying.
cede (ceed)	go, move, yield	The union *interceded* for him.
er (ar, or)	one who, that which	She is a good *employer* to work for.
ful	full of	He is a *careful* typist.
graph	written	*Telegraphs* are seldom used now.
ic	relating to, like	It is a truly *historic* occasion.
ion (ation, tion)	state of, result of	Find the *distinction* between them.
less	without, unable	A disorganized file is *useless.*
ment	state or action of	The joke gave *amusement* to us all.
ness	state or condition	She is known for her *politeness.*
ology	science or study of	Many people enjoy studying *biology.*
ous (tious)	the quality of	His laughter is *infectious.*
ship	condition of	Their *partnership* is working well.
wise	with regard to	Turn it *edgewise* to see it better.

Some words can be used as prefixes or suffixes or can stand alone. When these words are used in compound constructions, they keep their original meanings, simply adding those meanings to the base words.

Prefix/Suffix	**Definition**	**Example**
after	later, next, behind	My postscript is an *afterthought.*
by	near, beside, secondary	A *bystander* saw the accident.

extra	outside, beyond	He made an *extraordinary* statement.
out	external, greater	Our company can *outsell* any other.
over	excessive, above, beyond	Their payments are always *overdue*.
super	higher, greater, extra	We have a *superabundance* of pens.
under	below, too little	These items are *underpriced*.
up	raise	We *update* the lists weekly.

ADDITIONAL PREFIXES AND SUFFIXES

Prefix	Definition	Example
a (an)	without, not	asymmetric
ab (abs)	from, away	abstract
ad	to, toward	adjacent
ali	other	alias
ambi	both	ambidextrous
aqua (aque)	water	aquarium
aud (audio)	sound, hearing	audible
biblio	book	bibliomaniac
chron (chrono)	time	chronology
civ (civis)	citizen	civilize
dec	ten	decade
dia (di)	across, apart	diagonal
dic (dict)	speak, say	dictation
em, en	in, into	enclose
eu	well, good	euphemism
fid	trust, faith	fiducial
fin	end	finale
geo	earth	geology
homo	same	homogenized
hypno	sleep	hypnosis
infra	below, beneath	infrastructure
macro	long, large	macrocosm
mega	large, one million	megawatt
meta	changed	metamorphosis
mill	thousandth part	millennium
mono	one	monopoly
mort	death	mortality

neo	new	neophyte
nov	new	novice
peri	around, encircling	perimeter
phon	sound	phonics
poly	many	polychrome
pseudo	false	pseudonym
semi	half, twice in a period	semicircle
syn, sym	with, together	symphony

Suffix	**Definition**	**Example**
al	relating to	maternal
ary	pertaining to	stationary
dom	condition, state	freedom
ee	one who receives	trustee
fold	having parts	tenfold
gram	a record, something written	telegram
graph	written, recorded	telegraph
hood	condition, state	childhood
ish	like, about, belonging to	childish
ism	practice of, condition of	terrorism
ist	one who	psychiatrist
ity	quality, state, degree	possibility
ive	belonging to	native
ize	subject to, practice	philosophize
like	characteristic of	manlike
ly	characteristic of	womanly
meter	measure	kilometer
most	to the furthest extent	foremost
onym	name	synonym
pathy	feeling, suffering	empathy
phobia	fear	claustrophobia

phon	sound	telephone
port	carry	transport
proof	impervious to	fireproof
scope	means of seeing	telescope
some	tending to	loathsome
spect	see, view, observe	circumspect
ual	of, pertaining to	visual
ward	in a direction	backward

WORD DIVISION

In typing letters or other documents, it is sometimes necessary to divide a word at the end of a line in order to make a neatly aligned right-hand margin. Words are divided between syllables, a syllable being a word or part of a word pronounced as a single sound. A dictionary will show how words can be divided into syllables. While a dictionary is helpful, a number of special rules govern how words should be divided in writing.

The first rule is to avoid dividing words whenever possible. It is better to have a slightly uneven right margin than to have many lines that end with hyphens.

Dividing words is mainly a matter of common sense. When a word must be divided, divide it at a point least likely to disrupt its meaning for the reader.

BASICS

Divide words only between syllables. Check a dictionary for the correct syllable division of a word.

NOTE: It is not always acceptable to divide a word at every syllable break. For example, the words shown below should be broken only after the hyphen.

pho·to- graph   type- writ·er

Never divide one-syllable words, including one-syllable words that end in *ed*. Do not divide a word of less than six letters.

signed   debt   screened   new

Do not leave a syllable of only one letter at the end or beginning of a line.

a·live (*not* a- live)   o·per·a (*not* oper- a)

Divide a word only if a syllable of at least three characters (including the hyphen) is left at the end of the upper line and a syllable of at least three characters (including any punctuation marks) is left at the beginning of the lower line.

sub- tract   un- like·ly   fly- ing   here- to,

Do not divide contractions.

won't   o'clock   is·n't   would·n't

Never divide abbreviations unless they are hyphenated. Hyphenated abbreviations may be divided after the hyphen.

NASA   asst.   Ph.D.   rpm

BUT

AFL- CIO

PREFERRED PRACTICES

Avoid dividing a word at the end of the first line or the end of the last full line of a paragraph.

Do not divide the last word on a page.

Divide a word *after* a prefix, rather than within the prefix or within the base word.

in·ter- state re- in·vest
mis- cal·cu·late non- pay·ment

Divide a word *before* a suffix, rather than within the suffix or within the base word.

NOTE: Because of the way they are pronounced, some words containing suffixes are divided within the base word.

in·di·ca- tion sal- a·ble im·pec- ca·ble
gov·ern- ment in·vis- i·ble ad·mis- si·ble

If a word has a prefix *and* suffix or two suffixes, divide it so as to make the meaning clear.

pre- cau·tion·ary

OR

pre·cau·tion- ary

Divide a word after a vowel, especially if the vowel is a one-letter syllable. Do not divide after a vowel, however, if it would mean leaving a final syllable that has only a liquid "l" sound in it.

di·vi- sion pop·u- lar
busi- ness in·cor·po- rate

BUT

au- di·ble in·des·crib- a·ble

Divide a word between two adjacent vowels that are sounded separately.

re·li- a·ble pre- ar·range me·di- a·tion

Divide a solid compound word between the elements of the compound.

fin·ger- print air- mail sum·mer- time

Divide a hyphenated compound word at the hyphen.

dou·ble- space nar·row- mind·ed self- im·prove·ment

FIGURES, NAMES, AND PHRASES

A group of words that expresses a single fact should be kept on the same line whenever possible.

page 24	Mr. Burns	2:30 P.M.
60 miles	Ms. Kathryn Lewis	6 in.
July 6, 1982	John Chen, M.D.	New York, NY 10003

When it is impossible to keep these groups of words together, they may be divided (at slash marks) according to the following rules.

Divide dates between the day and the year.

January 5,/ 1976 April 19,/ 1980

Divide place names between the city and state or between the state and ZIP Code. If the name of a city or state is more than one word, you may divide the name between words.

Dallas,/ Texas 75221 Cincinnati, OH/ 45202

Costa/ Mesa, CA 92626

Divide a name, including a title, after the given name or the middle initial, if present. Divide between a long title and a person's name.

Arlene T./ Jackson Dr. Simon/ Grant

Secretary of State/ Cyrus Vance

Divide a telephone number after the area code.

(213)/ 223-7860

Divide a sentence containing a dash after the dash, not before the dash.

. . . at the start of the second quarter—/
the first day of April—for our annual meeting . . .

ABBREVIATIONS AND ACRONYMS

A

AA	Alcoholics Anonymous; American Airlines, Inc.
A.A.	Associate in Arts
AAA	American Automobile Association; American Accounting Association
AAU	Amateur Athletic Union
A.B., B.A.	Bachelor of Arts
ABA	American Bankers Association; American Bar Association
ABC	American Broadcasting Company
abr.	abridged; abridgment
abs.	absent
ac, a.c.	alternating current
a/c, A/C, acct.	account
A.C.	Air Corps
ACE	Amex Commodities Exchange
ACLD	Association for Children with Learning Disabilities
ACLU	American Civil Liberties Union
ACS	American Cancer Society
actg.	acting
ad	(pl. **ads**) advertisement
A.D.	(L. *anno Domini*) in the year of the Lord
ADC	Aid to Dependent Children; Air Defense Command
add.	addition
addl.	additional
adj.	adjective; adjustment
Adj. Gen., A.G.	Adjutant General
Adm.	Admiral; Admiralty
adm.	administration; administrative
ADP	Automatic Data Processing
adv.	ad valorem; adverb; (L. *adversus*) against
ad val., a/v, adv.	(L. *ad valorem*) according to the value
adv. chgs.	advance charges
advg., advtg.	advertising
advt.	(pl. **advts.**) advertisement
AEC	Atomic Energy Commission
AF	Air Force; Air France
Af., Afr.	African; Africa
a.f., AF	audio-frequency
AFA	Armed Forces Act; Air Force Academy
AFB	Air Force Base
AFDC	Aid to Families with Dependent Children
AFL	American Federation of Labor
AFL-CIO	American Federation of Labor and Congress of Industrial Organizations
AFT	American Federation of Teachers
agcy.	agency
agt.	agent; against; agreement
AK	Alaska (ZIP Code abbrev.)
aka, a.k.a.	also known as
AICPA	American Institute of Certified Public Accountants

AL	Alabama (ZIP Code abbrev.)
Ala.	Alabama
ALGOL	algorithmic language used in programming computers
alt.	alternate; alternating; altitude; alto
Am.	America; American; Associate Member
A.M., M.A.	Master of Arts
a.m., A.M.	(L. *ante meridiem*) before noon; amplitude modulation (radio)
AMA	American Management Association; American Medical Association
amb.	ambassador
Amex	American Stock Exchange
amt.	amount
A.N.	arrival notice (shipping)
anal.	analogous; analogy; analysis; analytic
anon.	anonymous
ans.	answer
A-1	first quality or first-class
AP	Associated Press
A.P.	Accounts Payable
APO	Army Post Office
app.	appendix; appointed; approved; applied
approx., ap.	approximate
appt.	appointed; appointment
apt.	(pl. **apts.**) apartment
AR	Arkansas (ZIP Code abbrev.); Army Regulation
ar.	arrives; arrival
A.R.	Accounts Receivable; (Fr. *Ans de reception*) return receipt
Arch. E.	Architectural Engineer
Ariz.	Arizona
Ark.	Arkansas
arr.	arrangements; arrival
A.S.	Associate of Science
asap, ASAP	as soon as possible
ASCAP	American Society of Composers, Authors, and Publishers
ASCE	American Society of Civil Engineers
ASME	American Society of Mechanical Engineers
assn.	(pl. **assns.**) association
asso., assoc.	associate; associated
asst.	assistant
AST	Atlantic Standard Time
AT&T	American Telephone and Telegraph Company
Atl.	Atlantic
ATM	automated teller machine
atm.	atmosphere; atmospheric
att., atch., attm.	attach; attached; attachment
attn.	attention
atty.	(pl. **attys.**) attorney
Atty. Gen.	Attorney General
at. wt.	atomic weight
au.	author
Aust.	Australia; Austria
aux.	auxiliary
AV	audiovisual
Ave., ave.	(pl. **Aves.**) Avenue
avg.	average

AWOL	absent without leave (military term)
AZ	Arizona (ZIP Code abbrev.)

B

B.A., A.B.	Bachelor of Arts
bal.	balance
bar.	barometer; barometric
BASIC	Beginner's All-purpose Symbolic Code (computer programming language)
B.B.A.	Bachelor of Business Administration
BBC	British Broadcasting Corporation
bbl.	(pl. **bbl.** or **bbls.**) barrel
B.C.	before Christ; British Columbia, Canada
B.C.E.	Bachelor of Civil Engineering; before the Common Era
bch.	(pl. **bchs.**) bunch
B.C.S.	Bachelor of Commercial Service
bd.	board; bond
B.D.	Bachelor of Divinity
b.d.	bank draft; bills discounted
B/E., b.e.	bill of exchange
B.E.	Bachelor of Education (also **B. Ed.**); Bachelor of Engineering
bet.	between
B/F	brought forward
bk.	(pl. **bks.**) bank; book
bkg.	banking
B/L	(pl. **BS/L**) bill of lading
B.L.	Bachelor of Laws
bldg.	building
B.L.S.	Bachelor of Library Science; Bureau of Labor Statistics
Blvd., Bv.	boulevard
b.o.	back order; bad order; branch office, broker's order; buyer's option
bor.	borough
bot.	(pl. **bots.**) bottle
B.O.T.	Board of Trade
BP	blood pressure
B.P.	bills payable
b.p., bp	boiling point
Br.	British; Branch; Brother
B.R., b. rec.	bills receivable
Brig. Gen.	Brigadier General
Brit.	British; Britain
bro.	(pl. **bros.**) brother
B.S.	Bachelor of Science; balance sheet; Bureau of Standards
b.s., B/S	bill of sale
B.t.u	British thermal unit
bu.	bushel(s)
bull.	(pl. **bulls.**) bulletin
bur.	bureau
bus.	business
b.v.	book value
BWI	British West Indies
bx	(pl. **bxs.**) box
BX	base exchange(s) (Air Force)

C

C, C.	Centigrade or Celsius; (L. *centum*) 100; Congress
c, c.	carat (metric); coupon; cent; copyright; cost
c., ca.	(L. *circa*) about

CA	California (ZIP Code abbrev.)
C.A.	chartered accountant; chief accountant; Central America; capital account; credit account; current account
CAA	Civil Aeronautics Administration
CAB	Civil Aeronautics Board
cal.	small calorie; calendar; caliber
Calif.	California
Can.	Canada; Canadian
canc.	cancel; canceled; cancellation
CAP, C.A.P.	Civil Air Patrol
cap.	capital; capitalize; capacity
Capt.	Captain
car.	carat
cat.	catalog
CATV	community antenna television
CBD, c.b.d.	cash before delivery
CBS	Columbia Broadcasting System
cc, c.c.	carbon copy; cubic centimeter
CD, C/D	(pl. **CDs**) Congressional District; Certificate of Deposit; Civil Defense
Cdr., Cmdr., Comdr.	Commander
C.E.	Chemical Engineer; Chief Engineer; Civil Engineer
c.e.	(L. *caveat emptor*) at buyer's risk
CEEB	College Entrance Examination Board
cen.	central; century
CEO	chief executive officer
cert., ct., ctf.	certificate; certification; certified
CETA	Comprehensive Employment Training Act
c. & f.	cost and freight
c/f	carried forward
cfm	cubic feet per minute
CFR	Code of Federal Regulations
cfs	cubic feet per second
cg, cg., cgm.	centigram(s)
Ch.	China; Chinese; Chaplain; Church
C.H., c.h.	clearinghouse; courthouse, customhouse
chap., ch.	(pl. **chaps.** or **chs.**) chapter
Ch. E., Chem. E.	Chemical Engineer
chem., ch.	chemical; chemist; chemistry
Chin.	China; Chinese
chron.	chronological; chronology
CIA	Central Intelligence Agency
Cia.	(Sp. *Compañía*) company
Cie	(Fr. *Compagnie*) company
CIO	Congress of Industrial Organizations
cir.	circa; circular; circumference
cit.	citation; cited; citizen
civ.	civil; civilian
ck.	(pl. **cks.**) check
cm	centimeter

CO	Colorado (ZIP Code abbrev.)
C/O	certificate of origin
c/o, c.o.	care of, carried over
Co., co.	(pl. **cos.**) company; county
C.O., CO	Commanding Officer; cash order
COBOL	common business-oriented language (computer programming language)
C.O.D., c.o.d.	cash on delivery
Col.	Colonel; Colombia
col.	column; colony
coll.	collection; collateral; college
colloq.	colloquial
Colo.	Colorado
com., comm.	commerce; commission; committee; communication; commonwealth
Comdr., Cdr., Cmdr.	Commander
Comdt.	Commandant
Cong., C.	Congress; Congressional
Conn.	Connecticut
contd., cont.	continued
cor.	corner; correct; corrected
Corp.	Corporal
corp., corpn.	corporation
corr.	corrected; corresponding; correspondence
cor. sec.	corresponding secretary
CPA, C.P.A.	Certified Public Accountant
CPFF	cost plus fixed fee
CPI	consumer price index
Cpl.	Corporal
cpm	cycles per minute
CPO	Chief Petty Officer
CPS	Certified Professional Secretary
cps	cycles per second
CRT	cathode-ray tube
CSC	Civil Service Commission
CST	Central Standard Time
CT	Connecticut (ZIP Code abbrev.)
ct.	(pl. **cts.**) cent; county; court
ctn.	carton
ctr.	center
cu.	cubic
cu. ft., cu ft	cubic foot or feet
cu. in., cu in	cubic inch or inches
cum.	cumulative
cur.	currency; current
cu. yd.	cubic yard or yards
CWO	chief warrant officer
c.w.o., C.W.O.	cash with order
cwt.	hundredweight

D

D.	Democrat; Democratic
d.	date; day
D.A.	District Attorney
db	decibel (unit of sound)
d.b.a.	doing business as (name of firm)
DC	District of Columbia (ZIP Code abbrev.)
D.C.	District of Columbia
d.c., dc	direct current

D.C.L.	Doctor of Civil Law
dd.	delivered
D.D.	Doctor of Divinity
D.D.S.	Doctor of Dental Surgery
DE	Delaware (ZIP Code abbrev.)
D.E., D. Eng.	Doctor of Engineering
Dec.	December
dec.	deceased; decrease
def.	defendant; defense; defined; definition; deferred
deg.	degree; degrees
Del.	Delaware
del.	delegate; delete
Dem.	Democrat; Democratic
Den.	Denmark
dep.	department; departure; deposit; depot; deputy
dept.	(pl. **depts.**) department; deponent
der.	derivation; derived
det.	detachment; detail
D.F.A.	Doctor of Fine Arts
dg	decigram
DHQ	Division Headquarters
di., dia., diam.	diameter
diag.	diagonal; diagram
dict.	dictator; dictionary
dir.	director
dis.	discount; distance
dist.	distance; district; distribution
div.	(pl. **divs.**) dividend; division
D.J., DJ	Dow Jones; district judge; disc jockey
DJI	Dow-Jones Index
dkg	decagram
dkl	decaliter
dkm	decameter
dl	deciliter
D/L	demand loan
D.Lit(t).	Doctor of Letters
D.L.S.	Doctor of Library Science
dlvy., dly.	delivery
dm	decimeter (metric)
D.O.	Doctor of Osteopathy
d.o., DO	delivery order; defense order
DOA	dead on arrival
doc.	document
DOD	Department of Defense
DOE	Department of Energy
dol., dl.	(pl. **dols.**) dollar
dom.	domestic; dominion
doz.	dozen; dozens
DP	(pl. **DPs**) displaced person; data processing
dp	depart
D.P.H.	Doctor of Public Health
dpt.	department
Dr.	(pl. **Drs.**) Doctor; Drive
D.S., D.Sc.	Doctor of Science
D.S.C.	Distinguished Service Cross
D.S.M.	Distinguished Service Medal
DST	daylight saving time
dstn.	destination
dtd.	dated
D.T.s, DTs	delirium tremens
Du.	Dutch
D.V.M.	Doctor of Veterinary Medicine

E

E., e.	east; eastern
ECC	European Economic Community
econ.	economic; economics; economy
ed.	(pl. **eds.**) edited; editor; edition; education
Ed.B.	Bachelor of Education
Ed.D.	Doctor of Education
Ed.M.	Master of Education
EDP	electronic data processing
EDT	Eastern Daylight Time
E.E.	Electrical Engineer
EFTS	electronic funds transfer system
e.g.	(L. *exempli gratia*) for example
elec.	electric; electrical; electricity
elev.	elevation
e.m.p.	end-of-month payment
enc., encl.	enclosure(s)
Eng.	England; English
eng., engr.	engineer; engineering; engraved
Ens.	Ensign
env.	(pl. **envs.**) envelope
e.o.m.	end of month
EPS	earnings per share
eq.	equal; equator; equivalent; equipment; equation
equiv.	equivalent
ERA	Equal Rights Amendment
ESOP	employee stock ownership plan
ESP	extrasensory perception
Esq.	(pl. **Esqs.**) Esquire
EST	Eastern Standard Time
est.	established; establishment; estimate; estate
ETA, e.t.a.	estimated time of arrival
et al.	(L. *et alii*) and others
etc.	(L. *et cetera*) and so forth
et seq.	(L. *et sequens*) and the following
ETV	educational television
Eur.	Europe; European
ex.	(pl. **exs.**) example; exchange; executive; exercise; express; exception; execute
exc., exch.	exchange
exec.	executive
exp.	expenses; express; export; experiment
exr.	executor
ext.	extension; exterior; extract; external; extra

F

F, Fahr.	Fahrenheit
f.	(pl. **ff.**) and the following [page]; female; father
FAA	Federal Aviation Administration
f.a.s.	free alongside ship
fax	facsimile
FBI	Federal Bureau of Investigation
FCC	Federal Communications Commission
FDA	Food and Drug Administration
FDIC	Federal Deposit Insurance Corporation
Feb.	February

Fed.	Federal; Federated; Federation
fem.	feminine
FET	federal excise tax
ff.	and the following [pages]; folio
FHA	Federal Housing Administration
FICA	Federal Insurance Contributions Act
FIFO	first in, first out
fig.	(pl. **figs.**) figure
Fin.	Finland; Finnish
fin.	finance; financial, finis; finished
FIT	federal income tax
FITW	Federal Income Tax Withholding
FL	Florida (ZIP Code abbrev.)
fl.	fluid; floor
Fla.	Florida
FM	frequency modulation
fm.	fathom; from
F.O.	field officer; Foreign Office
F.O.B., f.o.b.	free on board
fol.	folio; following
for.	foreign; forestry
FOR, f.o.r.	free on rail (or road)
FORTRAN	formula translation (computer programming language)
FOT, f.o.t.	free on truck
f.p., fp	freezing point
FPC	Federal Power Commission
f. pd.	full paid
fpm, f.p.m.	feet per minute
FPO	Fleet Post Office (U.S. Navy)
fps, f.p.s.	feet per second
FR	full rate (cables)
Fr.	France; French; Father; *Frau*
freq.	frequent; frequently; frequency
Fri.	Friday
FRS	Federal Reserve System
frt.	freight
FSLIC	Federal Savings and Loan Insurance Corporation
ft., ft	foot; feet; fort
FTC	Federal Trade Commission
fth., fthm.	fathom
furn.	furnished; furniture
fut.	future; futures (exchange)
fwd.	forward
FX	foreign exchange
FYI, fyi	for your information

G

g	gram(s)
g.	gravity
GA	General Agent; General Assembly; Georgia (ZIP Code abbrev.)
Ga.	Georgia
G.A., g.a.	general average
gal.	(pl. **gals.**) gallon
GAO	General Accounting Office
G.B.	Great Britain
g-cal.	gram calorie
GCT	Greenwich Civil Time
GD	general delivery

gds. goods
GDR German Democratic Republic
Gen. (pl. **Gens.**) General
gen. gender; general; generally; generator; genus
geog. geography; geographic; geographical; geographer
geol. geology; geologic; geological; geologist
Ger. Germany; German
GHQ General Headquarters
GI (pl. **GIs**) Government Issue
Gk. Greek
gloss. glossary
GM General Motors; general manager; guided missile
GMT Greenwich Mean Time
G.N. (pl. **G.N.s**) Graduate Nurse
GNP, G.N.P. gross national product
G.O.P. Grand Old Party (Republican)
Gov. (pl. **Govs.**) Governor
govt. government
G.P. Graduate in Pharmacy; general practitioner
GPA, g.p.a. grade point average
g.p.m., gpm gallons per mile
GPO Government Printing Office
Gr. Greece; Grecian
gr. gross; grade; gravity; graph
grad. graduate; graduated; graduation
gr. wt. gross weight
g.s. ground speed
GSA General Services Administration
gtd., gu., guar. guaranteed

H

h. hours
hdbk. handbook
hdlg. handling
hdw. hardware
hf. half
h-f., HF high-frequency (sound waves)
hg hectogram (metric)
HI Hawaii (ZIP Code abbrev.)
hist. history; historical; historian
hm hectometer (metric)
H.M.S. His (or Her) Majesty's Ship, or Service
hol. holiday
Hon. (pl. **Hons.**) Honorable

I

I. Island(s); Isle(s)
IA Iowa (ZIP Code abbrev.)
ib., ibid. (L. *ibidem*) in the same place
IBM International Business Machines Corporation
ICMB intercontinental ballistic missile
ICC Interstate Commerce Commission
ID Idaho (ZIP Code abbrev.)
id. (L. *idem*) the same
i.e. (L. *id est*) that is

IHS	monogram for Greek word for Jesus
IL	Illinois (ZIP Code abbrev.)
ILA	International Longshoremen's Association
ILGWU	International Ladies' Garment Workers' Union
Ill.	Illinois
ill., illus.	illustration; illustrated
ILO	International Labor Organization
imp.	imperative; imperfect; import; importing; imported; importer; imprimatur; imprint
IN	Indiana (ZIP Code abbrev.)
in., in	inch(es)
Inc.	Incorporated
inc.	increase; income; incoming
incl.	inclusive; including
incog.	(It. *incognito*) in secret; unknown
Ind.	Indiana
ind.	industry; industrial; independent
Ind. E.	Industrial Engineer
init.	initial
in re	in regard to (L.)
ins.	insurance; inspector
Inst.	Institute; Institution; Institutional
inst.	instant; installment
instr.	instructor; instruction(s); instrument; instrumental
int.	interest; international; interjection; interim; interior; internal; intransitive
Intl., Int.	International
inv.	invoice; investment; inventor; invention; invented
invt.	inventory
i.p.s., ips	inches per second
IQ, I.Q.	intelligence quotient
i.q.	(L. *idem quod*) the same as
Ir.	Irish
IRA	Individual Retirement Account
Ire.	Ireland
IRS, Int. Rev.	Internal Revenue Service
is., isl., i.	(pl. **is.** or **isls.**) island
iss.	issue
It.	Italian; Italy
ix.	index

J

J.	(pl. **JJ.**) Judge; Justice
J.A.	Judge Advocate
Jan.	January
JD	juvenile delinquency (or delinquent)
J.D.	(L. *Jurum Doctor*) Doctor of Laws
jnt. stk.	joint stock
jour., j.	journal
J.P.	Justice of the Peace
Jpn.	Japan; Japanese
Jr., jr.	(pl. **jrs.**) junior
J.S.D.	Doctor of Juristic (or Juridical) Science
Ju.	June
Jul.	July

K

K, k	karat (carat); kilo
k., kn.	knot

Kans.	Kansas
kc	kilocycle (radio)
K.C.	Knights of Columbus
kcal.	kilocalorie(s)
kg	keg(s), kilogram(s)
kgps, kg/s	kilograms per second
KKK, K.K.K.	Ku Klux Klan
kl	kiloliter
km	kilometer
KO	knockout
kph, k/h	kilometers per hour
KS	Kansas (ZIP Code abbrev.)
kt., K	karat
kw	kilowatt(s)
kwh, kw-hr., kwhr	kilowatt-hour
KY	Kentucky (ZIP Code abbrev.)
Ky.	Kentucky

L

L.	Latin
l	liter
l.	line (pl. **ll.**) league; left; length; lira; lire; liter(s)
LA	Louisiana (ZIP Code abbrev.)
La.	Louisiana
L.A.	Local Agent; Los Angeles
lab.	laboratory
lang.	language
lat.	latitude
lb., lb	(L. *libra;* pl. **lbs.**) pound
L/C	(pl. **Ls/C**) letter of credit
lc., l.c.	lower-case; left center
Lt. Cmdr.	Lieutenant Commander
lea.	league; leather
Leg.	Legislature, Legislative, Legislation
leg.	legal
LF, L.F., lf, l.f.	low frequency
lg.	large
L.H.D.	Doctor of the Humanities
L.I.	Long Island
lib.	library
Lieut., Lt.	(pl. **Lts.**) Lieutenant
LIFO	last in, first out
liq.	liquid
lit.	literature; literally
Litt.D.	Doctor of Letters or Literature
ll.	lines
LL.B.	Bachelor of Laws
LL.D.	Doctor of Laws
loc. cit.	(L. *loco citato*) in the place cited
long.	longitude
Lt., Lieut.	(pl. **Lts.**) Lieutenant
Lt. Col.	Lieutenant Colonel
Lt. Comdr.	Lieutenant Commander
Ltd., ltd.	limited
Lt. Gen.	Lieutenant General
Lt. Gov.	Lieutenant Governor
ltr.	letter
lv.	leave(s)

M

M	(L. *mille*) 1000
m	meter(s)
m^2	square meter
M.	(pl. **MM.** or **Messrs.**) Monsieur; Master; Monday

m.	male; married; masculine; medium; mile(s); mill(s); minute(s); month
MA	Massachusetts (ZIP Code abbrev.)
M.A.	Master of Arts
mach.	machine; machinery
mag.	magazine; magnitude
Maj.	Major
maj.	majority
Maj. Gen.	Major General
Man.	Manhattan; Manitoba (Canada)
Mar.	March
mar.	market; marine; maritime; married
masc., mas., m.	masculine
Mass.	Massachusetts
mat.	maturity; matinee
math.	mathematics; mathematician; mathematical
MATS	Military Air Transport Service
max.	maximum
M.B.A.	Master of Business Administration
MBS	Mutual Broadcasting System
mc	megacycle
M.C.	Master of Ceremonies; Member of Congress; Military Cross
MD	Maryland (ZIP Code abbrev.)
Md.	Maryland
M.D.	Doctor of Medicine
Mdm.	Madam
mdse.	merchandise
ME	Maine (ZIP Code abbrev.)
M.E.	Mechanical Engineer; Military Engineer; Mining Engineer; Managing Editor
meas.	measure, measurement
mech.	mechanic; mechanics; mechanical
med.	medical; medicine; medium
Messrs., MM.	Messieurs
met.	metropolitan; meteorological; metal
Mex.	Mexican; Mexico
mfd.	manufactured
mfg.	manufacturing
mfr.	(pl. **mfrs.**) manufacture; manufacturer
mg	milligram
m/g	miles per gallon
Mgm	(pl. **Mgms**) mailgram
mgm	milligram(s)
Mgr.	Manager; Monseigneur; Monsignor
mgt., mgmt.	management
M.H., MH	Medal of Honor
MI	Michigan (ZIP Code abbrev.)
mi.	mile(s); mill(s)
Mich.	Michigan
mid.	middle; midshipman
mil.	military; mileage; million
min.	minute(s); minimum; mineral; mining
Minn.	Minnesota
misc.	miscellaneous
Miss.	Mississippi
M.I.T.	Massachusetts Institute of Technology

mk. (pl. **mks.**) mark
mkt., mar. market
ml milliliter
Mlle (pl. **Mlles.**) Mademoiselle (Fr.)
mm millimeter
MM. Messieurs (Fr.)
Mme. Madame (Fr.)
Mmes. Mesdames (Fr.)
MN Minnesota (ZIP Code abbrev.)
Mn House (Fr., *maison*)
mng. managing
MO Missouri (ZIP Code abbrev.)
Mo. Missouri
mo. (pl. **mos.**) month
m.o. money order; mail order
mod. modified; moderate
mol. molecule
Mon., M., or Mo. Monday
Mont. Montana
MP (pl. **MPs**) Military Police; Member of Parliament; Mounted Police
mp, m.p. melting point
m.p.g., mpg, m/g miles per gallon
m.p.h., mph, m/h miles per hour
Mr. (pl. **Messrs.**) Mister
Mrs. (pl. **Mmes.**) Mistress
MS Mississippi (ZIP Code abbrev.)
m/s meters per second
Ms. (pl. **Mss.**) Miss or Mrs.
ms., MS (pl. **mss., MSS**) manuscript
M.S., M.Sc. Master of Science
msg. message
Msgr. Monsignor
msgr. messenger
M. Sgt., M/Sgt. Master Sergeant
MST Mountain Standard Time
MT Montana (ZIP Code abbrev.)
mt. (pl. **mts.**) mount; mountain; material
mtg. meeting; mortgage
mun. municipal
mus. music; musical; musician; museum
Mus.D. Doctor of Music
m.v. market value

N

N. Navy; north; noon
n. note; net; new; noun; noon; name
n/30 net in 30 days
n.a. no account (bank); not available (data)
NAACP National Association for the Advancement of Colored People
NAS National Academy of Sciences
NASA National Aeronautics and Space Administration
nat., natl. national
NATO North Atlantic Treaty Organization
naut. nautical
nav. naval; navigation
NB northbound; (L. *nota bene*) note well
N.B. New Brunswick, Canada

n.b., N.B.	(L. *nota bene*) note well
NBC	National Broadcasting Company
NBS	National Bureau of Standards
NC	North Carolina (ZIP Code abbrev.)
N.C.	North Carolina
n.c.	no charge
NCO	noncommissioned officer
ND	North Dakota (ZIP Code abbrev.)
n.d.	no date; next day's delivery
N. Dak.	North Dakota
NE	northeast; Nebraska (Zip Code abbrev.)
NEA	National Education Association; National Editorial Association
Nebr.	Nebraska
neg.	negative; negatively
Neth.	Netherlands
Nev.	Nevada
N.F.	no funds; Newfoundland
N.G., NG	National Guard
NH	New Hampshire (ZIP Code abbrev.)
N.H.	New Hampshire
NJ	New Jersey (ZIP Code abbrev.)
N.J.	New Jersey
NL	night letter
n.l.	(L., *non licet*) it is not permitted; (L., *non liquet*) it is not clear; new line
N.Lat., NL	north latitude
NLRB	National Labor Relations Board
NM	New Mexico (ZIP Code abbrev.)
N. Mex.	New Mexico
No., N.	North; northern
no., No.	(pl. **nos.**) number
n.o.c.	not otherwise classified
nol. pros.	(L., *nolle prosequi*) to be unwilling to prosecute
non. pros.	(L., *non prosequitur*) he does not prosecute
non. seq.	(L., *non sequitur*) it does not follow
Nor.	Norwegian; Norway
Nov.	November
N/P	notes payable
N.P.	Notary Public
n.p.	no place (of publication); net proceeds
NPO	Navy Post Office
NR	no ranking or rating
NRC	Nuclear Regulatory Commission
N.S.	Nova Scotia; not specified
N.S.F.	not sufficient funds
nt.wt., n.wt.	net weight
n.u.	name unknown
nuc.	nuclear
NV	no value; no valuation; nonvoting; Nevada (ZIP Code abbrev.)
N.V.D., nvd	no value declared
NW	northwest
NW.T.	Northwest Territories, Canada
NY	New York (ZIP Code abbrev.)
N.Y.	New York

NYC, N.Y.C.	New York City
NYSE	New York Stock Exchange
N.Z.	New Zealand

O

O.	Ocean
oa, OA	overall
o/a	on account; on or about
OAS	Organization of American States
ob.	(L., *obiit*) he or she died; obstetrics
obit.	(pl. **obits.**) obituary
obs.	obsolete; observation; observatory
ob.s.p.	(L., *obiit sine prole*) died without issue
O/C	over-the-counter; overcharge
oc.	overcharge; ocean
OCR	optical character recognition
Oct.	October
o.d.	on demand; overdraft
OED	Oxford English Dictionary
OEO	Office of Economic Opportunity
ofc., off.	office; official; officer
OH	Ohio (ZIP Code abbrev.)
OK	Oklahoma (ZIP Code abbrev.)
Okla.	Oklahoma
OMB	Office of Management and Budget
Ont.	Ontario, Canada
o.p., OP	out of print; open policy
op. cit.	(L., *opere citato*) in the work cited
OPEC	Organization of Petroleum Exporting Countries
opr.	operate; operating; operation(s)
opt.	optional; optician
OR	Oregon (ZIP Code abbrev.)
Or.	Oriental
ord.	ordinance; order; ordinary
Oreg.	Oregon
Org., Orgn.	Organization
orig.	original; originally
o/s, OS	out of stock
OSHA	Occupational Safety and Health Act
O/T	overtime
o.w., OW	one way (fare)
oz., oz	ounce(s)

P

p.	(pl. **pp.**) page; per; pressure; population
PA	Pennsylvania (ZIP Code abbrev.)
P/A	power of attorney
Pa.	Pennsylvania
pa.	paper
P.A.	(pl. **P.A.s**) Purchasing Agent; Press Agent; private account; public address system
p.a., per an.	per annum (by the year)
Pac.	Pacific
Pan-Am	Pan-American World Airways, Inc.
P. and L.	profit and loss

par.	(pl. **pars.**) paragraph; parallel; parenthesis
paren.	(pl. **parens.**) parenthesis
part.	particular
pat.	patent; patented
Pat. Off.	Patent Office
payt.	payment
PBX	private branch exchange
PC, P.C.	private corporation
pc.	(pl. **pcs.**) piece
pc., pct.	percent
pcl.	parcel
pd.	paid
P.E.	Professional Engineer
P.E.G.	prior endorsement guaranteed
perf.	perfect; performer; performance; perforated
perm.	permanent
perp.	perpetual; perpendicular
pet., petr.	petroleum
petn.	petition
pf.	perfect
pf., pfd., pref.	preferred (securities)
Pfc., PFC	Private First Class
Pg.	Portuguese; Portugal
ph., PH	phase
Phar.D.	Doctor of Pharmacy
Ph.C.	Pharmaceutical Chemist
Ph.D.	Doctor of Philosophy
P.I.	Philippine Islands
PJ	presiding judge
pk.	(pl. **pks.**) pack; packing; park
pkg.	(pl. **pkgs.**) package; parking
pky., pkwy.	parkway
PL	price list; public law
Pl.	Place
pl.	plural; place
Plf., Ptf.	(pl. **Plfs., Ptfs.**) plaintiff
PLO	Palestine Liberation Organization
PLS	Professional Legal Secretary
Plz.	Plaza
PM, P.M., p.m.	(L. *post meridiem*) afternoon
pm., prem.	premium
pmt., payt.	payment
p.n., PN	promissory note
P.O.	post office; Petty Officer (Navy)
p.o.d.	pay on delivery; payable on death
p.o.e., POE	port of entry; port of embarkation
Pol.	Polish; Poland
pol.	politics; political
pop.	population
Port.	Portuguese; Portugal
pos.	positive; possessive; position
pot.	potential
PP	Planned Parenthood
pp.	pages; privately printed; prepaid; postpaid
P.P., Per Pro.	(L. *per procurationem*) by authorization; by proxy
p.p.	parcel post
ppd.	postpaid; prepaid
p.p.i.	parcel post insured
P.Q.	Province of Quebec, Canada
PR	payroll; Public Relations
Pr.	Professor

pr. price; present; province; printed; printing; preferred (stock)

PRC People's Republic of China (mainland China)

pref., pf. preferred; preference; preface

prem., pm. premium

prep. preparatory; preposition

Pres. President

prim. primacy

prin. principal

prob. problem

prod. product; produce; produced

Prof. (pl. **Profs.**) Professor

pron. pronunciation; pronounced; pronoun

prop. property; proposition

Prot. Protestant

pro tem. (L. *pro tempore*) temporarily

prov. province; provision; provisional

prs. pairs

PS (pl. **PSS**) postscript

Ps. (pl. **Pss.**) Psalm

p.s.f., psf pounds per square foot

psgr., pass. passenger

p.s.i., psi pounds per square inch

P.S.T., PST Pacific Standard Time

pstg. postage

PT private terms

pt. part; payment; pint; point; port

p.t. pro tempore (L.)

P.T.A., PTA (pl. **P.T.A.s, PTAs**) Parent-Teacher Association

ptg. printing

ptr. printer

PU pickup

pub. public; publication; published; publishing; publisher

PUD pickup and delivery

pur. purchaser; purchasing

Pvt. Private (Army and Marines)

pwr., pow. power

PX (pl. **PXs**) post exchange (military)

Q

Q. Quebec; Question

q. (pl. **qq.**) quart; quarter; quarterly; query

Q.E.D. (L. *quod erat demonstrandum*) which was to be proved

QM., Q.M. quartermaster

qr. quarter; quarterly

qt., qt quart

Q.T., q.t. quiet: usually as **on the Q.T.** (or **q.t.**)

qtr., quar., qu. quarter, quarterly

qty. quantity

quad. quadrant; quadrangle

Que., Q. Quebec, Canada

que., Q., q., ques. question

R

R. Range; Republic; Republican

R.A. Rear Admiral; Royal Academy

rad. radio; radiant; radical

RAF, R.A.F. Royal Air Force

RAM random access memory

R & D Research and Development

RB Renegotiation Board

R.C. Red Cross; Roman Catholic

RCA Radio Corporation of America

rcpt. (pl. **rcpts.**) receipt

Rd., rd. Road; road

rd. rod; round

re in regard to (L.)

R.E. Real Estate

REA Railway Express Agency

Rear Adm., R.Adm. Rear Admiral

rec. record; recorded; recorder; recipe; receipt

recd., rcd. received

Rec. Sec. Recording Secretary

ref. reference; referee; refining; refunding

refr. refrigerate; refrigerated; refrigerating; refrigerator

reg. register; registered; regulation; regular

Rep. Republic; Republican; Representative

rep. repeat; report; repair

rept., rpt., rep. report

req. requisition; required

res. reserve; residence; resolution; research

ret. retired; return

retd. returned

Rev. (pl. **Revs.**) Reverend

rev. review; revenue; reverse; revise; revised; revision; revolve; revolving; revolution

Rev. Stat., R.S. Revised Statutes

rf., rfg. refunding (bonds); refining (oil)

r.f., RF radio frequency

R.F.D. rural free delivery

rg., reg. registered

RI Rhode Island (ZIP Code abbrev.)

R.I. Republik Indonesia; Rhode Island

R.I.P. (L. *requiescat in pace*) may he or may she rest in peace

rm. (pl. **rms.**) room

R.N. Registered Nurse; Royal Navy

R.N.R. Royal Naval Reserve

ROI return on investment

Rom. Roman; Romance

ROM read-only memory

ROTC Reserve Officers' Training Corps

R.P.D. (L. *Rerum Politicarum Doctor*) Doctor of Political Science

r.p.m., rpm, r/m revolutions per minute

RPO railway post office

r.p.s., rps, r/s revolutions per second

rpt. report

RR (pl. **RRs**) railroad

R.R. rural route

R.S. Revised Statutes; Recording Secretary

r.s. right side

R.S.V.P. (Fr. *Répondez s'il vous plaît*) please reply
rt. (pl. **rts.**) right; round trip
rte., rt. route
Rt. Hon. Right Honorable
Rt. Rev. Right Reverend
Rus. Russian; Russia
R/W right of way
Ry. (pl. **Rys.**) Railway

S

S Signed (before signature on typed copy of a document, original of which was signed)
S. south; science; Senate
s. silver; stock; steamer; second; seconds; section; see
s/a subject to approval
S.A. South America; South Africa; Salvation Army
SAE Society of Automotive Engineers
S. Afr. South Africa; South African
S. Am. South America; South American
San.D. Doctor of Sanitation
S & L (pl. **S & L's**) Savings and Loan
Sask. Saskatchewan, Canada
Sat. Saturday
Sav. Savings
SB southbound
S.B. Bachelor of Science
SBA Small Business Administration
SC South Carolina (ZIP Code abbrev.)
sc., sci. science
S.C. South Carolina
Sc.D. Doctor of Science
sch. school; schedule
Scot., Sc. Scottish; Scotch; Scotland
Script. Scripture(s)
script. scriptural
SD South Dakota (ZIP Code abbrev.)
s.d. special delivery
S. Dak. South Dakota
SE southeast
SEATO Southeast Asia Treaty Organization
SEC Securities and Exchange Commission
sec. section; second(s); security; secretary; sector
secy., sec. (pl. **secys., secs.**) secretary
sel. select; selected; selection
Sen. (pl. **Sens.**) Senate; Senator; Senior
Sep., Sept. September
sep. separate
seq. (L. *sequens*, pl. **seqq.**) the following
ser. series; serial; service
serv., svc. service
sess. session
S.F. Sinking Fund
SFC Sergeant First Class
Sgd., S signed
Sgt. Sergeant
sh. (pl. **shs.**) share; sheet
shpg. shipping
shpt. shipment
shtg. shortage
sic so written; thus
sig., sg. signature

sim. similar
sing. singular
S.J. Society of Jesus (the Jesuits)
S.J.D. Doctor of Juridical Science
S.Lat., SL south latitude
sld. sailed; sealed; sold
sltx, SLTX sales tax
sm small
S.M. Master of Science
SN Seaman
So., S. South; southern
s.o. shipping order
Soc. Society; Sociology; Socialist
sol. solution; solicitor
SOP standard operating procedure
SOR (pl. **SORs**) stockholder of record
Sp. Spanish; Spain; Specialist
sp. species; special; spelling; specimen; specific
s.p. (L. *sine prole*) without issue
spec. (pl. **specs**) specification; specimen
s.p.s. (L. *sine prole superstite*) without surviving issue
Sq., sq. square; squadron
sq. (L. *sequens*, pl. **sqq.**) the following
sq. ft., sq ft square foot or feet
sq. in., sq in square inch or inches
Sr. Senior; Sister; Sir
S.R. shipping receipt
S.R.O., SRO standing room only
S.S., SS steamship
S/S supersonic
SSA Social Security Administration
S. Sgt., S/Sgt. Staff Sergeant
SSR, S.S.R. Soviet Socialist Republic
SSS Selective Service System
St. Street; State; Store; (pl. **SS.**) Saint
Sta. Station
sta. stamped; stationary
stat. statistics; statutes
std. standard; seated
S.T.D. Doctor of Sacred Theology
Ste. (Fr. *Sainte*) Saint (feminine)
stge. storage
stk. stock
Stk. Ex., St. Ex. Stock Exchange
Stk. Mkt. Stock Market
stmt. statement
stp., st., sta. stamped
stud. student
sub. substitute; subway; subscriber; subscription; substance; submarine; suburb; suburban
subj., sub. subject
Sun. Sunday
sup. superior; supply
supp., sup. (pl. **supps.** or **sups.**) supplement; supplementary
Supt. Superintendent
sur. surface; surplus
surg. surgeon; surgery; surgical

surv. survey; surveying; surveyor; surviving

svc., svce., serv. service

svgs. savings

s.v.p. (Fr. *s'il vous plaît*) if you please

svy. survey

SW southwest

Sw., Swed. Swedish; Sweden

sw. switch

swbd. switchboard

syl. syllable(s)

sym. symbol; symphony; symptom; symmetrical

synd. syndicate; syndicated

syst., sys. system

T

T. Tablespoon(s); Territory

T., Tp., Twp. (pl. **Tps., Twps.**) township

t. temperature; time; teaspoon; ton

tab. table(s)

T.A.G. The Adjutant General

t.a.w. twice a week

TB tuberculosis

T.B. trial balance

tbsp., tbs., T. tablespoon(s)

TC Tax Court of the United States

T.C., TC travelers check

TD touchdown; time deposit; trust deed

tech. technical; technician

tel. telephone; telegraph; telegram

temp. temperature; temporary

Tenn. Tennessee

ter. territory; territorial; terrace

Tex. Texas

tg. telegraph

tgm. telegram

thou. thousand

Thurs., Thur. Thursday

TM, Tmk. (pl. **TMs, Tmks.**) trademark

tn., T. ton; town; train

TN Tennessee (ZIP Code abbrev.)

tonn. tonnage

t.p. title page

tph tons per hour

tpm tons per minute

tr. trust; trustee; transit; transfer; translated; translation; translator; treasurer

T.R. tons registered (shipping)

trans., tr. translated, translation, translator

treas., tr. treasurer; treasury

T. Sgt., T/Sgt. Technical Sergeant

tsp., t. teaspoon(s)

Tues., Tue. Tuesday

Turk. Turkish; Turkey

TV television; terminal velocity

TVA Tennessee Valley Authority

TWA Trans-World Airlines, Inc.

twp. township

TWX teletypewriter exchange

TX Texas (ZIP Code abbrev.)

tx. tax or taxes; text; textbook

U

U., Univ. University

UA United Air Lines, Inc.; United Artists

UAW United Automobile Workers

UCC Uniform Commercial Code

UFO (pl. **UFOs**) unidentified flying object

UGT urgent

UHF ultrahigh frequency

U.K. United Kingdom

UL Underwriters Laboratories

ult. ultimate, ultimately

UMW United Mine Workers

UN, U.N. United Nations

Un. Union; United

Univ. University

univ. universal; university

unl. unlimited; unlisted

UP United Press

up upper

UPI United Press International

UPS United Parcel Service

U.S., US United States

U.S.A., USA United States of America; United States Army

U.S.A.F., USAF United States Air Force

U.S.A.R., USAR United States Army Reserve

U.S.B.S. United States Bureau of Standards

U.S.C. University of Southern California; under separate cover

U.S.C.G. United States Coast Guard

U.S.D.J. United States District Judge

USIA United States Information Agency

U.S.M.C., USMC United States Marine Corps

U.S.N., USN United States Navy

U.S.N.G., USNG United States National Guard

U.S.N.R. United States Naval Reserve

U.S.S. United States Senate; United States Ship

U.S.S.R., USSR Union of Soviet Socialist Republics

UT Utah (ZIP Code abbrev.)

V

v volt

v. (pl. **vv.**) verse; verb; volume; versus

VA Virginia (ZIP Code abbrev.)

Va. Virginia

V.A., VA Veterans' Administration

vac. vacuum

val. value

var. variety; various

VDT video display terminal

vel. velocity

Ven. Venerable

vert. vertical
v.f., VF video frequency
V.G. Vicar General; very good
VHF very high frequency
V.I. Virgin Islands; Vancouver Island
Vice Adm., V.A., V.Adm. Vice Admiral
Vice-Pres., V.P., V. Pres. Vice-President
VIP (pl. **VIPs**) very important person
vis. visibility; visual
viz (L. *videlicet*) namely
vol. (pl. **vols.**) volume; volunteer
voy. voyage
V.P., Vice-Pres. Vice-President
vs., v. (L. *versus*) against; verse
V.S. Veterinary Surgeon
VT Vermont (ZIP Code abbrev.)
Vt. Vermont
vv. verses
v.v. vice versa

W

W, W., w, w. watt(s); west; western
W., w. warehouse; weight; width
WA Washington state (ZIP Code abbrev.)
WAC (pl. **WACs**) Women's Army Corps
Wash. Washington state
WB westbound
Wed. Wednesday
whs. warehouse
whsle. wholesale
WI Wisconsin (ZIP Code abbrev.)
W.I. West Indies
Wis. Wisconsin
wk. (pl. **wks.**) work; week
W.O., WO Warrant Officer; wait order
wpm words per minute
wps words per second
W.R. warehouse receipt
wt. (pl. **wts.**) weight; warrant
W/Tax withholding tax
WUX Western Union exchange
WV West Virginia (ZIP Code abbrev.)
W. Va. West Virginia
WY Wyoming (ZIP Code abbrev.)
Wyo. Wyoming

X

X movie rating: persons under 17 not admitted
x cross, as x-roads, x-ref.; extra, as x-hvy
Xch., X exchange
Xn. Christian
Xnty. Christianity
XP monogram for Greek word for Christ
XQ cross-question

Y

yb. yearbook
yd., yd yard

YMCA Young Men's Christian Association

YM-YWHA Young Men's and Young Women's Hebrew Association

YWCA Young Women's Christian Association

YWHA Young Women's Hebrew Association

Z

z., Z. zone; zero

ZIP Zone Improvement Plan

ZPG zero population growth

CAPITALS OF AMERICAN STATES, POSSESSIONS, AND TERRITORIES

State	Capital	Inhabitant
Alabama	Montgomery	Alabamian
Alaska	Juneau	Alaskan
Arizona	Phoenix	Arizonan or Arizonian
Arkansas	Little Rock	Arkansan
California	Sacramento	Californian
Colorado	Denver	Coloradan or Coloradoan
Connecticut	Hartford	Connecticuter
Delaware	Dover	Delawarean
District of Columbia		Washingtonian
Florida	Tallahassee	Floridian or Floridan
Georgia	Atlanta	Georgian
Hawaii	Honolulu	Hawaiian
Idaho	Boise	Idahoan
Illinois	Springfield	Illinoisan
Indiana	Indianapolis	Indianian
Iowa	Des Moines	Iowan
Kansas	Topeka	Kansan
Kentucky	Frankfort	Kentuckian
Louisiana	Baton Rouge	Louisianian or Louisianan
Maine	Augusta	Mainer
Maryland	Annapolis	Marylander
Massachusetts	Boston	Massachusettsan
Michigan	Lansing	Michigander or Michiganite
Minnesota	St. Paul	Minnesotan
Mississippi	Jackson	Mississippian
Missouri	Jefferson City	Missourian
Montana	Helena	Montanan
Nebraska	Lincoln	Nebraskan
Nevada	Carson City	Nevadan
New Hampshire	Concord	New Hampshirite
New Jersey	Trenton	New Jerseyite
New Mexico	Albuquerque	New Mexican
New York	Albany	New Yorker
North Carolina	Raleigh	North Carolinian
North Dakota	Bismarck	North Dakotan
Ohio	Columbus	Ohioan
Oklahoma	Oklahoma City	Oklahoman
Oregon	Salem	Oregonian
Pennsylvania	Harrisburg	Pennsylvanian
Rhode Island	Providence	Rhode Islander
South Carolina	Columbia	South Carolinian

State	Capital	Inhabitant
South Dakota	Pierre	South Dakotan
Tennessee	Nashville	Tennessean
Texas	Austin	Texan
Utah	Salt Lake City	Utahan
Vermont	Montpelier	Vermonter
Virginia	Richmond	Virginian
Washington	Olympia	Washingtonian
West Virginia	Charleston	West Virginian
Wisconsin	Madison	Wisconsinite
Wyoming	Cheyenne	Wyomingite
Possessions and Territories		
American Samoa	Pago Pago	Samoan
Guam	Agaña	Guamanian
Howland, Baker, and Jarvis Islands	none	(uninhabited)
Johnston Island	(none)	(uninhabited)
Midway Island	(none)	(uninhabited)
Navassa	(none)	(uninhabited)
Northern Mariana Islands	Saipan	Mariana Islander
Palmyra	(none)	(uninhabited)
Puerto Rico	San Juan	Puerto Ricans
Trust Territory of the Pacific Islands		
Marshalls, Republic of the	Majuro	Marshall Islander
Micronesia, Federated States of	Ponape	Micronesian
Palau, Republic of	Koror	Palauan
Virgin Islands	Charlotte Amalie	Virgin Islanders

CANADIAN PROVINCES AND CAPITALS

Province	Capital	Inhabitant
Alberta	Edmonton	Albertan
British Columbia	Victoria	British Columbian
Manitoba	Winnipeg	Manitoban
New Brunswick	Fredericton	New Brunswicker
Newfoundland	St. John's	Newfoundlander
Nova Scotia	Halifax	Nova Scotian
Ontario	Toronto	Ontarian
Prince Edward Island	Charlottetown	Prince Edward Islander
Quebec	Quebec	Quebecker or Québecois (pl. Québecois)
Saskatchewan	Regina	Saskatchewanian
Territories		
Northwest Territories	Yellowknife	Northwester
Yukon Territory	Whitehorse	Yukoner

FOREIGN COUNTRIES AND CAPITALS

Country	Capital	Inhabitant
Afghanistan	Kabul	Afghan
Albania	Tirana	Albanian
Algeria	Algiers	Algerian
Andorra	Andorra la Vella	Andorran
Angola	Luanda	Angolan
Argentina	Buenos Aires	Argentine
Australia	Canberra	Australian
Austria	Vienna	Austrian
Bahamas	Nassau	Bahamian
Bahrain	Manama	Bahraini (pl. Bahraini or Bahrainis)
Bangladesh	Dacca	Bangladeshi
Barbados	Bridgetown	Barbadian
Belgium	Brussels	Belgian
Benin (formerly Dahomey)	Porto Novo	Beninese (pl. Beninese)
Bhutan	Thimphu	Bhutanese (pl. Bhutanese)
Bolivia	La Paz and Sucre	Bolivian
Botswana	Gaborone	Botswana
Brazil	Brasília	Brazilian
Bulgaria	Sofia	Bulgarian
Burma	Rangoon	Burmese (pl. Burmese)
Burundi	Bujumbura	Burundian
Cambodia (see Kampuchea)		
Cameroun	Yaoundé	Camerounian
Canada	Ottawa	Canadian
Cape Verde	Praia	Cape Verdean
Central African Republic	Bangui	Central African
Ceylon (see Sri Lanka)		
Chad	N'Djamena	Chadian
Chile	Santiago	Chilean
China, People's Republic of	Peking	Chinese (pl. Chinese)
China, Republic of (Taiwan)	Taipei	Chinese (pl. Chinese) or Taiwanese (pl. Taiwanese)
Colombia	Bogotá	Colombian
Comoro Islands	Moroni	Comoran
Congo	Brazzaville	Congolese (pl. Congolese)
Costa Rica	San José	Costa Rican
Cuba	Havana	Cuban
Cyprus	Nicosia	Cypriot

Country	Capital	Inhabitant
Czechoslovakia	Prague	Czechoslovak or Czech
Dahomey (see Benin)		
Denmark	Copenhagen	Dane
Djibouti	Djibouti	Djiboutian
Dominica	Roseau	Dominican
Dominican Republic	Santo Domingo	Dominican
Ecuador	Quito	Ecuadorean
Egypt	Cairo	Egyptian
El Salvador	San Salvador	Salvadoran
England (United Kingdom)	London	Englishman
Equatorial Guinea	Malabo	Equatorial Guinean
Ethiopia	Addis Ababa	Ethiopian
Fiji	Suva	Fijian
Finland	Helsinki	Finn
France	Paris	Frenchman
Gabon	Libreville	Gabonese (pl. Gabonese)
Gambia, The	Banjul	Gambian
German Democratic Republic (East Germany)	East Berlin	German
Germany, Federal Republic of (West Germany)	Bonn	German
Ghana	Accra	Ghanaian
Greece	Athens	Greek
Great Britain (see United Kingdom)		
Grenada	St. George's	Grenadian
Guatemala	Guatemala	Guatemalan
Guinea	Conakry	Guinean
Guinea-Bissau	Bissau	Guinean
Guyana	Georgetown	Guyanese (pl. Guyanese)
Haiti	Port-au-Prince	Haitian
Honduras	Tegucigalpa	Honduran
Hungary	Budapest	Hungarian
Iceland	Reykjavik	Icelander
India	New Delhi	Indian
Indonesia	Jakarta	Indonesian
Iran	Tehran	Iranian
Iraq	Baghdad	Iraqi
Ireland (Republic of)	Dublin	Irishman
Israel	Jerusalem	Israeli
Italy	Rome	Italian
Ivory Coast	Abidjan	Ivoirian

Country	Capital	Inhabitant
Jamaica	Kingston	Jamaican
Japan	Tokyo	Japanese (pl. Japanese)
Jordan	Amman	Jordanian
Kampuchea (formerly Cambodia)	Phnom Penh	Kampuchean
Kenya	Nairobi	Kenyan
Kiribati	Tarawa	I Kiribati (pl. I Kiribati)
Korea, Republic of (South Korea)	Seoul	Korean
Korean People's Democratic Republic (North Korea)	Pyongyang	Korean
Kuwait	Kuwait	Kuwaiti
Laos	Vientiane and Luang	Laotian or Lao (pl. Lao)
Lebanon	Beirut	Lebanese (pl. Lebanese)
Lesotho	Maseru	Basuto
Liberia	Monrovia	Liberian
Libya	Benghazi and Tripoli	Libyan
Liechtenstein	Vaduz	Liechtensteiner
Luxembourg	Luxembourg	Luxembourger
Madagascar (formerly Malagasy Republic)	Antananarivo	Madagascan
Malawi	Lilongwe	Malawian
Malaysia	Kuala Lumpur	Malaysian
Maldives	Male	Maldivian
Mali	Bamako	Malian
Malta	Valletta	Maltese (pl. Maltese)
Mauritania	Nouakchott	Mauritanian
Mauritius	Port Louis	Mauritian
Mexico	Mexico City	Mexican
Monaco	Monaco	Monacan, Monegasque
Mongolia	Ulan Bator	Mongol
Morocco	Rabat	Moroccan
Mozambique	Maputo	Mozambican
Nauru	Uaboe District and Yaren District	Nauruan
Nepal	Katmandu	Nepalese (pl. Nepalese)
Netherlands	Amsterdam	Netherlander
New Zealand	Wellington	New Zealander
Nicaragua	Managua	Nicaraguan
Niger	Niamey	Nigerois
Nigeria	Lagos	Nigerian
Northern Ireland (see United Kingdom)		
Norway	Oslo	Norwegian
Oman	Muscat	Omani
Pakistan	Islamabad	Pakistani

Country	Capital	Inhabitant
Panama	Panama City	Panamanian
Papua New Guinea	Port Moresby	Papua New Guinean
Paraguay	Asunción	Paraguayan
Peru	Lima	Peruvian
Philippines	Manila	Filipino
Poland	Warsaw	Pole
Portugal	Lisbon	Portuguese (pl. Portuguese)
Qatar	Doha	Qatari
Rhodesia (see Zambia, Zimbabwe)		
Romania	Bucharest	Romanian
Rwanda	Kigali	Rwandan
St. Lucia	Castries	Lucian
St. Vincent	Kingstown	Vincentian
San Marino	San Marino	Sanmarinese
São Tomé and Príncipe	São Tomé	Sãotomense
Saudi Arabia	Riyadh	Saudi
Scotland (United Kingdom)	Edinburgh	Scot
Senegal	Dakar	Senegalese (pl. Senegalese)
Seychelles	Victoria	Seychellois (pl. Seychellois)
Sierra Leone	Freetown	Sierra Leonean
Singapore	Singapore	Singaporan
Solomon Islands	Honiari	Solomon Islander
Somalia	Mogadishu	Somali (pl. Somalis or Somali)
South Africa	Pretoria and Capetown	South African
Spain	Madrid	Spaniard
Sri Lanka (formerly Ceylon)	Colombo	Sri Lankan
Sudan	Khartoum	Sudanese (pl. Sudanese)
Surinam	Paramaribo	Surinamese (pl. Surinamese or Surinamer)
Swaziland	Mbabane	Swazi (pl. Swazis or Swazi)
Sweden	Stockholm	Swede
Switzerland	Bern	Swiss (pl. Swiss)
Syria	Damascus	Syrian
Taiwan (see China, Republic of)		
Tanzania	Dar es Salaam	Tanzanian
Thailand	Bangkok	Thai (pl. Thais or Thai)
Togo	Lomé	Togolese (pl. Togolese)

Country	Capital	Inhabitant
Tonga	Nukualofa	Tongan
Trinidad and Tobago	Port-of-Spain	Trinidadian, Tobagan
Tunisia	Tunis	Tunisian
Turkey	Ankara	Turk
Tuvalu	Funafuti	Tuvaluan
Uganda	Kampala	Ugandan
Union of Soviet Socialist Republics	Moscow	Soviet
United Arab Emirates	Abu Dhabi	Arabian
United Kingdom (Great Britain and Northern Ireland)	London	Briton or Britisher
United States of America	Washington, D.C.	American
Upper Volta	Ouagadougou	Upper Voltan
Uruguay	Montevideo	Uruguayan
Vanuatu	Vila	Vanuatuan
Venezuela	Caracas	Venezuelan
Vietnam	Hanoi	Vietnamese (pl. Vietnamese)
Wales (United Kingdom)	Cardiff	Welshman
Western Samoa	Apia	Western Samoan
Yemen Arab Republic	San'a	Yemenite or Yemeni
Yemen, People's Democratic Republic of	Aden	Yemenite or Yemeni
Yugoslavia	Belgrade	Yugoslav
Zaire	Kinshasa	Zairian
Zambia	Lusaka	Zambian
Zimbabwe	Harare	Zimbabwean

FOREIGN CURRENCIES

Country	Currency	Fractional Unit
Afghanistan	Afghani	100 Puls
Albania	Lek	100 Qintars
Algeria	Dinar	100 Centimes
American Samoa (US)	Dollar	100 Cents
Andorra	Franc	100 Centimes
	Peseta	100 Centimos
Angola	Kwanza	100 Lwei
Anguilla (UK)	Dollar	100 Cents
Antigua (UK)	Dollar	100 Cents
Argentina	Peso	100 Centavos
Armenia (USSR)	Ruble	100 Kopecks
Australia	Dollar	100 Cents
Austria	Schilling	100 Groschen
Azores (Portugal)	Escudo	100 Centavos
Bahamas	Dollar	100 Cents
Bahrain	Dinar	1000 Fils
Bangladesh	Takas	100 Paise
Barbados	Dollar	100 Cents
Belgium	Franc	100 Centimes
Benin	Franc	100 Centimes
Bermuda (UK)	Dollar	100 Cents
Belize (UK)	Dollar	100 Cents
Bhutan	Ngultrum	100 Chhetrums
Bolivia	Peso Boliviano	100 Centavos
Botswana	Pula	100 Thebe
Brazil	Cruzeiro	100 Centavos
British Honduras (see Belize)		
Brunei (UK)	Dollar	100 Cents
Bulgaria	Lev	100 Stotinki
Burma	Kyat	100 Pyas
Burundi	Franc	100 Centimes
Cambodia (see Kampuchea)		
Cameroun	Franc	100 Centimes
Canada	Dollar	100 Cents
Canary Islands (Spain)	Peseta	100 Centimos
Cape Verde	Escudo	100 Centavos
Cayman Islands (UK)	Dollar	100 Cents
Central African Republic	Franc	100 Centimes
Ceylon (see Sri Lanka)		
Chad	Franc	100 Centimes
Chile	Peso	100 Centavos
China, People's Republic of	Yuan	100 Fen
China, Republic of (Taiwan)	Dollar	100 Cents

Country	Currency	Fractional Unit
Colombia	Peso	100 Centavos
Comoro Islands	Franc	100 Centimes
Congo	Franc	100 Centimes
Cook Islands (New Zealand)	Dollar	100 Cents
Costa Rica	Colon	100 Centimos
Cuba	Peso	100 Centavos
Cyprus	Pound	1000 Mils
Czechoslovakia	Koruna	100 Halers
Dahomey (see Benin)		
Denmark	Krone	100 Øre
Djibouti	Franc	100 Centimes
Dominica	Dollar	100 Cents
Dominican Republic	Peso	100 Centavos
Ecuador	Sucre	100 Centavos
Egypt	Pound	100 Piasters
El Salvador	Colon	100 Centavos
Equatorial Guinea	Ekuele	100 Centimos
Estonia (USSR)	Ruble	100 Kopecks
Ethiopia	Birr	100 Santi motch
Faeroe Islands (Denmark)	Krone	100 Øre
Falkland Islands (UK)	Pound	100 Pence
Fiji	Dollar	100 Cents
Finland	Markka	100 Pennis
France	Franc	100 Centimes
French Guiana (France)	Franc	100 Centimes
French Polynesia (France)	Franc	100 Centimes
Gabon	Franc	100 Centimes
Gambia, The	Dalasi	100 Butut
German Democratic Republic (East Germany)	Mark	100 Pfennigs
Germany, Federal Republic of (West Germany)	Deutsche Mark	100 Pfennigs
Ghana	Cedi	100 Pesewa
Gibraltar	Pound	100 New Pence
Gilbert Islands (see Kiribati)		
Great Britain (see United Kingdom)		
Greece	Drachma	100 Lepta
Greenland (Denmark)	Krone	100 Øre
Grenada	Dollar	100 Cents
Guadeloupe (France)	Franc	100 Centimes
Guam (US)	Dollar	100 Cents
Guatemala	Quetzal	100 Centavos
Guinea	Syli	100 Kori
Guinea-Bissau	Peso	100 Centavos
Guyana	Dollar	100 Cents

Country	Currency	Fractional Unit
Haiti	Gourde	100 Centimes
Honduras	Lempira	100 Centavos
Hong Kong (UK)	Dollar	100 Cents
Hungary	Forint	100 Fillér
Iceland	Króna	100 Aurar
India	Rupee	100 Paise
Indonesia	Rupiah	100 Sen
Iran	Rial	100 Dinars
Iraq	Dinar	1000 Fils
Ireland, Republic of	Pound	100 Pence
Israel	Pound	100 Agorot
Italy	Lira	100 Centesimi
Ivory Coast	Franc	100 Centimes
Jamaica	Dollar	100 Cents
Japan	Yen	Yen
Jordan	Dinar	1000 Fils
Kampuchea	Riel	100 Sen
Kenya	Shilling	100 Cents
Kiribati	Dollar	100 Cents
Korea, Republic of (South Korea)	Won	100 Chon
Korean People's Democratic Republic (North Korea)	Won	100 Jeon
Kuwait	Dinar	1000 Fils
Laos	Kip	100 At
Latvia (USSR)	Ruble	100 Kopecks
Lebanon	Pound	100 Piasters
Lesotho	Loti	100 Lisente
Liberia	Dollar	100 Cents
Libya	Dinar	1000 Dirhams
Liechtenstein	Franc	100 Rappen
Lithuania (USSR)	Ruble	100 Kopecks
Luxembourg	Franc	100 Centimes
Macao (Portugal)	Escudo	100 Centavos
Madagascar	Franc	100 Centimes
Madeira (Portugal)	Escudo	100 Centavos
Malagasy Republic (see Madagascar)		
Malawi	Kwacha	100 Tambala
Malaysia	Ringgit	100 Sen
Maldives	Rupee	100 Cents
Mali	Franc	100 Centimes
Malta	Pound	100 Pence
Marshall Islands (US)	Dollar	100 Cents
Martinique (France)	Franc	100 Centimes
Mauritania	Ougiya	100 Khoms

Country	Currency	Fractional Unit
Mauritius	Rupee	100 Cents
Mayotte (France)	Franc	100 Centimes
Mexico	Peso	100 Centavos
Monaco	Franc	100 Centimes
Mongolia	Tugrik	100 Mongos
Montserrat	Dollar	100 Cents
Morocco	Dirham	100 Francs
Mozambique	Escudo	100 Centavos
Nauru	Dollar	100 Cents
Nepal	Rupee	100 Pice
Netherlands, The	Guilder	100 Cents
Netherlands Antilles	Guilder	100 Cents
New Caledonia (France)	Franc	100 Centimes
New Hebrides (see Vanuatu)		
New Zealand	Dollar	100 Cents
Nicaragua	Cordoba	100 Centavos
Nieu (New Zealand)	Dollar	100 Cents
Niger	Franc	100 Centimes
Nigeria	Naira	100 Kobo
Northern Ireland (see United Kingdom)		
Northwest Territories (Canada)	Dollar	100 Cents
Norway	Krone	100 Øre
Oman	Rial	1000 Baizas
Pakistan	Rupee	100 Paise
Panama	Balboa	100 Centesimos
Papua New Guinea	Kina	100 Toea
Paraguay	Guarani	100 Centimos
Peru	Sol	100 Centavos
Philippines	Peso	100 Centavos
Pitcairn Island (UK)	Dollar	100 Cents
Poland	Złoty	100 Groszy
Portugal	Escudo	100 Centavos
Portuguese Guinea (see Guinea-Bissau)		
Puerto Rico (US)	Dollar	100 Cents
Qatar	Riyal	100 Dirhams
Réunion Island (France)	Franc	100 Centimes
Rhodesia (see Zimbabwe)		
Romania	Leu	100 Bani
Rwanda	Franc	100 Centimes
St. Helena (UK)	Pound	100 Pence
St. Kitts-Nevis (UK)	Dollar	100 Cents
St. Lucia	Dollar	100 Cents

Country	Currency	Fractional Unit
St. Vincent	Dollar	100 Cents
St. Pierre and Miquelon (France)	Franc	100 Centimes
San Marino	Lira	100 Centesimi
São Tomé and Príncipe	Dobra	100 Centavos
Saudi Arabia	Riyal	20 Qursh
Senegal	Franc	100 Centimes
Seychelles	Rupee	100 Pence
Sierra Leone	Leone	100 Cents
Singapore	Dollar	100 Cents
Somalia	Shilling	100 Centesimi
South Africa	Rand	100 Cents
Spain	Peseta	100 Centimos
Sri Lanka	Rupee	100 Cents
Sudan	Pound	100 Piasters
Surinam	Guilder	100 Cents
Swaziland	Lilangeni	100 Cents
Sweden	Krona	100 Öre
Switzerland	Franc	100 Centimes
Syria	Pound	100 Piasters
Tahiti (France)	Franc	100 Centimes
Taiwan (see China, Republic of)		
Tanzania	Shilling	100 Cents
Thailand	Baht	100 Satangs
Togo	Franc	100 Centimes
Tokelau (New Zealand)	Dollar	100 Cents
Tonga	Pa'anga	100 Seniti
Trinidad and Tobago	Dollar	100 Cents
Tristan da Cunha (UK)	Pound	100 Pence
Tunisia	Dinar	1000 Millimes
Turkey	Lira	100 Piasters
Turks and Caicos Islands (UK)	Dollar	100 Cents
Tuvalu	Dollar	100 Cents
Uganda	Shilling	100 Cents
Union of Soviet Socialist Republics	Ruble	100 Kopecks
United Arab Emirates	Dirham	1000 Fils
United Kingdom	Pound	100 Pence
United States	Dollar	100 Cents
Upper Volta	Franc	100 Centimes
Uruguay	Peso	100 Centesimos
Vanuatu	Pound	100 Pence
	Franc	100 Centimes
Vatican City State	Lira	100 Centesimi

Country	Currency	Fractional Unit
Venezuela	Bolívar	100 Centimos
Vietnam	Dong	100 Xu
Virgin Islands (UK)	Dollar	100 Cents
Virgin Islands (US)	Dollar	100 Cents
Wallis and Futuna (France)	Franc	100 Centimes
Western Samoa	Tala	100 Sene
Yemen, People's Democratic Republic of	Dinar	1000 Fils
Yemen Arab Republic	Riyal	40 Bugshah
Yugoslavia	Dinar	100 Paras
Zaire	Zaire	100 Makuta
Zambia	Kwacha	100 Ngwee
Zimbabwe	Dollar	100 Cents

GUIDE TO REFERENCE SOURCES

ALMANACS

Information Please Almanac. New York: Simon & Schuster (published annually).

The World Almanac and Book of Facts. New York: Newspaper Enterprise Association (published annually).

ATLASES AND GAZETTEERS

The Columbia-Lippincott Gazetteer of the World, including 1961 supplement. New York: Columbia University Press, 1951.

Hammond's Ambassador World Atlas. New York: Hammond, 1977.

The New International Atlas. Chicago: Rand McNally & Company, 1980. Text is in English, French, German, Italian, and Spanish.

Rand McNally Cosmopolitan World Atlas, New Census Edition. Chicago: Rand McNally & Company, 1981.

The Times Atlas of the World, Comprehensive Edition. New York: Times Books, 1980.

Webster's New Geographical Dictionary. Springfield, Massachusetts: G. & C. Merriam Company, 1980.

BUSINESS WRITING

Brock, Luther A. *How to Communicate by Letter and Memo.* New York: Gregg Division, McGraw-Hill Book Company, 1974.

Brown, Leland. *Communicating Facts and Ideas in Business,* 3rd ed. Englewood Cliffs, New Jersey: Prentice-Hall, 1982.

DeVries, Mary A. *Guide to Better Business Writing.* Piscataway, New Jersey: New Century Publications, 1981.

Janis, J. Harold. *Writing and Communicating in Business.* 3rd ed. New York: Macmillan, 1978.

Krey, Isabelle A., and Metzler, Bernadette V. *Principles and Techniques of Effective Business Communications.* New York: Harcourt Brace Jovanovich, 1976.

Londo, Richard J. *Common Sense in Business Writing.* New York: Macmillan, 1982.

Paxson, William. *The Business Writing Handbook.* New York: Bantam Books, 1981.

Reid, James, and Silleck, Anne. *Better Business Letters: A Programmed Book to Develop Skill in Writing,* 2nd ed. Reading, Massachusetts: Addison-Wesley Publishing Co., 1978.

Shurter, Robert L. *Effective Letters in Business,* 2nd ed. New York: McGraw-Hill Book Company, 1954.

———. *Written Communication in Business,* 3rd ed. New York: McGraw-Hill Book Company, 1971

Treece, Malra. *Effective Reports.* Boston: Allyn and Bacon, 1982.

Turabian, Kate L. *A Manual for Writers,* 4th ed. Chicago: University of Chicago Press, 1973.

Wilkinson, C.W., and Clarke, Peter B. *Communicating Through Letters and Reports,* 7th ed. Homewood, Illinois: Richard D. Irwin, 1980.

DICTIONARIES

Desk Dictionaries

Funk & Wagnalls Standard College Dictionary. New York: Funk & Wagnalls, 1977.

The Random House College Dictionary, rev. ed. New York: Random House, 1980.

Webster's New Collegiate Dictionary, 8th ed. Springfield, Massachusetts: G. & C. Merriam Company, 1980.

Webster's New World Dictionary of the American Language, Second College Edition. New York: Simon and Schuster, 1982.

Unabridged Dictionaries

The American Heritage Dictionary of the English Language. New York: American Heritage Publishing Co., 1975.

The Random House Dictionary of the English Language. New York: Random House, 1967.

Webster's Third New International Dictionary. Springfield, Massachusetts: G. & C. Merriam Company, 1976.

Foreign Language Dictionaries

Cassell's dictionaries, in both single- and dual-language editions, in French, German, Italian, and Spanish are published by Macmillan Publishing Company, New York.

ENCYCLOPEDIAS AND YEARBOOKS

Single-Volume Encyclopedias

The Columbia Encyclopedia, 3rd ed., including 1976 supplement. New York: Columbia University Press, 1976.

The New Columbia Encyclopedia. Philadelphia: J.B. Lippincott Company, 1975.

Multivolume Encyclopedias

Collier's Encyclopedia. New York: Macmillan Educational Company, 1978.

Encyclopedia Britannica. Chicago: Encyclopedia Britannica, 1976. (Annual supplement, *The Britannica Book of the Year*)

The Random House Encyclopedia, 2 vols. New York: Random House, 1978.

Other useful yearbooks to be found in most libraries are: *New International Year Book, The Statesman's Yearbook, The Political Handbook of the World, The United States Government Manual, The Book of the States,* and the *Statistical Yearbook (Annuaire Statistique)* published by the United Nations.

ENGLISH GRAMMAR AND USAGE

Bernstein, Theodore M. *The Careful Writer: A Modern Guide to English Usage.* New York: Atheneum, 1965.

The Chicago Manual of Style. 13th ed. Chicago: University of Chicago Press, 1982.

Follett, Wilson. *Modern American Usage.* New York: Hill & Wang, 1966.

Harper Dictionary of Contemporary Usage, eds. William Morris and Mary Morris. New York: Harper & Row, 1975.

Hodges, John C., and Whitten, Mary E. *Harbrace College Handbook,* 7th ed. New York: Harcourt Brace Jovanovich, 1972.

Keithley, Edwin M., and Schreiner, Philip J. *A Manual of Style for the Preparation of Papers and Reports,* 2nd ed. Cincinnati: South-Western Publishing Company, 1971.

Strunk, William, and White, E.B. *The Elements of Style,* 3rd ed. New York: Macmillan, 1979.

U.S. Government Printing Office Style Manual, rev. ed. Washington, D.C.: U.S. Government Printing Office, 1973.

Warriner, John E., and Griffith, Francis. *Warriner's English Grammar and Composition: Complete Course.* New York: Harcourt Brace Jovanovich, 1977.

Words into Type, 3rd ed. Englewood Cliffs, New Jersey: Prentice-Hall, 1974.

Wentworth, Harold, and Flexner, Stuart B. *Dictionary of American Slang,* 2nd ed. New York: Thomas Y. Crowell, 1975.

LEGAL REFERENCE BOOKS

Black's Law Dictionary, 5th ed. St. Paul, Minnesota: West Publishing Co., 1979.

Martindale-Hubbell Law Directory. Summit, New York: Martindale-Hubbell (published annually).

Oceana Legal Almanac Series. Dobbs Ferry, New York: Oceana Publications. Multivolume series with each volume devoted to one area of the law.

PARLIAMENTARY PROCEDURE

Robert, Henry M., and Robert, Sarah Corbin. *Robert's Rules of Order*, rev. ed. Chicago: Scott, Foresman and Company, 1970. New York: Morrow Quill Paperback, 1979.

PUBLICATION GUIDES AND INDEXES

Books in Print. New York: R.R. Bowker Company.

Cumulative Book Index. New York: H.W. Wilson Company.

The New York Times Index. New York: The New York Times Company.

Readers' Guide to Periodical Literature. New York: H.W. Wilson Company.

United States Catalog. New York: H.W. Wilson Company.

The Wall Street Journal Index. New York: Dow Jones and Company.

Other indexes available in libraries are *Applied Science and Technical Index, Business and Periodical Index, Book Review Digest, Education Index, Funk & Scott's Index of Corporations and Industries.*

SECRETARIAL HANDBOOKS

Doris, Lillian, and Miller, Besse May. *Complete Secretary's Handbook*, 3rd ed., rev. by Mary A. DeVries. Englewood Cliffs, New Jersey: Prentice-Hall, 1977.

Hutchinson, Lois. *Standard Handbook for Secretaries*, 8th ed. New York: McGraw-Hill Book Company, 1979.

Quinn, Michelle. *Katharine Gibbs Handbook of Business English*. New York: The Free Press/Macmillan Publishing Co., 1982.

Sabin, William A. *The Gregg Reference Manual*, 5th ed. New York: Gregg Division, McGraw-Hill Book Company, 1979.

Tainton, Sarah Augusta; Monro, Kate M.; and Shertzer, Margaret D. *The Secretary's Handbook*, 9th ed. rev. New York: Macmillan Publishing Co., 1969.

Thompson, Margaret H., and Janis, J. Harold. *Revised Standard Reference for Secretaries and Administrators*. New York: Macmillan Publishing Co., 1980.

Webster's New World Secretarial Handbook, rev. ed. New York: Simon and Schuster, 1981.

Webster's Secretarial Handbook, ed. Anna L. Eckersley-Johnson. Springfield, Massachusetts: G. & C. Merriam Company, 1976.

SECRETARIAL MAGAZINES

Administrative Management. Geyer-McAllister Publications, 51 Madison Avenue, New York, New York 10010. Includes articles on office machines and supplies.

The Capstone. National Secretaries Association, 2440 Pershing Road, Suite G 10, Crown Center, Kansas City, Missouri 64108. Published once yearly.

The Secretary. National Secretaries Association.

Word Processing and Information Systems. Geyer-McAllister Publications.

Words. International Information/Word Processing Association, 1015 North York Road, Willow Grove, Pennsylvania 19090.

THESAURI AND WORDBOOKS

Devlin, Joseph. *A Dictionary of Synonyms and Antonyms.* New York: Fawcett Popular Library, 1961. Paperback.

Laird, Charlton. *Webster's New World Thesaurus.* New York: William Collins and World Publishing, 1971; Fawcett Popular Library, 1974 (paperback).

The Merriam-Webster Pocket Dictionary of Synonyms. New York: Pocket Books, 1972. Paperback.

The Random House Basic Dictionary of Synonyms and Antonyms, ed. Laurence Urdang. New York: Random House, 1960.

Roget's International Thesaurus, 4th ed., rev. by Robert L. Chapman. New York: Thomas Y. Crowell, 1977

Urdang, Laurence. *The Basic Book of Synonyms and Antonyms.* New York: Signet Books/New American Library, 1978.

Webster's Collegiate Thesaurus. Springfield, Massachusetts: G. & C. Merriam Company, 1976.

Webster's New Dictionary of Synonyms. Springfield, Massachusetts: G. & C. Merriam Company, 1978.

WORD PROCESSING

Bergerud, Marly, and Gonzalez, Jean. *Word Processing Concepts and Careers.* New York: John Wiley & Sons, 1978.

Cecil, Paula B. *Management and Word Processing Operations.* Menlo Park, California: Benjamin Cummings Publishing Co., 1980.

Ellis, Bettie Hampton. *Word Processing: Concepts and Applications.* New York: Gregg Division, McGraw-Hill Book Company, 1980.

Mathews, Anne, and Moody, Pat. *The Word Processing Correspondence Secretary.* Cincinnati: South-Western Publishing Company, 1981.

Rosen, Arnold, and Freiden, Rosemary. *Word Processing.* Englewood Cliffs, New Jersey: Prentice-Hall, 1982.

GENERAL REFERENCE

Bartlett's Familiar Quotations, 15th ed., rev. and enlarged by Emily Morrison Beck. Boston: Little, Brown and Company, 1980.

Encyclopedia of Associations, 2 vols. Detroit: Gale Research Company (published annually).

The Foundation Directory. 8th ed. New York: The Foundation Center, 1981.

Standard Periodical Directory, 7th ed. New York: Oxbridge Communications, 1982.

Trade Names Dictionary, 3rd ed., 2 vols. Detroit: Gale Research Company (published annually).

Ulrich's International Periodicals Directory, 20th ed. New York: R.R. Bowker Company, 1981.

Webster's Biographical Dictionary, Springfield, Massachusetts: G. & C. Merriam Company, 1972.

Who's Who in America, 41st ed., 2 vols. Chicago: Marquis Who's Who, 1981.